THE OLD TESTAMENT PSEUDEPIGRAPHA

EARLY JUDAISM AND ITS LITERATURE

Rodney A. Werline, General Editor

Editorial Board:
Randall D. Chesnutt
Kelley N. Coblentz Bautch
Maxine L. Grossman
Jan Joosten
James S. McLaren
Carol Newsom

Number 50

THE OLD TESTAMENT PSEUDEPIGRAPHA

Fifty Years of the Pseudepigrapha Section
at the SBL

Edited by

Matthias Henze and Liv Ingeborg Lied

SBL PRESS

Atlanta

Copyright © 2019 by Society of Biblical Literature

All rights reserved. No part of this work may be reproduced or transmitted in any form or by any means, electronic or mechanical, including photocopying and recording, or by means of any information storage or retrieval system, except as may be expressly permitted by the 1976 Copyright Act or in writing from the publisher. Requests for permission should be addressed in writing to the Rights and Permissions Office, SBL Press, 825 Houston Mill Road, Atlanta, GA 30329 USA.

Library of Congress Cataloging-in-Publication Data

Names: Henze, Matthias, editor. | Lied, Liv Ingeborg, editor. | Society of Biblical Literature. Pseudepigrapha Group.
Title: The Old Testament Pseudepigrapha : fifty years of the Pseudepigrapha Section at the SBL / edited by Matthias Henze and Liv Ingeborg Lied.
Description: Atlanta : SBL Press, [2019] | Series: Early Judaism and its literature; 50 | Includes bibliographical references and index.
Identifiers: LCCN 2019025814 (print) | LCCN 2019025815 (ebook) | ISBN 9781628372588 (paperback) | ISBN 9780884144113 (hardback) | ISBN 9780884144120 (ebook)
Subjects: LCSH: Apocryphal books (Old Testament)—Criticism, interpretation, etc. | Society of Biblical Literature. Pseudepigrapha Group—History.
Classification: BS1700 .O55 2019 (print) | LCC BS1700 (ebook) | DDC 229/.91007—dc23
LC record available at https://lccn.loc.gov/2019025814
LC ebook record available at https://lccn.loc.gov/2019025815

Printed on acid-free paper.

To the members of the Pseudepigrapha Breakfasts,

who introduced the Pseudepigrapha to the Society of Biblical Literature

Contents

Acknowledgments xi
Abbreviations xiii

1. The Pseudepigrapha and the Society of Biblical Literature
   Matthias Henze and Liv Ingeborg Lied 1

2. The Pseudepigrapha Project at the Society of Biblical Literature, 1969–1971
   Matthias Henze 11

   Remembering Fifty Years of the Pseudepigrapha
   at the Society of Biblical Literature

3. Let the Living Remember the Dead: Homage to the Departed Pioneers of the Pseudepigrapha Group—Father George W. MacRae, S.J.
   Robert A. Kraft 53

4. Early Days of the Society of Biblical Literature Pseudepigrapha Group: Pseudepigrapha Studies in the Second Half of the Twentieth Century
   Michael E. Stone 59

5. Memories of the Society of Biblical Literature Pseudepigrapha Group, 1970–1982
   James Hamilton Charlesworth 79

6. The Pseudepigrapha at the Society of Biblical Literature: The Early Growth of a Group
   George W. E. Nickelsburg 95

The History of the Study of the Pseudepigrapha

7. The History of the Study of the Pseudepigrapha
   Patricia D. Ahearne-Kroll 103

8. The Pseudepigrapha within and without Biblical Studies
   Benjamin G. Wright III 133

9. Dead Sea Scroll Scholarship and Pseudepigrapha Studies:
   From Józef Milik to Material Philology
   Eibert Tigchelaar 157

10. Pseudepigrapha and Gender
    Hanna Tervanotko 175

Topics in the Study of the Pseudepigrapha

11. Pseudepigrapha and Their Manuscripts
    Liv Ingeborg Lied and Loren T. Stuckenbruck..................................203

12. Manuscript Research in the Digital Age
    Lorenzo DiTommaso...231

13. The Pseudepigrapha in Greek: Translation, Composition, and the Diaspora
    Martha Himmelfarb..263

14. Origen and the Old Testament Apocrypha: The Creation of a Category
    William Adler 287

15. Pseudepigrapha between Judaism and Christianity: The Case of 3 Baruch
    John J. Collins 309

16. Pseudepigraphy as an Interpretative Construct
    Hindy Najman and Irene Peirano Garrison 331

The Future of the Study of the Pseudepigrapha

17. The More Old Testament Pseudepigrapha Project
    James R. Davila..359

18. *Encomium* or *Apologia*? The Future (?) of the Society of
    Biblical Literature Pseudepigrapha Section
    Randall D. Chesnutt..383

19. Looking Ahead: The Pseudepigrapha and the New Testament
    John R. Levison..399

20. Fifty More Years of the Society of Biblical Literature
    Pseudepigrapha Section? Prospects for the Future
    Judith H. Newman 407

21. Future Trends for the Study of Jewish Pseudepigrapha:
    Two Recommendations
    John C. Reeves 415

Contributors..423
Ancient Sources Index..427
Modern Scholars Index 439

Acknowledgments

This volume celebrates fifty years of the Pseudepigrapha at the Society of Biblical Literature. We wish to express our sincere appreciation to all who have helped make this book possible. Cindy Dawson helped with the editorial work. Rodney Werline encouraged us to pursue the project and kindly accepted the volume into the series. Nicole L. Tilford, Heather McMurray, and Bob Buller at SBL Press guided the book through the publication process. We are grateful to all of them.

Matthias Henze
Liv Ingeborg Lied

Abbreviations

Primary Sources

1 En.	1 Enoch
2 Esd	2 Esdras
3. Bar.	3 Baruch
A.J.	Josephus, *Antiquitates judaicae*
b.	Babylonian Talmud
B. Bat.	Bava Batra
Barn.	Barnabas
Bek.	Bekhorot
B.J.	Josephus, *Bellum judaicum*
C. Ap.	Josephus, *Contra Apionem*
CD	Damascus Document
Cels.	Origen, *Contra Celsum*
Comm. Cant.	Origen, *Commentarius in Canticum*
Comm. Isa.	Jerome, *Commentariorum in Isaiam libri XVIII*
Comm. Jo.	Origen, *Commentarii in evangelium Joannis*
Comm. Matt.	Jerome, *Commentariorum in Matthaeum libri IV*; Origen, *Commentarium in evangelium Matthaei*
Comm. ser. Matt.	Origen, *Commentarium series in evangelium Matthaei*
De Din.	Dionysius of Halicarnassus, *De Dinarcho*
Ecl.	Clement, *Eclogae propheticae*
Ep.	*Epistula*
Ep. Afr.	Origen, *Epistula ad Africanum*
Ep. Orig.	Africanus, *Epistula ad Origenem*
Expl. Dan.	Jerome, *Explanatio in Danielem*
Georg.	Virgil, *Georgics*
Hist. eccl.	Eusebius, *Historia ecclesiastica*
Hom. Num.	Origen, *Homiliae in Numeros*
Hypoth.	Philo, *Hypothetica*

LAB	Liber antiquitatum biblicarum
LAE	Life of Adam and Eve
Migr.	Philo, *De migration Abrahami*
Naz.	Nazir
Paed.	Clement, *Paedagogus*
Princ.	Origen, *De principiis*
Sib. Or.	Sibylline Oracles
Strom.	Clement, *Stromateis*
T. Mos.	Testament of Moses
T. Sol.	Testament of Solomon
Tract.	Priscillian, *Tractate*
Varia Hist.	Aelian, *Varia Historia*
Vit. Pyth.	Iamblichus, *De vita Pythagorica*
Vit. Verg.	Suetonius-Donatus, *Vita Vergiliana*
Yevam.	Yevamot

Secondary Sources

AAWG	Abhandlungen der Akademie der Wissenschaften zu Göttingen
AB	Anchor Bible
ABRL	Anchor Bible Reference Library
AbrN	*Abr-Nahrain*
ÄthF	Aethiopistische Forschungen
AGJU	Arbeiten zur Geschichte des antiken Judentums und des Urchristentums
AJSR	*Association for Jewish Studies Review*
ANRW	Temporini, Hildegard, and Wolfgang Haase, eds. *Aufstieg und Niedergang der römischen Welt: Geschichte und Kultur Roms im Spiegel der neueren Forschung.* Part 2, Principat. Berlin: de Gruyter, 1972–.
AOT	Sparks, Hedley F. D., ed. *The Apocryphal Old Testament.* Oxford: Clarendon, 1984.
BAC	Bible in Ancient Christianity
BCSR	*Bulletin of the Council on the Study of Religion*
BETL	Bibliotheca Ephermeridum Theologicarum Lovaniensium
Bib	*Biblica*
BibInt	Biblical Interpretation (series)

BibInt	*Biblical Interpretation*
BIOSCS	*Bulletin of the International Organization for Septuagint and Cognate Studies*
BJRL	*Bulletin of the John Rylands University Library of Manchester*
BkPh	Beiträge zur klassischen Philologie
BM	British Museum
BSNA	Biblical Scholarship in North America
BSOAS	*Bulletin of the School of Oriental and African Studies*
CBQ	*Catholic Biblical Quarterly*
CCCM	Corpus Christianorum: Continuatio Medaevalis
CdE	*Chronique d'Égypte*
CEJL	Commentaries on Early Jewish Literature
CQS	Companion to the Qumran Scrolls
CSCO	Corpus Scriptorum Christianorum Orientalium
CurBR	*Currents in Biblical Research*
DJD	Discoveries in the Judaean Desert
DSD	*Dead Sea Discoveries*
EDEJ	Collins, John J., and Daniel C. Harlow, eds. *The Eerdmans Dictionary of Early Judaism.* Grand Rapids: Eerdmans, 2010.
EJL	Early Judaism and Its Literature
EMEL	Early Manuscript Electronic Library
EMML	Ethiopian Manuscript Microfilm Library
ETL	*Ephemerides Theologicae Lovanienses*
frag.	fragment
GCS	Die griechischen christlichen Schriftsteller der ersten Jahrhunderte
Gnosis	*Gnosis: Journal of Gnostic Studies*
HTR	*Harvard Theological Review*
IES	Institute of Ethiopian Studies
JAAR	*Journal of the American Academy of Religion*
JAJSup	Journal of Ancient Judaism Supplements
JAOS	*Journal of the American Oriental Society*
JBL	*Journal of Biblical Literature*
JE	Singer, I., ed. *The Jewish Encyclopedia.* 12 vols. New York: Funk & Wagnalls, 1901–1906.
JECS	*Journal of Early Christian Studies*
JJS	*Journal of Jewish Studies*

JMRC	*Journal of Medieval Religious Cultures*
JR	*Journal of Religion*
JSAI	*Jerusalem Studies in Arabic and Islam*
JSJ	*Journal for the Study of Judaism in the Persian, Hellenistic, and Roman Periods*
JSJSup	Supplements to the Journal for the Study of Judaism in the Persian, Hellenistic, and Roman Periods
JSP	*Journal for the Study of the Pseudepigrapha*
JSPSup	Journal for the Study of the Pseudepigrapha Supplement Series
JSQ	*Jewish Studies Quarterly*
JTS	*Journal of Theological Studies*
LBS	Library of Biblical Studies
LHBOTS	Library of Hebrew Bible/Old Testament Studies
LSTS	Library of Second Temple Studies
MedLov	Mediaevalia Lovaniensia
MOTP	Bauckham, Richard, James R. Davila, and Alexander Panayotov, eds. *Old Testament Pseudepigrapha: More Noncanonical Scriptures*. 2 vols. Grand Rapids: Eerdmans, 2013–.
MTNA	Burke, Tony, and Brent Landau, eds. *New Testament Apocrypha: More Noncanonical Scriptures*. Grand Rapids: Eerdmans, 2016.
MTSRSup	Supplements to Method and Theory in the Study of Religion
NHS	Nag Hammadi Studies
NovT	*Novum Testamentum*
NPNF	Schaff, Philip, and Henry Wace, eds. *A Select Library of Nicene and Post-Nicene Fathers of the Christian Church*. 28 vols. in 2 series. 1886–1889. Repr., Buffalo, NY: Christian Literature, 1890.
NRSV	New Revised Standard Version
NTS	*New Testament Studies*
OLA	Orientalia Lovaniensia Analecta
OTP	Charlesworth, James H., ed. *Old Testament Pseudepigrapha*. 2 vols. New York: Doubleday, 1983–1985.
P.Oxy.	Grenfell, Bernard P., et al., eds. *The Oxyrhynchus Papyri*. London: Egypt Exploration Fund, 1898–.
postmedieval	*postmedieval: A Journal of Medieval Cultural Studies*

Abbreviations xvii

PVTG	Pseudepigrapha Veteris Testamenti Graece
RB	*Revue biblique*
Rbén	*Revue bénédictine*
RBS	Resources for Biblical Study
RelSRev	*Religious Studies Review*
RevQ	*Revue de Qumran*
RSV	Revised Standard Version
SANER	Studies in Ancient Near Eastern Records
SBLDS	Society of Biblical Literature Dissertation Series
SBLMS	Society of Biblical Literature Monograph Series
SBLSP	Society of Biblical Literature Seminar Papers
SBLTT	Society of Biblical Literature Texts and Translations
SC	Sources chrétiennes
SCS	Septuagint and Cognate Studies
Sem	*Semitica*
SNTSMS	Studiorum Novi Testamenti Societas Monograph Series
SPhiloA	*Studia Philonica Annual*
STDJ	Studies on the Texts of the Desert of Judah
StPB	Studia Post-biblica
SVTG	Septuaginta Vetus Testamentum Graecum
SVTP	Studia in Veteris Testamenti Pseudepigraphica
TBN	Themes in Biblical Narrative
TCS	Text Critical Studies
TDNT	Kittel, Gerhard, and Gerhard Friedrich, eds. *Theological Dictionary of the New Testament*. Translated by Geoffrey W. Bromiley. 10 vols. Grand Rapids: 1964–1976.
TSAJ	Texte und Studien zum antiken Judentum
TT	Texts and Translations
TUGAL	Texte und Untersuchungen zur Geschichte der altchristlichen Literatur
UCOP	University of Cambridge Oriental Publications
VC	*Virgilae Christianae*
VCSup	Virgilae Christianae Supplements
VTSup	Supplements to Vetus Testamentum
WUNT	Wissenschaftliche Untersuchungen zum Neuen Testament
ZAC	*Zeitschrift für Antikes Christentum*
ZDMG	*Zeitschrift der deutschen morgenländischen Gesellschaft*
ZTK	*Zeitschrit für Theologie und Kirche*

1
The Pseudepigrapha and the Society of Biblical Literature

Matthias Henze and Liv Ingeborg Lied

With this jubilee volume we celebrate fifty years of the study of the Pseudepigrapha at the Society of Biblical Literature and the pioneering scholars who introduced the Pseudepigrapha to the Society. In 1969, the same year in which the Society adopted a new constitution that restructured the Society's basic operations, Walter J. Harrelson, dean of the Divinity School at Vanderbilt University, convened the first Pseudepigrapha Breakfast. His goals for what he initially labeled the Pseudepigrapha Project were ambitious: to convene a cadre of international scholars who would work on the Old Testament pseudepigrapha; to photograph the most important manuscripts (Harrelson himself traveled to Ethiopia on multiple occasions); to produce new critical editions of the pseudepigrapha based on the best available manuscript evidence; and to publish an inexpensive English translation to make Israel's forgotten texts easily accessible. Harrelson was a visionary and a builder. His Pseudepigrapha Breakfasts in 1969 and 1970 were a great success, and the original team of pseudepigrapha scholars grew apace. Hence, the Pseudepigrapha Project marked the beginning of half a century of pseudepigrapha research at the Society of Biblical Literature.

The Pseudepigrapha at the Society of Biblical Literature

When Harrelson conceived of the Pseudepigrapha Project, he was careful to put a solid foundation into place that would support the unit for a long time to come. As early as during the first Pseudepigrapha Breakfast on November 17, 1969, a steering committee was appointed. It was chaired by Walter Harrelson (the Society's president in 1972) and included James

H. Charlesworth (who soon thereafter became the first secretary), Robert A. Kraft (president in 2006), George W. MacRae, Bruce M. Metzger (president in 1971), Harry M. Orlinsky (president in 1970), Michael E. Stone, and John Strugnell. Since much of the initial energy was spent on the study and publication of texts, a second, editorial board was formed. Before long other scholars joined, among them John J. Collins (president in 2002), Daniel J. Harrington, Martha Himmelfarb, George W. E. Nickelsburg, and James C. VanderKam.

The Pseudepigrapha unit at the Society of Biblical Literature soon became the flagship in pseudepigrapha research that changed scholarly perceptions of early Judaism. The sessions of the last half century tell the story of the academic contributions of the Pseudepigrapha unit at the Society of Biblical Literature. They also reflect some of the major trends and research developments in pseudepigrapha studies more broadly. In order to address Harrelson's goal to produce new text editions and English translations, throughout the 1970s members of the Pseudepigrapha unit began studying one specific text each year. The first of these texts was the Paralipomena of Jeremiah (1971), on which Robert A. Kraft and Ann-Elizabeth Purintun were working at the time. From 1972 to 1975, there followed a sequence of discussions on the testaments: the Testament of Abraham (1972), the Testament of Moses (1973), the Testament of Job (1974), and the Testament of Joseph (1975). In 1976, the focus was on Joseph and Aseneth, followed in 1977 by attention to Sethian and in 1978 to the Enochic traditions. Such sessions devoted to particular pseudepigraphic writings continued throughout the history of the unit: Judith (1989), the Testament of Abraham (2004), the Letter of Aristeas (2015), and Ben Sira (2016). Some texts have been discussed on several occasions. The book of Jubilees, for instance, was the subject of discussion in 1985, 2004, and 2013; 4 Ezra in 1981 and 2006; and Enochic texts in 1978, 1983, 1993, and 2003. Furthermore, the Pseudepigrapha unit has hosted several review sessions of newly published editions, translations, and commentaries on pseudepigraphical texts. For example, James H. Charlesworth's first volume of *Old Testament Pseudepigrapha* was reviewed in 1984, George W. E. Nickelsburg's Hermeneia commentary on 1 Enoch in 2001, and, more recently, at the 2013 meeting in Baltimore, the first volume of *Old Testament Pseudepigrapha: More Noncanoncial Scriptures*, edited by Richard Baukham, James R. Davila, and Alexander Panayotov.

In addition to preparing editions, translations, and commentaries on the pseudepigrapha, the unit devoted much attention to major themes and topics of the pseudepigrapha. Often such investigations required bringing the pseudepigrapha out of the shadows of the Bible in order to interpret them on their own terms. Now, instead of reading the pseudepigrapha only in service to other, mostly canonical writings, the pseudepigrapha became the center of attention. Thus, in 1979 and 1980, at the decennial meeting of the unit, sessions were devoted to the profiles and functions of righteous/ideal figures and the significance of ascribing texts to biblical luminaries. Both issues have remained central to the unit's history, which can be recognized in the discussions of pseudepigraphy and exemplarity in the 2000s and 2010s. Likewise, apocalypse and apocalypticism have been recurring foci. Although both pseudepigraphy and apocalypticism had become established topics of interest in the academy, the exploration of the ways in which they are articulated and put to use in the pseudepigraphic literature brought additional insights to the study of the intellectual and social world of Jewish antiquity.

On several occasions, the Pseudepigrapha unit explored the relationship between key historical events in ancient Judaism or the connections between pseudepigraphical texts, other literature, and the cultural milieu. For instance, at the 1982 Annual Meeting of the Society of Biblical Literature, the unit addressed reactions to the events of 70 CE. A 1983 session discussed the social setting of the Enoch literature. A 2017 session examined the pseudepigrapha within the context of Hellenistic Judaism.

Harrelson understood very well that close collaboration with other scholars working in adjacent fields was imperative for the success of the Pseudepigrapha Project. The Pseudepigrapha unit has always stayed in dialogue with other units that study the literatures of Jewish and Christian antiquity. The Pseudepigrapha and the Dead Sea Scrolls units at the Society of Biblical Literature repeatedly joined forces (in 1985, 1986, 1997, 2004, and 2008). The Nag Hammadi texts were also important interlocutors (1977, 1995, 1998). While the Dead Sea Scrolls and Nag Hammadi libraries have generated enormous energy and excitement among biblical scholars, the many ways in which these discoveries have complicated our perception of early Judaism and Christianity opened up new spaces for the pseudepigrapha to be heard and studied.

From the very beginnings of modern the Pseudepigrapha Project, scholars addressed methodological challenges associated with editing, interpreting, and categorizing pseudepigraphic texts. These discussions, associated early on with the oeuvre of Walter Harrelson, Robert A. Kraft, Michael E. Stone, Marinus de Jonge, and several others in recent decades, have included questions about the provenance of the texts (Jewish or Christian?), the predominantly Christian transmission history of the texts that are commonly perceived to be Jewish, and the anachronisms that have too often marred scholarly categorizations of these texts. In particular, the term *pseudepigrapha* itself has been debated from the very start, linked as it is to the same anachronistic and canon-dependent frames that the Pseudepigrapha unit set out to battle. Similar methodological issues have continued to be addressed during the 2000s and 2010s and can be detected in sessions such as one on the pitfalls of categorization in 2006, in a session devoted to problematizing the term *pseudepigrapha* in 2008, and again in 2018 in a session on hybrids, converts, and borders of Jewish and Christian identities.

The Pseudepigrapha unit has also addressed a range of theoretical and methodological concerns that are shared across the humanities. Such attention is observable, for instance, in the focus on intertextuality, a major debate in literary studies, at the Annual Meeting of the Society of Biblical Literature in San Francisco in 1992. We can see an awareness of the so-called linguistic turn at the Annual Meeting in 1996, where the move from text to social and historical contexts was debated. Rituals and religious experience were the topics in 2000 and 2008, and there was a session on the performative dimensions of the texts in 2008. Interest in materiality and media becomes palpable in the 2010s, for instance, in the sessions Ancient Media Culture in 2012, and Manuscripts, Scribal Culture, Scribal Change in 2016. Also, during the 2010s, finally, the digital turn slowly made its presence felt in individual papers but did not fully materialize in a special session until the Annual Meeting in Boston in 2017.

In its interactions with adjacent fields and the larger academic world, the Pseudepigrapha unit has sometimes been a pioneer and at other times a latecomer. Whereas the attention to the transmission and reception history of ancient texts remained underdeveloped in most humanistic scholarship until the 1990s, these issues were already on the radar of the Pseudepigrapha unit in the mid-1970s. By 1977, methodological aspects that concern the transmission and reception of the texts were already discussed by several members of the unit and have remained central throughout its history: "The Pseudepigrapha in Jewish, Christian and Manichean Transmission" appears on the program in 1990, "The Enochic Literature in Early Christianity" in 1993, and "The Jewish Pseudepigrapha in Egyptian Christianity" in 1995. A session on Jewish Pseudepigrapha and the Islamic World figures in the program in 2004, Daniel's Text Reception in 2013, and the Reception and Afterlife of Pseudepigrapha in Judaism, Christianity and Islam again in 2018.

In other fields of research, the Pseudepigrapha unit has been slow. As Hanna Tervanotko shows in her contribution to the present volume, attention to gender perspectives is only recent. Indeed, the unit explored texts ascribed to female figures already in the 1970s and 1980s—Joseph and Aseneth in 1976 and 1996, the Life of Adam and Eve in 1994, and the book of Judith in 1989—but an explicit interest in the experiences of women in antiquity, or more broadly in the role of female figures in the texts, is first found in the mid-2000s with sessions on Women's Religious Experience in Antiquity in 2006, The Parascriptural Dimensions of Biblical Women in 2007, and Women, Fire, and Dangerous Things in 2013. The first session to explore gender as a broader analytical category, embracing more than just women, appears as late as in 2017.

This brief sketch of some of the main academic tendencies of the sessions over the last half century shows that the Pseudepigrapha unit at the Society of Biblical Literature has provided a unique forum for scholarly discussions. Its aims have been ambitious and broad, from ensuring that the pseudepigrapha have their rightful place at the Society of Biblical Literature and are studied in their own right, to uncovering the relevance of the pseudepigrapha for understanding Judaism and Christianity more broadly and throughout their histories. New fields of inquiry continue to emerge as we gain a better understanding of the pseudepigrapha and their complex histories, not least the desire for more interdisciplinary inquiries in the various religious and linguistic traditions that have received, preserved, and transmitted the pseudepigraphic texts and that continue to revere them.

When Harrelson convened the first Pseudepigrapha Breakfast, one of his goals was to establish a community of scholars that would work in a collaborative spirit and make the little-known texts accessible to a larger audience by producing new text editions, translations, and commentaries. Looking back, the Pseudepigrapha unit at the Society of Biblical Literature has achieved and, in many regards, far surpassed Harrelson's goals. Today, it remains a stronghold that fosters the rigorous study of early Jewish and Christian literatures.

The Present Volume

The volume opens with an essay by Matthias Henze, "The Pseudepigrapha Project at the Society of Biblical Literature, 1969–1971," that tells the story of the inauguration and formative years of the Pseudepigrapha unit. Drawing upon documents from the Society of Biblical Literature archives at Drew University (now at Emory University) and supplemented by personal files of some of the unit's initial members, Henze describes the creation of the unit and the rationale for starting it, beginning with Harrelson's initial Pseudepigrapha Breakfast at the Annual Meeting in 1969 and leading up to the formal recognition of the Pseudepigrapha Seminar in 1971.

The volume consists of four sections. The first section, "Remembering Fifty Years of the Pseudepigrapha at the Society of Biblical Literature," collects the memories of four of the Pseudepigrapha unit's founding members. In "Let the Living Remember the Dead: Homage to the Departed Pioneers of the Pseudepigrapha Group—Father George W. MacRae, S.J.," Robert A. Kraft pays homage to those pseudepigrapha scholars of the very beginning who paved the way but have since died. In particular, he remembers Father George W. MacRae, S.J., dean of Harvard Divinity School and a charter member of the steering committee of the Pseudepigrapha Group. In his essay "Early Days of the Society of Biblical Literature Pseudepigrapha Group: Pseudepigrapha Studies in the Second Half of the Twentieth Century," Michael E. Stone brings the collaborative and productive atmosphere of the formative years to life. He identifies some of the main tendencies in the research on the pseudepigrapha since the early 1970s and directs our attention to some of the paths still not taken. James Hamilton Charlesworth recalls his involvement in the unit in the 1970s in his "Memories of the Society of Biblical Literature Pseudepigrapha Group, 1970–1982." In particular, he remembers the processes leading up to the publication of his *The Old Testament Pseudepigrapha* in 1983 and 1985. In his essay "The Pseudepigrapha at the Society of Biblical Literature: The Early Growth of a Group," George W. E. Nickelsburg shares his memories of the initial activities and academic priorities of the unit, paying particular attention to its wide-ranging publication initiatives and outcomes.

The second section of the book, "The History of the Study of the Pseudepigrapha," contains four essays that offer new perspectives on some of the main trajectories and decisive moments in the research history of the pseudepigrapha. Patricia D. Ahearne-Kroll's "The History of the Study of the Pseudepigrapha" explores the longstanding attention to texts labeled *pseudepigrapha*. The essay outlines both the modern history of a contested category and the longer lines of intellectual engagement with pseudepigraphal texts. In "The Pseudepigrapha within and without Biblical Studies,"

Benjamin G. Wright III tackles the categories and disciplinary dependencies that have shaped the study of early Jewish texts. Wright critically engages the organizational role the biblical canon has played in biblical studies and discusses how the past fifty years of scholarship on the Dead Sea Scrolls and the pseudepigrapha have challenged academic perceptions of the literatures of ancient Judaism. In his essay "Dead Sea Scroll Scholarship and Pseudepigrapha Studies: From Józef Milik to Material Philology," Eibert Tigchelaar explores moments of interaction between Dead Sea Scrolls and pseudepigrapha studies. He shows how scholarship in the two fields have both overlapped and diverged, each contributing to the broader general developments in biblical, textual, and religious studies in its own ways. Hanna Tervanotko's essay, "Pseudepigrapha and Gender," traces the use of feminist and gender studies in the history of pseudepigrapha research. Focusing on the development of the Pseudepigrapha unit during the last half decade, Tervantoko shows how the engagement with these perspectives is a relatively recent phenomenon.

The first two essays in the third section of the book, "Topics in the Study of the Pseudepigrapha," address the importance of manuscripts, technology, and communicative infrastructures. "Pseudepigrapha and Their Manuscripts," coauthored by Liv Ingeborg Lied and Loren T. Stuckenbruck, isolates six main tendencies that characterize the pool of surviving manuscripts of pseudepigraphal texts. Lied and Stuckenbruck discuss how manuscripts have typically been used and assessed in scholarship and how they can continue to be studied and engaged with, before suggesting some possible ways forward. Lorenzo DiTommaso's essay, "Manuscript Research in the Digital Age," reflects on the role of technology in the research on manuscripts containing pseudepigraphal texts. DiTommaso contends that available technology has always shaped the access to and the perception of these texts and explores how new digital technologies continue to transform the scholarship in the field.

The next three essays examine the complex relationships between the provenance and transmission of the pseudepigrapha, Jewish and Christian engagements with them, and the history of their academic treatment. In her essay, "The Pseudepigrapha in Greek: Translation, Composition, and the Diaspora," Martha Himmelfarb addresses the impact of exploring pseudepigrapha that survive in Greek. Himmelfarb asks us to consider how pseudepigrapha translated into Greek may shed light on the diaspora communities that translated them. William Adler's essay, "Origen and the Old Testament Apocrypha: The Creation of a Category," examines how a literary corpus is formed and assigned a name—in the past, as well as in the present. Taking Origen as his case, Adler discusses how categories such as *apocrypha* and *pseudepigrapha* are formed and how such categories influence research. In "Pseudepigrapha between Judaism and Christianity: The Case of 3 Baruch," John J. Collins revisits the longstanding debate of the provenance of the pseudepigrapha. Focusing on the research history of 3 Baruch, Collins highlights some key challenges to the study of the origins and transmission of pseudepigraphal texts, arguing that each text must be considered on its own merit. In the final essay of this section, "Pseudepigraphy as an Interpretative Construct," Hindy Najman and Irene Peirano Garrison articulate a new agenda for the study of pseudepigraphy. In constructive and critical dialogue with former research contributions in classics and biblical studies, Najman and Peirano offer an integrative approach to pseudepigraphy as an interpretative category.

The five essays in the fourth and final section of the volume, titled "The Future of the Study of the Pseudepigrapha," all look to the future and reflect on what the next steps in pseudepigrapha research might entail. In "The More Old Testament Pseudepigrapha Project," James R. Davila tells the story behind the first volume of *Old Testament Pseudepigrapha: More Noncanonical Scriptures* (2013) and discusses how that volume may contribute to a broadened chronological focus and richer repertoire of texts. Randall D. Chesnutt's "*Enconium* or *Apologia*? The Future (?) of the Society of Biblical Literature Pseudepigrapha Section" discusses the contested label *pseudepigrapha*, relating the debate about the term to the question of the future of a discrete Pseudepigrapha unit at the Society of Biblical Literature. The essay "Looking Ahead: The Pseudepigrapha and the New Testament" by John R. Levison presents two desiderata of pseudepigrapha studies. In the future, Levison would like to see studies that display the indispensability of pseudepigraphal literature to the study of the New Testament and studies that explore pseudepigraphal texts in their own right and in a one-to-one relationship with the texts of the New Testament. In her essay, "Fifty More Years of the Society of Biblical Literature Pseudepigrapha Section? Prospects for the Future," Judith H. Newman explores the potentials of the Pseudepigrapha unit, imagining an interdisciplinary future. She points out three promising avenues of inquiry: tracing traditions through the history of reception, the study of pseudepigrapha from the perspective of new (material) philology, and embodied approaches, that is, studying texts and manuscripts as intrinsically linked to the social contexts in which they were employed. John C. Reeves's "Future Trends for the Study of Jewish Pseudepigrapha: Two Recommendations," finally, is concerned with the *longue durée* transmission of pseudepigraphal writings. He encourages more studies of their reception, as well as of their continuing transmission and transformation, among Jewish, Christian, Manichean, and Muslim communities.

Celebrating Our Beginnings—Embracing the Future

It is with a deep sense of gratitude that the volume editors remember the pioneering scholars of the Pseudepigrapha Project, who launched what was to become one of the longest continuing program units at the Society of Biblical Literature. Some of these scholars are here with us today to celebrate half a century of pseudepigrapha research at the Society, while others have passed on. It is to all scholars of the Pseudepigrapha Project—with their unsurpassed vision, formidable scholarship, and great enthusiasm—that we dedicate this volume.

2

The Pseudepigrapha Project at the Society of Biblical Literature, 1969–1971

Matthias Henze

Changes at the Society of Biblical Literature in the 1960s

The formation of what during the early years of its existence was called the Pseudepigrapha Project coincided with and was largely made possible by a general restructuring of the Society of Biblical Literature in the late 1960s. Throughout the 1950s and early 1960s, the Annual Meetings of the Society of Biblical Literature were fairly small gatherings of senior scholars, mostly from the Northeast of the United States. In his centennial history of the Society, Ernest W. Saunders offers this description of the meetings.

> By and large the program forms and the organizational structure had made few departures from the form fixed in the earliest period. It was essentially an east coast establishment based in New York City consisting of a small staff of officers and a regional attendance at the meetings. Members convened in a forum style to present the results of solo research projects and to enjoy a pleasant comradeship on a first-name basis. In substance it was an amplified faculty club, benevolently presided over by a cadre of senior and highly respected scholars who enjoyed proprietary rights among awed but ambitious junior colleagues.[1]

I would like to thank Andrew D. Scrimgeour, dean of libraries emeritus at Drew University and Society of Biblical Literature archivist, and the library staff at Drew University, in particular Cassie Brand, for helping me access the Society of Biblical Literature archive. I also thank Randall D. Chesnutt, Liv Ingeborg Lied, and George W. E. Nickelsburg for reading drafts of this article.

1. Ernest W. Saunders, *Searching the Scriptures: A History of the Society of Biblical Literature, 1880–1980*, BSNA 8 (Chico, CA: Scholars Press, 1982), 41.

It was clear that the Society needed to change. One reason for the need to change was the rapid growth in membership. By 1968, the Society had 2,718 members, including many young and rising scholars.[2] Another reason was a general shift in higher education in North America, particularly in the study of religion in colleges and universities, both private and public. In 1963 the National Association of Biblical Instructors (NABI), originally founded in 1909 as the Association of Biblical Instructors in American Colleges and Secondary Schools, renamed itself the American Academy of Religion (AAR). In the 1960s the study of religion took on new momentum, leading, inter alia, to a rapid growth in departments of religious studies all over North America.[3]

In 1967, a committee of Society of Biblical Literature council members under the leadership of Robert W. Funk was established to consider changes to the constitution and by-laws of the Society.[4] Initially the committee consisted of Brevard S. Childs, Robert A. Kraft, and Norman E. Wagner, though later, Walter J. Harrelson and Bernhard W. Anderson joined. The committee's initial charge was modest, to consider some minor revisions in the Society's constitution, but their actual recommendations, presented at the 1968 Berkeley meeting, were far-reaching. Kraft and Funk were the driving forces behind the call for more substantive changes to the Society.[5]

The main turning point finally came in 1969 at the Toronto meeting, when the Society adopted a new constitution.[6] Three changes in particular

---

2. Saunders, *Searching the Scriptures*, 59.

3. The Religion Department at Rice University in Houston, Texas, my academic home, was founded in 1968.

4. Robert W. Funk played many important roles in the Society's transformation; now see Andrew D. Scrimgeour, ed., *Evaluating the Legacy of Robert W. Funk: Reforming the Scholarly Model*, BSNA 28 (Atlanta: SBL Press, 2018).

5. Saunders, *Searching the Scriptures*, 58–59, notes: "While there was resistance to radical change in the Council, it was not a standoff between the old guard and the young Turks, as they were dubbed. Had it not been for the support of members like Herbert G. May, Harry M. Orlinsky, and Frank W. Beare, who recognized that change was necessary and inevitable, the revisions would never have been accomplished. The document approved by the Council in 1968 went through further amendment by the Council and the Society and was finally adopted at the Toronto meeting in 1969."

6. The new constitution and by-laws were adopted on November 18, 1969 and amended on October 26, 1970. I am grateful to John F. Kutsko, executive director of the Society of Biblical Literature, for sending me a copy of the 1969 constitution.

stand out. First, articles iii and iv of the constitution impose term limits on all officers and council members of the Society and introduce a clear structure by which the leaders of the Society rotate. The Society president, for example, is not eligible for reelection, and the nine council members are elected to three-year terms. A consequence of these new policies was that the Society became much more transparent and inclusive in its organization, and the number of members who were actively involved in the Society's leadership grew. As Gene Tucker observes, "Far more persons are in active leadership positions today [2010] than actually attended the meetings before 1969."[7]

Second, article v of the new constitution lays down the rules for the establishment of various editorial boards, most significantly for our purpose that of the newly formed Committee on Research and Publications.[8] The Society thus came to see the publication of scholarship as one of its primary tasks. For example, in 1974 Scholars Press was founded by a consortium of learned societies, including the Society of Biblical Literature, the American Academy of Religion, the American Schools of Oriental Research, and others, again under the leadership of Funk, professor of religion at the University of Montana in Missoula, Montana. It may be indicative of the spirit of change that the press initially operated out of the University of Montana, where Funk was teaching, and not out of a university in the Northeast. As we will see below, for Harrelson, the father of the Pseudepigrapha Project, the publication of a new edition of the Old Testament pseudepigrapha, for which he sought the endorsement of the Society's Committee on Research and Publications, was the main reason why he convened the Pseudepigrapha Breakfast meetings in the first place. Thus, the Society's new self-understanding and the primary motivation for putting together a group of scholars working on the pseudepigrapha were

---

7. Gene M. Tucker, "The Modern (and Postmodern?) Society of Biblical Literature: Institutions and Scholarship," in *Foster Biblical Scholarship: Essays in Honor of Kent Harold Richards*, ed. Frank Ritchell Ames and Charles William Miller, BSNA 24 (Atlanta: Society of Biblical Literature, 2010), 33.

8. The Committee on Research and Publication consists of a chairman, three members elected by Council, an executive secretary, a treasurer, a delegate to the American Council of Learned Societies, and two editors. I mention this here because in his proposal to form the first Pseudepigrapha unit steering committee and editorial committee, Walter Harrelson recommended similar term limits. See below, Walter Harrelson, "Report to the Pseudepigrapha Breakfast Meeting: SBL, 26 October 1970." SBL Archive.

closely aligned from the very beginning: their shared interest was in the publication of texts.

The third change that was initiated in 1969 concerned the reorganization and structure of the Annual Meetings of the Society of Biblical Literature. The 1969 meeting in Toronto included a presidential address by Frank W. Beare, two invited lectures (by Yigael Yadin on "The Temple Scroll—Illustrated" and by Claude Welch on "Schleiermacher, Hegel, and the Curriculum in Religion"), and an unprecedented 109 papers.[9] The papers were classified under ten categories: apocrypha and pseudepigrapha; biblical archaeology; Nag Hammadi Library; Old Testament and New Testament theology; Hebrew and Greek grammar; history of American biblical interpretation; literary criticism and biblical criticism; eastern Mediterranean history and religions; textual criticism; and Septuagint and cognate studies. Soon after the Toronto meeting, the structure of the Annual Meetings was further revised, and six distinct program units were introduced: *sections* (first introduced in 1970); *groups* (intended for the exploration of new areas of research and methodologies); *seminars* (intended for a five-year period of intensive research);[10] *consultations* (for the preliminary exploration of a topic that might turn into a section, group, or seminar); and *plenary sessions* (for guest lectures and distinguished speakers).[11] In brief, "the years 1969 to 1971 were years of ferment, innovation, and restructuring, setting the Society on a new course."[12] One of these new courses was the formation of the Pseudepigrapha Project.

The Pseudepigrapha Breakfasts in 1969 and 1970

In September 1969, Walter J. Harrelson, dean of the Divinity School at Vanderbilt, proposed to Funk, executive secretary of the Society from 1968 to 1973, to put together a breakfast meeting at the 1969 Annual Meeting in Toronto. The purpose of the meeting was to organize what Harrelson in his letter to Funk called "the Pseudepigrapha Project."[13] Funk responded

---

9. "Titles of Papers at 1969 SBL Meetings," *JBL* 89 (1970): 132–36.
10. In 1971 the Pseudepigrapha Project turned into the Pseudepigrapha Seminar.
11. Saunders, *Searching the Scriptures*, 59–60.
12. Saunders, *Searching the Scriptures*, 61.
13. Harrelson's letter to Funk is dated September 9, 1969. SBL Archive.

promptly and pledged his support.[14] On October 1, 1969, Harrelson sent another letter of invitation to a number of colleagues (the letter does not provide their names) and invited them to the first Pseudepigrapha Project breakfast at the upcoming Toronto meeting. The body of the letter read:

> Bob Funk and I have been in conversation and correspondence about plans tentatively drawn up some time ago to see if we might find a way to get some new critical editions of pseudepigraphic Old Testament writings published, along with cheap copies of translations of the most important of these documents for student use.
> Enclosed is a sketch of what I have in mind thus far.
> Such an undertaking would require wide collaboration among specialists, plus considerable time from an editor and an editorial committee, I suspect. Obviously, my present assignment and commitments disqualify me from doing more than see to test the need for the project and lend a hand in its development.
> Would you be willing to meet with a few of us to discuss the matter? We have scheduled such meeting in connection with the SBL annual meeting in Toronto in November. The SBL program lists the time and place, Royal York Hotel, Monday, November 17, at 7:45 a.m. Dutch treat![15]

The letter also included a two-page proposal in which Harrelson described his rationale for putting together the group. Initially, his goal was twofold: to publish new critical editions of "the major Old Testament pseudepigraphs" and to produce inexpensive English translations of these texts, with brief introductions and notes. Harrelson further wrote in his letter: "Members of the faculty of Vanderbilt University Divinity School wish to propose such a project to be carried on by an international team of scholars. We seek the counsel and sponsorship of the new Committee on Research and Publications of the Society of Biblical Literature in the launching and oversight of this project."

With regard to the first part of his proposal, the publication of separate volumes of new critical editions of the pseudepigrapha, Harrelson included in his letter a tentative, though ambitious, list of the following works.

---

14. Letter from Robert W. Funk to Walter Harrelson, dated September 29, 1969. SBL Archive.

15. Letter from Walter Harrelson to an unspecified group of colleagues, dated October 1, 1969. SBL Archive.

1. Works Related to the Pentateuch:
   a. Jubilees (Ethiopic, plus portions in Latin and Hebrew)
   b. 1 Enoch (Ethiopic, Greek, Latin)
   c. Testaments of the Twelve Patriarchs (Greek, Armenian, Slavonic, Hebrew)
   d. Adam and Eve (Armenian, Slavonic, plus Ethiopic, Greek, and Latin)
2. Works Related to the Prophets:
   a. Martyrdom of Isaiah (Greek, Ethiopic, Latin)
   b. 2 Baruch (Syriac, Greek)
   c. 3 Baruch (Greek)
3. Works Related to the Writings:
   a. 4 Ezra (Latin, Syriac, Ethiopic, Arabic)
   b. Odes of Solomon (Syriac)
   c. Psalms of Solomon (Greek, Syriac)

In addition, Harrelson proposed "a one-volume, inexpensive edition of the above works in English translation with introductions, brief notes, and bibliographies, for the use of students and the general reader." Harrelson's proposal ends with the following note.

> This brief sketch is prepared for consideration by the new Committee on Research and Publications of the Society of Biblical Literature. An earlier form of the proposal has been discussed by several scholars (Robert M. Grant, Morton Smith, Bruce M. Metzger) and by several potential publishers (University of Chicago Press and Abingdon Press). No effort has been made thus far to secure a firm commitment from a publisher.

According to James H. Charlesworth, the first Pseudepigrapha Breakfast, which Harrelson convened on November 17, 1969, in the Royal York Hotel in Toronto, Ontario, was attended by "over forty persons."[16] Unfortunately, no list of attendees survives.[17] The group spoke about the critical editions

---

16. James H. Charlesworth, "The Renaissance of Pseudepigrapha Studies: The SBL Pseudepigrapha Project," *JSJ* 2 (1971): 107.

17. Harrelson included in his letter of October 1, 1969, a list of scholars "interested in the project and of those who have indicated that they will be present for the breakfast." His list consists of eighteen names: Hans Dieter Betz, School of Theology at Claremont; James H. Charlesworth, Duke University; Kenneth W. Clark, Duke Divinity School; Rolf Knierim, School of Theology at Claremont; Loren Fisher, School of

that were being prepared at the time, including editions by Charlesworth of the Odes of Solomon, Daniel J. Harrington of Pseudo-Philo, Robert A. Kraft of the Paralipomena of Jeremiah, John L. Sharpe III of the Assumption of Moses, and Michael A. Knibb with Edward Ullendorff of 1 Enoch.[18] The group also put together an initial Pseudepigrapha unit steering committee. The committee was chaired by Harrelson and included Charlesworth, who later became the group's first secretary, Robert A. Kraft, Harry M. Orlinsky, Michael E. Stone, and John Strugnell.[19]

In a letter dated April 16, 1970, Harrelson wrote Charlesworth that he was still waiting for the minutes of the Toronto breakfast meeting taken

---

Theology at Claremont; Herbert B. Huffmon, Drew University; Bruce M. Metzger, Princeton Theological Seminary; James Muilenburg, San Francisco Theological Seminary; Harry Orlinsky, Hebrew Union College; Jesse B. Renninger, Muhlenberg College; Erroll F. Rhodes (no academic affiliation given); James A. Sanders, Union Theological Seminary; David M. Scholer, Gordon-Conwell Theological Seminary; John L. Sharpe III, Duke University; Morton Smith, Columbia University; William F. Stinespring, Duke Divinity School; Hagen A. K. Staack (spelled "Strack" by Harrelson), Muhlenberg College; and W. Sibley Towner, Yale Divinity School.

18. James H. Charlesworth, *The Odes of Solomon* (Oxford: Clarendon, 1973); Daniel J. Harrington, "Text and Biblical Text in Pseudo-Philo's Liber Antiquitatum Biblicarum" (PhD diss., Harvard University, 1969); Robert A. Kraft and Ann-Elizabeth Purintun, ed., *Paraleipomena Jeremiou*, TT 1 (Missoula, MT: Society of Biblical Literature, 1972); Sharpe never published his work on the Assumption of Moses; Michael A. Knibb, in consultation with Edward Ullendorff, *The Ethiopic Book of Enoch: A New Edition in the Light of the Aramaic Dead Sea Fragments*, 2 vols. (Oxford: Clarendon; New York: Oxford University Press, 1978).

19. This list is found in Charlesworth, "Renaissance of Pseudepigrapha Studies," 107–8. In his contribution to this volume, "Memories of the Society of Biblical Literature Pseudepigrapha Group, 1970–1982," Charlesworth provides a slightly different list of committee members: Walter Harrelson, Bruce M. Metzger, John Strugnell, Robert A. Kraft, and George W. MacRae. George W. MacRae was part of the group from the beginning.

The steering committee did not meet in between the first and the second Pseudepigrapha Breakfast in 1969 and 1970. In his report to the attendees of the second Pseudepigrapha Breakfast on October 26, 1970, Harrelson apologized to the group that the steering committee that was appointed in Toronto did not have a formal meeting, "due to my neglect and my absence on leave during the fall. I apologize to you and to the committee members for that. I have been in correspondence with some of the committee members and have been helped greatly by their counsel" (Harrelson, "Report to the Pseudepigrapha Breakfast Meeting: SBL, 26 October 1970").

by Victor Gold.[20] Harrelson also informed Charlesworth that he had appointed him to the position of first secretary of the Pseudepigrapha Project and expressed his hope that Charlesworth would accept the invitation.

> Bob Kraft has been at work. He showed me a report that he has done recently for the LXX Bulletin. I took the liberty of listing you as Secretary of our Project and hope that you don't object. You know what a job it is for me to keep on top of the things I'm engaged in, and I would greatly appreciate your letting that designation stand. When Victor gets the minutes to us, we should (you and I) get to work to carry further our gathering of data on projects like our own and should enlist the cooperation of other groups. I'll be in touch with you soon.[21]

In the summer of 1970, Harrelson and Charlesworth exchanged their ideas for a second Pseudepigrapha Breakfast, scheduled for October 26, 1970, at the New Yorker Hotel in New York, again in connection with the Annual Meeting. Harrelson asked Charlesworth to serve as chairman and expressed his hope that Sharpe would become secretary.[22]

The letters from these early years of the Pseudepigrapha Project radiate with enthusiasm and a spirit of adventure that motivated these pioneering scholars. For example, Harrelson noted in passing to Charlesworth, "By the way, I'm eager to see John Sharpe's edition of the Assumption of Moses. That's a document that I have been much interested in for years. One of my goals for the fall is to discover another copy of it, including the Assumption, in some language or other!"[23]

---

20. "We're waiting to get the minutes of our Toronto meeting that Victor Gold kindly took for us. Victor will be getting them out very soon. He's been snowed, as have many of us, I'm sure." In his published report of the meeting, Charlesworth, "Renaissance of Pseudepigrapha Studies," does not refer to Gold's minutes, and the SBL Archive does not appear to have a copy of the minutes, either.

21. Letter from Walter Harrelson to James H. Charlesworth, dated April 16, 1970. SBL Archive.

22. Letter from Walter Harrelson to James H. Charlesworth, dated July 6, 1970. SBL Archive. Charlesworth accepted the assignment and was chair for one year (1970–1971). From 1971 to 1973 Harrelson became chair again, and after his resignation in 1973 George W. E. Nickelsburg took over from 1973 to 1979 (see Nickelsburg's essay "The Pseudepigrapha at the Society of Biblical Literature: The Early Growth of a Group" in this volume).

23. Letter from Walter Harrelson to James H. Charlesworth, dated July 6, 1970. SBL Archive. Harrelson was passionate about the church in Ethiopia, began to travel

Harrelson continued to devote considerable attention to the Pseudepigrapha Project through the fall of 1970. He exchanged letters with James M. Robinson, chair of the Society's Committee on Research and Publication, to secure the committee's endorsement. Robinson showed great interest in the Pseudepigrapha Project and asked Harrelson for more details, including a list of members. He also prompted Harrelson to think more about forming a steering committee and an editorial board.

> Are there other persons, in addition to you and Charlesworth, that should be envisaged for a steering comm. for the Seminar? Would it be useful to have an editorial board, and if so would it be wise for it to be identical with the steering comm.? I am anxious that seminars not be merely discussion groups, and therefore think they should be closely related to publication projects.[24]

In his response, Harrelson mentioned that he had conversations about his publication projects with Hedley F. D. Sparks, Matthew Black, Karl Heinrich Rengstorf, and Robert M. Wilson, as well as with Brill Publishers. He also sought the endorsement of Robinson's committee for the publication of a major edition of the Old Testament pseudepigrapha. Harrelson's timetable was ambitious:

> 1970: obtain the endorsement of the Society's Committee on Research and Publication and propose the project at the Pseudepigrapha Project at the next breakfast on October 26, 1970; 1971: put together an editorial and an advisory group by the Spring of 1971 and meet with an expanded group in Uppsala in connection with the meeting of the Society for Old Testament Study that year; and 1972: meet again with the editorial and advisory groups in Claremont, Cal., in connection with the Society's annual meeting in Los Angeles.

---

there, and worked on the preservation of Ethiopic manuscripts. In his contribution to this volume, "Pseudepigrapha at the Society of Biblical Literature," Nickelsburg points out that Harrelson continued to work on the biblical manuscripts from Ethiopia throughout the 1970s and 1980s and received about $400,000 in grant money from the National Endowment for the Humanities to microfilm the manuscripts. Note also a brief comment by Charlesworth in a letter to Harrelson dated June 9, 1970, "Congratulations on your fall trip to Sweden, Greece, Israel, and Ethiopia. Of course, you make us all envious."

24. Letter from James M. Robinson to Walter Harrelson, dated October 10, 1970. SBL Archive.

Finally, he mentioned to Robinson that he would be trying to raise funds for the project through the National Endowment for the Humanities to cover the expenses incurred by the meetings and contributing authors.[25]

In addition to his letter to Robinson, Harrelson also wrote a detailed, four-page report, titled "Report to the Pseudepigrapha Breakfast Meeting: SBL, 26 October 1970," dated October 19, 1970, one week prior to the second Pseudepigrapha Breakfast meeting.[26] The report was intended to provide the attendees of the breakfast with a quick overview of the work currently undertaken by colleagues in the field who were not (yet) formally affiliated with the Pseudepigrapha Project and to inform them of Harrelson's publication plans. The document has four parts. In the first part, Harrelson proposed three interrelated publication projects. First, he suggested that the Pseudepigrapha Project join forces with Albert-Marie Denis of the Université Catholique de Louvain and Marinus de Jonge of Leiden University, who were working on the Greek Old Testament pseudepigrapha.[27] The chief contribution of the Pseudepigrapha Project to the work of Denis and de Jonge, Harrelson explained, was the publication of the most important Old Testament pseudepigrapha, "including (where feasible) photographs of the major manuscript or manuscripts, a critical edition based upon the best manuscript or manuscripts, an English translation, notes, and introduction."[28]

Harrelson went on to describe a second publication project, a critical, annotated bibliography of the Old Testament pseudepigrapha. The bibliography was to begin with a brief definition of the term *Old Testament Pseudepigrapha* and a list of general works, followed by a bibliography for each of these works, including an exact description of the manuscript evidence, a list of modern critical editions, a survey of the scholarly as well as "popular treatments," and finally a list of desiderata. To this Harrelson

---

25. Handwritten letter from Walter Harrelson to James M. Robinson, dated October 19, 1970. SBL Archive.

26. Harrelson, "Report to the Pseudepigrapha Breakfast Meeting: SBL, 26 October 1970."

27. Albert-Marie Denis and Marinus de Jonge, "The Greek Pseudepigrapha of the Old Testament," *NovT* 7 (1965): 319–28; Denis, *Introduction aux pseuépigraphes grecs d'Ancien Testament*, SVTP 1 (Leiden: Brill, 1970).

28. Harrelson, "Report to the Pseudepigrapha Breakfast Meeting: SBL, 26 October 1970." With his keen interest in the Ethiopic manuscripts (for which he traveled to Ethiopia) and his effort to assemble an international team of leading scholars, Harrelson was well ahead of his time.

added a third project, the publication of an inexpensive English translation of the pseudepigrapha, based on the critical editions mentioned above.

In an effort to provide some international context for these publication projects, Harrelson added in the second part of his report a list of books that had just appeared or were in the process of being published. He began with the first two volumes that had already come out in Brill's Pseudepigrapha Veteris Testamenti Graece series, Marinus de Jonge's Testament of the Twelve Patriarchs, published in 1964, and Sebastian P. Brock's Testament of Job and J.-C. Picard's Apocalypse of Baruch, published in one volume in 1967.[29] Harrelson also mentioned Marc Philonenko's edition of Joseph and Aseneth and Pierre-Maurice Bogaert's two-volume "splendid and detailed study" of 2 Baruch.[30] Since Denis and de Jonge had no plans to publish any pseudepigrapha in languages other than Greek, Harrelson assured the group that there was no conflict between Denis, de Jonge, and the Pseudepigrapha Project. Furthermore, Harrelson reported that he had been in touch with European scholars and publishers, among them Hedley F. D. Sparks at Oxford, Erling Hammershaimb at Aarhus, Karl-Heinrich Rengstorf at Münster, and Matthew Black and Robert M. Wilson, both at St. Andrews, to avoid any possible duplication or conflict.

In part 3 of his report, Harrelson turned his attention to the organization of the Pseudepigrapha Project. He was clearly motivated to move the project forward quickly ("I present the following recommendations for consideration and possible action today") and thus made six specific recommendations worth citing in full.

  1. Designation of a Steering Committee as follows, the members of which would be asked to serve for a 3-year term:
    Chairman: Walter Harrelson or some other member
    Vice Chairman: Robert A. Kraft
    Secretary: James H. Charlesworth
    Additional Members: Bruce Metzger, Harry Orlinsky, John Strugnell, George MacRae

---

29. Marinus de Jonge, *Testament of the Twelve Patriarchs: Greek*, PVTG 1 (Leiden: Brill, 1964); Sebastian P. Brock, *Testament of Job: Greek*, and J.-C. Picard, *Apocalypsis Baruchi: Graece*, PVTG 2 (Leiden: Brill, 1967).

30. Marc Philonenko, *Joseph et Aséneth*, StPB 13 (Leiden: Brill, 1968); Pierre-Maurice Bogaert, *Apocalypse de Baruch: Introduction, Traduction du Syriaque et Commentaire*, SC 144–145, 2 vols. (Paris: Cerf, 1969).

2. Designation of an Editorial Committee with the following officers to serve for 3-year terms, the additional members to be appointed on the basis of consultation with the Steering Committee and the SBL Comm. on Research and Pub.:
Chairman: Robert A. Kraft
Secretary: James H. Charlesworth

3. Recommendation to the SBL Comm. on Research and Publications that our project be approved as a continuing Seminar of SBL and that the organization and publication plans be endorsed.

4. Recommendation that the Steering Committee be charged to plan and conduct seminar meetings at annual sessions of SBL and be responsible to propose to the SBL Program Committee the inclusion of a section if the Program Committee so desires. If held, such seminars and sectional meetings should be scheduled at a time that will not badly conflict with seminars and sections devoted to related literatures and subjects.

5. Recommendation that the Steering Committee be authorized, in consultation with the Editorial Committee and the SBL Comm. on Research and Publications, to seek funds to underwrite the publication of a major edition of the OT Pseudepigrapha and the support of related studies and meetings.

6. Recommendation that the Steering and Editorial Committees, in consultation with the SBL Comm. on Research and Publications, be empowered to negotiate an arrangement with Professors Denis and De Jonge that would bring our publication of major editions of the Pseudepigrapha into relationship with the Denis-De Jonge publications. Should this ensue, an expanded Advisory Committee and Editorial Board of the Denis-De Jonge venture would need to be created, in collaboration with Denis and De Jonge.

In the fourth and final part of his report, Harrelson proposed a rather strict timeline.

1. A meeting of our Steering and Editorial Committees with Professors Denis and De Jonge, plus others whom they may wish to invite, by late summer 1971, to seek to make arrangements for the joint undertaking referred to above. It may be that a September 1971 meeting in Uppsala could be arranged, in connection with the meeting of the SOTS meeting planned for that time and place.

2. Another breakfast meeting and a session of the Seminar on the OT Pseudepigrapha to be planned for the annual meeting of the SBL on 28–31 October 1971 in Atlanta.

3. A second meeting of the Steering and Editorial Committees in California on August/September 1972 in connection with the Congress planned for that time and place.

Harrelson ended his report by expressing his hope that, at the breakfast meeting, the group would make concrete plans for the publication projects, including drawing up a list of potential editors, discuss the layout and format of the publications, "and then begin with two or three of the writings that badly need to appear in the new major editions." He was thinking in particular of the Assumption of Moses, Jubilees, and 4 Ezra. Finally, Harrelson expressed his hope that the National Endowment for the Humanities or the Ford Foundation might provide financial support.[31]

Unfortunately, there are no minutes of the second Pseudepigrapha Breakfast, which took place on October 26, 1970, in the New Yorker Hotel in New York, New York during the Annual Meeting. Charlesworth writes that thirty-three people were in attendance.[32] Harrelson went through his report; others reported on related publication projects, both finished and ongoing; and Harrelson proposed that George W. MacRae and Bruce M. Metzger be added to the original steering committee, which was approved unanimously. In a separate session on the previous day, five pseudepigrapha papers were read at the Annual Meeting: William F. Stinespring, "The Contribution of C. C. Torrey to Intertestamental Studies"; Anitra B. Kolenkow, "The Cloud and Water Vision and Interpretation of II Baruch 53, 56–74"; John L. Sharpe, "The Apocalypse of Moses"; John Priest, "Wisdom in I Enoch"; and W. D. Davies, "The Concept of Land in the Apocrypha and Pseudepigrapha."

With the two Pseudepigrapha Breakfasts at the Society's Annual Meetings in 1969 and 1970, Harrelson laid a solid foundation for the study of the Old Testament pseudepigrapha at the Society of Biblical Literature to flourish.

---

31. Harrelson, "Report to the Pseudepigrapha Breakfast Meeting: SBL, 26 October 1970."

32. Charlesworth, "Renaissance of Pseudepigrapha Studies," 108.

Two Meetings of the Pseudepigrapha Seminar Steering Committee in 1971

The response from the Society to Harrelson's initiative was very positive. The Society embraced Harrelson's double emphasis on microfilming biblical manuscripts in Ethiopia and on producing new editions and translations of the Old Testament pseudepigrapha.

In a letter written by Funk, executive secretary of the Society, to Frederick Burkhardt, president of the American Council of Learned Societies, dated March 5, 1971, Funk pledged his support for Harrelson's endeavors to return to Ethiopia to look for more manuscripts.

> Dear President Burkhardt:
>
> The Pseudepigrapha Seminar and Research Project of the Society of Biblical Literature, chaired by Walter Harrelson, has been reviewed and approved by the Research and Publication Committee, of which Professor James M. Robinson is chairman. We have great hopes that this cooperative effort will produce significant results in an area to which little attention has been given in recent years.
>
> We are especially interested in the proposal to photograph unpublished manuscripts in Ethiopia. This proposal is a solid and promising first step in the long process of making inaccessible and virtually unknown materials available to the scholarly community.
>
> On behalf of the Society, I am pleased to endorse Walter Harrelson's request for assistance to enable him to return to Ethiopia, 21–28 March 1971, in order to make arrangements for the microfilming program. Any help you can give him will be most appreciated.[33]

In 1971, the Pseudepigrapha Project steering committee met twice. The first meeting took place on February 7, in the Hotel Baltimore in New York, New York, the first Pseudepigrapha unit meeting outside of the national Society of Biblical Literature conventions.[34] Six members were present: Harrelson, Charlesworth, MacRae, Kraft, Orlinsky, and Metzger. Following Harrel-

---

33. Letter from Robert W. Funk to Frederick Burkhardt, dated March 5, 1971. SBL Archive.

34. Charlesworth, "Renaissance of Pseudepigrapha Studies," 109–11; and James H. Charlesworth, "Minutes of the Pseudepigrapha Project Steering Committee." SBL Archive.

son's suggestion, the group decided for the next meeting later that year to address three topics: Charlesworth would present on ongoing work on the pseudepigrapha; Harrelson would offer some reflections on methodological problems associated with working on the pseudepigrapha; and Kraft would present on his ongoing work on the Paralipomena of Jeremiah.[35] After a discussion about an inquiry from Brill whether the seminar would recommend an English translation of Denis's *Introduction aux Pseudépigraphes grecs de l'Ancient Testament*, the group decided that such a translation would be appreciated by many readers.[36] Denis had suggested to the seminar to start a new series, Pseudepigrapha Veteris Testamenti Orientalia, that would contain manuscripts in Arabic, Armenian, Coptic, Ethiopic, Georgian, Hebrew, Latin, Rumanian, Slavonic, and Syriac, a proposal that was welcomed. Finally, Harrelson reported to the group about his plans to return to Ethiopia to microfilm more manuscripts in the monasteries.[37]

The steering committee met again on October 31, 1971, in the Regency Hyatt House in Atlanta, Georgia, during the Society's Annual Meeting.[38] Present were Charlesworth, Harrelson, Kraft, MacRae, Stone,

---

35. See the overview below, "The Pseudepigrapha Sessions at the Annual Meetings of the Society of Biblical Literature, 1970–2018."

36. Denis, *Introduction aux Pseudépigraphes grecs de l'Ancien Testament*. This proved to be controversial. In a letter to Walter Harrelson, John Strugnell, who was unable to attend the meeting of the steering committee, wrote that he would rather not see Denis's *Introduction* translated into English because of its "shortcomings" and suggested instead that the Seminar begin with "a Bibliography, done Book by Book, on our works each chapter by a man working on that work (e.g. Sharpe on Apoc. Mos., Harrington on Pseudo-Philo, Stone on IV Ezra, Nickelsburg on I Enoch, etc.—other names will come to mind)." Letter from John Strugnell to Walter Harrelson, dated June 15, 1971. Archive Michael E. Stone. In an undated note, James Charlesworth responded to, and agreed with, Strugnell's reservations. Archive Michael E. Stone. I thank Michael E. Stone for giving me access to his personal archive.

37. In 1971, plans for a collaboration between Albert-Marie Denis and Marinus de Jonge, on the one hand, and the members of the Pseudepigrapha Seminar, on the other, looked promising. In a letter to the members of the Seminar, dated March 27, 1971, Denis and de Jonge proposed three specific projects: an introduction, a critical edition of Greek texts, and concordances of the Greek and Latin pseudepigrapha. Letter from Albert-Marie Denis and Marinus de Jonge "A Messieurs les membres du Comité de Direction pour l'étude des Pseudépigraphes d'Ancien Testament," dated March 27, 1971. Archive of Michael E. Stone.

38. "Steering Committee Meeting. October 31, 1971. Agenda," and James H. Charlesworth, "Minutes of the Pseudepigrapha Project Steering Committee.

and Strugnell (Orlinsky and Metzger sent their apologies). The committee agreed to invite George W. E. Nickelsburg to join the steering committee. It was also decided to move ahead with the publication of a number of annotated bibliographies and to begin with six books: 4 Ezra (Michael E. Stone); Assumption of Moses (John L. Sharpe); Odes of Solomon (James H. Charlesworth); 1 Enoch (George W. E. Nickelsburg); Paraleipomena of Jeremiah (Ann-Elizabeth Purintun); and Ezekiel the Tragedian (John Strugnell). Independently, Stone and Strugnell proposed the publication of texts not found in R. H. Charles's *Apocrypha and Pseudepigrapha*.[39] Their proposal was to follow the format adopted in the Loeb Classical Library, with the edition of the text and the English translation on facing pages. The committee appointed an editorial board, consisting of Kraft, Nickelsburg, MacRae, Stone, and Strugnell, that was asked to present at the next meeting a list of works that could easily be produced. That meeting was set for January 23, 1972, in New Haven, Connecticut.

The Pseudepigrapha Seminar in the 1970s

The year 1971 marked a turning point for the Pseudepigrapha unit at the Society of Biblical Literature.[40] The Pseudepigrapha Project was renamed and became the Pseudepigrapha Seminar, before, in 1973, it became the Pseudepigrapha Group.[41] There were regular seminar sessions at the Annual Meetings (see the overview below). Harrelson had prepared the ground for the study of the pseudepigrapha at the Society of Biblical Literature to take off. He had established close ties between the Pseudepigrapha Project and the Society, particularly with the Committee on Research and Publication and the executive secretary, Funk. The members of the Pseudepigrapha Seminar steering committee and of

---

Regency Hyatt House. Atlanta, Georgia. October 31, 1971." Both in the archive of Michael E. Stone.

39. R. H. Charles, *The Apocrypha and Pseudepigrapha of the Old Testament*, 2 vols. (Oxford: Clarendon, 1913).

40. For descriptions of the various activities, see the essays by Michael E. Stone, James H. Charlesworth, and George W. E. Nickelsburg in this volume.

41. In his "Minutes of Pseudepigrapha Breakfast in Palmer House in Chicago, IL, on November 11, 1973," dated February 7, 1974, James H. Charlesworth wrote, "Walter Harrelson received due acclamation for his organization of the Pseudepigrapha Project, now called the Pseudepigrapha Group, and his leadership since 1969." Archive of Michael E. Stone.

the editorial committee were among the leading international scholars of the day, and only a short while later in the 1970s other members joined, including John J. Collins, Daniel J. Harrington, James C. VanderKam, and Martha Himmelfarb, the first woman to chair the Pseudepigrapha Seminar (1985–1988). In a collaborative spirit, Harrelson had begun from the very beginning to establish ties between the Pseudepigrapha Project and other colleagues in North America and abroad, particularly with Denis and de Jonge in Europe, but also with scholars who were working out of Addis Ababa, Ethiopia.[42]

The Pseudepigrapha Breakfasts at the Annual Meetings continued in the 1970s. There was obvious enthusiasm among the members of the Pseudepigrapha Seminar, and they wasted no time in getting to work. The main emphasis in the 1970s was on the publication of little-known texts. The first two volumes in the new Society of Biblical Literature Texts and Translation: Pseudepigrapha Series, with Kraft as series editor, came out in 1972, publishing texts that were discussed in the group's annual sessions.[43] That same year the Society initiated a new series, Septuagint and Cognate Studies, for which Kraft edited the first two volumes that contained the papers of the sessions of that year on the Greek Bible and the pseudepigrapha. Subsequently, volumes in the series appeared under the editorship of Orlinsky (Septuagint) and Nickelsburg (Cognate Studies). Four of the latter volumes contained papers presented in the annual sessions of the Pseudepigrapha Group (see below, appendix).[44] Charlesworth, the Pseudepigrapha Project's first secretary, continued to write about the progress of the Seminar. He published a series of articles, and

---

42. Charlesworth recorded in the minutes of the October 31, 1971, steering committee meeting, "Harrelson reported on the virtual certainty of receiving funds for the Ethiopia Project, and that Professors Sergew Hable Selassie and Taddesse Tamrat, both in Addis Ababa, are now heading the team in Ethiopia."

43. Texts and Translations came out of a proposal to publish the pseudepigrapha in single fasicles of texts and translations that would eventually be bound into one or two volumes. The proposal was worked out by Michael E. Stone and John Strugnell. Kraft and Purintun, *Paraleipomena Jeremiou*; Michael E. Stone, *Testament of Abraham, the Greek Recensions*, TT 2 (Missoula, MT: Society of Biblical Literature, 1972).

44. George W. E. Nickelsburg, ed., *Studies on the Testament of Moses*, SCS 4 (Cambridge, MA: Society of Biblical Literature, 1973); Nickelsburg, *Studies on the Testament of Joseph*, SCS 5 (Missoula, MT: Scholars Press, 1975); Nickelsburg, *Studies on the Testament of Abraham*, SCS 6 (Missoula, MT: Scholars Press, 1976).

he also produced the Pseudepigrapha Newsletter that included the call for papers to be read at the Annual Meetings.[45]

It would be difficult to overestimate the significance the Pseudepigrapha Project and its subsequent formations has had on the modern study of early Jewish literature. The vision, diligence, and expertise of these pioneering scholars has forever changed the ways in which we think about and read the pseudepigrapha. The collaborative spirit of these scholars is exemplary, as is their attention to the sources and the desire to make Israel's forgotten texts accessible to a broader audience. With their concern for the manuscripts and for the methodological issues associated with reading the pseudepigrapha, they were far ahead of their time. Such focused attention was clearly needed—and still is needed today—to move the pseudepigrapha out of the shadows of the apocrypha and the Hebrew Bible. Adventurous and determined, the scholars of the Pseudepigrapha Project laid a solid foundation for all future study of the pseudepigrapha at the Society of Biblical Literature.

Appendix 1: Chairs of the Pseudepigrapha Units at the Society of Biblical Literature, 1969–2018

The designation of the Pseudepigrapha unit changed over time, though the exact demarcations are difficult to reconstruct. The dates given in the list below are based on Annual Meeting years (as opposed to calendar or academic years).

1969–1970: Pseudepigrapha Project
1971–1972: Pseudepigrapha Seminar
1973–1977: Pseudepigrapha Group
1978–1996: A Pseudepigrapha Group and Pseudepigrapha Section coexisted.

---

45. James H. Charlesworth, "Some Reflections on Present Work on the Pseudepigrapha," *Society of Biblical Literature 2001 Seminar Paper*, 2 vols., SBLSP 40 (Missoula, MT: Society of Biblical Literature), 1:229–37; Charlesworth, "A History of Pseudepigraphal Research: The Re-emerging Importance of the Pseudepigrapha," *ANRW* 19.1:54–88; Charlesworth, "Reflections on the SNTS Pseudepigrapha Seminar at Duke on the Testament of the Twelve Patriarchs," *NTS* 23 (1976–1977): 296–304; Charlesworth, "The SNTS Pseudepigrapha Seminars at Tübingen and Paris on the Books of Enoch," *NTS* 25 (1978–1979): 315–23.

1996–1998: Pseudepigrapha Group
1999–today: Pseudepigrapha Section

1969–1970: Walter Harrelson, Vanderbilt Divinity School, convenes the first and second Pseudepigrapha Project Breakfast.
1971–1973: Walter Harrelson, Vanderbilt Divinity School, chair of the Pseudepigrapha Seminar
1973–1979: George W. E. Nickelsburg, University of Iowa, chair of the Pseudepigrapha Group
1979–1980: John J. Collins, De Paul University, and George W. E. Nickelsburg, University of Iowa, cochairs of the Pseudepigrapha Group
1981–1985: John J. Collins, De Paul University, chair of the Pseudepigrapha Group
1981–1984: James C. VanderKam, North Carolina State University, chair of the Pseudepigrapha Section
1985–1988: Martha Himmelfarb, Princeton University, chair of the Pseudepigrapha Section
1985–1989: James C. VanderKam, North Carolina State University, chair of the Pseudepigrapha Group
1989–1995: James R. Mueller, University of Florida, chair of the Pseudepigrapha Section
1989–1995: William Adler, North Carolina State University, chair of the Pseudepigrapha Group
1995–1998: Theodore A. Bergren, University of Richmond, and Randall D. Chesnutt, Pepperdine University, cochairs of the Pseudepigrapha Group
1998–2001: Theodore A. Bergren, University of Richmond, and Randall D. Chesnutt, Pepperdine University, cochairs of the Pseudepigrapha Section
2001–2003: Randall D. Chesnutt, Pepperdine University, and John C. Reeves, University of North Carolina, Charlotte, cochairs of the Pseudepigrapha Section
2003–2009: John C. Reeves, University of North Carolina, Charlotte, and John R. Levison, Seattle Pacific University, cochairs of the Pseudepigrapha Section
2009–2011: Hindy Najman, University of Toronto and Yale University, and Judith H. Newman, University of Toronto, cochairs of the Pseudepigrapha Section

2011–2017: Matthias Henze, Rice University, and Liv Ingeborg Lied, Norwegian School of Theology, cochairs of the Pseudepigrapha Section
2017–present: Kelley Coblentz-Bautch, St. Edward's University, and Jacques van Ruiten, University of Groningen, cochairs of the Pseudepigrapha Section

> Appendix 2: The Pseudepigrapha at the Annual Meetings of the Society of Biblical Literature, 1970–2018

1969   November 16–19; Royal York Hotel, Toronto, Canada
The first Pseudepigrapha Breakfast, convened by Walter Harrelson.

1970   October 22–27; Hotel New Yorker, New York, New York
The second Pseudepigrapha Breakfast, convened by Walter Harrelson.
Apocrypha and Pseudepigrapha. Session. Five papers: W. F. Stinespring; Anitra Bingham Kolenkow; John L. Sharpe III; John Priest; W. D. Davies.

1971   October 28–31; Regency Hyatt House, Atlanta, Georgia
Pseudepigrapha Seminar. Session 1. Three reports: James H. Charlesworth; Walter Harrelson; Robert A. Kraft.
Pseudepigrapha Seminar. Session 2. Two papers: George W. E. Nickelsburg; Michael E. Stone.

1972   September 1–5; Century Plaza Hotel, Los Angeles, California
Pseudepigrapha Seminar. Session 1. Symposium: The Testament of Abraham and Related Problems. Brief reports on "The Testament of Abraham in Recent and Forthcoming Studies": Marinus de Jonge; J. Smit Sibinga; Robert A. Kraft. Papers: Daniel J. Harrington; R. B. Ward; George W. E. Nickelsburg; Anitra Bingham Kolenkow. Respondent: J. Smit Sibinga, University of Amsterdam.
Pseudepigrapha Seminar. Session 2. Three papers: Albert-Marie Denis; Daniel J. Harrington; Robert B. Wright.

1973   November 8–11; The Palmer House, Chicago, Illinois
Pseudepigrapha Group. Sessions 1 and 2. Symposium: The Testament of Moses and Related Materials. Twelve papers: Daniel J. Harrington; Anitra Bingham Kolenkow; Paul D. Hanson; John J. Collins; Jonathan A. Goldstein; David M. Rhoads; Ralph W. Klein; David L. Tiede; Sheldon Isenberg; James D. Purvis; Harold

W. Attridge; Michael E. Stone. Respondent: George W. MacRae, Harvard Divinity School.
Pseudepigrapha Group. Session 3. Two papers: John G. Gammie; Daniel J. Harrington.

1974 October 24–27; The Washington Hilton, Washington DC
Pseudepigrapha Group. Symposium: The Testament of Job. Two papers: John J. Collins; Howard C. Kee. Respondent: Robert A. Kraft, University of Pennsylvania.

1975 October 30–November 2; Palmer House, Chicago, Illinois
Pseudepigrapha Group. Symposium: The Testament of Joseph and Related Joseph Traditions. Ten papers: Richard I. Pervo; Walter J. Harrelson; Anitra Bingham Kolenkow; Harm W. Hollander; Raymond A. Martin; Edgar W. Smith; Daniel J. Harrington; Barbara Geller; James D. Purvis; Michael E. Stone.

1976 October 28–31; Stouffer's Riverfront Towers, St. Louis, Missouri
Pseudepigrapha Group. Symposium: Perspectives on Joseph and Aseneth. Five papers: Edgar W. Smith; Richard I. Pervo; Jonathan Z. Smith; Howard C. Kee; Gary Vikan.

1977 December 28–31; San Francisco Hilton, San Francisco, California
Pseudepigrapha Group and Nag Hammadi. Symposium: Sethian Traditions in Judaism, Gnosticism, and the Chronographers. Four Papers: Anitra Bingham Kolenkow; William Adler; George W. MacRae; Birger A. Pearson.
Pseudepigrapha Group. Session.[46]

1978 November 18–21; Marriott Hotel, Monteleone Hotel, New Orleans, Louisiana
Pseudepigrapha Section. Session 1. Two papers: John J. Collins; Daniel J. Harrington.
Pseudepigrapha Group. Session 2. Symposium: The Enochic Book of the Watchers and Early Traditions about the Figure of Enoch. Four papers: Paul D. Hanson; George W. E. Nickelsburg; John J. Collins; Devorah Dimant.

1979 November 15–18; New York Statler Hotel, New York, New York

---

46. In a handwritten note, dated 27 November 2001, George W. E. Nickelsburg wrote Randall D. Chesnutt that there was a second session that year that is not included in the program.

Pseudepigrapha Group. Session 1. Symposium: Profiles of the Righteous Person. Four papers: Burton L. Mack; Robert A. Kraft; Henry Fischel; Michael Morgan.
Pseudepigrapha Group. Session 2. Symposium: Profiles of the Righteous Person. Six papers: Walter Harrelson; James C. VanderKam; John J. Collins; Dennis Berman; David Satran; Reuven Kimelman.

1980 November 5-9; Dallas, Texas
Pseudepigrapha Group. Symposium: Ideal Figures in Ancient Judaism: Profiles and Paradigms. Eleven papers: James C. VanderKam; John J. Collins; Gene L. Davenport; Anders Hultgard; Daniel J. Harrington; Susan Niditch; Sean Freyne; David Satran; Robert Doran; George W. E. Nickelsburg; James H. Charlesworth.

1981 December 19-22; San Francisco Hilton & Tower; San Francisco, California
Pseudepigrapha Group. Theme: 4 Ezra. Seven papers: Lester L. Grabbe; Wolfgang Harnisch; Howard Clark Kee; A. F. J. Klijn; André LaCocque; James R. Mueller; Pieter de Villiers.
Pseudepigrapha Section. Three papers: Martha Himmelfarb; Stephen E. Robinson; William Adler.

1982 December 19-22; The New York Hilton, New York, New York
Pseudepigrapha Section. Three papers: John R. Levison; Robert R. Hann; Carol Newsom.
Pseudepigrapha Group. Theme: Jewish Reactions to the Destruction of the Temple in 70 C.E. Eight papers: Alan J. Avery-Peck; Shaye Cohen; Anthony J. Saldarini; Walter Harrelson; André LaCocque; Anitra Bingham Kolenkow; Gwen Sayler; James R. Mueller.

1983 December 19-22; Loews Anatole Hotel, Dallas, Texas
Pseudepigrapha Group. Theme: Social Setting in the Enoch Literature. Six papers: Stephen B. Reid; Ephraim Isaac; Ted Lutz; James C. VanderKam; David Suter; George W. E. Nickelsburg. Respondent: Howard C. Kee, Boston University.
Pseudepigrapha Section. Four papers: Richard B. Vinson; John Kampen; Ronald A. Pascale; John C. Endres.

1984 December 8-11; Palmer House, Chicago, Illinois
Pseudepigrapha Group. Panel: *The Old Testament Pseudepigrapha*, ed. James H. Charlesworth. Panelists: James H. Charlesworth; Robert A. Kraft; Ross Kraemer; George W. E. Nickelsburg; James C. VanderKam.

Pseudepigrapha Section. Four papers: H. Dixon Slingerland; G. Tom Milazzo; Randall D. Chesnutt; R. Theodore Lutz.

1985 November 23–26; The Anaheim Hilton & Towers, Anaheim, California
Pseudepigrapha Group. Theme: The Temple Scroll and Its Relation to the Book of Jubilees. Five papers: James H. Charlesworth; Jacob Milgrom; Ben Zion Wacholder; Joseph Baumgarten; Lawrence H. Schiffman. Respondents: John Strugnell, Harvard University, and Phillip R. Callaway, Emory University.
Pseudepigrapha Section. Three papers: G. Tom Milazzo; William Adler; Frederic Murphy.

1986 November 22–25; Atlanta, Georgia
Pseudepigrapha Section. Six papers: Robert Doran; Randall D. Chesnutt; Frederick J. Murphy; Theodore Bergren; Benjamin G. Wright III; James R. Mueller. *Qumran Section and Pseudepigrapha Group.* Theme: Qumran Origins. Six papers: George W. E. Nickelsburg; Philip R. Davies; Jerome Murphy-O'Connor; John J. Collins; John C. Trever; Michael E. Stone. Respondents: Robert Doran, Amherst College, and John Kampen, Payne Theological Seminary.

1987 December 5–8; Boston, Massachusetts
Pseudepigrapha Section. Six papers: John R. Levison; Betsy Halpern Amaru; Gerbern S. Oegema; Daniel Merkur; Frederick Wisse; Stanley C. Pigué.
Early Christian Apocalyptic Seminar and Pseudepigrapha Group. Theme: Ascents to Heaven. Three papers: Martha Himmelfarb; James R. Mueller; David J. Halperin. Respondent: Carol Newsom, Emory University.
Panel: James D. Tabor, *Things Unutterable: Paul's Ascent to Paradise in Its Greco-Roman, Judaic, and Early Christian Contexts.* Panelists: James D. Tabor and Alan F. Segal.

1988 November 19–22; Chicago, Illinois
Pseudepigrapha Group. Six papers: Carey A. Moore; Irene Nowell; Paul Deselaers; Norman R. Petersen; William Soll; George W. E. Nickelsburg. Respondents: Robert Doran, Amherst College, and John Strugnell, Harvard University.
Pseudepigrapha Section. Six papers: Betsy Halpern-Amaru; David T. M. Frankfurter; Robert G. Hall; David P. Moesner; Gerbern S. Oegema; Michael E. Stone.

1989 November 18–21; Anaheim, California
Pseudepigrapha Group. Theme: The Book of Judith. Six papers: Adolfo D. Roitman; Toni Craven; Amy-Jill Levine; Sidnie Ann White; Nira Stone; Carey A. Moore. Respondents: George W. E. Nickelsburg, University of Iowa, and Richard I. Pervo, Seabury-Western Theological Seminary.
Pseudepigrapha Section. Six papers: J. Edward Wright; G. Tom Milazzo; L. M. Day; Randall D. Chesnutt; Gerbern S. Oegema; Theodore A. Bergren.

1990 November 17–20; New Orleans, Louisiana
Pseudepigrapha Section. Five papers: Patrick A. Tiller; Loren T. Stuckenbruck; Amy-Jill Levine; Adolfo D. Roltman; Albert Pietersma.
Pseudepigrapha Group. Panel: The Pseudepigrapha in Jewish/Christian/Manichean Transmission. Panelists: Martha Himmelfarb; Robert A. Kraft; John C. Reeves; David Satran; Michael E. Stone.

1991 November 23–26; Kansas City, Missouri
Pseudepigrapha Section. Four papers: Jonathan A. Draper; J. Edward Wright; David M. Freedholm; Elaine Pagels.
Pseudepigrapha Group. Theme: The Pseudepigrapha in Early Christianity. Three papers: Theodore A. Bergren; David Bundy; Rochus Zuurmond.
Panel: William Adler, *Time Immemorial: Archaic History and Its Sources in Christian Chronography from Julius Africanus to George Syncellus.* Panelists: Harold W. Attridge; George W. E. Nickelsburg; Gregory E. Sterling. Respondent: William Adler, North Carolina State University.

1992 November 21–24; San Francisco, California
Pseudepigrapha Section. Five papers: Randal A. Argall; James E. Bowley; Lawrence E. Frizzell; Lewis John Eron; J. Christian Wilson.
Intertextuality in Christian Apocrypha Seminar and Pseudepigrapha Group. Theme: "Intertextuality" in the Jewish Pseudepigrapha. Four papers: Devorah Dimant; Robert Hall; Carl R. Holladay; John C. Reeves. Respondents: James R. Mueller; Martha Himmelfarb; Philip Sellew; Patrick A. Tiller.

1993 November 20–23; Washington, DC

2. The Pseudepigrapha Project at the SBL, 1969–1971   35

Pseudepigrapha Section. Five papers: Theodore A. Bergren; J. Edward Wright; Gabriele Boccaccini; Susan Doty; Jan Willem van Henten.
Pseudepigrapha Group. Panel: The Enoch Literature in Early Christianity. Panelists: James C. VanderKam; Robert A. Kraft; George W. E. Nickelsburg; Jay C. Treat.

1994 November 19–22; Chicago, Illinois
Pseudepigrapha Section. Session 1. Five papers: Daniel C. Harlow; Robert Gnuse; Gabriele Boccaccini; J. Christian Wilson; G. Tom Milazzo.
Pseudepigrapha Section. Session 2. Five papers: Gideon Bohak; James E. Bowley; Benjamin G. Wright III; Sidnie A. White Crawford; Harry F. van Rooy.
Pseudepigrapha Group. Theme: Adam and Eve Literature. Four papers: Jeffrey A. Trumbower; Corrine L. Patton; Christiana de Groot van Houten; Gary A. Anderson. Respondent: Steven D. Fraade, Yale University.

1995 November 18–21; Philadelphia, Pennsylvania
Pseudepigrapha Section. Four papers: Theodore A. Bergren; Kenneth E. Pomykala; Cana Werman; John J. Collins.
Pseudepigrapha Group. Panel: The Jewish Pseudepigrapha in Egyptian Christianity. Panelists: William Adler; David Brakke; David Frankfurter; James E. Goehring.

1996 November 23–26; New Orleans, Louisiana
Pseudepigrapha Group. Session 1. Theme: Joseph and Aseneth: Moving from Text to Social and Historical Context. Four papers: Gideon Bohak; Randall D. Chesnutt; Ross S. Kraemer; Angela Standhartinger. Respondents: Amy-Jill Levine, Vanderbilt Divinity School, and Richard I. Pervo, Seabury-Western Theological Seminary.
Pseudepigrapha Group. Session 2. Five papers: Bruce N. Fisk; J. Bradley Chance; Hindy Najman; James E. Bowley; Kenneth Atkinson.

1997 November 22–25; San Francisco, California
Pseudepigrapha Group. Session 1. Theme: The Pseudepigrapha and Qumran. Four papers: Sidnie White Crawford; James L. Kugel; James C. VanderKam; John C. Reeves. Respondents: Martha Himmelfarb, Princeton University, and George W. E. Nickelsburg, University of Iowa.

Pseudepigrapha Group. Session 2. Five papers: Benjamin G. Wright III; John C. Endres; Ben Zion Wacholder; J. Edward Wright; Bruce Norman Fisk.

1998 November 21–24; Orlando, Florida
Pseudepigrapha Group. Session 1. Five papers: John R. Levison; Betsy Halpern-Amaru; Loren T. Stuckenbruck; Michael E. Stone; Jan Willem Van Henten.
Nag Hammadi and Gnosticism Section and Pseudepigrapha Group. Theme: Apocalyptic and Gnosticism. Four papers: Harold W. Attridge; Birger A. Pearson; Michael Roberge; Gordon Lyn Watley. Respondents: John J. Collins, University of Chicago, and David Frankfurter, University of New Hampshire.

1999 November 20–23; Boston, Massachusetts
Pseudepigrapha Section. Session 1. Theme: The Concept of Time in the Apocalypses. Four papers: George W. E. Nickelsburg; David E. Aune; Frances Flannery-Dailey; Robert G. Hall. Respondents: Michael A. Knibb, Kings College London, and Daniel C. Harlow, Calvin College.
Pseudepigrapha Section. Session 2. Five papers: Judith H. Newman; Michael E. Stone; Paul Owen; Bradford A. Kirkegaard; Ben Zion Wacholder.

2000 November 18–21; Nashville, Tennessee
Pseudepigrapha Section. Session 1. Theme: Rituals and Religious Experience in Early Judaism. Four papers: Robert A. Kugler; Frances Flannery-Dailey; Elaine H. Pagels; Dietmar Neufeld.
Pseudepigrapha Section. Panel: Ritual and Religious Experience in Early Judaism. Panelists: James R. Davila; David Frankfurter; Ross S. Kraemer; Rebecca Lesses; Stanley K. Stowers.
Pseudepigrapha Section. Session 2. Five papers: Andrei A. Orlov; Kenneth R. Atkinson; William K. Gilders; Kelley Coblentz Bautch; Crispin M.T. Fletcher-Louis.

2001 November 17–20; Denver, Colorado
Pseudepigrapha Section. Session 1. Panel: Review of George W. E. Nickelsburg, *1 Enoch 1: A Commentary on the Book of 1 Enoch.* Panelists: John J. Collins; Robert Doran; David Winston Suter; Patrick A. Tiller; James C. VanderKam. Respondent: George W. E. Nickelsburg, University of Iowa.

2. The Pseudepigrapha Project at the SBL, 1969–1971   37

Pseudepigrapha Section. Session 2. Five papers: Jan Willem van Henten; John Byron; Anathea Portier-Young; John R. Levison; Michael E. Stone.

2002　November 23–26; Toronto, Ontario, Canada
Pseudepigrapha Section. Session 1. Theme: Exploring the Afterlife of Early Jewish Pseudepigrapha. Five papers: Annette Yoshiko Reed; Sigrid Peterson; Heather McMurray; James E. Bowledy; Kirsti Barrett Copeland.
Pseudepigrapha Section. Session 2. Five papers: Jared Lodlow; Nathamiel Levtow; Rebecca Luft; Kenneth R. Atkinson; Andrei Orlov.

2003　November 22–25; Atlanta, Georgia
Pseudepigrapha Section. Session 1. Five papers: James R. Davila; Deborah Gera; John C. Poirier; William C. Gruen; Noah Hacham.
Pseudepigrapha Section. Session 2. Theme: Themes in the Study of Adamic and Enochic Literature. Six papers: John C. Reeves; Crispin H. T. Fletcher-Louis; Rebecca Luft; Tammie R. Wanta; Michael Segal; Kelley Coblentz Bautch.

2004　November 20–23; San Antonio, Texas
Pseudepigrapha Section. Session 1. Panel: Dale Allison, *The Testament of Abraham* (de Gruyter, 2003). Panelists: David E. Aune; Ann Jeffers; Jared Ludlow; Dale Allison.
Pseudepigrapha Section. Session 2. Three papers: Shani L. Berrin; Allen Kerkeslager; Andrei A. Orlov.
Qur'an and Biblical Literature and Pseudepigrapha Section. Theme: The Jewish Pseudepigrapha and the Islamic World. Panelists: Brannon M. Wheeler; David Cook; Fred Astren; Lucas van Rompay; Steve Wasserstrom.
Qumran and Pseudepigrapha Section. Theme: Re-presentations of History at Qumran. Panelists: Moshe J. Bernstein; Maxine Grossman; Cana Werman; James D. Tabor.

2005　November 19–22; Philadelphia, Pennsylvania
Pseudepigrapha Section. Session 1. Theme: Jewish Pseudepigrapha in the Slavonic Tradition. Six papers: Lorenzo DiTommaso; Christfried Böttrich; Nicolae Roddy; Basil Lourie; Alexander Golitzin; Andrei Orlov.
Aramaic Studies and Qumran and Pseudepigrapha Section. Theme: Two Recent Books on the Aramaic Levi Document. Cancelled.

2006　November 18–21; Washington, DC

Pseudepigrapha Section. Session 1. Panel: The Pitfalls of Categorization: A Panel Discussion of James R. Davila, *The Provenance of the Pseudepigrapha: Jewish, Christian, or Other?* (Brill, 2005). Panelists: Pierluigi Piovanelli; Chad Day; Magnar Kartveit; John C. Reeves.

Pseudepigrapha Section. Session 2. Five papers: Katy Valentine; Jared Ludlow; Andrew Teeter; Vered Hillel; Todd R. Hanneken.

Pseudepigrapha Section. Session 3. Theme: Rereading 4 Ezra. Four papers: Michael E. Stone; Hindy Najman; Robin Darling Young; Karina Martin Hogan.

Religious Experience in Early Judaism and Early Christianity Group and Pseudepigrapha Section. Theme: Women's Religious Experience in Antiquity. Four papers: Amy Hollywood; Sarah Iles Johnston; Patricia Ahearne-Kroll; John R. Levison.

2007 November 17–20; San Diego, California

Pseudepigrapha Section. Session 1. Theme: The Parascriptural Dimensions of Biblical Women. Five papers: Peter T. Lanfer; Vered Hillel; Mary Bader; Rivka Nir; Troy A. Miller.

Pseudepigrapha Section. Session 2. Panel: Addressing the Challenges of the *Commentaries on Early Jewish Literature* Series. Panelists: Dale Allison; David E. Aune; Randall D. Chesnutt; John Endres; Judith H. Newman; Pieter can der Horst; Loren T. Stuckenbruck.

Hellenistic Judaism Group and Pseudepigrapha Section. Theme: Exemplarity and Perfection in Hellenistic Judaism. Five papers: Erich Gruen; Annette Yoshiko Reed; Andrei Orlov; William Adler; Hindy Najman; Benjamin G. Wright III.

2008 November 22–25; Boston, Massachusetts

Religious Experience in Early Judaism and Early Christianity Group and Pseudepigrapha Section. Session 1. Theme: Spirit/s, Possession, Tongues, Dreams, Prayers, and other Performative Dimensions of Religious Experience. Four papers: Rebecca Lesses; Birger A. Pearson; Rodney A. Werline; John R. Levison.

Pseudepigrapha Section. Session 2. Five papers: Catherine Sider Hamilton; Ljubica Jovanovic; Mary R. D'Angelo; Françoise Mirguet; Hans Arneson.

Pseudepigrapha Section. Session 3. Theme: Problematizing "Pseudepigrapha." Three papers: Annette Yoshiko Reed; George J.

2. The Pseudepigrapha Project at the SBL, 1969–1971   39

Brooke; Martha Himmelfarb. Respondent: Robert Kraft, University of Pennsylvania, and Hindy Najman, University of Toronto.
Pseudepigrapha Section. Session 4. Theme: Qumran. Five papers: Hanna Tervanotko; Matthew E. Gordley; Ida Fröhlich; Hanne von Weissenberg; Ingrid Lilly.

2009 November 21–24; New Orleans, Louisiana
Pseudepigrapha Section. Session 1. Panel: The Inspired Production and Interpretation of Literary Texts in Antiquity. Panelists: Fritz Graf; Benjamin G. Wright III; Judith H. Newman; Annette Yoshiko Reed; John R. Levison; Hindy Najman; Ra'anan Boustan.
Pseudepigrapha Section. Session 2. Five papers: Michael Segal; Atar Livneh; Hans Arneson; Ted Erho; Ralph Korner.
Pseudepigrapha Section. Session 3. Five papers: James R. Davila; Stéphane Saulnier; John Strachan; John W. Fadden; Matthew W. Bates.

2010 November 20–23; Atlanta, Georgia
Pseudepigrapha Section. Session 1. Panel: Review of John J. Collins and Daniel C. Harlow, ed., *The Eerdmans Dictionary of Early Judaism* (Eerdmans, 2010). Panelists: Hindy Najman; Armin Lange; Eric Meyers; Tessa Rajak; Steven Weitzman. Respondent: Daniel Harlow, Calvin College, and John J. Collins, Yale University.
Pseudepigrapha Section. Session 2. Theme: The Inspired Production of Texts and Traditions. Seven papers: John R. Levison; Annette Yoshiko Reed; Eibert J. C. Tigchelaar; Hindy Najman; Benjamin G. Wright III; Ra'anan Boustan; Loren T. Stuckenbruck.
Pseudepigrapha Section. Session 3. Theme: Space and Time. Five papers: Jonathan Ben-Dov; Matthew Goff; Timothy Luckritz Marquis; Lutz Doering; Matthew E. Gordley.

2011 November 19–22; San Francisco, California
Pseudepigrapha Section. Session 1. Theme: Facing Death. Five papers: Jason M. Zurawski; Jan W. van Henten; Rodney A. Werline; Bernie H. Reynolds; Silviu Bunta.
Pseudepigrapha Section. Session 2. Theme: Preparing for Death in the Testamentary Literature. Four papers: Jacques van Ruiten; Vered Hillel; Annette Yoshiko Reed; James L. Kugel.

2012 November 16–20; Chicago, Illinois
Pseudepigrapha Section. Session 1. Theme: Ancient Media Culture. Five papers: Todd R. Hanneken; Jonathan Ben-Dov; Shayna Sheinfeld; Liv Ingeborg Lied; Robert A. Kraft.

Pseudepigrapha Section. Session 2. Panel: Review of Matthias Henze, *Jewish Apocalypticism in Late First Century Israel* (Mohr Siebeck, 2011). Panelists: Lutz Doering; Katrina Hogan; James L. Kugel; Liv Ingeborg Lied; Hindy Najman; Loren Stuckenbruck. Respondent: Matthias Henze, Rice University.
Pseudepigrapha Section. Session 3. Five papers: Kenneth Atkinson; Patricia Aherne-Kroll; Miryam T. Brand; Matthew E. Gordley; David Hamidovic.

2013 November 23–26; Baltimore, Maryland
Pseudepigrapha Section. Session 1. Theme: Women, Fire, and Dangerous Things. Five papers: Francoise Mirguet; Karina M. Hogan; Sonja Ammann; Hanna Tervanotko; Christopher E. J. Brenna.
Qumran and Pseudepigrapha Section. Theme: Composition, Authorship, and Reception of the Book of Jubilees. Five papers: Michael Segal; James L. Kugel; James C. VanderKam; Hindy Najman; Loren T. Stuckenbruck.
Pseudepigrapha Section. Session 2. Panel: Review of Richard Bauckham et al., eds., *Old Testament Pseudepigrapha: More Noncanonical Scriptures* (Eerdmans, 2013). Panelists: John J. Collins; Robert A. Kraft; Liv Ingeborg Lied; Hindy Najman. Respondent: James R. Davila, University of St. Andrews.
Book of Daniel Consultation and Pseudepigrapha Section. Theme: Daniel's Text Reception. Five papers: Devorah Dimant; Martin Rösel; Lorenzo DiTommaso; Sharon Pace; Carol Newsom.

2014 November 22–25; San Diego, California
Pseudepigrapha Section. Session 1. Five papers: Ted Erho; Jack Collins; G. Anthony Keddie; Brian W. Bunnell; Eva Mroczek.
Pseudepigrapha Section. Session 2. Panel: Honoring the Life and Work of Michael E. Stone. Panelists: Esther Chazon; Esther Eshel; Harold W. Attridge; George W. E. Nickelsburg; Abraham Terian. Respondent: Michael E. Stone, Hebrew University in Jerusalem.
Pseudepigrapha Section. Review of Andrei Orlov, *Heavenly Priesthood in the Apocalypse of Abraham* (Cambridge University Press, 2013). Panelists: Lorenzo DiTommaso; Gabrielle Boccaccini. Respondent: Andrei Orlov, Marquette University.
Pseudepigrapha Section. Session 3. Theme: Notions of Time in Early Judaism and Christianity. Four papers: Shayna Sheinfeld; Jan W. van Henten; Aaron Sherwood; Andrew B. Perrin.

2015 November 21–24; Atlanta, Georgia

Pseudepigrapha Section. Session 1. Five papers: Katell Berthelot; Veronika Hirschberger; Jackie Wyse-Rhodes; Ryan E. Stokes; John W. Fadden.
Pseudepigrapha Section. Session 2. Theme: Pseudepigrapha and Method. Six papers: Uta Heil; Nicholas A. Elder; Gavin McDowell; Benjamin G. Wright III; Eva Mroczek; Matthias Henze.
Pseudepigrapha Section. Session 3. Panel: Review of Benjamin G. Wright III, *The Letter of Aristeas* (de Gruyter, 2015). Panelists: Francis Borchardt; Sylvie Honigman; Timothy Michael Law; Maren Niehoff. Respondent: Benjamin G. Wright III, Lehigh University.

2016 November 19–22; San Antonio, Texas
Pseudepigrapha Section. Session 1. Theme: *Textual History of the Bible*, Vol. 2: *The Deuterocanonical Writings; Ben Sira*. Five papers: Armin Lange; Benjamin G. Wright III; Eric Reymond; Bradley Gregory; Daniel Assefa Kassaye.
Pseudepigrapha Section. Session 2. Five papers: Atar Livneh; Torleif Elgvin; Blake A. Jurgens; Aryeh Amihay; Bradley N. Rice.
Pseudepigrapha Section. Session 3. Theme: Violence. Six papers: Olivia Stewart Lester; Benjamin Lappenga; Robert Kugler; John Garza; Kyle Roark; Tim Wardle.
Hebrew Scriptures and Cognate Literature and Pseudepigrapha Section. Session 4. Theme: Manuscripts, Scribal Culture, Scribal Change. Five papers: Caroline Waerzeggers; Seth L. Sanders; Annette Yoshiko Reed; Ian Werrett; David Hamidovic.

2017 November 18–21; Boston, Massachusetts
Pseudepigrapha Section. Session 1. Theme: Pseudepigrapha and Gender. Five papers: Jill Hicks-Keeton; Francis Borchardt; Lee Sui Hung Albert; Tavis A. Bohlinger; Stephen L. Young.
Pseudepigrapha Section. Session 2. Five papers: Jeremiah Coogan; Caryn Tamber-Rosenau; Seth Adcock; Jonathan Klawans; Timothy A. Gabrielson.
Digital Humanities in Biblical, Early Jewish, and Christian Studies and Pseudepigrapha Section. Theme: Multi-spectral Imaging and the Recovery of "Lost" Texts from Palimpsests. Six papers: Michael Phelps; Keith T. Knox; Todd R. Hanneken; Ted Erho; Loren T. Stuckenbruck; Roger L. Easton.

2018 November 17–21; Denver, Colorado

Pseudepigrapha Section. Session 1. Five papers: Matthew L. Walsh; Joseph S. Khalil; Pierre J. Jordaan; Nicholas A. Elder; Eric Crégheur.
Pseudepigrapha Section. Session 2. Theme: The Reception and Afterlife of Pseudepigrapha in Judaism, Christianity, and Islam. Five papers: Liv Ingeborg Lied; Daniel M. Gurtner; Ashley L. Bacchi; Gavin McDowell; David Calabro.
Jewish Christianity/Christian Judaism and Pseudepigrapha Section. Theme: Hybrids, Converts, and Borders of Jewish and Christian Identities. Three papers: Michael Rosenberg; Carson Bay; Sunshee Jun.
Pseudepigrapha Section. Review panel: Jill Hicks-Keeton, *Arguing with Aseneth: Gentile Access to Israel's "Living God" in Jewish Antiquity* (Oxford University Press, 2018). Panelists: Patricia Ahearne-Kroll; Christopher Brenna. Respondent: Jill Hicks-Keeton, University of Oklahoma.
Pseudepigrapha Section. Review panel: John C. Reeves and Annette Yoshiko Reed, *Enoch from Antiquity to the Middle Ages: Sources from Judaism, Christianity, and Islam. Vol. 1* (Oxford University Press, 2018). Panelists: James VanderKam; Loren Stuckenbruck; Eva Mroczek; Andrei Orlov; Reuven Firestone. Respondents: Annette Yoshiko Reed, New York University, and John C. Reeves, University of North Carolina at Charlotte.

Appendix 3: The International Meetings of the
Society of Biblical Literature, 1983–2019

1983 First International Meeting of the Society of Biblical Literature in Salamanca, Spain
      No catalog available.
1984 August 16–17; Strasbourg, France
      Apocrypha and Pseudepigrapha.[47] Three papers: Devorah Dimant; André LaCocque; Frederick E. Brenk.
1985 August 14–16; Amsterdam, The Netherlands

---

47. The Apocrypha and Pseudepigrapha Section at the International Meetings has hosted sessions on both Jewish and Christian texts. The Old Testament pseudepigrapha have increasingly been discussed at the International Meetings in sections other than Apocrypha and Pseudepigrapha, e.g., in Slavonic Apocrypha (Berlin, 2017).

2. The Pseudepigrapha Project at the SBL, 1969–1971   43

       No Pseudepigrapha papers were read at the meeting.
1986   August 18–20; Jerusalem, Israel
       No Pseudepigrapha papers were read at the meeting.
1987   August 10–12; Heidelberg, Germany
       No Pseudepigrapha papers were read at the meeting.
1988   August 1–3; Sheffield, United Kingdom
       No Pseudepigrapha papers were read at the meeting.
1989   August 6–9; Copenhagen, Denmark
       No Pseudepigrapha papers were read at the meeting.
1990   August 5–8; Vienna, Austria
       No Pseudepigrapha papers were read at the meeting.
1991   July 14–17; Rome, Italy
       No Pseudepigrapha papers were read at the meeting.
1992   Melbourne, Australia
       No catalog available.
1993   Münster, Germany
       No catalog available.
1994   August 7–10; Katholieke Universiteit Lauven, Belgium
       No Pseudepigrapha papers were read at the meeting.
1995   July 23–26; Budapest, Hungary
       No Pseudepigrapha papers were read at the meeting.
1996   July 21–24; Dublin, Ireland
       No Pseudepigrapha papers were read at the meeting.
1997   July 27–30; Lausanne, Switzerland
       No Pseudepigrapha papers were read at the meeting.
1998   July 18–22; Cracow, Poland
       No Pseudepigrapha papers were read at the meeting.
1999   July 15–17; University of Helsinki, Helsinki, Finland; July 18–21; University of Helsinki, Lahti, Finland
       No Pseudepigrapha papers were read at the meeting.
2000   Cape Town, South Africa
       No catalog available.
2001   July 8–12; Rome, Italy
       No Pseudepigrapha papers were read at the meeting.
2002   Berlin, Germany
       No catalog available.
2003   July 20–25; Cambridge, United Kingdom
       No Pseudepigrapha papers were read at the meeting.
2004   July 25–28; Groningen, The Netherlands

Apocrypha and Pseudepigrapha. Session 1. Four papers: Mark A. Christian; Stefan Beyerle; Eric T. Noffke; Hanan Eshel.
Apocrypha and Pseudepigrapha. Session 2. Four papers: Heerak Christian Kim; Bradley Embry; James R. Davila; J. R. C. Cousland.
Apocrypha and Pseudepigrapha. Session 3. Four papers: Dilys Patterson; Kelley Coblentz Bautch; Petri Luomanen; Minna Laine.

2005 June 26–July 1; Singapore, Malaysia
Apocrypha and Pseudepigrapha. Six papers: Heerak Christian Kim; Mark Harding; Rivka Nir; Jon Ma; Jared W. Ludlow; Edna Israeli.

2006 July 2–6; Edinburgh, Scotland
Apocrypha and Pseudepigrapha. Session 1. Six papers: Michael Tait; David A. Fiensy; Ida Fröhlich; Pierre Johan Jordaan; Jacques van Ruiten; Jamal-Dominique Hopkins.
Apocrypha and Pseudepigrapha. Session 2. Five papers: Archie T. Wright; Markus H. McDowell; J. R. C. Cousland; James R. Davila; Kristian Heal.
Apocrypha and Pseudepigrapha. Session 3. Five papers: Bradley J. Embry; Rivka Nir; Edna Israeli; Pierluigi Piovanelli; Istvan Czachesz.

2007 July 22–26; Vienna, Austria
Biblical and Ancient Near Eastern Law. Session 3. Theme: Torah in the Second Temple Period and the Reuse of Torah in the Apocrypha and Pseudepigrapha. Five papers: Bruce Wells; Mark A. Christian; James L. Kugel; Benjamin G. Wright III; J. Cornelis de Vos.
Apocrypha and Pseudepigrapha. Four papers: Kelly J. Murphy; Ljubica Jovanovic; Friedrich Reiterer; Markus H. McDowell.

2008 July 6–11; Auckland, New Zealand
Apocrypha and Pseudepigrapha. Five papers: William R. G. Loader; Heike Omerzu; Gerhard van den Heever; Françoise Mirguet; Catherine Playoust.

2009 June 30–July 4; Rome, Italy
Apocrypha and Pseudepigrapha. Session 1. Five papers: Judith H. Newman; Edgar Kellenberger; Alex Samely; Edward Pillar; John Lorenc.
Apocrypha and Pseudepigrapha. Session 2. Panel: Why Study the Extra-Canonical Literature? Panelists: Michael Segal; Ida

Fröhlich; Joseph Sievers; Judith Newman; Jonathan Ben-Dov; Gabriele Boccaccini.
Apocrypha and Pseudepigrapha. Session 3. Theme: Enochic Literature. Six papers: Jonathan Ben-Dov; Veronika Bachmann; Luca Arcari; Rodney A. Werline; Henryk Drawnel; Stéphane Saulnier.
Apocrypha and Pseudepigrapha. Session 4. Theme: New Approaches to the Study of the Pseudepigrapha and Apocrypha. Six papers: Rebecca Raphael; Timothy B. Sailors; Pieter M. Venter; Tony Burke; Silviu N. Bunta; Yonata Moss.
Apocrypha and Pseudepigrapha. Session 5. Theme: When in Rome. Five papers: Francis Borchardt; Kenneth R. Atkinson; Jon Ma Asgeirsson; Ally Kateusz; Eric Noffke.

2010 June 25–29; Tartu, Estonia
Apocrypha and Pseudepigrapha. Session 1. Theme: Embodiment and the Construction of Identity. Six papers: Françoise Mirguet; Rebecca Raphael; Jonathan Knight; Angela Kim Harkins; Joel Gereboff; Nancy Tan.
Apocrypha and Pseudepigrapha. Session 2. Five papers: Randall D. Chesnutt; Rebecca Lesses; J. R. C. Cousland; Arthur Boulet; Mika Hynninen.
Apocrypha and Pseudepigrapha. Session 3. Joint session with Qumran and the Dead Sea Scrolls. Theme: Apocrypha and the Dead Sea Scrolls. Four papers: Ida Fröhlich; Edward Pillar; Maria Chrysovergi; Kim Papaioannou.

2011 June 3–7; London, United Kingdom
Apocrypha and Pseudepigrapha. Session 1. Theme: Pseudepigraphical Writings and Early Judaism. Four papers: Rivka Nir; Beniamin Pascut; Magdalena Diaz Araujo; Tom de Bruin.
Apocrypha and Pseudepigrapha. Session 2. Panel: Religious Experience in Apocryphal, Pseudepigraphal and Related Texts. Panelists: Frances Flannery; Robin Griffith-Jones; Angela Harkins; Bert Lietaert Peerbolte; Rodney A. Werline; Kelley Coblentz Bautch.
Apocrypha and Pseudepigrapha. Session 3. Panel: The Provenance of Pseudepigrapha: A Discussion of Methodology (Joseph and Aseneth, the Testament of Job, and 2 Enoch). Panelists: Lorenzo DiTommaso; Randall D. Chesnutt; Maria Haralambakis; Grant Macaskill. Respondent: Lorenzo DiTommaso, Concordia University.

Apocrypha and Pseudepigrapha. Session 4. Theme: Apocrypha/ Deuterocanonical Writings and Early Judaism. Three papers: Ruth Henderson; Woo Min Lee; Sean A. Adams.

2012 June 22–26; Amsterdam, The Netherlands
Apocrypha and Pseudepigrapha. Session 1. Review panel of Rivka Nir, *Joseph and Aseneth: A Christian Book* (Sheffield, 2012), and Veronika Bachmann, *Die Welt im Ausnahmezustand: Eine Untersuchung zu Aussagegehalt und Theologie des Wächterbuches* (de Gruyter, 2009). Panelists: Randall D. Chesnutt; Maria Haralambakis. Rivka Nir, Open University of Israel, responding. Panelists: Randall D. Chesnutt; Kelley Coblentz Bautch. Respondent: Veronika Bachmann, Universität Zürich.
Apocalyptic Literature and Apocrypha and Pseudepigrapha. Session 2. Theme: Monstrous Bodies, Gigantic Bodies, Session I. Four papers: Rebecca Raphael; Matthew A. Collins; Silviu Bunta; Tom de Bruin.
Apocrypha and Pseudepigrapha. Session 3. Five papers: Barbara Schmitz; Katell Berthelot; Christopher Begg; Johanna H. W. Dorman; Jason M. Zurawski.
Apocrypha and Pseudepigrapha. Session 4. Joint session with Apocalyptic Literature. Theme: Monstrous Bodies, Gigantic Bodies, Session II. Four papers: Matthew Goff; Ida Fröhlich; Rodney A. Werline; Ryan E. Stokes.
Apocrypha and Pseudepigrapha. Session 5. Five papers: Rivka Nir; Meghan Henning; Mika Hynninen; Matthew J. Lynch; Maria Haralambakis.

2013 June 7–11; St. Andrews, Scotland
Apocrypha and Pseudepigrapha. Session 1. Theme: *Old Testament Pseudepigrapha: More Noncanonical Scriptures.* Four papers: James R. Davila; Richard Bauckham; Martha Himmelfarb; Pierluigi Piovanelli.
Sacred Texts in Their Sociopolitical Context. Theme: Pseudepigrapha & Dead Sea Scrolls. Five papers: Loren T. Stuckenbruck (keynote); Nadov Sharon; Seth Bledsoe; Andrew R. Krause; Bernie Hodkin.
Apocrypha and Pseudepigrapha. Session 2. Theme: Deuterocanonical Books and Pseudepigrapha. Four papers: Angela Kim Harkins; Jason M. Zurawski; Michele Murray; P. Richard Choi.

Apocalyptic Literature and Apocrypha and Pseudepigrapha. Theme: Heavenly Bodies, Celestial Bodies. Five papers: Ida Fröhlich; Richard Bautch; Wolfgang Grünstäudl; Dominique Cote; Anne Gardner.

2014 June 6–10; Vienna, Austria
Apocrypha and Pseudepigrapha. Session 1. Theme: Old Testament Pseudepigrapha in the Ethiopic Tradition. Six papers: Michael A. Knibb; Loren T. Stuckenbruck; Jan Dochhorn; Martin Heide; Ted Erho; Daniel Assefa Kassaye.
Apocrypha and Pseudepigrapha. Session 2. Theme: Pseudepigrapha and Second Temple Judaism. Four papers: Phillip Muñoa; Claudia D. Bergmann; Andrew B. Perrin; Daniel Lanzinger.

2015 June 20–24; Buenos Aires, Argentina
Apocrypha and Pseudepigrapha. Session 1. Theme: Early Judaism I: Deuterocanonical Writings. Two papers: Nancy R. Bowen; Sung Soo Hong.
Apocrypha and Pseudepigrapha. Session 2. Theme: Early Judaism II. Three papers: Ida Fröhlich; Lydia Gore-Jones; Kenner Terra.
Apocrypha and Pseudepigrapha. Session 3. Theme: Between Jewish and Christian Apocryphal Literature. Four papers: Dominique Cote; Ezequiel Gustavo Rivas; Maria de los Angeles Roberto; Magdalena Diaz Araujo.
Hellenistic Judaism and Apocalyptic Literature and Apocrypha and Pseudepigrapha. Theme: Reception of the Scripture in Diaspora: Slavonic Apocrypha from Hellenistic Jewish Literature. Two papers: Laura Bizzarro; Silviu Bunta.

2016 June 2–7; Seoul, South Korea
Bible and Syriac Studies in Context and Apocrypha and Pseudepigrapha. Theme: Apocryphal and Canonical Traditions in West Asia. Three papers: Tamar Zewi; Satoshi Toda; Cornelia Horn.
Apocrypha and Pseudepigrapha. Session 1. Theme: Early Christian and Jewish Texts. Two papers: Jonathan Soyars; Mark Glen Bilby.
Apocrypha and Pseudepigrapha. Session 2. Theme: Early Jewish Texts. Three papers: Devorah Dimant; Ida Fröhlich; Matthew Goff.
Apocrypha and Pseudepigrapha. Session 3. Three papers: Randall D. Chesnutt; Sanglae Kim; Pierre Jordaan.

2017 August 7–11; Berlin, Germany

Apocrypha and Pseudepigrapha. Session 1. Three papers: Meredith Warren; Kaori Ozawa; Max Botner.
Apocrypha and Pseudepigrapha. Session 2. Theme: Is This a "Text"? Part 1. Three papers: Jonathan Henry; Francis Borchardt; James D. Moore.
Apocrypha and Pseudepigrapha. Session 3. Theme: Is This a "Text"? Part 2. Three papers: Dominique Cote; Ivan Miroshnikov; Janet Spitter.

2018 June 30–August 3; Helsinki, Finland
Apocrypha and Pseudepigrapha. Theme: Men, Mary, Magic. Four papers: Tom de Bruin; Susanna Asikainen; Bradley Rice; Shaily Shashikant Patel.

2019 July 1–5; Rome, Italy
Apocrypha and Pseudepigrapha. Section 1. Three papers: Ivan Miroshnikov; Elisa Uusimäki; R. Gillian Glass.
Apocrypha and Pseudepigrapha. Section 2. Three papers: Matthew J. Korpman; Jared Ludlow; Alexander McCarron.
Apocrypha and Pseudepigrapha. Section 3. Three papers: Maia Kotrosits; Tom de Bruin; Francis Borchardt.

Bibliography

Bogaert, Pierre-Maurice. *Apocalypse de Baruch: Introduction, Traduction du Syriaque et Commentaire.* SC 144–145. 2 vols. Paris: Cerf, 1969.

Brock, Sebastian P. *Testament of Job: Greek*, and J.-C. Picard, *Apocalypsis Baruchi: Graece.* PVTG 2. Leiden: Brill, 1967.

Charles, R. H. *The Apocrypha and Pseudepigrapha of the Old Testament.* 2 vols. Oxford: Clarendon, 1913.

Charlesworth, James H. "A History of Pseudepigraphal Research: The Reemerging Importance of the Pseudepigrapha." *ANRW* 19.1:54–88.

———. "Minutes of Pseudepigrapha Breakfast in Palmer House in Chicago, IL, on November 11, 1973." Archive of Michael E. Stone.

———. "Minutes of the Pseudepigrapha Project Steering Committee." SBL Archive.

———. "Minutes of the Pseudepigrapha Project Steering Committee. Regency Hyatt House. Atlanta, Georgia. October 31, 1971." Archive of Michael E. Stone.

———. *The Odes of Solomon.* Oxford: Clarendon, 1973.

———. "Reflections on the SNTS Pseudepigrapha Seminar at Duke on the Testament of the Twelve Patriarchs." *NTS* 23 (1976–1977): 296–304.

———. "The Renaissance of Pseudepigrapha Studies: The SBL Pseudepigrapha Project." *JSJ* 2 (1971): 107–14.

———. "The SNTS Pseudepigrapha Seminars at Tübingen and Paris on the Books of Enoch." *NTS* 25 (1978–1979): 315–23.

———. "Some Reflections on Present Work on the Pseudepigrapha." Pages 229–37 in vol. 1 of *Society of Biblical Literature 2001 Seminar Papers*. 2 vols. SBLSP 40. Missoula, MT: Society of Biblical Literature.

Denis, Albert-Marie. *Introduction aux pseuépigraphes grecs d'Ancien Testament*. SVTP 1. Leiden: Brill, 1970.

Denis, Albert-Marie, and Marinus de Jonge. "The Greek Pseudepigrapha of the Old Testament." *NovT* 7 (1965): 319–28.

Harrelson, Walter. "Report to the Pseudepigrapha Breakfast Meeting: SBL, 26 October 1970." SBL Archive.

Harrington, Daniel J. "Text and Biblical Text in Pseudo-Philo's *Liber Antiquitatum Biblicarum*." PhD diss., Harvard University, 1969.

Jonge, Marinus de. *Testament of the Twelve Patriarchs: Greek*. PVTG 1. Leiden: Brill, 1964.

Knibb, Michael A., with Edward Ullendorff. *The Ethiopic Book of Enoch: A New Edition in the Light of the Aramaic Dead Sea Fragments*. 2 vols. Oxford: Clarendon; New York: Oxford University Press, 1978.

Kraft, Robert A., and Ann-Elizabeth Purintun. *Paraleipomena Jeremiou*. TT 1. Missoula, MT: Society of Biblical Literature, 1972.

Nickelsburg, George W. E., ed. *Studies on the Testament of Abraham*. SCS 6. Missoula, MT: Scholars Press, 1976.

———. *Studies on the Testament of Joseph*. SCS 5. Missoula, MT: Scholars Press, 1975.

———. *Studies on the Testament of Moses*. SCS 4. Cambridge, MA: Society of Biblical Literature, 1973.

Philonenko, Marc. *Joseph et Aséneth*. StPB 13. Leiden: Brill, 1968.

Saunders, Ernest W. *Searching the Scriptures: A History of the Society of Biblical Literature, 1880–1980*. BSNA 8. Chico, CA: Scholars Press, 1982.

"Steering Committee Meeting. October 31, 1971. Agenda." Archive of Michael E. Stone.

Stone, Michael E. *Testament of Abraham, the Greek Recensions*. TT 2. Missoula, MT: Society of Biblical Literature, 1972.

"Titles of Papers at 1969 SBL Meetings." *JBL* 89 (1970): 132–36.

Tucker, Gene M. "The Modern (and Postmodern?) Society of Biblical Literature: Institutions and Scholarship." Pages 31–52 in *Foster Biblical Scholarship: Essays in Honor of Kent Harold Richards*. Edited by Frank Ritchell Ames and Charles William Miller. BSNA 24. Atlanta: Society of Biblical Literature, 2010.

Remembering Fifty Years of the
Pseudepigrapha at the Society of Biblical Literature

3

Let the Living Remember the Dead: Homage to the Departed Pioneers of the Pseudepigrapha Group—Father George W. MacRae, S.J.

Robert A. Kraft

The Pioneers of the Pseudepigrapha Unit at the Society of Biblical Literature

Since I was present when the Pseudepigrapha unit was started half a century ago, it made sense for me to try to remember some of the colleagues who also participated in the early discussions but are no longer with us. Initially, this seemed like a relatively easy task, with the help of Google and Wikipedia, my modern sources of basic truth and information—"Google is my Bible," I sometimes say. As it turned out, things were not so simple.

Memorable contributors in the early days of the Pseudepigrapha unit at the Society of Biblical Literature who are no longer with us included several established scholars. My own frail memory identified some major figures. Among them are Walter J. Harrelson (November 28, 1919–September 5, 2012), who maintained a "marginal" interest in the emerging activities of our Pseudepigrapha unit. We are fortunate to have his *Nachlass* at Vanderbilt Library. John Strugnell (May 25, 1930–November 30, 2007) was brilliant, tragic, and betrayed by manic depression and alcoholism. John was an early supporter and advisor. He would often come to steering committee meetings, usually held in someone's hotel room. Harry M. Orlinsky (March 14, 1908–March 21, 1992) was especially active in founding the Septuagint and Massoretic Studies units, while also maintaining contact with related endeavors such as the Pseudepigrapha unit. His life story is well told in the internet sources and the archival materials at Cincinnati. Bruce M. Metzger (February 9, 1914–February 13, 2007) headed the RSV and NRSV translation committees on which George MacRae and Orlinsky also served, as well as Harrelson and myself. Metzger also had an interest in pseudepigraphic matters, although his other involvements kept him very busy.

Many of these scholars were also involved in matters of the International Organization for Septuagint and Cognate Studies. Some of them served as presidents of the Society of Biblical Literature (Orlinsky, 1970; Metzger, 1971; Harrelson, 1972; and I myself in 2006). Of this early "late" group, Strugnell was most focused on pseudegraphic studies. One who was crucial during many of the formative years and has left his mark on much associated with the International Organization for Septuagint and Cognate Studies was John R. Abercrombie, who passed away from cancer in 2001. One of his first jobs was computer developer for the Center for Computer Analysis of Texts/Computer Assisted Tools for Septuagint/Scriptural Study (CCAT/CATSS).

There were no female scholars in leadership roles in the early days. However, to the best of my knowledge, there were women engaged in research on the pseudepigrapha during this time who are now deceased: Ann-Elizabeth Purintun (Jeremiah traditions, d. 2015), Zipora (Zipi) Talshir (Greek Jewish Scriptures, d. 2016), and Suzanne Daniel-Nataf (Greek Jewish Scriptures, d. 2004).

Father George Winsor MacRae, S.J.

Probably few people at the 2019 celebration remember Father George Winsor MacRae, S.J., who died suddenly in 1985 at the young age of fifty-seven. He was an important contributor to the formation of the Pseudepigrapha unit at the Society of Biblical Literature—not so much as a worker in the trenches, though he did that too, but as a voice of encouragement, planning, and organization. I fondly remember his sage counsels. Unfortunately, there is no Wikipedia summarization for George, and an internet search only yielded isolated obituary notices. What follows includes my attempt to correct that oversight.

Father George Winsor MacRae—I'll call him George—had his fingers in many pies, although somehow he has not achieved appropriate recognition in the online materials of the Wiki projects, which fail even to list and disambiguate his name successfully from other people of similar spellings and other claims of distinction. But George was indeed a person of distinction. George was born on July 27, 1928, in Lynn, Massachusetts. In 1948, he joined the Society of Jesus. After receiving his licentiate in philosophy in 1954 from Louvain and his artium magister (master of arts) in 1957 from Johns Hopkins University, he was ordained a priest in 1960. George taught at the Weston School of Theology, where he received his licentiate of sacred theology in 1961, and at Cambridge University, where he earned a doctorate in New Testament studies and the history of religions in 1966. His dissertation was on the relation of Jewish apocalyptic thought and gnostic literature.

George worked especially with the Nag Hammadi Coptic materials (e.g., on the Gospel of Mary, the Gospel of Truth, and Thunder, Perfect Mind). A scholar of the New Testament, he offered courses on gnosticism, the Gospel of John, the Letter to the Hebrews, and the biblical roots of Roman Catholic theology. George also assisted in the translation and interpretation of the Nag Hammadi Library and worked with Jewish, Catholic, Eastern Orthodox, and Protestant scholars on the New Revised Standard Version translation of the Bible. From 1954 until 1956 he taught at the Fairfield Preparatory School in Connecticut, from 1966 until 1973 at Weston School of Theology, and from 1973 to 1985 at Harvard Divinity School, where he was the first tenured Charles Chauncy Stillman Professor of Roman Catholic Studies and was appointed acting dean in 1985. From 1979 to 1980, George served as rector of the Ecumenical Institute for Theological Research in Tantur, Jerusalem. In 1957, George helped found the journal *New Testament Abstracts* and later served as its editor. He was the first Roman Catholic to be appointed executive secretary of the Society of Biblical Literature, a role he held from 1973 to 1976. George died suddenly in 1985. I remember him especially for his skills as a no-nonsense organizer and moderator of meetings and discussions.

His colleague Helmut Koester summarizes this well in a somewhat homiletic obituary, published in 1985 in *Harvard Theological Review*.

> It was at Harvard Divinity School that George participated every term, every week in the New Testament Graduate Seminar. He was often silent for an hour or more; but when he finally made a comment, it was incisive, clear, helpful, and always brought the discussion back to the essential questions of our work: "What text are you talking about?" and "What kind of criteria are you using for its interpretation?" It was also at Harvard that George spent hundreds of hours copyediting his colleagues' manuscripts as an editor of this journal [*Harvard Theological Review*], the *Hermeneia* commentary series, and many other scholarly publications. In this capacity George grappled with the stylistic and bib-

liographical difficulties inherent in academic publishing. He always gave willingly his time and energy to set things right....

If greatness in biblical scholarship is defined in terms of service to the scholarly community, George MacRae was the greatest in our generation. If leadership is understood as a faithful devotion to the well-being and intellectual and spiritual growth of others, George was truly a leader. If Christian life is defined as giving freely of one's knowledge, wisdom, talents, and critical insights to colleagues and students, friends, and strangers, George was truly a Christian.... During the two decades of his career as a scholar and teacher, ecumenicity has become a matter of course. George MacRae was a major contributor to an ecumenicity that is based upon the best standards of critical Biblical scholarship and upon open and unbiased inquiry and discourse—not only among Protestants and Catholics, but also with other religions of the world."[1]

We are fortunate to be able to access MacRae's well-organized *Nachlass* (his *Paralipomena*, if I may) at the Harvard Divinity School library, including some early correspondence regarding the formation of this Pseudepigrapha unit, as well as his many other academic activities (including his work on the *RSV* committee and much more).

Some of Father George MacRae's Contributions and Publications Relating to the Pseudepigrapha Unit

His numerous contributions to the study of the pseudepigrapha include:

- Society of Biblical Literature, Pseudepigrapha Seminar: proposals, papers, minutes, newsletters, correspondence (1971–1983);
- Society of Biblical Literature, Pseudepigrapha Seminar: the Testament of Abraham (1972);
- Society of Biblical Literature, Pseudepigrapha Group: the Testament/Assumption of Moses (1973);
- Society of Biblical Literature joint session of Nag Hammadi/Pseudepigrapha Groups: Seth in Jewish, Christian, and gnostic literature (1977);
- Duke University, the Doubleday Pseudepigrapha Translation: papers, correspondence (1973–1982).

---

1. Helmut Koester, "Obituary of George Winsor MacRae, SJ," *HTR* 78 (1985): 233–35.

3. Let the Living Remember the Dead

Selected Publications:

- "New Testament Theology: Some Problems and Principles," *Scripture* 16 (1964) 97–106;
- "Gnosis in Messina," *CBQ* 28 (1966): 322–33;
- "Gnosticism," *New Catholic Encyclopedia* 6 (New York: McGraw-Hill, 1967), 523–28;
- "Theodotus," *New Catholic Encyclopedia* 14 (New York: McGraw-Hill, 1967), 27;
- "Gnosis, Christian," *New Catholic Encyclopedia* 6 (New York: McGraw-Hill, 1967), 522–23;
- "Sleep and Awakening in Gnostic Texts," in *Le origini dello gnosticismo: Colloquio di Messina 13-18 Aprile 1966*, ed. Ugo Bianchi, Studies in the History of Religion 12 (Leiden: Brill, 1967), 496–507;
- "Gnosticism and New Testament Studies," *The Bible Today* 38 (1968): 2623–30;
- "The Jewish Background of the Gnostic Sophia Myth," *NovT* 12 (1970): 86–101;
- "The Thunder: Perfect Mind," in *The Thunder: Perfect Mind (Nag Hammadi Codex VI, Tractate 2)*, ed. W. Wuellmer (Berkeley: University of California Press, 1975), 1–9;
- "Seth in Gnostic Texts and Traditions," in *Society of Biblical Literature 1977 Seminar Papers*, ed. Paul J. Achtemeier, SBLSP 11 (Missoula, MO: Scholars Press, 1977), 17–24;
- "The Gospel of Truth: Introduced and translated by George W. MacRae," in *The Nag Hammadi Library in English*, ed. James McConkey Robinson, 2nd ed. (Leiden: Brill, 1984), 37–49;
- Robert McL. Wilson and George W. MacRae, "The Gospel of Mary," in *Nag Hammadi Codices V,2-5 and VI with Papyrus Berolinesis 8502,1 and 4*, ed. Douglas M. Parrott, NHS 11 (Leiden: Brill, 1979), 453–71;
- *Hebrews* (Collegeville, MN: Liturgical Press, 1983);
- "Apocalyptic Eschatology in Gnosticism," in *Apocalypticism in the Mediterranean World and the Near East: Proceedings of the International Colloquium on Apocalypticism, Uppsala, August 12-17, 1979*, ed. David Hellholm (Tübingen: Mohr Siebeck, 1983), 317–25;
- "Gnostic Sayings and Controversy Traditions in John 8:12–59," in *Nag Hammadi, Gnosticism and Early Christianity*, ed. Charles W. Hedrick and Robert Hodgson (Peabody, MA: Hendrickson, 1986), 97–110;

- George W. E. Nickelsburg and George W. MacRae, eds., *Christians among Jews and Gentiles: Essays in Honor of Krister Stendahl on His Sixty-Fifth Birthday* (Philadelphia: Fortress, 1986);
- Eldon Jay Epp and George W. MacRae, eds., *The New Testament and Its Modern Interpreters* (Atlanta: Scholars Press, 1989).

Bibliography

Koester, Helmut. "Obituary of George Winsor MacRae, SJ." *HTR* 78 (1985): 233–35.

4
Early Days of the Society of Biblical Literature Pseudepigrapha Group: Pseudepigrapha Studies in the Second Half of the Twentieth Century

Michael E. Stone

A Look Back

My first encounter with the Pseudepigrapha unit was at the Annual Meeting of the Society of Biblical Literature in Atlanta in 1971. It was during my first sabbatical year, and I was at Harvard as a Research Fellow in the Department of Near Eastern Languages and Civilizations (NELC). I remember traveling to Atlanta by plane, and on the return trip John Strugnell was on the plane with me. Although there had been a few Pseudepigrapha Breakfasts prior to 1971, the Atlanta conference was the first seminar gathering.

It was an exciting time. At Harvard I attended the New Testament Senior Seminar, where George W. MacRae, Krister Stendahl, Dieter Georgi, and Helmut Köster were reigning. James M. Robinson had the Nag Hammadi material in Claremont and was sending copies of the draft translations by mail when they were ready. Those were the days of dittos, duplications in purple type and smelling of chemicals. I recall once, in the spring term, Birger A. Pearson visited. We had been friends during our contemporary graduate work in the 1960's, and he was busy with the Melchizedek Codex IX from Nag Hammadi and very excited about apocryphal traditions—particularly concerning Noah's wife—and more broadly, about possible Jewish roots of gnosticism.

At the Atlanta meeting, George W. E. Nickelsburg and I became members of the steering committee. Others were John Strugnell, Bob Kraft, Walter J. Harrelson, and MacRae. James H. Charlesworth was secretary at that time. Under discussion was Paralipomena Ieremiou. Kraft and Betsy

Purintun had done a working edition, which we used as a basis of discussion.[1] This was an extraordinary time for our studies: this was a forum in which the pseudepigrapha were studied unabashedly as works in their own right, not merely as possible sources for Jewish background to the New Testament. The history of Judaism in the Second Temple period was coming into its own, stimulated by the Dead Sea Scrolls. It seemed to me then that the dual shackles of orthodoxies and their twin central streams of interest, apocalyptic literature (of concern to New Testament scholars) and protorabbinic traditions (of concern to scholars of rabbinic literature), were now contributing to a larger stream of the study of ancient Judaism and its literature as an historical venture. I was, I now think, a bit too optimistic, and the spectacles of orthodoxy still bedevil our field. At least, however, we know they exist.

This all was new to us: studying texts as wholes, the parallel material in the Dead Sea Scrolls and Nag Hammadi appearing (or, in the former instance, dribbling out), language traditions of transmission explored, and my own love affair with Armenian reinforced. It is hard to overestimate John Strugnell's influence, both in his contributions to our deliberations and in the extraordinarily enriching teaching that he bestowed on his own graduate students, such as Harry W. Attridge, John J. Collins, and others.

I knew John from long before. He came to Harvard in 1966–1967. I finished my doctorate. I had a job in the then newly established Department of Religious Studies at the University of California at Santa Barbara, a position subsequently held by Jonathan Z. Smith and Pearson. I held it for a year and resigned when I was invited to come to Jerusalem to the Hebrew University. I had flown cross-country for research purposes and met John in Cambridge, Massachusetts, where he had his office in the Center for the Study of World Religions. We found a great deal to talk about and lots of shared interests.

Later, after the Six Day War in 1967, I learned that John was often at the École Biblique in East Jerusalem. I would visit him quite often over subsequent years. Around the time of the Annual Meeting of the Society of Biblical Literature in Atlanta, I remember clearly being in John's room at the École. We were talking of the field of pseudepigrapha studies and decided between us that R. H. Charles's famous two volumes needed

---

1. The edition and translation were published eventually as the first volume of Texts and Translations: Robert A. Kraft and Ann-Elizabeth Purintun, *Paraleipomena Jeremiou*, SBLTT 1 (Missoula, MT: Society of Biblical Literature, 1972).

4. Early Days of the SBL Pseudepigrapha Group

replacing.[2] Things had changed since 1913! We developed an idea, initially formulated by John and quickly ratified by the steering committee: to produce new editions and translations in fascicles as they were ready and to make this work on texts and translations a focus of the Pseudepigrapha Seminar's activity. Each Annual Meeting would be devoted to one ancient document, the first having being Paralipomena Ieremiou mentioned above.[3]

For that, I wrote an article on the Armenian version.[4] Subsequently, we turned our attention to other works, to Joseph and Aseneth, for which I prepared an edition of the Armenian text of Testament of Joseph.[5] I associate a meeting in Washington with Testament of Job, another elsewhere with Testament of Moses, and so it went, with articles, text volumes, and seminar papers energetically produced as each work came up. Nickelsburg was an unfailing source of common sense, diligence, and insight, and he edited several of the volumes issuing from the seminar's deliberations.[6]

Long-time pseudepigrapha scholars will recognize in Strugnell's fascicles plan the origin of the Society's Texts and Translation series. Kraft took on the job of editor, and for that series I produced a translation of Testament of Abraham, wonderfully revised by MacRae.[7]

Those days had various spinoffs: Collins's initiative at the Society of Biblical Literature meetings that issued in *Semeia* 14 was one.[8] Charlesworth's *Old Testament Pseudepigrapha* was another.[9] The openness to the Dead Sea Scrolls and to Nag Hammadi proved to be fallow ground, and

---

2. R. H. Charles, *The Apocrypha and Pseudepigrapha of the Old Testament*, 2 vols. (Oxford: Clarendon, 1913).

3. This was directly connected with Kraft and Purintun, *Paralipomena Jeremiou*.

4. Michael E. Stone, "Some Observations on the Armenian Version of the Paralipomena of Jeremiah," *CBQ* 35 (1973): 47–59.

5. Michael E. Stone, *The Armenian Version of the Testament of Joseph: Introduction, Critical Edition, and Translation*, SBLTT 5 (Missoula, MT: Scholars Press, 1975).

6. George W. E. Nickelsburg, ed., *Studies on the Testament of Moses*, SCS 4 (Cambridge, MA: Society of Biblical Literature, 1973); Nickelsburg, ed., *Studies on the Testament of Joseph*, SCS 5 (Missoula, MT: Scholars Press, 1975); Nickelsburg, ed., *Studies on the Testament of Abraham*, SCS 6 (Missoula, MT: Scholars Press, 1976).

7. Michael E. Stone, *The Testament of Abraham: The Greek Recensions*, SBLTT 2 (Missoula, MT: Scholars Press, 1972).

8. John J. Collins, ed., *Apocalypse: The Morphology of a Genre*, Semeia 14 (1979).

9. James H. Charlesworth, ed., *The Old Testament Pseudepigrapha*, 2 vols. (New York: Doubleday, 1983–1985).

a number of other initiatives in the world of scholarship paired with the Pseudepigrapha Seminar, creating a long-term impetus that is still being worked out in our discipline.

Indeed, the time was ripe. That is shown by the fact that elsewhere a number of similar developments took place independently, mainly in the decade or fifteen years following that Atlanta meeting. For one, as I have mentioned, Nag Hammadi. Second, the Compendia rerum Iudaicarum ad Novum Testamentum project, centered in Western Europe, was coming into its own.[10] The Studiorum Novi Testamenti Societas (SNTS) had also established an equivalent group, with scholars like Marinus (Rein) de Jonge and Michael A. Knibb playing leading roles. De Jonge was an early scholar on the scene, the publication of his doctoral thesis on the Testaments of the Twelve Patriarchs as far back as 1953 being an informed and critical example.[11] He was also behind the establishment of two Brill series, Pseudepigrapha Veteris Testamenti Graece (PVTG) and Studia in Veteris Testamenti Pseudepigrapha (SVTP). Albert-Marie Denis published an introduction and his collection of Greek fragments of pseudepigrapha, and, somewhat later, Charlesworth published his *Pseudepigrapha and Modern Research*.[12] I clearly remember that in the summer of 1969, de

---

10. Compendia rerum Iudaicarum ad Novum Testamentum (Assen: Van Gorcum, 1974–present).

11. Marinus de Jonge, *The Testaments of the Twelve Patriarchs: A Study of Their Text, Composition and Origin* (Assen: Van Gorcum, 1953). Later he published *Studies on the Testaments of the Twelve Patriarchs: Text and Interpretation*, SVTP 3 (Leiden: Brill, 1975); de Jonge, *The Testaments of the Twelve Patriarchs: A Critical Edition of the Greek Text*, PVTG 1–2 (Leiden: Brill, 1978); Harm W. Hollander and Marinus de Jonge, *The Testaments of the Twelve Patriarchs: A Commentary*, SVTP 8 (Leiden: Brill, 1985).

12. Albert-Marie Denis, *Fragmenta Pseudepigraphorum quae supersunt graece una cum Historicorum et Auctorum Judaeorum Hellenistarum Fragmenti*, PVTG 3 (Leiden: Brill, 1970); observe the fully reworked form of this introduction, published as Albert-Marie Denis and J.-C. Haelewyck, *Introduction à la littérature religieuse Judéo-Hellénistique* (Turnhout: Brepols, 2000). Albert-Marie Denis, *Introduction aux Pseudépigraphes Grecs d'Ancient Testament* (Leiden: Brill, 1970); Denis, *Concordance Grecque des Pseudépigraphes d'Ancien Testament* (Louvain-la-Neuve: Université catholique de Louvain, Institut orientaliste, 1987). James H. Charlesworth, assisted by P. Dykers, *The Pseudepigrapha and Modern Research*, SCS 7 (Missoula, MT: Scholars Press, 1976). Charlesworth's work is now superseded by Lorenzo DiTommaso, *A Bibliography of Pseudepigrapha Research 1850–1999*, JSPSup 39 (Sheffield: Sheffield Academic, 2001), a most useful contribution.

4. Early Days of the SBL Pseudepigrapha Group 63

Jonge and Kraft came to visit me in Jerusalem and strong-armed a willing me into working on the Armenian version of the Testaments of the Twelve Patriarchs. It was, I believe, on occasion of a SNTS or some other meeting in Jerusalem and for me resulted in a series of publications culminating in the *editio minor* of this text.[13]

Work on the apocalypses was flourishing with Klaus Koch, David S. Russell (I remember discussing his *Method and Message* with Strugnell in 1966 in his Center for the Study of World Religions study), Paul Hanson's thesis and book *Dawn of Apocalyptic*, and then later Collins's influential work on the definition of apocalypse. These and other seminal contributions all appeared in the fifteen years or so following.[14] An attempt at summary was the influential conference held in Uppsala, with the proceedings edited by David Hellholm.[15] In addition, the Göttingen Septuagint editions of Maccabees and Ben Sira were underway.[16] Emanuel Tov wrote his doctoral thesis, proving that the second translator of LXX Jeremiah had also translated 1 Baruch.[17] The Hermeneia commentary series included apocryphal and pseudepigraphical works: I was commissioned in the mid-60s to write 4 Ezra, Nickelsburg at the end of that decade to write 1 Enoch.[18]

---

13. Michael E. Stone and in collaboration with Vered Hillel, *The Armenian Version of the Testaments of the Twelve Patriarchs: Edition, Apparatus, Translation and Commentary*, Hebrew University Armenian Series 11 (Leuven: Peeters, 2012).

14. Klaus Koch, *Ratlos vor der Apokalyptik: Eine Streitschrift über ein vernachlässigtes Gebiet der Bibelwissenschaften, und den schädlichen Auswirkungen auf Theologie und Philosophie* (Gütersloh: Gütersloher Verlagshaus, 1970); David S. Russell, *The Method and Message of Jewish Apocalyptic, 200 BC–AD 100* (Philadelphia: Westminster, 1964); Paul D. Hanson, *The Dawn of Apocalyptic: The Historical and Sociological Roots of Jewish Apocalyptic Eschatology* (Philadelphia: Fortress, 1979); Collins, *Apocalypse*.

15. David Hellholm, ed., *Apocalypticism in the Mediterranean World and the Near East: Proceedings of the International Colloquium on Apocalypticism, Uppsala, August 12–17, 1979* (Tübingen: Mohr Siebeck, 1983).

16. Joseph Ziegler, ed., *Sapientia Jesu Filii Sirach*, SVTG 12.2 (Göttingen: Vandenhoeck & Ruprecht, 1965).

17. Emanuel Tov, *The Septuagint Translation of Jeremiah and Baruch: A Discussion of an Early Revision of the LXX of Jeremiah 29–52 and Baruch 1:1–3:8*, HSM 8 (Missoula, MT: Scholars Press, 1976).

18. George W. E. Nickelsburg, *1 Enoch 1: A Commentary on the Book of 1 Enoch, Chapters 1–36, 81–108*, Hermeneia (Minneapolis: Fortress, 2001); George W. E. Nickelsburg and James C. VanderKam, *1 Enoch 2: A Commentary on the Book of 1 Enoch*

I tend to think that the attack on anachronistic reading back of modern orthodoxies into the past, led by Kraft, greatly influenced how things developed. Kraft and I worked together for a number of years in the late 1970s when I was adjunct professor at Penn. David Dumville (now in Aberdeen), who worked on Celtic pseudepigrapha, was there at that time.[19] Martin McNamara's work on the Old Irish pseudepigrapha was also fermenting.[20]

Just as Harvard was producing scholars who went on in the field in the late 1960s and the 1970s, Penn followed suit in the late 1970s and after. In the earlier group were scholars such as Nickelsburg, James C. VanderKam, and Collins; the Penn "hothouse," led by Kraft (who was at Harvard 1957–1961), became the matrix that produced folk such as William Adler, Benjamin G. Wright III, Martha Himmelfarb, and Steven D. Fraade (who came from Near Eastern studies, not religious studies, but wrote a fascinating thesis on Enosh).[21]

A Look Ahead

Looking back and thinking ahead, at present there are a number of topics that should be on the agenda.

Since pseudepigrapha studies have come into their own and the spectacles of orthodoxy are cracked, if not yet cast off, I think it is time to rid ourselves of the temporal constraints. Since our field now studies biblically associated works and traditions (recently I heard Kraft use the neologism "scripturesque,"[22] while John C. Reeves talks of "Abrahamic discourse"), it

---

37–82, Hermeneia (Minneapolis: Fortress, 2012); Michael E. Stone, *Fourth Ezra: A Commentary on the Book of Fourth Ezra*, Hermeneia (Minneapolis: Fortress, 1990).

19. David N. Dumville, "Biblical Apocrypha and the Early Irish: A Preliminary Investigation," *Proceedings of the Royal Irish Academy* 73C (1973): 299–338; Dumville, "Towards an Interpretation of Fís Adamnán," *Studia Celtica* 12/13 (1977): 62–77.

20. Martin McNamara, *The Apocrypha in the Irish Church* (Dublin: Institute for Advanced Studies, 1975). I also discussed some aspects of this in Michael E. Stone, "Jewish Tradition, the Pseudepigrapha and the Christian West," in *The Aramaic Bible: Targums in Their Historical Context*, ed. D. R. G. Beattie and M. J. McNamara (Sheffield: Sheffield Academic, 1994), 431–49.

21. Steven D. Fraade, *Enosh and His Generation: Pre-Israelite Hero and History in Postbiblical Interpretation*, SBLMS 30 (Chico, CA: Scholars Press, 1984).

22. See his recent work, Robert A. Kraft, *Exploring the Scripturesque: Jewish Texts and Their Christian Contexts* (Leiden: Brill, 2009); and his 2006 Society of Biblical Lit-

is time to follow the pseudepigrapha and their traditions down the centuries. The first millennium CE is coming to the fore as a rich and suggestive time. Reeves's pioneering work on the Book of the Giants, Gabriele Boccaccini's work on the medieval Enoch on the 4 Enoch website, and Annette Yoshiko Reed's also on the Enoch tradition, all show the way.[23] Nickelsburg included a substantial section on Roman and Byzantine uses of 1 Enoch in his Hermeneia commentary. Openness to the history of reception, then, is most important. Adler's works on the Byzantine chronicles and my own work on the Armenian apocryphal literature both are part of this stream of study.[24] It is also clear that Richard Bauckham, James R. Davila, and Alexander Panayotov's new collection, *Old Testament Pseudepigrapha*, reflects this development,[25] and there is more on the way.

Second, within the limits of the Second Temple period, the attempt to integrate the various subdisciplines seems to be a major challenge, and the historian of religion's job is central. Using the textual and conceptual data emerging from the studies of the pseudepigrapha, the Dead Sea Scrolls,

---

erature presidential address, "Para-Mania: Beside, before, and beyond Bible Studies," *JBL* 126 (2007): 5–27.

23. John C. Reeves, *Jewish Lore in Manichaean Cosmogony: Studies in the Book of Giants Traditions* (Cincinnati: Hebrew Union College Press, 1992); Annette Yoshiko Reed, *Fallen Angels and the History of Judaism and Christianity: The Reception of Enochic Literature* (Cambridge: Cambridge University Press, 2005).

24. William Adler, *Time Immemorial: Archaic History and Its Sources in Christian Chronography from Julius Africanus to George Syncellus* (Washington, DC: Dumbarton Oaks Research Library and Collection, 1989). For a complete bibliography of my work, see Lorenzo DiTommaso, Matthias Henze, and William Adler, eds. *The Embroidered Bible: Studies in Biblical Apocrypha and Pseudepigrapha in Honour of Michael E. Stone*, SVTP 26 (Leiden: Brill, 2018), xix–xlvi. In particular, see "The Apocryphal Literature in the Armenian Tradition," *Proceedings of the Israel Academy of Sciences and Humanities* 4 (1971): 59–77 [English], 153–67 [Hebrew]; "Jewish Apocryphal Literature in the Armenian Church," *Le Muséon* 95 (1982): 285–309; "Jewish Tradition, the Pseudepigrapha and the Christian West"; "The Armenian Apocryphal Literature: Translation and Creation," in *Il Caucaso: Cerniera fra culture dal mediterraneo alla Persia (secoli I–XI), 20–26 aprile 1995*, Settimane di studio dal centro italiano de studi sull'alto medioevo 43 (Spoleto: Presso la sede del centro, 1996), 612–46; "The Armenian Apocryphal Literature of the Old Testament in the Twentieth Century," in *Armenian Philology in the Modern Era: From Manuscript to Digital Text*, ed. Valentina Calzolari and Michael E. Stone (Leiden: Brill, 2014), 232–63.

25. Richard Bauckham, James R. Davila, and Alexander Panayotov, eds., *Old Testament Pseudepigrapha: More Noncanonical Scriptures*, vol. 1 (Grand Rapids: Eerdmans, 2013).

Jewish literature(s) in the Hellenistic world, the New Testament, epigraphy, and the earliest levels of the rabbinic corpus,[26] the history of Judaism in that age needs to be rewritten. In addition to the history of the exegesis of the Bible (which has been a focus of work in the last decades), we need to pay more attention to issues of the history of ideas and religion, using the sources now available.[27]

When we look at medieval Christian transmission of pseudepigraphical traditions, we can note, among others, that Alexander Kulik has worked on the Slavonic material; Sebastian P. Brock profoundly contributed to Syriac studies; Roger Cowley, Loren Stuckenbruck, and VanderKam have worked on the Ethiopic exegetical tradition; McNamara on the Irish traditions; Brian O. Murdoch on ancient German and Celtic biblical retellings; and more scholars and languages could be enumerated.[28]

---

26. Jacob Neusner, early in his career, set about trying to isolate pre-70 CE traditions preserved in rabbinic literature. See his *The Rabbinic Traditions about the Pharisees before 70*, 3 vols. (Leiden: Brill, 1971).

27. It should be noted that the German translation by Riessler had a wide focus, as does the new three-volume work edited by Feldman, Kugel, and Schiffman, *Outside the Bible*. See Paul Riessler, ed., *Altjüdisches Schrifttum ausserhalb der Bibel* (Heidelberg: Kerle, 1928); Louis H. Feldman, James L. Kugel, and Lawrence H. Schiffman, eds., *Outside the Bible: Ancient Jewish Writings Related to Scripture*, 3 vols. (Lincoln: University of Nebraska Press; Philadelphia: Jewish Publication Society, 2013).

28. Alexander Kulik, "Interpretation and Reconstruction: Retroverting the Apocalypse of Abraham," *Apocrypha* 13 (2002): 203–26; Kulik, *Retroverting Slavonic Pseudepigrapha: Toward the Original of the Apocalypse of Abraham*, TCS 3 (Atlanta: Society of Biblical Literature, 2004); Kulik, *3 Baruch: Greek-Slavonic Apocalypse of Baruch*, CEJL (Berlin: de Gruyter, 2010); Sebastian P. Brock, "Jewish Traditions in Syriac Sources," *JJS* 30 (1979): 212–32, and, among other publications, Brock, "A Fragment of Enoch in Syriac," *JTS* NS 19 (1968): 626–31; Brock, "Sarah and the Aqedah," *Le Muséon* 87 (1974): 67–77; Brock, "Abraham and the Ravens: A Syriac Counterpart to Jubilees 11–12 and Its Implications," *JSJ* 9 (1978): 135–52; Brock, "The Queen of Sheba's Questions to Solomon: A Syriac Version," *Le Muséon* 92.3-4 (1979): 331–45; James C. VanderKam, *Textual and Historical Studies in Jubilees*, HSM 14 (Missoula, MT: Scholars Press, 1977); Roger W. Cowley, *Ethiopian Biblical Interpretation: A Study in Exegetical Tradition and Hermeneutics*, University of Cambridge Oriental Publications 38 (Cambridge: Cambridge University Press, 1988); Loren T. Stuckenbruck and Ted M. Erho, "The *Book of Enoch* and the Ethiopian Manuscript Tradition: New Data," in *'Go Out and Study the Land' (Judges 18:2): Archaeological, Historical and Textual Studies in Honor of Hanan Eshel*, ed. Aren M. Maeir, Jodi Magness, and Lawrence H. Schiffman, JSJSup 148 (Leiden: Brill, 2012), 257–67; Loren T. Stuckenbruck, *1 Enoch 91–108*, CEJL (Berlin: de Gruyter, 2007); McNamara, *The*

All these philological disciplines need to be talking with one another, at least as far as the pseudepigrapha are concerned. Moreover, there are certain traditions that have been left out of consideration or little studied and that should be broached or investigated more profoundly (one thinks of Georgian, Bulgarian, Rumanian, Coptic, and Christian Arabic, at least).[29]

Other new and exciting avenues of research are also opening up. Liv Ingeborg Lied has worked on what the manuscripts themselves can contribute, using the tools of modern codicology and thinking of the manuscripts as artefacts deserving their own investigation.[30] The underlying Jewish and Christian traditions in Islam are also being unraveled again (some

---

Apocrypha in the Irish Church; Brian O. Murdoch, "Das Deutsche Adambuch und die Adamlegenden des Mittelalters," in *Deutsche Literatur des späten Mittelalters: Hamburger Colloquium 1973*, ed. Wolfgang Harms and L. Peter Johnson (Hamburg: Erich Schmidt Verlag, 1973), 209–24; Murdoch, *Commentary*, vol. 2 of *The Irish Adam and Eve Story from Saltair Na Rann* (Dublin: Dublin Institute for Advanced Studies, 1976); Murdoch, *The Apocryphal Adam and Eve in Medieval Europe*, Vernacular Translations and Adaptations of the Vita Adae et Evae (Oxford: Oxford University Press, 2009); and other works.

29. For Romanian, Bulgarian, Coptic, Georgian, and Christian Arabic. Some examples are M. Tarchnishvili, *Geschichte der kirchlichen georgischen Literatur von K. Kekelidze bearbeitet von P. M. Tarchnisvili in Verbindung mit J. Assfalg*, Studi e Testi 185 (Città del Vaticano, 1955); Anisava Miltenova, "The Apocryphon about the Struggle of the Archangel Michael with Satanail in Two Redactions" [Bulgarian], Старобългарска литература 9 (1981): 98–113; Nicolae Roddy, *The Romanian Version of the Testament of Abraham: Text, Translation, and Cultural Context*, EJL 19 (Atlanta: Society of Biblical Literature, 2001); Georg Graf, *Geschichte der christlichen arabischen Literatur: Erster Band, Die Übersetzungen*, Studi e Testi 118.1 (Vatican: Biblioteca Apostolica Vaticana, 1944).

In terms of scope, the field seems to be moving back, *mutatis mutandis*, to the scope of Fabricius and Migne's work (viewed critically, of course), though contemporary research benefits from the new discoveries and extraordinary volume of critical studies emerging since their publication. See J. A. Fabricius, *Codex Pseudepigrapha Veteris Testamenti* (Hamburg: Felginer, 1722); Fabricius, *Codicis Pseudepigraphi Veteris Testamenti Volumen Alterum Accedit Josephi Veteris Christiani Auctoria Hypomnesticon* (Hamburg: Felginer, 1723); Jacques-Paul Migne, *Dictionnaire des Apocryphes, Ou, Collection de tous les Livres Apocryphes relatifs à l'Ancient et au Nouveau Testament*, 2 vols. (1856; repr., Turnhout: Brepols, 1989).

30. Liv I. Lied, "Studying Snapshots: On Manuscript Culture, Textual Fluidity, and New Philology," in *Snapshots of Evolving Traditions: Jewish and Christian Manuscript Culture, Textual Fluidity, and New Philology*, ed. Liv I. Lied and Hugo Lundhaug, TUGAL 175 (Berlin: de Gruyter, 2017), 1–19. Compare also the fine study of Michael Langlois, *Le Premier Manuscrit du* Livre d'Hénoch (Paris: Cerf, 2008).

work was already done in the late nineteenth and early twentieth century): I think of studies by Reeves, among others.[31] Manicheism and Karaism, medieval Jewish, Muslim and Christian (often heretical) trends and sects, and more, studied from the perspective of pseudepigrapha studies, will contribute to the understanding of the reception of the pseudepigrapha. The study of magical traditions is also very promising for our field and has already revealed some remarkable information.[32] The mystical tradition in Judaism is another such potential arena for our research, as Gershom Scholem verbally stressed to me in the 1970s and has since been borne out by Philip S. Alexander's work.[33]

I cannot speak in detail here of Lorenzo DiTommaso's fascinating undertaking of following apocalyptic ideas and motifs from antiquity and down to our twenty-first century.[34] One could imagine similar studies of wisdom ideas and so forth. DiTommaso's project has already taken account of most of the caveats I mentioned above; it has gone beyond temporal and doctrinal constraints and, though I did not talk of it, beyond the geographic presuppositions that underlie the thinking of so many of us. It may (re)open for us an old/new path in the study of the human ésprit.

---

31. John C. Reeves, "The Reception and Reconfiguration of Earlier Scriptures in Islamic Traditions," unpublished essay; Reeves, "Jewish Pseudepigrapha in Manichean Literature: The Influence of the Enochic Library," in *Tracing the Threads: Studies in the Vitality of the Jewish Pseudepigrapha*, ed. John C. Reeves, EJL 6 (Atlanta: Scholars Press, 1994), 174–203; Reeves, *Jewish Lore in Manichaean Cosmogony*; Reeves, "Some Explorations of the Intertwining of Bible and Qur'ān," in *Bible and Qur'ān: Essays in Scriptural Intertextuality*, ed. John C. Reeves (Atlanta: Society of Biblical Literature, 1993), 43–60; Reeves, "Exploring the Afterlife of Jewish Pseudepigrapha in Medieval Near Eastern Religious Traditions: Some Initial Soundings," *JSJ* 30.2 (1999): 148–77; Reeves, "Jewish Apocalyptic Lore in Early Islam: Reconsidering Kaʿb Al-aḥbār," in *Revealed Wisdom: Studies in Apocalyptic in Honour of Christopher Rowland*, ed. John Ashton (Leiden: Brill, 2014), 200–216.

32. See, for example, J. Naveh and S. Shaked, *Amulets and Magical Bowls* (Jerusalem: Magnes, 1985); Naveh and Shaked, *Magical Spells and Formulae: Aramaic Incantations of Late Antiquity* (Jerusalem: Magnes, 1993); Gideon Bohak, *Ancient Jewish Magic: A History* (Cambridge: Cambridge University Press, 2008).

33. Philip S. Alexander, *Mystical Texts*, LSTS 61 (London: T&T Clark, 2006); Alexander, "Incantations and Books of Magic," in Emil Schürer, *The History of the Jewish People in the Age of Jesus Christ*, ed. Geza Vermes, Fergus Millar, and Martin Goodman (Edinburgh: Clark, 1986), 3.1:342–79; Alexander, "3 Enoch," *OTP* 1:223–315.

34. See particularly his forthcoming work, Lorenzo DiTommaso, *The Architecture of Apocalypticism* (Oxford: Oxford University Press, forthcoming).

4. Early Days of the SBL Pseudepigrapha Group 69

The above enumeration does not exhaust the things needing to be done, of course, but one matter that has been on the table for many years is of particular interest to me: the persistence and also the recuperation of apocryphal and pseudepigraphic traditions in Judaism down to the Enlightenment. The case of Pirqe di Rabbi Eliezer is well known.[35] How did the traditions known to it reach its author? The familiarity with Jubilees exhibited by Sefer Asaf HaRofe is another conundrum. The Hebrew translation of Prayer of Manasseh that Reimund Leicht has published was transmitted in the Jewish astrological tradition and offers hints at channels of transmission.[36] Nachmanides knew the Syriac of Wisdom of Solomon (after all, Syriac is an East Aramaic dialect, a congener of the Aramaic of the Babylonian Talmud). The Chronicle of Jeraḥmeel knows and preserves much, as do Josippon, Megillat Antiochus, the Hebrew of Pseudo-Callisthenes, and medieval Hebrew and Aramaic Judith and Tobit documents.[37]

This list is far from everything known, and the wealth that still remains only in manuscripts is hinted at by Adolph Jellinek's *Beth Ha-Midrasch* and in Oded Ir-Shai's recently issued reworking of Even Shmuel's *Midreshei Ge'ulah*.[38] Indeed, I have passed too quickly over the pseudepigraphical

---

35. Rachel Adelman, *The Return of the Repressed: Pirqe De-Rabbi Eliezer and the Pseudepigrapha*, JSJSup 140 (Leiden: Brill, 2009); S. A. Ballaban, "The Literature of the Second Temple in Pirqe D'Rabbi Eliezer and Josippon; The Enigma of the Lost Second Temple Literature: Routes of Recovery" (PhD diss., Hebrew Union College, 1994), 84–90; Menachem Kister, "Ancient Material in *Pirqe De-Rabbi Eli'Ezer*: Basilides, Qumran, the *Book of Jubilees*," in Maeir, Magness, and Schiffman, *'Go Out and Study the Land' (Judges 18:2)*, 69–93.

36. Reimund Leicht, "A Newly Discovered Hebrew Version of the Apocryphal 'Prayer of Manasseh,'" *JSQ* 3 (1996): 359–73.

37. L. Cohn, "Pseudo-Philo und Jerahmeel," in *Festschrift zum siebzigsten Geburtstage Jakob Guttmans* (Leipzig: Fock, 1915), 173–85; Howard Jacobson, "Thoughts on the Chronicles of Jerahmeel, Ps. Philo's Liber Antiquitatum Biblicarum and Their Relationship," *SPhiloA* 9 (1997): 239–63; Daniel J. Harrington, *The Hebrew Fragments of Pseudo-Philo's Liber Antiquitatum Biblicarum Preserved in the Chronicles of Jeraḥmeel*, SBLTT 3 (Missoula, MT: Society of Biblical Literature, 1974); Eli Yassif, *The Book of Memory, That Is the Chronicles of Jerahme'el (Sefer Ha-Zikronot Hu Divrei Ha-Yamim Le-Yerahmeel)* (Tel-Aviv: Tel Aviv University, 2001); David Flusser, *The Josippon [Josephus Gorionides]: Edited with Introduction and Notes*, 2 vols. (Jerusalem: Bialik Institute, 1981).

38. Adolph Jellinek, *Bet Ha-Midrasch*, 6 vols. (Leipzig: Friedrich Nies, 1853–1877); Yehudah Even-Shmuel, *Midreshei Ge'ulah: Chapters of Jewish Apocalypse Dating*

treasures of the Cairo Genizah, including Aramaic Levi Document, several manuscripts of Hebrew Ben Sira, the sectarian Damascus Document allied with the Qumran sect, and other possible ancient works preserved in manuscripts there. Moreover, there are works in medieval Hebrew literature with connections with antique documents, such as the Hebrew Testament of Naphtali and Midrash Wa-yissa'u, known for a century yet little studied. What a treasure such a study might be.

One final thought. In addition to the preservation of whole Jewish works from antiquity in Christian traditions, Christian works preserved a rich tradition of citations of testimonia to ancient pseudepigrapha, not otherwise known. This is something to which the Pseudepigrapha Group and its members turned their attention from time to time. J. A. Fabricius and Jacques-Paul Migne had first assembled such citations from much ancient literature, in the eighteenth and nineteenth centuries respectively.[39] In 1920, the learned and indefatigable M. R. James produced *The Lost Apocrypha of the Old Testament*.[40] The Greek fragmentary pseudepigraphic texts were collected by Denis and published, and he dealt with them in his introductory works.[41] The Pseudepigrapha Group took up this line of interest, resulting in a number of publications. Representative are the translations of the lists of canonical and uncanonical books given by Charlesworth, and some of my own publications of canon lists with annotations.[42] With Strugnell, I compiled a collection of fragmentary pseudepigrapha of Elijah in Texts and Translations.[43] My Jerusalem Senior Seminar produced two books, which include comprehensive

---

from the Completion of the Babylonian Talmud until the Sixth Millennium (Jerusalem: Carmel, 2016).

39. See note 29 above.

40. M. R. James, *The Lost Apocrypha of the Old Testament: Their Titles and Fragments*, Translations of Early Documents 1 (London: SPCK, 1920).

41. Denis, *Fragmenta Pseudepigraphorum*. See Denis, *Introduction aux pseudépigraphes grecs de l'Ancien Testament*; and Denis and Haelewyck, *Introduction à la littérature religieuse judéo-hellénistique*. Charlesworth, *Pseudepigrapha and Modern Research*, gives translations of various ancient lists of canonical and uncanonical works.

42. Charlesworth, *Pseudepigrapha and Modern Research*. See my publications in a series of articles in *Harvard Theological Review*, beginning in the 1970s.

43. Michael E. Stone and John Strugnell, *The Books of Elijah, Parts 1 and 2*, SBLTT 5 (Missoula, MT: Scholars Press, 1979). This was called "Parts 1 and 2" because our plan, never continued, was to include all the later apocryphal Elijah books, such as Sefer Eliyyahu, which we hoped would be edited by others. That has not yet happened.

presentations of testimonia, citations, and later reworkings of material attributed to Ezekiel and Noah.⁴⁴

To these lines of work, a number of further studies appertain. S. E. Robinson dealt with the Testament of Adam, extant in four substantial fragments; Wright, in addition to his excellent publications on Ben Sira, also published about Ezekiel fragments in the Dead Sea Scrolls, only two examples that represent many.⁴⁵ Finally, I will mention under this heading, Kraft's as yet incomplete reworking of James's *Lost Apocrypha*, online at http://ccat.sas.upenn.edu/rak/publics/mrjames/james.htm. This may well prove a harbinger of things to come.

Now the preparatory work has been done, and the possibilities the future offers are rich and enticing.

Bibliography

Adelman, Rachel. *The Return of the Repressed: Pirqe De-Rabbi Eliezer and the Pseudepigrapha*. JSJSup 140. Leiden: Brill, 2009.
Adler, William. *Time Immemorial: Archaic History and Its Sources in Christian Chronography from Julius Africanus to George Syncellus*. Washington, DC: Dumbarton Oaks Research Library and Collection, 1989.
Alexander, Philip S. "Incantations and Books of Magic." Pages 342–79 in vol. 3.1 of Emil Schürer, *The History of the Jewish People in the Age of Jesus Christ*. Edited by Geza Vermes, Fergus Millar, and Martin Goodman. Edinburgh: Clark, 1986.
———. *Mystical Texts*. LSTS 61. London: T&T Clark, 2006.
Ballaban, S. A. "The Literature of the Second Temple in Pirqe D'Rabbi Eliezer and Josippon; The Enigma of the Lost Second Temple Literature: Routes of Recovery." PhD diss. Hebrew Union College, 1994.

---

44. Michael E. Stone, Benjamin G. Wright III, and David Satran, eds., *The Apocryphal Ezekiel*, EJL 18 (Atlanta: Society of Biblical Literature, 2000); Michael E. Stone, Aryeh Amihai, and Vered Hillel, eds., *Noah and His Book(s)*, EJL 28 (Atlanta: Society of Biblical Literature, 2010).

45. S. E. Robinson, *The Testament of Adam: An Examination of the Syriac and Greek Traditions*, SBLDS 52 (Chico, CA: Scholars Press, 1982); Robinson, "The Testament of Adam: An Updated Arbeitsbericht," *JSP* 5 (1989): 95–100; Benjamin G. Wright III, "Qumran Pseudepigrapha and Early Christianity: Is 1 Clement 50:4 a Citation of 4QPseudo-Ezekiel (4Q385 12)?," in *Pseudepigraphic Perspectives: The Apocrypha and Pseudepigrapha in Light of the Dead Sea Scrolls*, ed. Michael E. Stone and Esther G. Chazon (Leiden: Brill, 1999), 183–93.

Bauckham, Richard, James R. Davila, and Alexander Panayotov, eds., *Old Testament Pseudepigrapha: More Noncanonical Scriptures*. Vol. 1. Grand Rapids: Eerdmans, 2013.

Bohak, Gideon. *Ancient Jewish Magic: A History*. Cambridge: Cambridge University Press, 2008.

Brock, Sebastian P. "Abraham and the Ravens: A Syriac Counterpart to Jubilees 11–12 and Its Implications." *JSJ* 9 (1978): 135–52.

———. "A Fragment of Enoch in Syriac." *JTS* NS 19 (1968): 626–31.

———. "Jewish Traditions in Syriac Sources." *JJS* 30 (1979): 212–32.

———. "The Queen of Sheba's Questions to Solomon: A Syriac Version." *Le Muséon* 92.3–4 (1979): 331–45.

———. "Sarah and the Aqedah." *Le Muséon* 87 (1974): 67–77.

Charles, R. H. *The Apocrypha and Pseudepigrapha of the Old Testament*. 2 vols. Oxford: Clarendon, 1913.

Charlesworth, James H. ed. *The Old Testament Pseudepigrapha*. 2 vols. New York: Doubleday, 1983–1985.

Charlesworth, James H., assisted by P. Dykers. *The Pseudepigrapha and Modern Research*. SCS 7. Missoula, MT: Scholars Press, 1976.

Cohn, L. "Pseudo-Philo und Jerahmeel." Pages 173–85 in *Festschrift zum siebzigsten Geburtstage Jakob Guttmans*. Leipzig: Fock, 1915.

Collins, John J. ed. *Apocalypse: The Morphology of a Genre*, Semeia 14 (1979).

Cowley, Roger W. *Ethiopian Biblical Interpretation: A Study in Exegetical Tradition and Hermeneutics*. University of Cambridge Oriental Publications 38. Cambridge: Cambridge University Press, 1988.

Denis, Albert-Marie. *Concordance Grecque des Pseudépigraphes d'Ancien Testament*. Louvain-la-Neuve: Université catholique de Louvain, Institut orientaliste, 1987.

———. *Fragmenta Pseudepigraphorum quae supersunt graece una cum Historicorum et Auctorum Judaeorum Hellenistarum Fragmenti*. PVTG 3. Leiden: Brill, 1970.

———. *Introduction aux Pseudépigraphes Grecs d'Ancient Testament*. Leiden: Brill, 1970.

Denis, Albert-Marie, and J.-C. Haelewyck. *Introduction à la littérature religieuse Judéo-Hellénistique*. Turnhout: Brepols, 2000.

DiTommaso, Lorenzo. *The Architecture of Apocalypticism*. Oxford: Oxford University Press, forthcoming.

———. *A Bibliography of Pseudepigrapha Research 1850–1999*. JSPSup 39. Sheffield: Sheffield Academic, 2001.

DiTommaso, Lorenzo, Matthias Henze, and William Adler, eds. *The Embroidered Bible: Studies in Biblical Apocrypha and Pseudepigrapha in Honour of Michael E. Stone*. SVTP 26. Leiden: Brill, 2018.

Dumville, David N. "Biblical Apocrypha and the Early Irish: A Preliminary Investigation." *Proceedings of the Royal Irish Academy* 73C (1973): 299–338.

———. "Towards an Interpretation of Fís Adamnán." *Studia Celtica* 12/13 (1977): 62–77.

Even-Shmuel, Yehudah. *Midrashei Ge'ulah: Chapters of Jewish Apocalypse Dating from the Completion of the Babylonian Talmud until the Sixth Millennium*. Jerusalem: Carmel, 2016.

Fabricius, J. A. *Codex Pseudepigrapha Veteris Testamenti*. Hamburg: Felginer, 1722.

———. *Codicis Pseudepigraphi Veteris Testamenti Volumen Alterum Accedit Josephi Veteris Christiani Auctoria Hypomnesticon*. Hamburg: Felginer, 1723.

Feldman, Louis H., James L. Kugel, and Lawrence H. Schiffman, eds. *Outside the Bible: Ancient Jewish Writings Related to Scripture*. 3 vols. Lincoln: University of Nebraska Press; Philadelphia: Jewish Publication Society, 2013.

Flusser, David. *The Josippon [Josephus Gorionides]: Edited with Introduction and Notes*. 2 vols. Jerusalem: Bialik Institute, 1981.

Fraade, Steven D. *Enosh and His Generation: Pre-Israelite Hero and History in Postbiblical Interpretation*. SBLMS 30. Chico, CA: Scholars Press, 1984.

Graf, Georg. *Geschichte der christlichen arabischen Literatur: Erster Band, Die Übersetzungen*. Studi e Testi 118.1. Vatican: Biblioteca Apostolica Vaticana, 1944.

Hanson, Paul D. *The Dawn of Apocalyptic: The Historical and Sociological Roots of Jewish Apocalyptic Eschatology*. Philadelphia: Fortress, 1979.

Harrington, Daniel J. *The Hebrew Fragments of Pseudo-Philo's Liber Antiquitatum Biblicarum Preserved in the Chronicles of Jeraḥmeel*. SBLTT 3. Missoula, MT: Society of Biblical Literature, 1974.

Hellholm, David, ed., *Apocalypticism in the Mediterranean World and the Near East: Proceedings of the International Colloquium on Apocalypticism, Uppsala, August 12–17, 1979*. Tübingen: Mohr Siebeck, 1983.

Hollander, Harm W., and Marinus de Jonge. *The Testaments of the Twelve Patriarchs: A Commentary*. SVTP 8. Leiden: Brill, 1985.

Jacobson, Howard. "Thoughts on the Chronicles of Jerahmeel, Ps. Philo's Liber Antiquitatum Biblicarum and Their Relationship." *SPhiloA* 9 (1997): 239–63.

James, M. R. *The Lost Apocrypha of the Old Testament: Their Titles and Fragments*. Translations of Early Documents 1. London: SPCK, 1920.

Jellinek, Adolph. *Bet Ha-Midrasch*. 6 vols. Leipzig: Friedrich Nies, 1853–1877.

Jonge, Marinus de. *Studies on the Testaments of the Twelve Patriarchs: Text and Interpretation*. SVTP 3. Leiden: Brill, 1975.

———. *The Testaments of the Twelve Patriarchs: A Critical Edition of the Greek Text*. PVTG 1–2. Leiden: Brill, 1978.

———. *The Testaments of the Twelve Patriarchs: A Study of Their Text, Composition and Origin*. Assen: Van Gorcum, 1953.

Leicht, Reimund. "A Newly Discovered Hebrew Version of the Apocryphal 'Prayer of Manasseh.'" *JSQ* 3 (1996): 359–73.

Menachem. Kister, "Ancient Material in *Pirqe De-Rabbi Eli'Ezer*: Basilides, Qumran, the *Book of Jubilees*." Pages 69–93 in *'Go Out and Study the Land' (Judges 18:2): Archaeological, Historical and Textual Studies in Honor of Hanan Eshel*. Edited by Aren M. Maeir, Jodi Magness, and Lawrence H. Schiffman. JSJSup 148. Leiden: Brill, 2012.

Koch, Klaus. *Ratlos vor der Apokalyptik: Eine Streitschrift über ein vernachlässigtes Gebiet der Bibelwissenschaften, und den schädlichen Auswirkungen auf Theologie und Philosophie*. Gütersloh: Gütersloher Verlagshaus, 1970.

Kraft, Robert A. *Exploring the Scripturesque: Jewish Texts and Their Christian Contexts*. Leiden: Brill, 2009

———. "Para-Mania: Beside, before, and beyond Bible Studies." *JBL* 126 (2007): 5–27.

Kraft, Robert A., and Ann-Elizabeth Purintun. *Paraleipomena Jeremiou*. SBLTT 1. Missoula, MT: Society of Biblical Literature, 1972.

Kulik, Alexander. *3 Baruch: Greek-Slavonic Apocalypse of Baruch*. CEJL. Berlin: de Gruyter, 2010.

———. "Interpretation and Reconstruction: Retroverting the Apocalypse of Abraham." *Apocrypha* 13 (2002): 203–26.

———. *Retroverting Slavonic Pseudepigrapha: Toward the Original of the Apocalypse of Abraham*. TCS 3. Atlanta: Society of Biblical Literature.

Langlois, Michael. *Le Premier Manuscrit du Livre d'Hénoch*. Paris: Cerf, 2008.

Lied, Liv I. "Studying Snapshots: On Manuscript Culture, Textual Fluidity, and New Philology." Pages 1–19 in *Snapshots of Evolving Traditions: Jewish and Christian Manuscript Culture, Textual Fluidity, and New Philology*. Edited by Liv I. Lied and Hugo Lundhaug. TUGAL 175. Berlin: de Gruyter, 2017.

McNamara, Martin. *The Apocrypha in the Irish Church*. Dublin: Institute for Advanced Studies, 1975.

Migne, Jacques-Paul. *Dictionnaire des Apocryphes, Ou, Collection de tous les Livres Apocryphes relatifs à l'Ancient et au Nouveau Testament*. 2 vols. 1856. Repr., Turnhout: Brepols, 1989.

Miltenova, Anisava. "The Apocryphon about the Struggle of the Archangel Michael with Satanail in Two Redactions" [Bulgarian]. Старобългарска литература 9 (1981): 98–113.

Murdoch, Brian O. *The Apocryphal Adam and Eve in Medieval Europe. Vernacular Translations and Adaptations of the Vita Adae et Evae*. Oxford: Oxford University Press, 2009.

———. *Commentary*. Vol. 2 of *The Irish Adam and Eve Story from Saltair Na Rann*. Dublin: Dublin Institute for Advanced Studies, 1976.

———. "Das Deutsche Adambuch und die Adamlegenden des Mittelalters." Pages 209–24 in *Deutsche Literatur des späten Mittelalters: Hamburger Colloquium 1973*. Edited by Wolfgang Harms and L. Peter Johnson. Hamburg: Erich Schmidt Verlag, 1973.

Naveh, J., and S. Shaked. *Amulets and Magical Bowls*. Jerusalem: Magnes, 1985.

———. *Magical Spells and Formulae: Aramaic Incantations of Late Antiquity*. Jerusalem: Magnes, 1993.

Neusner, Jacob. *The Rabbinic Traditions about the Pharisees before 70*. 3 vols. Leiden: Brill, 1971.

Nickelsburg, George W. E. *1 Enoch 1: A Commentary on the Book of 1 Enoch, Chapters 1–36, 81–108*. Hermeneia. Minneapolis: Fortress, 2001.

———, ed. *Studies on the Testament of Abraham*. SCS 6. Missoula, MT: Scholars Press, 1976.

———, ed. *Studies on the Testament of Joseph*. SCS 5. Missoula, MT: Scholars Press, 1975.

———, ed. *Studies on the Testament of Moses*. SCS 4. Cambridge, MA: Society of Biblical Literature, 1973.

Nickelsburg, George W. E., and James C. VanderKam. *1 Enoch 2: A Commentary on the Book of 1 Enoch 37–82*. Hermeneia. Minneapolis: Fortress, 2012.

Reed, Annette Yoshiko. *Fallen Angels and the History of Judaism and Christianity: The Reception of Enochic Literature*. Cambridge: Cambridge University Press, 2005.

Reeves, John C. "Exploring the Afterlife of Jewish Pseudepigrapha in Medieval Near Eastern Religious Traditions: Some Initial Soundings." *JSJ* 30.2 (1999): 148–77.

———. "Jewish Apocalyptic Lore in Early Islam: Reconsidering Kaʿb Al-aḥbār." Pages 200–216 in *Revealed Wisdom: Studies in Apocalyptic in Honour of Christopher Rowland*. Edited by John Ashton. Leiden: Brill, 2014.

———. *Jewish Lore in Manichaean Cosmogony: Studies in the Book of Giants Traditions*. Cincinnati: Hebrew Union College Press, 1992.

———. "Jewish Pseudepigrapha in Manichean Literature: The Influence of the Enochic Library." Pages 174–203 in *Tracing the Threads: Studies in the Vitality of the Jewish Pseudepigrapha*. Edited by John C. Reeves. EJL 6. Atlanta: Scholars Press, 1994.

———. "The Reception and Reconfiguration of Earlier Scriptures in Islamic Traditions." Unpublished essay.

———. "Some Explorations of the Intertwining of Bible and Qurʾān." Pages 43–60 in *Bible and Qurʾan: Essays in Scriptural Intertextuality*. Edited by John C. Reeves. Atlanta: Society of Biblical Literature, 1993.

Riessler, Paul, ed. *Altjüdisches Schrifttum ausserhalb der Bibel*. Heidelberg: Kerle, 1928.

Robinson, S. E. *The Testament of Adam: An Examination of the Syriac and Greek Traditions*. SBLDS 52. Chico, CA: Scholars Press, 1982.

———. "The Testament of Adam: An Updated Arbeitbericht." *JSP* 5 (1989): 95–100.

Roddy, Nicolae. *The Romanian Version of the Testament of Abraham: Text, Translation, and Cultural Context*. EJL 19. Atlanta: Society of Biblical Literature, 2001.

Russell, David S. *The Method and Message of Jewish Apocalyptic, 200 BC–AD 100*. Philadelphia: Westminster, 1964.

Stone, Michael E. "The Apocryphal Literature in the Armenian Tradition." *Proceedings of the Israel Academy of Sciences and Humanities* 4 (1971): 59–77 (English), 153–67 (Hebrew).

———. "The Armenian Apocryphal Literature: Translation and Creation." Pages 612–46 in *Il Caucaso: Cerniera fra culture dal mediterraneo alla Persia (secoli I–XI), 20–26 aprile 1995*. Settimane di studio dal centro italiano de studi sull'alto medioevo 43. Spoleto: Presso la sede del centro, 1996.

———. "The Armenian Apocryphal Literature of the Old Testament in the Twentieth Century." Pages 232–63 in *Armenian Philology in the Modern Era: From Manuscript to Digital Text*. Edited by Valentina Calzolari and Michael E. Stone. Leiden: Brill, 2014.

———. *The Armenian Version of the Testament of Joseph: Introduction, Critical Edition, and Translation*. SBLTT 5. Missoula, MT: Scholars Press, 1975.

———. *Fourth Ezra: A Commentary on the Book of Fourth Ezra*. Hermeneia. Minneapolis: Fortress, 1990.

———. "Jewish Apocryphal Literature in the Armenian Church." *Le Muséon* 95 (1982): 285–309.

———. "Jewish Tradition, the Pseudepigrapha and the Christian West." Pages 431–49 in *The Aramaic Bible: Targums in Their Historical Context*. Edited by D. R. G. Beattie and M. J. McNamara. Sheffield: Sheffield Academic, 1994.

———. "Some Observations on the Armenian Version of the Paralipomena of Jeremiah." *CBQ* 35 (1973): 47–59.

———. *The Testament of Abraham: The Greek Recensions*. SBLTT 2. Missoula, MT: Scholars Press, 1972.

Stone, Michael E., Aryeh Amihai, and Vered Hillel, eds. *Noah and His Book(s)*. EJL 28. Atlanta: Society of Biblical Literature, 2010.

Stone, Michael E., with Vered Hillel. *The Armenian Version of the Testaments of the Twelve Patriarchs: Edition, Apparatus, Translation and Commentary*. Hebrew University Armenian Series 11. Leuven: Peeters, 2012.

Stone, Michael E., and John Strugnell, *The Books of Elijah, Parts 1 and 2*. SBLTT 5. Missoula, MT: Scholars Press, 1979.

Stone, Michael E., Benjamin G. Wright III, and David Satran, eds. *The Apocryphal Ezekiel*. EJL 18. Atlanta: Society of Biblical Literature, 2000.

Stuckenbruck, Loren T. *1 Enoch 91–108*. CEJL. Berlin: de Gruyter, 2007.

Stuckenbruck, Loren T., and Ted M. Erho. "The *Book of Enoch* and the Ethiopian Manuscript Tradition: New Data." Pages 257–67 in *'Go Out and Study the Land' (Judges 18:2): Archaeological, Historical and Tex-*

tual Studies in Honor of Hanan Eshel. Edited by Aren M. Maeir, Jodi Magness, and Lawrence H. Schiffman. JSJSup 148. Leiden: Brill, 2012.

Tarchnishvili, M. *Geschichte der kirchlichen georgischen Literatur von K. Kekelidze bearbeitet von P. M. Tarchnisvili in Verbindung mit J. Assfalg*. Studi e Testi 185. Città del Vaticano, 1955.

Tov, Emanuel. *The Septuagint Translation of Jeremiah and Baruch: A Discussion of an Early Revision of the LXX of Jeremiah 29–52 and Baruch 1:1–3:8*. HSM 8. Missoula, MT: Scholars Press, 1976.

Wright, Benjamin G., III, "Qumran Pseudepigrapha and Early Christianity: Is 1 Clement 50:4 a Citation of 4QPseudo-Ezekiel (4Q385 12)?" Pages 183–93 in *Pseudepigraphic Perspectives: The Apocrypha and Pseudepigrapha in Light of the Dead Sea Scrolls*. Edited by Michael E. Stone and Esther G. Chazon. Leiden: Brill, 1999.

VanderKam, James C. *Textual and Historical Studies in Jubilees*. HSM 14. Missoula, MT: Scholars Press, 1977.

Yassif, Eli. *The Book of Memory, That Is the Chronicles of Jerahme'el (Sefer Ha-Zikronot Hu Divrei Ha-Yamim Le-Yerahmeel)*. Tel-Aviv: Tel Aviv University, 2001.

Ziegler, Joseph, ed. *Sapientia Jesu Filii Sirach*. SVTG 12.2. Göttingen: Vandenhoeck & Ruprecht, 1965.

5
Memories of the Society of Biblical Literature Pseudepigrapha Group, 1970–1982

James Hamilton Charlesworth

The editors of this volume asked me to share my reflections on the proceedings of the Society of Biblical Literature Pseudepigrapha Group. In the following pages, I shall share my own memories with a particular focus on the developments that helped produce the publication of *The Old Testament Pseudepigrapha* (*OTP*). The first volume appeared in 1983; the second volume was on our shelves in 1985.[1]

The Society of Biblical Literature Pseudepigrapha Sessions

In November of 1969, in Toronto during the Annual Meeting of the Society of Biblical Literature, Walter J. Harrelson invited a selection of scholars devoted to the study of the Old Testament pseudepigrapha to attend a breakfast. The agenda was to chart a way for these pseudepigraphal documents that constituted a *terra incognita*, to use a term shared with me by W. D. Davis, who counseled me during the early years of preparing the *The Old Testament Pseudepigrapha*. I recall that Jonathan Z. Smith suggested that I serve on the steering committee. Near the end of the breakfast, a steering committee was chosen by all present. Eventually, Harrelson was chosen chairman, and later I was appointed secretary.

I hope that my memory serves me well as I ponder the erudition and kindness of those on the steering committee, most importantly, Harrelson, Bruce M. Metzger, John Strugnell, Robert A. Kraft, and George W.

---

1. James H. Charlesworth, ed., *The Old Testament Pseudepigraha*, 2 vols. (Garden City, NY: Doubleday, 1983–1985).

MacRae. Soon three special friends and now internationally renowned specialists on the Old Testament pseudepigrapha, then PhD candidates at Harvard, joined us. They are John J. Collins, George W. E. Nickelsburg, and Michael E. Stone.

The Pseudepigrapha Newsletter and Other Publications

About two years after the selection of the steering committee of the Pseudepigrapha Group, I was chosen to edit and produce the Pseudepigrapha Newsletter. It was sent to a vast number of international experts. The costs were covered by the Religion Department at Duke University. The purpose was to share with other biblical scholars the discussions in our sessions. My other publications that announced the discussions in the Society of Biblical Literature Pseudepigrapha Group, in the Studiorum Novi Testamenti Societas Pseudepigrapha Seminars, the American Schools of Oriental Research Ancient Biblical Manuscript Committee, and the perception of the importance of the corpus are placed in an appendix to this chapter.

The Invitation from Doubleday

Based on my publication at Clarendon Press of the Syriac, Greek, and Coptic manuscripts of the Odes of Solomon and the Latin quotation by Lactantius,[2] I received a letter from John Delaney of Doubleday. He informed me of some long developments at Doubleday focused on the publication of a new edition of the Old Testament pseudepigrapha and the New Testament apocrypha and pseudepigrapha. On the advice of Ray Brown, he and his subeditors had chosen me to be the editor of this massive task. After discussions that occupied over six months between scholars and lawyers at Duke University and Doubleday, I finally signed the contract with Doubleday. My work on the Odes had been accepted for publication in 1968, on the advice of John Emerton and Geza Vermes, but the setting of all exotic texts delayed the publication until 1973. Such detailed research brought into focus the need to have a more inclusive and historically defined concept of the Old Testament pseudepigrapha than the editions supplied by Emil F. Kautzsch, R. H. Charles, and even Paul Riessler.[3]

---

2. James H. Charlesworth, *The Odes of Solomon* (Oxford: Clarendon, 1973), xv, 167.
3. Emil F. Kautzsch, ed., *Die Apokryphen und Pseudepigraphen des Alten Testaments* (Freiburg: J. C. B. Mohr, 1898–1900); R. H. Charles, ed., *The Apocrypha and*

Defining the Documents in *The Old Testament Pseudepigrapha*

What should be included in the new edition of *The Old Testament Pseudepigrapha*? Works well known in other collections did not need to be included, unless attractive reasons loomed large, like those for including Jewish pseudepigraphical documents in the *Papyri Graecae Magicae* and the Nag Hammadi Codices. No writings in the Old Testament (= Hebrew Scriptures) and New Testament should be included, but we needed to stress that many compositions in both parts of the canon were definitely pseudepigraphical, and the New Testament works were almost always composed by Jews and represented a sect within early Judaism.

In the 1970s, none of us knew the problems that would be generated by the vast amount of apocryphal and pseudepigraphical works found in the eleven Qumran caves. In the Princeton Dead Sea Scrolls Project, I have called these pseudepigrapha "Qumran Pseudepigrapha" to distinguish them from compositions that appear in collections of the Old Testament pseudepigrapha, which are now called "biblical pseudepigrapha."

It was widely known that R. H. Charles's collection was too inclusive and too exclusive. That is, Charles included the Zadokite Document and Pirke Aboth; but all experts know that these compositions belonged in other collections, respectively among the Qumran Scrolls and rabbinics. Far more important was the exclusion of early Jewish works that were considered authoritative and inspired by many early Jews from about 300 BCE to at least 200 CE. Charles did not include many early Jewish compositions that must be included in a complete edition of the Old Testament pseudepigrapha. Now, we should include Joseph and Aseneth, Pseudo-Philo, the Testament of Solomon, the History of the Rechabites, and the Testament of Adam.

Charles also did not include the documents cited by Alexander Polyhistor that are included in the second volume of *The Old Testament Pseudepigrapha*. Unique also to *The Old Testament Pseudepigrapha* is the inclusion of the Prayer of Joseph, and the Prayer of Jacob.

Discussions within the Society of Biblical Literature Pseudepigrapha Group and within other meetings, notably the Studiorum Novi Testamenti Societas, focused on collections of ancient Jewish documents. Conflicting

---

Pseudepigrapha of the Old Testament in English, 2 vols. (Oxford: Clarendon, 1963); Paul Riessler, ed., *Altjüdisches Schrifttum ausserhalb der Bibel* (Augsburg: Filser, 1928).

criteria were unconsciously employed, a fact clarified during discussions with Kraft during the Society's Pseudepigrapha Group's discussions. Some ancient documents, like the Dead Sea Scrolls (defined inclusively) and the Nag Hammadi Codices, were defined by the place of discovery. Others were defined by the canon, but it was receiving new attention from many scholars, including specialists on the pseudepigrapha and the Qumran Scrolls. Following the insights of James Sanders, biblical scholars began to perceive that the canon was not defined at Jamnia and remained open, at least with the text of the Torah and Prophets and the inclusion of psalms in the Writings.

With Metzger, we included all the chapters of a document we renamed the Fourth Book of Ezra. With Stone, we placed other documents attributed to Ezra next in the first volume. With William Stinespring, we chose to highlight a new selection: The Testaments of the Three Patriarchs, thus framing Ed Sanders's Testament of Abraham. With Collins, we included all the Sibylline Oracles and only now ventured on to ponder how the ancient scribes and priests who copied the Greek texts collected the ancient writings attributed to the sibyl together but never thought it pertinent to decide what was Jewish, what was edited by Jews, what was Jewish with later Christian editing, and what was a Christian creation. With H. Lunt and F. Andersen, we dove into the complex whirlpool represented by the Slavonic pseudepigrapha, crafting a path ahead for more explorations.

Imagined borders had for centuries hindered the perception of the importance of the so-called pseudepigrapha. One of these borders was the assumption of a closed canon by 200 CE, a myopia that still stains the publications of some biblical scholars. Our group recognized from the beginning that these were fictitious borders for historians, as evidenced by insights shared freely by Nickelsburg, MacRae, Strugnell, Harrelson, Kraft, Stone, Collins, and a coterie of young scholars who were given new vistas for conquest. As a scholar in my thirties, I learned much from so many older specialists and friends. If I have obtained some international prominence, it is because greater minds lifted me up.

The Appearance of Tools for the Study of the Old Testament Pseudepigrapha

Due to the success and importance of *The Old Testament Pseudepigrapha*, scholars around the world recognized the need for a journal and monograph series devoted to the corpus. Hence, in the mid-1980s, I was asked by Sheffield Press to organize and edit two new series. One was the *Journal for the Study of the Pseudepigrapha and Related Literature* and its supplement series. I continued as editor of both publications until I needed to devote my time to being editor of the Princeton Dead Sea Scrolls Project.

Insightful Sharing about Ancient Collections of Early Jewish Compositions

I recall fondly, during the 1981 sessions of the Studiorum Novi Testamenti Societas in Rome, the time George MacRae and I slipped away from the sessions and found a quiet place to talk about the pseudepigrapha and all the ancient literary creations. We found some good wine and sat around the swimming pool at the Holiday Inn during a late evening, feeling the delightful air of Rome in August. George could converse about the Hebrew Scriptures, the Dead Sea Scrolls, the gnostic codices, and the Old Testament pseudepigrapha. I matured under such tutelage.

George and I turned our thoughts to the Testament of Adam. We agreed that there were many Baptist groups around the Jordan River, and the most famous was led by John the Baptizer whose disciples included Jesus from Nazareth. We concurred that somehow the Testament of Adam evolved from such beginnings through early Jewish traditions and perhaps documents. We agreed that some gnostic treatises developed not from Christian or christological sources but directly from Judaism.

George was one of the finest interlocutors I have enjoyed. He shared insights with thoughtful reflection and wondered about issues that never can be resolved because we have so few unedited ancient works to study. How can we really recreate the Jewish environment of first-century Palestinian Judaism when we have only a small percentage of the scrolls placed in the eleven Qumran caves, and so many other texts, mentioned but not yet found, are possibly lost forever? I decided to draw attention to these lost works, known only by name, in my introduction to *The Old Testament Pseudepigrapha*.

I developed dialogues with editors of other collections of Jewish apocryphal documents in progress or preparation into many modern languages, including Danish, Dutch, French, German, Greek, Italian, Japanese, and Spanish. The most important collections were Erling Hammershaimb's *De gammeltestamentlige pseudepigrafer*, Marc Philonenko's *Pseudépigraphes de l'Ancien Testament*, Paolo Sacchi's *Apocrifi dell'Antico*

Testamento and *Antico testament, apocrifi e nuovo testamento*, and W. G. Kümmel's *Jüdische Schriften aus hellenistisch-römisher Zeit*.[4]

How can I ever forget the symposium on the Old Testament pseudepigrapha in Strasbourg in the fall of 1983; it was chaired by Philonenko. Scholars from France, the United States, Spain, Great Britain, the Netherlands, Germany, Italy, and elsewhere shared their insights regarding the importance of the Old Testament pseudepigrapha and announced their own series and editions. Afterwards, Philonenko wined and dined each of us in his home. Then he placed a piglet in front of me in full bodily form with an apple in its mouth. The colleague to my left almost fainted, and I shared similar feelings; but thanks to God's graciousness, we tasted succulent meat and special wine.

Scholars from Many Countries Influence What Should Be Included

With the insight of many experts, especially the Board of Advisors of *The Old Testament Pseudepigrapha*, namely, R. E. Brown, W. D. Davies, B. M. Metzger, R. E. Murphy, and J. Strugnell, I began to define *The Old Testament Pseudepigrapha* by including or excluding ancient documents. Many others met with me and discussed the Old Testament pseudepigrapha, notably George W. MacRae, John Priest, Geza Vermes, Michael E. Stone, Shemaryahu Talmon, and Pierre Benoit. I became slowly convinced how the new edition of the Old Testament pseudepigrapha should be far more extensive than those by E. Kautzsch and R. H. Charles; as Strugnell confided in me, it would be more like Riessler's collection.

A large amount of previously excluded early Jewish works needed to be included. First, gnostic texts emanating from Judaism should find a home, and that search led me to appreciate the Jewish Baptist groups possibly behind the Testament of Adam.

---

4. E. Hammershaimb, *De gammeltestamentlige pseudepigrafer i oversaettelse med indledning og noter*, 2 vols. (Copenhagen: Gad, 1953-1976); Marc Philonenko, *Pseudépigraphes de l'Ancien Testament et manuscrits de la Mer morte*, Cahiers de la Revue d'histoire et de philosophie religieuses 41 (Paris: Presses universitaries de France, 1967-); Paolo Sacchi, *Apocrifi dell'Antico Testamento*, Biblica Testi e studi 5, 7-8, 3 vols. (Brescia: Paideia editrice, 1997-2000); and Sacchi, *Antico testament, apocrifi e Nuovo Testamento: Un viaggio autobiografico* (Brescia: Morcelliana, 2015); Werner Georg Kümmel, with Christian Habicht, ed., *Jüdische Schriften aus hellenistisch-römischer Zeit* (Gütersloh: G. Mohn, 1973-).

Second, early Jewish works in the *Papyri Graecae Magicae* should be included. That drew attention to the Prayer of Jacob.

Third, documents that are fundamentally Jewish but interpolated or redacted by Christians must be included. That meant the Martyrdom and Ascension of Isaiah, the Apocalypse of Adam, and the Testaments of the Twelve Patriarchs were attractive candidates for inclusion. I well remember the positive responses to Nickelsburg when he opined that if a Testament of Naphtali had been identified among the Dead Sea Scrolls it should follow that all twelve testaments of the sons of Jacob had been composed before 68 CE. Indeed, a scholar easily imagines that a Testament of Joseph, a Testament of Levi, and a Testament of Judah could have circulated independently since these men were prominent biblical luminaries. But no scholar can readily imagine a testament created solely for Naphtali, not the most prominent of Jacob's sons; but such a testament would be needed in a collection of testaments attributed to Jacob's sons.

Fourth, documents that are late but may include prerabbinic traditions should be present. Thus, we wisely excluded 5 Maccabees because it is a medieval work but included 3 Enoch, the Apocalypse of Sedrach, and the Apocalypse of Daniel to emphasize the continuity of apocalyptic speculation and, hopefully, of some early Jewish traditions.

Too many reviewers of *The Old Testament Pseudepigrapha* expressed being lost with too many documents to master and in too many unfamiliar languages. From the moment the first volume appeared, I was convinced more documents needed to be included and expressed that thought in many places.

The Borders of Collections Are Not Barriers

This broad focus proved that the borders of the Old Testament pseudepigrapha are not barriers. To study these early Jewish or early Jewish-Christian documents demanded a mastery of other fields of research, particularly the Dead Sea Scrolls, the Nag Hammadi Codices, and the *Papyri Graecae Magicae*, as well as—of course—the writings of Philo and Josephus. The late documents in the Hebrew Scriptures and all the writings in the New Testament should be in focus to avoid a myopic view. Thus, much discussion was heard and echoed in the Society of Biblical Literature Pseudepigrapha Group regarding the uselessness or anachronism of such terms as *canon*, *Jewish Christianity*, and *extracanonical*. All of us in the Pseudepigrapha Group emphasized that *Christianity* was a most inappropriate term for first-century compositions, since all or nearly all of the authors of New Testament books were Jews. In *Jesus within Judaism*, I attempted to prove that Jesus and Paul were devout Jews and should be studied not only within the history of Christianity but also within the history of early Judaism.[5] This term was chosen to represent the vast varieties of Judaism from about 300 BCE, the date for the earliest traditions or composition within Ethiopic Enoch, to circa 200 CE, the date for the first edition of the Mishnah.

The Old Testament Pseudepigrapha would be defined by the so-called Old Testament; it would be a biblical Old Testament pseudepigrapha. In contrast, the Qumran Pseudepigrapha would include such previously unknown documents as (titles used in the Princeton Dead Sea Scrolls Project), Aramaic Apocryphal Work (4Q310), Birth of Noah (4Q534-536), Book of Giants (1Q23-24, 2Q26, 4Q203, 4Q530-533, 6Q8), Daniel Apocryphon (4Q246), David Apocryphon (2Q22), Genesis Apocryphon (1Q20, 6Q8), Jeremiah Apocryphon A-C (4Q383, 384, etc.), Joseph Apocryphon (Mas1m), Joshua Apocryphon [a-b] (4Q378-379), Melchizedek (11Q13), Midrash Sefer Moses (4Q249, 4Q445), Testament of Jacob (4Q537), Pseudepigraphon of Testament of Benjamin (4Q538), Testamnent of Naphtali (4Q215), Testament of Judah (3Q7 and 4Q484), Testament of Joseph (4Q539), Testament of Levi (1Q21, 4Q213, etc.), the Testament (Visions) of 'Amram (4Q543, 544, 546, 547, 548), Testament of Qohath (4Q542), and so many other similar, so-called apocryphal documents unknown until the discovery of ancient Jewish documents found in the Qumran Caves beginning in the late 1940s. These Qumran Pseudepigrapha appear in Discoveries in the Judaean Desert and the Princeton Dead Sea Scrolls Project. Scholars are debating how and in what way the Testaments are sources for the Greek Testaments of the Twelve Patriarchs.

Previous Abbreviations Needed Revisions

Defining the contents of *The Old Testament Pseudepigrapha* meant creating a new list of abbreviations for these compositions. To be consistent and clear meant focusing on the works in the New Testament apocrypha and

---

5. James H. Charlesworth, *Jesus within Judaism: New Light from Exciting Archaeological Discoveries*, ABRL (New York: Doubleday, 1988).

the New Testament pseudepigrapha and devising distinct abbreviations. This focus meant organizing a list of works to be included in the New Testament apocrypha and the New Testament pseudepigrapha. This tedious work eventually produced the following two publications (my work was completed with the help of devoted assistants):

The New Testament Apocrypha and Pseudepigrapha: A Guide to Publications, with Excurses on Apocalypses. ALTA Bibliography Series 17. Metuchen, NJ: Scarecrow, 1987.

"Research on the New Testament Apocrypha and Pseudepigrapha." *ANRW* 25.5: 3919–68.

The Corpus and the Relation among Jews and Christians

During the time I was preparing *The Old Testament Pseudepigrapha*, Samuel Sandmel asked me to travel with him to speak about the complex relation between Jews and Christians. We often spoke to a church full of ministers and priests. I recall him saying that as a Jew he would go 50 percent of the way and maybe 51 percent but not all the way to achieve a better relationship among Jews and Christians. We shared a rare love and respect. As Talmon emphasized some years later, when we study the book of the people, we also study the people of the book. I chose Sandmel to write the "Foreword for Jews" in *The Old Testament Pseudepigrapha*. He wisely began his foreword with these words: "By the strangest quirk of fate respecting literature that I know of, large numbers of writings by Jews were completely lost from the transmitted heritage."[6]

Stone, famous for his work on the Armenian pseudepigrapha, was an engaging member of the Pseudepigrapha Group. He emphasized his surprise at learning about the creative compositions produced within early Judaism. He became as energized about the Old Testament pseudepigrapha as he had been about the Hebrew Bible and rabbinics. Eventually, the Pseudepigrapha Group realized that all the books in the Hebrew Bible had passed through the copying and editing of early Jews. The borders between copies of the Hebrew Bible, in various versions found at Qumran, blurred the borders between Bible, Rewritten Bible, and biblically inspired herme-

---

6. Samuel Sandmel, "Foreword for Jews," *OTP* 1:xi.

neutical creations. That led to the perception that virtually every book in the New Testament was composed by Jews and that Jesus must be understood within Judaism, a claim I emphasized in *Jesus within Judaism*.[7]

The Biblical Canon Is Revisited

Slowly we in the Pseudepigrapha Group, along with many other biblical scholars, obtained a consensus that the canon of the Old Testament, especially the Davidic Psalter, remained open long after the destruction of Qumran in 68 CE and Jerusalem in 70 CE. Gradually, we tended to agree that many documents in the so-called pseudepigrapha were considered replete with God's Word by numerous early Jews. Thus, almost all the documents in the pseudepigrapha and some works among the Qumran Scrolls, notably the Temple Scroll, were assumed to be *sacra scriptura* by Jews during the time of Hillel and Jesus. I remember Ephrem E. Urbach and Menahem Stern telling me that they knew that their own historical works must include the documents collected into the Old Testament pseudepigrapha, but they were not clear how to incorporate them or how to evaluate the claims in these compositions. It was evident to me that the approach that privileged the Mishnah and Tosefta was being recognized as not sufficiently scientific and objective. We all agreed that Josephus was tendentious and the New Testament authors selectively based their compositions on messianic exegesis and enthusiastic confession. Only the apocrypha, many pseudepigrapha, and Dead Sea Scrolls provided primary texts for reconstructing the intellectual world of Judaism before 200 CE and the codification of the Mishnah.

Thinking back to the years of preparing *The Old Testament Pseudepigrapha* without the aid of computers helps me appreciate the tedious work of so many. Bob Heller of Doubleday was professional and became a good friend. Many students and others helped in numerous ways for years at Duke, notably Trisha Dykstra, Amy Jill Levine, Jean Hamilton Charlesworth, Steve Robinson, David Fiensy, Randy Chesnutt, George Zervos, and especially Jim Mueller.

Many of my reflections were shaped by conversations with William Stinespring, Roland Murphy, W. D. Davies, Frank Moore Cross, Martin Hengel, Doron Mendels, and Hugh Anderson. Anderson's work on 3 Mac-

---

7. Charlesworth, *Jesus within Judaism*.

cabees and especially 4 Maccabees in *The Old Testament Pseudepigrapha* helped many understand the place of pseudepigraphic writings within the history of world literature. No one could exceed the eloquence and brilliance Hugh brought to seminars and conversations. During a seminar in Philadelphia featuring Talmon, Hengel, Mendels, and Anderson, I recall Paul Hanson publically admitting that Hugh's control of English was exceptional.

Studiorum Novi Testamenti Societas Pseudepigrapha Seminars

In the early 1970s, I was asked to coconvene the Studiorum Novi Testamenti Societas Diatessaron Seminar. Focus was directed to Semitics, notably Old Syriac, and the "problem of the canon." It became clear that Tatian had used more gospels than the so-called canonical gospels. In 1976, the bicentennial of the founding of the United States, I was often quoted referring to the lost bicentennial of the Bible: the apocryphal compositions and the Dead Sea Scrolls. During August 1976, the first session of the Studiorum Novi Testamenti Societas Pseudepigrapha Seminar met at Duke University. I had been chosen convener. I well remember the contributions during this seminar by Matthew Black, Howard Kee, John Priest, Rien de Jonge, and Kraft.

I shall never forget the long discussions with Strugnell, beginning in 1962 in Durham, NC, at Duke University, in Jerusalem at the École Biblique and Rockefeller Museum, and many other locations in the world. He was the one who introduced me to the Odes of Solomon and to Alexander Polyhistor and who taught me ancient palaeography. Strugnell loved the varieties of early Judaism and the freedom that we inherited to explore all sources and to ask any question. I was with him in Jerusalem the year he reedited the texts assigned to John Allegro.

From the beginnings in 1970 of the Society of Biblical Literature Pseudepigrapha Group we confronted the problems with the term *pseudepigrapha*. In contrast to Fabricius, none of us thought of these masterpieces as false. For me, to put my name on this memory or on any publication seems misrepresentative as it reflects the insights of many savants. To attribute a document to Enoch, Elijah, or a psalm to David was to honor the biblical hero. To offer a poem to Sheila, Jeptha's daughter, or Aseneth, Pharaoh's daughter, is to honor the luminary. And for many early Jews, such divinely gifted persons were sometimes imagined to be alive and present to guide and support God's people on this tiny earth.

The American Academy of Religion Group on the Relevance of Sociology for Biblical Research

From 1969 to 1982, I and my colleagues were enriched by many research groups and international seminars that deepened discussions in the Society of Biblical Literature Pseudepigrapha Group. These related sessions helped me obtain global perspectives, and they helped inform me how to define the new edition of the Old Testament pseudepigrapha.

In the early 1970s, when Lee Keck was still at Emory University, he invited me to serve on the steering committee of a new American Academy of Religion group. We were to discuss how and in what ways, if at all, sociological studies could benefit biblical research, which many thought had become too theological and repetitive. We decided to focus on Antioch in antiquity. During discussions with Lee, Jonathan Z. Smith, and many archaeologists, I began to see how the study of the Old Testament pseudepigrapha could benefit from sociological studies on pilgrimages to Jerusalem, purity and danger, liminality, borders and walls that keep some out and others in, and sacred space. For example, archaeologists proved that most families slept in the same room. Anthropological and sociological reflections revealed crises related to intimacy and awakening to a dead person in a common bed or carpet. I pointed out that some texts in *The Old Testament Pseudepigrapha* mention a person awakening to feeling a loved one had become cold and passed on. Such groups and seminars helped me comprehend the new world that would be created by the publication of ancient Jewish and Christian texts.

Intermittently, I was asked to clarify why the documents in *The Old Testament Pseudepigrapha* were so important. So, in 1987, thanks to a major grant from the National Endowment for the Humanities, I convened a large group of international experts to explore what we could know about early Jewish messianic concepts. The proceedings were published in *The Messiah*.[8] Our major contribution was the discovery that too often nonmessianic passages were assumed incorrectly to be a reference to "the Messiah." Sometimes the person was anonymous, nonmessianic, or an angel. It was clarified that kings, priests, and prophets were announced

---

8. James H. Charlesworth, et al., eds., *The Messiah: Developments in Earliest Judaism and Christianity*, Princeton Symposium on Judaism and Christian Origins (Minneapolis: Fortress, 1992).

as "the Anointed One." No grammatical clues helped an exegete move from "the Anointed One" to "the Messiah."

Since 1970, the Old Testament pseudepigrapha have become a cottage industry, and many careers were made by focusing on these writings that before 1970 were too often considered noncanonical and misleading, aberrant, and heretical. It was certain that *heresy* and *orthodoxy* were terms defined much later than 200 CE; and these concepts were placed on documents by rabbinic authorities and ecclesiastical leaders. Both used selective theology as the norm.

The American Schools of Oriental Research Ancient Manuscript Committee

Because of my work with the Holy Council in Saint Catherine's Monastery and the discovery of over three hundred ancient uncials, I was invited to serve on the American Schools of Oriental Research Ancient Manuscript Committee. Discussions on the pseudepigrapha took on wider dimensions, as confidentially we shared knowledge about over thirty scrolls—perhaps two full scrolls—taken eastward from the Qumran Caves. Obviously, these discussions have been and continue to be secret in the hope of our search may prove fruitful.

Often the members of the American Schools of Oriental Research Ancient Manuscript Committee discussed one question crucial for preparing the new edition of the Old Testament pseudepigrapha: how and in what significant ways were the documents in the Old Testament pseudepigrapha related to the Dead Sea Scrolls? The discovery of numerous copies of Old Testament pseudepigrapha writings among the Qumran Scrolls proved that the relationship was deep. No historical distinction should be attempted since these ancient Jewish works were composed not at Qumran but in Judea or Galilee. Each collection, the Old Testament pseudepigrapha and Qumran Scrolls, preserved sacred compositions by early Jews. As editor of *The Old Testament Pseudepigrapha*, I became dependent in many ways on discussions with Jim Sanders, John Strugnell, Frank Moore Cross, and Noel Freedman. I doubt few scholars had or will possess the experience and wisdom of these older colleagues. My memory takes me back to the years discussing early Judaism, the Bible, and Christian origins with Roland de Vaux, Pierre Benoit, and Jerome Murphy O'Connor in the late 1960s and early 1970s in the École Biblique. Hence, the edition of *The Old Testament Pseudepigrapha* is a tribute to all those I have named previously.

These are my selected memories of a time long ago, sometimes last millennium and sometimes over two millennia. Deep insights are often obtained during private discussions. For example, Doron Mendels convinces me that memories are subjectively selective but are our only way back to historical events, and Dale Allison reminds all of us that memories can be accurate in providing general impressions.

Appendix: Publications by James H. Charlesworth Announcing the Discussions in the Society of Biblical Literature Pseudepigrapha Group and Related Groups and Seminars

- "The SBL Pseudepigrapha Project." *BCSR* 2 (1971): 24–25.
- "The Renaissance of Pseudepigrapha Studies: The SBL Pseudepigrapha Project." *JSJ* 2 (1971): 107–14.
- "Some Reflections on Present Work on the Pseudepigrapha." Pages 229–37 in *Society of Biblical Literature 1971 Seminar Papers*. Edited by John Lee White. SBLSP. Atlanta: Society of Biblical Literature, 1971.
- "A Clearing House for the Publication of Jewish Apocryphal Literature." *RevQ* 8 (1972): 160.
- "Concerning the Study of the Pseudepigrapha." Pages 129–35 in *1972 Proceedings: IOSCS, Pseudepigrapha*. Edited by Robert A. Kraft. SCS 2. Missoula, MT: Society of Biblical Literature, 1972.
- "Some Cognate Studies to the Septuagint." *BIOSCS* 6 (1973): 10–11.
- *The Pseudepigrapha and Modern Research*. SCS 7. Missoula, MT: Scholars Press, 1976.
- "Reflections on the *SNTS* Pseudepigrapha Seminar at Duke on the Testaments of the Twelve Patriarchs." *NTS* 23 (1977): 296–304.
- "'Lost Books' May Give New Insights into Jesus' Time." *The Ohio Wesleyan Magazine* 54.4 (1977): 14–16.
- "Jewish Astrology in the Talmud, Pseudepigrapha, the Dead Sea Scrolls, and Early Palestinian Synagogues." *HTR* 70 (1977): 183–200.
- "Translating the Apocrypha and Pseudepigrapha: A Report of International Projects," *BIOSCS* 10 (1977): 11–21.
- "Focus on the Pseudepigrapha." *The Circuit Rider* 2 (1978): 6–8.
- "Rylands Syriac MS 44 and a New Addition to the Pseudepigrapha: The Treatise of Shem, Discussed and Translated." *BJRL* 60 (1978): 376–403.
- "New Developments in the Study of the *Écrits Intertestamentaires*." *BIOSCS* 11 (1978): 14–18.

- "The *SNTS* Pseudepigrapha Seminars at Tübingen and Paris on the Books of Enoch." *NTS* 25 (1979): 315–23.
- "A History of Pseudepigrapha Research: The Re-emerging Importance of the Pseudepigrapha." *ANRW* 19.1:54–88.
- "The Concept of the Messiah in the Pseudepigrapha." *ANRW* 19.1:188–218.
- *The Pseudepigrapha and Modern Research: With A Supplement*. SCS 7. Chico, CA: Scholars Press, 1981.
- "Christian and Jewish Self-Definition in Light of the Christian Additions to the Apocryphal Writings." Pages 27–55, 310–15 in *Aspects of Judaism in the Graeco-Roman Period*. Vol. 2 of *Jewish and Christian Self-Definition*. Edited by E. P. Sanders, Albert I. Baumgarten, and Alan Mendelson. Philadelphia: Fortress, 1981.
- *The Greek Recension*. Vol. 1 of *The History of the Rechabites*. SBLTT 17. Chico, CA: Scholars Press, 1982.
- "A Prolegomenon to a New Study of the Jewish Background of the Hymns and Prayers in the New Testament." *JSJ* 33 (1982): 265–85.
- "The Historical Jesus in Light of Writings Contemporaneous with Him." *ANRW* 25.1:451–76.

Bibliography

Charlesworth, James H. *Jesus within Judaism: New Light from Exciting Archaeological Discoveries*. ABRL. New York: Doubleday, 1988.

———. *The New Testament Apocrypha and Pseudepigrapha: A Guide to Publications, with Excurses on Apocalypses*. ALTA Bibliography Series 17. Metuchen, NJ: Scarecrow, 1987.

———. *The Odes of Solomon*. Oxford: Clarendon, 1973.

———. "Research on the New Testament Apocrypha and Pseudepigrapha." *ANRW* 25.5:3919–68.

Charlesworth, James H., et al., eds. *The Messiah: Developments in Earliest Judaism and Christianity*. Princeton Symposium on Judaism and Christian Origins. Minneapolis: Fortress, 1992.

Hammershaimb, E. *De gammeltestamentlige pseudepigrafer i oversaettelse med indledning og noter*. 2 vols. Copenhagen: Gad, 1953–1976.

Kautzsch, Emil F., ed. *Die Apokryphen und Pseudepigraphen des Alten Testaments*. Freiburg: J. C. B. Mohr, 1898–1900.

Kümmel, Werner Georg, with Christian Habicht, ed. *Jüdische Schriften aus hellenistisch-römischer Zeit*. Gütersloh: G. Mohn, 1973–.

Philonenko, Marc. *Pseudépigraphes de l'Ancien Testament et manuscrits de la Mer morte*. Cahiers de la Revue d'histoire et de philosophie religieuses 41. Paris: Presses universitaries de France, 1967–.

Riessler, Paul, ed. *Altjüdisches Schrifttum ausserhalb der Bibel*. Augsburg: Filser, 1928.

Sacchi, Paolo. *Antico testament, apocrifi e Nuovo Testamento: Un viaggio autobiografico*. Brescia: Morcelliana, 2015.

———. *Apocrifi dell'Antico Testamento*. Biblica Testi e studi 5, 7–8. 3 vols. Brescia: Paideia editrice, 1997–2000.

6
The Pseudepigrapha at the Society of Biblical Literature: The Early Growth of a Group

George W. E. Nickelsburg

Credit for being the patriarch of pseudepigrapha study at the Society of Biblical Literature belongs to Walter J. Harrelson, dean of the Vanderbilt Divinity School, who in 1969 convened what was announced in the Toronto Annual Meeting program book as a Pseudepigrapha Project breakfast. Arriving late from Iowa, I missed the event, but I was present at the second breakfast in the 1970 New York Annual Meeting, when a decision was made to seek formal status as a unit in the Society's new structure, which had been adopted the previous year in the Toronto meeting. With the Society's formal recognition of that group's first year as 1970-1971, the Pseudepigrapha unit is not only nearing its fiftieth year; it may also be the longest continuing unit in the Society of Biblical Literature.[1]

Walter's leadership continued to sustain the group over the years. In addition to arranging two breakfasts, Walter chaired the group from 1970-1971 to 1972-1973. Just as important, in the 1970s and into 1980s,

---

1. In a memo to the chairman of the Society's Research and Publications Committee, dated 13 November 1973, Walter Harrelson recommended "that the Group's five-year period be identified as beginning with the year 1970-71, with the first annual meeting of the group for formal seminar work commencing with 1971." I assume the recommendation was accepted. At the 1970 Annual Meeting in New York, a group publicly convened to discuss Robert Tomson Fortna's *The Gospel of Signs: A Reconstruction of the Narrative Source Underlying the Fourth Gospel*, SNTSMS 11 (London: Cambridge University Press, 1970). Whether this was a formally constituted John Seminar under the Society's rules and/or whether such a group continued and for how long, I do not know. But I do recall its existence being recognized as a first.

he successfully wrote grants (more than $400,000 from the National Endowment for the Humanities) to initiate the microfilming of biblical manuscripts in Ethiopia and to begin their accession in the Monastic Microfilm Library at Saint John's University in Collegeville, Minnesota.

Early on, the group's steering committee consisted of: Harry M. Orlinsky, Bruce M. Metzger, and Harrelson, presidents of the Society in successive years (1970, 1971, 1972); Robert A. Kraft, later a Society president (2006); George W. MacRae, executive secretary of the Society (1973–1976), whose premature death likely prevented him from being elected a Society president; James H. Charlesworth; Daniel J. Harrington; John Strugnell; Michael E. Stone; and myself; and as corresponding members, Albert-Marie Denis (Louvain) and Marinus de Jonge (Leiden). Later additions to the committee included, *inter aliis*, Harold W. Attridge and John J. Collins, both of whom also served as Society presidents (2001, 2002); and James C. VanderKam, later the *Journal of Biblical Literature* editor (2006–2012). There was a great deal of intellectual power in the committee, as well as a breadth of scholarly experience that our long late-evening meetings and our daylight sessions reflected.

One of the roles that Bob Kraft, Michael Stone, and John Strugnell played was to keep us focused on texts. This was for the simple reason that the texts of the pseudepigrapha were by-and-large unfamiliar to the world of biblical studies and, indeed, to most of *us*, but they promised much new light on the ancient cultures. To make this study possible, Michael and John invented the idea of Texts and Translations, a series that Bob was instrumental in bringing to life and that continues to be published under a different name forty-six years later. This fact is significant because today the series ties Michael's, Bob's, and John's work to scholarship that is more or less *not* in the purview of this unit. Presumably a series like Texts and Translations would inevitably have been launched somewhere in the Society by someone. But in point of historical fact, it was this trio (along with, lest we forget him, its facilitator, Bob Funk, the Society's executive secretary) that was responsible for starting up a series that has published far and away more texts that we in this group do *not* count among the so-called pseudepigrapha of the Old Testament.

In the 1973 steering committee meeting, Harrelson announced his resignation as chairman of the group, and the committee recommended to the Society's Research and Publications Committee that I replace him and that Jim Charlesworth continue formally as the steering committee's secretary.² I served in this capacity from 1973 to 1979 and then during the following year as cochairman along with John Collins. What follows are my memories of the group's activities from its inception through my tenure as chairman.

In the 1971 Annual Meeting—after two annual breakfasts—the newly named Pseudepigrapha Seminar took up the Paraleipomena of Jeremiah with Bob Kraft and Betsy Purintun providing the first volume of Texts and Translations and with Michael and me presenting papers.³

The following year, in 1972, Michael provided our seminar with volume 2 of Texts and Translations, a reprint of M. R. James's text of the Testament of Abraham together with Michael's own translation of the work.⁴ Papers discussed in the year's sessions were printed first in volume 2 of Septuagint and Cognate Studies, a series newly launched by Bob Funk, as it turned out in anticipation of the creation of Scholars Press in 1975. The papers were later republished with a dozen others as volume 6 of Septuagint and Cognate Studies, entitled *Studies on the Testament of Abraham*.⁵ Beginning already in our second year of activity, we scheduled not only a seminar session, but also a section for the reading of submitted papers that did not fit in the seminar's specific topic. Interest in our subject matter was catching fire.

Success with the Testament of Abraham led us (now the Pseudepigrapha Group in the Society's parlance) to a series of sessions on other texts of testamentary character: Testament of Moses (1973); Testament of Job (1974); Testament of Joseph (1975). The interest in the figure of Joseph suggested another apocryphon, Joseph and Aseneth (1976). With the imminent appearance of J. T. Milik's publication of the Qumran Aramaic fragments of the Enochic literature, it seemed feasible to look first at literature relating to Seth (1977) and then at the figure of Enoch and the

---

2. Walter Harrelson's aforementioned memo.

3. Robert A. Kraft and Ann-Elizabeth Purintun, *Paraleipomena Jeremiou*, SBLTT 1 (Missoula, MT: Society of Biblical Literature, 1972). Both papers were published in the *Catholic Biblical Quarterly* two years later: Michael E. Stone, "Some Observations on the Armenian Version of the Paraleipomena of Jeremiah," *CBQ* 35 (1973): 47–59; George W. E. Nickelsburg, "Narrative Traditions in the Paraleipomena of Jeremiah and 2 Baruch," *CBQ* 35 (1973): 60–68.

4. Michael E. Stone, *The Testament of Abraham*, SBLTT 2 (Missoula, MT: Society of Biblical Literature, 1972).

5. George W. E. Nickelsburg, ed., *Studies on the Testament of Abraham*, SCS 6 (Missoula, MT: Scholars Press, 1976).

literature attributed to him (1978).[6] When the Society's centennial celebration of 1980 presented an appropriate opportunity for a two-year synthetic study, we broadened the topic to "Profiles of the Righteous Person." After the first year's drafts required that we change the narrow notion of "righteous persons" to "ideal figures," the papers and some others were published in Septuagint and Cognate Studies 12.[7]

So, early on, the Pseudepigrapha Group was closely connected with two printed series. Texts and Translations published the texts we were to study from year to year, and its editorial board consisted of a handful of us pseudepigraphers. The first number of Septuagint and Cognate Studies contained papers devoted to issues in the Greek Old Testament, and so the series editorship was placed in the hands of Harry Orlinsky, one of the Society's premier Septuagint scholars. In 1973, the call for papers on the Testament of Moses got fourteen responses totaling 110 pages, much more than we had expected. George MacRae, who had just begun as the Society's executive secretary and was thus in charge of publication, was a member of the Harvard faculty. With me on leave in Cambridge at the time, he asked me to edit and write an introduction to what would be bound separately as Septuagint and Cognate Studies 4.[8] After I had served as editor of two more volumes, Harry proposed that the two of us split editorial duties, and so I became coeditor of the series for manuscripts dealing with the pseudepigrapha, while he was responsible for volumes relating to the Septuagint.

The sessions of the group were lively, exciting, and super-stimulating; we were dealing with texts that were, by and large, outside the radar of the biblical guild. This was evident in 1973 when the Society was considering reprinting three volumes of the *Journal of Biblical Literature* articles as part of its 1980 centennial celebration. George MacRae deputized me to search through ninety-four volumes of *the Journal of Biblical Literature* for articles relating to the pseudepigrapha. I found many on the Qumran Scrolls and a few pieces on the apocrypha, but only one on the noncanonical

---

6. See Józef T. Milik, *The Books of Enoch: Aramaic Fragments of Qumrân Cave 4* (Oxford: Clarendon, 1976).

7. George W. E. Nickelsburg and John J. Collins, eds., *Ideal Figures in Ancient Judaism*, SCS 12 (Chico, CA: Scholars Press, 1980).

8. George W. E. Nickelsburg, ed., *Studies on the Testament of Moses*, SCS 4 (Cambridge: Society of Biblical Literature, 1973).

pseudepigrapha published in 1973.⁹ So we were on a cutting edge of biblical scholarship, dealing with primary sources attesting Judaism in the Greco-Roman period and, as we would acknowledge some years later, Christianity in the late Roman and Byzantine periods. The reprint proposal eventually transmogrified into a trio on *The Bible and Its Modern Interpreters*, with Bob Kraft and me editing the volume on *Early Judaism* that covered not only the pseudepigrapha, but the broad range of Jewish literature, material remains, and history.[10]

Also contributing to the character of the sessions was the fact that we were discussing noncanonical texts in which none of us had any existential investment. During a meeting I could walk down the hall and pause at an open door to listen to a couple of my New Testament colleagues in locked combat over some point or another in a canonical text. Conversely, our sessions were relaxed and, at times, fun. We were discovering new things about texts long forgotten, writings that some of us had not even read prior to our commitment to the sessions. The conversation, moreover, was enhanced by the varied personalities and scholarly experience of the participants. And occasionally we invited a paper by someone outside our group. For example, when we discussed Joseph and Aseneth, Jonathan Z. Smith, in his typical way, brought a new and unexpected vector to the text. Evidently, we were doing something right, because we drew sizable audiences; in 1972 I counted around fifty in the room.

The publication of Texts and Translations and Septuagint and Cognate Studies extended our work beyond the North American continent. Our discussions were being heard in Europe and perhaps elsewhere. And the action was reciprocal; on occasion, European scholars contributed to our publications. Harm Hollander, a student of Rien de Jonge, contributed a major paper to *Studies on the Testament of Joseph*, and the following year Francis Schmidt at the Sorbonne, Bob Kraft, Raymond Martin, and I exchanged at length our ideas on the recensions of the Testament of Abraham in *Studies on the Testament of Abraham*.[11]

---

9. Earl Breech, "These Fragments I Have Shored against My Ruins: The Form and Function of 4 Ezra," *JBL* 92 (1973): 267–74.

10. Robert A. Kraft and George W. E. Nickelsburg, eds., *Early Judaism and Its Modern Interpreters* (Atlanta: Scholars Press, 1986); a second edition, edited by Matthias Henze and Rodney Werline, is scheduled to come out in 2020.

11. Harm W. Hollander, "The Ethical Character of the Patriarch Joseph," in *Studies on the Testament of Joseph*, ed. George W. E. Nickelsburg, SCS 5 (Missoula, MT:

It is beyond the scope of my essay and beyond my experience to reflect on the Society's almost fifty years of delving into pseudepigrapha, but in retrospect, I am gratified to have had the opportunity to have been present at the birth and infancy of a significant field of study within the Society of Biblical Literature. For many years, along with my university, the group—by whatever name—was my intellectual home.

Bibliography

Breech, Earl. "These Fragments I Have Shored against My Ruins: The Form and Function of 4 Ezra." *JBL* 92 (1973): 267–74.

Hollander, Harm W. "The Ethical Character of the Patriarch Joseph." Pages 47–104 in *Studies on the Testament of Joseph*. Edited by George W. E. Nickelsburg. SCS 5. Missoula, MT: Scholars Press, 1975.

Jonge, Marinus de, and Th. Korteweg. "The New Edition of the Testament of Joseph." Pages 125–26 in *Studies on the Testament of Joseph*. Edited by George W. E. Nickelsburg. SCS 5. Missoula, MT: Scholars Press, 1975.

Kraft, Robert A., and Ann-Elizabeth Purintun. *Paraleipomena Jeremiou*. SBLTT 1. Missoula, MT: Society of Biblical Literature, 1972.

Kraft, Robert A., and George W. E. Nickelsburg, eds. *Early Judaism and Its Modern Interpreters*. Atlanta: Scholars Press, 1986.

Milik, Józef T. *The Books of Enoch: Aramaic Fragments of Qumrân Cave 4*. Oxford: Clarendon, 1976.

Nickelsburg, George W. E. "Narrative Traditions in the Paraleipomena of Jeremiah and 2 Baruch." *CBQ* 35 (1973): 60–68.

———, ed. *Studies on the Testament of Abraham*. SCS 6. Missoula, MT: Scholars Press, 1976.

———, ed. *Studies on the Testament of Moses*. SCS 4. Cambridge: Society of Biblical Literature, 1973.

Nickelsburg, George W. E., and John J. Collins, eds. *Ideal Figures in Ancient Judaism*. SCS 12. Chico, CA: Scholars Press, 1980.

Stone, Michael E. "Some Observations on the Armenian Version of the Paraleipomena of Jeremiah." *CBQ* 35 (1973): 47–59.

Scholars Press, 1975): 47–104. See also a note by Marinus de Jonge and Th. Korteweg, "The New Edition of the Testament of Joseph," in Nickelsburg, *Studies on the Testament of Joseph*, 125–26. Nickelsburg, *Testament of Abraham*, 23–137.

# The History of the Study of the Pseudepigrapha

7
The History of the Study of Pseudepigrapha

Patricia D. Ahearne-Kroll

In the *Cyclopaedia of Biblical, Theological, and Ecclesiastical Literature*, published in 1887, Bernhard Pick identifies pseudepigrapha of the Old Testament as one class of biblical literature (the other two being canonical literature and Protestant apocrypha) that was composed and transmitted during the Hellenistic era. Pseudepigraphic texts related to the canonical books in form and content, and they were created to "instruct, exhort, and console" much like the biblical prophets had done in previous times. The production of this literature was needed, Pick asserts, because the Babylonian exile issued the beginnings of "the inner rupture in the spiritual life of the Jews," who by Second Temple times had a "broken national spirit" under foreign rule and for whom divine revelation had ended (with the "Holy Spirit having withdrawn"). But when Christianity arose, "sects and heretics" utilized this literature for "dangerous purposes," and in a nutshell, "later, this class of literature was used for worldly and evil purposes, and stood in the service of quackery, witchcraft, and sorcery."[1]

The *Cyclopaedia* that published Pick's essay was heralded at the time as impressive in its depth and scope; it was meant to be a comprehensive resource for Christian ministers, students, and lay readers, and its influence in North America remains to this day.[2] It is noteworthy, then, that

---

1. Bernhard Pick, "Pseudepigrapha of the Old Testament," in *Supplement to the Cyclopaedia of Biblical, Theological, and Ecclesiastical Literature*, ed. John McClintock and James Strong (New York: Harper & Brothers, 1887), 2:784–86.

2. See the anonymous review of *Cyclopaedia of Biblical, Theological, and Ecclesiastical Literature*, edited by John McClintock and James Strong, *The North American Review* 105 (1867): 682–88; and Milton S. Terry, "Biblical Scholars of the United States in 1882," *The Biblical World* 39 (1912): 227. Logos Bible Software offers a download-

Pick's entry provides an instructive synopsis of how this literature that was later labeled as *pseudepigrapha* has been studied in the West for much of the past millennia. The actual category, pseudepigrapha, was coined by Johann Albert Fabricius, who published a collection of pseudepigraphic texts in 1713 (*Codex pseudepigraphus Veteris Testamenti*), but the historical study of so-called pseudepigrapha did not gain footing in Western European scholarship until the nineteenth century. Pick reflects how many Christian scholars in the nineteenth and early twentieth centuries viewed this literature. For them, pseudepigrapha provided proof of a perceived shift in Judaism, when it supposedly no longer plugged into the inspired production of literature (as it had creating the canonical texts) and when it could ultimately be construed as a failing religion replaced by Jesus. Even for Jewish scholars like Abraham Geiger and Louis Ginzberg, the seeming oddity of pseudepigrapha gave them pause.[3] They had difficulty reconciling the apocalyptic and messianic worldviews of some of these texts with their own assessments of first-century Judaism, so assigning such traditions to fringe groups seemed reasonable to them. More than anything, these texts were utilized to defend and describe particular pictures of Judaism during the Hellenistic age and how that Judaism compared with Jesus, early Christians, and the rabbinic sages.[4] It was not until the discovery of the Dead Sea Scrolls, and the academic contributions that poured in decades afterwards, that pseudepigrapha studies began to shift its focus. Postcolonial analyses of European scholarship and greater attention to the historical contexts of versions (such as Armenian, Latin, Slavonic, and Syriac) have also had an impact.[5] Since the historical study of pseudepigrapha has primarily been conducted in the West, this essay will focus on the transmission and study of this literature in Western academic circles, although pertinent connections will be made regarding the transmission of pseudepigrapha in the Christian East.

---

able version of the entire twelve-volume set, and StudyLamp Software provides a free online link to the encyclopedia.

3. See the section on Fabricius and the historical study of pseudepigrapha below.

4. This part of the essay has been highly influenced by Michael E. Stone's discussion, "Categorization and Classification of the Apocrypha and Pseudepigrapha," *AbrN* 24 (1986): 167–77; and Annette Yoshiko Reed, "The Modern Invention of 'Old Testament Pseudepigrapha,'" *JTS* 60 (2009): 408–14.

5. Examples are Christian Wiese, *Challenging Colonial Discourse: Jewish Studies and Protestant Theology in Wilhelmine Germany* (Leiden: Brill, 2005) and related essays in this volume.

7. The History of the Study of Pseudepigrapha

Even though Johann Albert Fabricius created the scholarly classification of pseudepigrapha, the history of the study of this literature precedes him. For centuries, pseudepigrapha were transmitted by scribes who were affiliated with different (mostly Christian) religious traditions in distinct languages.[6] As this survey will demonstrate, in some historical eras and locations, pseudepigraphic texts were treated as enlightened or revelatory literature, but at other times, as Fabricius saw them, they were thought to be fraudulent or misleading. Furthermore, in both the pre- and post-Fabricius periods, the religious sensibilities of educated elite men framed how these men applied the scholarly reasoning of their contemporary times to the study of these texts.[7] Especially when we examine the study of pseudepigrapha in the West, we can identify a blending of objective and subjective analyses that scholars have exercised. On the one hand, scholars studied this literature in accordance with the linguistic knowledge of their respective eras and in conjunction with whatever ancient data was available to them. But on the other hand, scholars' views about Judaism, Christianity, and divine revelation defined how they interpreted this literature.

When we simply consider the literal meaning of the word, pseudepigrapha (sg., pseudepigraphon) denote falsely attributed writings, but most pseudepigrapha do not fit this definition and some canonical texts do (such as the book of Daniel or Qoheleth). For this reason, the term's heuristic value continues to be debated, which is a point that will be further discussed below. This essay will adapt the definition of pseudepigrapha provided by Richard Bauckham, James R. Davila, and Alexander

---

6. Applying the definition for pseudepigrapha that is used in this essay, there are examples of pseudepigrapha that were transmitted or composed by Jewish scribes, such as a medieval Hebrew version of The Testament of Naphtali. On this and other applicable examples, see Eli Yassif, "The Hebrew Narrative Anthology in the Middle Ages," trans. Jacqueline S. Teitelbaum, *Prooftexts* 17 (1997): 153–75. The vast majority of pseudepigrapha at our disposal, however, were transmitted or composed by Christian scribes.

7. I am unaware of a verifiable example of an educated female interpreting and discussing pseudepigrapha prior to the twentieth century. It is likely, however, that there were educated, elite women who read and even copied pseudepigraphic texts (especially in monasteries), as we have evidence of female scribal activity in the Middle Ages. For a recent discussion of the latter, see A. Radini et al., "Medieval Women's Early Involvement in Manuscript Production Suggested by Lapis Lazuli Identification in Dental Calculus," *Science Advances* 5.1 (2019): https://doi.org/10.1126/sciadv.aau7126.

Panayotov, whereby *biblical* signifies the content of (most) Christian Old Testaments or Jewish Bibles and pseudepigrapha refers to ancient literature that "claims to be written by a character in [biblical literature] or set in the same time period as [that literature] and recounts narratives related to it, but which does not belong to Jewish, Catholic, Orthodox, or Protestant biblical canons."[8] My discussion, then, leaves out the history of the study of Protestant apocrypha/Catholic deuterocanonical texts, the content of which overlaps with the use of pseudepigrapha in scholarship but has been viewed with less skepticism.[9]

Early Stages of Pseudepigrapha Studies: The Transmission and Study of Texts

The literary texts that are now referred to as pseudepigrapha have a varied past. Too large a topic to treat in this essay, I will summarize three interrelated circumstances that influenced the study and transmission of these texts prior to Fabricius. First, before the discovery of the Dead Sea Scrolls, the vast majority of pseudepigraphic texts had been preserved by Christian scribes, and over the centuries the reception of this material from within Christian circles has been mixed. During the first several centuries of defining canonical and instructive literature in the Christian West, pseudepigrapha were treated with interest, caution, and

---

8. Richard Bauckham, James R. Davila, and Alexander Panayotov, *Old Testament Pseudepigrapha: More Noncanonical Scriptures*, vol. 1 (Grand Rapids: Eerdmans, 2013). The editors use "Old Testament" in lieu of "biblical literature" and "that literature," and they provide their reasons for maintaining the term (xvii–xviii).

9. The following texts are typically classified as apocrypha/deuterocanonical literature in modern Christian Bibles that employ either category: Tobit, Judith, Additions to the Book of Esther, Wisdom of Solomon, Ecclesiasticus (Sirach), Baruch, The Letter of Jeremiah, Additions to the Book of Daniel (the Prayer of Azariah and the Song of the Three Young Men, Susanna, and Bel and the Dragon), 1 and 2 Maccabees, 1 Esdras (3 Ezra), 2 Esdras (4, 5, and 6 Ezra), Prayer of Manasseh, and sometimes Psalm 151, 3 and 4 Maccabees. See Loren T. Stuckenbruck, "Apocrypha and Pseudepigrapha," in *Early Judaism: A Comprehensive Overview*, ed. John J. Collins and Daniel C. Harlow (Grand Rapids: Eerdmans, 2012), 179–83. Fourth Ezra and Prayer of Manasseh have interesting histories, in that they also have been designated as pseudepigrapha in scholarship, such as by Pick, "Pseudepigrapha of the Old Testament," 785–86; and in modern collections like James H. Charlesworth, ed., *The Old Testament Pseudepigrapha*, 2 vols. (New York: Doubleday, 1983–1985).

sometimes contempt. In his *Stromateis*, Clement of Alexandria viewed traditions from 4 Ezra, 1 Enoch, and possibly the Assumption of Moses as secret, yet instructive Jewish works; Origen sometimes found pseudepigrapha insightful and sometimes considered them as Jewish attempts to undermine Christianity; and Tertullian defended the importance of 1 Enoch when Christian contemporaries were rejecting it (clearly indicating popular suspicion of 1 Enoch).[10] Into the early Middle Ages, scholars continued to debate the merit of pseudepigrapha, with several advocating for its instructive purposes but also using it with caution. The Byzantine chronicler, George Syncellus, for example, cited and discussed passages from 1 Enoch and Jubilees, but he advised that only learned Christians could understand pseudepigrapha since it was "corrupted by Jews and heretics," and contain[ed] material at odds with ecclesiastical teachings."[11] At the same time, however, there are examples from the Christian East that indicate that pseudepigraphic texts were incorporated into authoritative collections. Notably by the Middle Ages, Syriac Christian communities had adopted the Epistle of Baruch into their literary and liturgical traditions, and Ethiopic Christian communities treated Jubilees and portions of what is now called 1 Enoch as instructive if not inspired.[12]

---

10. William Adler, "The Pseudepigrapha in the Early Church," in *The Canon Debate*, ed. Lee Martin McDonald and James A. Sanders (Peabody, MA: Hendrickson, 2002), 211–28. In this essay, the title 1 Enoch will refer to one or more portions that constitute the Ethiopic version of 1 Enoch (in Geʿez), which scholars divide as follows: the Book of the Watchers (chs. 1–36); the Book of Parables (37–71); the Astronomical Book (72–82); The Book of Dreams (83–90); the Epistle of Enoch (91–107); and an extra composition attributed to Enoch (108). Historically speaking, these portions were produced by different writers and at different times in antiquity.

11. Adler, "Pseudepigrapha in the Early Church," 224–28. Syncellus's quote is taken from his, *Ecloga Chronographica*, 27.12–18, quoted in Adler, "Pseudepigrapha in the Early Church," 227.

12. The Epistle of Baruch was transmitted as an independent document, but a copy is also preserved in 2 Baruch (as chs. 78–87 of that work). On the epistle, see Liv Ingeborg Lied, "Between 'Text Witness' and 'Text on the Page': Trajectories in the History of Editing the Epistle of Baruch," in *Snapshots of Evolving Traditions: Jewish and Christian Manuscript Culture, Textual Fluidity, and New Philology*, ed. Liv Ingeborg Lied and Hugo Lundhaug, TUGAL 175 (Berlin: de Gruyter, 2017), 272–96; and on 2 Baruch, see Lied, "Recent Scholarship on *2 Baruch*: 2000–2009," *CurBR* 9 (2011): 238–76 (despite the title, Lied provides a helpful summary of the manuscript evidence as well as the historical research on 2 Baruch since the nineteenth century). For the use of Jubilees in Ethiopic tradition, see James C. VanderKam, *The Book of Jubilees*

Second, the dissemination of pseudepigrapha was in part motivated by scholars' expanding intellectual interests in ancient texts. With traces identifiable in late antiquity but especially into the Middle Ages and the Renaissance period, academics (scholastics or humanists, formally or informally educated) carefully studied and transmitted ancient texts, and some engaged in extensive philological work, which included the examination of religious texts.[13] It is during this period that Greek manuscripts from the Byzantine East caught the attention of the Latin West and influenced the literary production of Slavic lands.[14] Armenian scholars engaged with Syriac, Greek, and Latin writings and also created new pseudepigraphic texts, and Syriac scholars translated Greek sources, composed new pseudepigraphic works, and incorporated some of this material in liturgical, Christian practice.[15] The continuation and enhancement of manuscript production from the tenth to the seventeenth centuries yielded much of the data that later scholarship analyzed, and Christians produced the vast majority of it.

An illustrative example of a pseudepigraphon's transmission history—both in terms of its mixed reception and in terms of its manuscript production—is the textual evidence for the narrative Joseph and Aseneth (hereafter referred to as Aseneth), which exists in ninety-one manuscripts in six languages and of differing lengths. The earliest witness is in Syriac and from the sixth century CE; Aseneth is placed near the beginning of a

---

(Sheffield: Sheffield Academic, 2001). For 1 Enoch, see George W. E. Nickelsburg, *1 Enoch 1: A Commentary on the Book of 1 Enoch, Chapters 1–36; 81–108*, Hermeneia (Minneapolis: Fortress, 2001). For the use of both in Ethiopic Christianity, see also Leslie Baynes, "*Enoch* and *Jubilees* in the Canon of the Ethiopian Orthodox Church," in *A Teacher for All Generations: Essays in Honor of James C. VanderKam*, ed. Eric F. Mason, 2 vols., JSJSup 153 (Leiden: Brill, 2012), 2:799–818.

13. On this basic point, see Robert A. Kraft, "The Pseudepigrapha in Christianity," in *Tracing the Threads: Studies in the Vitality of Jewish Pseudepigrapha*, ed. John C. Reeves, EJL 6 (Atlanta: Scholars Press, 1994), 55–86. See also Reed, "Modern Invention," 408–15, and Anthony Grafton, *Defenders of the Text: The Traditions of Humanism in an Age of Science, 1450–1800* (Cambridge: Harvard University Press, 1991).

14. Reed, "Modern Invention," 408–14; Andrei Orlov, *Selected Studies in the Slavonic Pseudepigrapha*, SVTP 23 (Leiden: Brill, 2009), 1–18.

15. Michael E. Stone, "The Armenian Apocryphal Literature: Translation and Creation," in *Apocrypha, Pseudepigrapha, and Armenian Studies: Collected Papers*, vol. 1 (Leuven: Peeters, 2006), 105–37. For an example of the transmission life of Syriac sources, see Lied's discussion of the Epistle of Baruch in the manuscript tradition ("Between 'Text Witness' and 'Text on the Page'").

chronicle attributed to Pseudo-Zachariah Rhetor, and attached copies of correspondence indicate that Moses of Aggel translated Aseneth from the Greek. Chronologically, the next manuscripts are in Greek dating between the tenth and eleventh centuries; two are part of menologia, one is in a hagiographical collection, and one is a palimpsest, the initial use of which is indecipherable. Between the twelfth and fourteenth centuries, Aseneth began to be translated into Latin in the West (twelve witnesses exist from this time period) and into Armenian in the East (six witnesses). The most complete version among the Armenian witnesses dates to this time period (MS 332^f), and it was compiled in a volume that includes the Old Testament, the New Testament, the writings of Philo, and the Testaments of the Twelve Patriarchs. By the fifteenth century, six Greek manuscripts were copied from earlier witnesses; three Latin manuscripts were copied from their predecessors; more Armenian manuscripts were produced (at least five exist); and two Slavonic witnesses were translated from the Greek. During the sixteenth and seventeenth centuries, more Greek manuscripts were produced (including a translation into Modern Greek), but most notably the importance of this narrative grew in Armenia. The bulk of the fifty Armenian manuscripts of Aseneth come from the seventeenth century (at least twenty-five), sixteen of which are in Bibles. Beginning in the thirteenth century, Aseneth was included in Armenian Bibles, amounting to at least half of the Armenian evidence. During the eighteenth and nineteenth centuries, the narrative was also translated into Romanian (four witnesses).[16] Aseneth travelled far and wide across languages and cultural systems that although were Christian, were not identical.

We can also detect the mixed reception of Aseneth in these distinct Christian circles. A good portion of the evidence places the narrative in authoritative, Christian collections, thereby associating it more closely with perceived inspired literature. In part, what gave weight to pseudepigraphic texts was their association with canonical literature; the expansions of biblical characters and scenes appealed to scribes, scholars, and other educated recipients. Yet, not all the evidence yields such a positive picture of Aseneth's revelatory import. Certainly the transmission and study of

---

16. Christoph Burchard, *Joseph und Aseneth* (Leiden: Brill, 2005), 1–65. See also Burchard, "Der jüdische Asenethroman und seine Nachwirkung: Von Egeria zu Anna Katharina Emmerick oder von Moses aus Aggel zu Karl Kerényi," *ANRW* 20.1:543–667. There are indications that Aseneth was known in Ethiopic, but no manuscripts have been found, and references to it are sparse.

these texts were driven by how the texts resonated with religious worldviews, but pseudepigrapha sometimes were viewed as rich resources that particularly evoked sharp distinctions between Judaism and Christianity. One Latin manuscript of Aseneth could demonstrate such a purpose.

Manuscript 288 of Cambridge, Corpus Christi College, preserves a Latin version of Aseneth along with Latin versions of the well-known Vindicta Salvatoris (Vengeance of the Savior, which narrates the fall of Jerusalem) and a Pseudo-Augustine sermon on the Jews; the Life of Adam and Eve; Infancy Gospels of Matthew and Thomas; and apocalyptic narratives including Matthew Paris's rendering of the Mongol invasion of 1241 from his *Chronica Majora*.[17] These texts were compiled in the thirteenth century, prior to the British expulsion of Jews in 1290, and the manuscript was likely produced at the Benedictine monastery of Christ's Church Canterbury. Ruth Nisse persuasively argues that this anthology possibly served as a collection of "alternative narratives" that helped monks to redescribe the impact of the Crusades, the contemporary escalating hostility against Jews in England, and the monks' perception of the end times. In this context, Aseneth offered an authentic story of conversion that echoed motifs about foreign female conversion and fed allegorical, eschatological readings (with Aseneth as the location of refuge).[18] Although we cannot verify whether Aseneth was precisely used in this way, the particular provenance and compilation of the entire MS 288 (beyond Aseneth) suggests the likelihood of Nisse's basic argument.

An even stronger example of how pseudepigrapha fueled Jewish-Christian distinctions is Robert Grosseteste's discovery of a tenth-century Greek manuscript of the Testaments of the Twelve Patriarchs, his translation of it into Latin, and the reception of his text.[19] In thirteenth-century England, Grosseteste's interest to circulate the Testaments of the Twelve Patriarchs to a broad audience fit his agenda of denigrating and disempowering local Jews.[20] In the Testaments of the Twelve Patriarchs, patriarchs of Judaism

---

17. Ruth Nisse, *Jacob's Shipwreck: Diaspora, Translation, and Jewish-Christian Relations in Medieval England* (Ithaca, NY: Cornell University Press, 2017), 107–8.

18. Nisse, *Jacob's Shipwreck*, 102–26.

19. H. J. de Jonge, "La bibliothèque de Michel Choniatès et la tradition occidentale des Testaments des XII Patriarches," in *Studies on the Testaments of the Twelve Patriarchs: Text and Interpretation*, ed. Marinus de Jonge, SVTP 3 (Leiden: Brill, 1975), 97–106.

20. Most telling of Grosseteste's views about Judaism are his treatise *De cessatione*

prophesize about Christ, thus seemingly declaring the ultimate superiority of the Christian Church, and contemporaries of Grosseteste noticed. In his popular work, *Chronica Majora*, Paris praised Grosseteste's achievement in bringing the Testaments of the Twelve Patriarchs to light and accused Jews of hiding it for centuries from Christian leaders; and Vincent of Beauvais included Christ-centered portions of the Testaments of the Twelve Patriarchs in his equally influential *Speculum Historiale*.[21] Even though the Testaments of the Twelve Patriarchs did not have the same inspired authority as canonical texts did for Vincent, its emphasis on Christ from the mouths of the Hebrew patriarchs compelled him to include portions of Grosseteste's translation in his work.[22] Grosseteste's translation of the Testaments of the Twelve Patriarchs or Vincent's abridged portions of it exist in over eighty manuscripts and in an undetermined number of printed editions; the perception that the Testaments of the Twelve Patriarchs was a Jewish text that promoted the superiority of Christianity clearly had an impact in educated, Christian circles in the West.[23]

These examples of MS 288 of Aseneth and of Grosseteste's Latin translation of the Testaments of the Twelve Patriarchs lead to my final point. Christian scholars into the Renaissance period made significant contributions within their learned circles and more popular domains, yet they operated within the religious systems of their environments. The proliferation of pseudepigrapha was inextricably tied with interests—whether favorable or not—in Christianity and/or Judaism. Even those who seemed more objective in their analysis were not impervious to unfalsifiable assumptions. By a close analysis of several manuscripts, for example, the sixteenth century scholar Johannes Opsopoeus exposed that the composition of the Sibylline Oracles was later than had been assumed, but parts of

---

legalium (*On the Cessation of the Ritual Torah*) in 1213, and his disapproving letter to the Countess of Winchester, who wanted to allow Jews who had been expelled from Leicester to live on her property. Marinus de Jonge, "Robert Grosseteste and The Testaments of the Twelve Patriarchs," *JTS* 42 (1991): 115–25; Nisse, *Jacob's Shipwreck*, 111–12.

21. Nisse, *Jacob's Shipwreck*, 127–47.

22. According to Nisse, Vincent also included abbreviated portions of the Latin version of Aseneth (*Jacob's Shipwreck*, 5–8).

23. de Jonge, "La bibliothèque de Michel Choniatès," 105. The manuscripts date between the fourteenth and sixteenth centuries. S. H. Thomson, *The Writings of Robert Grosseteste, Bishop of Lincoln 1235–1253* (Cambridge: Cambridge University Press, 2013), 43–44.

his reasoning betrayed his religious sentiments. The vagueness of Isa 7:14, for example, indicated prophetic authenticity (the nameless boy whom the anonymous virgin would bear persuasively referred to Jesus), but the sibyl's explicit mention of Mary bearing Jesus indicated a fraudulent text.[24] God would not have provided more prophetic information to pagans (through the sibyl) than to God's own people (through Isaiah).[25] The study of pseudepigrapha, then, remained in dialogue with religious thought and activity even as scholars before Fabricius and the Enlightenment became more critically engaged with religious texts.

The proliferation of texts that later became labelled as pseudepigrapha was motivated by a set of circumstances that oftentimes were interrelated. Although some Christian communities fully embraced particular pseudepigrapha as revelatory and authoritative, in the West, pseudepigrapha was received with a mixture of caution and interest. Western scholars from the early Christian centuries up through the Renaissance combed the possibilities of pseudepigrapha's instructive value, which oftentimes was interpreted as distinguishing Christianity from Judaism. It is significant that the ambiguous nature of pseudepigrapha in the West (e.g., that pseudepigrapha were instructive but not as revelatory as canonical texts) coincided with scholarly interpretations of pseudepigrapha that implied Christian distinction. If it were not for these centuries of discussions and circulation of pseudepigrapha in the West, Fabricius would never have compiled his collection. He would not have had the material to gather nor the motivation to distinguish it from more authoritative texts. As we will also see, well into the twentieth century, pseudepigrapha scholarship continued to be plagued by the motivation to use this literature to differentiate between Judaism and Christianity.

Fabricius and the Historical Study of Pseudepigrapha

In 1713, Fabricius published a collection of texts that he identified as pseudepigrapha (*Codex pseudepigraphus Veteris Testamenti*).[26] Having

---

24. Grafton, *Defenders of the Text*, 162–77.
25. Rieuwerd Buitenwerf, *Book Three of the Sibylline Oracles and Its Social Setting* (Leiden: Brill, 2003), 11.
26. Johann Albert Fabricius, *Codex pseudepigraphus Veteris Testamenti: Collectus, castigatus, testimoniisque, censuris et animaduersionibus illustrates* (Hamburg: Lieberzeit, 1713), with a second volume entitled, *Codicis pseudepigraphi Veteris Testamenti:*

completed anthologies of Greek and Latin writings, Fabricius next turned his attention to collecting extracanonical literature about Jesus and the apostles[27] and then to compiling his pseudepigrapha volumes. According to Fabricius, his apocryphal and pseudepigraphic collections were meant for historical study but nonetheless remained inferior to canonical literature. His pseudepigraphic volumes consisted of over three hundred texts (non-Protestant apocryphal) that were associated with Old Testament patriarchs and prophets, and he particularly designated the corpus as a collection of *"pseudepigrapha," "fabula[e],"* and *"fraudes"* (falsely attributed texts, tales, and forgeries).[28] Fabricius worked in a post-Reformation period when the delineation of scripture was still debated (i.e., about the role of Protestant apocrypha and other ancient texts in the church), and his pseudepigrapha volumes provided source material for counter-ecclesiastical claims. A notable example is William Whiston's *A Collection of Authentik Records Belonging to the Old and New Testament* (1728), in which he argued for the authenticity of the Testaments of the Twelve Patriarchs, Psalms of Solomon, 4 Ezra, the Epistle of Baruch, and "Extracts out of the Book of Enoch."[29] Otherwise, Fabricius's volumes had little impact in academic circles.

By the nineteenth century, however, interest in such pseudepigraphic works gained more momentum in European scholarship for several reasons, two of which will be highlighted here.[30] First, by this point more pseudepigraphic works were becoming known, which led to the increased attention of Fabricius's collection. This century witnessed the publication of commentaries on manuscripts of 1 Enoch and Jubilees in expanded forms, a translation of the Slavonic 2 Enoch, and the text of and commentaries on the Latin palimpsest of the Assumption of Moses.[31] Second,

---

Volumen Alterum Accedit Josephi Veteris Christiani Auctoria Hypomnesticon (Hamburg: Felginer, 1723). The description of Fabricius's work and the reception of it in this remaining paragraph is taken from Reed, "Modern Invention," especially 415–30.

27. Johan Albert Fabricius, *Codex apocryphus Novi Testamenti* (Hamburg: Schiller, 1703).

28. Fabricius, *Codex pseudepigraphus Veteris Testamenti* (1713), folio 3ᵛ, as cited and discussed in Reed, "Modern Invention," 425–26 and n.74.

29. William Whiston, *A Collection of Authentik Records Belonging to the Old and New Testament* (London, 1728), iii–iv.

30. The key points of this paragraph are taken from Reed's discussion, "Modern Invention," especially 430–33.

31. Examples include: (1) by the beginning of the twentieth century, twenty-nine

challenges to common assumptions about the historicity of New Testament texts intensified, and soon pseudepigrapha were incorporated into academic discourse about Second Temple Judaism. In France, Ernest Renan's *Vie de Jésus* (*Life of Jesus*, 1863) and in Germany, David Strauss's *Das Leben Jesu* (*Life of Jesus*, 1835) were provocative in rationalizing the supernatural and sensational presentations of Jesus in the gospels, but at the same time, these works enhanced scholarly distinctions between Jesus, first-century Judaism, and the early Christians.[32] Debates ensued among Christian scholars about the religiopolitical setting of Jesus's time and his relationship with Judaism, and the *Wissenschaft des Judentums* (Jewish Studies) movement entered the fray to challenge contemporary scholars' perceptions of the Hebrew Bible, Second Temple Judaism, and the rabbinic period. The most prominent example is Abraham Geiger,

---

Ethiopic manuscripts of 1 Enoch were known, and two editions were published in the nineteenth century, one by Richard Laurence in 1838 and another by August Dillmann in 1851. Richard Laurence, *Libri Enoch Versio Aethiopica* (Oxford, 1838), and August Dillmann, *Liber Henoch, Aethiopice, ad quinque codicum fidem editus cum variis lectionibus* (Leipzig, 1851). See also Ephraim Isaac, "New Light Upon the Book of Enoch from Newly-Found Ethiopic MSS," *JAOS* 103 (1983): 399–411; (2) Greek Codex Panopolitanus (dated to the eighth century CE or later) was discovered in 1886–1887 in Egypt and contains 1 En. 1:1–32:6 (Isaac, "1 [Ethiopic Apocalypse of] Enoch," *OTP* 1:6); (3) in 1859, Dillmann produced the first scholarly edition of Jubilees in Ethiopic: Maṣḥafa Kufālē *sive Liber Jubilaeorum* (Kiel: C. G. L. van Maack, 1859); and R. H. Charles produced his edition in 1895: *Maṣḥafa Kufālē or the Ethiopic Version of the Hebrew Book of Jubilees* (Oxford: Clarendon, 1895); see also James C. VanderKam, "The Jubilees Fragments from Qumran Cave 4," in *The Madrid Qumran Congress: Proceedings of the International Congress on the Dead Sea Scrolls*, ed. Julio Trebolle Barrera and Luis Vegas Montaner (Leiden: Brill, 1992), 635–36; (4) in 1861, Antonio M. Ceriani published a Latin palimpsest of Jubilees that predated Ethiopic manuscripts by one thousand years: *Monumenta Sacra et Profana* (Milan: Bibliotheca Ambrosiana, 1861), 1:9–64; (5) R. H. Charles and William R. Morfill published Slavonic 2 Enoch in translation in 1896: *The Book of the Secrets of Enoch* (Oxford, 1896); and (6) Ceriani is credited with discovering the Latin palimpsest of The Assumption of Moses in 1861 (Ambrosian Library in Milan) and published it in his *Monumenta Sacra* volumes; several editions and commentaries followed in that century, most especially one by R. H. Charles, *The Assumption of Moses* (London, 1897); see also J. Priest, "Testament of Moses," *OTP* 1:919–26.

32. Ernest Renan, *Vie de Jésus* (Paris: Michel Lévy frères, 1863); David Strauss, *Das Leben Jesu*, 2 vols. (Tübingen: C. F. Osiander, 1835–1836); Susannah Heschel, *Abraham Geiger and the Jewish Jesus* (Chicago: Chicago University Press, 1998), 106–61.

7. The History of the Study of Pseudepigrapha 115

who debated Christian scholars' rendering of the Assumption of Moses (Geiger argued that the author was anti-Sadducean, not anti-Pharisean as contemporary, Christian scholars purported), and he critiqued Christian scholars' methodologies in discerning the source of the Testaments of the Twelve Patriarchs (he argued for careful consideration of rabbinic literature for understanding the Jewish influences of so-called Jewish-Christian sects).[33] By the end of the nineteenth century, an increasing number of scholars relied on pseudepigraphic texts in their constructions of Second Temple Judaism.[34] This interest laid the groundwork for new pseudepigrapha collections in translation, such as that of William John Deane who published the following texts into English: Psalms of Solomon, 1 Enoch, Assumption of Moses, 2 Baruch, the Testaments of the Twelve Patriarchs, Jubilees, Ascension of Isaiah, and Sibylline Oracles.[35]

In the early twentieth century, more collections of pseudepigrapha in translation were published, which made these texts more accessible to scholars and more prominent in their work.[36] For Christian scholars, though, the dominant object of study was the historical Jesus and origins of early Christianity, and pseudepigrapha (and apocrypha) were gleaned to explain these phenomena. This interest is notable, for example, in R. H. Charles's introduction to his edited volume of the pseudepigrapha. He summarizes the volume as primarily exhibiting an "apocalyptic Judaism" that was intertwined with "legalistic Judaism" but broke away when

---

33. Abraham Geiger, "Apokryphische Apokalypsen und Essäer," *Jüdische Zeitshrift für Wissenschaft und Leben* 6 (1868): 41–47; Geiger, "Apokryphen zweiter Ordnung," *Jüdische Zeitshrift für Wissenschaft und Leben* 7 (1869): 116–35; and Geiger, "Die Testamente der zwölf Patriarchen," *Jüdische Zeitshrift für Wissenschaft und Leben* 9 (1871): 123–25. See Heschel, *Abraham Geiger and the Jewish Jesus*, 170–72, 174–76.

34. Most influential are (1) Emil Schürer's *Geschichte des jüdischen Volkes im Zeitalter Jesu Christi*, 2nd ed. (Leipzig: Hinrichs, 1886–1890) and its publication in English: *A History of the Jewish People in the Time of Jesus Christ* (Edinburgh: T&T Clark, 1886–1891); and (2) the contemporary work of the history of religions school in Germany (Christian Wiese, *Challenging Colonial Discourse*, 159–215). Reed also mentions that by the 1890s, sections on "der Apokryphen und der Pseudepigraphen" became standard in German introductory books in biblical studies ("Modern Invention," 432).

35. William John Deane, *Pseudepigrapha: An Account of Certain Apocryphal Sacred Writings of the Jews and Early Christians* (Edinburgh, 1891). See Reed, "Modern Invention," 403–4.

36. For more, see the essay by William Adler in this volume.

it "passed over into Christianity." This apocalyptic Judaism also communicated ethical teachings, but it was more inspiring than what rabbinic teachings provided.[37] Stereotyped views about Jewish observance of torah and Jewish leadership (especially regarding the Pharisees, Sadducees, and later rabbis) were pillars in Christian scholars' construction of first-century Judaism and the rise of Christianity, and pseudepigrapha provided stock data pieces that demonstrated other Jewish voices that later rabbinic writers did not preserve.[38] This is clear in Wilhelm Bousset's influential book, *Religion des Judentums im neutestamentlichen Zeitalter* (*Religion of Judaism in the New Testament Period*) (1903), which utilized several pseudepigraphic sources to describe developments in Judaism during the Hellenistic period. Texts like the Assumption of Moses, 2 Baruch, 1 Enoch, Jubilees, Psalms of Solomon, and Sibylline Oracles were seen to provide the evidence for a postexilic Judaism (most especially in its messianic and apocalyptic hopes) that not only foregrounded how Christianity arose but also exposed what later rabbis supposedly had eliminated. As Bousset explained to his contemporaries, scholars had a vast quantity of literary portions that were "products of a more heretical, unofficial Judaism" or had been declared by "official Judaism" as "spurious (apocryphal)."[39]

---

37. R. H. Charles, *The Apocrypha and Pseudepigrapha of the Old Testament*, vol. 2 (Oxford: Clarendon, 1913), vii–xi. Charles's edited volume provides the following texts in translation: Jubilees, the Letter of Aristeas, the Books of Adam and Eve, the Martyrdom of Isaiah, 1 Enoch, the Testaments of the Twelve Patriarchs, the Sibylline Oracles, the Assumption of Moses, 2 Enoch, 2 Baruch, 3 Baruch, 4 Ezra, the Psalms of Solomon, 4 Maccabees, Pirkē Aboth, the story of Aḥiqar, and the Fragments of a Zadokite Work. Charles explains in his introduction that he added Pirkē Aboth as a point of comparison: "It will be obvious even to the most cursory reader that a great gulf divides the Ethics of the Testaments of the XII Patriarchs, and even those of 2 Enoch, from these excellent but very uninspiring sayings of Jewish sages belonging to the legalistic wing of Judaism" (xi).

38. As Wiese and Heschel convincingly show, Jewish scholars consistently critiqued such stereotyped views in New Testament scholarship, and Christian scholars were aware of their arguments, but little changed in the overall tenor of Christian biblical scholarship (Wiese, *Challenging Colonial Discourse*; Heschel, *Abraham Geiger and the Jewish Jesus*). The Christian scholar George F. Moore also offered a blistering critique of New Testament scholars in this regard. George F. Moore, "Christian Writers on Judaism," *HTR* 14 (1921): 197–254. See also Stone, "Categorization and Classification of the Apocrypha and Pseudepigrapha," 170.

39. "Giebt es nun eine Unmasse kleinerer Schriften und Stücke, die zum Teil Erzeugnisse eines mehr härestischen inofficiellen Judentums sind, zum Teil auch

7. The History of the Study of Pseudepigrapha 117

That pseudepigrapha were the product of unorthodox Jewish voices no longer holds up according to current academic standards, but this impression of pseudepigrapha lasted for decades in scholarship. For many, pseudepigraphic texts were awkward and did not quite fit into reconstructions of the past, a point made regardless of religious affiliation. Abraham Geiger and his colleagues viewed apocalyptic literature like 1 Enoch as representative of unconventional Jewish opinion.[40] Felix Perles, who advocated for the study of pseudepigrapha in Jewish Studies, nonetheless critiqued Bousset's book for focusing too little on texts that reflected every day Judaism (i.e., as represented in rabbinic literature) and too much on marginal concepts (i.e., as represented in pseudepigrapha).[41] Even though Louis Ginzberg demonstrated weaknesses in the hypothesis that the rabbis rejected pseudepigrapha, he, too, expressed discomfort with apocalyptic literature in particular. The rabbis must have concluded that the "vagaries and fantasmagoria of the apocalypses of creation" and the fixation on angels and demons were unhelpful because such narratives and ideas were impractical and elitist in content.[42] Although in his multivolume, *The Legends of the Jews*, Ginzberg presented summaries of several pseudepigraphic sources, he claimed that his renditions were at best reflecting the kernels of Jewish content that Christian scribes preserved.[43] For Ginzberg,

---

wie die frühere Litteratur vom officiellen Judentum für apokryph erklärt." Wilhelm Bousset, *Religion des Judentums im neutestamentlichen Zeitalter* (Berlin: Reuther & Reichard, 1903), 45.

40. Heschel, *Abraham Geiger and the Jewish Jesus*, 168–69.

41. Felix Perles, *Bousset's Religion des Judentums im neutestamentlichen Zeitalter kritisch untersucht* (Berlin: Peiser, 1903), 22–24. See Wiese, *Challenging Colonial Discourse*, 170–215 and 395–97.

42. Louis Ginzberg, "Some Observations on the Attitude of the Synagogue towards the Apocalyptic-Eschatological Writings," *JBL* 41 (1922): 135–36. Stone, "Categorization and Classification of the Apocrypha and Pseudepigrapha," 175.

43. In Henrietta Szold's translation of the German manuscript of *The Legends of the Jews*, the index includes: Apocalypse of Abraham, 2 Baruch, Ascension of Isaiah, Assumption of Moses, 1 Enoch, 2 Enoch, Jubilees, Life of Adam (and Eve), Sibylline Oracles, the Testaments of the Twelve Patriarchs, and other texts from Fabricius's *Codex pseudepigraphicus* of 1722. Louis Ginzberg, *The Legends of the Jews*, trans. Henrietta Szold (Philadelphia: Jewish Publication Society of America, 1909), 7:531–41. In his preface to the same translated volumes, Ginzberg explains his caution with Jewish literature that was solely preserved by Christians (1:xii–xiii). See also, Stone, "Categorization and Classification of the Apocrypha and Pseudepigrapha," 175–76.

then, Jewish pseudepigrapha was too fragmentary to be used to reconstruct Second Temple Judaism.

The overarching scholarly interest in Christian origins, however, framed how dominant academic discourse analyzed pseudepigrapha in the West. Special emphasis was placed on texts that expressed apocalyptic and/or messianic ideas, which, paired with the book of Daniel, could be compared with New Testament texts and could be used to construct scenarios how Christianity came to be. The momentum in pseudepigrapha studies diminished, however, in the wake of human atrocities in the West (World Wars I and II, the Holocaust, and economic depressions).[44] But with the discovery of the Dead Sea Scrolls, all past presumptions about Judaism and early Christianity were challenged, reworked or abandoned, and the evidence for ancient pseudepigrapha grew.

Discovery of the Dead Sea Scrolls and Its Effect on Pseudepigrapha Studies

Between 1947 and 1956, scrolls were discovered in caves near the Dead Sea at Qumran and close to where ruins of an inhabited site were also excavated (Khirbet Qumran). Evidence for more than nine hundred manuscripts were found, written mostly in Hebrew, with some in Aramaic and a small fraction in Greek. Almost all of it, too, consists of Jewish religious content. A little over two hundred manuscripts preserve portions of Hebrew biblical texts, and all biblical books other than Esther are represented; there are commentaries on or expositions about biblical content; liturgical texts; halakhic writings; wisdom texts; community rules of a religious nature; eschatological texts; and copies of known apocrypha and pseudepigrapha. Portions of 1 Enoch (what was known from the Ethiopic version) in Aramaic and, at the least, literary traditions in Hebrew that are associated with Jubilees were discovered in a considerable number of manuscripts.[45] Although no copies of the Testaments of

---

44. James H. Charlesworth rehearses scholarly interest in pseudepigrapha from Fabricius forward and particularly mentions this time gap in Western scholarship. James H. Charlesworth, "The *Parables of Enoch* and the Apocalypse of John," in *The Pseudepigrapha and Christian Origins: Essays from the Studiorum Novi Testamenti Societas*, ed. Gerbern S. Oegema and James H. Charlesworth (New York: T&T Clark, 2008), 200–220.

45. On recent discussions of the Jubilees's evidence at Qumran, see Matthew Phil-

the Twelve Patriarchs were found, there were Aramaic fragments of testament narratives that share affinities with the Testaments of the Twelve Patriarchs, most notably one according to Levi (4Q213-214 and 1Q21). Equally noteworthy, however, are the works that had been unknown in scholarship and that fit the broader definition of pseudepigrapha used in this essay. Examples are a retelling of Genesis stories in Aramaic (Genesis Apocryphon, 1Q20); expansions of the Daniel narrative in Aramaic (Prayer of Nabonidus and Four Kingdoms, 4Q242, 4Q552, 4Q553); testaments by several Hebrew ancestors (Jacob, Judah, Joseph, Levi, Qahat, and Amram; 4Q537-548); and expansions on the deeds of the prophets (e.g., about Moses [1Q22, 4Q375-376], Jeremiah [4Q385b] and Ezekiel [4Q385-389]).[46]

This evidence has become a catalyst for reviewing the categories of apocrypha and pseudepigrapha that have been used in scholarship. By the twentieth century in the West, apocrypha typically referred to literature that some Christian Bibles preserved but Jewish Bibles did not, and pseudepigrapha referred to nonauthoritative but canon-related material. The terms, then, have been canon-oriented, but the Dead Sea Scrolls' evidence complicates these distinctions. The book of Tobit, for example, may not be as apocryphal as once thought. The fragments of one Hebrew and several Aramaic copies of Tobit at Qumran (4Q200, 4Q196-199) confirm the narrative's existence prior to versions in Christian Bibles. As for pseudepigrapha, our list of texts has grown so considerably that the classification is losing its clarity.[47] If we recalibrate our analysis of the evidence according to the definition of pseudepigrapha given at the start of this essay, then the scrolls (of either the apocryphal or pseudepigraphic sort) expand our list even further. A good example is the Temple Scroll (11QT), which is typically absent from academic lists of pseudepigrapha. The pseudepigraphon par excellence, the Temple Scroll purports itself to be a dictation from the mouth of God; there is no mediating person like

---

lip Monger, "4Q216 and the State of 'Jubilees' at Qumran," *RevQ* 26 (2014): 595-612; and Eibert J. C. Tigchelaar, "The Qumran 'Jubilees' Manuscripts as Evidence for the Literary Growth of the Book," *RevQ* 26 (2014): 579-94.

46. Devorah Dimant, "Apocrypha and Pseudepigrapha at Qumran," *DSD* 1 (1994): 151-59; Michael E. Stone, "The Dead Sea Scrolls and the Pseudepigrapha," *DSD* 3 (1996): 270-95. For a more complete, updated list see Stuckenbruck, "Apocrypha and Pseudepigrapha," 188 and 197-98.

47. Stone, "Dead Sea Scrolls and Pseudepigrapha," 270-71.

Moses or even an angel, only the first-person speech of God at Sinai.[48] This text, above of all else, portrays itself as revelation, which challenges Pick's notion (given at the start of this essay) that divine revelation was perceived to have ended during Second Temple times.

Dead Sea Scrolls' pseudepigrapha (broadly defined), then, have also led scholars to review assumptions about canon and the authority of scripture in ancient Judaism.[49] As presented in the previous sections, scholars for centuries pitted their contemporary religious canons (Hebrew or Christian Bibles, corpora of rabbinic or Christian traditions) against pseudepigrapha in trying to discern the value of the latter, but this method began to fade with the discovery of the scrolls. Discussions about why biblically-related texts were composed have often been interrelated with questions about authoritative purpose; what kind of revelatory value, scholars have asked, did this extrabiblical material have in comparison with the authoritative quality of biblical texts?[50] Yet, the weight of the evidence has brought about a more nuanced understanding of authoritative texts, or scripture, in Second Temple Judaism. The idea of a closed collection of particular texts that were precisely copied and disseminated never existed in Second Temple times. Specific texts were authoritative to individual communities, but as Hindy Najman argues, texts that were authoritative served as catalysts for generating new texts and interpretations so as to "sustain the vitality" of that scripture.[51] We must consider, then, that during the Second Temple period, so-called pseudepigraphic literature was a part of authoritative traditions for some or even many Jews.

The scrolls are dated between the mid-third century BCE and late first century CE, with most dated to the first century BCE, and their rich array of sectarian views, poetry, wisdom instruction, and narratives contributed to a change in how scholars discussed Second Temple

---

48. Lawrence H. Schiffmann, "The *Temple Scroll* and the Halakhic Pseudepigrapha of the Second Temple Period," in *Pseudepigraphic Perspectives: The Apocalyptic and Pseudepigrapha in the Light of the Dead Sea* Scrolls, ed. Esther G. Chazon and Michael E. Stone, STDJ 31 (Leiden: Brill, 1999), 121–31.

49. Dimant, "Apocrypha and Pseudepigrapha at Qumran"; James C. VanderKam, "Questions of Canon Viewed through the Dead Sea Scrolls," in McDonald and Sanders, *Canon Debate*, 91–109.

50. Dimant, "Apocrypha and Pseduepigrapha"; Sidnie White Crawford, *Rewriting Scripture in Second Temple Times* (Grand Rapids: Eerdmans, 2008).

51. Hindy Najman, "The Vitality of Scripture Within and Beyond the 'Canon,'" *JSJ* 43 (2012): 515–17.

Judaism and its relationship with Jesus and early Christianity. For one thing, the deconstruction of categories like biblical texts, pseudepigrapha, and apocrypha have led to new approaches in analyzing Judaism during the Hellenistic and early Roman periods. For example, the book of Daniel, 4 Ezra, Jubilees, Sirach, and Wisdom of Solomon have all been analyzed together with portions of 1 Enoch to ascertain the meanings and societal functions of certain Enochic traditions.[52] The former works use motifs, literary styles, and/or intellectual traditions that 1 Enoch shares regardless of later canonical or noncanonical designations. For about a half-century, there has also been an emerging hermeneutical shift in Second Temple studies that encourages more self-awareness and transparency in scholarly analysis (more on this below), which has led to greater emphasis on the historically contingent settings of ancient texts. Now, the Enochic Apocalypse of Weeks or Book of Dreams, Psalms of Solomon, 4 Ezra, and 2 Baruch reflect debates and power struggles, concerns and cultural data from the authors' perspectives during particular times of Judea under imperial control; these theories focus primarily on the literary content alone, mostly diminishing the impulse to distinguish them from New Testament or rabbinic writings.[53] Sociohistorical settings of Greek pseudepigrapha garnered renewed attention as well (such as the Letter of Aristeas, Artapanus, and Aristobulus), and in conjunction with papyrological studies, a rich investigation into Judaism in Hellenistic Egypt ensued.[54] Particularly noteworthy to the growth in pseudepigrapha studies is the two-volume collection, *The Old Testament Pseudepigrapha*, edited by James H. Charlesworth, and the professional society sessions that encouraged further study and debate of this material.[55] Overall, the study of pseudepigrapha and related Dead Sea and

---

52. Nickelsburg, *1 Enoch 1*, 68–82.

53. Anathea Portier-Young, *Apocalypse against Empire: Theologies of Resistance in Early Judaism* (Grand Rapids: Eerdmans, 2011); Kenneth Atkinson, *I Cried to the Lord: A Study of the Psalms of Solomon's Historical Background and Social Setting* (Leiden: Brill, 2004); Karina Martin Hogan, *Theologies in Conflict in 4 Ezra: Wisdom Debate and Apocalyptic Solution*, JSJSup 130 (Leiden: Brill, 2008); and Liv Ingeborg Lied's summary in "Recent Scholarship on *2 Baruch*."

54. For a summary of scholarship up until 2000, see John J. Collins, *Between Athens and Jerusalem: Jewish Identity in the Hellenistic Diaspora*, 2nd ed. (Grand Rapids: Eerdmans, 2000). See also John M. G. Barclay, *Jews in the Mediterranean Diaspora from Alexander to Trajan (323 BCE—117 CE)* (Edinburgh: T&T Clark, 1996).

55. Such as the Society of Biblical Literature's Pseudepigrapha program unit,

apocryphal texts have fostered a range of thematic studies (e.g., apocalypticism, messianism, narrative genres, and scribal interpretation practices).[56] These ancient texts have been employed as resources for describing Jewish practices and worldviews during the Hellenistic and early Roman periods, as several handbooks from the past fifty years demonstrate.[57] Unlike the work of Bousset over a century ago, however, these introductory books do not make claims of differentiating between Christianity and Judaism. This shift in purpose cannot be understated. Critiques about Jewish stereotyping and Christian supersessionism in scholarship have had a valuable impact on pseudepigrapha studies, helping scholarship to be more precise and transparent in discussing the evidence.[58]

So, studying the text in its environment became the key focus, but the location of that environment began to be questioned. As Ginzberg had observed, since most pseudepigrapha were preserved by Christian scribes, recovering the Jewish composition becomes harder to do. After the discovery of the Dead Sea Scrolls, more scholars wondered whether pseudepigrapha that was only preserved in later, Christian-produced

---

which this current volume commemorates. On the impact of *The Old Testament Pseudepigrapha* in pseudepigrapha studies, see James H. Charlesworth, "The *Old Testament Pseudepigrapha*—Thirty Years Later," in *New Vistas on Early Judaism and Christianity: From Enoch to Montreal and Back*, ed. Lorenzo DiTommaso and Gerbern S. Oegema (London: Bloomsbury, 2016), 3–24.

56. For example, John J. Collins, *The Apocalyptic Imagination: An Introduction to Jewish Apocalyptic Literature*, 2nd ed. (Grand Rapids: Eerdmans, 1988); Collins, *The Scepter and the Star: The Messiahs of the Dead Sea Scrolls and Other Ancient Literature* (New York: Doubleday, 1995); Lawrence M. Wills, *The Jewish Novel in the Ancient World* (Ithaca, NY: Cornell University Press, 1995); and the collection of essays in Matthias Henze, ed., *A Companion to Biblical Interpretation in Early Judaism* (Grand Rapids: Eerdmans, 2012).

57. A list of formative works includes the revised edition by Geza Vermes, Fergus Millar, and Matthew Black of Emil Schürer's *The History of the Jewish People in the Age of Jesus Christ* (Edinburgh: T&T Clark, 1973); George W. E. Nickelsburg, *Jewish Literature between the Bible and the Mishnah: A Historical and Literary Introduction* (Philadelphia: Fortress, 1981); Michael E. Stone, *Jewish Writings of the Second Temple Period: Apocrypha, Pseudepigrapha, Qumran Sectarian Writings, Philo Josephus* (Philadelphia: Fortress, 1984); and Robert A. Kraft and George W. E. Nickelsburg, eds., *Early Judaism and Its Modern Interpreters* (Atlanta: Scholars Press, 1986).

58. George W. E. Nickelsburg, "Why Study the Extra-canonical Literature? A Historical and Theological Essay," *Neot* 28 (1994): 181–204.

manuscripts should be identified as Christian compositions.[59] No other pseudepigraphon captures this altered opinion better than the Testaments of the Twelve Patriarchs, which had been valued in scholarship for centuries as an ancient Jewish text. As early as 1953, Marinus de Jonge posited that the Testaments of the Twelve Patriarchs was best understood as a Christian document, and his critical studies published in the 1970s and 1980s persuasively changed scholarly opinion.[60] Although Jewish texts akin to Aramaic Levi likely served as source material for the Testaments of the Twelve Patriarchs, the so-called Christian interpolations into the text are best understood as original to the composition. Whoever wrote the Testaments of the Twelve Patriarchs was deeply knowledgeable in Old Testament traditions, and unlike the Testaments of the Twelve Patriarchs, most pseudepigrapha lack explicit Christian references. The question arises, then, whether Christian writers would have intentionally composed literature that replicated Old Testament genres and storylines (instead of simply adapting or transmitting Jewish material).[61] For the past two decades, several challenges have been made about the Jewish origin of particular pseudepigrapha (such as Aseneth and 2 Baruch), but the debate about those texts continue; the arguments on both sides depend upon educated guesses given the limitations of the evidence (e.g., surmising either the value of the manuscripts for Christians or the value of the text for Jews in earlier times).[62]

---

59. Synthesized best by Robert A. Kraft, "The Multiform Jewish Heritage of Early Christianity," in *Christianity, Judaism and Other Greco-Roman Cults: Studies for Morton Smith at Sixty*, ed. Jacob Neusner (Leiden: Brill, 1975), 174–99; Kraft, "Pseudepigrapha in Christianity," 55–86; and Kraft, "Setting the Stage and Framing Some Central Questions," *JSJ* 32 (2001): 371–95.

60. De Jonge provides a summary of his contributions in, "Defining the Major Issues in the Study of the Testaments of the Twelve Patriarchs," in *Pseudepigrapha of the Old Testament as Part of Christian Literature: The Case of the Testaments of the Twelve Patriarchs and the Greek Life of Adam and Eve*, SVTP 18 (Leiden: Brill, 2003), 71–83.

61. See the systematic treatment of this question in James R. Davila, *The Provenance of the Pseudepigrapha: Jewish, Christian, or Other?*, JSJSup 105 (Leiden: Brill, 2005).

62. Ross S. Kraemer argues that Aseneth is a Christian composition from the third to fourth centuries CE. Ross S. Kraemer, *When Aseneth Met Joseph: A Late Antique Tale of the Biblical Patriarch and His Egyptian Wife, Reconsidered* (New York: Oxford University Press, 1998); and Rivka Nir argues for both 2 Baruch and Aseneth as Christian compositions. Rivka Nir, *The Destruction of Jerusalem and the Idea of Redemption in the Syriac Apocalypse of Baruch* (Atlanta: Society of Biblical Literature, 2003), and

Pseudepigrapha Studies Going Forward

The past half-century has seen the evaporation of dichotomies such as canonical/noncanonical, normative/sectarian, Jewish/Christian that have been used in pseudepigrapha scholarship, so the usefulness of the term pseudepigrapha has increasingly been questioned.[63] What does such a corpus look like when we extend the time range or even religious associations of the texts, providing a selection that date up to the early seventh century CE or that map out the literary traditions of a particular biblical motif?[64] If anything, by virtue of the actual manuscript evidence, we can trace the trajectories of literary traditions regardless of their supposed origin (as Jewish or Christian, early or late centuries). The focus on the manuscript evidence has also yielded more discussion about the medium of a pseudepigraphon's transmission (as liturgical material, codex of arranged texts, or other), which at the very least can indicate the intended use of that pseudepigraphon in a particular place and time.[65]

In closing, a word must be said about how institutional, cultural, and political limitations in pseudepigrapha studies directed the history of scholarship. For one thing, the preferential treatment of Christian Western traditions has made the academic research incomplete and one-sided. The very definitions of pseudepigrapha and apocrypha are mostly Western European distinctions, and the untreated manuscript evidence from Armenian pseudepigrapha alone is striking.[66] Another sober point is that in addition to the tragic events of the Holocaust, there were times when

---

Nir, *Joseph and Aseneth: A Christian Book* (Sheffield: Sheffield Phoenix, 2012). See the summaries of the respective debates in Angela Standhartinger, "Recent Scholarship on *Joseph and Aseneth* (1988–2013)," *CurBR* 12 (2014): 353–406; and Lied, "Recent Scholarship on *2 Baruch*."

63. Marinus de Jonge, "Pseudepigrapha of the Old Testament: An Ill-Defined Category of Writings," in *Pseudepigrapha of the Old Testament as Part of Christian Literature*, 9–17; Reed, "Modern Invention," 434–36.

64. As done, respectively, by Bauckham, Davila, and Panayotov, *Old Testament Pseudepigrapha*, and by John C. Reeves and Annette Yoshiko Reed, *Sources from Judaism, Christianity, and Islam*, vol. 1 of *Enoch from Antiquity to the Middle Ages* (Oxford: Oxford University Press, 2018).

65. See Lied on 2 Baruch in "Recent Scholarship on *2 Baruch*," and my discussion above ("Early Stages of Pseudepigrapha Studies").

66. The work of Michael E. Stone has been dedicated to correcting this oversight in scholarship. Examples of his contributions can be found in Michael E. Stone,

Jewish scholars were ignored, belittled, or even prevented from dominant academic venues.[67] Pseudepigrapha studies continues to improve partially because of greater inclusion of skilled academics, regardless of their affiliations or, for that matter, gender.

The study of pseudepigrapha will undergo even more transformations, but against Pick's assessment, the texts associated with this category might best be remembered for their creativity and vision to regenerate traditions, rework cosmologies, and rewrite history, no matter their value to religious traditions.

Bibliography

Adler, William. "The Pseudepigrapha in the Early Church," Pages 211–28 in *The Canon Debate*. Edited by Lee Martin McDonald and James A. Sanders. Peabody, MA: Hendrickson, 2002.

Atkinson, Kenneth. *I Cried to the Lord: A Study of the Psalms of Solomon's Historical Background and Social Setting*. Leiden: Brill, 2004.

Barclay, John M. G. *Jews in the Mediterranean Diaspora from Alexander to Trajan (323 BCE—117 CE)*. Edinburgh: T&T Clark, 1996.

Bauckham, Richard, James R. Davila, and Alexander Panayotov. *Old Testament Pseudepigrapha: More Noncanonical Scriptures*. Vol. 1. Grand Rapids: Eerdmans, 2013.

Baynes, Leslie. "*Enoch* and *Jubilees* in the Canon of the Ethiopian Orthodox Church." Pages 799–81 in *A Teacher for All Generations: Essays in*

Apocrypha, Pseudepigrapha, and Armenian Studies: Collected Papers, 3 vols. (Leuven: Peeters, 2006).

67. See Wiese on Felix Perles's critique that Bousset was ignorant of contemporary Jewish scholarship and about Emil Schürer's infamous asterisks beside the names of Jewish scholars in his bibliography of *Geschichte des jüdischen Volkes* (see Wiese, *Challenging Colonial Discourse*, 177–90). In response to the editor's (Adolf Hilgenfeld) refusal to publish non-Protestant scholarship in the journal, *Zeitschrift für wissenschaftliche Theologie*, Abraham Geiger created his own journal (*Jüdische Zeitshrift für Wissenschaft und Leben*) so to contribute to academic discussions of his time (Heschel, *Abraham Geiger and the Jewish Jesus*, 42–43). In the mid-twentieth century, the Jordanian government prohibited the participation of Jewish scholars in the initial study of the Dead Sea Scrolls by virtue of the discovery occurring in Jordanian territory. John J. Collins, *The Dead Sea Scrolls: A Biography* (Princeton: Princeton University Press, 2013), 18.

Honor of James C. VanderKam. Edited by Eric F. Mason. Vol. 2. JSJSup 153. Leiden: Brill, 2012.

Bousset, Wilhelm. *Religion des Judentums im neutestamentlichen Zeitalter*. Berlin: Verlag von Reuther & Reichard, 1903.

Buitenwerf, Rieuwerd. *Book Three of the Sibylline Oracles and Its Social Setting*. Leiden: Brill, 2003.

Burchard, Christoph. "Der jüdische Asenethroman und seine Nachwirkung: Von Egeria zu Anna Katharina Emmerick oder von Moses aus Aggel zu Karl Kerényi." ANRW 20.1:543–667.

———. *Joseph und Aseneth*. Leiden: Brill, 2005.

Charles, R. H. *The Apocrypha and Pseudepigrapha of the Old Testament*. Vol. 2. Oxford: Clarendon, 1913.

———. *The Assumption of Moses*. London, 1897.

———. *Maṣḥafa Kufālē or the Ethiopic Version of the Hebrew Book of Jubilees*. Oxford: Clarendon, 1895.

Charles, R. H., and William R. Morfill. *The Book of the Secrets of Enoch*. Oxford, 1896.

Charlesworth, James H., ed. *The Old Testament Pseudepigrapha*. 2 vols. New York: Doubleday, 1983–1985.

———. "The *Old Testament Pseudepigrapha*—Thirty Years Later." Pages 3–24 in *New Vistas on Early Judaism and Christianity: From Enoch to Montreal and Back*. Edited by Lorenzo DiTommaso and Gerbern S. Oegema. London: Bloomsbury, 2016.

———. "The *Parables of Enoch* and the Apocalypse of John." Pages 200–220 in *The Pseudepigrapha and Christian Origins: Essays from the Studiorum Novi Testamenti Societas*. Edited by Gerbern S. Oegema and James H. Charlesworth. New York: T&T Clark, 2008.

Ceriani, Antonio M. *Monumenta Sacra et Profana*. Vol. 1. Milan: Bibliotheca Ambrosiana, 1861.

Collins, John J. *The Apocalyptic Imagination: An Introduction to Jewish Apocalyptic Literature*. 2nd ed. Grand Rapids: Eerdmans, 1988.

———. *Between Athens and Jerusalem: Jewish Identity in the Hellenistic Diaspora*. 2nd ed. Grand Rapids: Eerdmans, 2000.

———. *The Dead Sea Scrolls: A Biography*. Princeton: Princeton University Press, 2013.

———. *The Scepter and the Star: The Messiahs of the Dead Sea Scrolls and Other Ancient Literature*. New York: Doubleday, 1995.

Crawford, Sidnie White. *Rewriting Scripture in Second Temple Times*. Grand Rapids: Eerdmans, 2008.

Davila, James R. *The Provenance of the Pseudepigrapha: Jewish, Christian, or Other?* JSJSup 105. Leiden: Brill, 2005.
Deane, William John. *Pseudepigrapha: An Account of Certain Apocryphal Sacred Writings of the Jews and Early Christians.* Edinburgh, 1891.
Dillmann, August. *Liber Henoch, Aethiopice, ad quinque codicum fidem editus cum variis lectionibus.* Leipzig, 1851.
———. *Maṣḥafa Kufālē sive Liber Jubilaeorum.* Kiel: C. G. L. van Maack, 1859.
Dimant, Devorah. "Apocrypha and Pseudepigrapha at Qumran." *DSD* 1 (1994): 151–59.
Fabricius, Johann Albert. *Codex apocryphus Novi Testamenti.* Hamburg: Schiller, 1703.
———. *Codex pseudepigraphus Veteris Testamenti: Collectus, castigatus, testimoniisque, censuris et animaduersionibus illustrates.* Hamburg: Lieberzeit, 1713.
———. *Codicis pseudepigraphi Veteris Testamenti: Volumen Alterum Accedit Josephi Veteris Christiani Auctoria Hypomnesticon.* Hamburg: Felginer, 1723.
Geiger, Abraham. "Apokryphische Apokalypsen und Essäer." *Jüdische Zeitshrift für Wissenschaft und Leben* 6 (1868): 41–47.
———. "Apokryphen zweiter Ordnung." *Jüdische Zeitschrift für Wissenschaft und Leben* 7 (1869): 116–35.
———. "Die Testamente der zwölf Patriarchen." *Jüdische Zeitshrift für Wissenschaft und Leben* 9 (1871): 123–25.
Ginzberg, Louis. *The Legends of the Jews.* Translated by Henrietta Szold. Philadelphia: Jewish Publication Society of America, 1909.
———. "Some Observations on the Attitude of the Synagogue towards the Apocalyptic-Eschatological Writings." *JBL* 41 (1922): 115–36.
Grafton, Anthony. *Defenders of the Text: The Traditions of Humanism in an Age of Science, 1450–1800.* Cambridge: Harvard University Press, 1991.
Isaac, Ephraim. "New Light Upon the Book of Enoch from Newly-Found Ethiopic MSS." *JAOS* 103 (1983): 399–411.
Henze, Matthias, ed. *A Companion to Biblical Interpretation in Early Judaism.* Grand Rapids: Eerdmans, 2012.
Heschel, Susannah. *Abraham Geiger and the Jewish Jesus.* Chicago: Chicago University Press, 1998.
Hogan, Karina Martin. *Theologies in Conflict in 4 Ezra: Wisdom Debate and Apocalyptic Solution.* JSJSup 130. Leiden: Brill, 2008.

Isaac, Ephraim. "1 (Ethiopic Apocalypse of) Enoch." Pages 5–89 in vol. 1 of *The Old Testament Pseudepigrapha*. Edited by James H. Charlesworth. 1 vols. New York: Doubleday, 1983–1985.

Kraemer, Ross S. *When Aseneth Met Joseph: A Late Antique Tale of the Biblical Patriarch and His Egyptian Wife, Reconsidered*. New York: Oxford University Press, 1998.

Jonge, H. J. de. "Defining the Major Issues in the Study of the Testaments of the Twelve Patriarchs." Pages 71–83 in *Pseudepigrapha of the Old Testament as Part of Christian Literature: The Case of the Testaments of the Twelve Patriarchs and the Greek Life of Adam and Eve*. SVTP 18. Leiden: Brill, 2003.

———. "La bibliothèque de Michel Choniatès et la tradition occidentale des Testaments des XII Patriarches." Pages 97–106 in *Studies on the Testaments of the Twelve Patriarchs: Text and Interpretation*. Edited by Marinus de Jonge. SVTP 3. Leiden: Brill, 1975.

———. "Pseudepigrapha of the Old Testament: An Ill-Defined Category of Writings." Pages 9–17 in *Pseudepigrapha of the Old Testament as Part of Christian Literature: The Case of the Testaments of the Twelve Patriarchs and the Greek Life of Adam and Eve*. SVTP 18. Leiden: Brill, 2003.

Jonge, Marinus de. "Robert Grosseteste and The Testaments of the Twelve Patriarchs." *JTS* 42 (1991): 115–25.

Kraft, Robert A. "The Multiform Jewish Heritage of Early Christianity." Pages 174–99 in *Christianity, Judaism and Other Greco-Roman Cults: Studies for Morton Smith at Sixty*. Edited by Jacob Neusner. Leiden: Brill, 1975.

———. "The Pseudepigrapha in Christianity." Pages 55–86 in *Tracing the Threads: Studies in the Vitality of Jewish Pseudepigrapha*. Edited by John C. Reeves. EJL 6. Atlanta: Scholars Press, 1994.

———. "Setting the Stage and Framing Some Central Questions." *JSJ* 32 (2001): 371–95.

Kraft, Robert A., and George W. E. Nickelsburg, eds. *Early Judaism and Its Modern Interpreters*. Philadelphia: Fortress; Atlanta: Scholars Press, 1986.

Laurence, Richard. *Libri Enoch Versio Aethiopica*. Oxford, 1838.

Lied, Liv Ingeborg. "Between 'Text Witness' and 'Text on the Page': Trajectories in the History of Editing the Epistle of Baruch." Pages 272–96 in *Snapshots of Evolving Traditions: Jewish and Christian Manuscript*

Culture, Textual Fluidity, and New Philology. Edited by Liv Ingeborg Lied and Hugo Lundhaug. TUGAL 175. Berlin: de Gruyter, 2017.

———. "Recent Scholarship on *2 Baruch*: 2000–2009." *CurBR* 9 (2011): 238–76.

Monger, Matthew Phillip. "4Q216 and the State of 'Jubilees' at Qumran." *RevQ* 26 (2014): 595–612.

Moore, George F. "Christian Writers on Judaism." *HTR* 14 (1921): 197–254.

Najman, Hindy. "The Vitality of Scripture Within and Beyond the 'Canon.'" *JSJ* 43 (2012): 497–518.

Nickelsburg, George W. E. *1 Enoch 1: A Commentary on the Book of 1 Enoch, Chapters 1–36; 81–108*. Hermeneia. Minneapolis: Fortress, 2001.

———. *Jewish Literature between the Bible and the Mishnah: A Historical and Literary Introduction*. Philadelphia: Fortress, 1981; 2nd ed., 2005.

———. "Why Study the Extra-canonical Literature? A Historical and Theological Essay." *Neot* 28 (1994): 181–204.

Nir, Rivka. *The Destruction of Jerusalem and the Idea of Redemption in the Syriac Apocalypse of Baruch*. Atlanta: Society of Biblical Literature, 2003.

———. *Joseph and Aseneth: A Christian Book*. Sheffield: Sheffield Phoenix, 2012.

Nisse, Ruth. *Jacob's Shipwreck: Diaspora, Translation, and Jewish-Christian Relations in Medieval England*. Ithaca, NY: Cornell University Press, 2017.

Orlov, Andrei. *Selected Studies in the Slavonic Pseudepigrapha*. SVTP 23. Leiden: Brill, 2009.

Perles, Felix. *Bousset's Religion des Judentums im neutestamentlichen Zeitalter kritisch untersucht*. Berlin: Peiser, 1903.

Pick, Bernhard. "Pseudepigrapha of the Old Testament." Pages 784–86 in vol. 2 of *Supplement to the Cyclopaedia of Biblical, Theological, and Ecclesiastical Literature*. Edited by John McClintock and James Strong. New York: Harper & Brothers, 1887.

Portier-Young, Anathea. *Apocalypse against Empire: Theologies of Resistance in Early Judaism*. Grand Rapids: Eerdmans, 2011.

Priest, J. "Testament of Moses." Pages 919–34 in vol. 1 of *The Old Testament Pseudepigrapha*. Edited by James H. Charlesworth. 2 vols. New York: Doubleday, 1983–1985.

Radini, A., et al. "Medieval Women's Early Involvement in Manuscript Production Suggested by Lapis Lazuli Identification in Dental Calculus." *Science Advances* 5.1 (2019): https://doi.org/10.1126/sciadv.aau7126.

Reed, Annette Yoshiko. "The Modern Invention of 'Old Testament Pseudepigrapha.'" *JTS* 60 (2009): 403–36.

Reeves, John C., and Annette Yoshiko Reed. *Sources from Judaism, Christianity, and Islam*. Vol. 1 of *Enoch from Antiquity to the Middle Ages*. Oxford: Oxford University Press, 2018.

Renan, Ernest. *Vie de Jésus*. Paris: Michel Lévy frères, 1863.

Review of *Cyclopaedia of Biblical, Theological, and Ecclesiastical Literature*, edited by John McClintock and James Strong. *The North American Review* 105 (1867): 682–88.

Schiffmann, Lawrence H. "The *Temple Scroll* and the Halakhic Pseudepigrapha of the Second Temple Period." Pages 121–31 in *Pseudepigraphic Perspectives: The Apocalyptic and Pseudepigrapha in the Light of the Dead Sea Scrolls*. Edited by Esther G. Chazon and Michael E. Stone. STDJ 31. Leiden: Brill, 1999.

Schürer, Emil. *Geschichte des jüdischen Volkes im Zeitalter Jesu Christi*. 2nd ed. Leipzig: Hinrichs, 1886–1890.

———. *A History of the Jewish People in the Time of Jesus Christ*. Edinburgh: T&T Clark, 1886–1891. Rev. ed. 1973.

Standhartinger, Angela. "Recent Scholarship on *Joseph and Aseneth* (1988–2013)." *CurBR* 12 (2014): 353–406.

Stone, Michael E. *Apocrypha, Pseudepigrapha, and Armenian Studies: Collected Papers*. 3 vols. Leuven: Peeters, 2006.

———. "The Armenian Apocryphal Literature: Translation and Creation." Pages 105–37 in vol. 1 of *Apocrypha, Pseudepigrapha, and Armenian Studies: Collected Papers*. Leuven: Peeters, 2006.

———. "Categorization and Classification of the Apocrypha and Pseudepigrapha." *AbrN* 24 (1986): 167–77.

———. "The Dead Sea Scrolls and the Pseudepigrapha." *DSD* 3 (1996): 270–95.

———. *Jewish Writings of the Second Temple Period: Apocrypha, Pseudepigrapha, Qumran Sectarian Writings, Philo Josephus*. Philadelphia: Fortress, 1984.

Strauss, David. *Das Leben Jesu*. 2 vols. Tübingen: C. F. Osiander, 1835–1836.

Stuckenbruck, Loren T. "Apocrypha and Pseudepigrapha." Pages 179–83 in *Early Judaism: A Comprehensive Overview*. Edited by John J. Collins and Daniel C. Harlow. Grand Rapids: Eerdmans, 2012.

Terry, Milton S. "Biblical Scholars of the United States in 1882." *The Biblical World* 39 (1912): 227.

Thomson, S. H. *The Writings of Robert Grosseteste, Bishop of Lincoln 1235–1253*. Cambridge: Cambridge University Press, 2013.

Tigchelaar, Eibert J. C. "The Qumran 'Jubilees' Manuscripts as Evidence for the Literary Growth of the Book." *RevQ* 26 (2014): 579–94.

VanderKam, James C. *The Book of Jubilees*. Sheffield: Sheffield Academic, 2001.

———. "The Jubilees Fragments from Qumran Cave 4." Pages 635–48 in *The Madrid Qumran Congress: Proceedings of the International Congress on the Dead Sea Scrolls*. Edited by Julio Trebolle Barrera and Luis Vegas Montaner. Leiden: Brill, 1992.

———. "Questions of Canon Viewed through the Dead Sea Scrolls." Pages 91–109 in *The Canon Debate*. Edited by Lee Martin McDonald and James A. Sanders. Peabody, MA: Hendrickson, 2002.

Whiston, William. *A Collection of Authentik Records Belonging to the Old and New Testament*. London, 1728.

Wiese, Christian. *Challenging Colonial Discourse: Jewish Studies and Protestant Theology in Wilhelmine Germany*. Leiden: Brill, 2005.

Wills, Lawrence M. *The Jewish Novel in the Ancient World*. Ithaca, NY: Cornell University Press, 1995.

Yassif, Eli. "The Hebrew Narrative Anthology in the Middle Ages." Translated by Jacqueline S. Teitelbaum. *Prooftexts* 17 (1997): 153–75.

8
The Pseudepigrapha within and without Biblical Studies

Benjamin G. Wright III

In the modern academy, those of us who study Judaism and Christianity in the ancient world have gotten used to certain categories that have become normative ways of sorting in our field, most of which were created initially with some conscious relationship to the Bible and/or biblical studies as organizing principles.[1] As a field, biblical studies traditionally has had a somewhat fraught relationship with the broader study of religion—thus the separate entities of the American Academy of Religion and the Society of Biblical Literature—as if in recognition that these fields of study actually did things fundamentally different from one another.[2] Indeed, for many years they did do different things. More and more, however, scholars who study ancient Judaism and Christianity have begun to reposition themselves within the study of religion and to employ shared or similar methods and interdisciplinary approaches with scholars of religion more generally, although that is by no means an across-the-board shift.[3] With

---

This essay is a heavily revised version of a paper originally delivered at Collaborations: Directions in the Study of Religion at Lehigh University in 2014 and revised again for presentation in the Pseudepigrapha Section at the Annual Meeting of the Society of Biblical Literature in Atlanta 2015. I am grateful to both audiences for their questions and comments on these earlier versions. Many thanks to Matthias Henze, Liv Ingeborg Lied, and Michael Legaspi for their comments on earlier drafts of this article.

1. For the pseudepigrapha, see Patricia Ahearn-Kroll's essay in this volume. See also Annette Yoshiko Reed, "The Modern Invention of 'Old Testament Pseudepigrapha,'" *JTS* 60 (2009): 403–36.

2. So, for example, the two organizations met for many years concurrently in the same city, but in 2008–2011 they went through a period of separation. They are now back to concurrent meetings.

3. I hesitate to use the category *religious studies*, since whatever else we do, I

this movement have come three significant developments that in my mind are related and that have had a profound impact on the study of Jewish literature that did not find its way into the Jewish and Christian canons of scripture: (1) the explicit recognition that the Bible (in one or another of its Jewish and/or Christian iterations) historically has been and in many places continues to be the organizing framework in which scholarly study of early Judaism and Christianity takes place; (2) the increasing awareness that this frame traditionally has obscured the value of studying what we now call early or Second Temple Judaism on its own terms and in its own right; and (3) the continuing debates over the extent to which that framework presents an obstacle to making the best sense of early Jewish and Christian literature.[4] As I was thinking about how I might approach writing this essay, I was listening to the song "Fountain of Sorrow" on Jackson Browne's album *Late for the Sky*, in which he sings at one point, "What I was seeing wasn't what was happening at all." As I reflected on the work that we scholars of early Judaism do particularly when it comes to the pseudepigrapha, I was reminded that what we *see* metaphorically might not be what is happening, and I was reminded that we never *see*—and here I mean what the scholar of religion sees in her research—without certain constraints or blinders that condition what we are able to see. In other words, accepting the Bible *de facto* as the normative standard prevented scholars from seeing what was happening; that is, even as it presumably illuminates, the framework of Bible obscures a great deal.

The Field of Biblical Studies and the Old Testament Pseudepigrapha

In his introductory essay in *A Modest Proposal on Method*, Russell T. McCutcheon highlights the importance of how we label or name what we do—not just the disciplinary homes in which we live, although I think

---

would suggest our scholarly interest ought not to be religious. We can leave that part to confessional religious professionals.

4. That so much literature that is *not* the Bible or only tangentially related to the Bible falls under the Society of *Biblical* Literature is to my mind symptomatic of the historical situation and the analytical problem. Moreover, the category *religion* itself has come under fire in recent times within the study of religion. See, for example, Russell T. McCutcheon, *Manufacturing Religion: The Discourse on Sui Generis Religion and the Politics of Nostalgia* (Oxford: Oxford University Press, 1997); and Kevin Schilbrack, "Religions: Are There Any?," *JAAR* 78 (2010): 1112–38 as different examples of this contestation.

such titles significant—since the labels that we use go a long way toward determining how we know and what we can know about the objects of our inquiry.[5]

The academic study of the Bible and the development of the field of biblical studies has had a long and complex history. While Philip R. Davies has observed that a field that was explicitly titled biblical studies within humanistic study only came along in the 1970s and beyond, the humanistic/academic study of the Bible extends back well into the eighteenth century with roots in the German Enlightenment.[6] The persistence of the Bible and biblical studies as the frame of reference for the study of other early Jewish texts, then, might be accounted for via two different paths, both of which have affected contemporary scholarship on the pseudepigrapha: (1) focus on the Bible within confessional contexts where, quite naturally, biblical studies serves the interests of studying the Bible as sacred scripture; and (2) the persistence of the Bible as a vestige of the Bible's long-standing cultural authority within which biblical studies remains focused on and framed by the Bible, even if the central concern is not on the Bible as scripture *per se*.

Even in its incarnation as a form of humanistic study within the larger study of religion in which the object of biblical studies inquiry has been the Bible, that Bible has taken mostly, but not exclusively, its Protestant form of an Old Testament conterminous with the Hebrew Bible and the New Testament. Even the so-called deuterocanonical or apocryphal books, which appear in Catholic collections of scripture, often do not get included. So, for example, studies of Old Testament Wisdom treat Job, Proverbs, Qoheleth, maybe the so-called wisdom psalms, and less frequently Song of Songs.

---

5. Russell T. McCutcheon, "Introduction: Plus ça Change ...," in *A Modest Proposal on Method: Essaying the Study of Religion*, MTSRsup 2 (Leiden: Brill, 2015), 1–16.

6. Davies writes: "Yet, in few other academic disciplines has there been quite such a fundamental shift as in ours. What I have observed is nothing other than the creation of a new discipline, or rather multidiscipline. I do not recall the name 'biblical studies' being used in the 1970s, nor would it have been recognized as the name of an autonomous branch of the human sciences. The Bible was not studied in Europe apart from theology or divinity, and hardly anywhere else outside the context of religious discourse." Philip R. Davies, "Biblical Studies: Fifty Years of a Multi-discipline," *CurBR* 13 (2014): 36. For a detailed intellectual history of the development of the humanistic study of the Bible, see Michael C. Legaspi, *The Death of Scripture and the Rise of Biblical Studies* (Oxford: Oxford University Press, 2010).

However, the Wisdom of Ben Sira, the Wisdom of Solomon, or Tobit rarely appear, even though Ben Sira and Tobit, at least, date from the same general period as a work such as Qoheleth.[7] In short, biblical wisdom usually has been defined by a theological category that imposes significant limitations that determine the various possibilities for inquiry into this literature. The subdivision into specialties of Old Testament and New Testament further narrows the field into ancient Israel and early Christianity. I will note here for the moment that ancient Judaism, as a field of study, does not enter the picture explicitly.

Yet, although study of the Bible has moved into the secular academy, the humanistic field of biblical studies inherited and retained the methods and more critically the theological and cultural framework of earlier scholarship. Before the middle of the twentieth century, ancient Jewish and Christian works that did not make it into the Protestant canon of scripture were divided and subdivided into different categories: apocrypha—both Old Testament and New Testament; pseudepigrapha—Old Testament and New Testament as well; or, for early Jewish literature, the older, more encompassing designation intertestamental literature. These categories still serve to organize the discipline, as can be seen in titles like James H. Charlesworth's two-volume *The Old Testament Pseudepigrapha* and H. F. D. Sparks's *The Apocryphal Old Testament* from the mid-1980s to its expansion *Old Testament Pseudepigrapha: More Noncanonical Scriptures* in 2013 or even the enormous three-volume collection from 2014 entitled *Outside the Bible*, which began its life with the title *The Lost Bible*.[8]

---

7. There is a debate about what constitutes wisdom literature or even if such a thing exists. See, for instance, Stuart Weeks, *An Introduction to the Study of Wisdom Literature* (New York: T&T Clark International, 2010); and Will Kynes, "The Nineteenth-Century Beginnings of 'Wisdom Literature,' and Its Twenty-First-Century End?," in *Perspectives on Israelite Wisdom: Proceedings of the Oxford Old Testament Seminar*, ed. John Jarick, LHBOTS 618 (London: Bloomsbury T&T Clark, 2016), 83–108. In some cases, Ben Sira does get included, largely, I think, because we have at least some Hebrew text of his book.

8. James H. Charlesworth, ed., *The Old Testament Pseudepigrapha*, 2 vols. (Garden City, NY: Doubleday, 1983–1985); H. F. D. Sparks, *The Apocryphal Old Testament* (Oxford: Clarendon, 1984); Richard Bauckham, James R. Davila, and Alexander Panayotov, eds., *Old Testament Pseudepigrapha: More Noncanonical Scriptures*, vol. 1 (Grand Rapids: Eerdmans, 2013); Louis H. Feldman, James L. Kugel, and Lawrence H. Schiffman, eds., *Outside the Bible: Ancient Jewish Writings Related to Scripture*, 3 vols. (Lincoln: University of Nebraska Press; Philadelphia: The Jewish Publication

This latter collection even includes selections from the Septuagint, as if this collection of translations somehow existed outside the Bible.[9] Moreover, not only the texts but the practices connected with them that we call early or Second Temple Judaism often bear the qualifying adjective *intertestamental*, and in German scholarship on Second Temple Judaism they were often referred to as representing *Spätjudentum* ("late Judaism"), a term that became more widely used and that set up Judaism as a foil to the early Jesus movement and implied a static and largely legalistic tradition—usually identified with the Pharisees and later rabbinic Judaism—which the advent of Jesus and early Christianity supplanted. While such assessments of early Judaism certainly reflect a classic anti-Semitism in the study of the Bible, they also had the effect of marginalizing early or Second Temple Jewish literature, inasmuch as Judaism in this period served as both a source of and a foil for the development of early Christianity, while at the same time its literature could be mined for backgrounds of the development of Jesus and early Christianity.[10]

Up through the middle of the twentieth century and even in some corners all the way into the twenty-first century, these Jewish texts came under scholarly scrutiny for the value that they had for the study of the biblical books, and the developing discipline of biblical studies did nothing materially to change that state of affairs. So, scholars in biblical studies looked at the Jewish apocrypha and pseudepigrapha because they provided a background for the emergence of Christianity, if they looked at them at all. In making this critique, I do not intend to minimize the contributions of earlier scholars, such as R. H. Charles, who edited the first convenient collection and translation of some of these texts in English under the title *The Apocrypha and Pseudepigrapha of the Old Testament* or Emil F. Kautzsch,

---

Society, 2013). This latter set contains many more texts than those usually designated apocrypha, such as selections from the Septuagint (!), Philo, Josephus, fragments of Hellenistic Jewish authors, and selections from the Dead Sea Scrolls. On Charlesworth and Sparks, see the reviews by Robert Kraft and Michael Stone in *RelSRev* 14 (1988): 111, 113–17.

9. Even though the recent encyclopedia project, *The Encyclopedia of the Bible and Its Reception* published by de Gruyter, has articles on topics from Second Temple/Hellenistic Judaism, the focus is on the Bible. As a result, works such as Ezra, Nehemiah, Chronicles, and Daniel are treated in the Hebrew Bible/Old Testament area, even though they originated in the Second Temple period.

10. For a recent, perceptive discussion of these issues, see Michael E. Stone, *Ancient Judaism: New Visions and Views* (Grand Rapids: Eerdmans, 2011), 1–30.

who did the same for German in *Die Apokryphen und Pseudepigraphen des Alten Testaments*,[11] but these collections came into being in the service of the study of the Bible (and sometimes as the result of an incipient anti-Semitism on the part of the mostly Christian scholars who studied them). Almost as important, the social landscape of ancient Judaism was broken down along the lines that the first-century Jewish historian Josephus laid out in *A.J.* 18.11–22 and *B.J.* 2.119–166, when he described Judaism as comprised of three major groups, Pharisees, Sadducees, and Essenes, and a good deal of scholarly energy got expended trying to see which of these nonbiblical books fit into which of Josephus's groups. For example, the Wisdom of Ben Sira was associated variously with both Saducean and Pharisaic ideas.[12] Those works that did not fit the categories easily either got forced into one of them, no matter how ill fitting, or neglected altogether. A good example of the latter case is the Letter of Aristeas, which has received comparatively scant scholarly attention in the last three centuries.

Of course, the Bible formed the main category of study and the focus of research because these texts had utility—that is, they formed the basis for Christian belief and practice, and the modern scholarly study of the Bible inherited a centuries-old interest in determining what the Bible said. Moreover, many, if not most, of the Christian scholars who studied these Jewish texts were ordained clergy. Thus, for these scholars, the history and literature of ancient Judaism was not the primary interest; the emergence of Christianity and its subsequent replacement of that Judaism was. So, while dozens of commentaries have been written on, say, Romans or Deuteronomy, only a very few full-length treatments have appeared on Aristeas.[13] As a general rule, then, in this period the category of Bible

---

11. R. H. Charles, *The Apocrypha and Pseudepigrapha of the Old Testament*, 2 vols. (Oxford: Clarendon, 1913); Emil F. Kautzsch, *Die Apokryphen und Pseudepigraphen des Alten Testaments* (Tübingen: Mohr Siebeck, 1900).

12. On the connection of Ben Sira to Sadduceean ideas, see Jonathan Klawans, "Sadducees, Zadokites, and the Wisdom of Ben Sira," in *Israel's God and Rebecca's Children, Christology and Community in Early Judaism and Christianity: Essays in Honor of Larry W. Hurtado and Alan F. Segal*, ed. David B. Capes, April D. DeConick, and Helen K. Bond (Waco, TX: Baylor University Press, 2008), 261–76. For the claim that Ben Sira anticipates certain Pharisaic ideas, see Gabriele Boccaccini, *Middle Judaism: Jewish Thought 300 B.C.E. to 200 C.E.* (Minneapolis: Fortress, 1991), 117.

13. For the most recent commentary, Benjamin G. Wright III, *The Letter of Aristeas: 'Aristeas to Philocrates' or 'On the Translation of the Law of the Jews'*, CEJL (Berlin: de Gruyter, 2015).

remained regnant, despite the fact that the Bible as *we* know it did not exist at least until, at the earliest, the late second century in Judaism and the fourth century for Christianity. There was first and foremost the Bible and then anything else outside of Bible, the latter category being of lesser value, since these texts were included neither in the canon of Christianity nor that of Judaism. The biblical canon constituted the lens through which ancient Judaism was viewed, and the pseudepigrapha (and other ancient Jewish texts that did not find inclusion in the canon) first and foremost provided evidence for understanding a developing Christianity and rabbinic Judaism. Of course, such study enhances understanding the Hebrew Bible, the New Testament, or early Christianity, but as Michael E. Stone has noted, "problems arise when the exegetical task is confused with the historical."[14]

The Dead Sea Scrolls and the Study of Pseudepigrapha

The chance discovery of the Dead Sea Scrolls in the late 1940s had the potential to transform this state of affairs. The initial revelation of what we now know was comprised of over 1000 (by the latest count) mostly fragmentary but in some cases relatively complete scrolls sent shock waves through the biblical studies scholarly community. Among these scrolls, written in Hebrew, Aramaic, and Greek, were the oldest manuscripts of biblical books ever found, but in addition scores of ancient Jewish works that scholars had heretofore not known also came to light. In one momentous discovery, scholarly knowledge of ancient Jewish literature increased almost exponentially and thereby the potential to revise or even scrap older models in favor of new ones that would take into full consideration this plethora of new texts. Importantly for my account, the scrolls drew renewed attention to those earlier works contained in the categories of the apocrypha and pseduepigrapha. So, for example, even though the compendium of texts in Ethiopic that make up 1 Enoch had long been known to scholars—Charles included them in his collection of pseudepigrapha—their current centrality to reconstructions of early Judaism results directly from the discovery at Qumran of the Aramaic fragments of four of the five major components of 1 Enoch. Yet, the reign of the Bible and the canon continued—and in some circles continues—to dominate how these

---

14. Stone, *Ancient Judaism*, 13.

texts were studied and explained, even to the extent that we often speak of the biblical books found at Qumran—even though the Qumranites seem to have held a wide variety of works as authoritative, probably including 1 Enoch, Jubilees, and the Temple Scroll.[15]

On the positive side, these newly discovered texts, which included a number of pseudepigraphic texts, demonstrated that previous characterizations of Judaism that had been put forward were simply wrong. Whether intertestamental Judaism had been described as apocalyptic, sapiential, legal/halakic, or covenantal, the Qumran texts offered abundant evidence that early Judaism was a much more diverse and vibrant tradition than scholars had imagined. Indeed, it became clear that some apocryphal or pseudepigraphal texts were constitutive for the identity of some Jewish groups in the Second Temple period. In this sense, then, the Dead Sea Scrolls gave impetus to the study of early Judaism, and along with it interest in the Jewish pseudepigrapha, as a scholarly concern in its own right, although it would be a while yet before it would fully flourish. Thus, the discovery of the scrolls provided impetus for studying Judaism—and hence its literature—for its own sake, and it propelled the study of the pseudepigrapha as part of that effort rather than relegating these texts to a supporting role to the study of the Bible.

At least two factors help to explain why the burgeoning scholarly study of the scrolls, which certainly extended then to the apocrypha and pseudepigrapha that had now become ineluctably tied to the scrolls, did not result sooner in a flowering of new theoretical or methodological models and approaches to the texts and the Judaism to which they witnessed. The story is well known. First, since the site of Qumran was located in Jordanian territory, the first group of scholars to edit the scrolls had no Jews as members and a significant number of them were Christian. This situation was emblematic of scrolls scholarship in the early years, which tilted significantly towards Christian interests and theology as scholars worked out comprehensive theories of the Qumran community's beliefs and how they related to Christianity and rabbinic Judaism. Second, work on the Dead Sea Scrolls from the beginning was subsumed under the umbrella of the historical-critical methods that characterized biblical studies, and, even more specifically, since the vast majority of the scrolls were written

---

15. See Timothy H. Lim, "Authoritative Scriptures and the Dead Sea Scrolls," in *The Oxford Handbook of the Dead Sea Scrolls*, ed. Timothy H. Lim and John J. Collins (Oxford: Oxford University Press, 2010), 303–22.

in Hebrew and Aramaic, the early generations of scrolls scholars were specialists in these languages trained largely in biblical studies.[16] This situation was analogous to the earlier study of the apocrypha and pseudepigrapha, since other than Greek and Latin, many of these texts had survived in languages such as Geʾez, Syriac, or Armenian, and the scholars who had the specialized knowledge of those languages tended to be Christian and interested in the pseudepigrapha for the reasons I have outlined above.

That biblical scholars were called on to do the work is not the issue, however. These people were the natural choice to begin the enormous task of sorting, transcribing, and ultimately publishing the scrolls.[17] As I see it, because the study of the scrolls, as with the apocrypha and pseudepigrapha previously, was located in the discipline of biblical studies with its central focus of the Bible as the regnant organizing category, the literary remains of early Judaism, which had expanded so dramatically with the discovery of the scrolls, continued to be viewed through the lens of the Bible. So, for example, at the basic level of labeling and categorizing, the Bible, whether explicitly or implicitly, persisted as the touchstone for how to organize the scrolls, as it had for the apocrypha and pseudepigrapha before them, and thus for how to read them. One paradigmatic example is 4QReworked Pentateuch (4Q364, 4Q365, 4Q366, 4Q367, and 4Q158), which contained the complete Pentateuch in the same order as in the biblical corpus: Genesis, Exodus, Leviticus, Numbers, and Deuteronomy. It is characterized, however, by substantial harmonizations and the insertion of new material from outside the Pentateuch. The name *reworked Pentateuch* suggests that this text has taken the biblical Pentateuch and refashioned it to produce a new text that presents the Pentateuch along with interpretations of it. Recently, however, one of 4QReworked Pentateuch's initial editors, Sidnie White Crawford, has argued that the scribes of at least 4Q364 and 4Q365

---

16. I do not intend this as a criticism. Of course, this state of affairs was hard to avoid, since only scholars with the necessary language expertise could undertake the mammoth task of deciphering and reassembling the thousands of fragments that now lay in the vaults of the Palestine Archaeological Museum, soon to be renamed the Rockefeller.

17. I cannot discuss the matter of the way that politics (both international and scholarly) affected work in the scrolls throughout the last seventy years. The interactions of politics and scholarship on the scrolls has been chronicled in numerous publications. See, for a general overview, Philip R. Davies, George J. Brooke, and Phillip R. Callaway, *The Complete World of the Dead Sea Scrolls* (London: Thames & Hudson, 2002), 14–35, "The Scrolls Revealed."

regarded these manuscripts as pentateuchal texts rather than as something else.[18] Somewhat ironically, the shift from understanding these manuscripts as comprising *interpretations of* a set of biblical texts to viewing them as authoritative texts *in themselves* dramatically changes the way one might read them; that is, we might see with more nuance what comprised Bible for those at Qumran as well as what constituted authoritative scripture for this ancient Jewish sectarian community. In a similar way, movement away from seeing Jewish pseudepigrapha as fundamentally interpretations of or somehow related to the Bible, that is, removing the Bible as the primary lens for understanding the pseudepigrapha, broadens the kinds of productive questions we might ask of these texts as literary products in their own right and as witnesses to Judaism in the Second Temple period.

Beyond the labeling of individual texts, the totality of the texts was organized with the Bible as the main organizing principle. Essentially there were two categories, Bible and non-Bible, the latter subdivided into subdivisions of apocrypha and pseudepigrapha and sectarian texts. In this schema, though, one is hard pressed to decide where to put 4QReworked Pentateuch or works like 1 Enoch or Jubilees, for example. Moreover, perpetuating the distinction between biblical and nonbiblical texts risks projecting contemporary notions of sacrality or canonicity onto an ancient community that did not make those distinctions in the same way, potentially obscuring that community's attitudes toward and use of a variety of texts, including the pseudepigrapha. Maintaining biblical as an organizing category already predisposes us to regard that category as inherently authoritative and other text outside of it as lacking that same authority—or at least that the status of texts within the category biblical does not have to be established while those in other categories require some justification for their authority, even when the Qumran community might not have recognized the difference. So, for example, in the Damascus Document, the speaker encourages the reader in the manner of a wisdom sage to consider God's deeds "so that you can choose what he is pleased with and repudiate what he hates" (II, 15).[19] The speaker then gives a paradigmatic example, that of the Watchers:

---

18. Sidnie White Crawford, *Rewriting Scripture in Second Temple Times* (Grand Rapids: Eerdmans, 2008), 56.

19. Translations for the Damascus Document follow Florentino García Martínez, *The Dead Sea Scrolls Translated*, 2nd ed., trans. Wilfred G. E. Watson (Leiden: Brill; Grand Rapids: Eerdmans, 1996).

> For many have wandered off after these matters (i.e., the guilty inclination and lascivious eyes); brave heroes yielded on account of them, from ancient times until now. For having walked in the stubbornness of their hearts the Watchers of the heavens fell; on account of it they were caught, for they did not follow the precepts of God. And their sons, whose height was like that of cedars and whose bodies were like mountains, fell. (CD II, 17-19)

The speaker offers the version of the Watchers story as we know it from 1 Enoch; it is paradigmatic and authoritative as a negative example. In this sense, the story—and perhaps the Book of the Watchers as the source of that story—gets treated as scripture, that is, as carrying authority within the community.

Later, in column XVI, the speaker is discussing membership in the group as a return to the law of Moses. The implicit question regarding Israel's repentance is answered with: "And the exact interpretation of their ages about the blindness of Israel in all these matters, behold, it is defined in the book of the divisions of the periods according to the jubilees and their weeks" (XVI, 2-4) here likely referring to the book of Jubilees.[20] The conceit of this text is that the angel of the presence dictates the law to Moses from heavenly tablets, and it narrates events that we also see in Genesis and Exodus, which are organized into periods of jubilees of forty-nine years. Yet in the Damascus Document, it is quoted in the same way as biblical texts are elsewhere. For the group at Qumran, at least, Jubilees apparently stood alongside other books attributed to Moses as authoritative, perhaps even qualifying as Bible, if we want to retain that terminology.[21]

I hope at this juncture that I have made my general point clear, but let me summarize briefly. Biblical studies as a field of humanistic study found

---

20. While most scholars accept this view, Devorah Dimant has challenged it. See her article, "Two 'Scientific' Fictions: The So-Called Book of Noah and the Alleged Quotation from Jubilees in the Damascus Document XVI, 3-4," in *Studies in the Hebrew Bible, Qumran, and the Septuagint Presented to Eugene Ulrich*, ed. Peter W. Flint, Emanuel Tov and James C. VanderKam, VTSup 101 (Leiden: Brill, 2006), 230-49.

21. For the way that Jubilees and other pseudepigrapha participate in discourses tied to founders—and how such discourses might change the way that we think about biblical books and their interpretation—see Hindy Najman, *Seconding Sinai: The Development of Mosaic Discourse in Second Temple Judaism*, JSJSup 77 (Leiden: Brill, 2003).

in colleges and universities emerged out of a primarily theological and religious environment, which it has never really been able to shed fully. One major consequence of this inability was the devaluation of Jewish works that did not make it into the Hebrew Bible or Christian Old Testament, which were accorded value inasmuch as they helped to support certain pictures of early Christianity for Christians and rabbinic Judaism for Jews. The discovery of the Dead Sea Scrolls constituted a moment when the sudden explosion of new data held out the possibility of transcending those older categories and understanding the literature of Judaism of the Persian, Hellenistic, and Roman periods in a new light.

The Pseudepigrapha within Their Contexts of Preservation and Transmission

The discovery of the scrolls, then, provided an important impetus to the development of the study of early Judaism for its own sake, and the pseudepigrapha in particular, even if for a long while the Bible remained the frame for that study. Part of that momentum came from the discovery, as I noted above, of Hebrew and Aramaic texts, however fragmentary, of pseudepigrapha that scholars had only known in translation and sometimes tertiary translations at that.[22] We now know, for instance, that the Aramaic form of the Enochic Astronomical Book at Qumran was longer than the Ge'ez translation (made from a Greek translation) in 1 Enoch that comprises the fullest known form of the text. The appearance of important pseudepigrapha in their original languages and the identification of new pseudepigraphical texts also spurred a renewed scholarly conversation about the phenomenon of pseudepigraphy in antiquity.[23] In each case,

---

22. See Michael E. Stone, *Scriptures, Sects, and Visions: A Profile of Judaism from Ezra to the Jewish Revolts* (Philadelphia: Fortress, 1980), 63, where he connects a revival of the study of pseudepigrapha with the discovery of the scrolls.

23. See, for example, Najman, *Seconding Sinai*; Najman, "How Should We Contextualize Pseudepigrapha? Imitation and Emulation in 4 Ezra," in *Flores Florentino: Dead Sea Scrolls and Other Early Jewish Studies in Honour of Florentino García Martínez*, ed. Anthony Hilhorst, Émile Puech, and Eibert Tigchelaar, JSJSup 122 (Leiden: Brill, 2007), 529–36; Karina Martin Hogan, "Pseudepigraphy and the Periodization of History," in *Pseudepigraphie und Verfasserfiktion in frühchristlichen Briefen*, ed. Jörg Frey, WUNT 246 (Tübingen: Mohr Siebeck, 2009), 61–83; see also the essays in the section on pseudepigraphy in John J. Collins, *Apocalypse, Prophecy, and Pseudepigraphy: On Jewish Apocalyptic Literature* (Grand Rapids: Eerdmans, 2015).

the new discoveries at Qumran propelled scholars to turn their attention to the pseudepigrapha for what these texts could reveal about Judaism in the Second Temple period and about important textual and religious phenomena connected with Judaism in that period.

At approximately the same time as the first scrolls were being published, some scholars began to question whether many pseudepigrapha that had hitherto been assumed to be the products of early Judaism were actually Christian in origin, inaugurating a significant and continuing debate about how scholars ought to think about pseudepigrapha that had been preserved by Christians, as most of them had. In his 1953 PhD dissertation on the Testaments of the Twelve Patriarchs, Marinus de Jonge brought the issue to the fore by asking the extent to which the Testaments might be thought of as a Christian text.[24] In 1976, Robert Kraft reflected in a broader methodological way on the issue of "The Pseudepigrapha in Christianity."[25] Kraft expressed his "discontent" in three "problem areas": (1) "Comparative Linguistic Analysis"; (2) "The Role of the Pseudepigrapha in Christian Thought"; and (3) "Formulation of Satisfactory Hypotheses Regarding Origins and Transmission of Pseudepigrapha."[26] One of the more pressing questions he asked concerned what criteria might be used to distinguish Jewish from Christian features, and he identified important methodological caveats to the criterion often used to identify a text as being Jewish—"Whatever is not clearly Christian is Jewish"[27]—essentially turning this axiom on its head:

> From my perspective, "the *Christianity* of the Pseudepigrapha" is not the hidden ingredient that needs to be hunted out and exposed in contrast

---

24. Marinus de Jonge, *The Testaments of the Twelve Patriarchs: A Study of Their Text, Composition, and Origin* (Assen: Van Gorcum, 1953).
25. Kraft delivered this paper at the Studiorum Novi Testamenti Societas meeting in 1976, but it was published much later in Kraft, "The Pseudepigrapha in Christianity," in *Tracing the Threads: Studies in the Vitality of Jewish Pseudepigrapha*, ed. John C. Reeves, EJL 6 (Atlanta: Scholars Press, 1994), 55–86.
26. Kraft, "Pseudepigrapha in Christianity," 56–57.
27. Kraft, "Pseudepigrapha in Christianity," 57. He uses scare quotes around the terms *Jewish* and *Christian*. He cites this form of the criterion from Adolf von Harnak in *Geschichte der altchristlichen Literatur bis Eusebius*, although it has become the most used criterion. Kraft notes that some earlier scholars, most notably, M. R. James, were more cautious about ascribing Jewish origins to many pseudepigrapha, although that caution does not seem to have prevailed for the most part in scholarship.

to a supposed native *Jewish* pre-Christian setting. On the contrary, when the evidence is clear that only Christians preserved the material, the Christianity of it is the given, it is the setting, it is the starting point for delving more deeply into this literature to determine what, if anything, may be safely identified as originally Jewish. And even when the label "originally Jewish" can be attached to some material in the pseudepigrapha, that does not automatically mean pre-Christian Jewish, or even pre-rabbinic Jewish.[28]

Like de Jonge before him on the Testaments of the Twelve Patriarchs, Kraft emphasized and privileged the setting of the text within the manuscript tradition and its textual history as it has come down to modern scholars, whether one can identify specifically Christian features in the text or not. So, for example, we might look at Daniel Harlow's and Alexander Kulik's differing assessments of 3 Baruch as a case that exemplifies the methodological difficulty that de Jonge, Kraft, and others have highlighted.[29]

Third Baruch survives in Greek and Slavonic, whose earliest witnesses are Slavonic manuscripts from the thirteenth–fourteenth centuries.[30] The Greek textual tradition contains several passages that are clearly Christian redactions, since the Slavonic, which was translated from a Greek parent text, does not have those Christian passages and almost certainly represents the older form of the text.[31] On the basis of this evidence, Harlow remarks in line with Kraft's methodological caveats: "Even granting this point [i.e., that the Christian elements in 3 Baruch are redactional], however, the secondary character of the overtly Christian elements in the extant Greek version *does not definitively establish* [emphasis added] that 3 Baruch was originally a *Jewish* [emphasis original] composition....

---

28. Kraft, "Pseudepigrapha in Christianity," 75, emphasis original. In 2005, James R. Davila built explicitly on Kraft's article and suggested a number of criteria. James R. Davila, *The Provenance of the Pseudepigrapha: Jewish, Christian, or Other?*, JSJSup 105 (Leiden: Brill, 2005); see, for example, 10–73.

29. For discussions of some other texts, see, Marinus de Jonge, *Pseudepigrapha of the Old Testament as Part of Christian Literature: The Case of the Testaments of the Twelve Patriarchs and the Greek Life of Adam and Eve*, SVTP 18 (Leiden: Brill, 2003), 39–68.

30. Alexander Kulik, *3 Baruch: Greek-Slavonic Apocalypse of Baruch*, CEJL (Berlin: de Gruyter, 2010), 7.

31. Kulik, *3 Baruch*, 13–14; and Daniel C. Harlow, *The Greek Apocalypse of Baruch (3 Baruch) in Hellenistic Judaism and Early Christianity*, SVTP 12 (Leiden: Brill, 1996), 83.

The remaining work might still be Christian—only one lacking *overtly* [emphasis original] Christian terminology."[32] Yet, about the same text and evidence, Kulik remarks, "In the case of *3 Baruch* we are delivered from the vicious circle of the assumptions that the Christian passages must be interpolations, since the text is Jewish, and that the text *must be Jewish* [emphasis added], since all that is Christian is interpolated."[33] Here the axiom that what is not Christian is Jewish underlies Kulik's position. In Kulik's estimation, since the best form of the text does not have Christianizing interpolations and thus is not explicitly Christian, it must be Jewish by default. While Harlow does not deny that 3 Baruch is Jewish, he resists the assumption of its Jewish origins simply because the overtly Christian elements are redactional.

Kulik, on the other hand, has no doubt about its Jewish character precisely because the Christian elements are not part of the best form of the text.[34] Moreover, the desire to push texts like 3 Baruch back into the Second Temple period, often skipping over a long history of transmission represents an attempt to recover some earlier version of a text, something close to an *Urtext*, and hypothetical versions of that text (that is, for instance, a possible Semitic-language original that does not exist) over the concrete manuscripts and contexts that make up our evidence for them. Certainly, scholars ought to attempt to recover a form of the text that is close to the time period of its composition. Yet the assumption that Kraft identifies, that the pseudepigrapha preserved in Christian contexts originated in Second Temple Jewish contexts, also tacitly privileges periods connected with the Bible, which makes it possible to seek out a relationship between those pseudepigrapha and the Bible, which remains the de facto lens through which these texts are viewed, whether the importance of that connection is construed as seeing how the text interprets biblical texts or how to understand the thought world of biblical books.[35]

---

32. Harlow, *Greek Apocalypse of Baruch*, 83.
33. Kulik, *3 Baruch*, 13.
34. See the essay by John J. Collins in this volume.
35. So, for instance, although Kulik does not explicitly spell out such an agenda, a quick look at his commentary reveals that the Bible is his most frequent point of comparison for the language of 3 Baruch. See, for example, his comment on 2:1 (in the Greek) that the phrase, "And having taken me, he brought me," "must be of biblical origin" (122). He compares this with the Hebrew of Ezekiel but otherwise does not comment on the significance of that origin.

As Harlow pointed out in 2001, however, it was only recently that "the climate in early Jewish and Christian studies has become really favorable" to the approach championed for so long by de Jonge.[36] He makes the important point that scholars in the early twentieth century "showed little hesitation in adducing texts among the Old Testament Pseudepigrapha to fill in our picture of Judaism in the pre-Christian era."[37] Of course, that picture played an important role in how early Judaism, especially the pseudepigrapha, served as a source of ideas in the New Testament and as a foil for a supersessionist view of Jesus and early Christianity. The scholar who takes seriously the Christian context and transmission of these texts, though, confronts methodological and multidisciplinary challenges on a host of levels that require a more nuanced view of Second Temple Judaism and its literature. If scholars are to have greater confidence in their conclusions about the Second-Temple roots of certain pseudepigrapha, then a multidisciplinary approach seems necessary. To cite just one example, the languages and Christian contexts alone in which pseudepigrapha are preserved can be dizzying—for example, Greek, Latin, Syriac, Coptic, Ethiopic, Armenian, Slavonic, Georgian, Arabic, to name the most prominent ones—and these point to other issues that scholars of pseudepigraphical texts have to engage. I want to point to just a few here as exempla.

Many pseudepigrapha only survive in translation, and sometimes in tertiary translation and in multiple translation into different languages.[38] In whatever contexts these texts survive, such pseudepigrapha reflect the context into which they were translated, and even if the text can be shown to be a Second Temple Jewish text, we cannot assume, as so often happens, that the translated form of the text represents accurately the text in its original language. A great example is the Enochic Astronomical Book (1 En. 72–82), which was originally composed in Aramaic, was translated into Greek, and then into Ethiopic, the language in which the complete text

---

36. Daniel C. Harlow, "The Christianization of Early Jewish Pseudepigrapha: The Case of 3 *Baruch*," *JSJ* 32 (2001): 419.

37. Harlow, "Christianization of Early Jewish Pseudepigrapha," 416.

38. Some texts like 1 Enoch and Jubilees, which found their way into the canon of the Ethiopian church, survive in complete form in only one language. Others, like the Books of Adam and Eve, which survives in Greek, Latin, Armenian, Slavonic, and Georgian, might come down to us in numerous translations. For the Life of Adam and Eve, see Gary A. Anderson and Michael E. Stone, eds. *A Synopsis of the Books of Adam and Eve*, EJL 5 (Atlanta: Scholars Press, 1994).

has come down to modern scholars. The Aramaic fragments discovered at Qumran have shown that the Astronomical Book in both the Aramaic version and the Ethiopic version "has reached us in garbled form," as Jonathan Ben-Dov has put it, one that has been simplified and abridged, and thus, we cannot blithely accept that the Ethiopic Astronomical Book is the same as the Qumran Astronomical Book.[39] Moreover, in Septuagint studies, a greater engagement with the discipline of translation studies has helped scholars to think with more theoretical clarity about how translations work and what we might be able to say about ancient translations.[40] Within the study of pseudepigrapha, a more explicit attention to the phenomenon of translation would bring into greater relief the differences between a text in its originating cultural milieu and that of its translated version(s) and thus of its use within the context into which the translation was received.[41]

In a 1986 article "Categorization and Classification of the Apocrypha and Pseudepigrapha," Stone asked: "Are we justified in establishing the Jewish or Christian character of a pseudepigraphon found only in a Christian manuscript without first making a careful study of how it functioned within the Christian tradition that preserved it, unless the evidence from content is totally compelling?"[42] He answers his own question: "Nevertheless, before the Pseudepigrapha and similar writings can be

---

39. Jonathan Ben-Dov, *Head of All Years: Astronomy and Calendars in Qumran in Their Ancient Context*, STDJ 78 (Leiden: Brill, 2008), 73. Of course, once the text was translated into Ethiopic, it had its own transmission history in that language, which must be taken into account. As Loren Stuckenbruck's recent work has shown, that history still has numerous lacunae. See Ted M. Erho and Loren T. Stuckenbruck, "A Manuscript History of *Ethiopic Enoch*," *JSP* 23 (2013): 1–47.

40. See, for example, the articles in *BIOSCS* 39 (2006): Albert Pietersma, "LXX and DTS: A New Archimedean Point for Septuagint Studies?" (1–11); Gideon Toury, "A Handful of Methodological Issues in DTS: Are They Applicable to the Study of the Septuagint as an Assumed Translation?" (13–25); Cameron Boyd-Taylor, "Toward the Analysis of Translational Norms: A Sighting Shot" (27–46); Benjamin G. Wright III, "The Letter of Aristeas and the Reception History of the Septuagint" (47–67); and Steven D. Fraade, "Locating Targum in the Textual Polysystem of Rabbinic Pedagogy" (69–91).

41. So, for example, in Septuagint studies, for many years the Septuagint was primarily of interest for its text-critical evidence for the development of the biblical text. With increased attention to the text as a translation and a product of Second Temple Judaism, more scholarly attention is being paid to what the Septuagint can tell us about Jews and Jewish thought in that period.

42. Michael E. Stone, "Categorization and Classification of the Apocrypha and Pseudepigrapha," *AbrN* 24 (1986): 172–73.

used as evidence for that more ancient period, they must be examined in the Christian context in which they were transmitted and utilized." Only after this kind of study can scholars reach conclusions about whether any text can serve as a source for understanding Second Temple Judaism or if it reworks Jewish material from that period and thus transmits important traditions for studying ancient early Judaism and Christianity.[43] Moreover, studying these texts in their Christian contexts contributes to understanding the history of Christianity and perhaps to the relationships between Jews and Christians in late antiquity and beyond. This latter point becomes especially significant if we recognize that even if we can identify Jewish sources and/or traditions in these pseudepigrapha, what criteria do we apply to determine that this material originated in the Second Temple period and not in late antiquity or the Byzantine period?

David Satran's analysis of the *vita* of Daniel in the Lives of the Prophets exemplifies how study of pseudepigrapha within their Christian contexts complicates and illuminates using these texts as direct sources for Second Temple Judaism. Satran demonstrates that Nebuchadnezzar's penitence in the *vita* of Daniel "enables us to speak confidently of the narrative as a fourth- or fifth-century composition, representative of aspects of early Byzantine piety."[44] Satran uncovers one element of that construction in the detail that after Nebuchadnezzar's repentance Daniel enjoins the king to eat nothing but "soaked beans and herbs." While this diet recalls Daniel's own diet in the biblical book of Daniel, Satran points out that the adjective *soaked* does not occur at all in early Jewish or Christian sources, but rather it appears after the fourth century in the context of monastic dietary practices. That is, all the way down to the smallest details, the narrative turns Nebuchadnezzar into an exemplar of repentance modeled on Christian monastic practice.[45] Satran has successfully shown that the Lives of the Prophets "as it stands is in the fullest sense a text of early Byzantine Christianity.... The text is, therefore, far more than the sum of its parts: even if it could be proven to consist entirely of earlier Jewish tradition, the *Lives of the Prophets* is in every respect a new composition."[46]

---

43. Stone offers these possibilities in "Categorization and Classification of the Apocrypha and Pseudepigrapha," 172–73.

44. David Satran, *Biblical Prophets in Byzantine Palestine: Reassessing the* Lives of the Prophets, SVTP 11 (Leiden: Brill, 1995), 91.

45. Satran, *Biblical Prophets in Byzantine Palestine*, 90–91.

46. Satran, *Biblical Prophets in Byzantine Palestine*, 120.

Finally, in many cases, pseudepigrapha, such as 2 Baruch, which is extant in a single Syriac manuscript (Codex Ambrosianus), survive in a very few manuscripts; others, such as 1 Enoch, might appear in dozens. We can learn much about the lives of these texts and the communities that used them by studying them through the lenses of manuscripts studies, book history, or the new philology. These approaches study the manuscripts within their literary cultures of production and reception, focusing on their materiality and their functions as inscribed cultural artifacts. Although relatively new in the study of pseudepigrapha, these disciplines seem poised to make a critical impact of the study of the pseudepigrapha.[47]

To treat the pseudepigrapha in the way that de Jonge, Kraft, Stone, and others have insisted requires a wide-ranging set of disciplinary engagements that set aside the primacy of the Bible as the standard of analysis and that range outside of the traditional historical-critical methods that have characterized biblical studies especially as they have been employed to reinforce that primacy. Indeed, in some respects—while also noting a hint of irony—the Bible as a category becomes less anachronistic and more relevant the farther away that we move from the periods that have traditionally occupied biblical studies, even though what comprised the Bible continued to vary in different time periods, geographical regions, and communities. At least in later periods the category is not inherently anachronistic. The scholarly study of Second Temple Judaism began with those who argued that Judaism in this period should be studied for its own sake as one part of the broader history of Judaism, and it has matured as scholars have moved outside of traditional biblical studies methods, models, and time periods and have adopted theories and approaches used more widely in the study of religion. One only need look at recent publications to see the shift that has taken place. As the study of Second Temple Judaism has incorporated other disciplinary approaches such as literary theory, colonial and postcolonial studies, feminist theory, culture studies, or gender theory, among others—approaches that have become more

---

47. On the new philology, see most recently Liv Ingeborg Lied and Hugo Lundhaus, eds., *Snapshots of an Evolving Tradition: Jewish and Christian Manuscript Culture, Textual Fluidity, and New Philology*, TUGAL 175 (Berlin: de Gruyter, 2017), as well as the recently formed Book History and Biblical Literatures Consultation at the Society of Biblical Literature. See also Liv Ingeborg Lied, "2 Baruch and the Syriac Codex Ambrosianus (7a1): Studying Old Testament Pseudepigrapha in Their Manuscript Context," *JSP* 26 (2016): 67–107.

usual in the broader field of religious studies—and has moved away from relying primarily on the historical-critical method, new avenues have opened up for understanding the past that have, for example, expanded our understanding of texts as literary creations and as repositories of different kinds of knowledge, and they have complicated how we look at the production and transmission of texts in the ancient world.[48] By letting go of the Bible as studied primarily through the traditional methods of biblical studies as the sine qua non for understanding ancient Judaism, scholars of early Judaism are beginning to grasp that what we were seeing was not all that was happening. In this sense the very idea of studying the past and realizing what we can understand of it has changed. This certainly seems to be the case when it comes to those texts that have been labeled Jewish pseudepigrapha.

Bibliography

Anderson, Gary A., and Michael E. Stone, ed. *A Synopsis of the Books of Adam and Eve*. EJL 5. Atlanta: Scholars Press, 1994.

Bauckham, Richard, James R. Davila, and Alexander Panayotov, eds. *Old Testament Pseudepigrapha: More Noncanonical Scriptures*. Vol. 1. Grand Rapids: Eerdmans, 2013.

Ben-Dov, Jonathan. *Head of All Years: Astronomy and Calendars in Qumran in Their Ancient Context*. STDJ 78. Leiden: Brill, 2008.

Boccaccini, Gabriele. *Middle Judaism: Jewish Thought 300 B.C.E. to 200 C.E.* Minneapolis: Fortress, 1991.

Boyd-Taylor, Cameron. "Toward the Analysis of Translational Norms: A Sighting Shot." *BIOSCS* 39 (2006): 27–46.

Charles, R. H. *The Apocrypha and Pseudepigrapha of the Old Testament*. 2 vols. Oxford: Clarendon, 1913.

---

48. I give here only four recent examples that treat Jewish pseudepigrapha among many that could be marshaled: Hindy Najman, *Losing the Temple and Recovering the Future: An Analysis of* 4 *Ezra* (Cambridge: Cambridge University Press, 2014) (trauma theory, philosophical ethics, literary theory); Ronald Charles, "Hybridity and the *Letter of Aristeas*," *JSJ* 40 (2009): 242–59 (postcolonial theory); Rebecca Raphael, "Monsters and the Crippled Cosmos: Construction of the Other in *Fourth Ezra*," in *The "Other" in Second Temple Judaism: Essays in Honor of John J. Collins*, ed. Daniel C. Harlow (Grand Rapids: Eerdmans, 2011), 279–301 (disability studies and monster theory); Jill Hicks-Keeton, "Aseneth between Judaism and Christianity: Reframing the Debate," *JSJ* 49 (2018): 189–222 (ethnicity and identity).

Charles, Ronald. "Hybridity and the *Letter of Aristeas*." *JSJ* 40 (2009): 242–59.
Charlesworth, James H., ed. *The Old Testament Pseudepigrapha*. 2 vols. Garden City, NY: Doubleday, 1983–1985.
Collins, John J. *Apocalypse, Prophecy, and Pseudepigraphy: On Jewish Apocalyptic Literature*. Grand Rapids: Eerdmans, 2015.
Crawford, Sidnie White. *Rewriting Scripture in Second Temple Times*. Grand Rapids: Eerdmans, 2008.
Davies, Philip R. "Biblical Studies: Fifty Years of a Multi-discipline." *CurBR* 13 (2014): 34–66.
Davies, Philip R., George J. Brooke, and Phillip R. Callaway. *The Complete World of the Dead Sea Scrolls*. London: Thames & Hudson, 2002.
Davila, James R. *The Provenance of the Pseudepigrapha: Jewish, Christian, or Other?* JSJSup 105. Leiden: Brill, 2005.
Dimant, Devorah. "Two 'Scientific' Fictions: The So-Called Book of Noah and the Alleged Quotation from Jubilees in the Damascus Document XVI, 3–4." Pages 230–49 in *Studies in the Hebrew Bible, Qumran, and the Septuagint Presented to Eugene Ulrich*. Edited by Peter W. Flint, Emanuel Tov and James C. VanderKam. VTSup 101. Leiden: Brill, 2006.
Feldman, Louis H., James L. Kugel, and Lawrence H. Schiffman, eds. *Outside the Bible: Ancient Jewish Writings Related to Scripture*. 3 vols. Lincoln: University of Nebraska Press; Philadelphia: The Jewish Publication Society, 2013.
Fraade, Steven D. "Locating Targum in the Textual Polysystem of Rabbinic Pedagogy." *BIOSCS* 39 (2006): 69–91.
Harlow, Daniel C. "The Christianization of Early Jewish Pseudepigrapha: The Case of 3 Baruch." *JSJ* 32 (2001): 416–44.
———. *The Greek Apocalypse of Baruch (3 Baruch) in Hellenistic Judaism and Early Christianity*. SVTP 12. Leiden: Brill, 1996.
Hicks-Keeton, Jill. "Aseneth between Judaism and Christianity: Reframing the Debate." *JSJ* 49 (2018): 189–222.
Hogan, Karina Martin. "Pseudepigraphy and the Periodization of History." Pages 61–83 in *Pseudepigraphie und Verfasserfiktion in frühchristlichen Briefen*. Edited by Jörg Frey. WUNT 246. Tübingen: Mohr Siebeck, 2009.
Jonge, Marinus de. *Pseudepigrapha of the Old Testament as Part of Christian Literature: The Case of the Testaments of the Twelve Patriarchs and the Greek Life of Adam and Eve*. SVTP 18. Leiden: Brill, 2003.

———. *The Testaments of the Twelve Patriarchs: A Study of Their Text, Composition, and Origin*. Assen: Van Gorcum, 1953.

Legaspi, Michael C. *The Death of Scripture and the Rise of Biblical Studies*. Oxford: Oxford University Press, 2010.

Kautzsch, Emil F. *Die Apokryphen und Pseudepigraphen des Alten Testaments*. Tübingen: Mohr Siebeck, 1900.

Klawans, Jonathan. "Sadducees, Zadokites, and the Wisdom of Ben Sira." Pages 261–76 in *Israel's God and Rebecca's Children, Christology and Community in Early Judaism and Christianity: Essays in Honor of Larry W. Hurtado and Alan F. Segal*. Edited by David B. Capes, April D. DeConick, and Helen K. Bond. Waco, TX: Baylor University Press, 2008.

Kraft, Robert A. "The Pseudepigrapha in Christianity." Pages 55–86 in *Tracing the Threads: Studies in the Vitality of Jewish Pseudepigrapha*. Edited by John C. Reeves. EJL 6. Atlanta: Scholars Press, 1994.

———. Review of *The Old Testament Pseudepigrapha*, by J. H. Charlesworth; review of *The Apocryphal Old Testament*, by H. F. D. Sparks. *RelSRev* 14 (1988): 113–17.

Kulik, Alexander. *3 Baruch: Greek-Slavonic Apocalypse of Baruch*. CEJL. Berlin: de Gruyter, 2010.

Kynes, Will. "The Nineteenth-Century Beginnings of 'Wisdom Literature,' and Its Twenty-First-Century End?" Pages 83–108 in *Perspectives on Israelite Wisdom: Proceedings of the Oxford Old Testament Seminar*. Edited by John Jarick. LHBOTS 618. London: Bloomsbury T&T Clark, 2016.

Lied, Liv Ingeborg. "2 Baruch and the Syriac Codex Ambrosianus (7a1): Studying Old Testament Pseudepigrapha in Their Manuscript Context." *JSP* 26 (2016): 67–107.

Lied, Liv Ingeborg, and Hugo Lundhaus, eds. *Snapshots of an Evolving Tradition: Jewish and Christian Manuscript Culture, Textual Fluidity, and New Philology*. TUGAL 175. Berlin: de Gruyter, 2017.

Lim, Timothy H. "Authoritative Scriptures and the Dead Sea Scrolls." Pages 303–22 in *The Oxford Handbook of the Dead Sea Scrolls*. Edited by Timothy H. Lim and John J. Collins. Oxford: Oxford University Press, 2010.

McCutcheon, Russell T. "Introduction: Plus ça Change …." Pages 1–16 in *A Modest Proposal on Method: Essaying the Study of Religion*. MTSRsup 2. Leiden: Brill, 2015.

———. *Manufacturing Religion: The Discourse on Sui Generis Religion and the Politics of Nostalgia*. Oxford: Oxford University Press, 1997.
Najman, Hindy. "How Should We Contextualize Pseudepigrapha? Imitation and Emulation in 4 Ezra." Pages 529–36 in *Flores Florentino: Dead Sea Scrolls and Other Early Jewish Studies in Honour of Florentino García Martínez*. Edited by Anthony Hilhorst, Émile Puech, and Eibert Tigchelaar. JSJSup 122. Leiden: Brill, 2007.
———. *Losing the Temple and Recovering the Future: An Analysis of* 4 Ezra. Cambridge: Cambridge University Press, 2014.
———. *Seconding Sinai: The Development of Mosaic Discourse in Second Temple Judaism*. JSJSup 77. Leiden: Brill, 2003.
Pietersma, Albert. "LXX and DTS: A New Archimedean Point for Septuagint Studies?" *BIOSCS* 39 (2006): 1–11.
Raphael, Rebecca. "Monsters and the Crippled Cosmos: Construction of the Other in *Fourth Ezra*." Pages 279–301 in *The "Other" in Second Temple Judaism: Essays in Honor of John J. Collins*. Edited by Daniel C. Harlow. Grand Rapids: Eerdmans, 2011.
Reed, Annette Yoshiko. "The Modern Invention of 'Old Testament Pseudepigrapha.'" *JTS* 60 (2009): 403–36.
Satran, David. *Biblical Prophets in Byzantine Palestine: Reassessing the Lives of the Prophets*. SVTP 11. Leiden: Brill, 1995.
Schilbrack, Kevin. "Religions: Are There Any?" *JAAR* 78 (2010): 1112–38.
Sparks, H. F. D., ed. *The Apocryphal Old Testament*. Oxford: Clarendon, 1984.
Stone, Michael E. *Ancient Judaism: New Visions and Views*. Grand Rapids: Eerdmans, 2011.
———. "Categorization and Classification of the Apocrypha and Pseudepigrapha." *AbrN* 24 (1986): 167–77.
———. Review of *The Old Testament Pseudepigrapha*, by J. H. Charlesworth; review of *The Apocryphal Old Testament*, by H. F. D. Sparks. *RelSRev* 14 (1988): 111–13.
———. *Scriptures, Sects, and Visions: A Profile of Judaism from Ezra to the Jewish Revolts*. Philadelphia: Fortress, 1980.
Toury, Gideon. "A Handful of Methodological Issues in DTS: Are They Applicable to the Study of the Septuagint as an Assumed Translation?" *BIOSCS* 39 (2006): 13–25.
Weeks, Stuart. *An Introduction to the Study of Wisdom Literature*. New York: T&T Clark International, 2010.

Wright, Benjamin G., III. "The Letter of Aristeas and the Reception History of the Septuagint." *BIOSCS* 39 (2006): 47–67.

———. *The Letter of Aristeas: 'Aristeas to Philocrates' or 'On the Translation of the Law of the Jews'*. CEJL. Berlin: de Gruyter, 2015.

9
Dead Sea Scrolls Scholarship and Pseudepigrapha Studies: From Józef Milik to Material Philology

Eibert Tigchelaar

1. Dead Sea Scrolls and Pseudepigrapha Studies

The discoveries of the Dead Sea Scrolls from 1947 onwards were one of the main triggers for an academic focus on early Judaism in the second part of the twentieth century. The renaissance of Old Testament pseudepigrapha studies in the 1960s and 1970s could thus be seen as forming part of this scholarly interest in early Judaism.[1] This assumption is strengthened by some direct connections between the Dead Sea Scrolls and the pseudepigrapha. By the mid-1950s it was clear that, among the Dead Sea Scrolls fragments, some of the well-known pseudepigrapha were preserved (Jubilees, parts of 1 Enoch, and a version of the Testament of Levi). These texts could now be studied in a more concrete historical and literary context, while the pseudepigrapha provided a welcome background for the new but often fragmentary texts and data of the Dead Sea Scrolls.

However, this close correspondence with the Dead Sea Scrolls holds true for only a few of the pseudepigrapha, and the rebirth of pseudepigrapha studies was largely initiated by the editing and textual study of Greek pseudepigrapha, be they Jewish or Christian. Additional developments aside from the discovery of new corpora of texts—the Dead Sea Scrolls or the Nag Hammadi Codices—also contributed to the interest in both

---

1. For terms such as *rebirth* or *renaissance*, see James H. Charlesworth, "The Renaissance of Pseudepigraphy Studies: The SBL Pseudepigrapha Project," *JSJ* 2 (1971): 107–14.

early Judaism and the pseudepigrapha.² Other studies in this volume may highlight some of these developments, such as the increase in the number of religious studies departments in American universities and the remodelling of the Annual Meetings of the Society of Biblical Literature in the late 1960s, both of which promoted the study of religious texts beyond the biblical canons. The rising interest in the pseudepigrapha during the 1960s was also a move away from biblical-theological approaches, which dominated New Testament studies in the preceding decades, towards more historical and literary approaches.³ These developments in biblical studies can aptly be illustrated by the trajectory leading from Ernst Käsemann's biblical-theological treatment of apocalyptic in the early 1960s, through Klaus Koch's 1970 insistence that a study of apocalyptic should be based on a description of the genre and an analysis of the most important apocalypses, to John Collins's 1979 *Semeia* 14 description of a genre based on a morphological analysis of a multitude of apocalypses, many of which we would now call Old Testament pseudepigrapha or ancient Christian apocrypha.⁴

The first meeting of the Pseudepigrapha Project at the 1969 Annual Meeting of the Society of Biblical Literature was one of many initiatives that led to the gradual creation of a range of subdisciplines within biblical studies. The creation of the different sections of the Annual Meetings, the founding of journals focusing on specific corpora, book series—initially especially with Brill—for studies in specific areas, the foundation of international organizations for the study of such corpora, the funding of specialized research centers at European universities, as well as the publication of text editions or translations of specific collections of texts, all led to the creation of separate scholarly areas, differentiated not only by their distinct textual corpora, but occasionally also by different approaches or interests, thus resulting, in a sense, in differing fields of scholarship.

---

2. See Charlesworth, "Renaissance of Pseudepigraphy Studies," and especially George W. MacRae, "Foreword," *OTP* 1:ix–x.

3. Suggestion by John J. Collins (personal communication).

4. Ernst Käsemann, "Die Anfänge christlicher Theologie," *ZTK* 57 (1960): 162–85; Käsemann, "Zum Thema der urchristlichen Apokalyptik," *ZTK* 59 (1962): 257–84; Klaus Koch, *Ratlos vor der Apokalyptik: Eine Streitschrift über ein vernachlässigtes Gebiet der Bibelwissenschaft und die schädlichen Auswirkungen auf Theologie und Philosophie* (Gütersloh: Gütersloher Verlagshaus, 1970); John J. Collins, ed., *Apocalypse: The Morphology of a Genre, Semeia* 14 (1979).

9. Dead Sea Scrolls Scholarship and Pseudepigrapha Studies

Dead Sea Scrolls scholarship and pseudepigrapha studies both form part of broader general developments in biblical, textual, and religious studies. Hence, more or less simultaneously, they have experienced the same developments and the introduction of new approaches. For example, in the past decade both fields have embraced aspects of material philology, or a focus on cognition and emotions. Moreover, ever since the discovery of the scrolls, many scholars have worked in both areas. However, from a different perspective, over the past fifty years the two fields of scholarship have also expanded in opposite directions. In particular, once all the Dead Sea Scrolls had been published in the 1990s, there was a challenge to interpret the entirety of the Dead Sea Scrolls as a collection or library, frozen in time and space, which can give insight into the textual practices of a specific textual microcommunity. Within pseudepigrapha studies, there has never been a consensus about the definition and demarcation of the collection, which in recent decades has been extended with respect to provenance and date, and that field of scholarship may be determined more by its scholarly perspectives than by its corpus.

The interaction of Dead Sea Scrolls and pseudepigrapha studies may be illustrated concretely by three different, largely chronologically successive, examples: first, the discovery and analysis of fragmentary Dead Sea Scrolls manuscripts related to three pseudepigrapha, Jubilees, 1 Enoch, and the Testaments of the Twelve Patriarchs; second, discussions since the 1990s about the labeling of texts as pseudepigrapha, related to the literary classification of the many Dead Sea Scrolls published in the 1990s and to the project of collecting more Old Testament pseudepigrapha; and, third, recent material philology approaches and their different impacts on scrolls and pseudepigrapha studies.

2. Józef Milik and Pseudepigrapha Studies

The small scrolls team that was formed to publish the Qumran Cave 4 materials divided the types of texts to be published by its members. The two American scholars, Frank Moore Cross and Patrick Skehan, were responsible for the publication of the so-called biblical texts; the nonbiblical texts were assigned to the European scholars. Altogether, the largest lot was entrusted to Józef Milik, who was also responsible for the publication of the Cave 4 manuscripts of Jubilees, Enoch, and the Testament of Levi. As early as 1955 and 1956 (published from 1956 to 1959), within a decade after the discovery of the Dead Sea Scrolls from Qumran Cave 1 and less than five years after the discovery of the more than ten thousand fragments from Qumran Cave 4, Milik briefly discussed the Qumran manuscript forms of several pseudepigrapha, proffered some implications for the study of those texts, and gave a brief description of other hitherto unknown pseudepigrapha from Qumran Caves 1 and 4.[5] His report on these manuscripts answered many introductory questions that had haunted earlier scholarship (such as language of composition). More interestingly, these reports do not merely present the first results of Milik's work, but they also reflect his approaches and insights. However, one had to wait until the 1970s for Milik's further discussion and publication of the Enoch material and until the 1990s for the final publication of the Jubilees and Aramaic Levi manuscripts, which by then had been entrusted to other scholars.[6]

In these first descriptions,[7] Milik emphasizes that it is only in the case of Jubilees that the textual form found in the Qumran manuscripts is largely similar to that found in the early Ethiopic and Latin versions. In contrast, as early as the mid-1950s, he points to the compositional differences

---

5. Józef T. Milik, "Le travail d'édition des fragments manuscrits de Qumrân," *RB* 63 (1956): 60; Milik, *Dix ans de découvertes dans le désert de Juda* (Paris: Cerf, 1957), 29-34; Milik, *Ten Years of Discovery in the Wilderness of Judaea* (London: SCM, 1959), 32-37.

6. Józef T. Milik, "Problèmes de la littérature Hénochique à la lumière des fragments araméens de Qumrân," *HTR* 64 (1971): 333-78; Milik, "Fragments grecs du livre d'Hénoch (P. Oxy. XVII 2069)," *CdE* 46 (1971): 32-43 (with references to the Aramaic fragments); Milik, "Turfan et Qumran: Livre des Géants juif et manichéen," in *Tradition und Glaube: Das frühe Christentum in seiner Umwelt: Festgabe für Karl Georg Kuhn zum 65. Geburtstag*, ed. Gert Jeremias, Heinz-Wolfgang Kuhn, and Hartmut Stegemann (Göttingen: Vandenhoeck & Ruprecht, 1971), 118-27; Milik, *The Books of Enoch: Aramaic Fragments of Qumrân Cave 4* (Oxford: Clarendon, 1976). For later scholars, see James C. VanderKam and Józef T. Milik, "Jubilees," in *Qumran Cave 4.XIII: Parabiblical Texts; Part 1*, ed. Harold Attridge et al., DJD 13 (Oxford: Clarendon, 1994), 1-185 (some Cave 4 manuscripts had been prepublished in articles from 1991 onward); Michael E. Stone and Jonas C. Greenfield (with contributions by Matthew Morgenstern), "Aramaic Levi Document," in *Qumran Cave 4.XVII: Parabiblical Texts; Part 3*, ed. George J. Brooke and James C. VanderKam, DJD 22 (Oxford: Clarendon, 1996), 1-72 (the Cave 4 manuscripts were also published separately in articles from 1994 onward).

7. Note that there are some differences between the reports, clearly reflecting ongoing work and interpretation.

between the Aramaic Enochic manuscripts and the Ethiopic version.[8] The Aramaic fragments attest to a separate work consisting of the first, fourth, and fifth section of the Ethiopic version. However, the second part of the Ethiopic version (the Similitudes) had apparently not been written before the first century CE, while the Ethiopic text of the third part (the Astronomical Book) is an abridgment of an independent Aramaic work, parts of which were also found at Qumran. As for the Testaments of the Twelve Patriarchs, Milik regards it as a first- or second-century CE work that used and adapted some already existing testaments, of which those of Levi and Naphtali were found at Qumran, and completed a full set of testaments for all the twelve patriarchs. In the same overview, Milik mentions several other, hitherto unknown, pseudepigrapha found among the Dead Sea Scrolls, such as the so-called Genesis Apocryphon, and, for example, the Psalms of Joshua, a Vision of Amram, and the Prayer of Nabonidus. Other narrative texts among the Cave 4 manuscripts were mentioned by John Strugnell and included a Pseudo-Jeremianic work and a possibly related Apocalypse of Jubilees, both of which were only fully published in 2001 by Devorah Dimant.[9]

In these first reports we can already see the specific concerns of Milik as a scholar. Although he was probably the most gifted scholar ever with respect to the reading, decipherment, and identification of scrolls fragments, and the most perceptive with regard to the material and scribal aspects of the scrolls,[10] his real concerns were historical and cultural, with a special focus on the transmission and transformation of texts and traditions, more than, for example, on an analysis of the literary form or theological meaning of individual works or manuscripts. Perhaps for that reason, he did not show much interest in the Qumran manuscripts of Jubilees, of which the text seemed to be largely identical to that of

---

8. In "Le travail d'édition," 60, Milik stated that the Aramaic version of the Book of Watchers contained sections omitted by the versions, such as the letter by Enoch to Shemihazah, before he discovered that some of the Enoch fragments were actually part of the Book of Giants.

9. John Strugnell in Milik, "Le travail d'édition," 65; Devorah Dimant, *Parabiblical Texts, Part 4: Pseudo-Prophetic Texts*, DJD 30 (Oxford: Clarendon, 2001). The Apocalypse of Jubilees is 4Q390, which has now been incorrectly published as another copy or version of Apocryphon of Jeremiah C.

10. See, e.g., Józef T. Milik, "Fragment d'une source du Psautier (4QPs 89) et fragments des Jubilés, du Document de Damas, d'un phylactère dans la grotte 4 de Qumrân," *RB* 63 (1966): 94–106.

the later Ethiopic and Latin versions; his most extensive publication on Jubilees concerns quotations of and references to the book of Jubilees by later Christian authors.[11] His brief comments of the mid-1950s about the works attributed to Enoch and Levi particularly address the relation of the Dead Sea Scrolls manuscript to the later works of 1 Enoch and the Testaments of the Twelve Patriarchs. In the same period, Milik had already written an article on a major Cave 4 Levi fragment (now published as 4Q213a 1–2), arguing, just as Marinus de Jonge had done a few years earlier, that the Aramaic text, which was already known from a Genizah manuscript, was one of the sources adapted by the author of the Testaments of the Twelve Patriarchs.[12] In virtually all his subsequent works on the scrolls his primary aim was not to publish the manuscripts allotted to him, but rather to explore the relationships with later Jewish and Christian texts and traditions, especially those written in Greek, and to trace trajectories. Thus, in his only more or less full edition of any of the works assigned to him, *The Books of Enoch*, Milik gives ample attention not only to the Aramaic books of Enoch, but also to the early versions in other languages of those books, and on works attributed to Enoch in Roman-Byzantine and medieval times. Likewise, most of Milik's work on other Dead Sea Scrolls manuscripts and fragments scrutinizes the possible literary or thematic links with later Greek texts or Christian authors, and more attention is often given to these later texts than to the fragmentary Aramaic materials.[13]

Milik's *The Books of Enoch* (incorporating several fragments published earlier) gave a boost to studies of 1 Enoch, even though several of his central arguments and proposals have been dismissed by subsequent

---

11. Józef T. Milik, "Recherches sur la version grecque du livre des Jubilés," *RB* 78 (1971): 545–57.

12. Józef T. Milik, "Le Testament de Lévi en araméen: Fragment de la Grotte 4 de Qumrân," *RB* 62 (1955): 398–406. Cf. Marinus de Jonge, *The Testaments of the Twelve Patriarchs: A Study of Their Text, Composition and Origin* (Assen: Van Gorcum, 1953).

13. This is often expressed even in the titles of Milik's works, such as "Milkî-ṣedeq et Milkî-reša' dans les anciens écrits juifs et chrétiens," *JJS* 33 (1972): 95–144, and "4QVisions de 'Amram et une citation d'Origène," *RB* 79 (1972): 77–97. For an example, see Milik's "Daniel et Susanne à Qumran?," in *De la Torah au Messie: Études d'exégèse et d'herméneutique bibliques offertes à Henri Cazelles*, ed. Maurice Carrez, Joseph Doré, and Pierre Grelot (Paris: Desclée, 1981), 337–59, where the first part deals with the LXX and only the last three pages with the possible fragment dealing with Daniel and Susanna.

scholarship. Most influential have been the data provided by the manuscript evidence. First, Milik's publication and early palaeographic dating to the "first half of the second century B.C."[14] for 4Q201 (with remnants of 1 En. 1–12), suggested that 1 En. 1–5, which had often been seen as an introduction to the entire collection of 1 Enoch, served even at an early stage as an introduction to the Book of Watchers and suggested that the core of the Book of Watchers goes back to an even earlier period. This revised dating also affected the discussions on the origins of apocalyptic, a topic very popular in the 1970s and 1980s. Second, the publication of the old 4Q208, palaeographically dated by Milik to "the end of the third century or else to the beginning of the second century B.C.,"[15] and 4Q209—the first exclusively with fragments of a so-called synchronistic calendar, the second with fragments of this synchronistic calendar as well as fragments corresponding to 1 En. 76–79 and 82—prompted a reevaluation of the Astronomical Book in 1 En. 72–82, and of the provenance and importance of astronomical knowledge and calendrical issues in early Judaism. Third, the manuscript evidence of all the Enochic manuscripts together demonstrates that from a material, and perhaps also a literary, point of view, there were different Enochic booklets that could be copied both independently and as a collection. This evidence, together with the absence of any copy of the second part of 1 Enoch, the Similitudes, but the presence among these collections of the so-called Book of Giants,[16] challenged the scholars of 1 Enoch to reconsider the nature of the Ethiopic collection. Among the interpretive proposals of Milik, sev-

---

14. Milik, *Books of Enoch*, 22. It should be noted, however, that Milik's palaeographic datings are more intuitive (and often older) than those based on the typological approach of Frank Moore Cross, as developed in Cross's "The Development of the Jewish Scripts," in *The Bible and the Ancient Near East: Essays in Honor of William Foxwell Albright*, ed. G. E. Wright (Garden City, NY: Doubleday, 1961), 133–202. On the basis of Cross's typological approach, Michaël Langlois dates the hand to the middle of the second century BCE. Michaël Langlois, *Le premier manuscrit du Livre d'Hénoch: Étude épigraphique et philologique des fragments araméens de 4Q201 à Qumrân* (Paris: Cerf, 2008), 62–68.

15. Milik, *Books of Enoch*, 273.

16. Milik's proposal that, in the case of 4Q203 (4QEnGiants^a)–4Q204 (4QEn^c), the Book of Giants fragments derived from the same manuscript as other Enochic booklets has been disputed. I do not see any material or scribal grounds to contest Milik's view that 4Q203 and 4Q204 formed one and the same manuscript, even though the order of the booklets in this manuscript cannot be ascertained on the

eral have encountered criticism or even downright dismissal. This holds for Milik's suggestion of an original fourth-century BCE or older Enochic booklet consisting of 1 En. 6–19, for his hypothesis of an Enochic Pentateuch originally containing the Book of Giants which was later replaced by the Similitudes, and for his late dating of the Similitudes (around 270 CE) and 2 Enoch (ninth or tenth centuries).

Regardless of some of his more problematic suggestions, Milik's publication and interpretations have greatly influenced both early Jewish studies and the study of 1 Enoch. His work on the manuscripts introduced a kind of material philology approach within Dead Sea Scrolls studies. His survey of a range of Enochic books and versions, from antiquity up to medieval times, has initiated an entire branch of Enochic studies. His book, as well as his other studies, also put forward an approach that studies discrete literary texts or versions not in isolation but as part of larger trajectories of versions and traditions. He also drew attention, albeit more implicitly than explicitly, to the problem of the concept of the literary work. He emphasized that, in several respects, the Ethiopic version of the Book of Enoch is not identical with the various forms of the Aramaic books of Enoch from the Hellenistic and early Roman period. This raises the issue of how one should actually deal with 1 Enoch: by focusing on the Aramaic booklets and collections or by focusing on the Ethiopic book. Nickelsburg's major commentary of 1 Enoch in the Hermeneia series does neither, taking as its organizing principle a hypothesized original literary form of a collection of Enochic booklets that is substantially different from both the present Ethiopic collection and the attested collections in the Qumran manuscripts.[17]

3. More Old Testament Pseudepigrapha

Even in the first decade of Dead Sea Scrolls studies, the term *pseudepigrapha* was employed (in anglophone scholarship) as a label for a range of

---

grounds of materials. See Eibert Tigchelaar, "Notes on 4Q206/206a, 4Q203–4Q204, and Two Unpublished Fragments (4Q59?)," *Meghillot* 5–6 (2008): *187–99.

17. George W. E. Nickelsburg, *1 Enoch 1: A Commentary on the Book of 1 Enoch Chapters 1–36; 81–108*, Hermeneia (Minneapolis: Fortress, 2001). For a critical discussion, see Michael A. Knibb, "Interpreting the Book of Enoch: Reflections on a Recently Published Commentary," in *Essays on the Book of Enoch and Other Early Jewish Texts and Traditions* (Leiden: Brill, 2009), 77–90.

hitherto unknown texts among the Dead Sea Scrolls.[18] It was sometimes used conveniently as a category for those works that were neither canonical or deuterocanonical nor sectarian. Or, alternatively, as a literary label for works that displayed a form of pseudepigraphy, or, more generally, for narrative works that had something in common with the traditional Old Testament pseudepigrapha. In Milik's survey,[19] all three aspects play a role.[20] He describes the text that is now known as the Cave 1 Genesis Apocryphon as "a collection of pseudepigraphical material concerning the Patriarchs arranged in a chronological order."[21] Most of these so-called pseudepigrapha, such as a range of Aramaic texts attributed to the pre-Mosaic patriarchs, the Hebrew Apocryphon of Joshua, several Moses apocrypha or pseudepigrapha, the texts now known as Pseudo-Ezekiel and the Apocryphon of Jeremiah C, and the Aramaic work labeled Pseudo-Daniel, were first published in the 1990s.[22] However, by that time the difficult label pseudepigrapha was no longer used as a broad category, and Dead Sea Scrolls scholars preferred other classifying terms, such as *parabiblical*; some of these texts were specified as *rewritten Bible* and others as *apocalypses*.[23] Such recategorizations also challenged Dead Sea Scrolls scholars

---

18. The literature on the use of the term *pseudepigrapha* is extensive. See, e.g., Eibert Tigchelaar, "Old Testament Pseudepigrapha and the Scriptures," in *Old Testament Pseudepigrapha and the Scriptures*, ed. Eibert Tigchelaar (Leuven: Peeters, 2014), 1–18.

19. Milik, *Ten Years of Discovery*, 35–37.

20. However, Milik distinguishes in French between "apocryphes de l'Ancient Testament" for the category and "pseudépigraphe" as a literary label (*Dix ans de découvertes*, 32–34).

21. Milik, *Ten Years of Discovery*, 31.

22. There is no exhaustive list of the texts that might be called pseudepigrapha among the Dead Sea Scrolls, in part because of the different understandings of the term. See, for example, the list offered in Loren T. Stuckenbruck, "Apocrypha and Pseudepigrapha," in *EDEJ*, 143–62, esp. 150 (Dead Sea Scrolls texts entitled apocrypha by modern scholars) and 157–58 (pseudepigrapha), which does not, for example, mention some of the texts named by scholars with the infelicitous prefix "pseudo-" (such as Pseudo-Ezekiel). See also Devorah Dimant, "Hebrew Pseudepigrapha at Qumran," in Tigchelaar, *Old Testament Pseudepigrapha and the Scriptures*, 89–103.

23. For discussions of pseudepigraphy in the Dead Sea Scrolls, see, especially, Michael E. Stone, "The Dead Sea Scrolls and the Pseudepigrapha," *DSD* 3 (1996): 270–95; Moshe J. Bernstein, "Pseudepigraphy in the Qumran Scrolls: Categories and Functions," in *Pseudepigraphic Perspectives: The Apocrypha and Pseudepigrapha in Light of the Dead Sea Scrolls*, ed. Esther G. Chazon and Michael E. Stone (Leiden: Brill,

to consider both the appropriateness of existing labels, or the introduction of new labels, and the heuristic value of such labels in helping to give an understanding of the literary production of the Second Temple period.

However, while Dead Sea Scrolls scholars avoided the classificatory use of the term pseudepigrapha within pseudepigrapha studies, the More Old Testament Pseudepigrapha Project expanded its use and reconsidered the criteria for inclusion of additional works in its new, more expansive, collection of Old Testament pseudepigrapha, also including Dead Sea Scrolls works.[24] The criteria set out in the foreword of the first volume are more traditional and restrictive than those voiced in the introduction.[25] The description and discussion in the introduction, however, by focusing largely on formal elements (books from outside the Jewish and Christian canons, claimed to be written by characters appearing in the Old Testament, or containing narratives set in the period covered by the narrative texts of the Old Testament) disregard its anachronistic and basically ahistorical approach, resulting in the inclusion of texts with entirely different historical backgrounds and hence with different functions.

The introduction does, however, feature perspectives and questions similar to those raised by Dead Sea Scrolls scholars with regard to parabiblical literature or rewritten scriptures. First, both fields raise the question of the different literary forms by which such parabiblical or pseudepigraphic texts relate to the Old Testament: the two kinds of literature described in the introduction, "ancient books that claim to be written by a character in the Old Testament or set in the same time period as the Old Testament and recount narratives related to it," largely

---

1999), 1–26; Eibert Tigchelaar, "Forms of Pseudepigraphy in the Dead Sea Scrolls," in *Pseudepigraphie und Verfasserfiktion in frühchristlichen Briefen*, ed. Jörg Frey, Jens Herzer, Martina Janßen, and Clare K. Rothschild (Tübingen: Mohr Siebeck, 2009), 85–101; Stuckenbruck, "Apocrypha and Pseudepigrapha." Armin Lange and Ulrike Mittmann-Richert simply dismiss the use of the term *pseudepigrapha* and use instead a range of other terms. See Armin Lange with Ulrike Mittmann-Richert, "Annotated List of the Texts from the Judaean Desert Classified by Content and Genre," in *The Texts from the Judaean Desert: Indices and an Introduction to the Discoveries in the Judaean Desert Series*, ed. Emanuel Tov, DJD 39 (Oxford: Clarendon, 2002), 117.

24. Richard Bauckham, James R. Davila, and Alexander Panayotov, eds., *Old Testament Pseudepigrapha: More Noncanonical Scriptures* [*MOTP*], vol. 1 (Grand Rapids: Eerdmans, 2013).

25. James H. Charlesworth, "Foreword," *MOTP* 1:xi–xvi; Richard Bauckham and James R. Davila, "Introduction," *MOTP* 1:xvii–xxxviii.

coincide with the two sets of parabiblical literature described by Daniel Falk for the Dead Sea Scrolls, "interpretative rewritings of earlier scriptures, sometimes with expansions" and "new compositions ... which are attributed or closely related to scriptural figures."[26] One may note that these distinctions also roughly overlap with Loren Stuckenbruck's distinction between apocrypha and pseudepigrapha.[27] Second, both in the introduction to the first volume of the More Old Testament Pseudepigrapha Project and in the field of Dead Sea Scrolls studies, the question of the relationship between parabiblical texts or pseudepigrapha and authoritative or canonical scriptures comes to the fore. The Dead Sea Scrolls have contributed strongly to the modern model of the canonical process, with the implication that there may not have been a clear or qualitative distinction between some of the scriptures that ultimately became canonical and texts that one now would call rewritten scripture or parabiblical. The More Old Testament Pseudepigrapha Project rather flippantly dismisses the distinction between canonical scriptures and other texts as tangential for historical purposes.[28] I would dispute that: for historians, the question should be how the creation and transmission of these other texts relates, historically, culturally, and sociologically, to the existence and function of a canon of scriptures.

Of course, the field of the study of the pseudepigrapha and that of the study of the Dead Sea Scrolls are both influenced by, and sometimes contribute to, broader discussions in the humanities: about textual production in general, or, more specifically, about pseudepigraphy and authorial attribution, which explore more subtly and broadly the various functions of forms of pseudepigraphy in literary cultures. One model, developed by Hindy Najman when working on the Hebrew Bible, Dead Sea Scrolls, and pseudepigrapha, in which pseudepigraphic works form part of discourses linked to founders or to other figures, has been adopted heuristically in both fields of scholarship.[29] Both fields of scholarship have not yet sufficiently, in my opinion, taken into account the developments in the study of the ancient Christian apocrypha, with its discussions about the textual

---

26. Daniel K. Falk, *The Parabiblical Texts: Strategies for Extending the Scriptures among the Dead Sea Scrolls* (London: T&T Clark, 2007), 21.

27. Stuckenbruck, "Apocrypha and Pseudepigrapha."

28. Bauckham and Davila, "Introduction," xix–xx.

29. Initially in Hindy Najman, *Seconding Sinai: The Development of Mosaic Discourse in Second Temple Judaism*, JSJSup 77 (Leiden: Brill, 2003), 1–16.

and cultural interrelationship between canonical collections and transmissions of apocryphal texts.[30]

4. Material Philology

Material philology serves as an umbrella term for a range of philological practices that have in common a focus on texts exclusively, or primarily, in their specific manuscript contexts.[31] For example, editions of texts would aim not to construct with text critical methods an original or older textual form, but to register and discuss the texts as found in specific manuscripts. Likewise, material philologists would want to interpret texts, even if they were versions of much older texts, within their present manuscript context or their actual textual communities. Depending on the texts and on the philologist, such approaches are either alternative or complementary to traditional interpretive practices.

The special character of the Dead Sea Scrolls, consisting of an enormous range of often very fragmentary manuscripts, mostly stemming from the same period and found at one location and often associated with a very specific community, has required an approach comparable to material philological practices.[32] The fragmentary nature of the manuscripts necessitated the application of methods with special attention to material aspects, as a means to construct manuscripts and obtain more knowledge of often unknown texts. Since, apart from the biblical texts and the few pseudepigrapha, none of the texts were hitherto known to scholarship, their primary interpretive context was exactly this "one time, one space" manuscript context. Moreover, from the 1990s onwards it became evident that most of the texts, both biblical and nonbiblical, were copied in

---

30. See references in Tigchelaar, "Old Testament Pseudepigrapha and the Scriptures," 1, 17.

31. For a recent introduction, applied to the field of ancient Jewish and Christian studies, see Hugo Lundhaug and Liv Ingeborg Lied, "Studying Snapshots: On Manuscript Culture, Textual Fluidity, and New Philology," in *Snapshots of Evolving Traditions: Jewish and Christian Manuscript Culture, Textual Fluidity, and New Philology*, ed. Liv Ingeborg Lied and Hugo Lundhaug, TUGAL 175 (Berlin: de Gruyter, 2017), 1–19.

32. On the relation between material philology and the fragmentary nature of the Dead Sea Scrolls, see Eibert Tigchelaar, "Editing the Dead Sea Scrolls: What Should We Edit and How Should We Do It?," *Zenodo* (February 2019): http://doi.org/10.5281/zenodo.2560997.

variant literary editions and that even within this temporally and locally limited collection of texts variance was the rule, rather than the exception. Therefore, most manuscripts and their texts—with the partial exception of the biblical manuscripts—were interpreted primarily within their very specific Qumran context, and more recently also within the broader eastern Mediterranean Hellenistic-Roman context.[33] This even holds true, to some extent, for the pseudepigrapha. More and more, the book of Jubilees has been interpreted within the context, or even as a product, of the Dead Sea Scrolls collection, with questions being raised about the extent to which the manuscript evidence entirely supports the Ethiopic and Latin texts or also signals the possibility of variant editions, and with other Dead Sea Scrolls manuscripts forming the first interpretive key to its interpretation, and Hellenistic texts the broader secondary window.[34] As such, these research contributions on the Dead Sea Scrolls are an example of material philological practice, interpreting texts within a very concrete matrix, even though many details remain disputed or unclear.

Traditional pseudepigrapha studies have often focused on retrieving original ancient Jewish texts, ideas, concepts or traditions from works that were generally copied, reworked or even composed by Christians. Scholars of ancient Judaism have frequently divorced purportedly original ancient Jewish texts from their Christian manuscript context and used these texts as evidence for ancient Jewish concepts, practices or literary forms, even though since the 1950s this scholarly practice has been questioned.[35] More

---

33. Exemplary are Mladen Popović, *Reading the Human Body: Physiognomics and Astrology in the Dead Sea Scrolls and Hellenistic-Early Roman Period Judaism* (Leiden: Brill, 2007); and Pieter B. Hartog, *Pesher and Hypomnema: A Comparison of Two Commentary Traditions from the Hellenistic-Roman Period* (Leiden: Brill, 2017).

34. See, e.g., Cana Werman's work, culminating in her *The Book of Jubilees: Introduction, Translation, and Interpretation* (Jerusalem: Ben-Zvi, 2015). Werman regards the book of Jubilees as a Qumranic rewriting. More cautiously, e.g., Michael Segal, *The Book of Jubilees: Rewritten Bible, Redaction, Ideology and Theology* (Leiden: Brill, 2007). Cf. Eibert Tigchelaar, "The Qumran *Jubilees* Manuscripts as Evidence for the Literary Growth of the Book," *RevQ* 26 (2014): 579–94; Matthew Phillip Monger, "4Q216 and the State of *Jubilees* at Qumran," *RevQ* 26 (2014): 595–612.

35. De Jonge, *The Testaments of the Twelve Patriarchs*; see also the work of Robert A. Kraft, beginning with "The Multiform Jewish Heritage of Early Christianity," in *Christianity, Judaism and Other Greco-Roman Cults: Studies for Morton Smith at Sixty*, ed. Jacob Neusner, 4 vols. (Leiden: Brill, 1975), 3:174–99; Michael E. Stone, "Categorization and Classification of the Apocrypha and Pseudepigrapha," *AbrN* 24 (1986):

recent pseudepigrapha research has focused instead on one of the features that characterizes many pseudepigraphic writings, namely, the lack of fixity of the texts and of literary versions of the pseudepigrapha, where texts and traditions are often transmitted and transformed and used differently in successive contexts. These texts and traditions are particularly subject to variance and mouvance, requiring an analysis that takes account of their ongoing development through different contexts and pays attention to how these texts were actually used, for example in liturgy.[36]

Although many scholars may deal with only a few texts from the Dead Sea Scrolls or the Old Testament pseudepigrapha, the nature of the corpora and the development of these two fields have resulted in different and complementary scholarly approaches: the first aims to read the scrolls as a discrete and variegated collection of one or perhaps a few textual communities, while the second challenges the idea of the pseudepigrapha as a discrete collection and aims instead to place them in broader matrixes.

Bibliography

Adler, William. "The Story of Abraham and Melchizedek in the *Palaea Historica*." Pages 47–63 in *The Embroidered Bible: Studies in Biblical Apocrypha and Pseudepigrapha in Honour of Michael E. Stone*. Edited by Lorenzo DiTommaso, Matthias Henze, and William Adler. SVTP 26. Leiden: Brill, 2018.

167–77; James R. Davila, *The Provenance of the Pseudepigrapha: Jewish, Christian, or Other?*, JSJSup 105 (Leiden: Brill, 2005).

36. Cf., e.g., Liv Ingeborg Lied, "Nachleben and Textual Identity: Variants and Variance in the Reception History of 2 Baruch," in *Fourth Ezra and Second Baruch: Reconstruction after the Fall*, ed. Matthias Henze and Gabriele Boccaccini, JSJSup 164 (Leiden: Brill, 2013), 403–28; Maria Cioată, "Medieval Hebrew Tellings of Tobit: 'Versions' of the Book of Tobit or New Texts?," in *Is There a Text in This Cave? Studies in the Textuality of the Dead Sea Scrolls in Honour of George J. Brooke*, ed. Ariel Feldman, Maria Cioată, and Charlotte Hempel (Leiden: Brill, 2017), 334–67; William Adler, "The Story of Abraham and Melchizedek in the *Palaea Historica*," in *The Embroidered Bible: Studies in Biblical Apocrypha and Pseudepigrapha in Honour of Michael E. Stone*, ed. Lorenzo DiTommaso, Matthias Henze, and William Adler, SVTP 26 (Leiden: Brill, 2018), 47–63; Matthew Phillip Monger, "The Many Forms of Jubilees: A Reassessment of the Manuscript Evidence from Qumran and the Lines of Transmission of the Parts and Whole of Jubilees," *RevQ* 30 (2018): 191–211. See also Lorenzo DiTommaso's essay in the current volume.

9. Dead Sea Scrolls Scholarship and Pseudepigrapha Studies 171

Bauckham, Richard, and James R. Davila. "Introduction." *MOTP* 1:xvii–xxxviii.

Bauckham, Richard, James R. Davila, and Alexander Panayotov, eds. *Old Testament Pseudepigrapha: More Noncanonical Scriptures*. Vol. 1. Grand Rapids: Eerdmans, 2013.

Bernstein, Moshe J. "Pseudepigraphy in the Qumran Scrolls: Categories and Functions." Pages 1–26 in *Pseudepigraphic Perspectives: The Apocrypha and Pseudepigrapha in Light of the Dead Sea Scrolls*. Edited by Esther G. Chazon and Michael E. Stone. Leiden: Brill, 1999.

Charlesworth, James H. "Foreword," *MOTP* 1:xi–xvi.

———. "The Renaissance of Pseudepigraphy Studies: The SBL Pseudepigrapha Project." *JSJ* 2 (1971): 107–14.

Cioată, Maria. "Medieval Hebrew Tellings of Tobit: 'Versions' of the Book of Tobit or New Texts?" Pages 334–67 in *Is There a Text in This Cave? Studies in the Textuality of the Dead Sea Scrolls in Honour of George J. Brooke*. Edited by Ariel Feldman, Maria Cioată, and Charlotte Hempel. Leiden: Brill, 2017.

Collins, John J., ed. *Apocalypse: The Morphology of a Genre*. Semeia 14 (1979).

Cross, Frank Moore. "The Development of the Jewish Scripts." Pages 133–202 in *The Bible and the Ancient Near East: Essays in Honor of William Foxwell Albright*. Edited by G. E. Wright. Garden City, NY: Doubleday, 1961.

Davila, James R. *The Provenance of the Pseudepigrapha: Jewish, Christian, or Other?* JSJSup 105. Leiden: Brill, 2005.

Dimant, Devorah. "Hebrew Pseudepigrapha at Qumran," Pages 89–103 in *Old Testament Pseudepigrapha and the Scriptures*. Edited by Eibert Tigchelaar. Leuven: Peeters, 2014.

———. *Parabiblical Texts, Part 4: Pseudo-Prophetic Texts*. DJD 30. Oxford: Clarendon, 2001.

Falk, Daniel K. *The Parabiblical Texts: Strategies for Extending the Scriptures among the Dead Sea Scrolls*. London: T&T Clark, 2007.

Hartog, Pieter B. *Pesher and Hypomnema: A Comparison of Two Commentary Traditions from the Hellenistic-Roman Period*. Leiden: Brill, 2017.

Jonge, Marinus de. *The Testaments of the Twelve Patriarchs: A Study of Their Text, Composition and Origin*. Assen: Van Gorcum, 1953.

Käsemann, Ernst. "Die Anfänge christlicher Theologie." *ZTK* 57 (1960): 162–85.

———. "Zum Thema der urchristlichen Apokalyptik." *ZTK* 59 (1962): 257–84.
Knibb, Michael A. "Interpreting the Book of Enoch: Reflections on a Recently Published Commentary." Pages 77–90 in *Essays on the Book of Enoch and Other Early Jewish Texts and Traditions*. Leiden: Brill, 2009.
Koch, Klaus. *Ratlos vor der Apokalyptik: Eine Streitschrift über ein vernachlässigtes Gebiet der Bibelwissenschaft und die schädlichen Auswirkungen auf Theologie und Philosophie*. Gütersloh: Gütersloher Verlagshaus, 1970.
Kraft, Robert A. "The Multiform Jewish Heritage of Early Christianity." Pages 174–99 in *Christianity, Judaism and Other Greco-Roman Cults*. Edited by Jacob Neusner. 4 vols. Leiden: Brill, 1975.
Lange, Armin, with Ulrike Mittmann-Richert. "Annotated List of the Texts from the Judaean Desert Classified by Content and Genre." Pages 115–64 in *The Texts from the Judaean Desert: Indices and an Introduction to the Discoveries in the Judaean Desert Series*. Edited by Emanuel Tov. DJD 39. Oxford: Clarendon, 2002.
Langlois, Michaël. *Le premier manuscrit du Livre d'Hénoch: Étude épigraphique et philologique des fragments araméens de 4Q201 à Qumrân*. Paris: Cerf, 2008.
Lied, Liv Ingeborg. "Nachleben and Textual Identity: Variants and Variance in the Reception History of 2 Baruch." Pages 403–28 in *Fourth Ezra and Second Baruch: Reconstruction after the Fall*. Edited by Matthias Henze and Gabriele Boccaccini. JSJSup 164. Leiden: Brill, 2013.
Lundhaug, Hugo, and Liv Ingeborg Lied. "Studying Snapshots: On Manuscript Culture, Textual Fluidity, and New Philology." Pages 1–19 in *Snapshots of Evolving Traditions: Jewish and Christian Manuscript Culture, Textual Fluidity, and New Philology*. Edited by Liv Ingeborg Lied and Hugo Lundhaug. TUGAL 175. Berlin: de Gruyter, 2017.
MacRae, George W. "Foreword." *OTP* 1:ix–x.
Milik, Józef T. "4QVisions de ʿAmram et une citation d'Origène." *RB* 79 (1972): 77–97.
———. *The Books of Enoch: Aramaic Fragments of Qumrân Cave 4*. Oxford: Clarendon, 1976.
———. "Daniel et Susanne à Qumran?" Pages 337–59 in *De la Torah au Messie: Études d'exégèse et d'herméneutique bibliques offertes à Henri Cazelles*. Edited by Maurice Carrez, Joseph Doré, and Pierre Grelot. Paris: Desclée, 1981.

———. *Dix ans de découvertes dans le désert de Juda*. Paris: Cerf, 1957.

———. "Fragment d'une source du Psautier (4QPs 89) et fragments des Jubilés, du Document de Damas, d'un phylactère dans la grotte 4 de Qumrân." *RB* 63 (1966): 94–106.

———. "Fragments grecs du livre d'Hénoch (P. Oxy. XVII 2069)." *CdE* 46 (1971): 32–43.

———. "Le Testament de Lévi en araméen: Fragment de la Grotte 4 de Qumrân." *RB* 62 (1955): 398–406.

———. "Le travail d'édition des fragments manuscrits de Qumrân." *RB* 63 (1956): 49–67.

———. "Milkî-ṣedeq et Milkî-rešaʿ dans les anciens écrits juifs et chrétiens." *JJS* 33 (1972): 95–144.

———. "Problèmes de la littérature Hénochique à la lumière des fragments araméens de Qumrân." *HTR* 64 (1971): 333–78.

———. "Recherches sur la version grecque du livre des Jubilés." *RB* 78 (1971): 545–57.

———. *Ten Years of Discovery in the Wilderness of Judaea*. London: SCM, 1959.

———. "Turfan et Qumran: Livre des Géants juif et manichéen." Pages 118–27 in *Tradition und Glaube: Das frühe Christentum in seiner Umwelt: Festgabe für Karl Georg Kuhn zum 65. Geburtstag*. Edited by Gert Jeremias, Heinz-Wolfgang Kuhn, and Hartmut Stegemann. Göttingen: Vandenhoeck & Ruprecht, 1971.

Monger, Matthew Phillip. "4Q216 and the State of *Jubilees* at Qumran." *RevQ* 26 (2014): 595–612.

———. "The Many Forms of Jubilees: A Reassessment of the Manuscript Evidence from Qumran and the Lines of Transmission of the Parts and Whole of Jubilees." *RevQ* 30 (2018): 191–211.

Najman, Hindy. *Seconding Sinai: The Development of Mosaic Discourse in Second Temple Judaism*. JSJSup 77. Leiden: Brill, 2003.

Nickelsburg, George W. E. *1 Enoch 1: A Commentary on the Book of 1 Enoch Chapters 1–36; 81–108*. Hermeneia. Minneapolis: Fortress, 2001.

Popović, Mladen. *Reading the Human Body: Physiognomics and Astrology in the Dead Sea Scrolls and Hellenistic-Early Roman Period Judaism*. Leiden: Brill, 2007.

Segal, Michael. *The Book of Jubilees: Rewritten Bible, Redaction, Ideology and Theology*. Leiden: Brill, 2007.

———. "Categorization and Classification of the Apocrypha and Pseudepigrapha." *AbrN* 24 (1986): 167–77.

———. "The Dead Sea Scrolls and the Pseudepigrapha." *DSD* 3 (1996): 270–95.

Stone, Michael E., and Jonas C. Greenfield (with contributions by Matthew Morgenstern). "Aramaic Levi Document." Pages 1–72 in *Qumran Cave 4.XVII: Parabiblical Texts; Part 3*. Edited by George J. Brooke and James C. VanderKam. DJD 22. Oxford: Clarendon, 1996.

Stuckenbruck, Loren T. "Apocrypha and Pseudepigrapha." *EDEJ*, 143–62.

Tigchelaar, Eibert. "Editing the Dead Sea Scrolls: What Should We Edit and How Should We Do It?" *Zenodo* (February 2019): http://doi.org/10.5281/zenodo.2560997.

———. "Forms of Pseudepigraphy in the Dead Sea Scrolls." Pages 85–101 in *Pseudepigraphie und Verfasserfiktion in frühchristlichen Briefen*. Edited by Jörg Frey, Jens Herzer, Martina Janßen, and Clare K. Rothschild. Tübingen: Mohr Siebeck, 2009.

———. "Notes on 4Q206/206a, 4Q203–4Q204, and Two Unpublished Fragments (4Q59?)." *Meghillot* 5–6 (2008): *187–99.

———. "Old Testament Pseudepigrapha and the Scriptures." Pages 1–18 in *Old Testament Pseudepigrapha and the Scriptures*. Edited by Eibert Tigchelaar. Leuven: Peeters, 2014.

———. "The Qumran *Jubilees* Manuscripts as Evidence for the Literary Growth of the Book." *RevQ* 26 (2014): 579–94.

Werman, Cana. *The Book of Jubilees: Introduction, Translation, and Interpretation*. Jerusalem: Ben-Zvi, 2015.

VanderKam, James C., and Józef T. Milik. "Jubilees." Pages 1–185 in *Qumran Cave 4.XIII: Parabiblical Texts; Part 1*. Edited by Harold Attridge et al. DJD 13. Oxford: Clarendon, 1994.

10
Pseudepigrapha and Gender

Hanna Tervanotko

During the last few decades, the field of critical gender studies has demonstrated how gender is much more than women seeing gender and gendered structures as intrinsic to social life. We have come to learn that gender is present everywhere and in all spheres of life. While the scholars of ancient Jewish texts have been aware of some of these insights for a long time, the present climate in academia calls us to analyze our material with an even more critical eye. This essay addresses the relationship between the Old Testament pseudepigrapha, understood as a collection of early Jewish writings often pseudonymously attributed to figures from the biblical narrative,[1] and gender studies. I will assess previous research on the pseudepigrapha that has addressed gender and examine the ways in which gender has been analyzed in the study of the pseudepigrapha.

I am particularly grateful to the participants of the Enoch seminar Nangeroni meeting in Rome in June 2018 for the fruitful conversations during the conference on gender and Second Temple Judaism. They influenced this essay in many ways. I would like to thank Dr. Shayna Sheinfeldt and Dr. Kathy Ehrensperger for inviting me to join the meeting. I would also like to thank MA Katharine Fitzgerald and MA Channah Fonseca-Quezada for their help in the writing process.

1. Typically, the term *pseudepigrapha* refers to the texts that are published in the two-volume set edited by James H. Charlesworth, *The Old Testament Pseudepigrapha*, 2 vols. (Garden City, NY: Doubleday, 1983, 1985). This article focuses on the so-called Old Testament pseudepigrapha referred to as the pseudepigrapha. Note that although scholars focus on the Jewish compositions, the pseudepigrapha have a long history of transmission within Christian communities. Even more so, at times it is not easy to distinguish between Jewish and Christian compositions. For this, see, e.g., Charlesworth, "Introduction for the General Reader," *OTP* 1:xxi–xxxiv; Annette Yoshiko Reed, "The Modern Invention of Old Testament Pseudepigrapha," *JTS* 60 (2009): 403–36.

While doing this, I will take into consideration the developments of academic gender studies and ask how the pseudepigrapha studies relates to them. The present study does not attempt to be an exhaustive review of the research history. Rather, I will take some key publications and the program of the Society of Biblical Literature Pseudepigrapha unit in the period 1970–2017 as my case, exploring broader trends and aiming at highlighting developments that have influenced scholarship on gender in this field. In light of this modest survey, I will pinpoint areas of research that have not yet been covered or that cause particular challenges for scholarship today and tentatively explore some future avenues of study.

The term *gender* derives from Latin *gener-*, *genus*, which attests to birth, race, and kind.[2] In contemporary usage, the term carries similar significances. On the one hand, gender can denote the sex of a person (i.e., male, female, or other). On the other hand, it pertains to a broad range of behavioral, cultural, or psychological features stereotypically associated with one sex.[3] This is the way it is commonly understood in academic studies. In academic gender studies, it is now generally accepted that gender is a cultural construct because characteristics connected with masculinity and femininity vary in different cultural contexts.[4] In other words,

---

2. *Merriam-Webster's Online Dictionary*, s.v. "gender."

3. The World Health Organization says that "gender refers to the socially constructed characteristics of women and men—such as norms, roles and relationships of and between groups of women and men. It varies from society to society and can be changed. While most people are born either male or female, they are taught appropriate norms and behaviors—including how they should interact with others of the same or opposite sex within households, communities and work places. When individuals or groups do not 'fit' established gender norms they often face stigma, discriminatory practices or social exclusion—all of which adversely affect health. It is important to be sensitive to different identities that do not necessarily fit into binary male or female sex categories." World Health Organization, "Gender, Equity and Human Rights," https://tinyurl.com/SBL3550a. For the term *gender* in the field of biblical and related studies, see e.g., Laura Nasrallah and Elisabeth Schüssler Fiorenza, eds., *Prejudice and Christian Beginnings: Investigating Race, Gender, and Ethnicity in Early Christian Studies* (Minneapolis: Fortress, 2009); Birgitta L. Sjöberg, "More than Just Gender: The Classical Oikos as a Site of Intersectionality in Families in the Greco-Roman World," in *Families in the Greco-Roman World*, ed. Ray Laurence and Agneta Strömberg (London: Continuum, 2012), 48–59.

4. See, e.g., Judith Butler, *Gender Trouble: Feminism and the Subversion of Identity*, 2nd ed. (New York: Routledge, 2010), 8–10.

cultural contexts influence the ways in which masculinity and femininity are played out.

While the term gender does not appear anywhere in ancient Jewish literature, as an analytical concept it is relevant for the study of ancient texts. Masculinity and femininity are portrayed in different ways not only in contemporary cultural contexts but also in the ancient world. Moreover, there is evidence that, similarly to today, gender was not viewed as something fixed in antiquity. Rather, ancient people seem to have been well aware about the fluidity of gender categories and that both masculinity and femininity had several types of variations.[5]

Apart from the gender representations in texts, gendered perspectives are also present in scholars' ideas about ancient texts. For instance, a stereotypical understanding of gender continues to influence the social structures and identities that the scholars read into the texts they study, and these stereotypical understandings may affect the overall understanding of the pseudepigrapha. Therefore, when we explore the pseudepigrapha, gender is not only a topic in its own right but also an issue interwoven with other issues, our perspectives, and the questions we ask. In order to analyze critically how gender is present in the pseudepigrapha or in the study of the pseudepigrapha, both aspects—the gendered representations in the texts and the gendered perspectives of the scholars who study the texts—need to be addressed.

1. Feminist Studies, Gender Studies, and Biblical Scholarship

The feminist movement has deeply impacted the development of academic gender studies. The movement began in the late 1800s as a social and political project that advocated women's rights, with the goal of equality between men and women. The first feminists (or first wave) especially called women to fight for the right to vote and to represent themselves. Later, the second wave of the feminist movement (ca. 1960s–1980s) broadened the discussion to include domestic aspects of women's rights,

---

5. Luc Brisson, *Sexual Ambivalance: Androgyny and Hermaphroditism in Graeco-Roman Antiquity*, trans. Janet Lloyd (Berkeley: University of California Press, 2002). These views on gender variations are present for instance in rabbinic literature. The Talmud refers to a possibility that a boy turned to be a girl in b. Bekh. 42b. The rabbis also discuss *tumtum* (טומטום), which is an individual whose sex cannot be determined, see b. Naz. 12b; b. Yevam.72a; b. B. Bat. 140b.

including women's employment, equality issues within the family, reproductive rights, and legal inequalities between men and women. The third wave of the feminist movement started in the early 1990s and continues to the present. This wave claims no singular focus, nor does it concentrate only on women.[6] Rather, it consists of different ideas of micropolitics.[7] Third-wave feminists acknowledge the intersectionality of gender and propose that it influences everything, including race, class, sexual orientation, religion, and age. They maintain that people experience aspects of their identity collectively and that the significance of different features of identity evolve in connection to each other. People interpret an individual's gender in connection with other traits of identity, such as race and age. For instance, a young black female is not interpreted the same way as a young white female. In this case, the racial interpretation impacts how womanhood is viewed.[8]

The efforts of the feminist movement have led to the establishment of academic fields of study such as women's studies or feminist studies, which have gained a prominent place in academic institutions. These subject areas place women's lives and experiences at the center of study, for example, by analyzing history from a women's perspective. By focusing on women, these fields of study also contribute to debates regarding equality. Initially feminist researchers employed the term gender to address the social divide between men and women, but later scholars established gender studies as an academic field of its own.[9] This partly shared history between feminist studies and gender studies explains how both disciplines

---

6. For the history of the feminist movement, see e.g., Sarah Gamble, ed., *The Routledge Companion to Feminism and Postfeminism* (London: Routledge, 2001). The third wave feminist movement acknowledges that also men face challenges due to their sex. For instance, in many countries military service is compulsory for men alone.

7. See Yvonne Sherwood, "Introduction: The Bible and Feminism: Remapping the Field," in *The Bible and Feminism: Remapping the Field*, ed. Yvonne Sherwood with the assistance of Anna Fisk (Oxford: Oxford University Press, 2017), 1–14; Hanna Tervanotko, "Feminist Interpretation of the Bible in Retrospect," *lectio difficilior* 2 (2016): https://tinyurl.com/SBL3550b.

8. Kimberle Crenshaw, "Demarginalizing the Intersection of Race and Sex: A Black Feminist Critique of Antidiscrimination Doctrine, Feminist Theory and Antiracist Politics," *University of Chicago Legal Forum* 140 (1989): 139–67, coined the term *intersectionality*.

9. See Gamble, *Routledge Companion to Feminism and Postfeminism*, esp. the chapters by Stephanie Hodgson-Wright, "Early Feminism," 3–14; Valerie Sanders,

at times ask similar types of research questions.[10] Whereas many scholars no longer use the term gender as it was earlier (i.e., to address the hierarchy between men and women), it now serves as an analytical term that addresses social and cultural differences.

Turning to the field of biblical studies, of which I consider studies of the pseudepigrapha to be a part, feminist studies goes back to Elizabeth Cady Stanton. Cady Stanton made important connections between the political climate of her own time in the 1800s and biblical interpretation. The first wave of feminists and their debates about legislation inspired Cady Stanton to ask to what extent the Bible was used as a tool to silence women and to legitimate women's inferiority in relation to men.[11] In her mind, this stood in contradiction to a belief in a just and fair divine being who treats everyone equally. These observations led Cady Stanton and women close to her to inquire more closely about the presence of women in the biblical corpus. The result of their efforts was the publication of the two-volume *The Women's Bible*.[12] Women who contributed to the volume were inspired by the political agenda of the first-wave feminists. By recovering the voices of women in the Bible and demonstrating the unjust treatment of men and women in various biblical passages, they sought to change the uneven dealing between men and women in their own social contexts, for example, the church and the state.[13]

"First Wave Feminism," 15–24; Sue Thornham, "Second Wave Feminism," 25–35; and Sarah Gamble, "Postfeminism," 36–45.

10. See Beatrice Lawrence, "Gender Analysis: Gender and Method in Biblical Studies," in *Method Matters: Essays on the Interpretation of the Hebrew Bible in Honor of David L. Petersen*, ed. Joel M. LeMon and Kent Harold Richards, RBS 56 (Atlanta: Society of Biblical Literature, 2009), 335.

11. Luise Schottroff, Silvia Schroer, and Marie-Theres Wacker, *Feminist Interpretation: The Bible in Women's Perspective*, trans. Martin and Barbara Rumscheidt (Minneapolis: Fortress, 1998), esp. 3–35.

12. Elizabeth Cady Stanton, *The Women's Bible* (New York: European Publishing Company, 1895–1898).

13. Schottroff, Schroer, and Wacker, *Feminist Interpretation*, 4–5. For the history of the feminist biblical studies, see, e.g., Carolyn De Swarte Gifford, "American Women and the Bible: The Nature of Woman as a Hermeneutical Issue," in *Feminist Perspectives on Biblical Scholarship*, ed. Adela Yarbro Collins, BSNA 10 (Atlanta: Scholars Press, 1985), 11–33.

2. Gender and Pseudepigrapha: Review of the Research History

Scholars have paid attention to some gendered portrayals for a long time. The prime example in this regard is the book of Jubilees. Early studies of Jubilees in the beginning of the twentieth century noticed that the book's depiction of the role of women differs from that portrayed in Genesis and Exodus. R. H. Charles pointed out that the author of Jubilees elaborates on women especially when highlighting the importance of endogamic marriages.[14] Other scholars agreed with Charles's observations on the portrayal of women and the role that women play in the text. Despite this focus on the significance of the female figures in Jubilees, their role was not studied in more detail until Betsy Halpern-Amaru's important 1999 monograph, *The Empowerment of Women in Jubilees*, which analyzes the female figures of Jubilees with respect to the Genesis accounts that its author reworks.[15] Regarding gender, Halpern-Amaru shows how the author of Jubilees depicts female figures as ideal mothers and spouses and thereby portrays them in their part as important enablers of the covenant.[16]

Scholars have dealt similarly with other pseudepigraphic works. For example, scholars have long recognized that the author of Liber antiquitatum biblicarum emphasizes female figures.[17] As with Jubilees, the literary

---

14. Robert H. Charles, *The Book of Jubilees or the Little Genesis* (London: Black, 1902), lix, lxi.

15. Betsy Halpern-Amaru, *Empowerment of Women in the Book of Jubilees*, JSJSup 60 (Leiden: Brill, 1999). Note that here my study is restricted exclusively to scholarly interest in the texts. Thinking more broadly about the interest in the pseudepigrapha texts one can, for instance, pinpoint artistic interest in them. One of the most famous example in this regard is Artemisia Gentileschi (1593–1654), whose paintings are based on pseudepigrapha narratives such as Susanna and the Elders. Gabriele Boccacini pointed this out in his opening presentation at the Enoch Nangeroni seminar on Gender and Second Temple Judaism in Rome in June 2018.

16. Halpern-Amaru explained at the Enoch Nangeroni seminar on Gender and Second Temple Judaism in Rome in June 2018 that she does not think that *Empowerment of Women in the Book of Jubilees* makes use of any method of feminist or gender studies.

17. E.g., M. R. James, *The Biblical Antiquities of Philo with Prolegomenon by Louis H. Feldman*, LBS (New York: Ktav, 1971); Pieter Willem van der Horst, "Portraits of Biblical Women in Pseudo Philo's Liber Antiquitatum Biblicarum," *JSP* 5 (1989): 29–46; Betsy Halpern-Amaru, "Portraits of Women in Pseudo-Philo's Antiquities," in *'Women Like This': New Perspectives on Jewish Women in the Greco-Roman World*, ed. Amy-Jill Levine, EJL 1 (Atlanta: Scholars Press, 1991), 83–106; Frederick J. Murphy,

female figures of Liber antiquitatum biblicarum have typically been compared to representations preserved in the Hebrew Bible. The author's exceptional interest in female figures has been difficult to explain—or better, scholars have seldom addressed it.

Despite these early acknowledgments of the significance of gender in the pseudepigraphal writings, only a few publications explored gender within them in any depth.[18] More recently, this situation has changed. Amy-Jill Levine points out in her introduction to *'Women Like This': New Perspectives on Jewish Women in the Greco-Roman World* that, whereas scholars once lamented the lack of literature that would critically analyze women "between the Bible and the Mishnah," by the 1990s the situation had improved.[19]

One reason behind this change is the publication of new material, most significantly the Dead Sea Scrolls. When this material became available to the wider scholarly community in the 1990s, the various compositions of this collection demonstrated the diversity of early Judaism and the importance of a variety of texts during the late Second Temple period.[20] The Dead Sea Scrolls preserve numerous copies of various pseudepigrapha writings, for example, the book of Jubilees, and this sparked new interest in the pseudepigrapha. Further, previously unknown texts shed new light on men and women and thus challenged scholars to rethink earlier assumptions about their gendered roles. In what follows I will explore these developments more closely.

2.1. Pseudepigrapha Unit of the Society of Biblical Literature

In order to get a better idea of the developments in the study of the pseudepigrapha and gender, I will focus on the programs of the Pseudepigrapha

---

Pseudo-Philo: Rewriting the Bible (New York: Oxford University Press, 1993), 258–59; Howard Jacobson, *A Commentary of Pseudo-Philo's Liber Antiquitatum Biblicarum with Latin Text and English Translation 1-2*, AGJU 31 (Leiden: Brill, 1996).

18. See Elisabeth Schüssler Fiorenza, *In Memory of Her: A Feminist Theological Reconstruction of Christian Origins* (London: SCM, 1985), 108.

19. Amy-Jill Levine, preface to *'Women Like This*,' xi–xvii, xi.

20. See, e.g., Annette Yoshiko Reed, "Old Testament Pseudepigrapha and Post-70 Judaism," in *Les Judaïsmes dans tous leur états aux Ier-IIIe siècles*, ed. Simon Claude Mimouni, Bernard Pouderon, and Claire Clivas (Turnhout: Brepols, 2015), 117. For the significance of the Dead Sea Scrolls for the study of the pseudepigrapha, see the essays of Patricia Ahearne-Kroll and Eibert Tigchelaar in the current volume.

unit at the Annual Meetings of the Society of Biblical Literature from 1970 to 2017. This section focuses on the pseudepigrapha, and, as it turns out, its program is representative of how the study of the pseudepigrapha and gender has developed in the last couple of decades. Since I cannot review the entire history of the program unit (some papers are no longer available), I will pay attention to those meetings that either focus on texts where women play a notable role or otherwise seemingly elaborate on gender, such as by referring to it in the title of the session.

Several meetings of the Pseudepigrapha unit have significantly contributed to the analysis of gender. The records of the unit begin in 1970.[21] The earliest reference to a session that addressed a gender-themed pseudepigrapha composition is from 1976, when the seminar papers analyzed Joseph and Aseneth. Various papers in this session analyzed Joseph and Aseneth as a novella, asked about its connections to ancient romance, and examined its socioreligious context.[22] The next reference to a gendered topic is from the 1989 SBL Annual Meeting, in which various papers were presented in a session that examined the book of Judith. In this case a few of the papers focused on the portrayal of Judith as a hero.[23] In 1994 the Pseudepigrapha unit focused on Adam and Eve literature.[24] No further information is preserved from these meetings, so it remains open as to *how* the various papers contributed to the study of gender.

Two years later, in 1996, the theme was for a second time (although with twenty years between the two meetings!) Joseph and Aseneth. This

---

21. I thank Matthias Henze and Liv Ingeborg Lied for sharing these records with me.

22. The meeting took place in Saint Louis, MO, and the symposium was titled Perspectives on Joseph and Aseneth. The following scholars presented papers: Edgar W. Smith, Richard I. Pervo, Jonathan Z. Smith, Howard C. Kee, and Gary Vikan. See George MacRae W., ed., *Society of Biblical Literature 1976 Seminar Papers*, SBLSP 10 (Missoula, MT: Scholars Press, 1976).

23. This meeting took place in Anaheim, CA, and the following presenters gave papers in the session: Adolfo D. Roitman, Toni Craven, Amy-Jill Levine, Sidnie Ann White, Nira Stone, and Carey A. Moore. George W. E. Nickelsburg and Richard I. Pervo offered responses to the papers. See David J. Lull, ed., *Society of Biblical Literature 1989 Seminar Papers*, SBLSP 28 (Atlanta: Scholars Press, 1989). Especially the papers by Levine and White focus on Judith as a literary character.

24. Four papers by Jeffrey A. Trumbower, Corrine L. Patton, Christiana de Groot van Houten, and Gary A. Anderson were presented. Steven D. Fraade responded them. The papers are available in Eugene H. Lovering Jr., ed., *Society of Biblical Literature 1994 Seminar Papers*, SBLSP 33 (Atlanta: Scholars Press, 1994).

10. Pseudepigrapha and Gender   183

program also contained a separate subtitle: Moving from Text to Social and Historical Context. The papers of this session explored theories concerning the constructed original context of the text and its audiences.[25]

These topics and some of the published papers allow us to make some observations. The themes of these sessions suggest that, in the early history of the Pseudepigrapha unit, most of the gendered attention was given to pseudepigraphic works that feature female figures in their titles. Some scholars were particularly keen to discuss the images of women in these texts. It is of interest that the attempt to advance research on female figures parallels the goals of the broader feminist movement, which aims at establishing women on the same level as men.[26] These tendencies in the research find affinities in the goals of the second wave of the feminist movement.[27] Therefore, several scholars have argued that focusing on a marginal figure who is not seemingly powerful in the text is a feminist method. This method has been actively emphasized by scholars who combine the feminist/gender approach with the instruments of historical-critical methodology.[28] Whereas several papers in the sessions of the Pseudepigrapha unit seem to align with the goals of the feminist reading of

---

25. Four papers were presented by Gideon Bohak, Randall D. Chesnutt, Ross S. Kraemer, and Angela Standhartinger. Amy-Jill Levine and Richard I. Pervo responded to them. See Society of Biblical Literature, *Society of Biblical Literature 1996 Seminar Papers*, SBLSP 35 (Atlanta: Scholars Press, 1996).

26. Depending on the definition of gender studies, this field of research shares such a goal. See section 1 of this article.

27. The second wave of feminism influenced feminist biblical studies. Scholars who associate with the principles of the second wave advocate that female figures should be placed in the center of the biblical analysis even when the biblical texts preserve only marginal references to them. By various methodological approaches scholars have attempted to recover the seemingly missing female figures of the ancient texts. See Marie-Theres Wacker, "Methods of Feminist Exegesis," in Schottroff, Schroer, and Wacker, *Feminist Interpretation*, 63–82; Athalya Brenner and Carole Fontaine, eds., *A Feminist Companion to Reading the Bible: Approaches, Methods and Strategies* (Sheffield: Sheffield Academic, 1997).

28. Bernadette Brooten, "Early Christian Women and Their Cultural Context: Issues of Method in Historical Reconstruction," in *Feminist Perspectives in Biblical Scholarship*, ed. Adela Yarbro Collins (Atlanta: Scholars Press, 1985), 65. See also Wacker, "Methods of Feminist Exegesis," 63–82. More recently, Cecilia Wassen, *Women in the Damascus Document* (Leiden: Brill, 2005), 14–15; Hanna Tervanotko, *Denying Her Voice: The Figure of Miriam in Ancient Jewish Literature*, JAJSup 23 (Göttingen: Vandenhoeck & Ruprecht, 2016), 38–39. Both Wassen and I explain that the

biblical texts methodologically, it is noteworthy that none of these sessions explicitly refers to a feminist approach as a methodology. In contrast, the terms *feminism* and *gender* appear only seldom, if at all, in the texts and titles.[29] I will discuss feminist language more in detail below.

More recently, the Pseudepigrapha unit has focused on more precise gendered topics. The theme at the 2006 SBL Annual Meeting in Washington, DC, was Women's Religious Experience in Antiquity.[30] The 2007 meeting in San Diego analyzed how interpretations of the Jewish biblical traditions that portray women vary. The presenters addressed Jewish biblical female figures in texts such as the pseudepigrapha and Pauline literature.[31] Once more, in 2013, in Baltimore, the focus was on women; the theme of the session was Women, Fire and Dangerous Things, inspired by George Lakoff's book.[32]

Whereas these sessions notably featured the term *women* in their titles and focused on women, their interest went beyond analyzing them on the level of the narrative in the texts. The meeting of 2013, which broadly engaged Lakoff's theory, deserves further remarks. While the book itself deals with cognitive linguistics, the title *Women, Fire and Dangerous Things* drew feminist attention. Some were offended by the way the title of the book associates women with danger; others loved it because it clarifies the irrationality between categories.[33] The papers in the meeting of the Pseudepigrapha unit studied femininity from various linguistic perspectives: women's emotions, feminine personification of places, polemical use of female imaginary, women's leadership, and metaphors. Hence we can observe that, instead of focusing on women as literary figures, which was the focus of most of the relevant sessions up until 2013, there was now a

---

feminist approach allows us to focus on female figures, which is an addition to the historical-critical method we use.

29. I refer to the records of n. 21 and the published Seminar Papers.

30. This was a joint session organized with the program unit Religious Experience in Early Judaism and Early Christianity. Papers were presented by Amy Hollywood, Sarah Iles Johnston, Patricia Ahearne-Kroll, and John R. Levison.

31. The presenters in this meeting were Peter T. Lanfer, Vered Hillel, Mary Bader, Rivka Nir, and Troy A. Miller.

32. George Lakoff, *Women, Fire and Dangerous Things: What Categories Reveal about the Mind* (Chicago: University of Chicago Press, 1987). The presenters of the session were Françoise Mirguet, Karina M. Hogan, Sonja Ammann, Hanna Tervanotko, and Christopher E. J. Brenna.

33. Lakoff, *Women, Fire, and Dangerous Things*, 5–6.

growing interest in looking into language that makes use of female images. This shift can be seen as a concrete move to analyze specifically gender in the Pseudepigrapha unit at the Society of Biblical Literature.[34]

A few years later, in the meeting of 2017, the theme was Pseudepigrapha and Gender, which did not restrict the thematic and methodological approaches to the theme gender but instead allowed for a variety of gendered perspectives to come to the fore.[35] These studies offered more insights for female identities and contributed to the discussion of female characteristics. What they seem to share is a more conscious engagement with methods, for example, analyzing Aseneth's symbolic motherhood, exploring male mediators of female knowledge, and reading the texts through Bakhtin's theory of dialogism.[36] While the term gender in the title did not restrict the discussion only to female identities, it is interesting to point out that just one of the papers in the session focused on masculinities in the pseudepigrapha. This may be an indication as to how the gender approach is not yet fully incorporated into the study of the pseudepigrapha. It may also reflect the close contact between the academic gender and feminist studies and the fact that gender is still often understood through the lens of feminism.

It seems to me that the present state of research on gender and the pseudepigrapha in many ways reflects the third wave of feminism, which is characterized by pluriformity and diversity of approaches. Most evidently, scholars who study the pseudepigrapha through the lens of gender do not focus on one topic or make use of one interpretative method. Apart

---

34. Hanna Tervanotko, "Obey Me Like Your Mother: Deborah's Leadership in Light of *Liber antiquitatum biblicarum* 33," *JSP* 24 (2015): 301–23.

35. The following scholars presented papers at this meeting: Jill Hicks-Keeton, "Genesis, Gender, and Gentiles: Aseneth as Mythic Mother"; Francis Borchardt, "The Framing of Female Knowledge in the Prologue of the Sibylline Oracles"; Lee Sui Hung Albert, "A Dialogical Reading of Judith through the Lens of Bakhtin's Dialogism"; Tavis A. Bohlinger, "Faith in a Silent God: The Characterization of Hannah in Pseudo-Philo"; Stephen L. Young, "'Undergird Him with Strength': Masculine Eschatological Agents in Ancient Jewish Sources." I have included the titles of the talks here because interestingly, while the majority of them deal with female figures or feminine characteristics, the call for papers invited the scholars to address any gender-related matter present in the pseudepigrapha. Therefore, the titles demonstrate the slow change to study gender instead of focusing on women.

36. Abstracts of this session are available through the Society of Biblical Literature website.

from addressing femininity from multiple angles (e.g., emotions, female images, and symbolism), studies also deal with topics such as biblical masculinities, sexual violence, and LGBT people.[37] The overarching goal of these studies seems to be to gain a better understanding on how gender is constructed in the texts. The history of gender research in the biblical field is still relatively young, and the incorporation of gendered aspects into the research of Old Testament pseudepigrapha is only in its beginning.

2.2. Demographics in the Field

Scholarship does not evolve in a vacuum, so paying attention to the demographics of the guild can reveal important insights about academic research cultures. Thus, as important as it is to analyze the questions that have been asked, it is also vital to consider the people who pose the questions. The records of the Pseudepigrapha unit demonstrate an evident bias. In general, and consistent with the gender distribution in the field and among the members of the Society of Biblical Literature, a large majority of the presenters in this section have been men. However, in years when the title of the program includes terms such as *women* or *gender*, the majority of the presenters have been women.[38] Moreover, even today it is easy to note that most of the publications that analyze the role of women in the pseudepigrapha are written by female scholars (including this one!). These statistics are both interesting and revealing when compared to the makeup of the Society of Biblical Literature itself, in which 76 percent of all members are male.[39]

---

37. See, e.g., Rhiannon Graybill, *Are We Not Men? Unstable Masculinity in the Hebrew Prophets* (Oxford: Oxford University Press, 2016). Also, the interdisciplinary Shiloh Project that studies Rape Culture, Religion, and the Bible at the University of Sheffield connects with third wave feminism. See https://www.sheffield.ac.uk/siibs/sresearch/the-shiloh-project. Apart from the study of the Hebrew Bible, this approach finds parallels in other subfields of biblical studies. I have in mind for instance the study of the Dead Sea Scrolls that closely relates to the pseudepigrapha. In this regard, only recently scholars have started to pay attention to the gendered aspects present in the Dead Sea Scrolls. See, e.g., the recent important study by Jessica M. Keady, *Vulnerability and Valour: A Gendered Analysis of Everyday Life in the Dead Sea Scrolls Communities*, LSTS 91 (London: T&T Clark, 2017).

38. I take into consideration that the names do not necessarily align with gender identities.

39. The Society Report of 2017 states that "women make up 24.37 percent of our

This imbalance between the gendered makeup of the Society and those who engage in gender analysis requires more reflection. To begin, these numbers suggest that female scholars are more invested in gender-related questions than their male counterparts. Feminist scholarship began as a women's enterprise, and, while the movement has grown and includes men who are concerned on equality-related matters, in some ways it still remains women-driven. Strikingly, the present situation contributes to the status of gender as a theme and methodology applied in the studies of the pseudepigrapha. Given that most of the research in this field is done by women, it appears that gender studies is not yet regarded as a viable alternative or an equally valued addition to historical-critical methodology. All in all, the result may be that people who aim at gender equality and inclusivity in their research find themselves alienated from mainstream scholarship.[40]

While the historical-critical method remains the dominant approach to the study of biblical and related texts, its place with respect to other methods raises questions. Interestingly, scholars often present the historical-critical method as a timeless and neutral approach to the texts, in contrast to a feminist or gender-studies approach, which is considered an ideology-based perspective, thus seemingly distancing themselves from and contrasting themselves with the politically driven gender studies.[41] Surprisingly, many scholars who employ the historical-critical method seldom question its use and do not acknowledge that, in the end, it is like any other approach to the text: it has its own gendered caveats. For instance, this method assumes that, by posing text-critical questions, the text's history can be somehow uncovered. However, the questions asked are those that the specific researcher wants to pose. Moreover, scholars who make use of this method often refer to reading the text "in its own

---

membership today, men make up 75.57 percent, and transgender members represent .06 percent."

40. Sara Parks, "Nixing the Niche: Moving Women from the Margins in Second Temple Jewish Scholarship" (paper presented at the Tenth Enoch Nangeroni Meeting, Rome, 18 June 2018), puts it well, and my paper is inspired by her remarks. When this article was going to the press I learned that Parks has published some of the arguments of her paper in the journal article "Historical-Critical Ministry? The Biblical Studies Classroom as Restorative Secular Space," *New Blackfriars* 100 (2018): 229–44.

41. Francis Borchardt, "A Gender Theory Critique of the Historical-Critical Method," *CSTT and Gender ebooklet* (2017): 5. The booklet is available via zenodo: https://zenodo.org/record/998282#.W8jPM2hKhyw.

right," thus entirely neglecting the fact that the text was not produced in a vacuum, that it represents the voice of its author. Although the historical-critical method may present itself as the timeless approach to the text, it is assuredly not. It was established in a specific historical context, that of the Enlightenment and Reformation, and it reflects the ideals of at least some people of that time.[42]

Finally, feminist biblical scholars have pointed out how the different treatments of the two methods itself reflects a gender bias: the historical-critical method is valued as the objective and primary approach to texts; the feminist and gender studies approach represents the Other. In a recent article Francis Borchardt claims that this situation itself reflects the dichotomy between masculine and feminine: the first is the dominant and the most powerful method within the field of biblical studies; the gendered reading is often treated as the marginal phenomenon next to it.[43] All in all, these critical ideological aspects concerning the historical-critical approach call scholars to evaluate the methods from the perspective of gender studies.

3. Some Future Directions

As I pointed out above, it has long been recognized that some of the pseudepigrapha texts significantly elaborate on the gendered images preserved in the corpus of the Hebrew Bible. This recognition has resulted in numerous studies in which figures or passages preserved in the pseudepigrapha are compared with those in the Hebrew Bible. On the basis of a comparative reading, scholars draw conclusions as to how the later authors reworked already-existing traditions.[44]

---

42. Elisabeth Schüssler Fiorenza has outlined this in *Sharing Her Word: Feminist Biblical Interpretation in Context* (Edinburgh: T&T Clark, 1998), 33–34, where she calls this approach to the ancient texts "malestream" to indicate its affinities with white Euro-American male scholarship

43. Borchardt, "Gender Theory Critique of the Historical-Critical Method," 9–12. The examples that demonstrate Borchardt's point are numerous, from thematic conferences to textbooks and rewards that biblical scholars receive. For further data, see Liv Ingeborg Lied's blogpost on this matter: "Who Is Reviewed at the SBL Annual Meeting," Religion-Manscripts-Media Culture, 5 January 2016, https://tinyurl.com/SBL3550c. Lied concludes that on average about 13 percent of the honorary sessions of the Society of Biblical Literature celebrate women's contributions.

44. For the terminology between a base text and its elaboration, see, e.g., Robert A. Kraft, "Para-mania: Beside, Before, and Beyond Bible Studies," *JBL* 126 (2007):

Highlighting the role and status of women in the pseudepigrapha offers alternatives to the images of women derived strictly from the biblical texts and sheds further light on multiple interpretations of the role and status of women in antiquity. However, this methodology emphasizes certain characters and passages, illuminating in particular texts where women play prominent roles. The attention given to women is notable (especially from the comparative approach described above) in the texts where they are seemingly present. Meanwhile, other texts that may contribute equally to our understanding of gender roles remain understudied. Elisabeth Schüssler Fiorenza has argued that texts may talk about women even when women are not explicitly present in them.[45] For example, texts that do not talk explicitly about women may use women's bodies or social domains metaphorically or may refer to gendered stereotypes and assessments. Further, whereas the comparative analysis referenced above helps scholars to see the distinct features in both the pseudepigrapha and Hebrew Bible corpora, we should acknowledge that scholars may unconsciously present the Hebrew Bible as the more original and timeless version and pseudepigrapha as the more folkloristic version of the existing literary traditions.[46]

One example of the assumed secondary nature of the pseudepigrapha vis-à-vis the biblical corpus is reflected in scholars' ideas about authorial intention. Interestingly, some studies on the pseudepigrapha refer to an ancient author's feminism. One sees this with texts such as Liber antiquitatum biblicarum and the Testament of Job, where women play more

---

3–27; Armin Lange, "In the Second Degree: Ancient Jewish and Paratextual Literature in the Context of Graeco-Roman and Ancient Near Eastern Literature," in *In the Second Degree: Paratextual Literature in Ancient Near Eastern and Ancient Mediterranean Culture and Its Reflections in Medieval Literature*, ed. Philip Alexander, Armin Lange, and Renate Pillinger (Leiden: Brill, 2010), 3–40, esp. 16–19.

45. This theory is fundamental for Schüssler Fiorenza's "hermeneutics of suspicion" set forth in *But She Said: Feminist Practices of Biblical Interpretation* (Boston: Beacon Press, 1992). A brilliant example of this method is the Wisdom commentary series that writes a feminist commentary on texts that do not even refer to women. See, e.g., Stacy Davis, *Haggai and Malachi*, Wisdom Commentary 39 (Collegeville, MN: Liturgical Press, 2015).

46. Already the title *pseudepigrapha*, which denotes "with false superscription," implies something inauthentic. For the term, see James H. Charlesworth, "Introduction for the General Reader," *OTP* 1:xxv. Also the continuing use of the term *intertestamental literature* implies that pseudepigrapha texts are often regarded as secondary to canonical ones.

visible roles than in the literary traditions that they elaborate. Scholars have called attention to the unusual ways authors emphasize female figures as the "feminism of the author."[47] Such a labeling is problematic for several reasons. Most significantly, the challenge lies in applying to antiquity a modern term that was not used before the beginning of the feminist movement.[48] Therefore, it remains questionable how this term can clarify a phenomenon of the Second Temple era. Further, none of the scholars who refer to the feminism of ancient authors has explained what is meant by this term. Feminism is a broad term used to denote different ideas and movements depending on the time period and context.[49] In light of the challenges related to the use of the term, it seems evident that the term feminism has been used in a rather unsystematic manner and mostly due to a lack of a better term that would explain the presence of women in the texts.

The use—and the neglect—of the term feminism in various scholarly contributions illustrates the present state of pseudepigrapha and gender studies. Individual analysis of specific texts rarely mentions feminism as a methodological approach, nor does the term appear in the titles of the studies.[50] The absence of this term, which can broadly refer to one's methodological starting points, is striking when one takes into account the great number of studies that explicitly address female figures in the pseudepigrapha. Moreover, as pointed out above, numerous studies focus on a female figure, yet they do not explicitly identify feminism as the methodological starting point. This indicates that there is at some level discomfort with the use of the term.

---

47. E.g., Charles Perrot and Pierre-Maurice Bogaert, *Pseudo-Philon: Les antiquités bibliques*, vol. 2, SC 230 (Paris: Cerf, 1976), 52–53, who discuss the emphasis the author puts on some female characters. Daniel J. Harrington writes: "There are [in Liber antiquitatum biblicarum] some interesting plays on Old Testament clichés from what would now be described as a feminist perspective" ("Pseudo-Philo," *OTP* 2:300). In this context Harrington specifically mentions LAB 33.1 and its reference to the "woman of God" and LAB 40.4, which refers to "the bosom of her mothers."

48. I have dealt with these questions extensively in Tervanotko, "Obey Me Like Your Mother," 301–23.

49. For a study of feminism and how the term has been understood in different historical eras, see, e.g., Gamble, *Routledge Companion to Feminism and Postfeminism*.

50. An exception in this regard is the Feminist Companion to the Bible series (first and second series) edited by Athalya Brenner-Idan.

On the one hand, the scholarly contributions rarely mention feminism; on the other hand, when they do, the use of the term is peculiar. This reluctance is particularly evident when *feminism* is juxtaposed with *gender*. Schüssler Fiorenza argues that gender comes across as a more value-neutral term than feminism. It communicates an idea that gender is a cultural construct and can be studied scientifically, with approaches grounded in the social sciences.[51] Therefore, Schüssler Fiorenza maintains that gender studies provides a hermeneutical lens that can more easily win the approval of mainstream and male-dominant audiences than politically oriented feminist interpretation.[52]

Deciding which terminology to use when addressing gender is a matter of some consequence. Analyzing the pseudepigrapha texts through the lens of gender instead of feminism has both benefits and disadvantages in relation to feminism. There is no doubt that addressing different types of gendered matters from intersectional perspectives will advance our understanding of the multifaceted nature of gender in antiquity. Meanwhile, the risk in this approach is that seemingly male aspects of study overtake the female perspectives and experiences. Consequently, the theory that initially was established to emphasize women and their gendered experience vis-à-vis men may risk losing its purpose.[53]

Studies on women in ancient Jewish history have suggested for a long time that different groups perceived women differently.[54] Incorporation of intersectionality into the studies on pseudepigrapha and gender can significantly add to this observation, and analyzing texts through the lens of intersectionality can provide new nuances to this paradigm. For instance, not all women were perceived in a same way in antiquity; depending on status and age, for example, women had different identities.

---

51. Schüssler Fiorenza, *Sharing Her Word*, 33–34. She points to the work of Peggy L. Day, where the two approaches "feminist interpretation" and "gender studies" are distinctly separated. See, e.g., Peggy L. Day, "Introduction," in *Gender and Difference*, ed. Peggy L. Day (Minneapolis: Fortress, 1989), 1–11.

52. Cf. Graybill, *Are We Not Men*, 12–13, where the author explicitly states that her gendered reading of the prophetic texts, which focuses on the bodies of the prophets, i.e., "turning the scrutinizing gaze onto the bodies of men" is a feminist act.

53. This section in particular is inspired by the conversations at the Nangeroni seminar.

54. Most importantly, the studies by Tal Ilan, esp. *Jewish Women in Greco Roman Palestine: An Inquiry into Image and Status*, TSAJ 44 (Tübingen: Mohr Siebeck, 1995).

When analyzing ancient texts, we are often confronted with the challenge that the ancient authors seem not to be interested in the questions we pose to those texts. The authors of the pseudepigrapha do not, for instance, directly address various types of gender roles and statuses. When trying to build a more complete image of the past offered by our literary sources, scholars turn to other related fields of study so that may offer a broader spectrum to matters overlooked in the ancient Jewish texts. For instance, studies of gender in the fields of classics, early Christianity, and the ancient Near East all demonstrate that a wider range of identities and roles were available for women than are preserved in the pseudepigrapha.[55] These sources, deriving from the neighboring cultural contexts, depict the roles and statuses of both men and women in complex ways and suggest that perhaps the ancient Jewish texts only reflect in a partial way the realities of their authors.

One example of this concerns women's education in antiquity. Scholars of ancient Jewish literature have long argued that the Jewish Scriptures were composed by men.[56] Meanwhile, it has been argued that the biblical corpus does not witness to women being educated, let alone functioning as scribes. Significantly, the cognate cultures of the ancient Near East and the Greco-Roman world both attest to women writings. These observations encourage scholars to reconsider women's education reflected in the biblical and related texts. This inquiry is particularly relevant for the study of the pseudepigrapha, because this corpus contains at least two works that have been at times associated with female authors. Specifically, scholars have argued that Liber antiquitatum biblicarum and the Testament of Job, which notably highlight women, were authored by women.[57] While

---

55. For classical studies and gender, see, e.g., Nancy Sorkin Rabinowitz and Amy Richlin, eds., *Feminist Theory and the Classics* (New York: Routledge, 1993). Moreover, numerous textbooks and the series Oxford Studies in Classical Literature and Gender Theory demonstrate the ample interest in this topic. For the ancient Near East, see, e.g., Brigitte Lion and Cécile Michel, eds., *The Role of Women in Work and Society in the Ancient Near East*, SANER 13 (Berlin: de Gruyter, 2016).

56. See Karel van der Toorn, *Scribal Culture and Making of the Hebrew Bible* (Cambridge: Harvard University Press, 2007), 285 n. 5.

57. Mary Therese DesCamps, "Why Are These Women Here? An Examination of the Sociological Setting of Pseudo-Philo through Comparative Reading," *JSP* 16 (1997): 53–80; and DesCamps, *Metaphor and Ideology: Liber Antiquitatum Biblicarum and Literary Methods through a Cognitive Lens*, BibInt 97 (Leiden: Brill: Brill, 2007), 4 n. 9, 347–48. Note that While DesCamp's study is the most complex on this issue, she

women's presence in the text is an important indicator about a possible audience of the text, their presence should also be weighed against the evidence of women's roles in neighboring cultures. Insights from cognate cultures can help fill those gaps that the pseudepigrapha contain in their portrayal of women.[58]

Finally, whereas the question of women's literacy may seem to pertain exclusively to the study of historical women, in light of intersectional reading it is crucial to see its implications for other fields of research. A scholar who asks whether women could read and write in antiquity also engages with broader questions, including those related to ancient education and text production. Therefore, gender is not an isolated topic that can be studied alone; it always bears consequences for other themes. Rather than studying gender as a field of its own, its relevance to any research question requires full recognition. When intersectional identities are generally acknowledged, the significance of gender in them should be fully recognized.[59]

---

is not the first to propose a female authorship for Liber antiquitatum biblicarum. This was earlier proposed by Pieter Willem van der Horst, "Images of Women in the Testament of Job," in *Studies in the Testament of Job*, ed. Michael A. Knibb and Pieter W. van der Horst (Cambridge: Cambridge University Press, 1989), 93–116; and van der Horst, "Portraits of Biblical Women in Pseudo-Philo's *Liber Antiquitatum Biblicarum*," 44–46, who argues that these compositions that highlight women could hardly be written by men. Van der Horst proposes they originated in a Jewish movement in which women played the leading role. More recently, Gerbern Oegema, "Female Authorship in Jewish Antiquity" (paper presented at the Enoch Nangeroni Meeting, 18 June 2018, Rome), suggests that 2 Macc 7 was composed by a woman because it describes emotions that relate closely to a female experience. While I do not think that emotions that seem to match with ideas on women alone offer enough support for Oegema's theory, I agree that female authorship remains to be further explored.

58. Concerning women's authorship, see Ross S. Kraemer, "Women's Authorship of Jewish and Christian Literature in the Greco-Roman Period," in Kraemer, *'Women Like This'*, 221–42, who points out female authorship in the Christian texts of the first centuries CE.

59. See, e.g., Candace West and Don H. Zimmerman, "Doing Gender," *Gender and Society* (1987): 125–51; West and Zimmerman, "Accounting for Doing Gender," *Gender and Society* (2009): 112–22. I have been inspired to look at the work of these sociologists by Saana Svärd, who refers to their work in, e.g., Svärd, "Studying Gender: A Case Study of Female Administrators in Neo-Assyrian Palaces," in *The Role of Women in Work and Society in the Ancient Near East*, 447–58.

4. Conclusions

In this essay I have reviewed some of the history of research pertaining to the study of the pseudepigrapha and gender. This research history demonstrates how scholarship does not develop in an intellectual vacuum. Rather, throughout the essay I outlined how research on the pseudepigrapha and gender has evolved methodologically in connection with developments in the feminist movement. In particular, the second-wave feminist movement has been influential in bringing the female figures from the margins of the texts to the center of analysis.

With regard to future research on the pseudepigrapha and gender, it is necessary for the sake of methodological clarity that the relationship between feminist and gender studies be expressed more explicitly. There is a need for both feminist and gender perspectives. Gender is not the same as women's studies and does not restrict the discussion to women scholars and topics. Scholars should be conscious about choosing between feminist and gender perspectives, acknowledging that their goals are somewhat different but that both are needed. Moreover, it is necessary to assess critically all hermeneutical perspectives. Given the particular status that the historical-critical method enjoys, this hermeneutical lens should be cautiously evaluated.

A particular challenge that modern researchers face is that, while we are interested in gender, we cannot tell to what extent our ancient authors were. The ancient texts do not give any indication of such an interest. Rather, the focus of the ancient authors often lies on other matters, such as cult and law. Therefore, in order to trace potential functions of gender in the texts, we must ask our texts the right questions, questions that reveal any gendered aspect underlying the text. Although scholars have long paid attention to various gendered elements in the pseudepigrapha, the analyses have so far focused mostly on women on a literary level, whereas questions pertaining to social realities remain understudied. In order to address this deficiency, we can look for inspiration, for instance, from studies of cognate cultures or social-scientific methods. Scholarship gains its inspirations from the political and intellectual atmosphere of the time. Therefore, when I evaluate the study of the pseudepigrapha and gender in a broader historical and cultural context, I am positive that the present situation offers new inspiration to this field. The silence on gender that our material features cannot be changed, but the questions we pose can.

Bibliography

Borchardt, Francis. "A Gender Theory Critique of the Historical-Critical Method." *CSTT and Gender ebooklet* (2017): 5–12.

Brenner, Athalya, and Carole Fontaine, eds. *A Feminist Companion to Reading the Bible: Approaches, Methods and Strategies*. Sheffield: Sheffield Academic, 1997.

Brisson, Luc. *Sexual Ambivalance: Androgyny and Hermaphroditism in Graeco-Roman Antiquity*. Translated by Janet Lloyd. Berkeley: University of California Press, 2002.

Brooten, Bernadette. "Early Christian Women and Their Cultural Context: Issues of Method in Historical Reconstruction." Pages 65–91 in *Feminist Perspectives in Biblical Scholarship*. Edited by Adela Yarbro Collins. BSNA 10. Atlanta: Scholars Press 1985.

Butler, Judith. *Gender Trouble: Feminism and the Subversion of Identity*. 2nd ed. New York: Routledge, 2010.

Cady Stanton, Elizabeth. *The Women's Bible*. New York: European Publishing Company, 1895–1898.

Charles, R. H. *The Book of Jubilees or the Little Genesis*. London: Black, 1902.

Charlesworth, James H. "Introduction for the General Reader." *OTP* 1:xxi–xxxiv.

———, ed. *Old Testament Pseudepigrapha*. 2 vols. New York: Doubleday, 1983–1985.

Crenshaw, Kimberle. "Demarginalizing the Intersection of Race and Sex: A Black Feminist Critique of Antidiscrimination Doctrine, Feminist Theory and Antiracist Politics." *University of Chicago Legal Forum* 140 (1989): 139–67.

Davis, Stacy. *Haggai and Malachi*. Wisdom Commentary 39. Collegeville, MN: Liturgical Press, 2015.

Day, Peggy L. "Introduction." Pages 1–11 in *Gender and Difference*. Edited by Peggy L. Day. Minneapolis: Fortress, 1989.

DesCamps, Mary Therese. *Metaphor and Ideology: Liber Antiquitatum Biblicarum and Literary Methods through a Cognitive Lens*. BibInt 97. Leiden: Brill: Brill, 2007.

———. "Why Are These Women Here? An Examination of the Sociological Setting of Pseudo-Philo through Comparative Reading." *JSP* 16 (1997): 53–80.

Gamble, Sarah. "Postfeminism." Pages 36–46 in *The Routledge Companion to Feminism and Postfeminism*. Edited by Sarah Gamble. London: Routledge, 2001.

———, ed. *The Routledge Companion to Feminism and Postfeminism*. London: Routledge, 2001.

Gifford, Carolyn De Swarte. "American Women and the Bible: The Nature of Woman as a Hermeneutical Issue." Pages 11–33 in *Feminist Perspectives on Biblical Scholarship*. Edited by Adela Yarbro Collins. BSNA 10. Atlanta: Scholars Press, 1985.

Graybill, Rhiannon. *Are We Not Men? Unstable Masculinity in the Hebrew Prophets*. Oxford: Oxford University Press, 2016.

Halpern-Amaru, Betsy. *Empowerment of Women in the Book of Jubilees*. JSJSup 60. Leiden: Brill, 1999.

———. "Portraits of Women in Pseudo-Philo's Antiquities." Pages 83–106 in *'Women Like This': New Perspectives on Jewish Women in the Greco-Roman World*. Edited by Amy-Jill Levine. EJL 1. Atlanta: Scholars Press, 1991.

Harrington, Daniel J. "Pseudo-Philo." *OTP* 2:297–377.

Hodgson-Wright, Stephanie. "Early Feminism." Pages 3–14 in *The Routledge Companion to Feminism and Postfeminism*. Edited by Sarah Gamble. London: Routledge, 2001.

Horst, Pieter W. van der. "Images of Women in the Testament of Job." Pages 93–116 in *Studies in the Testament of Job*. Edited by Michael A. Knibb and Pieter W. van der Horst. Cambridge: Cambridge University Press, 1989.

———. "Portraits of Biblical Women in Pseudo Philo's Liber Antiquitatum Biblicarum." *JSP* 5 (1989): 29–46.

Ilan, Tal. *Jewish Women in Greco Roman Palestine: An Inquiry into Image and Status*. TSAJ 44. Tübingen: Mohr Siebeck, 1995.

Jacobson, Howard. *A Commentary of Pseudo-Philo's Liber Antiquitatum Biblicarum with Latin Text and English Translation 1–2*. AGJU 31. Leiden: Brill, 1996.

James, M. R. *The Biblical Antiquities of Philo with Prolegomenon by Louis H. Feldman*. LBS. New York: Ktav, 1971.

Keady, Jessica M. *Vulnerability and Valour: A Gendered Analysis of Everyday Life in the Dead Sea Scrolls Communities*. LSTS 91. London: T&T Clark, 2017.

Kraft, Robert A. "Para-mania: Beside, Before, and Beyond Bible Studies." *JBL* 126 (2007): 3–27.

Kraemer, Ross S. "Women's Authorship of Jewish and Christian Literature in the Greco-Roman Period." Pages 221–42 in *'Women Like This': New Perspectives on Jewish Women in the Greco-Roman World*. Edited by Amy-Jill Levine. EJL 1. Atlanta: Scholars Press, 1991.

Lakoff, George. *Women, Fire and Dangerous Things: What Categories Reveal about the Mind*. Chicago: The University of Chicago Press, 1987.

Lange, Armin. "In the Second Degree: Ancient Jewish and Paratextual Literature in the Context of Graeco-Roman and Ancient Near Eastern Literature." Pages 3–40 in *In the Second Degree: Paratextual Literature in Ancient Near Eastern and Ancient Mediterranean Culture and Its Reflections in Medieval Literature*. Edited by Philip Alexander, Armin Lange, and Renate Pillinger. Leiden: Brill, 2010.

Lawrence, Beatrice. "Gender Analysis: Gender and Method in Biblical Studies." Pages 333–48 in *Method Matters: Essays on the Interpretation of the Hebrew Bible in Honor of David L. Petersen*. Edited by Joel M. LeMon and Kent Harold Richards. RBS 56. Atlanta: Society of Biblical Literature, 2009.

Levine, Amy-Jill. Preface to *'Women Like This': New Perspectives on Jewish Women in the Greco-Roman World*. Edited by Amy-Jill Levine. EJL 1. Atlanta: Scholars Press, 1991.

Lion, Brigitte, and Cécile Michel, eds. *The Role of Women in Work and Society in the Ancient Near East*. SANER 13. Berlin: de Gruyter, 2016.

Lovering, Eugene H., Jr., ed. *Society of Biblical Literature 1994 Seminar Papers*. SBLSP 33. Atlanta: Scholars Press, 1994.

Lull, David J., ed. *Society of Biblical Literature 1989 Seminar Papers*. SBLSP 28. Atlanta: Scholars Press, 1989.

MacRae, George W., ed. *Society of Biblical Literature 1976 Seminar Papers*. SBLSP 10. Missoula, MT: Scholars Press, 1976.

Murphy, Frederick J. *Pseudo-Philo: Rewriting the Bible*. New York: Oxford University Press, 1993.

Nasrallah, Laura, and Elisabeth Schüssler Fiorenza, eds. *Prejudice and Christian Beginnings: Investigating Race, Gender, and Ethnicity in Early Christian Studies*. Minneapolis: Fortress, 2009.

Parks, Sara. "Historical-Critical Ministry? The Biblical Studies Classroom as Restorative Secular Space." *New Blackfriars* 100 (2018): 229–44.

———. "Nixing the Niche: Moving Women from the Margins in Second Temple Jewish Scholarship." Paper presented at the Tenth Enoch Nangeroni Meeting. Rome, 18 June 2018.

Perrot, Charles, and Pierre-Maurice Bogaert. *Pseudo-Philon: Les antiquités bibliques*. Vol. 2. SC 230. Paris: Cerf, 1976.

Rabinowitz, Nancy Sorkin, and Amy Richlin, eds. *Feminist Theory and the Classics*. New York: Routledge, 1993.

Reed, Annette Yoshiko. "The Modern Invention of Old Testament Pseudepigrapha." *JTS* 60 (2009): 403–36.

———. "Old Testament Pseudepigrapha and Post-70 Judaism." Pages 117–48 in *Les Judaïsmes dans tous leur états aux Ier-IIIe siècles*. Edited by Simon Claude Mimouni, Bernard Pouderon, and Claire Clivas. Turnhout: Brepols, 2015.

Sanders, Valerie. "First Wave Feminism." Pages 15–24 in *The Routledge Companion to Feminism and Postfeminism*. Edited by Sarah Gamble. London: Routledge, 2001.

Schottroff, Luise, Silvia Schroer, and Marie-Theres Wacker. *Feminist Interpretation: The Bible in Women's Perspective*. Translated by Martin and Barbara Rumscheidt. Minneapolis: Fortress, 1998.

Schüssler Fiorenza, Elisabeth. *But She Said: Feminist Practices of Biblical Interpretation*. Boston: Beacon Press, 1992.

———. *In Memory of Her: A Feminist Theological Reconstruction of Christian Origins*. London: SCM, 1985.

———. *Sharing Her Word: Feminist Biblical Interpretation in Context*. Edinburgh: T&T Clark, 1998.

Sherwood, Yvonne. "Introduction: The Bible and Feminism: Remapping the Field." Pages 1–14 in *The Bible and Feminism: Remapping the Field*. Edited by Yvonne Sherwood with the assistance of Anna Fisk. Oxford: Oxford University Press, 2017.

Sjöberg, Birgitta L. "More than Just Gender: The Classical Oikos as a Site of Intersectionality in Families in the Greco-Roman World." Pages 48–59 in *Families in the Greco-Roman World*. Edited by Ray Laurence and Agneta Strömberg. London: Continuum, 2012.

Society of Biblical Literature. *Society of Biblical Literature 1996 Seminar Papers*. SBLSP 35. Atlanta: Scholars Press, 1996.

Svärd, Saana. "Studying Gender: A Case Study of Female Administrators in Neo-Assyrian Palaces." Pages 447–58 in *The Role of Women in Work and Society in the Ancient Near East*. Edited by Brigitte Lion and Cécile Michel. SANER 13. Berlin: de Gruyter, 2016.

Tervanotko, Hanna. *Denying Her Voice: The Figure of Miriam in Ancient Jewish Literature*. JAJSup 23. Göttingen: Vandenhoeck & Ruprecht, 2016.

———. "Feminist Interpretation of the Bible in Retrospect." *lectio difficilior* 2 (2016): https://tinyurl.com/SBL3550b.
———. "Obey Me Like Your Mother: Deborah's Leadership in Light of *Liber antiquitatum biblicarum* 33." *JSP* 24 (2015): 301–23.
Thornham, Sue. "Second Wave Feminism." Pages 25–35 in *The Routledge Companion to Feminism and Postfeminism*. Edited by Sarah Gamble. London: Routledge, 2001.
Toorn, Karel van der. *Scribal Culture and Making of the Hebrew Bible*. Cambridge: Harvard University Press, 2007.
Wassen, Cecilia. *Women in the Damascus Document*. Leiden: Brill, 2005.
West, Candace, and Don H. Zimmerman. "Accounting for Doing Gender." *Gender and Society* (2009): 112–22.
———. "Doing Gender." *Gender and Society* (1987): 125–51.
World Health Organization. "Gender, Equity and Human Rights." https://tinyurl.com/SBL3550a.

Topics in the Study of the Pseudepigrapha

11
Pseudepigrapha and Their Manuscripts

Liv Ingeborg Lied and Loren T. Stuckenbruck

Introduction

The most well-attested medium for pseudepigraphal texts is late antique and medieval manuscripts.[1] A birds-eye view on the surviving manuscripts containing the pseudepigrapha[2] shows that these texts come down to us in various material shapes and textual combinations, in a broad variety of linguistic traditions, dating as early as the third or second century BCE and, in some traditions, as late as the twentieth century. It is helpful, sometimes, to state the obvious: many pseudepigraphal texts, which have traditionally been assumed to originate in and to some degree belong to

---

1. By *manuscript* we refer to inscribed artefacts produced and copied by hand, excluding the use of any printing press or electronic means.

2. In this essay, we understand *pseudepigraphal texts* etically, referring to the writings that have been characterized as such in scholarly discourse since Johan A. Fabricius's 1713/1722 publication of *Codex Pseudepigraphus Veteris Testamenti: Collectus, castigatus, testimoniisque, censuris et animaduersionibus illustres* (Hamburg: Felginer, 1713); second edition: *Codicis pseudepigraphi Veteris Testamenti: Volumen Alterum Accedit Josephi Veteris Christiani Auctoria Hypomnesticon* (Hamburg: Felginer, 1722–1723); and in common usages since the nineteenth century. The term *pseudepigrapha* typically refers to texts that neither were part of the Hebrew Bible nor the (Protestant) apocrypha, but which contain narratives about figures and events known from the Hebrew Bible/the Old Testament and which are typically assumed to originate in the Jewish Second Temple period. The use of the category in scholarship is widely debated and rightfully so. For problematizing accounts regarding pseudepigrapha as a special and descriptive category for ancient literature that is distinguishable from other collections of sacred writings, see Annette Yoshiko Reed, "The Modern Invention of 'Old Testament Pseudepigrapha,'" *JTS* 60 (2009): 403–36; and Loren T. Stuckenbruck, "Apocrypha and Pseudepigrapha," *EDEJ* 152–56.

the Second Temple period (i.e., between, roughly, the third century BCE and the second century CE), are known to us today only because later generations continued to find it worth the effort to copy and engage with them. Thus, to a large extent, our access to pseudepigraphal writings both depends on and is restricted by the manuscript materials that survive. A significant corollary to this is that our knowledge about these texts is shaped by their mediating capacity.

In discussing the role of manuscripts in the preservation of pseudepigraphal writings, the present essay consists of two main parts, followed by a conclusion. The first part presents a number of notable tendencies that characterize the pool of surviving manuscripts, which include pseudepigraphal texts. These tendencies will be accompanied, as appropriate by examples that shall chiefly, though not exclusively, take the manuscript history of two texts into account: 1 Enoch and 2 Baruch. In the second section, we discuss how manuscripts have typically been used and assessed in scholarship and how they can continue to be studied and engaged with, while suggesting some important ways forward.

Before we outline characteristics that apply to manuscript traditions containing pseudepigrapha, it is appropriate to begin with some general observations that contextualize the scope of what we are considering. The mapping of manuscripts that preserve pseudepigraphal texts is a daunting task, whether conceptually or materially. For one thing, so-called pseudepigrapha never made up a collection of literature in its own right that can be distinguished from other categories of writings; in manuscript traditions, they were hardly segregated and collected in late antiquity and the middle ages.[3] Instead, these texts were most commonly preserved as part of other bound collections and copied in different manuscript genres produced for various purposes. Moreover, pseudepigraphal texts were transmitted in most major languages of the Middle East, the Mediterranean world, and Central Asia, as well as in European and African linguistic traditions. Furthermore, as already suggested, the chains of copying of pseudepigraphal texts span many centuries. We find such texts among the Dead Sea Scrolls, while many of them are copied by hand in manuscripts produced in the twentieth century, as, for instance, in Ethiopia. Finally, we find pseudepigraphal texts in a wide variety of material shapes

---

3. See the essay of Benjamin Wright in the present volume. Also see the bibliography in n. 2 above.

and constitutions. The term *manuscript* as we apply it here covers a wide range of forms and materials, most commonly scrolls and codices, or their fragmented remains, carrying texts inscribed on papyrus, parchment (or prepared skins), paper, and other. Manuscripts may refer to everything from rough notepads to valuable deluxe artefacts, produced for various reasons and sometimes playing different roles during the course of their circulation. Hence, the most notable feature that characterizes the pool of manuscripts containing pseudepigraphal texts is its multivalence and complexity. And since these texts never made up a collection that was copied as such, a generalizing picture thereof is in vain. Nevertheless, based on available material, it is possible to describe some six major tendencies and particularly salient factors that both complicate and illuminate our perception of the texts the manuscripts contain.

1. Manuscripts Preserving the Pseudepigrapha: Six Main Tendencies

The *first* tendency we wish to highlight is that the manuscripts containing pseudepigrapha are generally late. Of course, there are notable exceptions that remind us that many of these texts were produced at a much earlier time, though not always in entirely the same form. For example, pseudepigraphal texts attested among the Dead Sea Scrolls, prominent among them parts of Jubilees and Enoch-related literature, survive in manuscripts dated to the periods between the third century BCE and the first century CE.[4] Some other, still relatively early exceptions were found among the heaps of fragments at Oxyrhynchus, for instance, a late fourth-century CE Greek fragment of 2 Baruch (P.Oxy. 3.403).[5] Further manuscripts can probably also be dated to the first seven centuries of the Common Era, such as the fifth-century palimpsest containing Latin Jubilees and the Testament/Assumption of Moses, the early seventh-century Syriac Codex Ambrosianus with complete texts of 2 Baruch and 4 Ezra, and Greek materials covering sizeable portions of the Enochic Book of Watch-

---

4. On the dates of the early manuscripts to these writings, see the discussions by Józef T. Milik, *The Books of Enoch: Aramaic Fragments of Qumrân Cave 4* (Oxford: Clarendon, 1976); and James C. VanderKam, e.g., in "The Manuscript Tradition of Jubilees," in *Enoch and the Mosaic Torah: The Evidence of Jubilees*, ed. Gabriele Boccaccini and Giovanni Ibba (Grand Rapids: Eerdmans, 2009), 3–22.

5. See Bernhard P. Grenfell and Arthur S. Hunt, "403. Apocalypse of Baruch, XII–XIV," in *The Oxyrhynchus Papyri* (London: Egypt Exploration Fund, 1903), 3:3–7.

ers and Epistle of Enoch.⁶ Still, it remains a fact that the large majority of manuscripts preserving copies of pseudepigraphal texts are much younger than this. Most of the surviving manuscripts are copied no earlier than the eighth century, and many of them date from the period between the twelfth and the sixteenth century.⁷ This situation implies that the manuscripts furnishing text for studying pseudepigrapha may often be, give or take a few hundred years, a millennium younger than the time they were assumedly composed, first translated, or even initially received and translated in a tertiary language. Recognition of this raises fundamental questions regarding scholarly approaches that have commonly focused on the texts in the ancient contexts in which they were first generated.⁸

A *second* tendency that characterizes manuscripts that preserve pseudepigraphal texts is that they are frequently the products of Christian communities. Many pseudepigraphal writings, in whole or in excerpted parts, were transmitted by Christians in order to be used by Christians. Several features of the manuscripts point us in this direction. Sometimes colophons and marginal notes in the manuscripts provide explicit information about the identities of the scribe, the commissioner, and/or the community for which the manuscript was copied, identifying them as Christian.⁹ Examples for this phenomenon are multiple. Here, it suffices

---

6. Todd R. Hanneken, "The Book of Jubilees in Latin," in *Deuterocanonical Writings*, vol. 2 of *The Textual History of the Bible*, ed. Frank Feder and Matthias Henze (Leiden: Brill, forthcoming); Liv Ingeborg Lied, "2 Baruch and the Syriac Codex Ambrosianus (7a1): Studying Old Testament Pseudepigrapha in Their Manuscript Context," *JSP* 26 (2016): 67–107. The Enochic Greek texts, respectively dateable to the fourth and fifth centuries CE, are preserved in Codex Panopolitanos (1 En. 1:1–32:6a, with duplicate in 19:3–21:9) and the Chester-Beatty Michigan Papyrus (1 En. 94:7–107:3, missing ch. 105), texts brought together in Matthew Black, *Apocalypsis Henochi Graece*, PVTG 3 (Leiden: Brill, 1970).

7. When comparing this situation with the set of manuscripts preserving other collections of texts, there is nothing special to the transmission history of pseudepigraphal texts. The profile is quite common. See, for instance, the transmission of texts ascribed to Philo of Alexandria and Josephus and, even to some extent, writings from the Hebrew Bible.

8. See the introduction and contributions to the edited volume *Snapshots of Evolving Traditions: Jewish and Christian Manuscript Culture, Textual Fluidity, and New Philology*, ed. Liv Ingeborg Lied and Hugo Lundhaug, TUGAL 175 (Berlin: de Gruyter, 2017).

9. This kind of information is commonly found in, for instance, Syriac, Armenian, and Georgian manuscripts; see Adam Bremer-McCollum, "Notes and Colophons of

to note in some detail the way 1 En. 105.2 is transmitted in a Geʿez manuscript from Hayq Ǝstifanos (EMML 2080) that some have regarded as significant for text-critical purposes. The text reads: "For I and my son will join ourselves with them forever on the ways of righteousness during their lives." The phrase "ways of righteousness" resonates with the same phrase found in both the Exhortation of 1 Enoch at 1 En. 91.18–19, the Apocalypse of Weeks at 91.14 (so the Ethiopic; the Aramic reads with the singular "way"), and the Epistle of Enoch itself at 92.3 and 94.1; therefore, this part of the text is likely ancient. However, the phrase "I and my son" is surprising, in that it envisions an eschatological return of Enoch and his son Methuselah to earth. Thus August Dillmann, in attempting to reconcile the text's content with ancient Jewish tradition, maintained that it is concerned with God and the Messiah and argued that this interpretation is made plausible by the Epistle's appearance after the messianic references in the Book of Parables that come earlier in the book of Enoch (1 En. 48.10; 52.4; cf. also 65.5; 69.29).[10] Such a connection is possible, but not if one is thinking about the original context of the Epistle, which was composed centuries before the Parables and initially and certainly in the Greek tradition, likely copied separately. In addition, in the Parables "my son" is not so much "the Son of Man" of the Parables or even Methuselah, who is never mentioned there, but rather the figure of Noah (1 En. 65.11). Thus, rather than deriving the text's interpretation from another part of 1 Enoch, it is possible that it has been shaped in a way that fits with Christian tradition, whether its precise content owes to editorial work at the level of Christian Geʿez transmission or goes back to a nonextant Greek *Vorlage*. The fit with Christian tradition is reflected rather transparently in a marginal note to the text found in the sixteenth-century Hayq Ǝstifanos manuscript, which, commenting on "I and my son," states: "the Father and the Son, or Enoch and Methuselah." At this level, that is, the transmission of the text in the Ethiopian context, a literary connection with the Parables would be possible to imagine on the part of the comment (not to mention to Christian tradition more generally). Remote from a Second Temple context, in which "Father" as a title for God, together with a Messiah "son," never

---

Scribes and Readers in Georgian Biblical Manuscripts from Saint Catherine's Monastery (Sinai)," in *Bible as Notepad: Tracing Annotations and Annotation Practices in Late Antique and Medieval Biblical Manuscripts*, ed. Liv Ingeborg Lied and Marilena Maniaci, Manuscripta Biblica 3 (Berlin: de Gruyter, 2018), 111–24.

10. August Dillmann, *Das Buch Henoch* (Leipzig: Vogel, 1853), 325.

occurs together,[11] the text may, in its present form, have cast the Enoch-Methuslah paradigm in language that echoes Christian tradition (God the Father, Jesus the Son), with the marginal note openly declaring the text's meaning in this way.

In other instances, pseudepigraphal texts can be found in manuscripts containing collections of texts that are distinctly Christian, in the sense that they may be regarded as Christian scriptures (for instance, Old or New Testament codices) or as specialized books dedicated to be used in Christian reading—or worship practices (for instance, catenae, historiographical works, homilies, and lectionary manuscripts).[12] From yet another perspective, the fact that the texts were copied in ecclesiastical languages (such as Greek, Latin, Arabic, Armenian, Slavonic, Syriac and Ge'ez) in areas that were predominantly Christian strongly *suggests* that the manuscripts themselves reflect this provenience. Based on the surviving materials, these texts seem to have circulated among and put to use by Christians. Some manuscripts contain notes from active readers that came across them,[13] and many of the manuscripts have been kept in churches, cathedrals, or in the libraries and storerooms of monasteries.

There are, nonetheless, interesting exceptions to the dominant Christian preservation. Some manuscripts preserving pseudepigraphal texts are to be identified as Jewish. In addition to the Dead Sea Scrolls, the most well-known examples consist of the fragmented manuscripts found in the Cairo Genizah. In addition to the Damascus Document associated with the community behind many of the much earlier Dead Sea Scrolls, this genizah held fragments of medieval copies of Sirach, the Aramaic Levi Document, the Prayer of Manasseh, and the Testament of Naphtali.[14] In addition, one could think of Enochic traditions preserved—whether whole, excerpted, or variously adumbrated—among medieval manuscripts, such as the so-called 3 Enoch or Hebrew Enoch

---

11. Apart from writings of the New Testament (see, e.g., Mark 1:11 // Matt 3:17 // Luke 3:22; Matt 12:18b; 17:5; Heb 5:5; 2 Pet 2:17).

12. See the examples below.

13. See Loren T. Stuckenbruck and Ted M. Erho, "EMML 8400 and Notes on the Reading of *Hēnok* in Ethiopia," in Lied and Maniaci, *Bible as Notepad*, 125–29.

14. For a convenient summary of these, see Ida Fröhlich, "The Dead Sea Scrolls and Geniza Studies," in *David Kaufmann Memorial Volume: Papers Presented at the David Kaufmann Memorial Conference, November 29 1999*, ed. Éva Apor (Budapest: Library of the Hungarian Academy of Sciences, 2002), 61–67.

and related texts,[15] though their date of origin in relation to the Second Temple period is debated. Yet another, though less clear-cut example may be some of the manuscripts produced within the Jewish Beta Israel community of Ethiopia.[16] As the above exceptions indicate, some medieval Jewish communities were familiar with and engaged with several of these texts or with traditions associated with them, and this familiarity is also reflected in the reception of traditions, if not in textual manuscripts of the works themselves, in texts that draw on interpretative solutions based on Enoch literature, Jubilees, the Testaments of the Twelve Patriarchs and Ben Sira.[17] It remains, nevertheless, that the relatively low number of examples of explicitly Jewish manuscripts containing pseudepigraphal texts is interesting in its own right, and examples of Jewish *manuscripts* dedicated to, or including, copies of pseudepigraphal texts are rare.[18]

---

15. As edited, e.g., by Hugo Odeberg, *3 Enoch or the Hebrew Book of Enoch* (Cambridge: Cambridge University Press, 1923) or in manuscripts such as the early printed 1516 Constantinople as found in the British Library, shelfmark 1952.c.22 (which itself picks up on manuscript traditions), which contained, alongside the book of Tobit, works in adumbrated form called Eldad ha-Dani, Proverbs of Sandabar, the book of Enoch, Fables of Aesop, Proverbs of Solomon, and Speech of Aphar and Dinah. The latter and related collections are worthy of further research.

16. So, e.g., the preservation of 1 Enoch in the Faitlovitch collection (MS 5) at the Sourasky Central Library, Tel Aviv University. However, the strict separation of manuscripts as Jewish (as opposed to Christian), even when they have been copied in the Beta Israel community, cannot be assumed in each instance; for example, though rare, texts of the psalms produced in the community are appended by Christian materials (e.g., homilies or meditations on Mary or even on the Trinity), so, e.g., in the EMML collection nos. 7868 and 7869 from Gonder.

17. That is, as can be found in rabbinic literature and *hekhalot* texts. See, e.g., John R. Reeves, "Exploring the Afterlife of Jewish Pseudepigrapha in Medieval Near Eastern Religious Traditions: Some Initial Soundings," *JSJ* 30 (1999): 148–77; Jenny R. Labendz, "The Book of Ben Sira in Rabbinic Literature," *AJSR* 30 (2006): 347–92; Michael E. Stone, "The Testament of Naphtali," *JJS* 47 (1996): 311–21; Menachem Kister, "Ancient Material in *Pirqe De-Rabbi Eli'Ezer*: Basilides, Qumran, the Book of Jubilees," in *'Go Out and Study the Land' (Judges 18:2): Archaeological, Historical and Textual Studies in Honor of Hanan Eshel*, ed. Aren M. Maeir, Jodi Magness, and Lawrence H. Schiffman, JSJSup 148 (Leiden: Brill, 2012), 69–93; Martha Himmelfarb, "Preservation of Second Temple Texts and Traditions in Rabbinic and Post-Rabbinic Jewish Transmission," in *A Guide to Early Jewish Texts and Traditions in Christian Transmission*, ed. Alexander Kulik, Gabriele Boccaccini, Lorenzo DiTommaso, David Hamidovic, and Michael E. Stone (Oxford: Oxford University Press, forthcoming).

18. The history of the Jewish transmission of these texts is a much-debated issue.

Another instance of transmission outside an avowedly Christian context occurs in the Manichaean text tradition, which received ancient Enochic tradition. Specifically, Manichaean manuscript fragments in Middle Persian, Sogdian, Uyghur, and Coptic preserve text that recognizably transmits the Book of Giants (known from ten manuscripts among the Dead Sea Scrolls), albeit in a heavily edited form.[19] In Muslim manuscripts the occurrences of pseudepigraphal texts are rare.[20] Although examples of independently circulating story lines and narrative clusters associated with these texts such as stories about the fall of Adam and Eve or the fallen angels are relatively commonly found in Muslim literatures,[21]

See, Reeves, "Exploring the Afterlife"; Himmelfarb, "Preservation of Second Temple Texts and Traditions"; Stuckenbruck, "Apocrypha and Pseudepigrapha"; Arye Edrei and Doron Mendels, "A Split Jewish Diaspora: Its Dramatic Consequences," *JSP* 16 (2007): 91–137. We also cannot rule out that some of the manuscripts have a more complex affiliation. It is also important to remember that the simplistic categories *Jewish* and *Christian* may not serve as fruitful labels for the various individuals, groups, and communities that engaged with apocryphal and pseudepigraphal texts and traditions.

19. On these materials, which have not yet been published in full, see W. B. Henning, "The Book of Giants," *BSOAS* 11 (1943): 52–74; Werner Sundermann, "Ein weiteres Fragment aus Manis Gigantenbuch," in *Orientalia J. Duchesne-Guillemin emerito oblata*, Acta Iranica 23 (Leiden: Brill, 1984), 491–505; Jens Wilckens, "Neue Fragmente aus Manis Gigantenbuch," *ZDMG* 150 (2000): 133–76; Enrico Morano, "Sogdian Tales in Manichean Script," in *Literarische Stoffe und ihre Gestaltung in mitteliranischer Zeit*, ed. D. Durkin-Meisterernst, C. Reck, and D. Weber (Wiesbaden: Harrassowitz, 2009), 173–200; Jens Wilckens, "Funktion und gattungsgeschichtliche Bedeutung des manichäischen Gigantenbuchs," in *Der östliche Manichäismus: Gattungs- und Werkgeschichte*, ed. Z. Özertural and J. Wilckens, AAWG NS 17 (Berlin: de Gruyter, 2011), 63–88; and Enrico Morano, "New Research on Mani's Book of Giants," in Özertural and Wilckens, *Der östliche Manichäismus*, 101–12. See overviews and prospects for the study of additional material in Matthew J. Goff, Loren T. Stuckenbruck, and Enrico Morano, eds., *Ancient Tales of Giants from Qumran and Turfan*, WUNT 360 (Tübingen: Mohr Siebeck, 2016).

20. Christian Arabic manuscripts containing pseudepigraphal texts are relatively well attested. One example is Mount Sinai Arabic MS 589, which includes 2 Baruch and 4 Ezra. See P. Sj. van Koningsveld, "An Arabic Manuscript of the Apocalypse of Baruch," *JSJ* 6 (1974–1975): 205–7.

21. Cf., e.g., Michael Pregill, "Isra'iliyyat, Myth, and Pseudepigraphy: Wahb b. Munabbih and the Early Islamic Version of the Fall of Adam and Eve," *JSAI* 34 (2008): 215–84; Annette Yoshiko Reed, "Fallen Angels and the Afterlives of Enochic Traditions in Early Islam," in *Early Islam: The Sectarian Milieu of Late Antiquity? Proceedings of the Fourth Nangeroni Meeting*, ed. G. Dye (Chicago: The Oriental Institute, forthcoming).

discrete copies of pseudepigraphal text are apparently not. Occasionally, Muslim manuscripts may contain excerpted parts of pseudepigraphal texts. This is the case with the twelfth-century Arabic manuscript Berol. Sprenger 30, kept in the Staatsbibliothek in Berlin. This manuscript, which still remains unpublished, includes 4 Ezra 14:38–50.[22]

Third, we can observe that the largely Christian transmission of pseudepigrapha seems to have flourished in the East. This is not to diminish the significance of western scribal traditions for the preservation of such material,[23] but rather to acknowledge that the Slavic, Armenian, and Ethiopic manuscript traditions not only preserve writings shared with other Christian contexts, but also have unique portions of texts to which there would otherwise be no access at all.[24] Furthermore, it could be noted that

---

22. See Adrina Drint, "The Mount Sinai Arabic Version of IV Ezra: Text, Translation and Introduction" (PhD diss., Rijksuniversitet Groningen, 1995).

23. Doron Mendels and Aryeh Edrei have argued that for ancient Judaism the apocrypha and pseudepigrapha flourished in the West but were ignored in the East. They have further maintained that Jews, whose writings of this sort were taken up by Christians in the West, were absorbed into the Christian tradition, while in the East they retained a more narrowly defined identity. Doron Mendels and Aryeh Edrei, *Zweierlei Diaspora: Zur Spaltung der antiken jüdischen Welt* (Göttingen: Vandenhoeck & Ruprecht, 2009). We thus offer a corrective to this picture; namely, that the flourishing of pseudepigraphal literature in the East cannot be ignored. If one retains the argument by Mendels and Edrei as it relates to Jews in the East, then we are to imagine a stricter drawing of socioreligious boundaries there from the middle of the First Millennium than may have been the case in the West. This question, in any case, should be regarded as open and requires research in more details.

24. For a collection of the Slavonic texts, see Alexander Kulik and Sergey Minov, *Biblical Pseudepigrapha in Slavonic Tradition* (Oxford: Oxford University Press, 2016) and the authors' discussion of unique and shared books in that tradition (xvi–xxii). See also the transmission history of writings such as 2 Enoch, 3 Baruch, and the Apocalypse of Abraham in Slavonic traditions: Andrei Orlov, *Selected Studies in the Slavonic Pseudepigrapha*, SVTP 23 (Leiden: Brill, 2009); Alexander Kulik, *3 Baruch: Greek-Slavonic Apocalypse of Baruch*, CEJL (Berlin: de Gruyter, 2010). On the Armenian tradition, see the collection of ground-breaking studies by Michael E. Stone, *Apocrypha, Pseudepigrapha, and Armenian Studies: Collected Papers*, OLA, 3 vols. (Leuven: Peeters, 2006); see further, Stone, "Jewish Apocalyptic Literature in the Armenian Tradition"; Lorenzo DiTommaso, "The Armenian *Seventh Vision of Daniel* and the Historical Apocalyptica of Late Antiquity"; and Annette Yoshiko Reed, "Enoch in Armenian Apocrypha," in *The Armenian Apocalyptic Tradition: A Comparative Perspective*, ed. Kevork B. Bardakjian and Sergio La Porta (Leiden: Brill, 2014), 29–40, 126–48, 149–87, respectively. Within 1 Enoch, only the Ge'ez manuscripts preserve

many pseudepigraphal texts have been copied and preserved in monastic circles. This *may* indicate that the circulation of many of the pseudepigraphal texts was predominantly monastic and that monastic readers have been among their primary readers. However, it is also possible that the circulation has once been more comprehensive, but that substantial parts of the traces of such a broader circulation has been lost due to less fortunate conditions of preservation. Indeed, even if we assume a monastic production, this did not prevent manuscripts from being read and used in other settings as well. Monastic communities were never islands, and it well known that manuscripts were borrowed by others, for instance, to facilitate copying.

Fourth, as pointed out above, before the published collections of modern scholars,[25] pseudepigrapha never existed as a historically identifiable *collection* of writings in the sense that they were traditionally copied together in dedicated, bound volumes. On occasion, singular writings, or pairs of writings, were copied on their own.[26] On most occasions, though, copies of pseudepigraphal texts are found in conjunction

---

text from chs. 37–71 (Book of Parables), chs. 83–84 (the first vision of the Book of Dreams), and ch. 108 (Eschatological Admonition). In addition, the Ge'ez traditions preserves valuable additional material relating to texts found in other languages such as Jubilees, the Ascension of Isaiah, the Testament of Joseph, the Testaments of the Three Patriarchs, and Jannes and Jambres.

25. The category was introduced by Fabricius in 1713/1722. Well-known modern collections with varying numbers of writings and content have been made by E. Kautzsch, R. H. Charles, H. F. D. Sparks, and James H. Charlesworth. See also the more recent collection of additional (or neglected) works by Richard Bauckham, James R. Davila, and Alex Panayotov, eds., *Old Testament Pseudepigrapha: More Noncanonical Scriptures*, vol. 1 (Grand Rapids: Eerdmans, 2013).

26. Among examples of this would be the Arabic manuscript that contains (only) 2 Baruch and 4 Ezra (Mount Sinai Arabic 587), but this codex is probably best understood as one volume in a multivolume copying of the Old Testament. Among the many Ge'ez, examples of single copies of, e.g., 1 Enoch include Gunda Gunde 151, Remnant Trust, Petermann II Nachtrag 29, Parma 3843, while combinations with one other text are extant in EMML 8400 (with Dersane Gabriel, though secondary), IES 392 (with Jubilees), BM 485 (with Jubilees), and EMML 7922 (with Isaiah). As for Jubilees, in addition to the above examples, it could be combined with Daniel—so a bifolium at Adigrat Catholic Seminary no. 17 (fifteenth/sixteenth century). It should be noted, though, that many Old Testament codices would also contain just a selection of texts, sometimes just one writing (as is the case, for instance, with several codices containing the book/compendium of Jeremiah).

with writings scholars commonly identify as part of other corpora. Some writings identified today as pseudepigrapha were copied in biblical manuscripts of various sorts, most commonly Old Testament codices, and most commonly interspersed with other Old Testament writings. This is, for instance, the case with Jubilees, 4 Baruch, and 1 Enoch in the Ethiopian tradition; 2 Baruch and 4 Ezra in one preserved Syriac Old Testament manuscript; and the Testaments of the Twelve Patriarchs and Joseph and Aseneth in several Armenian biblical manuscripts.[27] Other pseudepigraphal texts, such as 3 Baruch and the Testament of Job, are preserved in manuscripts collecting hagiographical and homiletical writings.[28] Some collections of thematically related writings, or writings of similar genre, as, for instance, apocalypses, also include pseudepigraphal texts. Again, 3 Baruch is an example of a text that has been included in a manuscript in this capacity.[29] Some liturgical manuscripts

---

27. The Ethiopic tradition is replete with examples of all sorts of combinations of Old Testament/Hebrew Bible writings with one or more pseudepigrapha that include these texts. The book of Enoch (1 Enoch), for example, if not copied on its own or with one other work (such as Job, Jubilees, or a homily), could be combined with other prophetic texts (e.g. EMML 8292 = Tana 9, EMML 8433) and in many different combinations—and after the seventeenth century often at the beginning of manuscripts—with Old Testament texts and a smattering of other Second Temple literature (BM 491, AB 35, AB 55, EMML 1768, EMML 2080, EMML 2436, EMML 7584, EMML 8703, Church of Zion Aksum, Cambridge 1570), or even with a Christian text (i.e., with Qälementos in EMML 6281, with Dersane Gabriel in EMML 8400). On the presence of 4 Baruch alongside other writings (including 1 Enoch), see, e.g., EMML 6686, EMML 6706, and EMML 7584. Jubilees can appear alongside the Octateuch (EMML 7862, seventeenth century) or alongside at least Isaiah, the cycle of Jeremiah works in secondary combination (EMML 8671, sixteenth century?). For this and further information on Ge'ez Jubilees manuscripts, see Ted M. Erho and James Hamrick, "Ethiopic [Jubilees]," in Feder and Henze, *Deuterocanonical Writings*. For the Syriac, see Milan, Biblioteca Ambrosiana B. 21 Inf and bis Inf (Syriac Codex Ambrosianus). Cf. Lied, "2 Baruch and the Syriac Codex Ambrosianus." For the Armenian, see, Michael E. Stone, "The Armenian Apocryphal Literature: Translation and Creation," in *Apocrypha, Pseudepigrapha and Armenian Studies: Collected Papers*, 3 vols. (Leuven: Peeters, 2006), 1:105–37.

28. On this, see Daniel C. Harlow, "The Christianization of Early Jewish Pseudepigrapha: The Case of 3 Baruch," *JSJ* 32 (2001): 416–44; Kulik, *3 Baruch*, 7–8; Maria Haralambakis [Chioată], *The Testament of Job: Text, Narrative and Reception History*, LSTS 80 (London: Bloomsbury, 2012).

29. Daniel C. Harlow, *The Greek Apocalypse of Baruch (3 Baruch) in Hellenistic Judaism and Early Christianity*, SVTP 12 (Leiden: Brill, 1996).

contain pseudepigraphal texts, in the sense that they preserve copies of excerpted parts of these texts identified in headings as stemming from the larger writing. For instance, excerpts from Jubilees are found in Latin catena manuscripts; portions of 2 Baruch and 4 Ezra are found in Syriac lectionary manuscripts.[30] Manuscripts containing historiographical treatises display a similar practice. The excerpt from 4 Ezra in a Muslim manuscript, mentioned above, is part of an Arabic chronicle.[31] Excerpts from 1 Enoch can be explicitly identified as such: (1) EMML 2063 (late fifteenth century), among a number of other calendrically related and further texts, excerpts 1 En. 72; and (2) a Latin manuscript from the British Library (Royal MS 5 E XIII), excerpts 1 En. 106.1–18 alongside a list of notorious evildoers from the time of Adam until the crucifixion of Jesus, Josephus's account of cannibalism during the siege of Jerusalem in 70 CE (taken from *B.J.* 6.196, 201–213), and an account of the siege of Samaria in 2 Kgs 6:24–8:3. Aside from the very rare attempts to gather into a manuscript an entirety of the sacred tradition, no concerted effort can be discerned that transmits pseudepigrapha as a separate category. As the above examples suggest, the scribal traditions transmitting pseudepigraphal writings hardly reflect, if at all, a fixed literary- or collection-affiliation: they are often copied as part of and in conjunction with various collections of writings.

A *fifth* point, which a birds-eye view at manuscripts containing pseudepigrapha clearly demonstrates, is that these writings circulated in different formats. In scholarly communication, pseudepigraphal writings tend to be talked about as discrete works and compositional wholes—as "books." Accordingly, they are often listed by commentators or in introductory articles as texts that are extant in this or that manuscript, without information offered on their literary and, in this case, physical presentation.[32] Indeed, some of the pseudepigraphal texts are fruitfully approached

---

30. Jeremiah Coogan, "The Reception of Jubilees in a Fifth Century Catena of Genesis," in *Zeitschrift für antikes Christentum*, forthcoming; Liv Ingeborg Lied, "Nachleben and Textual Identity: Variants and Variance in the Reception History of 2 Baruch," in *Fourth Ezra and Second Baruch: Reconstruction after the Fall*, ed. Matthias Henze and Gabriele Boccaccini, JSJSup 164 (Leiden: Brill, 2013), 403–28. The Prayer of Manasseh is found, in full, for instance, in the Greek Books of Hours; see Ariel Gutman and Wido van Peursen, *The Two Syriac Versions of the Prayer of Manasseh*, Gorgias Eastern Christian Studies 30 (Piscataway NJ: Gorgias, 2012), 10.

31. Berlin, Staatsbibliothek, MS Berol. Sprenger 30.

32. This is the case, for instance, with the so-called Syriac manuscript of Jubi-

as such, or at least they exist in the book format in some surviving manuscripts. However, in many cases the book format may only account for one of the formats in which these writings are preserved. In surviving manuscripts, they often (also) appear in the shape of smaller layout units—identified, or not, with the larger book-entities. Smaller sections of writings, such as prayers, lists, lections, and autonomously circulating narrative units, were circulating independently or attached to other writings.[33] Adding to the complexity, several of the writings were transmitted in more than one form. Writings were copied in differing formats or with different interpretative solutions to parts of the storyline.[34] Sometimes, as is the case with the transmission of popular stories, such as the so-called Story of Melchizedek, the variation is substantial, and it would make more

---

lees (Alain Desreumaux, "Esquisse d'une liste d'œvres apocryphes syriaques," in *Les apocryphes syriaques*, ed. M. Debié, A. Desreumaux, C. Jullien, and F. Jullien, Études Syriaques 2 [Paris: Geuthner, 2005], 217–25), which is not a manuscript containing a copy of Jubilees, but rather a composite codex (London, British Library Add. 12154) containing a collection of various treatises, among them one that includes a list of the wives of the patriarchs ascribed to Jubilees in its rubric.

33. Prayers: See the Prayer of Manasseh, which is found attached to a wide range of other texts in differing collections. See Gutman and van Peursen, *Two Syriac Versions of the Prayer of Manasseh*, 6 and 10. This is potentially also the case with the prayer in 4 Ezra 8 in Paris, Bibliothèque nationale de France, Supplément turc 983 (folios 113/126). Lists: The names of the wives of the patriarchs, associated with Jubilees, are listed in London, British Library, 12154. Lections: Readings from 4 Ezra are, for instance, included in both Syriac and Georgian lectionary manuscripts. See Adam McCollum, "On 4 Ezra in Old Georgian, with a Synoptic Text Example of 5:22–30," hmmlorientalia, 12 September 2015, https://tinyurl.com/SBL3550d; Liv Ingeborg Lied and Matthew Phillip Monger, "Look to the East: New and Forgotten Sources of 4 Ezra," in *The Embroidered Bible: Studies in Biblical Apocrypha and Pseudepigrapha in Honour of Michael E. Stone*, ed. Lorenzo DiTommaso, Matthias Henze, and William Adler, SVTP 26 (Leiden: Brill, 2018), 639–52. Narrative units: One example is the story of the Maccabean mother (Shamuni) and her sons in Syriac transmission, in, e.g., London, British Library Add. 14732 and 12172. Another potential example is the Jubilees creation account which may have circulated independently; see Matthew Phillip Monger, "4Q216 and the State of Jubilees at Qumran," *RevQ* 104 (2014): 595–612.

34. This is the case with, for instance, the Testament of Solomon (Ryan Bailey, "Greek Manuscripts of the Testament of Solomon in the Biblioteca Apostolica Vaticana," in DiTommaso, Henze, and Adler, *Embroidered Bible*, 170–212) and the Prayer of Manasseh (Gutman and van Peursen, *The Two Syriac Versions of the Prayer of Manasseh*, 24–26).

sense to imagine them as clusters of texts, or compendia, rather than singular books.[35]

Sixth and finally, we must assume that a large part of the manuscripts that once contained pseudepigraphal texts are lost and that the manuscripts that remain only give us a very incomplete picture of any conceivable totality. Although papyrus and parchment have turned out to be surprisingly durable media, chemical decay, wear and tear, destructive events such as fire and flooding, and manuscripts going out of use and becoming irrelevant have by necessity done away with substantial numbers of the manuscripts that were once circulating. In general, manuscript preservation typically depends on a combination of factors such as climatic conditions; stable stewardship; the economic, traditional, or ritual value of the inscribed artefact; and the perceived religious or cultural importance of the texts copied in it. This means that manuscripts kept in the dry climate of Egypt or at the shores of the Dead Sea will have a greater chance of surviving than manuscripts circulating in regions subject to the vicissitudes of seasonal change. In other words, it is not a coincidence that many of the manuscripts that survive come from these regions. Likewise, manuscripts kept in curated archives, for instance, in monastic keeps, have a larger chance of coming down to us.[36] A substantial part of the surviving Syriac manuscripts, for instance, were for a long time preserved in the keeps of the Monastery of the Syrians in the Wadi al-Natrun (Scetis) in Egypt.[37] As most of the Geʿez manuscript in churches and monasteries of Ethiopia are dated to a thousand or more years after the initial translations were made from Greek, without there being much evidence for them during the intervening period, the ways writings were combined with one another in the earlier period are largely lost, while developing combinations of writings reflect the sociopolitical and religious exigencies sparked by events from the fourteenth to the seventeenth centuries (a period of particular interest for the scribal development of sacred tradition). The survival of pseudepigraphal texts may also have depended on the value and relevance ascribed to them and/or the material artefacts in which they were copied by those who engaged

---

35. William Adler, "The Story of Abraham and Melchizedek in the *Palaea Historica*," in DiTommaso, Henze, and Adler, *Embroidered Bible*, 48.

36. Himmelfarb, "Preservation of Second Temple Texts and Traditions."

37. Sebastian Brock, "Without Mushē of Nisibis, Where Would We Be? Some Reflections on the Transmission of Syriac Literature," *JECS* 56 (2004): 15–24.

the manuscripts. In other words, and as a general precaution, we must factor in that there is much we do not know and that we may not even know what we do not know.

If we still were to say something about the quantitative measures of the manuscripts containing pseudepigraphal texts based on the materials that have in fact survived (and not aiming for an impossible comprehensiveness), some features could be pointed out. A fair share of pseudepigraphal texts are singularly attested (e.g., the Testament of Moses) or surviving in a relatively limited number of manuscripts (e.g., 2 Baruch). Some of the texts have been preserved predominantly in one linguistic and cultural tradition (e.g., the Slavonic attestations of 2 Enoch), or, although attested elsewhere, seem to have played a particular role in one tradition (again, 2 Baruch among Syriac Christians). Yet other texts seem to have enjoyed a certain popularity and relevance, being copied in a broad range of languages and being adapted to a wide span of usages (1 Enoch). In other words, the manuscript attestation of various pseudepigraphal texts is varied. This is not surprising, given that these texts never constituted a historically identifiable collection, nor were ever copied as such.

2. Exploring the Manuscripts of the Pseudepigrapha: Challenges and Ways Forward

In many ways, manuscript copies have always played a key role in the history of research of pseudepigrapha as they were the very media that provided access to the literary texts in the first place. On several occasions a new manuscript find, or the retrieval of a manuscript in a known collection, marked the starting point of the study of a writing. And often, the work of scholars on a text is intimately linked to the history of study of a particular manuscript or a group of manuscripts. However, the scholarly use of and engagement with the manuscripts of pseudepigrapha is still relatively limited. The last decades have shown that new technological tools are allowing us to study manuscripts in new ways, while developing methodological and theoretical sensitivities hold the promise of engaging them with fresh perspectives and insights. With these developments in view, we conclude by indicating some of the gains and challenges that, beyond printed texts and editions, are associated with closer attention to manuscripts themselves. We also point out some ways forward.

2.1. Manuscripts as Witnesses to an Early Text Tradition or to a Complex Textual History

By far the most common scholarly usage of the manuscripts that preserve the pseudepigrapha has been to apply them as witnesses to an (assumedly) early text, or alternatively, to the history of a text. The manuscripts have been, and continue to be, studied primarily for the sake of recovering something external to them, that is, to texts so far not extant, or to versions, recensions, or shapes of texts hitherto unknown. The engagement with increasing numbers of manuscripts for given works may both aid and challenge this use of manuscripts.

First, the number of manuscripts that scholars can consult and study is steadily increasing. Thus far, the study of pseudepigraphal texts has often been based on a relatively small number of manuscripts. Many of the first critical editions of pseudepigraphal texts were produced in the mid- to late nineteenth and early twentieth century. At the time of their production, scholars generally had to rely on the manuscripts that were at hand in their national libraries or in other local collections, sometimes assisted by colleagues in other countries providing access to additional materials.[38] These early editions have turned out to be highly influential on the later imagination of the pseudepigraphal texts,[39] which in effect means that the scholarly conception of given writings that has developed in the field depends on the manuscripts that happened to be at hand to the pioneering scholars who published the first editions more than a century ago. During the last seventy years, however, a significant number of manuscripts has come to light, manuscripts that at times preserve versions, recensions and formats of the pseudepigraphal texts that were unknown

---

38. See, for instance, Antonio M. Ceriani's description of the manuscripts "qui ad manus erant" in "Apocalypsis Baruch Syriacae," in *Monumenta sacra et profana ex codicibus praesertim Bibliothecae Ambrosianae*, vol. 5.2 (Milan: Bibliotheca Ambrosianae Mediolani, 1868), 167. For a presentation of early manuscript acquisitions, see e.g., Columba Stewart, "Mine, Yours, or Theirs? Historical Observations on the Use, Collection and Sharing of Manuscripts in Western Europe and the Christian Orient," *Analecta Gorgiana* 126 (2009): 1–29. For a description of the technological and infrastructural constraints, see DiTommaso's essay in the current volume. See also Annette Yoshiko Reed's description of a transnational "Republic of Letters" in "The Modern Invention of 'Old Testament' Pseudepigrapha," 14.

39. See Eva Mroczek, *The Literary Imagination in Jewish Antiquity* (Oxford: Oxford University Press, 2016).

11. Pseudepigrapha and Their Manuscripts

to the first editors. The Dead Sea Scrolls are, of course, a primary example, but scholars have also increasingly gained access to collections containing additional Ethiopic, Armenian, and Slavonic manuscripts.[40] Untold numbers of Ethiopic manuscripts are still kept *in situ*, and some of the more significant of them that contain 1 Enoch and Jubilees have only been consulted since 2010. Other manuscript traditions, such as Arabic and Coptic, represent frontiers for research that deserve more attention.

Sometimes the seeming discovery of evidence has been a matter of gaining access to texts in manuscripts that have already been subjected to study. This has more recently been the case in particular with palimpsests as photographic, digitalization, and imaging techniques have undergone marked improvements. Two more recent instances of the recovery of erased texts have been carried out by the Early Manuscript Electronic Library team under the direction of Michael Phelps. In addition to its important work (2011–2017) on palimpsests at Saint Catharine's Monastery in the Sinai and in Vienna (2013),[41] Todd R. Hanneken's scholarly and organizational work, financed partly through a grant from the National Endowment of Humanities, has made it possible for the Early Manuscript Electronic Library, in 2016–2017 to recover (partly) unreadable fifth-century Latin undertexts for the Testament of Moses and Jubilees in Milan, Biblioteca Ambrosiana C 73 inf that, moreover, are leading to many improved readings of those texts.[42] Another manuscript in the Staatsbibliothek zu Berlin photographed by the Early Manuscript Electronic Library team, with funding provided by the Deutsche Forschungsgemeinschaft, carries the signature Petermann II Nachtrag 29. The upper text, dated to the seventeenth century, was identified and catalogued by August Dillmann in 1878. However, the undertext revealed by advanced imaging has been found for portions of 1 En. 82–84, 89, 99–100, and 103–104 (paleographically datable to the early sixteenth century) alongside remains of some further twelve writings (twelfth to fifteenth centuries).[43]

---

40. See, in particular, Stone, *Apocrypha, Pseudepigrapha and Armenian Studies*; Lorenzo DiTommaso and Christfried Böttrich, eds., *Old Testament Apocrypha in the Slavonic Traditions: Continuity and Diversity*, TSAJ 140 (Tübingen: Mohr Siebeck, 2011); Loren T. Stuckenbruck and Ted M. Erho, "The Manuscript History of *Ethiopic Enoch*," JSP 23 (2013): 87–133. For the Dead Sea Scrolls, see note 4, above.

41. For overviews of this work, see http://emel-library.org/projects-2.

42. Hanneken, "Book of Jubilees in Latin."

43. See Loren T. Stuckenbruck and Ira Rabin, "Die Entdeckung verlorener Texte:

When the increase of evidence for a given writing is significant, the question sometimes rises whether or not to attempt new reconstructions of earlier text-traditions. The new witnesses may for instance present better readings or solutions to textual problems. On yet other occasions, an increased amount of manuscripts may generate a larger repertoire of textual forms that in consequence may challenge the representation in previous editions of these writings as discrete works. Sometimes, the variation is so substantial that it may be more helpful to represent them as evolving stories, literary clusters, or plural books rather than to represent the variance in the shape of as a singular book.[44] Lorenzo DiTommaso has argued that digital editions may provide a solution to the challenges of editing texts that are too fluid to present in stemmatic or synoptic form, allowing the variance to be represented in digital mediation.[45] In both instances, the increased amount of manuscripts expands our knowledge about the ways in which pseudepigraphal texts were circulating and engaged and promises to enrich our understanding of them.

2.2. Manuscripts: Snapshots of Reception History and Circulation

The use of the manuscripts as witnesses to potential early texts remains their most common application. However, this is just one way in which a meaningful study of the manuscripts can be conducted. Since the 1990s, an increasing interest in manuscript transmission of texts *as reception* has developed. These studies explore the paths on which the texts circulated as intrinsic parts of surviving manuscript—that is, the material and social contexts in which they themselves were received.[46] Some of these

---

Foto- und Textarbeiten am Untertext einer altäthiopischen Handschrift," *Bibliotheksmagazin* 2/18 (2018): 72–76.

44. See Liv Ingeborg Lied, "Text—Work—Manuscript: What Is an 'Old Testament Pseudepigraphon'?," *JSP* 25 (2015): 150–65; Adler, "Story of Abraham and Melchizedek in the *Palaea Historica*," 57.

45. See DiTommaso's essay in the current volume.

46. See, in particular, Marinus de Jonge, *The Testament of the Twelve Patriarchs: A Study of Their Text Composition and Origin*, 2nd ed. (Assen: Van Gorcum, 1975); Michael E. Stone, "Methodological Issues in the Study of the Text of the Apocrypha and Pseudepigrapha," in *Selected Studies in Pseudepigrapha And Apocrypha, with Special Reference to the Armenian Tradition*, SVTP 9 (Leiden: Brill, 1991), 124–30; Reeves, "Exploring the Afterlife of Jewish Pseudepigrapha," 148–77; Harlow, *Greek Apocalypse of Baruch (3 Baruch) in Hellenistic Judaism*; David Satran, *Biblical Prophets in Byzan-*

studies have focused on the manuscripts as production objects, asking how a better understanding of the practices that shaped the manuscript may aid our study of the texts included in them. Scribal copies are among our primary sources to the diachronic process of circulation, adoption, and adaption of these texts. Close attention, where relevant, to different scribal hands that contributed to the text, notes on the content (whether commentary, alternative readings, or corrections, whether supralinear or in the margins), instructions on the text's use (e.g., for liturgical reading), and further indicators about the writing in its textual and codicological environment can reveal a great deal about the work as a living tradition and its importance to the community that received it. Even illumination styles that decorate the beginning of manuscripts can provide clues about the region or scribal tradition in which the works were transmitted; in some cases, it is possible that the common style (e.g., of harags) among different manuscripts reflects on a similar relationship among the texts they contain.[47] Such contextualizing factors, when they can be discerned, throw meaningful light on the times and socioreligious contexts in which the manuscripts were copied; indeed, before they can be used as referents to an external reality to be reconstructed, recognition of their contiguous and conditional nature opens windows into the relative value they were held to embody.

The manuscripts in which pseudepigraphal texts were copied may indicate some reasons for the circulation and spread of these writings, as well as provide some indications as to how they were identified, assessed, and interpreted in select communities and in particular historical settings. As the above-mentioned examples suggest, some of the writings are likely to have been perceived as biblical/scriptural, at least to those who produced the manuscripts that have them inscribed as such. For instance, and as suggested above, 2 Baruch's inclusion in an Old Testament codex and in lectionary manuscripts probably means that at least some of the Syriac Christian communities that copied it regarded it as an Old Testa-

---

tine Palestine: Reassessing the Lives of the Prophets, SVTP 11 (Leiden: Brill, 1995); Lied, "2 Baruch and the Syriac Codex Ambrosianus (7a1)."

47. For a nuanced correspondence between illuminatory style and a textual family, see Loren T. Stuckenbruck, "Witnesses to the Ethiopic I Recension of *Mashafa Henok* from Gunda Gunde: A Comparison," in *Studies in Ethiopian Languages, Literature and History: Festschrift for Getatchew Haile*, ed. Adam Carter McCollum, ÄthF 83 (Wiesbaden: Harrassowitz, 2017), 473–92.

ment text. Manuscripts including 1 Enoch (and other pseudepigrapha) alongside one or more sacred writings associated with the Old Testament suggest the same.[48] Likewise, when we come across pseudepigraphal writings as part of hagiographical or homiletic collections, it is indeed likely that they have been understood as such by those who decided to include them in those collections.[49]

Some other studies of manuscript transmission as reception have explored the manuscripts as circulation objects. Manuscripts are movable objects, and at times the history of a manuscript in time and space can be traced. Studies of manuscripts as circulation objects take interest in verbal and other traces of active readers of the texts, asking how the texts may have been engaged by later readers who came across the texts in this particular material embodiment. For instance, active readers have sometimes added liturgical notes in the margins of texts where there originally were none to aid the liturgical use of the text. This is the case in an Ethiopic manuscript containing 1 Enoch (EMML 8400), suggesting that later readers facilitated the liturgical reading of sections of this text.[50] At other occasions, we can trace the history of a manuscript over several centuries and explore the variety of functions former owners ascribed to it. Notes in the Syriac Old Testament manuscript that includes 2 Baruch and 4 Ezra suggest that over the years this codex has been considered a valuable donation, a treasure worth protecting, an aid for monastic study, a liturgical artefact, a Muster codex, and an efficient medium of prayer requests ensuring the afterlives of the note writers—in addition to being an Old Testament. The texts inscribed in the manuscripts were not foreign to the practices in which the manuscripts were a part. They were intrinsic to the inscribed artefacts, and the various sematic, performative, and iconic functions their stewards ascribed to them. Studies of such materialized circulation of and engagement with pseudepigraphal texts are still in an early phase but may add more and other knowledge about the engagement with these writings.

---

48. See note 27, above.

49. This is less certain, of course, in the case of secondary compilations of texts in which writings copied by different scribes and times have been assembled into a manuscript due, for example, to comparable size rather than a match in genre or status.

50. Stuckenbruck and Erho, "EMML 8400 and Notes on the Reading of Hēnok in Ethiopia."

Conclusion

The discussion above has underscored the significance of manuscripts of pseudepigraphal writings as witnesses not only to diachronic but also to synchronic realities. With this in mind, we are in a position to conclude by highlighting two important methodological points. First, it should be noted that the manuscripts we study as sources to the reception of the text are the same manuscripts that for generations have been applied as witnesses to the early text. In other words, and in effect, we apply the same source to talk about the received text as we do to talk about an assumed ancient text, or put differently, the only sources available to us are the received texts and their development cannot easily be disentangled from their receiving contexts.[51] The burden on interpretation lies, then, in the extent to which a plausible case can be made for the contextualization of such writings in a more ancient setting than the one to which they, as much later copies, are more immediately linked. Such dedicated studies of the manuscripts address the longstanding debate about the Christian transmission of pseudepigrapha,[52] highlighting the methodological challenges involved in using predominantly medieval Christian manuscripts as sources to texts assumed to have originated in Jewish antiquity. As pointed out above, the manuscripts can sometimes be more than a millennium younger than the assumed composition or even initial translation of the writing. These considerations are especially significant when such late manuscripts comprise our only potential witnesses to a work.

Second, the ethical consequences of applying the manuscripts primarily as detached witnesses to earlier texts should also be acknowledged. As pointed out initially, the manuscripts that contain pseudepigrapha are typically the cultural products of medieval, Christian, communities, whereas scholars of these texts have typically been interested in exploring the texts as ancient and Jewish. Such use does not match the nature of the manuscript and the context to which it points, with scholars depending thoroughly on the cultural products of other communities than the ones to which the literary texts are commonly ascribed.[53] As these manuscripts

---

51. Adler, "Story of Abraham and Melchizedek," 56–58.
52. See, emblematically, Robert A. Kraft, "The Pseudepigrapha in Christianity," in *Tracing the Threads: Studies in the Vitality of the Jewish Pseudepigrapha*, ed. John C. Reeves, EJL 6 (Atlanta: Scholars Press, 1994), 55–86.
53. See Liv Ingeborg Lied, "Textual Scholarship, Ethics, and Someone Else's Man-

have a role to play in learning about living traditions, their significance amounts to much more than haphazard containers of detached texts.

To be sure, more recent approaches to interpret manuscripts as windows into *their own* material and socioreligious and cultural settings do not render their use as sources for more ancient traditions obsolete. Those who copied texts were participating in a long-standing and sometimes vast and complicated process of transmission, much of which they may not have been aware. At the same time, if the first point of departure for scholarship is to determine what can be known about a manuscript and to take it seriously *in itself*, then it is precisely here where study has to begin and, when there is a dearth of evidence otherwise, perhaps to find its conclusion.

Bibliography

Adler, William. "The Story of Abraham and Melchizedek in the *Palaea Historica*." Pages 47–63 in *The Embroidered Bible: Studies in Biblical Apocrypha and Pseudepigrapha in Honour of Michael E. Stone*. Edited by Lorenzo DiTommaso, Matthias Henze, and William Adler. SVTP 26. Leiden: Brill, 2018.

Bailey, Ryan. "Greek Manuscripts of the Testament of Solomon in the Biblioteca Apostolica Vaticana." Pages 170–212 in *The Embroidered Bible: Studies in Biblical Apocrypha and Pseudepigrapha in Honour of Michael E. Stone*. Edited by Lorenzo DiTommaso, Matthias Henze, and William Adler. SVTP 26. Leiden: Brill, 2018.

Bauckham, Richard, James R. Davila, and Alex Panayotov, eds. *Old Testament Pseudepigrapha: More Noncanonical Scriptures*. Vol. 1. Grand Rapids: Eerdmans, 2013.

Black, Matthew. *Apocalypsis Henochi Graece*. PVTG 3. Leiden: Brill, 1970.

Bremer-McCollum, Adam. "Notes and Colophons of Scribes and Readers in Georgian Biblical Manuscripts from Saint Catherine's Monastery (Sinai)." Pages 111–24 in *Bible as Notepad: Tracing Annotations and Annotation Practices in Late Antique and Medieval Biblical Manuscripts*. Edited by Liv Ingeborg Lied and Marilena Maniaci. Manuscripta Biblica 3. Berlin: de Gruyter, 2018.

---

uscripts" (paper presented at the Annual Meeting of the Society of Biblical Literature, Denver, CO, 18 November 2018).

Brock, Sebastian. "Without Mushē of Nisibis, Where Would We Be? Some Reflections on the Transmission of Syriac Literature." *JECS* 56 (2004): 15–24.

Ceriani, Antonio M., ed. *Monumenta sacra et profana ex codicibus praesertim Bibliothecae Ambrosianae*. Vol. 5.2. Milan: Bibliotheca Ambrosianae Mediolani, 1868.

Desreumaux, Alain. "Esquisse d'une liste d'œvres apocryphes syriaques." Pages 217–25 in *Les apocryphes syriaques*. Edited by M. Debié, A. Desreumaux, C. Jullien, and F. Jullien. Études Syriaques 2. Paris: Geuthner, 2005.

Dillmann, August. *Das Buch Henoch*. Leipzig: Vogel, 1853.

DiTommaso, Lorenzo. "The Armenian *Seventh Vision of Daniel* and the Historical Apocalyptica of Late Antiquity." Pages 126–48 in *The Armenian Apocalyptic Tradition: A Comparative Perspective*. Edited by Kevork B. Bardakjian and Sergio La Porta. Leiden: Brill, 2014.

DiTommaso, Lorenzo, and Christfried Böttrich, eds. *Old Testament Apocrypha in the Slavonic Traditions: Continuity and Diversity*. TSAJ 140. Tübingen: Mohr Siebeck, 2011.

Drint, Adrina. "The Mount Sinai Arabic Version of IV Ezra: Text, Translation and Introduction." PhD diss., Rijksuniversitet Groningen, 1995.

Edrei, Arye, and Doron Mendels. "A Split Jewish Diaspora: Its Dramatic Consequences." *JSP* 16 (2007): 91–137.

Fabricius, Johan A. *Codex Pseudepigraphus Veteris Testamenti: Collectus, castigatus, testimoniisque, censuris et animaduersionibus illustrates*. Hamburg: Felginer, 1713); 2nd ed., *Codicis pseudepigraphi Veteris Testamenti: Volumen Alterum Accedit Josephi Veteris Christiani Auctoria Hypomnesticon*. Hamburg: Felginer, 1722–1723.

Fröhlich, Ida. "The Dead Sea Scrolls and Geniza Studies." Pages 61–67 in *David Kaufmann Memorial Volume: Papers Presented at the David Kaufmann Memorial Conference, November 29 1999*. Edited by Éva Apor. Budapest: Library of the Hungarian Academy of Sciences, 2002.

Goff, Matthew J., Loren T. Stuckenbruck, and Enrico Morano, eds. *Ancient Tales of Giants from Qumran and Turfan*. WUNT 360. Tübingen: Mohr Siebeck, 2016.

Grenfell, Bernhard P., and Arthur S. Hunt. "403. Apocalypse of Baruch, XII–XIV." Pages 3–7 in vol. 3 of *The Oxyrhynchus Papyri*. London: Egypt Exploration Fund, 1903.

Gutman, Ariel, and Wido van Peursen. *The Two Syriac Versions of the Prayer of Manasseh*. Gorgias Eastern Christian Studies 30. Piscataway NJ: Gorgias, 2012.

Hanneken, Todd R. "The Book of Jubilees in Latin." In *Deuterocanonical Writings*, vol. 2 of *The Textual History of the Bible*. Edited by Frank Feder and Matthias Henze. Leiden: Brill, forthcoming.

Haralambakis [Chioată], Maria. *The Testament of Job: Text, Narrative and Reception History*. LSTS 80. London: Bloomsbury, 2012.

Harlow, Daniel C. "The Christianization of Early Jewish Pseudepigrapha: The Case of 3 Baruch." *JSJ* 32 (2001): 416–44.

———. *The Greek Apocalypse of Baruch (3 Baruch) in Hellenistic Judaism and Early Christianity*. SVTP 12. Leiden: Brill, 1996.

Henning, W. B. "The Book of Giants." *BSOAS* 11 (1943): 52–74.

Himmelfarb, Martha. "Preservation of Second Temple Texts and Traditions in Rabbinic and Post-rabbinic Jewish Transmission." In *A Guide to Early Jewish Texts and Traditions in Christian Transmission*. Edited by Alexander Kulik, Gabriele Boccaccini, Lorenzo DiTommaso, David Hamidovic, and Michael E. Stone. Oxford: Oxford University Press, forthcoming.

Jonge, Marinus de. *The Testament of the Twelve Patriarchs: A Study of Their Text Composition and Origin*. 2nd ed. Assen: Van Gorcum, 1975.

Kister, Menachem. "Ancient Material in *Pirqe De-Rabbi Eli'Ezer*: Basilides, Qumran, the Book of Jubilees." Pages 69–93 in *'Go Out and Study the Land' (Judges 18:2): Archaeological, Historical and Textual Studies in Honor of Hanan Eshel*. Edited by Aren M. Maeir, Jodi Magness, and Lawrence H. Schiffman. JSJSup 148. Leiden: Brill, 2012.

Koningsveld, P. Sj. van. "An Arabic Manuscript of the Apocalypse of Baruch." *JSJ* 6 (1974–1975): 205–7.

Kraft, Robert A. "The Pseudepigrapha in Christianity." Pages 55–86 in *Tracing the Threads: Studies in the Vitality of the Jewish Pseudepigrapha*. Edited by John C. Reeves. EJL 6. Atlanta: Scholars Press, 1994.

Kulik, Alexander. *3 Baruch: Greek-Slavonic Apocalypse of Baruch*. CEJL. Berlin: de Gruyter, 2010.

Kulik, Alexander, and Sergey Minov. *Biblical Pseudepigrapha in Slavonic Tradition*. Oxford: Oxford University Press, 2016.

Labendz, Jenny R. "The Book of Ben Sira in Rabbinic Literature." *AJSR* 30 (2006): 347–92.

Lied, Liv Ingeborg. "2 Baruch and the Syriac Codex Ambrosianus (7a1): Studying Old Testament Pseudepigrapha in Their Manuscript Context." *JSP* 26 (2016): 67–107.

———. "Nachleben and Textual Identity: Variants and Variance in the Reception History of 2 Baruch." Pages 403–28 in *Fourth Ezra and Second Baruch: Reconstruction after the Fall*. Edited by Matthias Henze and Gabriele Boccaccini. JSJSup 164. Leiden: Brill, 2013.

———. "Text—Work—Manuscript: What Is an 'Old Testament Pseudepigraphon'?" *JSP* 25 (2015): 150–65.

———. "Textual Scholarship, Ethics, and Someone Else's Manuscripts." Paper presented at the Annual Meeting of the Society of Biblical Literature, Denver, CO, 18 November 2018.

Lied, Liv Ingeborg, and Hugo Lundhaug, eds. *Snapshots of Evolving Traditions: Jewish and Christian Manuscript Culture, Textual Fluidity, and New Philology*. TUGAL 175. Berlin: de Gruyter, 2017.

Lied, Liv Ingeborg, and Matthew Phillip Monger. "Look to the East: New and Forgotten Sources of 4 Ezra." Pages 639–52 in *The Embroidered Bible: Studies in Biblical Apocrypha and Pseudepigrapha in Honour of Michael E. Stone*. Edited by Lorenzo DiTommaso, Matthias Henze, and William Adler. SVTP 26. Leiden: Brill, 2018.

McCollum, Adam. "On 4 Ezra in Old Georgian, with a Synoptic Text Example of 5:22–30." hmmlorientalia, 12 September 2015. https://tinyurl.com/SBL3550d.

Mendels, Doron, and Aryeh Edrei. *Zweierlei Diaspora: Zur Spaltung der antiken jüdischen Welt*. Göttingen: Vandenhoeck & Ruprecht, 2009.

Milik, Józef T. *The Books of Enoch: Aramaic Fragments of Qumrân Cave 4*. Oxford: Clarendon, 1976.

Monger, Matthew Phillip. "4Q216 and the State of Jubilees at Qumran." *RevQ* 104 (2014): 595–612.

Morano, Enrico. "New Research on Mani's Book of Giants." Pages 101–12 in *Der östliche Manichäismus: Gattungs- und Werkgeschichte*. Edited by Z. Özertural and J. Wilckens. AAWG NS 17. Berlin: de Gruyter, 2011.

———. "Sogdian Tales in Manichean Script." Pages 173–200 in *Literarische Stoffe und ihre Gestaltung in mitteliranischer Zeit*. Edited by D. Durkin-Meisterernst, C. Reck, and D. Weber. Wiesbaden: Harrassowitz, 2009.

Mroczek, Eva. *The Literary Imagination in Jewish Antiquity*. Oxford: Oxford University Press, 2016.

Odeberg, Hugo. *3 Enoch or the Hebrew Book of Enoch*. Cambridge: Cambridge University Press, 1923.

Orlov, Andrei. *Selected Studies in the Slavonic Pseudepigrapha*. SVTP 23. Leiden: Brill, 2009.

Pregill. Michael "Isra'iliyyat, Myth, and Pseudepigraphy: Wahb b. Munabbih and the Early Islamic Version of the Fall of Adam and Eve." *JSAI* 34 (2008): 215–84.

Reed, Annette Yoshiko. "Enoch in Armenian Apocrypha." Pages 149–87 in *The Armenian Apocalyptic Tradition: A Comparative Perspective*. Edited by Kevork B. Bardakjian and Sergio La Porta. Leiden: Brill, 2014.

———. "Fallen Angels and the Afterlives of Enochic Traditions in Early Islam." In *Early Islam: The Sectarian Milieu of Late Antiquity? Proceedings of the Fourth Nangeroni Meeting*. Edited by G. Dye. Chicago: The Oriental Institute, forthcoming.

———. "The Modern Invention of 'Old Testament Pseudepigrapha.'" *JTS* 60 (2009): 403–36.

Reeves, John R. "Exploring the Afterlife of Jewish Pseudepigrapha in Medieval Near Eastern Religious Traditions: Some Initial Soundings." *JSJ* 30.2 (1999): 148–77.

Satran, David. *Biblical Prophets in Byzantine Palestine: Reassessing the Lives of the Prophets*. SVTP 11. Leiden: Brill, 1995.

Stewart, Columba. "Mine, Yours, or Theirs? Historical Observations on the Use, Collection and Sharing of Manuscripts in Western Europe and the Christian Orient." *Analecta Gorgiana* 126 (2009): 1–29.

Stone, Michael E. *Apocrypha, Pseudepigrapha, and Armenian Studies: Collected Papers*. OLA. 3 vols. Leuven: Peeters, 2006.

———. "Jewish Apocalyptic Literature in the Armenian Tradition." Pages 29–40 in *The Armenian Apocalyptic Tradition: A Comparative Perspective*. Edited by Kevork B. Bardakjian and Sergio La Porta. Leiden: Brill, 2014.

———. "Methodological Issues in the Study of the Text of the Apocrypha and Pseudepigrapha." Pages 124–30 in *Selected Studies in Pseudepigrapha And Apocrypha, with Special Reference to the Armenian Tradition*. SVTP 9. Leiden: Brill, 1991.

———. "The Testament of Naphtali." *JJS* 47 (1996): 311–21.

Stuckenbruck, Loren T. "Apocrypha and Pseudepigrapha." *EDEJ* 152–56.

———. "Witnesses to the Ethiopic I Recension of *Mashafa Henok* from Gunda Gunde: A Comparison." Pages 473–92 in *Studies in Ethiopian*

Languages, Literature and History: Festschrift for Getatchew Haile. Edited by Adam Carter McCollum. ÄthF 83. Wiesbaden: Harrassowitz, 2017.
Stuckenbruck, Loren T., and Ted M. Erho. "EMML 8400 and Notes on the Reading of *Hēnok* in Ethiopia." Pages 125–29 in *Bible as Notepad: Tracing Annotations and Annotation Practices in Late Antique and Medieval Biblical Manuscripts*. Edited by Liv Ingeborg Lied and Marilena Maniaci. Manuscripta Biblica 3. Berlin: de Gruyter, 2018.
———. "The Manuscript History of *Ethiopic Enoch*." *JSP* 23 (2013): 87–133.
Stuckenbruck, Loren T., and Ira Rabin. "Die Entdeckung verlorener Texte: Foto- und Textarbeiten am Untertext einer altäthiopischen Handschrift." *Bibliotheksmagazin* 2/18 (2018): 72–76.
Sundermann, Werner. "Ein weiteres Fragment aus Manis Gigantenbuch." Pages 491–505 in *Orientalia J. Duchesne-Guillemin emerito oblata*. Acta Iranica 23. Leiden: Brill, 1984.
VanderKam, James C. "The Manuscript Tradition of Jubilees." Pages 3–22 in *Enoch and the Mosaic Torah: The Evidence of Jubilees*. Edited by Gabriele Boccaccini and Giovanni Ibba. Grand Rapids: Eerdmans, 2009.
Wilckens, Jens. "Funktion und gattungsgeschichtliche Bedeutung des manichäischen Gigantenbuchs." Pages 63–88 in *Der östliche Manichäismus: Gattungs- und Werkgeschichte*. Edited by Z. Özertural and J. Wilckens. AAWG NS 17. Berlin: de Gruyter, 2011.
———. "Neue Fragmente aus Manis Gigantenbuch." *ZDMG* 150 (2000): 133–76.

12
Manuscript Research in the Digital Age

Lorenzo DiTommaso

In memoriam M. R. James

Normally overlooked in accounts of the history of manuscript research, technological innovation in fact constitutes a deep change that informs every level of investigation. The outstanding illustration is the digital revolution, which has transformed manuscript studies in the twenty-first century.[1]

This paper investigates the effects of the digital revolution on the practice and results of manuscript research.[2] Its lens is apocryphal literature,

---

I presented an early version of this paper at the Herzog August Bibliothek in 2016. I am indebted to Dr. Jill Bepler for facilitating the talk and arranging my stay as a research fellow. Research for this paper was underwritten by 2011–2016 and 2018–2023 grants from the Social Sciences and Humanities Research Council of Canada. Garrick Allen, David Calabro, Todd Hanneken, Brandon W. Hawk, Matthias Henze, Michael Johnson, Matthias Kaup, Liv Ingeborg Lied, Hugo Lundhaug, Andrew W. Perrin, Ira Rabin, Enrico Raffaelli, Loren Stuckenbruck, Michael E. Stone, Alin Suciu, and Charles D. Wright each read early drafts and offered valuable suggestions and comments, for which I am grateful. Any inaccuracies that remain are my own. Internet links cited in this paper are current as of 1 October 2018.

1. The bedrock change is from analog computing, storage, and communication technologies to digital ones and its knock-on economic, social, and cultural effects. *Digital* here refers both to the technologies and to their applications and outcomes. *Digitalization* is the process of converting information into digital form.

2. This topic has largely escaped scholarly notice, despite much fine work on the impact of the new technologies on other aspects of medieval manuscripts and manuscript culture. I have found the following studies to be particularly useful: Stilyana Batalova, "Manuscript Catalogues and Manuscripts via Internet," *Scripta & e-Scripta* 3–4 (2006): 25–28; Kristian S. Heal, "Digital Humanities and the Study of Christian Apocrypha: Resources, Prospects and Problems," in *Forbidden Texts on the Western*

with a focus on the pseudepigrapha specifically. This large and diverse aggregate of texts and traditions offers an ideal test case by which the transformative impact of the new communications technologies on manuscript research may be identified and measured.

My approach is that of an end-user scholar.[3] The primary objects of my examination are the literary contents of the manuscripts. Digital technology has, of course, also transformed the study of palaeography, codicology, pastedowns, bindings, and so on, as well as how manuscripts are archived, stored, and curated. These subjects fall outside my expertise, however, and my comments on them are therefore minimal.

Pseudepigrapha scholars are above all literary specialists.[4] The subjects of their research are the apocryphal texts and traditions that are attributed to or associated with figures from the Hebrew Bible/Old Testament.[5] The

---

Frontier, ed. Tony Burke (Eugene, OR: Cascade, 2015), 270–78; and the essays in W. Th. van Peursen, Ernst D. Thoutenhoofd, and Adriaan van der Weel, eds., *Text Comparison and Digital Creativity: The Production of Presence and Meaning in Digital Text Scholarship* (Leiden: Brill, 2010); Tara Andrews and Caroline Macé, eds., *Analysis of Ancient and Medieval Texts and Manuscripts: Digital Approaches*, Lectio 1 (Turnhout: Brepols, 2014); Claire Clivaz, et al., eds., *Digital Humanities in Ancient Jewish, Christian and Arabic Traditions, Journal of Religion, Media and Digital Culture* 5.1 (2016); Jennifer E. Boyle and Helen J. Burgess, eds., *The Routledge Research Companion to Digital Medieval Literature* (New York: Routledge, 2017); and David J. Birnbaum, Sheila Bonde, and Mike Kestemont, eds., *The Digital Middle Ages: An Introduction*, *Speculum* 92.S1 (2017). See also Liv Ingeborg Lied, "Digitization and Manuscripts as Visual Objects: Reflections from a Media Studies Perspective" (paper presented at the Annual Meeting of the Society of Biblical Literature, Atlanta, GA, 24 November 2015), which the author kindly shared with me. Among the many research projects, see the University of Toronto's Digital Tools for Manuscript Study (digitaltoolsmss.library.utoronto.ca) and the sources cited in note 18, below.

3. The observations made in this paper are based on my experience with Latin, Greek, and Western vernacular manuscripts, plus some Slavonic and Hebrew/Aramaic ones. For the record, insofar as it informs my observations, I have visited over one hundred manuscript libraries in Europe and North America, many of them multiple times. I have photographed at half these libraries and ordered or downloaded images from virtually all of them, and also from over one hundred other libraries. My experience with non-Western manuscripts is as an amateur only, as is my sense of the effects of the digital revolution on research in those areas.

4. This (and what follows) is true also for scholars of the New Testament apocrypha/Écrits apocryphes chrétiens, as well as pseudonymous writings in general (e.g., spurious tracts of Plato, Augustine, Joachim of Fiore).

5. These works are either Second-Temple Jewish in origin (but were preserved

principal medium for these texts and traditions is the medieval manuscript (ca. 500–1500 CE). *Manuscript* here describes a spectrum of media on which these writings are preserved. This includes codices, bound quires, and loose sheets; rolls (open up-down) and scrolls (open sideways); and fragments, flyleaves, old bindings, cartonnage, and other scraps. The writing material is typically animal skin, prepared for the purpose. Also common are papyrus and, in the West from the fifteenth century, paper.[6]

The foundational task of pseudepigrapha research is to locate and consult the manuscripts in order to identify texts and traditions that might be germane to one's investigation and to disseminate the results of research via scholarly channels. The task may be formulated in informational terms, that is, the identification, verification, and transfer of relevant literary data (the writings) from their source (the manuscripts) to a personal storage medium, followed by broadcast via academic books and articles.

The history of pseudepigrapha research (and biblical apocrypha, generally) can be divided into four phases that reflect major shifts in the concept of the pseudepigrapha as a category and corpus: (1) the age of Scipione Sgambati, Johann Fabricius, and the maximalist origins of the category (early 1700s to the 1850s);[7] (2) the golden age of research and the

---

and often reworked in later Christian milieus) or early Christian. In both cases, the main vehicle for their survival is the medieval Christian manuscript. Notable premedieval exceptions are the apocryphal texts preserved in the Dead Sea Scrolls or late-antique Christian papyri. For more on these texts, see my comments in the section on "Dissemination" below. Apocryphal traditions in the premodern world are also expressed in graphic formats, including manuscript illumination, engraving and woodcut illustration, painting, wall fresco, mosaic, paving stone, stone and wood sculpture, *pietra dura*, stained glass, porcelain, and tile. Short texts sometimes accompany such illustrations.

6. Apocryphal works are also preserved in early print- and block-books, whose emergence in the fifteenth century coincides with the invention and widespread use of paper in western Europe and in pamphlets and broadsheets, particularly in the two centuries that followed. In private conversation, Michael E. Stone informs me about Armenian books constituted from long sheets of paper that have been folded concertina-wise. In very rare cases the writing material is stone or metal. The study of early print culture has been affected by the digital revolution no less than that of manuscripts.

7. Scipione Sgambati, *Archiuorum Veteris Testamenti libri tres; De rebus ad Deum spectantibus; De primis patribus; De uiris illustribus in Veteri Testamento* (Napoles: Mutio, 1703); Johann A. Fabricius, *Codex apocryphus Novi Testamenti* (Hamburg: Schiller, 1703; second, rev. ed. 1719); and Fabricius, *Codex pseudepigraphus Veteris*

minimalist drift (the 1850s to 1914); (3) the silver age renaissance and its controlled reexpansion of the category (late 1960s to mid-1990s);[8] and (4) the age of reception history and a return to an uncontrolled, maximalist corpus of the pseudepigrapha (mid-1990s to the present day).[9]

Each phase in the research is marked by an approach to the manuscripts that was determined in part by the available technology. Eighteenth-century pioneers such as Sgambati and Fabricius had access to manuscript collections where they lived and worked, supplemented by rare trips to consult manuscripts in other regions. Mainly, however, they relied on prodigious amounts of reading and tended not to approach the manuscripts (or the texts that they preserved) in a diagnostic fashion. Finding aids, including manuscript catalogues,[10] took the form of index cards or ledgers and were typically hand-written and meant to be consulted *in situ*. Scholarly research was communicated mainly via printed books (often massive, multivolume works) and copious personal correspondence with their peers in the Republic of Letters.

The golden age of pseudepigrapha research that followed was animated by the text-critical spirit that developed during the second half of the nineteenth century. Its focus was on the scrupulous examination of old sources and the recovery of new ones.[11] This methodology is exemplified in the work of Constantin von Tischendorf, August Dillmann, Nikolai Tikhonravov, Paul Meyer, Nathaniel Bonwetsch, Robert Henry Charles, and Montague Rhodes James, among many others. James also was a

---

Testamenti: Collectus, castigatus, testimoniisque, censuris et animaduersionibus illustratus (Hamburg: C. Liebezeit, 1713).

8. See Michael E. Stone's contribution to this volume for a first-hand reflection of the excitement that scholars felt during the heady first decade of the rediscovery of the pseudepigrapha.

9. Lorenzo DiTommaso, "The 'Old Testament Pseudepigrapha' as Category and Corpus," in *A Guide to Early Jewish Texts and Traditions in Christian Transmission*, ed. Alexander Kulik (Oxford: Oxford University Press, 2019), 253–79.

10. These tend to be hand-lists instead of true catalogues and are often organized by topic rather than class- or shelf-mark, the latter an obstacle to research that was overcome only with digitalization. Many old catalogues of manuscripts in Italian libraries are available online courtesy of the Istituto Centrale per il Catalogo Unico delle Biblioteche Italiane e per le Informazioni Bibliografiche (cataloghistorici.bdi.sbn.it).

11. So Arnaldo D. Momigliano, "A Hundred Years after Ranke," *Studies in Historiography* (1966): 105–11, referring to historical studies in general.

manuscript cataloguer, and it is no coincidence that the first modern catalogues appeared during this period, part of a concentrated effort to make the manuscript holdings of libraries known to scholars.[12] Meanwhile, the steam engine expedited research travel by rail and by ship, while emerging state postal systems and the advent of the scientific journal aided the acquisition of information and the dissemination of results.

And the manuscripts were there, awaiting discovery—in the monasteries, in the private collections, and, above all, in the new national libraries. James's exhortation to his colleagues in the preface to the first volume of his *Apocrypha Anecdota* (1893) captures the excitement of the age:

> This collection of documents represents the result of three years' gleaning in English and foreign libraries, carried on by no means continuously, and extending over no very wide field. Oxford, London, Cheltenham, Paris and Trèves have furnished all the material, and even under these conditions more has been collected than appears here. The moral of these remarks is plain: if a not very systematic research adds as many as thirteen new documents to the apocryphal literature, how much more may be waiting in very accessible places for future explorers![13]

In the late 1960s, after a fifty-year stretch of academic indifference, pseudepigrapha research underwent a second resurgence, one that has continued unabated to the present day. Technological advancement was one of the many contributing factors that led to this silver age. Most significant was the widespread use of image reproduction in microfilm/fiche formats. Scholars of that era were able to consult scans of pages from microfilmed manuscripts that could be sent by post or consulted at new, large microfilm libraries in North America.[14] Microfilm technology also

---

12. The era witnessed the wholescale cataloguing of the public, private, and university manuscript collections, as well as the appearance of the first national catalogues. In France, the publication of the first series of the *Catalogue général des manuscrits des bibliothèques publiques de France* commenced in 1849, followed by the more comprehensive second series in 1886. In Britain, the Historical Manuscripts Commission, appointed under Royal Warrant in 1869, oversaw the publication of multiple volumes, mostly involving manuscripts in the great private collections. In Italy, the first volume of the *Inventari dei manoscritti delle biblioteche d'Italia* appeared in 1890.

13. M. R. James, preface to *Apocrypha Anecdota I* (Cambridge: Cambridge University Press, 1893), vii. Cheltenham was the location of the great Phillipps collection, now dispersed. Trèves is, of course, Trier.

14. The British Manuscripts Project was undertaken in 1941–1945 by the Ameri-

facilitated the reproduction and circulation of manuscript catalogues and multivolume reference works to university libraries. A parade example is F. Edward Cranz's *Microfilm Corpus of Unpublished Inventories of Latin Manuscripts before 1600*.[15] At the same time, xerographic machines enabled scholars to photocopy material in their university libraries for use in their offices or at their homes, while the advent of reliable library inter-lending systems offered them access to libraries elsewhere, especially across North America. Increasing access to jet travel, in part a result of the deregulation of the industry, along with the integration of rail networks, particularly in western Europe, enabled a greater number of scholars (in no small part a result of the postwar hiring boom and the slew of newly created PhD programmes) to visit manuscript libraries and examine their holdings.[16]

Yet for all this, the silver age was an analog age. Scholars consulted paper reference volumes and catalogues, transcribed manuscript texts onto paper notes, made paper photocopies, ordered paper scans of microfilm images, typed their research on sheets of paper, distributed papers at conferences, read society transactions on paper newsletters, published their work in paper volumes and articles, and did the bulk of their research in libraries while consulting paper books and journals. The inertial drag of all this paper imposed a speed-limit on research that was enforced by the

---

can Council of Learned Societies under the direction of L. K. Born and was followed by similar projects in the libraries and monasteries of postwar Europe. The great international delegate microfilm repositories also took shape during this period. The Institute of Microfilmed Hebrew Manuscripts at the National Library of Israel traces its history to 1950. In the United States, the Vatican Film Library (VFL) at Saint Louis University was established in 1959 ("in case of an atomic attack on Europe," so I was told when a research fellow there), the first of the Biblioteca Ambrosiana microfilms arrived at the Notre Dame's Medieval Institute in 1962, and the Hill Museum and Manuscript Library (HMML) was founded in 1965. This also was the period when major European manuscript libraries began to microfilm their collections and establish reliable imaging and reproduction departments.

15. F. Edward Cranz, in consultation with Paul Oskar Kristeller, *A Microfilm Corpus of the Indexes to Printed Catalogues of Latin Manuscripts before 1600 A.D.*, 3rd ed. (New London, CT: n.p, 1982), consisting of 38 reels; and Cranz, *A Microfilm Corpus of Unpublished Inventories of Latin Manuscripts before 1600* (New London, CT: Renaissance Society of America, 1987), consisting of 340 reels (in 347), plus one volume.

16. I thank Robert A. Kraft and Michael E. Stone for our discussions over the years regarding the processes of manuscript investigation in the analog age.

necessity on the part of manuscript scholars to conduct the vast majority of these tasks in-person and on-site.[17]

The wholescale application of digital technologies in the twenty-first century has transformed everything in the world of apocryphal texts and traditions except the foundational task of research, which remains the recovery and study of hitherto unknown texts and unknown states or versions of extant texts and works from manuscripts.[18] What has changed over the past two decades are the various processes by which this task is accomplished and, I would argue, how it is envisioned.[19] As with virtually

---

17. Heralds of the digital age appeared in the mid-1980s and through the 1990s in the form of the first successful mass-market PCs. These were supported by early text-based e-mail applications (such as Pine) as well as first-generation computer programs (such as Peter Robinson's Collate!) that could be applied to textual studies and database compilation, the production of concordances and critical editions, and the composition and printing of research results.

18. Back-dropping this task is the broader world of scholarship on medieval manuscripts in the digital age. *Manuscript Studies*, published by the University of Pennsylvania's Schoenberg Institute for Manuscript Studies, is an important vector for information, as is its annual Symposium on Manuscript Studies in the Digital Age (www.library.upenn.edu/exhibits/lectures/ljs_symposium.html), first held in 2008. See also the journal *Digital Philology: A Journal of Medieval Cultures* and the Digital Medievalist (digitalmedievalist.wordpress.com), hosted by the University of Lethbridge and part of the European Alliance for Social Science and Humanities (www.eassh.eu). Sessions devoted to medieval digital humanities now regularly appear at the International Congress on Medieval Studies (wmich.edu/medievalcongress), hosted by the Medieval Institute at Western Michigan University, among other venues.

19. These two decades mirror my own history as a manuscript scholar, beginning in 1999 with my initial manuscript research trip as a PhD student to the Bibliothèque nationale de France (Richelieu). At the time, the Bibliothèque nationale de France employed a wonderfully arcane system of 10 x 12 cm green and red plaques. After entry into the *salle de lecture*, readers carried their green plaques between their desks and the central island where the librarians and curators were seated and the manuscripts were requested and distributed. Green plaques were exchanged for red when consulting a manuscript. One could not leave the *salle* without first returning the manuscript and reacquiring his or her green plaque from the central island and then handed over to the staff member at the front desk. Manuscripts were requested by completing and submitting paper forms; microfilm copies, if extant, had to be consulted first. Today's analogue is the fully electronic system at the Biblioteca Apostolica Vaticana. Readers who wish to consult manuscripts must present their Biblioteca Apostolica Vaticana identification cards first to the Swiss Guards at the Porta sant'Anna (or else obtain a temporary permit at the gatehouse) and at two further points to the police before reaching the front door of the library (the Secret Library has a different entrance). The

all activities in the twenty-first century involving information acquisition, storage, and transfer, manuscript research has become unfettered from all the traditional restrictions on time and place.

A useful way to highlight the nature and effects of these changes is to group the processes in three stages: preparation, examination, and dissemination. *Preparation* here refers to the set of procedures that a scholar undertakes before viewing the manuscripts. *Examination* refers to the acts associated with the actual consultation of the manuscripts, based on the information that the scholar has uncovered during the preparation stage. *Dissemination* involves the distillation and communication of research results. In practice, these stages are not always so discrete, a segregation that has been further eroded by the effects of the digital revolution, as we shall see.

1. Preparation

The extensive digitalization and uploading of source material to the internet has enabled scholars to conduct filtered, Boolean searches[20] at a comprehensive level. For manuscript researchers, *source material* means, above all, the manuscript catalogues,[21] as well as scholarly books,[22] articles

---

porter inside scans cards electronically, which also assigns readers a daily personal locker that is opened by a card-scanner inside the change-room. After bags and personal items are stowed, readers proceed through another gated scanner to access the elevator or stairs that leads to the manuscript and rare books reading rooms (these are separate). Cards are scanned yet again by the duty librarian at the front desk, where readers sign the log book record the numbers of their lockers and reading desks. Only then may they request manuscripts, a process that begins by tapping one's card at one of two dedicated terminals located at the front desk, where manuscripts are deposited after being requested and fetched. Exiting the library requires readers to go through the entire process in reverse. The system might appear baroque, but in reality it works smoothly and provides layers of security for manuscripts and researchers, the latter assisted by a staff of extremely competent librarians.

20. A Boolean search is one that allows users to combine meaningful key-words or -phrases with control operators such as "and," "not," and "or" in order to generate more relevant results.

21. Thousands of manuscript catalogues that were once difficult or impossible to access on account of their age or limited distribution are now available and searchable online. Although a dramatic improvement in the descriptive quality of catalogues occurred in the 1970s and 1980s, their full research potential was not realized until their digitalization in tandem with OCR technologies. Charles D. Wright has com-

12. Manuscript Research in the Digital Age 239

in academic journals,[23] conference papers,[24] and, now, digital images. The development of reliable optical character recognition (OCR)[25] technology has aided this process immensely, not only in terms of time, labor, and efficiency, but also in expanding the search from the metadata (such as indexes) to the information itself.[26]

---

piled a superb online bibliography of Medieval and Modern Manuscript Catalogues and Digitized Manuscripts (bibliography.arc-humanities.org/medieval-modern-manuscript-catalogues), with links. See also syri.ac/manuscripts and the sites listed in note 42, below. Unfortunately, access to the online version of P. O. Kristeller's sprawling and indispensable *Iter Italicum* is by subscription only, along with the Iter Bibliography (www.itergateway.org).

22. Paramount here has been the widespread digitalization of books both in and out of the public domain (including many dating from the seventeenth through the nineteenth centuries), and their free access online, by Google, large publishers, and nonprofit digital libraries such as the Internet Archive. The benefits for manuscript research are immense. For example, upon encountering an unfamiliar text in manuscript, a scholar need only type a short phrase into Google's advanced search engine to discover its source (if known) and editions and studies (if any).

23. These are available via specialist digital archives such as JSTOR or the bundling and sale of current and past issues of academic journals to university libraries on the part of major publishers.

24. Standout here is the appearance of networking websites such as academia.edu or researchgate.net, onto which scholars are able to upload their books, articles, and conference papers, and the online newsletters and blogs, which among other things offer virtually instantaneous notification of news, publications, and events. Many of the latter are devoted to manuscript studies. A parade example is Manuscripts on My Mind (www.slu.edu/arts-and-sciences/medieval-renaissance-studies/publications.php), edited by Susan L'Engle at Saint Louis University. Active blogs include the British Library's Medieval Manuscripts Blog (blogs.bl.uk/digitisedmanuscripts) and Roger Pearse's Thoughts on Antiquity, Patristics, Information Access, and More (www.roger-pearse.com/weblog). James Davila's PaleoJudaica.com (paleojudaica.blogspot.com) and Tony Burke's Apocryphicity (www.apocryphicity.ca) blogs have a special interest in biblical apocrypha.

25. The utility of OCR technology has been augmented by developments in the field of artificial intelligence, which have transformed handwritten texts to machine-readable form. I thank Brandon Hawk for this information. See the comments on HTR in the text below, and the HIMANIS project (HIstorical MANuscript Indexing for user-controlled Search, himanis.hypotheses.org). On paleography and dating of manuscripts, see DigiPal: Digital Resource and Database of Paleography, Manuscripts Studies and Diplomatic (www.digipal.eu).

26. Indexes in older catalogues are rarely accurate or comprehensive. One may verify this claim by downloading the digital versions of the catalogues of the Oxford

The net increase in speed and efficiency has been transformative. Preparatory research for projects that used to require months of often intermittent work (including find- and fetch-times, and travel to consult sources) has been consolidated and its duration cut significantly, even as its exploratory depth has increased.[27] In addition, manuscript scholars are now able to be conduct searches from virtually any connected location on the globe.

Other applications of new communications technologies have further streamlined the task of preparatory research. Electronic library catalogues, initially on-site and later available online, have overcome the physical and informational limitations inherent to the old card-catalogue system.[28] An array of online bibliographies coordinates and expedites research searches.[29] E-mail permits researchers to contact manuscript libraries in advance,

---

University manuscripts, including the volumes of the *Summary Catalogues*, searching for words or phrases relevant to one's research in the pages, and comparing the results with what is listed in the indexes. In the old days, I would hot-read printed catalogues (a mode of speed-reading, the brain seeking patterns of relevant words, titles, and phrases, with much back-and-forth page-flipping) in addition to consulting the indexes. The practice was time-consuming but necessary and frequently rewarding.

27. Here the ongoing utility of repositories such as the Hill Museum and Manuscript Library (notes 14, above, and 81, below) cannot be overestimated, especially for scholars in North America, as I underscored in "Microform Manuscript Collections in the United States," *Bulletin de l'Association pour l'étude de la littérature apocryphe chrétienne* 17 (2007): 14–16. Such repositories enable scholars to conduct a large part of their primary research on site, often with manuscripts from libraries or places that are difficult to visit, and to triage their preliminary research before ordering images or consulting manuscripts elsewhere.

28. Prior to digital catalogues, the most reliable way to discover what a library actually contained in the ways of books and journals was to scour the stacks at the appropriate call numbers. For *rats d'archives*, a library unvisited was *terra incognita*. Since at least 2010, the Annual Conferences of the Ligue des Bibliothèques Européennes de Recherche—Association of European Research Libraries (LIBER, libereurope. eu) have hosted sessions of papers devoted to all aspects of librarianship in the digital age. The group's journal, *Liber Quarterly* (www.liberquarterly.eu), is also a fine source in this regard.

29. Open sites include the Orion Dead Sea Scrolls Bibliography (covering early Judaism), RAMBI—Index of Articles on Jewish Studies, and Regesta Imperii (medieval studies), as well as bibliographic websites created by Charles Conroy (www.cjconroy.net/bibliog.htm), Robert A. Kraft (ccat.sas.upenn.edu/rak/publics/0index.htm), Andrei Orlov (www.marquette.edu/maqom/pseudepigrapha.html), and Charles D. Wright (bibliography.arc-humanities.org), among others. Comprehensive

in order to set visitation dates and establish whether items are available for consultation.[30]

Advanced imaging technologies, including multi- and hyper-spectral imaging and x-ray fluorescence, have assisted in recovering text in manuscripts from the ancient Dead Sea Scrolls to medieval palimpsests.[31] The carbonized Herculaneum scrolls, the Archimedes palimpsest, and the Jubilees palimpsest are only a few of the triumphs in this area.[32]

Sites such as retroReveal[33] provide documentation and web-based image-processing algorithms that aim to illuminate obscure or hidden content in manuscripts and other media. Other digital applications appear to be solving the problem of electronic handwritten text recognition (HTR).[34]

---

subscription sites include the International Medieval Bibliography (www.brepolis. net), the Index of Medieval Art (ima.princeton.edu), and the Oxford Bibliographies series (www.oxfordbibliographies.com). The number of specialist and thematic sites, open or subscriber, is staggering.

30. This is hardly a trivial benefit. Many libraries still set an upper limit on the number of items that a researcher may consult daily (below, note 47). The practice is imposed, in part, by the time it takes to fetch and process the material. For this reason, preordering items via e-mail or online ordering systems can facilitate manuscript work greatly, particularly if one is photographing. On a research trip, each day saved represents funds not spent and time that can be allocated for another task.

31. The Scripta Qumranica Electronica (www.uni-goettingen.de/en/441241. html) is a new joint project of the Göttingen Academy of Sciences and Humanities, the Israel Antiquities Authority, Haifa University, and Tel Aviv University. One of its goals is to facilitate "the virtual joining of the 'puzzle pieces' of thousands of ancient scrolls fragments." I thank James Tucker for bringing this project to my attention, and for clarifying its dynamic capabilities regarding the digital presentation of macrotexts or works (below, note 78) such as 1Q/4QHodayot.

32. See the Papyrological Indexing Network (PINAX, 163.1.169.40/cgi-bin/lib rary?a=p&p=home&l=en&w=utf-8) of the Faculty of Classics at Oxford University, with also a database of the Oxyrhynchus papyri (POxy); The Archimedes Palimpsest Project (www.archimedespalimpsest.org); and The Jubilees Palimpsest Project (jubi lees.stmarytx.edu), under the direction of Todd Hanneken and of special import to pseudepigrapha scholars. I thank Todd Hanneken and Ira Rabin for clarifying the technological data in this paragraph.

33. See retroreveal.org.

34. Examples include the EU project Transkribus (read.transkribus.eu/transkri bus), part of the Recognition and Enrichment of Archival Documents, whose goal is "to revolutionize access to archival documents with the support of cutting-edge technology such as Handwritten Text Recognition (HTR) and Keyword Spotting (KWS)." Fragmentarium (fragmentarium.ms) is a digital research laboratory that aims to facil-

This potentially opens a new vista in manuscript research. It should also enable researchers to conduct lexicographic searches in a manuscript based on any word or group of words, as opposed to the *incipits* or *explicits* only, which can be highly variable, particularly in apocryphal works.

2. Examination

The tasks associated with the activity of manuscript examination may be divided into two categories, off-site (remote access) and on-site.

Off-Site

The standout development here has been the wholescale creation of websites that present online versions of manuscript catalogues and/or digitalized images of the manuscripts themselves. Such sites bridge the activities of preparation and examination. Collectively, they represent the most significant application of the technological innovations generated by the digital revolution as they apply to manuscript studies.

Most libraries today have their own websites.[35] Those with manuscripts typically present information about their collections on dedicated webpages, where information for readers is detailed, including contact data and reading-room hours. Many libraries also present manuscript researchers with two of the most valuable resources of all: (1) the electronic reproductions service; and (2) the digital library.

Reproduction services enable scholars to order digital images of manuscript pages[36] and to receive them within a reasonable time as e-mail attachments or via a file-transfer application. Prices vary among the libraries—most are reasonable—and usually correlate to the quality of the images. These range from low-resolution scans made from microfilms to

---

itate the publication, cataloguing, and transcription of manuscript fragments (I thank Torsten Schaßan for this information). Another application, In codice ratio (www.inf.uniroma3.it/db/icr/index.html), aims for the same objectives, using material from the Vatican's secret archives as a test case. I have received a spectrum of opinions regarding the ultimate feasibility and utility of such endeavors.

35. One barometer of change: many French municipal libraries have recently rebranded themselves as "mediathèques."

36. This is normally accomplished by means of a dedicated website or a downloadable form that is completed and sent as an e-mail attachment. Many smaller libraries will take informal orders via e-mail message.

JPEG photographs useful for most purposes to publication-quality TIFFs.³⁷ Payment is handled by internet bank transfer, online payment systems, or telephone. The net savings in time and money (in contrast with the old, analog procedures) is extraordinary.³⁸

Digital libraries are essentially free, remote-access reproductions services.³⁹ The websites of most major manuscript libraries today have dedicated pages with links to downloadable, digitalized images of their manuscripts,⁴⁰ as do many of the minor ones. Many libraries also make available online digitalized versions of their manuscript catalogues or, better still, dedicated websites that link catalogue data with each manuscript according to its shelf-mark. Digitalization and internet access have also enabled libraries that have been outside the academic mainstream to introduce their holdings to scholarship.⁴¹

---

37. The use of images for purposes other than personal research (e.g., in publication) normally requires explicit permission. The processes of ordering manuscript images and obtaining reproduction permissions were more difficult prior to the digital age. Not only was the mind-set of libraries proprietary, but connecting with the correct person or office was not easy: there was no internet to search for a library's contact information or e-mail address to which one could send requests for reproductions.

38. Reproduction costs can mount, but if one knows what one wants (here the research preparation stage is instrumental), the net savings can be immense as compared with travelling to examine manuscripts in person. Reproduction services also eliminate time spent on-site. Rather than transcribing texts by hand (and double-checking the results—who knew when one might return to the library?), one can view the manuscripts, verify the texts, and order reproductions (assuming here that reader photography is not permitted).

39. What is said in the following paragraphs regarding manuscripts pertains also to early print- and block-books.

40. Commercial sites (e.g., Les Enluminures, www.textmanuscripts.com) and personal webpages (e.g., using the image hosting service Flikr) represent a secondary yet useful source of manuscript images.

41. A good example is the National Library of the Czech Republic (Národní knihovna České republiky), the manuscript holdings of which are comparatively unmined. Many of these are available for viewing on the Manuscriptorium website (next note, below). Another is the Biblioteca Digital del Patrimonio Iberoamericano (www.iberoamericadigital.net/es/Inicio), which went online in August 2018. It was created with the collaboration of fourteen national libraries in Iberia and Latin America, including their large (and largely unknown) manuscript collections, including medieval codices.

Augmenting the websites of these individual libraries are the many hundreds of internet sites that collate and present catalogue and manuscript data at the regional, thematic (linguistic, topical, and commercial), state, and global levels.[42] Each site has its niche in the online ecology, since

---

42. For regional examples: see, e.g., the sites that catalogue the medieval manuscripts in Wallonia (www.cicweb.be/en/recherche.php), the Veneto (www.nuovabibliotecamanoscritta.it), Upper Austria (digi.landesbibliothek.at), and so on. For linguistic thematic examples: see, e.g., Pinakes | Πίνακες (pinakes.irht.cnrs.fr), for manuscripts in Greek and hosted by the Institut de Recherche et d'histoire des textes (IHRT), the Digitized Hebrew Manuscripts Catalogue (web.nli.org.il/sites/NLI/English/library/news/Pages/dig-heb-manus-catalog.aspx) for manuscripts in Hebrew, the Repertorium of Old Bulgarian Literature and Letters (repertorium.obdurodon.org) for manuscripts in Old Bulgarian, and the Handschriftencensus (www.handschriftencensus.de/forschungsliteratur/kataloge) for manuscripts in German. For manuscripts in French, see below. For topical thematic examples: see Les Archives de littérature du Moyen Âge (ARLIMA, www.arlima.net), Mirabile: Archivio digitale della cultura medievale (www.mirabileweb.it/index.aspx), Earlier Latin Manuscripts (elmss.nuigalway.ie), the Islamic Manuscript Association (www.islamicmanuscript.org/extresources/manuscriptcatalogues.aspx), and the Avestan Digital Archive (ada.usal.es/), among many others. For commercial thematic examples: see past and present catalogues of auction houses (e.g., Christie's, Sotheby's, Hôtel Drouot) and booksellers (Bernard Quaritch, H. P. Kraus, etc.) who deal in manuscripts and early books. For state examples, the quality of websites varies widely. Among the more comprehensive and current sites are those that detail manuscript and/or catalogue data in the Austrian (manuscripta.at/m1), Dutch (www.mmdc.nl/static/site), German (www.manuscripta-mediaevalia.de/#|4), Italian (manus.iccu.sbn.it), Swedish (www.manuscripta.se), and Swiss (www.codices.ch) libraries. The Digital Scriptorium, a consortium of American libraries with medieval manuscript holdings (vm136.lib.berkeley.edu/BANC/digitalscriptorium), is wide-ranging, but gaps remain. De Ricci's *Census* of manuscripts in North America is available as an ACLS Humanities E-Book (quod.lib.umich.edu/cgi/t/text/text-idx?c=acls;cc=acls;view=toc;idno=heb05703.0001.001). For global examples, see the Monastic Manuscript Project (www.earlymedievalmonasticism.org/index.html) and the Universitätsbibliothek Kassel's Handschriftenkataloge (www.uni-kassel.de/ub/historisches-erbe/sondersammlungen/handschriftenkataloge/kataloge-international.html) are the most comprehensive and thus the most useful. See also Manuscriptorium (www.manuscriptorium.com), an ever-expanding consortium of researchers, libraries, and historical and cultural institutions; the Europeana manuscript pages (www.europeana.eu/portal/en/collections/manuscripts), part of the Europeana Collections suite of sites; the Digitized Medieval Manuscripts App (digitizedmedievalmanuscripts.org/app), now under the aegis of European Association for Digital Humanities; and the Bibliothèque virtuelle des manuscrits médiévaux (bvmm.irht.cnrs.fr), hosted by the IHRT and essential for items in French or in French librar-

each offers researchers different services. Many provide links to electronic images of manuscripts and/or manuscript catalogues, supported occasionally with bibliographic information.[43] Many also contain advanced search engines, amplifying research results. Still others provide scholars with searchable editions of the ancient and medieval texts.[44]

The online presence of a significant percentage of the digitalized images of the manuscripts and incunabula of the world's libraries, supported by integrated online versions of their catalogues and other relevant data, have substantively decreased research time and increased scholarly productivity. In my view, we are approximately one-third of the way to achieving what should be the logical end-point of this technological trajectory, which is free online access to high-resolution images of all or nearly all of the world's medieval manuscripts.[45]

---

ies. Also useful is the Leuven Database of Ancient Books (www.trismegistos.org/ldab/index.php). Analogue sites for the study of incunabula include the Gesamtkatalog der Wiegendrucke (http://www.gesamtkatalogderwiegendrucke.de), hosted by the Staatsbibliothek zu Berlin, and the Incunabula Short Title Catalogue (data.ccrl.org/istc/_search), hosted by the British Library.

43. E.g., TLION MSS—Bibliografia dei manoscritti citati in rivista (tlion.sns.it/mssb/index.php) and FAMA—Œuvres latines médiévales à succès (fama.irht.cnrs.fr), again, among many others, including integrative sites such as International Image Interoperability Framework (http://iiif.io).

44. E.g., the Corpus corporum—Repositorium operum Latinorum, hosted by the Universität Zürich (www.mlat.uzh.ch/MLS). Useful sites for scholars of biblical apocrypha are the North American Society for the Study of Christian Apocryphal Literature (www.nasscal.com) and the Online Critical Pseudepigrapha (ocp.tyndale.ca). See also the Leon Levy Dead Sea Scrolls Digital Library (www.deadseascrolls.org.il/home) and the digital library of the Genizah manuscripts (fjms.genizah.org/?eraseCache=true), hosted by the Friedberg Jewish Manuscript Society of Toronto.

45. The leaders among the Big Twelve manuscript libraries (below, note 47) are the Bibliothèque nationale de France (including the super-site Gallica [gallica.bnf.fr/accueil]), the Berlin Staatsbibliothek, and especially the Bayerische Staatsbibliothek. The Biblioteca Apostolica Vaticana, the Biblioteca Medicea Laurenziana, the British Library, and the Biblioteca Nacional de España also have digitalized and uploaded significant portions of their manuscript collections. The recent decision to upload digitalized images of the manuscripts in the Parker Library (Corpus Christi College, Cambridge University), previously available only as a subscription service, is a sign of the times.

On-Site

Paramount here is reader photography by means of a digital camera or a hand-held device with this capability and, importantly, the opening of manuscript collections to the practice.[46] Approximately half of the one hundred-plus libraries that I have visited permit readers to photograph manuscripts for private study (no publication).[47] The use of the flash func-

---

46. Despite the ever-increasing popularity and widespread availability of digital cameras by the turn of the century, reader photography was rarely permitted until the 2010's. My first encounter came in January 2012. While preparing for the day's research at the Pierpont Morgan Library in New York, I was informed that photographs were permitted—and immediately rushed out to Fifth Avenue to purchase a digital camera.

47. I have consulted with librarians at many institutions that prohibit the practice. One reason is monetary—libraries sell manuscript images in order to generate funds that help defray their operating costs. Another is the lack of dedicated space or oversight staff. There is also an entrenched belief that reader photography will damage the manuscript. This, of course, is preposterous: a reader prepares a manuscript in the same fashion whether s/he intends to read, transcribe, or photograph its pages. The real dangers are cramped or improperly lit study spaces, which compel inexperienced scholars to force open tight bindings or otherwise damage the manuscripts in order to read (or photograph) their texts. In my view, the new, state-of-the-art manuscripts reading room at the Weston (New Bodleian) Library in Oxford is perfect in all technical respects and stands in wonderful modernist counterpoint to the traditional verbal oath that one must still recite when admitted to the library for the first time. Of the Big Twelve manuscript libraries, the Bayerische Staatsbibliothek (München), Biblioteca Apostolica Vaticana (Città del Vaticano), Biblioteca Medicea Laurenziana (Firenze), Biblioteca Ambrosiana (Milano), Biblioteca Nacional de España (Madrid), and Österreichische Nationalbibliothek (Wien) prohibit reader photography. However, each one has an excellent online digital library, except the Ambrosiana. The Biblioteca nazionale Marciana (Venezia) and the Berlin Staatsbibliothek allow readers to consult/photograph up to four and six manuscripts per day, respectively, with only a few restrictions. The Bodleian Library (Oxford), which also holds a high number of manuscripts from the College Libraries, and the Bibliothèque nationale de France (Paris), allow ten manuscripts daily, again with few restrictions. The British Library (London) also allows ten manuscripts per day, but a significant portion of their collections is classified as "restricted" or "select" and cannot be photographed, even though select manuscripts may be consulted. Cambridge University Library has no daily limit, though the libraries of its Colleges that retain their manuscripts vary in these policies. This information is current as of July 2018, based on website information and personal experience; however, policies tend to change without notice. Broadly speaking,

tion and tripods are not permitted.[48] Over time, the benefits of reader photography will decrease as the percentage of high-resolution images of manuscripts that are freely available online increases.[49] At this point, however, the practice offers tremendous economic advantages for those who have conducted their preparatory research with due diligence.[50]

A Cumulative Advantage

The aggregate of the effects of the digital revolution on manuscript research described above is augmented by an extra, cumulative advantage that accrues to scholars who focus on apocryphal writings specifically. The simple reason is that, until recently, scholarship has virtually ignored these writings. Even in times when interest in the pseudepigrapha waxed, as it did during the golden age, they were investigated primarily to explain the backdrop of Christian origins.[51] This attitude is reflected in the older manuscript catalogues, which tend to neglect or marginalize apocryphal writings, apocalyptic texts, prognostic tracts, and other kinds of what was once considered low or popular literature. Apocalyptic texts, for example, are commonly indexed in these catalogues under generic rubrics such as "apocalypses," "oracles," "prognostics," "prophecies," "revelations," "signs," and "visions" (and their equivalents in other languages). Such catalogues represent gold mines for pseudepigrapha scholars with the inclination to

---

the same proportion of these twelve libraries that do not allow or allow with/without restrictions is reflected across the other libraries, large and small.

48. Professional photographers who work on behalf of the library or special projects are permitted devices.

49. Certain items are deemed too fragile, precious, or historically important for reader consultation and/or photography without a compelling reason. But these are often the first items that libraries digitalize and upload images to their websites.

50. In April 2015, I visited the Biblioteca Estense Universitaria in Modena to photograph texts in ten manuscripts that I had identified via preliminary catalogue searches. I moved quickly through the material, photographing the items on my list (and thumbing through the rest of each codex to ensure that I had not overlooked other items). The librarian brought me the codices one by one. After handing me the last codex, she remarked, "*velocissimo*" ("very fast"). That was the moment when I began to consider how digital technologies had transformed manuscript research.

51. One corollary of this objective was the *terminus ante quem* of ca. 200 CE that generations of editors set on the date of the writings they admitted to their pseudepigrapha collections. See DiTommaso, "'Old Testament Pseudepigrapha' Category and Corpus."

manuscript research, but it is digital technology that provides them with the best tools by which to excavate the ore. It is my experience that one of every ten manuscripts identified via online catalogue searches will contain something useful,[52] while one of every three or four of these useful finds will be of sufficient import to warrant publication.

The cumulative advantage imparted by the new digital technologies on manuscript investigation into apocryphal texts and traditions is measurable in the research output. Three examples, drawn from my own experience, demonstrate the *quantitative* results.[53] Each also illustrates a specific *qualitative* effect.

The first example is the Penitence of Solomon. It is a short catena of patristic excerpts in Latin on the subject of the penitence of King Solomon after his idolatry with the foreign gods of his wives. The first scholarly edition of the text was printed in the late nineteenth century on the basis of one manuscript. Subsequent studies appeared on a steady basis; the last, in 2010, listed fifty-nine manuscripts. None of the studies, however, recognized the nature or extent of the textual variation, principally because a sufficient number of manuscripts had yet to be consulted and read. In 2018, I published an article-length study of the Penitence of Solomon.[54] The article identifies 146 extant manuscript exemplars. These collectively demonstrate ten major versions of the catena, with a host of minor versions and subtypes. Each version is composed of two or more excerpts that are drawn from a total set of twenty-four, eight of which may be considered core. No excerpt, though, appears in every version. In a remarkable example, two versions of the Penitence of Solomon appear in a single manuscript, yet share no excerpts (and therefore no text!). This is all the

---

52. E.g., a new copy or version of a known work.

53. Every serious manuscript scholar working today will be able to cite examples of his or her own demonstrating the cumulative advantage in the ways outlined above and perhaps in other ways also. Three reasons prompt my assertion. (1) My own experience in this regard cannot be unique. (2) The scholarship published today seems to be a quantum leap ahead of older studies in the extent and depth of its manuscript research results. (3) Other manuscript scholars have confirmed in private conversation that the digital revolution has similarly transformed the ways, means, and results of their research.

54. Lorenzo DiTommaso, "The *Penitence of Solomon (Poenitentia Salomonis)*," in *The Embroidered Bible: Studies in Biblical Apocrypha and Pseudepigrapha in Honour of Michael E. Stone*, ed. Lorenzo DiTommaso, Matthias Henze, and William Adler, STVP 26 (Leiden: Brill, 2018), 371–452.

more remarkable given that the later version (thirteenth century), which is titled, is written on the same page as the earlier one (tenth century).[55] The manuscript research for this article occupied only two or three years of study, "carried on by no means continuously," in the words of James quoted above. The same research, had it been conducted without the cumulative advantage of the new digital technologies, would have required at least three times the time, labor, and costs. I make the comparison with confidence: the 2010 study, also mine, is constituted of work largely undertaken before the digital revolution.[56]

The second case involves the *Revelations* of Pseudo-Methodius. This text was composed in Syriac in the late seventh century and translated shortly afterwards into Greek and then from Greek into Latin. The *Revelations* of Pseudo-Methodius is the most important apocalyptic text composed in the Middle Ages in terms of its subsequent influence on apocalyptic speculation. Yet, until just a few decades ago, our knowledge of its manuscript evidence was negligible. The situation with the Latin manuscripts did not improve until 1988, when Marc Laureys and Daniel Verhelst published their list of 196 copies, disposed in four versions.[57] Given the age in which they worked, theirs was a Herculean effort. It also represented the labor of decades: Verhelst had spent that long on compiling the manuscripts of Adso's *De Antichristo* and other apocalyptic works and must have noted the copies of the *Revelations* of Pseudo-Methodius as he went along from library to library.[58] Even so, he and Laureys were able to classify only two-thirds of the 196 manuscripts, and even here errors suggest that they relied frequently on catalogue references. James Palmer

---

55. See the section on "Dissemination" below for additional comments.

56. Lorenzo DiTommaso, "Pseudepigrapha Notes III: 4. Old Testament Pseudepigrapha in the Yale University MS Collection," *JSP* 20 (2010): 3–80.

57. Marc Laureys and Daniel Verhelst, "Pseudo-Methodius, *Revelationes*: Textgeschichte und kritische Edition. Ein Leuven-Groninger Forschungsprojekt," in *The Use and Abuse of Eschatology in the Middle Ages*, ed. Wernner Verbeke, Daniel Verhelst, and Andries Welkenhuysen, MedLov 15 (Leuven: Leuven University Press, 1988), 122–36. The Greek text has been less fortunate; the last major studies, by Anastasios Lolos, *Die Apokalypse des Ps.-Methodios*, BkPh 83 (Meisenheim am Glan, 1976), and Lolos, *Die dritte und vierte redaktion des Ps.-Methodios*, BkPh 94 (Meisenheim am Glan, 1978), cite forty-five manuscripts between them. I estimate that fifty to one hundred additional manuscript copies are extant.

58. Adso Dervensis, *De ortu et tempore Antichristi*, CCCM 45 (Turnhout: Brepols, 1976).

and I are presently revising and updating their list of Latin manuscripts, preparatory to a new volume on the texts and reception history of the *Revelations* of Pseudo-Methodius in the West.[59] We have now identified and verified over seventy new manuscript versions of the work and a few new abbreviated versions. We also have examined nearly all the 196 manuscripts cited by Laureys and Verhelst, removing or reclassifying fifty items. In short, the shift in research techniques enabled by digital technologies not only has opened the door to the discovery of new copies, but also has facilitated the reexamination of nearly all the known copies, all within a relatively short period of time.

The final example is the Fifteen Signs of Doomsday. This short text is preserved in several versions and a dozen languages that range from Old Welsh to Armenian, but most notably Latin. In 1952, William Heist published what remains the definitive study of the Fifteen Signs of Doomsday.[60] In it, he records 120 manuscript copies and early printed versions, two dozen of which he leaves unexamined. My research over the past six years—conducted, again, "by no means continuously"—has increased the total number of witnesses of the Fifteen Signs of Doomsday to over 500, including illustrated exemplars in manuscripts and stained glass. I have located and verified most of these exemplars myself, either *in situ* (photographing, where possible) or, more commonly, via images that I have obtained. This nearly fivefold increase in numbers, however, is overshadowed by the fact that a significant proportion of these four hundred-odd so-called new finds are not new at all. Rather, approximately half had already been cited among the sixty years of scholarly publications since Heist, which is to say, I did not discover them personally. The cumulative advantage in this case allowed me to locate and collate this previous research far more efficiently than it would have been possible in a predigital environment.

3. Dissemination

Scholars in every field have come to enjoy the benefits of the digital revolution as it applies to the dissemination of their work, from its initial

---

59. To appear in the Brepols series Corpus Christianorum Series Apocryphorum. See my preliminary study, "The *Apocalypse* of Pseudo-Methodius: Notes on a Recent Edition," *Medioevo greco* 17 (2017): 311–21.

60. William W. Heist, *The Fifteen Signs before Doomsday* (East Lansing, MI: Michigan State Press, 1952).

preparation to the final product.⁶¹ These processes are underwritten by fundamental changes in publishing and the increasing use of personal webpages and social-networking websites.⁶² Issues related to academic publishing in the electronic age, which cannot be isolated from the suite of topics comprising the field of digital humanities,⁶³ have been the subject of much scholarly discussion and extend beyond the scope of this paper.

That being said, certain benefits related to research dissemination accrue to manuscript researchers in general and to scholars of apocryphal writings in particular. For example, high-resolution digital images of manuscript folia can be procured efficiently and inexpensively, to be included in one's published work as a matter of course. In addition, specialized electronic font types permit scholars to reproduce the multitude of ancient and medieval languages in which apocryphal texts are preserved in manuscript. Most important, digital platforms allow scholars to graphically represent groups of compositions that exhibit a literary coherence over time but a textual affiliation that is too fluid to describe in stemmatic or synoptic form.⁶⁴ This kind of compositional relationship is characteristic of apocryphal literature as a class (the Penitence of Solomon and the

---

61. Scholars of previous generations would check the library stacks before submitting their work for publication in order to ensure that they did not overlook any new books or journal articles. Now this task is accomplished with far greater speed and efficiency online. See also the next note.

62. Academia.edu is the best-known of these websites. Combined with the mighty search capabilities of Google, it and similar sites provide a platform for the global dissemination of research (from entire books to preliminary research reports) for full-time and part-time academics, independent scholars, and graduate students.

63. Most universities or university libraries have webpages on manuscripts and the digital humanities. Specialized sites such as Michael Johnson's website (michaelbrooksjohnson.com) are typically more useful.

64. See Liv Ingeborg Lied, "Text—Work—Manuscript: What is an 'Old Testament Pseudepigraphon'?," *JSP* 25 (2015): 150–65, and my comments in Lorenzo DiTommaso, "The Apocryphal Daniel Apocalypses: Works, Manuscripts, and Overview," *ETL* 94 (2018): 309–12. The points in these articles have been made independently elsewhere; see, e.g., Elaine Treharne, "Fleshing out the Text: The Transcendent Manuscript in the Digital Age," *postmedieval* 4 (2013): 465–78, and, from the solution to the plight, in Dean Sakel, "The Manuscripts of the *Chronicle of 1570*," *Byzantion* 83 (2013): 363–74. An earlier study that identifies the basic problem is Mark J. Clark, "How to Edit *The Historia Scholastica* of Peter Comestor?," *RBén* 116 (2006): 83–91. A good testcase is outlined in Hugo Lundhaug, "An Illusion of Textual Stability: Textual Fluidity, New Philology, and the Nag Hammadi Codices," in *Snapshots of Evolving Traditions: Jewish*

Fifteen Signs of Doomsday are examples) and is virtually impossible to display on a traditional printed page. But digital technology permits its expression, along with a dynamic component that charts the historical evolution of the work.

Digital platforms also enable scholars of apocryphal texts and traditions to pursue large-scale manuscript research projects that are open-ended, collaborative, and stable. Consider, for example, the possibility of a comprehensive database of apocryphal traditions related to the apostles or of the vernacular "embroidered Bibles" such as the *Bible historiale*, each coordinated to catalogue data, manuscript images, and secondary studies.[65] By their nature, such projects would be able to overcome obstacles that vex manuscript websites today: the inherently limited scope of any project tied to a single library or manuscript collection (no matter how extensive); the bottleneck in time and labor as solitary scholars receive, filter, and upload new data to personal websites; the close-ended nature of project research funding, which has prompted websites to shutter or become dormant;[66] and the fact that shifts in research direction, personnel changeover, and sometimes merely the desire to appear *au courant* (buttressed by the latest buzz-words) can prompt even the largest and most stable websites to change their e-addresses like electronic jackrabbits. I see such large, collaborative projects evolving in conjunction with formal academic publishing, rather than superseding it.[67]

---

and *Christian Manuscript Culture, Textual Fluidity, and New Philology*, ed. Liv Ingeborg Lied and Hugo Lundhaug, TUGAL 175 (Berlin: de Gruyter, 2017), 20–54.

65. This is already becoming a reality. The Insitut für neutestamentliche Textforschung at the Universitäts Münster (egora.uni-muenster.de/intf) aims to reconstruct the Greek initial text of the New Testament on the basis of its complete manuscript tradition, the early translations, and the patristic citations. The ongoing publication of the *Editio critica maior* (ECM) is coordinated with the project. The data on this site is now the engine for revisions of the Nestle-Aland editions and the new ECM fascicles. I thank Garrick Allen for this information.

66. E.g., the Europeanea Regia project (www.europeanaregia.eu) terminated in June 2012, and the Digital Scholarly Editions Initial Training Network (dixit.uni-koeln.de) ended in August 2017. Scriptorium: Medieval and Early Modern Manuscripts Online (scriptorium.english.cam.ac.uk), a website hosted by Cambridge University's Faculty of English and announced with some fanfare (Agnus Vine, "Scriptorium: When to Build a Digital Archive Rather than a Digital Edition," in *A Handbook of Editing Early Modern Texts*, ed. Claire Loffmann and Harriet Phillips [New York: Routledge, 2017], no. 3.2.2), has been offline for over a year.

67. The Scriptorium project (www.rch.uky.edu/project_scriptorium.html),

4. Observations

The net effect of the digital revolution on manuscript studies is this: *research is where you are.*[68] Scholars are now able to study high-resolution electronic images of manuscript pages on a personal electronic device at any time and in almost any location. This state of affairs was unimaginable only fifteen or twenty years ago.[69] It has been made possible by a suite of technological innovations that have transformed the processes of research

---

hosted by the University of Kentucky's Collaboratory for Research in Computing for Humanities, is a tool that might make such websites possible. Its online description is worth quoting: "Scriptorium is a digital environment for collaborative research on manuscripts, of any era or language. Scriptorium offers a powerful and flexible viewer for studying manuscript images: zoom, pan, compare multiple images on a single screen, annotate the images to draw attention to specific features in script, layout, illumination, etc. Scriptorium also allows collaborators to work together in real time on documents relating to their project, and to display to each other their discoveries in real time. Scholarly resources related to the project can be uploaded, stored, shared, and opened for viewing alongside manuscript images." See also Humanities Research and Continuous Publishing (humarec.org), using "the test-case of the edition of a unique trilingual Greek, Latin and Arabic New Testament manuscript."

68. Here again one must underscore the role of Google as a vector for information and a means by which to search it, and how it has changed the expectations and results of research, at every level. David Bell states the point well in his review of Ronald Schechter, *A Genealogy of Terror in Eighteenth-Century France* (Chicago: University of Chicago Press, 2018). Bell remarks that the book mostly "consists of a close analysis of the uses of the word 'terror' in France in the century before the Revolution of 1789. [Schechter] does not comment on his research methods, but this is the sort of project that would have been almost impossible to carry out before the Great Digitization of the past two decades, and particularly the extraordinary work carried out by Google in scanning tens of millions of books previously accessible only in research libraries. Thanks to the Google Books database, supplemented by several other, more specialized online collections, it is now possible, sitting in the comfort of one's home, to track virtually every single occurrence of the word *terreur* in print during the period in question" (*New York Review of Books* [28 June 2018]: 75).

69. "Unimaginable" is not hyperbole. Andy Clark and David Chalmers's theory of the extended mind proposes that human cognition is integrated with its larger, extra-somatic environment. But the theory gained traction only as individuals increasingly came to rely on personal electronic devices in order to augment or amplify their mental functions (e.g., GPS). Chalmers quotes the verdict of philosopher Ned Block: "the thesis *was false in 1995* ... but it *has since become true* with the advent of smartphones and the like" [italics mine]. David J. Chalmers, "Extended Cognition and Extended Consciousness," in *Andy Clark and His Critics*, ed. Matteo Colombo, Elizabeth Irvine, and Mog

preparation, manuscript examination, and the dissemination of results. No facet has been left unchanged. Manuscript researchers today stand at one end of a long and ongoing history of technological change that has proceeded along multiple trajectories—from chained books to the internet, from repositories to users, from analog to digital, and from closed stacks to open-access.

(1) Technological change has expanded the horizon of the possible. For field ornithologists, "the bird must be in the mind before it is seen in the bush." The lesson is particularly acute for pseudepigrapha scholars. As we have seen, apocryphal writings were either overlooked in older manuscript catalogues or regarded as sources for the study of Christian origins rather than as early Jewish texts. This also meant that their complicated reception histories in later Christian contexts were largely ignored. Recent research has revealed the full extent and depth of apocryphal texts and traditions in myriad postbiblical milieus[70]—as well as their true identity: they are *received* works, having been embroidered, reworked, and adapted to their later cultural settings, which are, of course, *manuscript* cultures.[71] What once went unseen has become the center of attention. The text must be in the mind before it is recognized on the page.[72]

Stapleton (Oxford: Oxford University Press, 2019), 9–20. In other words, the state of human cognition proposed by the theory was realized only with the digital revolution.

70. The digital revolution has also facilitated the identification of clusters of short apocryphal or apocalyptic writings that appear together in manuscripts either in sequence or else in close proximity to each other. Tracing the transmission history of such clusters allows scholars to map the geographic and cultural contexts of the use and reuse of apocryphal writings. This task is informed by the broader effort to reconstruct the manuscript contents of early libraries and scriptoria, an important area of research that predates the digital revolution but has been no less profoundly affected by it.

71. Paramount here is the social function of the apocryphal texts in their received settings. Two recent studies: Brandon W. Hawk, "The Literary Contexts and Early Transmission of the Latin *Life of Judas*," *JMRC* 44 (2018): 60–76, and Liv Ingeborg Lied and Matthew Phillip Monger, "Look to the East: New and Forgotten Sources of *4 Ezra*," in DiTommaso, Henze, and Adler, *Embroidered Bible*, 639–52. The study of manuscript cultures extends well beyond the boundaries of this paper. See the book series, Studies in Manuscript Cultures, published by de Gruyter, which boasts eighteen volumes that are now in press or on deck in only five years since the publication of the first installment, Jörg Quenzer, Dmitry Bondarev, and Jan-Ulrich Sobisch, eds., *Manuscript Cultures: Mapping the Field* (Berlin: de Gruyter, 2014).

72. For this reason, I identify digital revolution as one of the major factors that

(2) Technological change has shifted the boundaries of the expected. Until recently, manuscript research flowed in a linear fashion, moving from the preparation stage to the examination of the evidence by autopsy. Tasks had to be accomplished at the right time and in their proper order. They required a huge investment of labor, funds, and, above all, time. Researchers were hamstrung by all the limitations of the analog age. Every task had to be carried out *in situ*. Manuscript travel could only be arranged during summer vacations or the rare sabbatical leave. It took decades of intermittent research to acquire a critical mass of manuscript information even within the limits of one's specialty.[73] The digital revolution has largely overturned this research sequence. The critical mass of manuscript data that is necessary to stretch one's research expectations is now at one's fingertips. *If research is where you are, so are its results.* Research results along one trajectory can initiate research along another, often in a matter of hours or even minutes.[74] Moreover, its impact is potentially greater, insofar as it affects not only a small, related collection of works (Verhelst's Antichrist texts, for example) but a scholar's entire research profile, be it apocryphal writings, apocalyptic texts, Syriac literature, medieval lectionaries, picture Bibles, and on and on. Scholars of apocryphal texts and traditions are now

---

have combined to transform the pseudepigrapha as a category and corpus over the past decades The other factors are (1) the readmission into the corpus of apocryphal works that were composed in post-biblical settings, (2) the recognition of the inadequacy of standard notions of a text to describe the full range of evidence (this has been discussed in passing above), and (3) the ongoing reexpansion of the category beyond its traditional boundaries of form and medium. See DiTommaso, "'Old Testament Pseudepigrapha' as Category and Corpus."

73. The exceptions prove the rule. Over their long careers, golden age scholars such as Angelo Mai, Léopold Delisle, and Montegue Rhodes James could bring sustained attention to bear on one or two great manuscript collections, the data in mind or at their fingertips. Their modern analogues are more likely to be specialists in one area of study rather than a single collection.

74. Time and again I have unexpectedly encountered new texts while consulting manuscripts either on- or off-site. Internet connection allows for a quick identification via Boolean searches (note 20, above). The process is supported by 90 GB of digital images representing over 3,500 manuscripts from 200-plus libraries and stored on my laptop computer. This data is summarized on an 800-page searchable master list and supplemented by a further 15 GB of PDF scans of secondary sources that have been organized into coherent files. Safe storage involves three 128 GB flash drives, one at home, another in the office, and a third in my travel carry-on. If research is where you are, so too is one's library.

able to pursue multiple projects simultaneously or on a rolling basis,[75] the latter with an eye to establishing a research platform for the next funding application. The availability of digital images of manuscripts also causes us to ask new questions of the materials. It contributes to a greater focus on the producers and readers of the texts and works in the forms that actually appear in the manuscripts and not merely on the original text.[76]

(3) Finally, technological change has expanded the pale of inclusion. During the era of Sgambati and Fabricius, manuscript research (not to mention literacy itself) was beyond all but an exceedingly thin slice of the population. Over the next three centuries, a series of interconnected political, technological, economic, and social changes culminated in the democratization of higher education in North America and Western Europe after 1945. This process was gradual and partial, yet still unprecedented, and had the correlative benefit of an equally unprecedented faculty hiring boom. Now the digital revolution has democratized information itself and with it research scholarship. These demographic and economic effects cannot be overstated. Hitherto, manuscript research was restricted to those who could afford it and had the time and position to pursue it. Now it can be undertaken today by all persons with a certain level of training and an internet connection, regardless of their academic rank or financial situation.[77] *If research is where you are, it is also now available to all.* The field has grown to encompass not only a far greater percentage of full-time professors, but their advanced graduate students, along with librarians, curators, editors, independent scholars, sessional instructors, and members of research teams.[78]

---

75. Once inside a library and working with its manuscripts, researchers will note copies of texts that, although not the immediate subject of their investigation, are nonetheless interesting from the perspective of future projects.

76. Hugo Lundhaug brought this seminal point to my attention in private communication.

77. Junior scholars are not usually in a position to apply for the major grants that are necessary for sustained research travel and the purchase of manuscript reproductions. Many have reported in private conversation that they are able to continue their research as a result of the digital revolution and the cumulative advantages it has imparted.

78. The *elenchi* provide a good indication of the expansion of the field. An *elenchus* is a sheet that is delivered to a researcher along with the requested manuscript, on which are the names of the scholars who have consulted the manuscript previously and to which the present researcher is required to add his or her name. *Elenchi* are

This paper began by qualifying its approach as that of an end-user scholar, rather than a librarian, archivist, curator, or technical specialist. But the digital revolution has begun to blur and even collapse such distinctions. This, too, represents a transformation, in this case the categories that are used to structure information, which in turn re-orders the ways that we receive and assimilate this information.[79] We are what we know—and when this changes, we change.

5. A Coda

Despite the manifold advantages imparted by the digital revolution, there remain good reasons for researchers to continue to visit libraries in person and consult the manuscripts by autopsy.[80] As noted, we are only one-third of the way to having full, free online access to high-resolution images of the world's medieval manuscripts. Hence the ongoing need to visit manuscript collections, particularly to investigate generic catalogue references to apocryphal works, apocalyptic texts, and other neglected literature, as discussed. It should also be noted that the digital revolution has transformed the study of writings that are preserved in Latin and the western vernacular manuscripts more profoundly than those preserved in manuscripts in other languages and cultural traditions.[81]

---

rare today, although one still encounters them in libraries, particularly in Italy. Many stretch back to the late nineteenth century. I always take the time to see who has consulted the manuscript previously. Such lists reinforce the sense that we in the present are building upon the work of those who came before us, just as those who are yet to come will build upon our own work. Over the years I have read and signed several hundred *elenchi*. In my experience, the number of names that have been recorded over the past two decades is equal or greater to those recorded in the entire century beforehand.

79. I am grateful to Michael Johnson for highlighting this point to me in private communication.

80. On the deleterious effects of the digital revolution on scholarly activity beyond information loss caused by dead links and vanished websites, see Paul Gooding, "Mass Digitization and the Garbage Dump: The Conflicting Needs of Quantitative and Qualitative Methods," *Literary and Linguistic Computing* 28 (2013): 425–31.

81. Many manuscripts in these other traditions have not been catalogued, much less photographed and digitalized. Consider the Ethiopian Manuscript Microfilm Library (EMML) collection, which is housed at HMML (notes 18 and 31, above). HMML also preserves a major microfilm collection of Syriac manuscripts, as well as the world's largest repository of digital images of Eastern manuscripts, many of which

Other, more specialized tasks still demand on-site investigation: counting quires, searching for watermarks, dry-point ruling and glosses, and so on.[82] Likewise, pages damaged by iron-gall ink corrosion do not reproduce well in digital images and thus require on-site examination.[83] (3-D imaging technology may eventually prove to be of profit for all these tasks and issues.) Onsite consultation permits researchers to examine the in-house copies of the catalogues of a library's own manuscript holdings. These often contain unique handwritten annotations and emendations that have been made by generations of past librarians.[84] Some libraries, such as the Biblioteca Apostolica Vaticana, permit on-site access to digitalized manuscripts, manuscript catalogues, and hand-lists that are unavailable to those who access the databases remotely.

Beyond these things, there is also something to be said about physically working with manuscripts—holding a codex in one's hands, thumbing through its pages, discovering its contents, inspecting its bindings, discovering its secrets. Over time, a sensitive researcher will acquire a certain feel for manuscripts and their contents that expresses itself in educated hunches about codices that are likely to contain certain types of material,[85] even if this information is unrecorded in a catalogue. I am not suggesting that there is anything mystical about the phenomenon. Rather, it should be understood more in terms of experience—analogous to the state that a master woodworker attains by working constantly with the material or a field ornithologist achieves with a lifetime's experience watching birds.

In February 2018, I was photographing some fire-scorched manuscripts at the Biblioteca Nazionale Universitaria in Torino, relics of the disastrous 1904 inferno. At a long table beside me, a professor was direct-

---

were photographed *in situ* in the Middle East. Such films and images, however, represent only a fraction of the total number of manuscripts.

82. I am indebted to Andreas Nievergelt, who in June 2015 introduced me to dry-point glosses and kindly demonstrated striking illustrations in some eighth and ninth-century codices at the Stiftsbibliothek Saint Gallen. I thank Alberto Campagnolo for devoting the good part of a lunch together to enlightening me on the benefits of the digital revolution on codicological research.

83. This effect is quite pronounced in paper manuscripts of the sixteenth and seventeenth centuries, with their flowing cursive script. Portions of such texts are often illegible, even under close examination. Digital photographs are often worse.

84. Even some of these (e.g., many of the Bodleian catalogues) have now been digitalized and uploaded to the internet.

85. "Textual truffles," so one colleague described them in personal conversation.

ing a seminar on manuscripts, surrounded by a group of perhaps a dozen undergraduate students. Several codices were on the table, the objects of great fascination. The students were using their smartphones to photograph the manuscript pages for private study as their professor explained their contents and contexts. This is the future of manuscript research in the digital age.

Bibliography

Adso Dervensis. *De ortu et tempore Antichristi*. CCCM 45. Turnhout: Brepols, 1976.
Andrews, Tara, and Caroline Macé, eds. *Analysis of Ancient and Medieval Texts and Manuscripts: Digital Approaches*. Lectio 1. Turnhout: Brepols, 2014.
Birnbaum, David J., Sheila Bonde, and Mike Kestemont, eds. *The Digital Middle Ages: An Introduction. Speculum* 92.S1 (2017).
Boyle, Jennifer E., and Helen J. Burgess, eds. *The Routledge Research Companion to Digital Medieval Literature*. New York: Routledge, 2017.
Chalmers, David J. "Extended Cognition and Extended Consciousness." Pages 9–20 in *Andy Clark and His Critics*. Edited by Matteo Colombo, Elizabeth Irvine, and Mog Stapleton. Oxford: Oxford University Press, 2019.
Clark, Mark J. "How to Edit *The Historia Scholastica* of Peter Comestor?" *RBén* 116 (2006): 83–91.
Clivaz, Claire, Paul Dilley, David Hamidović, Mladen Popović, Caroline T. Schroeder, and Joseph Verheyden, eds. *Digital Humanities in Ancient Jewish, Christian and Arabic Traditions. Journal of Religion, Media and Digital Culture* 5.1 (2016).
Cranz, F. Edward. *A Microfilm Corpus of Unpublished Inventories of Latin Manuscripts before 1600*. New London, CT: Renaissance Society of America, 1987.
Cranz, F. Edward, in consultation with Paul Oskar Kristeller. *A Microfilm Corpus of the Indexes to Printed Catalogues of Latin Manuscripts before 1600 A.D*. 3rd ed. New London, CT: n.p, 1982.
Batalova, Stilyana. "Manuscript Catalogues and Manuscripts via Internet." *Scripta & e-Scripta* 3–4 (2006): 25–28.
Bell, David. Review of *A Genealogy of Terror in Eighteenth-Century France*, by Ronald Schechter, *New York Review of Books* (28 June 2018): 75–76.

DiTommaso, Lorenzo. "The *Apocalypse* of Pseudo-Methodius: Notes on a Recent Edition." *Medioevo greco* 17 (2017): 311–21.

———. "The Apocryphal Daniel Apocalypses: Works, Manuscripts, and Overview." *ETL* 94 (2018): 275–316.

———. "Microform Manuscript Collections in the United States." *Bulletin de l'Association pour l'étude de la littérature apocryphe chrétienne* 17 (2007): 14–16.

———. "The 'Old Testament Pseudepigrapha' as Category and Corpus." Pages 253–79 in *A Guide to Early Jewish Texts and Traditions in Christian Transmission*, ed. Alexander Kulik. Oxford: Oxford University Press, 2019.

———. "The *Penitence of Solomon* (*Poenitentia Salomonis*)." Pages 371–452 in *The Embroidered Bible: Studies in Biblical Apocrypha and Pseudepigrapha in Honour of Michael E. Stone*. Edited by Lorenzo DiTommaso, Matthias Henze, and William Adler. SVTP 26. Leiden: Brill, 2018.

———. "Pseudepigrapha Notes III: 4. Old Testament Pseudepigrapha in the Yale University MS Collection." *JSP* 20 (2010): 3–80.

Fabricius, Johann A. *Codex apocryphus Novi Testamenti*. Hamburg: Schiller, 1703; second, rev. ed. 1719.

———. *Codex pseudepigraphus Veteris Testamenti: Collectus, castigatus, testimoniisque, censuris et animaduersionibus illustrates*. Hamburg: C. Liebezeit, 1713.

Gooding, Paul. "Mass Digitization and the Garbage Dump: The Conflicting Needs of Quantitative and Qualitative Methods." *Literary and Linguistic Computing* 28 (2013): 425–31.

Hawk, Brandon W. "The Literary Contexts and Early Transmission of the Latin *Life of Judas*." *JMRC* 44 (2018): 60–76.

Heal, Kristian S. "Digital Humanities and the Study of Christian Apocrypha: Resources, Prospects and Problems." Pages 270–78 in *Forbidden Texts on the Western Frontier*. Edited by Tony Burke. Eugene, OR: Cascade, 2015.

Heist, William W. *The Fifteen Signs before Doomsday*. East Lansing, MI: Michigan State Press, 1952.

James, M. R. Preface to *Apocrypha Anecdota I*. Cambridge: Cambridge University Press, 1893.

Laureys, Marc, and Daniel Verhelst, "Pseudo-Methodius, *Revelationes*: Textgeschichte und kritische Edition. Ein Leuven-Groninger Forschungsprojekt." Pages 122–36 in *The Use and Abuse of Eschatology in the Middle Ages*. Edited by Wernner Verbeke, Daniel Verhelst, and

Andries Welkenhuysen. MedLov 15. Leuven: Leuven University Press, 1988.

Lied, Liv Ingeborg. "Digitization and Manuscripts as Visual Objects: Reflections from a Media Studies Perspective." Paper presented at the Annual Meeting of the Society of Biblical Literature. Atlanta, GA, 24 November 2015.

———. "Text—Work—Manuscript: What Is an 'Old Testament Pseudepigraphon'?" *JSP* 25 (2015): 150–65.

Lied, Liv Ingeborg, and Matthew Phillip Monger. "Look to the East: New and Forgotten Sources of *4 Ezra*." Pages 639–52 in *The Embroidered Bible: Studies in Biblical Apocrypha and Pseudepigrapha in Honour of Michael E. Stone*. Edited by Lorenzo DiTommaso, Matthias Henze, and William Adler. SVTP 26. Leiden: Brill, 2018

Lolos, Anastasios. *Die Apokalypse des Ps.-Methodios*. BkPh 83. Meisenheim am Glan: Hain, 1976.

———. *Die dritte und vierte Redaktion des Ps.-Methodios*. BkPh 94. Meisenheim am Glan: Hain, 1978.

Lundhaug, Hugo. "An Illusion of Textual Stability: Textual Fluidity, New Philology, and the Nag Hammadi Codices." Pages 20–54 in *Snapshots of Evolving Traditions: Jewish and Christian Manuscript Culture, Textual Fluidity, and New Philology*. Edited by Liv Ingeborg Lied and Hugo Lundhaug. TUGAL 175. Berlin: de Gruyter, 2017.

Momigliano, Arnaldo D. "A Hundred Years after Ranke." *Studies in Historiography* (1966): 105–11.

Peursen, W. Th. van, Ernst D. Thoutenhoofd, and Adriaan van der Weel, eds. *Text Comparison and Digital Creativity: The Production of Presence and Meaning in Digital Text Scholarship*. Leiden: Brill, 2010.

Quenzer, Jörg, Dmitry Bondarev, and Jan-Ulrich Sobisch, eds. *Manuscript Cultures: Mapping the Field*. Berlin: de Gruyter, 2014.

Sakel, Dean. "The Manuscripts of the *Chronicle of 1570*." Byzantion 83 (2013): 363–74.

Schechter, Ronald. *A Genealogy of Terror in Eighteenth-Century France*. Chicago: University of Chicago Press, 2018.

Sgambati, Scipione. *Archiuorum Veteris Testamenti libri tres; De rebus ad Deum spectantibus; De primis patribus; De uiris illustribus in Veteri Testamento*. Napoles: Mutio, 1703.

Treharne, Elaine. "Fleshing out the Text: The Transcendent Manuscript in the Digital Age." *postmedieval* 4 (2013): 465–78.

Vine, Agnus. "Scriptorium: When to Build a Digital Archive Rather Than a Digital Edition." Number 3.2.2 in *A Handbook of Editing Early Modern Texts*. Edited by Claire Loffmann and Harriet Phillips. New York: Routledge, 2017.

13

The Pseudepigrapha in Greek: Translation, Composition, and the Diaspora

Martha Himmelfarb

In the second part of the Second Temple period, the language of the Jews of the western diaspora was Greek. It was the primary language that they read, though perhaps some could read Hebrew and Aramaic as well, and, as far as we can tell, Greek was the only language in which they wrote. In this essay, I consider the significance of the pseudepigrapha in Greek for the diaspora from two different angles: translation and composition. (Henceforth, unless otherwise indicated, *diaspora* means the western diaspora and primarily Egypt, home to virtually all the diaspora literature we can locate with any confidence.)

In the first part of the essay, I discuss the implications of the translation into Greek of pseudepigrapha written in Hebrew or Aramaic for our understanding of the diaspora. The Aramaic or Hebrew fragments of pseudepigrapha—the Book of the Watchers and Jubilees found among the Dead Sea Scrolls, for example—have given us a better understanding of the contexts in which those works were composed and have provided insight into a range of textual issues. But they should also remind us that, prior to the discovery of the Dead Sea Scrolls, the only reason the Book of the Watchers and Jubilees (as well as most other pseudepigrapha) were known to us is that they had been translated into Greek, at least some of them, for Jews in the diaspora. They were thus available to Christians, who continued to transmit them in daughter translations after Jews stopped using them.[1] In contrast, the New Jerusalem text, to offer just one example,

---

1. See Robert A. Kraft, "The Multiform Jewish Heritage of Early Christianity," in *Christianity, Judaism and Other Greco-Roman Cults: Studies for Morton Smith at Sixty*,

was unknown before the discovery of the Dead Sea Scrolls, although it is attested among them in more copies than the Book of the Watchers, either because it was never translated or because the translation failed to catch on with Christians. Once Jews lost interest in it, it ceased to be transmitted.

Yet despite the probability that diaspora Jews comprised the earliest audience for many of the pseudepigrapha translated into Greek, scholarship on the pseudepigrapha has had very little to say about the implications of these translations for our understanding of the diaspora. Of course, the possibility that Christians were responsible for the translations into Greek of Hebrew and Aramaic pseudepigrapha deserves consideration, especially since the works were eventually transmitted by Christians, and without evidence for a pre-Christian date for a translation, it is rarely possible to be certain whether a translation was undertaken by Jews or Christians. But for the Book of the Watchers in particular there is strong evidence for an early date for the translation, and I believe that there are persuasive arguments in favor of Jewish translation for other works as well, as I will discuss shortly.[2]

In the second part of the essay I discuss what it would mean if a work widely assumed to have been composed in Hebrew or Aramaic, such as Judith, the Psalms of Solomon, or Baruch, were instead shown to have been composed in Greek, as some recent scholarship has argued on linguistic grounds for each of these texts. To be sure, given the evidence that Jews from Palestine were active as translators, Greek composition does not necessarily require origin in the diaspora. My discussion will focus on Judith, for which I think there is a case to be made for diaspora provenance, with a few words about the Psalms of Solomon. At the very least, it is a worthwhile exercise to consider how origin in the diaspora of either or both of those works would change our picture of diaspora Judaism.

---

ed. Jacob Neusner, 4 vols. (Leiden: Brill, 1975), 3:174–99; Kraft, "The Pseudepigrapha in Christianity," in *Tracing the Threads: Studies in the Vitality of Jewish Pseudepigrapha*, ed. John C. Reeves, EJL 6 (Atlanta: Scholars Press, 1994), 55–86; and Kraft, "Setting the Stage and Framing Some Central Questions," *JSJ* 32 (2001): 371–95.

2. Matthew Black suggests that translation by Christians is the default assumption: "There is no reason to doubt that this Greek version [the *Vorlage* of Ethiopic 1 Enoch], like other such Greek translations of intertestamental writings, was made by Christian scribes for Christians, in some cases probably for Jewish-Christian congregations." Matthew Black, *The Book of Enoch or 1 Enoch: A New English Edition with Commentary and Textual Notes*, SVTP 7 (Leiden: Brill, 1985), 4. He does not, however, offer any support for this claim.

Translation

In the Second Temple period, Jews engaged in translation in order to make Hebrew and Aramaic works available to the Greek-speaking diaspora. We have considerable evidence about their activity. The most famous Jewish translation, and probably also the first, was the Torah. Scholarly opinion is divided about the plausibility of the Letter of Aristeas's picture of the translators as natives of Jerusalem brought to Alexandria to undertake the translation.[3] But whether or not the picture is accurate, by the second century BCE there can be no doubt of the role of Jews from Palestine in translating Hebrew texts into Greek. Ben Sira's grandson tells us that he undertook the translation of his grandfather's work after arriving in Egypt from Palestine in 132 BCE, and the colophon to the Greek translation of Esther, which records the delivery of the translation to Egypt in 114 BCE, identifies the translator as Lysimachus son of Ptolemy of Jerusalem. For most translations of books of the prophets and other works that would become part of the Hebrew canon, there is not enough evidence to locate the translation geographically with any confidence. The elements of language and interpretation invoked in favor of origin in Palestine or Egypt are rarely decisive. But there is little evidence for knowledge of Hebrew or Aramaic among Egyptian Jews in the Hellenistic era, which means that even if some translations were made in Egypt, the translators, like Ben Sira's grandson, are likely to have been Jews from Palestine.[4] The work of the kaige-Theodotion translators and revisers around the turn of the era is also widely viewed as having taken place in Palestine.[5]

---

3. See the discussion of Gilles Dorival and the references there in Marguerite Harl, Gilles Dorival, and Olivier Munnich, *La Bible grecque des Septante: Du judaïsme hellénistique au christianisme ancient* (Paris: Éditions du Cerf/Éditions du C.N.R.S., 1988), 58–62. Jan Joosten has recently argued that the character of the Greek of the translation of the Torah fits best with translators of Egyptian origin who belong to a community dominated by soldiers. Jan Joosten, "Language as Symptom: Linguistic Clues to the Social Background of the Seventy," in *Collected Studies on the Septuagint* (Tübingen: Mohr Siebeck, 2012), 185–94.

4. Emanuel Tov, "Reflections on the Septuagint with Special Attention Paid to Post-Pentateuchal Translations," in of *Textual Criticism of the Hebrew Bible, Qumran, Septuagint: Collected Essays*, vol. 3 (Leiden: Brill, 2015), 429–48.

5. Olivier Munnich in Harl, Dorival, and Munnich, *La Bible grecque des Septante*, 150–61, and references there.

The first translation I would like to discuss, and the one I shall treat in greatest detail, is the Book of the Watchers.[6] The Book of the Watchers was completed sometime around the turn of the third to the second century BCE, and its impact is already evident in the second century in the Apocalypse of Weeks, the Book of Dreams, and Jubilees.[7] It would thus not be surprising if Jews in Palestine in the centuries before the turn of the era wanted to make it available to Greek-speaking Jews in the diaspora just as they made other highly valued texts available. It is true that the Book of the Watchers embraces a piety that might appear out of tune with diaspora Judaism or at least its Alexandrian version, but we shall see that it is not the only such text to have been translated into Greek during the Second Temple period.

Only a single manuscript of the Greek of the Book of the Watchers survives: the Codex Panopolitanus, also known as the Akhmim or Gizeh manuscript. Current scholarship dates the codex to the fifth or sixth century, earlier than previous opinions but far too late to establish the translation in the Second Temple period.[8] It contains almost the entire Book of the Watchers as it is known in Ethiopic together with excerpts from the Gospel of Peter and the Apocalypse of Peter. Its text of the Book of the Watchers begins with 19.3–21.9, ending in mid-sentence, and continues with 1.1–32.6a, including 19.3–21.9 in its expected place. The copy is the work of two scribes; the second one takes over in the middle of 14.22, at the top of a new page of the codex. The standard scholarly view understands the placement of 19.3–21.9 at the beginning as reflecting error or confusion on the part of the scribe, so much so that Matthew Black's publication of the text ignores the passage and begins

---

6. For a thorough and up-to-date presentation of the state of the question for the Greek of the Book of the Watchers with an extensive bibliography, see Kelly Coblentz Bautch, "5.2.1 The Book of the Watchers-Greek," in *Deuterocanonical Scriptures*, vol. 2 of *Textual History of the Bible*, ed. Frank Feder and Matthias Henze (Leiden: Brill, forthcoming). I would like to thank Matthias Henze and Kelly Coblentz Bautch for allowing me access to the article before its publication.

7. I refer to the Apocalypse of Weeks rather than to the Epistle of Enoch, the larger work in which it is embedded, because a second century date for the Epistle of Enoch as a whole is possible but by no means certain. See George W. E. Nickelsburg, *1 Enoch 1: A Commentary on the Book of 1 Enoch, Chapters 1–36, 81–108*, Hermeneia (Minneapolis: Fortress, 2001), 427–28.

8. Nickelsburg, *1 Enoch 1*, 12.

with chapter 1.[9] A more positive interpretation of the scribe's activity is possible, but in any case the codex is by no means a straightforward witness to the Greek translation.[10] The other major source for the Greek text of the Book of the Watchers is the chronography of George Syncellos from the beginning of the ninth century. It contains a significant body of extracts from the Book of the Watchers, which reached Syncellos as found in earlier chronographies.[11]

The strongest evidence for a Second Temple date for the translation of the Book of the Watchers comes from allusions and quotations, which appear in Greek and Latin texts from as early as the late first or early second century.[12] The texts in question are all Christian, but the early dates make it likely that the translation was already in existence in the Second Temple period. Second Enoch's debt to the Book of the Watchers would also provide evidence for the Greek in the Second Temple period—on the assumption that 2 Enoch dates to the turn of the era, an assumption that I accept but that is by no means certain.[13]

---

9. Matthew Black, *Apocalypsis Henochi Graece*, PVTG 3 (Leiden: Brill, 1970), 19; he refers to the codex as containing 19:3-21:9 "in duplicate" (8). See also, e.g., Nickelsburg, *1 Enoch 1*, 12; Black, *The Book of Enoch or 1 Enoch*; and Erik W. Larson, "The Translation of Enoch from Aramaic into Greek" (PhD diss., New York University, 1995).

10. For a reading of the placement of 19:3-21:9 at the beginning of the Book of the Watchers as meaningful, see the Princeton dissertation-in-progress of Elena Dugan.

11. On Synkellos's extracts, see Nicklesburg, *1 Enoch 1*, 12-13. Luca Arcari, "Il *Nachleben* del testo greco del *1Enoc* in alcuni scritti del Christianesimo antico: É esistita 'una' traduzione greca di *1Enoc*?," *Materia giudaica* 10 (2005): 57-72 (English summary, 72), argues that the text preserved by Synkellos reflects a different translation from that of Codex Panopolitanus.

12. For the citations and allusions, Nickelsburg, *1 Enoch 1*, 87-95.

13. The debt is most apparent in Enoch's ascent (2 En. 3-9 [*AOT*]; 2 En. 3-22 [*OTP*]). Although 2 Enoch is almost universally treated as a work of the Second Temple era, it is preserved only in Slavonic, and the earliest manuscripts date to the fourteenth century. I am not convinced that the Coptic fragments identified by Joost L. Hagen as part of 2 Enoch really belong to the work, but even if they do, they date from the eighth century, still a long distance from the Second Temple period. For the identification of the fragments, see Joost L. Hagen, "No Longer 'Slavonic' Only: 2 Enoch Attested in Coptic from Nubia," in *New Perspectives on 2 Enoch: No Longer Slavonic Only*, ed. Andrei A. Orlov and Gabriel Boccaccini (Leiden: Brill, 2012), 7-34. For criticism of the identification, see Christfried Böttrich, "The Angel of Tartarus and the Supposed Coptic Fragments of 2 Enoch," *Early Christianity* 4 (2013): 509-21.

A Second Temple dating for the translation of the Book of the Watchers also finds support in the similarity of its language to that of the Greek of specific books of the LXX. Not long after József T. Milik's publication of the Aramaic, James Barr suggested that there are particular points of contact between the Greek of the Enochic works and the Greek of Daniel, particularly LXX Daniel, although he noted that some similarity was to be expected since Daniel is written partly in Aramaic and contains apocalyptic material.[14] Erik Larson's more systematic study of the Greek of the Enochic corpus some years later agreed with Barr's findings.[15] LXX Daniel is usually dated around the turn of the second to the first century BCE.[16] The close relationship of the Greek of the Book of the Watchers to that of LXX Daniel thus strengthens the case for a date before the turn of the era for the translation of the Book of the Watchers.

Barr assumes without discussion that the translation of the Book of the Watchers was part of a larger translation, dating from the Second Temple period, of an Enochic corpus that he does not define. Larson also embraces the picture of a single translation of early date, arguing that the Greek translators worked on a collection of three Enochic works—the Book of the Watchers, the Book of Dreams, and the Epistle of Enoch—that are attested together in one of the manuscripts from the Dead Sea Scrolls.[17] He admits, however, that the Greek evidence demonstrates that both the Book of the Watchers and the Epistle of Enoch circulated separately well into the Christian era. Thus neither Barr nor Larson separates his consideration of the Greek of the Book of the Watchers from the Greek evidence for the other Enochic works found among the Dead Sea Scrolls.

Barr and Larson may be correct that the other Enochic works were translated together with the Book of the Watchers during the Second Temple period. Of course, even if the works were translated one by one

---

14. József T. Milik, *The Books of Enoch: Aramaic Fragments of Qumrân Cave 4* (Oxford: Clarendon, 1976); James Barr, "Aramaic-Greek Notes on the Book of Enoch (I)," *JSS* 23 (1978): 184–98; Barr, "Aramaic-Greek Notes on the Book of Enoch (II)," *JSS* 24 (1979): 179–92. For the conclusion, see Barr, "Aramaic-Greek Notes (II)," 191.

15. Larson, "Translation of Enoch," 203, 345.

16. Larson, "Translation of Enoch," 203, and references there.

17. Erik W. Larson, "The Relation between the Greek and Aramaic Texts of Enoch," in *The Dead Sea Scrolls Fifty Years after Their Discovery: Proceedings of the Jerusalem Congress, July 25–27, 1997*, ed. Lawrence H. Schiffman, Emanuel Tov, and James C. VanderKam (Jerusalem: Israel Exploration Society in cooperation with the Shrine of the Book, 2000), 437; Larson, "Translation of Enoch," 191–98, 346–48.

rather than as part of a single project, it does not rule out a Second Temple date for the individual translations. But the nature of the evidence makes it impossible to be confident about either claim.[18] Apart from the Book of the Watchers, the only Enochic work for which a significant amount of Greek is preserved is the Epistle of Enoch, and only a very brief passage from the Noah chapters (106–107) overlaps with the Aramaic fragments. A few lines of the Greek of the Book of Dreams survive in two separate witnesses. The Astronomical Book is attested in a very small fragment from Oxyrhynchus, but it seems likely that the Greek was a revision of the Aramaic rather than a translation since the Aramaic fragments differ from the Ethiopic in fundamental ways.[19] In other words, comparison of the Greek and Aramaic versions of Enochic literature is primarily a discussion of the translation of the Book of the Watchers, so the connections to LXX Daniel established on this basis and the dating they imply may not apply to the other Enochic works.

The patristic allusions to the other Enochic works are neither as early nor as frequent as those to the Book of the Watchers, which means that they do not as strongly favor a Second Temple date.[20] Second Enoch's debt to the Astronomical Book as well as to the Book of the Watchers suggests that some form of the Astronomical Book was available in the Second Temple period, again, on the assumption that 2 Enoch belongs to the Second Temple period.[21] If the identification of several papyrus fragments from Qumran Cave 7 as part of a Greek translation of the Epistle of Enoch is correct, it would settle the question in favor of an early translation for that work at least.[22] But it is hard to be confident when, as George Nickelsburg notes, the

---

18. For a brief discussion of the Greek evidence for the Astronomical Book, the Book of Dreams, and the Epistle of Enoch, Nickelsburg, *1 Enoch 1*, 13–14, with references to the relevant editions. Black, *Apocalypsis Henochi Graece*, publishes all the evidence except the Oxyrhynchus fragments of the Astronomical Book and the Book of Dreams.

19. For a persuasive case for the identity of the fragment, see Randall D. Chesnutt, "*Oxyrhynchus Papyrus* 2069 and the Compositional History of *1 Enoch*," *JBL* 129 (2010): 491–95.

20. For the allusions, Nickelsburg, *1 Enoch 1*, 82–95.

21. Thus VanderKam in George W. E. Nickelsburg and James C. VanderKam, *1 Enoch 2: A Commentary on the Book of 1 Enoch 37–82*, Hermeneia (Minneapolis: Fortress, 2012), 348. The relevant passage is 2 En. 6 (*AOT*) or 2 En. 11–16 (*OTP*).

22. G.-Wilhelm Nebe, "'7Q4'—Möglichkeit und Grenze einer Identifikation," *RQ* 13 (1988): 629–33; Ernest A. Muro Jr., "The Greek Fragments of Enoch from Qumran

fragments preserve only seven percent of the text they are alleged to have contained.²³ The Oxyrhynchus fragments of the Astronomical Book and the Book of Dreams probably date to the early fourth century.²⁴ Altogether, then, there is nothing to exclude a Second Temple date for the translations of these Enochic works, but there is nothing to require it.

The translation of the Book of the Watchers into Greek presumably reflects enthusiasm for the work outside Qumran since it seems unlikely that members of the Qumran sect would have been interested in undertaking a translation for the benefit of Jews of the diaspora. It also seems reasonable to assume that the translators of the Book of the Watchers would not have engaged in a time-consuming and difficult task if they had not expected the work to find an audience in the diaspora. In addition to 2 Enoch, some scholars would point to 3 Baruch and the Testament of Abraham, which also recount their heroes' ascents to heaven, as evidence that the translators were correct. My view is that both the Testament of Abraham and 3 Baruch should be understood as Christian compositions,²⁵ but even if it is difficult to document its Jewish reception beyond 2 Enoch, the wide knowledge of the Greek version of the Book of the Watchers in early Christian literature indicates that it was popular enough to remain in circulation.

Now let me consider briefly the significance of the Greek translations of several other Aramaic works with points of contact with the Book of the Watchers. One such work is the book of Tobit. Devorah Dimant makes a powerful case that Tobit's status as part of the Greek canon has obscured its connections to a group of interrelated Aramaic texts found among the Dead Sea Scrolls that includes the Book of the Watchers and Aramaic Levi.²⁶ She also argues that Tobit reflects distinctive features of the laws found in sectarian texts.²⁷ Tobit's place in the Greek canon means that the Greek is very well attested, but the larger textual situation is extremely complex.

Cave 7 (7Q4, 7Q8, & 7Q12 = 7QEn gr = Enoch 103:3–4, 7–8)," *RevQ* 18 (1997): 307–12; Émile Puech, "Sept fragments grecs de la *Lettre d'Hénoch* (*1 Hén* 100, 103, et 105) dans la grotte 7 de Qumrân (=7QHéngr)," *RevQ* 18 (1997): 313–23.

23. George W. E. Nickelsburg, "The Greek Fragments of *1 Enoch* from Qumran Cave 7: An Unproven Identification," *RevQ* 21 (2004): 631–34.

24. Chesnutt, "*Oxyrhynchus Papyrus* 2069," 487.

25. See below, n.58, for references.

26. Devorah Dimant, "Tobit and the Qumran Aramaic Texts," in *From Enoch to Tobit: Collected Studies in Ancient Jewish Literature* (Tübingen: Mohr Siebeck, 2017), 173–91.

27. Dimant, "Book of Tobit and the Qumran Aramaic Texts."

Tobit's original language was likely Aramaic, the language of most of the fragments from the Dead Sea Scrolls, but the Dead Sea Scrolls preserve a Hebrew fragment as well.[28] There are also two different forms of the Greek translation, one apparently a revision of the other, with a third form preserved for part of the work.[29] It is the widespread assumption that at least the original translation is owed to Jews in the Second Temple period, and the assumption seems plausible, although undoubted allusions to the work are not early enough to make it certain.[30]

Aramaic Levi is another work with a worldview close to that of the Book of the Watchers. Although it appears to embrace a 364-day calendar (as indicated by the dates of the birth of Levi's sons and the use of numbered as opposed to named months), it is not a sectarian composition; its sacrificial laws, for example, show no evidence of distinctively sectarian rules.[31] Unlike the Book of the Watchers and Tobit, however, Aramaic Levi did not circulate in translation for very long. Apart from the evidence to be discussed momentarily, it survives only in Aramaic fragments from the Dead Sea Scrolls and the Cairo Genizah;[32] the Testament of Levi, which is deeply indebted to Aramaic Levi throughout, is an independent composition and

---

28. Thus Dimant, "Tobit and the Qumran Aramaic Texts," 175; see also Andrew B. Perrin, "An Almanac of Tobit Studies: 2000–2014," *CurBR* 13 (2014): 111–13. For the view that it is impossible to determine whether the original language was Aramaic or Hebrew, see Loren Stuckenbruck and Stuart Weeks, "Tobit," in *The T&T Clark Companion to the Septuagint*, ed. James K. Aitken (London: Bloomsbury, 2015), 239–41; they are similarly agnostic about the language from which the Greek was translated, noting that it need not have been the original language (240–41).

29. Carey A. Moore, *Tobit*, AB (New York: Doubleday, 1996), 53–60.

30. Thus Moore: "Tobit, like other books of the Apocrypha, was translated into Greek for the benefit of those Jews who could not read the Semitic text" (*Tobit*, 52). For possible allusions, Moore, *Tobit*, 46–48.

31. On the calendar, see Jonas C. Greenfield and Michael E. Stone, "Remarks on the Aramaic Testament of Levi from the Geniza," *RB* 86 (1979): 224. On the sacrificial laws, see Martha Himmelfarb, "Earthly Sacrifice and Heavenly Incense: The Law of the Priesthood in *Aramaic Levi* and *Jubilees*," in *Between Temple and Torah: Essays on Priests, Scribes, and Visionaries in the Second Temple Period and Beyond* (Tübingen: Mohr Siebeck, 2013), 62–72; Lawrence H. Schiffman, "Sacrificial Halakhah in the Fragments of the *Aramaic Levi Document* from Qumran, the Cairo Geniza, and the Mt. Athos Monastery," in *Reworking the Bible: Apocryphal and Related Texts at Qumran*, ed. Esther G. Chazon, Devorah Dimant, and Ruth A. Clements (Leiden: Brill, 2005), 177–202.

32. For a complete listing and brief discussion of the witnesses, see Jonas C.

not a translation. The evidence for a translation consists of two substantial passages corresponding to preserved portions of Aramaic Levi inserted into the Testament of Levi at appropriate points in an eleventh-century manuscript of the Testaments of the Twelve Patriarchs from Mount Athos.[33] One passage reports Levi's prayer; the other, Isaac's instructions for priestly practice. The most likely explanation for the presence of these passages is that the scribe of the Mount Athos manuscript, or the scribe of an unknown manuscript on which he drew, had access to a Greek translation of Aramaic Levi. If the author of the Testaments of the Twelve Patriarchs made use of a Greek translation of Aramaic Levi in composing the Testament of Levi, the translation dates to no later than the middle of the second century. In any case, the subject matter of Aramaic Levi makes translation by Jews in the Second Temple period likely; the brief career of the translation suggests that Christians lost interest in it rather quickly.

The book of Jubilees is another notable example of a text indebted to the Book of the Watchers that was translated into Greek. Jubilees differs from the Enochic corpus, Tobit, and Aramaic Levi in having been composed in Hebrew. As for the Enochic corpus, the full text reaches us because it was taken up by the Ethiopic Church. The Greek version survives only in citations; the most important sources for them are Epiphanius and the chronographers Synkellos and Kedrenos. The passages used by the chronographers are usually understood to go back to Julius Africanus, which would mean that the Greek translation was available by the early third century.[34] It seems likely to me that the translation is the work of Christians, a case I plan to argue elsewhere.

Greenfield, Michael E. Stone, and Esther Eshel, *The Aramaic Levi Document: Edition, Translation, Commentary* (Leiden: Brill, 2004), 1–6.

33. Marinus de Jonge refers to the manuscript in question as MS e (Marinus de Jonge, *The Testaments of the Twelve Patriarchs: A Critical Edition of the Greek Text*, in cooperation with H. W. Hollander, H. J. de Jonge, and Th. Korteweg [Leiden: Brill, 1978], xvii). The stemma proposed in this edition suggests that MS e is not descended from any known manuscript (xxxiii). Greenfield, Stone, and Eshel refer to it as MS Athos, Monastery of Kouloumous, Cod. 39 (*Aramaic Levi Document*, 5). Henryk Drawnel refers to it as MS Athos Kouloumousiou 39 (*An Aramaic Wisdom Text from Qumran: A New Interpretation of the Levi Document* [Leiden: Brill, 2004], 31). To the best of my knowledge, the most extensive discussion of the passages and their implications is Marinus de Jonge, *The Testaments of the Twelve Patriarchs: A Study of Their Text, Composition, and Origin* (Assen: Van Gorcum, 1953), 129–31.

34. On the Greek evidence, see James C. VanderKam, *Book of Jubilees*, CSCO 511,

Even if we cannot be certain, it is probable that the translations of some of the works just discussed were made during the Second Temple period, and, as already noted, it seems reasonable to assume that no one would have expended the effort involved in translating compositions of considerable length and complexity without confidence that there was an audience for them. Some Greek-speaking Jews must have been curious to read works by authors from Palestine who embraced a form of piety that as far as we know was not shared in the diaspora. The evidence for translation activity in Palestine makes it reasonable to assume that the translators of these works came from Palestine, whether they undertook the translations there or, like Ben Sira's grandson, in the diaspora. While it comes as no surprise that there were Jews from Palestine who were capable of translating Hebrew and Aramaic into Greek, it is noteworthy that some of them were sufficiently taken with the Book of the Watchers and likely other such works to undertake their translation. Nor was their knowledge of Greek merely linguistic: Larson points to several instances in which the translation of the Book of the Watchers makes use of vocabulary associated with Greek mythology, while Luca Arcari argues that the terminology related to knowledge in the Book of the Watchers reflects knowledge of Greek literature and philosophy.[35] Perhaps we should have assumed that countercultural piety or at least respect for it does not preclude knowledge of Greek culture, but it is nonetheless instructive to have such compelling evidence for this point. The translations should thus have an impact on our pictures not only of the Jews of the diaspora but also the Jews of Palestine.

Composition?

My goal thus far has been to consider the implications of the translation into Greek of a group of interrelated works attested among the Dead Sea Scrolls that have concerns quite distant from those usually associated with diaspora Jews. I turn now to the problem of texts preserved in Greek

---

Scriptores Aethiopici 88 (Leuven: Peeters, 1989), 2:xi–xiv; and VanderKam, *Jubilees 1: A Commentary on the Book of Jubilees Chapters 1–21*, Hermeneia (Minneapolis: Fortress, 2018), 10–14.

35. Larson, "Relation between the Greek and Aramaic Texts of Enoch," 41–44; Luca Arcari, "Il vocabolario della conoscenza nel testo greco del *Libro dei Vigilanti*: Per una definizione del *Sitz im Leben* della versione greca di *1 Enoc*," *Materia giudaica* 8 (2003): 95–104 (English summary, 103–4).

that are usually understood to have been translated from a Hebrew original and to reflect the concerns of Palestinian Jews, though without any traces of the sectarian affinities of the texts discussed in the first part of the paper. Judith, the Psalms of Solomon, and Baruch are leading examples of such works. Yet despite the widespread assumption, no evidence for Hebrew originals has been found among the Dead Sea Scrolls, and recent scholarship on each work has raised the possibility that Greek is its original language.[36] In the second part of the paper I consider the way our picture of Judaism in the diaspora would be affected if we understood Judith or, more briefly, the Psalms of Solomon, to have been composed in Greek, as some recent scholarship has proposed. It is, of course, dangerous to build arguments on the basis of absence. It is not impossible that the Dead Sea Scrolls contain fragments of the Hebrew originals of Judith, the Psalms of Solomon, Baruch, or other works known only in translation but that the fragments in which they survive are too small to identify. Furthermore, while it is true that the Dead Sea Scrolls preserve works that do not show obvious points of contact with the views of the Qumran community, such as Ben Sira and several Aramaic court tales, some works assumed to have Hebrew or Aramaic originals that are not found among the Dead Sea Scrolls would clearly have been objectionable to the community. It is not surprising, for example, that there is no evidence at Qumran for 1 Maccabees, a work of Hasmonean propaganda, and it is possible that Judith too was distasteful to the sectarians. The book of Esther is the only book included in the Hebrew canon not attested among the Dead Sea Scrolls, and if the sectarians did not want to read Esther, they might also have preferred to avoid Judith, although Judith's behavior reflects more attention to the standards of contemporary piety than does Esther's. Still, for putatively Second Temple era works transmitted by Christians in Greek, Latin, and other languages, fragments from the Dead Sea Scrolls normally constitute the only certain evidence that they were composed in Hebrew or Aramaic. The garbled Hebrew title for 1 Maccabees that Eusebius attributes to Origen makes 1 Maccabees an exception to the rule (Eusebius, *Hist. eccl.* 6.25.2). For other works, the absence of Hebrew or Aramaic fragments among the Dead Sea Scrolls

---

36. On Judith and the Psalms of Solomon, see below. On Baruch, see Sean A. Adams, *Baruch and the Epistle of Jeremiah: A Commentary Based on the Texts in Codex Vaticanus*, Septuagint Commentary Series (Leiden: Brill, 2014), 11–12, for the possibility of a Greek original for all of Baruch rather than just the psalms.

leaves the way open for arguments in favor of a Greek original although it certainly does not require it.

In a thoughtful discussion of the problem of the original language of Judith, Deborah Levine Gera points out that while its Greek displays a number of features common in works translated from Hebrew, it sometimes uses idiomatic Greek for which it is difficult to reconstruct a Hebrew original.[37] Weighing in favor of a Greek original is the fact that Judith's many quotations or near quotations of passages from works that became part of the biblical canon almost always follow the Greek rather than the Hebrew.[38] But no matter which language he wrote in, the author of Judith participated in both cultures, displaying familiarity with Greek literature and the works of what would become the Hebrew Bible.[39] Gera concludes by expressing a cautious preference for a Greek original, an opinion with some support in recent scholarship.[40] Yet she also argues that Judith was composed in Palestine, pointing to its interest in the temple and the geography of the land of Israel and its differences from court tales set in the eastern diaspora.[41] But each of these factors could be interpreted differently; it is worth noting that Jan Joosten cites the peculiarities of Judith's geography as evidence for Egyptian provenance in an article arguing for a Greek original.[42]

I am not sure that I find Joosten's arguments on this point persuasive. But since Egypt is the place where the vast majority of Greek works by Jews in the Second Temple period were written, in the absence of compelling evidence for Palestinian provenance, Egypt seems to me the more likely

---

37. Deborah Levine Gera, *Judith*, CEJL (Boston: de Gruyter, 2014), 79–89.
38. Gera, *Judith*, 89–91.
39. Gera, *Judith*, 93–94.
40. For references, Gera, *Judith*, 79 n. 296.
41. Gera, *Judith*, 96–97.
42. Jan Joosten, "The Original Language and Historical Milieu of the Book of Judith," in *Collected Studies on the Septuagint*, 195–209; arguments for Egyptian origin, 203–8. Joosten also finds evidence for Egyptian provenance in Achior's account of Israel's history, which he sees as reflecting "the traditional Alexandrian narrative of Jewish origins" (206) and as defending against the Egyptian claim that the Jews are descended from lepers expelled from Egypt, and in Judith's ownership of her late husband's property, for which he finds a parallel in the Elephantine papyri. Joosten's reading of Achior's speech is so subtle that I am not sure it can testify to provenance, and the relevance of Aramaic legal material from Elephantine for a work composed by a Greek-speaking Jew centuries later is open to question.

place for Judith's composition if the original language was in fact Greek. The evidence for translation activity in Palestine, to be sure, means that there were Palestinian Jews with a mastery of Greek that would have made it possible for them to compose works in Greek as well as to translate. As Gera notes, Ben Zion Wacholder argued some decades ago that Jews from Palestine started writing books in Greek not long after Alexander's conquest of the near east and continued to do so into the decades following the destruction of the Second Temple.[43] But Wacholder understood the use of Greek to reflect the audience at which particular types of works were directed: gentiles or diaspora Jews. Why would a Palestinian author have chosen to write Judith in a language that would have limited its circulation in Palestine to those capable of reading Greek? That is, why would he be more interested in reaching an audience in the diaspora than in Palestine?

It is true that neither the location of Judith's narrative in the land of Israel nor its genre finds many parallels in works of Egyptian provenance. Yet there is one Egyptian work with which Judith has a great deal in common: 3 Maccabees. Both 3 Maccabees and Judith recount a story of miraculous deliverance from foreign oppression. Furthermore, while most of the action in 3 Maccabees takes place in Egypt, the event that sets the narrative in motion is the Ptolemaic king's sacrilegious desire to enter the holy of holies in the Jerusalem temple (1:10). Both 3 Maccabees (1:16–25) and Judith (4:8–15) describe public mourning in the temple environs in the face of a foreign threat in terms that recall a similar scene in 2 Maccabees (3:14–21). Third Maccabees also differs from most of Egyptian Jewish literature in its negative depiction of the Ptolemaic king, although at the end of the work the king becomes a friend of the Jews, apparently as the result of divine intervention, but Judith too depicts the foreign king as a villain and his most important representative as well. The negative attitude sets 3 Maccabees and Judith apart from the book of Esther (to which both are indebted) and from other court tales such as those in the book of Daniel, in which it is not the foreign king who is the villain but a courtier or courtiers.

Third Maccabees' debt to Esther can be seen in the royal decrees and drunken banquets that play a crucial role in the story. Furthermore, like Esther, 3 Maccabees serves as the foundation legend for a festival. Judith's

---

43. Gera, *Judith*, 96; Ben Zion Wacholder, *Eupolemus: A Study of Judaeo-Greek Literature* (Cincinnati: Hebrew Union College-Jewish Institute of Religion, 1974).

debt to Esther is evident in the role it gives to a woman in securing the salvation of the Jews through her beauty. But like the additions to the Greek Esther, both Judith and 3 Maccabees worry about aspects of pious behavior, a concern that the book of Esther ignores. Thus, Judith manages to save her people without eating foreign food or having to pollute herself by actually sleeping with a foreigner, while 3 Maccabees insists that the Jews "kept their separateness with respect to foods" (3 Macc 3:4).[44]

Scholarly sentiment in favor of a Greek original for the Psalms of Solomon is more limited than for Judith. The broadest discussion I know is that of Joosten, who points to aspects of its Greek that are difficult to understand as the result of translation and to its allusions to works that would become part of the Hebrew Bible, of which some display distinctive features of the Greek translations of those works.[45] Eberhard Bons argues from a different point of view and a narrower textual base, focusing on usage in a single verse of the Psalms of Solomon that he sees reflecting Stoic vocabulary; he suggests that his argument has wider implications.[46]

---

44. Addition C to Greek Esther displays a similar anxiety about the Hebrew book's apparent acceptance of Esther's status as the king's concubine and lack of concern for the dietary laws, and some scholars have detected the influence of the book of Judith on additions C and D (Gera, *Judith*, 12, and references there [n. 25]). These additions, however, are generally understood to have been composed in Hebrew, which means that if Judith was in fact composed in Greek, the path by which it made its influence felt would have to be somewhat different from the one assumed by scholars who understand its original language as Hebrew. On the other hand, the points of contact between Judith and the additions do not necessarily require influence of one text on the other rather than a shared set of concerns. It is worth noting that 3 Maccabees too shows points of contact with the additions to Greek Esther, but unlike addition C, the additions in question, B and E, the two royal letters, do not serve to revise Esther in keeping with contemporary norms. Additions B and E were likely composed in Greek, and they share distinctive vocabulary and phrases with 3 Maccabees. Noah Hacham, "3 Maccabees and Esther: Parallels, Intertextuality, and Diaspora Identity," *JBL* 126 (2007): 765–85, has argued that the shared elements point to the use of 3 Maccabees by the author of these additions (on shared vocabulary and direction of influence, 772–80). The significance of the relationship between Judith and 3 Maccabees and the additions to Esther requires further consideration.

45. Jan Joosten, "Reflections on the Original Language of the Psalms of Solomon," in *The Psalms of Solomon: Language, History, Theology*, ed. Eberhard Bons and Patrick Pouchelle, EJL 40 (Atlanta: SBL Press, 2015), 31–47; arguments for Greek original, 33–42.

46. Eberhard Bons, "Philosophical Vocabulary in the Psalms of Solomon: The Case of Ps. Sol. 9:4," in Bons and Pouchelle, *Psalms of Solomon*, 49–58.

It is also worth noting that Géza G. Xeravits, who argues for a Greek original for the psalms of Baruch, views the relationship between Pss Sol 11 and the second psalm of Baruch (4:30–5:6, in his view) as sufficiently close to require the Psalms of Solomon's use either of the psalm in Baruch or of a common source and to indicate that Pss Sol 11 was composed in Greek.[47]

Recent scholarship has been virtually unanimous in asserting a Palestinian provenance for the Psalms of Solomon, which fits well with the widely presumed Hebrew original. Benedikt Eckhardt has recently criticized scholarly use of the Psalms of Solomon for historical purposes, thus calling into question the assumptions that undergird the assignment of the work to Palestine, but he nonetheless appears to accept Palestinian origin for the work, perhaps because he assumes a Hebrew original.[48] So also, despite their preference for a Greek original, both Joosten and Bons continue to understand the Psalms of Solomon as written in Palestine. Joosten points to vocabulary the Psalms of Solomon shares with the kaige-Theodotion revision and Aquila.[49] Bons admits that his arguments require him to make reference to Stoic ideas known only from texts that postdate the first century BCE, the usual date for the Psalms of Solomon, but he defends his procedure with the observation that their attestation only later does not exclude the possibility that the ideas were available in Jerusalem when the Psalms of Solomon was written.[50] The only possible exception to the consensus for Palestinian provenance is Joshua Efron, whose reading of the Psalms as a Christian work presumably implies composition in Greek (although Efron does not make this point explicit) and is compatible with a location anywhere in the eastern Mediterranean.[51]

But if, as Joosten and Bons argue, the original language of the Psalms of Solomon was Greek, surely it demands that we examine the assumption of Palestinian provenance. Indeed, Joosten admits that if the Psalms of Solomon was composed in Palestine, "the motivation for writing in Greek

---

47. Géza G. Xeravits, *"Take Courage, O Jerusalem...": Studies in the Psalms of Baruch 4–5* (Berlin: de Gruyter, 2015), 121–25.

48. Benedikt Eckhardt, "The Psalms of Solomon as a Historical Source for the Late Hasmonean Period," in Bons and Pouchelle, *Psalms of Solomon*, 7–29.

49. Joosten, "Reflections on the Original Language," 44–46.

50. Bons, "Philosophical Vocabulary in the Psalms of Solomon," 52–53.

51. Joshua Efron, *Studies on the Hasmonean Period* (Leiden: Brill, 1987), 219–86. Efron's position has been rejected or ignored, although I think Eckhardt is correct that it raises important questions (Eckhardt, "Psalms of Solomon as a Historical Source for the Late Hasmonean Period," 8–9).

remains somewhat obscure."[52] Furthermore, he points out that the Psalms of Solomon shows considerable interest in the diaspora.[53] Nor is the focus of the Psalms of Solomon on Jerusalem and the temple out of place in Alexandria, where not only 3 Maccabees but also the more typically Alexandrian Letter of Aristeas and works of Philo manifest such concern. It is also worth remembering that Stoic ideas were available in Alexandria at the turn of the era alongside the Platonism that was the city's dominant philosophical tradition, as the presence of Chaeremon demonstrates.

Implications for Diaspora Judaism

The questions of the original language of Judith and the Psalms of Solomon and their place of composition will benefit from further discussion, but they are unlikely ever to be resolved with certainty. Still it seems to me worth considering how our picture of diaspora Judaism would be different if we understood one or both of the works as written in Egypt or even as composed in Greek in Palestine and thus directed at a readership in the Greek-speaking diaspora. Both works can be integrated without much difficulty into John Barclay's picture of diaspora Judaism as constituted by an "ethnic bond" maintained and expressed through the symbols and practices of the Torah.[54] But neither work fits well with John Collins's description of diaspora Judaism as "a religion of ethical monotheism" that "downplay[s] its ethnic and particularistic aspects."[55]

There are many reasons Collins and Barclay arrive at different pictures of diaspora Judaism, but one is surely that they base their pictures on different bodies of evidence. That is, they have somewhat different understandings of the contents of the corpus of works composed by Jews in the Greek-speaking diaspora. For Collins, Joseph and Aseneth, the Testament of Job, the books of Adam and Eve (the Apocalypse of Moses and Life of Adam and Eve), the Testament of Abraham, and 3 Baruch are part of that corpus, although he notes that 3 Baruch reaches us in Christian redaction. Collins also makes use of the Testaments of the Twelve Patriarchs, with

---

52. Joosten, "Reflections on the Original Language," 46.
53. Joosten, "Reflections on the Original Language," 43–44.
54. John M. G. Barclay, *Jews in the Mediterranean Diaspora from Alexander to Trajan (323 BCE–117 CE)* (Edinburgh: T&T Clark, 1996), esp. 402–13.
55. John J. Collins, *Between Athens and Jerusalem: Jewish Identity in the Hellenistic Diaspora*, 2nd ed. (Grand Rapids, MI: Eerdmans, 2000), 259.

attention to its problematic status.⁵⁶ Of the works just mentioned, Barclay uses only Joseph and Aseneth. He mentions the Testament of Abraham as likely a Jewish work from the diaspora and considers it possible that the Testament of Job is one, but he does not include them in his discussion.⁵⁷

For each of the works mentioned in the preceding paragraph, scholars have made serious arguments in favor of Christian authorship in the second century or later.⁵⁸ It is not surprising, then, that Collins's picture of diaspora Judaism appears to provide more fertile soil for the emergence of Christianity than does Barclay's. My own preference is for a picture that looks more like Barclay's than like Collins's. But my point here is not substantive but methodological: the decisions we make about which works to include in the corpus of literature of the diaspora inevitably shapes the way we understand diaspora Judaism.⁵⁹ The determination of whether the works in question are Jewish or Christian is extremely challenging, and for most of them there are strong arguments to be made for both position and sometimes for intermediate positions as well. There is no easily identifiable essence of Judaism and Christianity that allows works to be sorted into the correct category. Furthermore, it is clearly impossible to

---

56. All page references are to Collins, *Between Athens and Jerusalem*. Joseph and Aseneth: 103–10, 230–39; Testament of Job: 240–46; books of Adam and Eve: 246–48; Testament of Abraham: 248–51; 3 Baruch: 255–59; Testaments of the Twelve Patriarchs: 174–83.

57. Barclay, *Jews in the Mediterranean Diaspora*, 12 and n. 4 there.

58. Joseph and Aseneth: Ross S. Kraemer, *When Aseneth Met Joseph: A Late Antique Tale of the Biblical Patriarch and His Egyptian Wife, Reconsidered* (New York: Oxford University Press, 1998); James R. Davila, *The Provenance of the Pseudepigrapha: Jewish Christian, or Other?* JSJSup 105 (Leiden: Brill, 2005), 190–95. Testament of Job: Davila, *Provenance of the Pseudepigrapha*, 195–99 and references there. Books of Adam and Eve: Marinus de Jonge, "The Christian Origin of the Life of Adam and Eve," in *Pseudepigrapha of the Old Testament as Part of Christian Literature: The Case of the Testaments of the Twelve Patriarchs and the Greek Life of Adam and Eve*, SVTP 18 (Leiden: Brill, 2003), 181–200; Testament of Abraham: Davila, *Provenance of the Pseudepigrapha*, 199–207 and references there. 3 Baruch: Martha Himmelfarb, "3 Baruch Revisited: Jewish or Christian Composition, and Why It Matters," ZAC 20 (2016): 41–62. Testaments of the Twelve Patriarchs: de Jonge, *Testaments of the Twelve Patriarchs*; de Jonge, "The Pre-Mosaic Servants of God in the Testaments of the Twelve Patriarchs and in the Writings of Justin and Irenaeus," VC 39 (1985): 157–70. These references are illustrative rather than exhaustive.

59. See Kraft, "Pseudepigrapha in Christianity," and Davila, *Provenance of the Pseudepigrapha*.

understand the growth of early Christianity without sustained attention to diaspora Judaism.

It is also important to recognize that the impact of those decisions goes beyond the inclusion of a particular work in the corpus of diaspora texts since our reading of any text in the corpus is inevitably and rightly influenced by our understanding of the other texts in it. One way to illustrate this point is to consider the difference between Collins's reading of 3 Maccabees and Barclay's. Barclay treats 3 Maccabees as an example of what he terms "cultural antagonism" and suggests that its praise of the Greeks (3:8–10) is intended to deny that honorable identity to the non-Jewish inhabitants of Alexandria.[60] Collins takes the praise of the Greeks as one of the most important features of 3 Maccabees and uses it as evidence that 3 Maccabees' outlook "is not very different from [that of] the so-called 'apologetic' writings of Egyptian Judaism."[61]

The addition of Judith to the corpus of diaspora literature would strengthen the case for Barclay's understanding by adding to the evidence for the type of Judaism exemplified by 3 Maccabees as read by Barclay. Even if we continue to understand Judith as written in Hebrew in Palestine, the fact of its translation emphasizes the existence of diaspora Jews who embraced an understanding of Judaism in which ethnic identity and ritual law played a central role. The genre of the Psalms of Solomon makes it harder to compare to 3 Maccabees, but overall the assumption of a Greek original would have a similar impact, and even the more common assumption that it was translated into Greek points in the same direction. Nor should we forget the Jews who formed the audience for the translations of the Book of the Watchers, Tobit, and Aramaic Levi. The concerns of these works are different from those of 3 Maccabees, Judith, and the Psalms of Solomon, but they are not incompatible with them.

There is, of course, an unavoidable circularity to the process of deciding which works count as evidence for diaspora Judaism. If we include the Testament of Abraham and the Testament of Job, it is easier to make the case for 3 Baruch. If we include Judith, it is easier to make the case for the Psalms of Solomon. Nor can we entirely avoid the problem by basing our picture on works that are undoubtedly products of the Greek-speaking diaspora in the Second Temple period. The nature of the preservation

---

60. Barclay, *Jews in the Mediterranean Diaspora*, 192–203; on the Greeks, 196–97.
61. Collins, *Between Athens and Jerusalem*, 127–31; quotation, 130; importance of attitude toward the Greeks, 131.

and transmission of Jewish texts written in Greek means that there are few works about which certainty is possible, and it would be arbitrary to limit the corpus to them since our knowledge of their provenance is the result of more or less accidental factors. Furthermore, as we have seen for 3 Maccabees, our understanding of particular texts and their implications for how we read other texts are inevitably tied to larger assumptions. The same would be no less true for texts for which the diaspora provenance is certain.

Given the nature of the evidence and the different concerns scholars bring to the subject, disagreements about the nature of diaspora Judaism in the Second Temple period will never be fully resolved. But I hope that I have succeeded in making the case for the importance of careful attention to the Greek translations of works attested in Aramaic and Hebrew as well as to works of the Second Temple period generally understood to be of Palestinian provenance but likely composed in Greek. Both types of evidence have the potential to shed further light on the interests of Jews in the diaspora, and the first type will serve to illumine the culture of Palestinian Jews as well.

Bibliography

Adams, Sean A. *Baruch and the Epistle of Jeremiah: A Commentary Based on the Texts in Codex Vaticanus.* Septuagint Commentary Series. Leiden: Brill, 2014.

Arcari, Luca. "Il *Nachleben* del testo greco del *1Enoc* in alcuni scritti del Christianesimo antico: É esistita 'una' traduzione greca di *1Enoc*?" *Materia giudaica* 10 (2005): 57–72.

———. "Il vocabolario della conoscenza nel testo greco del *Libro dei Vigilanti*: Per una definizione del *Sitz im Leben* della versione greca di *1 Enoc.*" *Materia giudaica* 8 (2003): 95–104.

Barclay, John M. G. *Jews in the Mediterranean Diaspora from Alexander to Trajan (323 BCE–117 CE).* Edinburgh: T&T Clark, 1996.

Barr, James. "Aramaic-Greek Notes on the Book of Enoch (I)." *JSS* 23 (1978): 184–98.

———. "Aramaic-Greek Notes on the Book of Enoch (II)." *JSS* 24 (1979): 179–92.

Black, Matthew. *Apocalypsis Henochi Graece.* PVTG 3. Leiden: Brill, 1970.

———. *The Book of Enoch or 1 Enoch: A New English Edition with Commentary and Textual Notes.* SVTP 7. Leiden: Brill, 1985.

Bons, Eberhard. "Philosophical Vocabulary in the Psalms of Solomon: The Case of Ps. Sol. 9:4." Pages 49–58 in *The Psalms of Solomon: Language, History, Theology*. Edited by Eberhard Bons and Patrick Pouchelle. EJL 40. Atlanta: SBL Press, 2015.

Böttrich, Christfried "The Angel of Tartarus and the Supposed Coptic Fragments of 2 Enoch." *Early Christianity* 4 (2013): 509–21.

Chesnutt, Randall D. "*Oxyrhynchus Papyrus* 2069 and the Compositional History of *1 Enoch*." *JBL* 129 (2010): 491–95.

Coblentz Bautch, Kelly. "5.2.1 The Book of the Watchers-Greek." In *Deuterocanonical Scriptures*. Vol. 2 of *Textual History of the Bible*. Edited by Armin Lange and Matthias Henze. Leiden: Brill, forthcoming.

Collins, John J. *Between Athens and Jerusalem: Jewish Identity in the Hellenistic Diaspora*. 2nd ed. Grand Rapids, MI: Eerdmans, 2000.

Davila, James R. *The Provenance of the Pseudepigrapha: Jewish, Christian, or Other?* JSJSup 105. Leiden: Brill, 2005.

Dimant, Devorah. "Tobit and the Qumran Aramaic Texts." Pages 173–91 in *From Enoch to Tobit: Collected Studies in Ancient Jewish Literature*. Tübingen: Mohr Siebeck, 2017.

Drawnel, Henryk. *An Aramaic Wisdom Text from Qumran: A New Interpretation of the Levi Document*. Leiden: Brill, 2004.

Eckhardt, Benedikt. "The Psalms of Solomon as a Historical Source for the Late Hasmonean Period," Pages 7–29 in *The Psalms of Solomon: Language, History, Theology*. Edited by Eberhard Bons and Patrick Pouchelle. EJL 40. Atlanta: SBL Press, 2015.

Efron, Joshua. *Studies on the Hasmonean Period*. Leiden: Brill, 1987.

Gera, Deborah Levine. *Judith*. CEJL. Boston: de Gruyter, 2014.

Greenfield, Jonas C., and Michael E. Stone. "Remarks on the Aramaic Testament of Levi from the Geniza." *RB* 86 (1979): 224.

Greenfield, Jonas C., Michael E. Stone, and Esther Eshel. *The Aramaic Levi Document: Edition, Translation, Commentary*. Leiden: Brill, 2004.

Hacham, Noah. "3 Maccabees and Esther: Parallels, Intertextuality, and Diaspora Identity." *JBL* 126 (2007): 765–85.

Hagen, Joost L. "No Longer 'Slavonic' Only: 2 Enoch Attested in Coptic from Nubia." Pages 7–34 in *New Perspectives on 2 Enoch: No Longer Slavonic Only*. Edited by Andrei A. Orlov and Gabriel Boccaccini. Leiden: Brill, 2012.

Harl, Marguerite. Gilles Dorival, and Olivier Munnich. *La Bible grecque des Septante: Du judaïsme hellénistique au christianisme ancient*. Paris: Éditions du Cerf/Éditions du C.N.R.S., 1988.

Himmelfarb, Martha. "*3 Baruch* Revisited: Jewish or Christian Composition, and Why It Matters." *ZAC* 20 (2016): 41–62.

———. "Earthly Sacrifice and Heavenly Incense: The Law of the Priesthood in *Aramaic Levi* and *Jubilees*." Pages 62–72 in *Between Temple and Torah: Essays on Priests, Scribes, and Visionaries in the Second Temple Period and Beyond*. Tübingen: Mohr Siebeck, 2013.

Jonge, Marinus de. "The Christian Origin of the Life of Adam and Eve." Pages 181–200 in *Pseudepigrapha of the Old Testament as Part of Christian Literature: The Case of the Testaments of the Twelve Patriarchs and the Greek Life of Adam and Eve*. SVTP 18. Leiden: Brill, 2003.

———. "The Pre-Mosaic Servants of God in the Testaments of the Twelve Patriarchs and in the Writings of Justin and Irenaeus." *VC* 39 (1985): 157–70.

———. *The Testaments of the Twelve Patriarchs: A Critical Edition of the Greek Text*. In cooperation with H. W. Hollander, H. J. de Jonge, and Th. Korteweg. Leiden: Brill, 1978.

———. *The Testaments of the Twelve Patriarchs: A Study of Their Text, Composition, and Origin*. Assen: van Gorcum, 1953.

Joosten, Jan. "Language as Symptom: Linguistic Clues to the Social Background of the Seventy." Pages 185–94 in *Collected Studies on the Septuagint*. Tübingen: Mohr Siebeck, 2012.

———. "The Original Language and Historical Milieu of the Book of Judith." Pages 195–209 in *Collected Studies on the Septuagint*. Tübingen: Mohr Siebeck, 2012.

———. "Reflections on the Original Language of the Psalms of Solomon." Pages 31–47 in *The Psalms of Solomon: Language, History, Theology*. Edited by Eberhard Bons and Patrick Pouchelle. EJL 40. Atlanta: SBL Press, 2015.

Kraft, Robert A. "The Multiform Jewish Heritage of Early Christianity." Pages 174–99 in vol. 3 of *Christianity, Judaism and Other Greco-Roman Cults: Studies for Morton Smith at Sixty*. Edited by Jacob Neusner. Leiden: Brill, 1975.

———. "The Pseudepigrapha in Christianity." Pages 55–86 in *Tracing the Threads: Studies in the Vitality of Jewish Pseudepigrapha*. Edited by John C. Reeves. EJL 6. Atlanta: Scholars Press, 1994.

———. "Setting the Stage and Framing Some Central Questions." *JSJ* 32 (2001): 371–95.

Kraemer, Ross S. *When Aseneth Met Joseph: A Late Antique Tale of the Biblical Patriarch and His Egyptian Wife, Reconsidered.* New York: Oxford University Press, 1998.

Larson, Erik W. "The Relation between the Greek and Aramaic Texts of Enoch." Pages 434–44 in *The Dead Sea Scrolls Fifty Years after Their Discovery: Proceedings of the Jerusalem Congress, July 25–27, 1997.* Edited by Lawrence H. Schiffman, Emanuel Tov, and James C. VanderKam. Jerusalem: Israel Exploration Society in cooperation with the Shrine of the Book, 2000.

———. "The Translation of Enoch: From Aramaic into Greek." PhD diss., New York University, 1995.

Milik, Józef T. *The Books of Enoch: Aramaic Fragments of Qumrân Cave 4.* Oxford: Clarendon, 1976.

Moore, Carey A. *Tobit.* AB. New York: Doubleday, 1996.

Muro, Ernest A., Jr. "The Greek Fragments of Enoch from Qumran Cave 7 (7Q4, 7Q8, & 7Q12 = 7QEn gr = Enoch 103:3–4, 7–8)." *RevQ* 18 (1997): 307–12.

Nebe, G.-Wilhelm. "'7Q4'—Möglichkeit und Grenze einer Identifikation." *RQ* 13 (1988): 629–33.

Nickelsburg, George W. E. *1 Enoch 1: A Commentary on the Book of 1 Enoch, Chapters 1–36, 81–108.* Hermeneia. Minneapolis: Fortress, 2001.

———. "The Greek Fragments of *1 Enoch* from Qumran Cave 7: An Unproven Identification." *RevQ* 21 (2004): 631–34.

Nickelsburg, George W. E., and James C. VanderKam. *1 Enoch 2: A Commentary on the Book of 1 Enoch 37–82.* Hermeneia. Minneapolis: Fortress, 2012.

Perrin, Andrew B. "An Almanac of Tobit Studies: 2000–2014." *CurBR* 13 (2014): 111–13.

Puech, Émile. "Sept fragments grecs de la *Lettre d'Hénoch* (*1 Hén* 100, 103, et 105) dans la grotte 7 de Qumrân (=7QHéngr)." *RevQ* 18 (1997): 313–23.

Schiffman, Lawrence H. "Sacrificial Halakhah in the Fragments of the *Aramaic Levi Document* from Qumran, the Cairo Geniza, and the Mt. Athos Monastery." Pages 177–202 in *Reworking the Bible: Apocryphal and Related Texts at Qumran.* Edited by Esther G. Chazon, Devorah Dimant, and Ruth A. Clements. Leiden: Brill, 2005.

Stuckenbruck, Loren, and Stuart Weeks. "Tobit." Pages 239–41 in *The T and T Clark Companion to the Septuagint*, ed. James K. Aitken. London: Bloomsbury, 2015.

Tov, Emanuel. "Reflections on the Septuagint with Special Attention Paid to Post-Pentateuchal Translations." Pages 429–48 in vol. 3 of *Textual Criticism of the Hebrew Bible, Qumran, Septuagint: Collected Essays*. Leiden: Brill, 2015.

VanderKam, James C. *Book of Jubilees*. CSCO 511; Scriptores Aethiopici 88. Leuven: Peeters, 1989.

———. *Jubilees 1: A Commentary on the Book of Jubilees Chapters 1–21*. Hermeneia. Minneapolis: Fortress, 2018.

Wacholder, Ben Zion. *Eupolemus: A Study of Judaeo-Greek Literature*. Cincinnati: Hebrew Union College-Jewish Institute of Religion, 1974.

Xeravits, Géza G. *"Take Courage, O Jerusalem…": Studies in the Psalms of Baruch 4–5*. Berlin: de Gruyter, 2015.

14
Origen and the Old Testament Apocrypha: The Creation of a Category

William Adler

Whenever a new collection of Old Testament pseudepigrapha appears in print, reviewers tend to question the selection criteria and the continued use of misleading nomenclature like *pseudepigrapha* and *noncanonical*. The persistence of what are generally acknowledged as anachronistic and pejorative categories has at least something to do with the homogenizing tendencies of any collection. The act of assembling and assigning a name to any literary corpus implies that the sources included in it constitute a fixed body of works connected to one another temporally, by genre or origins, or in some other way. But a collection is by nature a composite. As its contents expand, labels, terminology, and the criteria for inclusion often wind up looking arbitrary or meaningless.

While R. H. Charles was not the first to apply the term *pseudepigrapha* to a miscellany of mostly Second Temple Jewish sources, use of that label in collections of English translations has become commonplace since the publication of his two-volume edition of *Apocrypha and Pseudepigrapha of the Old Testament*.[1] As Charles recognized, several of the sources in the second volume are not, *strictu sensu*, pseudepigraphic, that is, falsely attributed to a sage, prophet, or some other notable figure of the biblical past. The use of the term was mainly a device to distinguish these works from the contents of the first volume. Nor was Charles's

---

1. R. H. Charles, *The Apocrypha and Pseudepigrapha of the Old Testament*, 2 vols. (Oxford: Clarendon, 1913). For the history of the label *Old Testament pseudepigrapha* in modern scholarship, see Annette Yoshiko Reed, "The Modern Invention of Old Testament Pseudepigrapha," *JTS* 60 (2009): 403–36.

description of the contents of volume two as noncanonical meant as a sweeping statement about the formal rejection of these works by some authorizing body. He only wanted to let readers know that, since these works were mostly absent from official lists of recognized books, they were comparatively unfamiliar.[2]

In recognizing what now seems to be its arbitrarily imposed limitations, new volumes have been more expansive, including sources falling well outside the chronological boundaries of Charles's volume. But the widened scope has also exposed problems and assumptions extending beyond the continued use of pseudepigrapha and noncanonical. One of them, examined at length by Liv Ingeborg Lied, is that a pseudepigraphon is "by default an ancient book."[3] Making the disparate source material in these newer collections conform to that conception often required the application of questionable analytical methods, including the postulation of the existence of an Ur-text that may in fact have never even existed. And to what end? Even if it were possible to recover a lost text or a single work lying behind widely divergent witnesses, Lied questioned the value of what she considered a counter-productive methodology. "Is it relevant to talk about a given passage as 'a passage excerpted from' another work, or are we better off understanding that passage as integral to the work that the manuscripts seem to suggest it belongs to?"[4] In posing this question, Lied called attention to a broader issue, again foreshadowed in Charles's collection. One of the criteria for a work's inclusion in volume two of Charles's edition was its demonstrated value in "throwing light on a lost chapter of Jewish religious history."[5] But to what exactly are the pseudepigrapha in these later editions witnesses: the context in which these works survive or some putative older setting in Second Temple Judaism?

When Origen, the early Christian biblical scholar and Platonist, set about defining a body of works broadly equivalent to what today are called

---

2. See Charles, *Apocrypha and Pseudepigrapha*, 2:iii–iv. Volume 1, the "Apocrypha Proper," constituted the "excess of the Vulgate over the Hebrew Old Testament, which was in turn borrowed from the LXX." He then consigned to the volume of pseudepigrapha all remaining "extant non-Canonical Jewish Books written between 200 B.C. and 100 A.D."

3. See Liv Ingeborg Lied, "Text—Work—Manuscript: What Is an 'Old Testament Pseudepigraphon'?," *JSP* 25 (2015): 164.

4. Lied, "Text—Work—Manuscript," 158.

5. Charles, *Apocrypha and Pseudepigrapha*, 2:iv.

Old Testament pseudepigrapha, he had to confront problems not all that dissimilar to those encountered in modern scholarship: How does one decide what belongs in the corpus? What does it mean to think of them as a collection of texts? What are the conditions, if any, under which they might be read, for what purpose, and by whom? Because Origen is the first Christian author of record to undertake this project, the discussion that follows will deal mainly with his formulation of the category and its subsequent impact.[6]

Origen and the Creation of the Category of Apocrypha

Origen's designation of these sources by the collective name *apocrypha* marked a watershed in the Christian treatment of this literature. There is little to suggest that previous Christian authors citing them ever understood them as part of a literary corpus or even conceived of them as written texts, at least in the way that Origen did. Without further qualification, the Epistle of Jude (v. 14) prefaces its citation from the book of Enoch with the words "Enoch prophesied" (προεφήτευσεν ... Ἐνώχ; cf. 1 En. 1.9). A citation from Enoch in the epistle of (Pseudo-) Barnabas introduces the work with the same formula the author uses elsewhere of biblical books: "concerning which it has been written, as Enoch says" (περὶ οὗ γέγραπται, ὡς Ἐνὼχ λέγει) (Barn. 4.3a). The case of Clement of Alexandria is most instructive, if only by way of contrast with Origen. In his *Stromateis*, Clement often ascribes parabiblical traditions to some biblical authority: Enoch, Ezra, Ham, Ezekiel, or Zephaniah.[7] But he never locates them in a written work, much less identify a broader class of writings to which the work belongs.[8]

---

6. For previous studies of Origen's concept of apocrypha, see, among others, Gustave Bardy, "Les traditions juives dans l'oeuvre d'origène," *RB* 34 (1925): 217–52; Adolf von Harnack, *Der kirchengeschichtliche Ertrag der exegetischen Arbeiten des Origenes*, TUGAL 42.3 (Leipzig: Hinrichs, 1918), 42–50; Edmon L. Gallagher, *Hebrew Scriptures in Patristic Biblical Theory*, VCSup 114 (Leiden: Brill, 2012), 19–49; Albrecht Oepke, "Βίβλοι ἀπόκρυφοι in Christianity," *TDNT* 3:987–1000, esp. pp. 994–95; J. Ruwet, "Les *apocryphes* dans les œuvres d'Origène," *Bib* 25 (1944): 143–66; Theodor Zahn, *Geschichte des Neutestamentlichen Kanons* (Erlangen: Deichert, 1888), 1:126–34.

7. See, for examples, Clement, *Ecl.* 53.4, Ἐνὼχ φησιν; *Strom.* 3.16.100.4, Ἔσδρας ὁ προφήτης λέγει; *Strom.* 6.6.53: ἀπὸ τῆς τοῦ Χὰμ προφητείας τὴν ὑπόθεσιν; *Strom.* 5.11.77: τοῖς ὑπὸ Σοφονία λεχθεῖσι τοῦ προφήτου; *Paed.* 1.9.84.2: Φησὶν γοῦν διὰ Ἰεζεκιὴλ.

8. When Clement does use the term apocrypha as a description of a written work, it is in reference to books used to promote false doctrines. See *Strom.* 3.4.29.1, where

Given his fluid understanding of the sources of religious authority, Clement's general indifference to the textual origins of a Jewish tradition is unsurprising. Religious wisdom, he writes in his *Stromateis*, is a living tradition of "ineffable teachings, entrusted to logos, not to writing [λόγῳ πιστεύεται, οὐ γράμματι]" (1.1.13.2–3).[9] But it is a perspective far removed from Origen's. The underpinning of Origen's thinking about an apocryphal book is that it is a written text, part of a defined corpus, and clearly distinguishable from Jewish writings constituting what Origen variously calls "the common and widely circulated books" (τὰ κοινὰ καὶ δεδημευμένα βιβλία) or the "publicly known books" (τὰ φανερὰ βιβλία).[10]

Origen's acquaintance with works making up this corpus reaches beyond mere references, in many cases reflecting a real engagement with the text. Recognition of their disputed status does not deter him from consulting them either as an aid to interpretation of the evangelists and apostles or in support of some article of doctrine. In his massive commentary on the Gospel according to John, Origen alerts readers to a passage from the otherwise unknown Prayer of Joseph, recounting how, when wrestling with the archangel Uriel, the patriarch Jacob revealed himself as the chief angel Israel. Its underlying premise—that an angel could descend into human form—lent support to Origen's own identification of John the Baptist as an angel who assumed a body for the sake of "bearing witness to the light" (cf. John 1:18) (Origen, *Comm. Jo.* 2.31).[11] In the same commentary, he appeals to the book of Enoch to elaborate his allegorical reading of John's baptismal ministry. From Enoch's account of the fallen Watchers, Origen had learned that the event occurred in the days of the patriarch Jared, a name derived from the Hebrew word for "descend" (cf. 1 En. 6.6). The etymological links with the word *Jordan* suggested that John's ministry at the Jordan and Enoch's account of the Watchers' intercourse with women could be read in the same way: as allegories of the fall of souls into bodies. Origen does not claim credit for this explanation of Enoch's nar-

---

Clement derives the source of the antinomian error from "some apocryphal work" (ἔκ τινος ἀποκρύφου).

9. For discussion, see R. P. C. Hanson, *Origen's Doctrine of Tradition* (London: SPCK, 1954), 57–58.

10. See, for example, Origen, *Comm. Matt.* 10.18: ἐν τοῖς κοινοῖς καὶ δεδημευμένοις βιβλίοις, εἰκὸς δ' ὅτι ἐν ἀποκρύφοις φερομένη.

11. For English translation of the surviving fragments, see J. Z. Smith, "Prayer of Joseph, a New Translation with Introduction," *OTP* 2:699–714.

14. Origen and the Old Testament Apocrypha   291

rative of the fallen Watchers. He attributes its inspiration instead to other unnamed interpreters. "Some have supposed," he writes, that the story "hints at the descent of souls into bodies." They likewise understood the phrase "daughters of men" "more figuratively" (τροπικώτερον), as a symbol of "the earthly tabernacle" (Origen, *Comm. Jo.* 6.42.217).[12] Already known to and cited approvingly by his predecessor Clement (see Clement, *Ecl.* 2.1; 53.4), the book of Enoch had by Origen's time apparently become a staple of the Alexandrian exegetical school.[13]

Although more guarded in his assessment elsewhere, Origen quotes Enoch here with the same formula he uses of recognized scriptures: "As has been written in the book of Enoch" (ὡς ἐν τῷ Ἐνὼχ γέγραπται). But he also predicates his citation from Enoch on the condition that his readers "might be willing to accept the book as holy [ὡς ἅγιον]" (Origen, *Comm. Jo.* 6.42.217). A similar stipulation accompanies his treatment of the Prayer of Joseph. Readers will find his appeal to the work valid only if they are willing to embrace one of the "apocryphal works current among the Hebrews" (καὶ τῶν παρ' Ἑβραίοις φερομένων ἀποκρύφων) (Origen, *Comm. Jo.* 2.31.188). Qualifications like these typically complement Origen's appeal to apocryphal books. But about one thing Origen was assured. If used judiciously, these writings might offer real insight into the teachings of Jesus and the apostles, especially when examination of better-known Jewish scriptures proved unavailing.

Judging from the number of places in which he enlarges on this theme, Origen's favorite illustration of his principle of selective reading of apocrypha involved a recurring motif in the New Testament: the harassment and persecution of biblical prophets by Jewish authorities. Especially in Matthew's Gospel, Jesus discoursed at length about prophets "dishonored in their own country" (Matt 13:57). He also held to account the scribes and Pharisees, "sons of those who murdered the prophets" (23:31), for killing and crucifying the prophets, scourging them in the synagogues and persecuting them from town to town (23:35). In his own synopsis of Jewish history, Stephen asked the members of the Sanhedrin whether

---

12. For Origen's classification of the book of Enoch, see further below, 294–95.
13. On the later use and interpretation of the book of Enoch, see Annette Yoshiko Reed, *Fallen Angels and the History of Judaism and Christianity: The Reception of Enochic Literature* (New York: Cambridge University Press, 2005); John C. Reeves and Annette Yoshiko Reed, *Sources from Judaism, Christianity, and Islam*, vol. 1 of *Enoch from Antiquity to the Middle Ages* (Oxford: Oxford University Press, 2018).

there "was ever a prophet whom your ancestors did not persecute" (Acts 7:52). And who were the prophets and other exemplars of faith said in the epistle to the Hebrews to have been "sawn in two and killed with the sword" (Heb 11:37)?

While mindful that verification of these claims was largely lacking in "the ancient scriptures read in their synagogues," Origen believed that he could find the incriminating evidence in apocrypha, both real and conjectural. In a book he identifies as the "Isaiah Apocryphon" (ἐν τῷ ἀποκρύφῳ Ἡσαΐᾳ), Origen discovered a historical detail recorded in "none of the 'public books'" (ἐν οὐδενὶ τῶν φανερῶν βιβλίων γεγραμμένα) of the Jews. According to this work, the prophet Isaiah died after having been sawn in two (Origen, *Comm. Matt.* 10.18.50–53). Origen also held out hope that an as yet undiscovered source might confirm and elaborate Jesus's own enigmatic account of the death of the prophet Zechariah, "son of Barachiah," between the "sanctuary and the altar" (Matt 23:35). There were good reasons why this passage disquieted Christian interpreters: the biblical prophet Zechariah was not known as the son of Barachiah, nor was Jesus's report of his murder attested in Jewish scriptures. Considering it likely that confirmation of Jesus's words might be found among the apocrypha, Origen urges readers to look beyond "the common and widely circulated books" (*Comm. Matt.* 10.18.56–60).

For Origen, these examples did more than attest to the potential benefits of apocryphal books in amplifying a theme in the New Testament. They also demonstrated why they were to be treated cautiously. The integrity of the text of many of these works was in doubt—blame for which he lays squarely at the feet of leaders in the Jewish community. Fearful that the mistreatment of prophets by "elders, rulers, and judges" recounted in works like the Apocryphon of Isaiah might prove damaging to their image, Jewish officials removed them from wider circulation, at the same time eroding their credibility by deliberately adulterating the textual witnesses with "certain unseemly phrases" (λέξεις τινὰς τὰς μὴ πρεπούσας) (see Origen, *Ep. Afr.* 9 [PG 11:65]). For that reason, apocrypha had to be read with discernment.

The most detailed exposition of this principle appears in Origen's *Commentariorum in Matthaeum Series*, a work that survives only in Latin translation. After a learned discussion of the value of apocrypha as testimony to the mistreatment of the prophets, he appends the following admonition: "We have said all of this … not unaware of the fact that many of the apocrypha (*secretorum*) have been invented by impious men and those speaking 'iniquity on high' (cf. Ps 72:8), and that the Hypythiani use some of these fabrications, and the followers of Basilides others." It is therefore necessary "to examine them cautiously so that we might not embrace all the apocrypha that circulate in the name of holy men—this is because of the Jews, who in confirming false doctrines have fabricated certain things to destroy the truth of our scriptures." Above all, readers unable to differentiate between true content and later corruptions would do well to avoid apocrypha altogether; nor should anyone consult these works for instruction in doctrine. But textual corruptions did not discredit these sources altogether. Readers equipped to deal with the mixed contents of apocrypha should observe the advice of the apostle Paul: "Test all things; hold fast to what is good" (1 Thess 5:21) (Origen, *Comm. ser. Matt.* 28 on Matt 23:37–39).

Such measured appraisals about works labeled as apocrypha are hard to find in other Christians writers of the second and third centuries. For heresiologists and other champions of orthodoxy, the term was virtually a code-word for falsehoods disguised as secret wisdom. Not long before Origen, Irenaeus had warned readers to steer clear of the "countless mass of apocrypha and spurious fictions [ἀποκρύφων καὶ νόθων γραφῶν] … meant to bewilder the minds of foolish men, and of such as are ignorant of the Scriptures of truth" (Irenaeus, *Haer.* 1.13.1). Irenaeus was obviously in no mood to sift through "spurious fictions" decorously called apocrypha in search of "what is good" in them.

Where necessary, Origen was fully prepared to assume the role of the churchman in policing apocrypha for corrupt and potentially harmful content. But dismissing them as fabrications of heretics would have been at odds with his own counsel on the selective value of these works. What he does instead is to circumscribe the meaning and scope of the word apocrypha. No longer works of value in their own right, they have now been subordinated to a largely exegetical role: how much light do they cast on the writings of the "evangelists and apostles"? By restricting the corpus of apocrypha to works not read publicly in the synagogue services of the Jews, Origen also excluded from this class of literature the gnostic apocrypha that by Origen's time had earned the scorn of the heresiologists.[14] Basilides and other teachers of false doctrines may have exploited apocrypha for

---

14. See Ruwet, "Les apocryphes dans les œuvres d'Origène," 152–53; Harnack, *Der kirchengeschichtliche Ertrag,* 44.

their own advantage; but they were not their authors. Nor should anyone suppose that the removal of apocrypha from public reading had anything to do with restricting access to religious elites. The reasons why Jewish leaders set them apart were far more venal and self-serving.[15]

In the zero-sum ideological struggles of the second and third centuries, the contours of the controversy over secret books were typically cast in the most polarizing language. Works known as apocrypha were either sources of hidden wisdom or fabrications of heretics. Origen's own treatment of apocrypha seems deliberately calculated to steer the conversation away from the all-or-nothing approach of the heresiologist and into the domain of biblical scholarship and exegesis. Rather than a wholesale verdict on the truthfulness or value of all the works belonging to this class of writings, the term apocrypha has been transformed into a formal designation of a class of writings defined by the circumstances of their preservation.

Refining the Categories

In Origen's usage, the term apocrypha is not a tightly bounded category. He avoids producing a definitive list of the works making up this class of literature. Nor does he always clearly differentiate between and among "apocrypha," "widely-circulating," and "disputed" writings. In the early and speculative *de Principiis*, citations from parabiblical sources are not subject to the fine distinctions he introduces later. The Ascension of Moses is called only a "little treatise of which Jude makes mention in an epistle," without further elaboration (Origen, *Princ.* 3.2.1). Origen's position on the status of the book of Enoch, a work which he never explicitly assigns to the class of apocrypha, is anything but stable. In *de Principiis*, he cites from the book of Enoch unapologetically, quoting it here with the same formula he uses of inspired scriptures.[16] While he continues to think well of the work in his *Commentary on John*, he acknowledges its disputed standing in the churches. In his *Homilies on Numbers*, his enthusiasm for the Enoch corpus had clearly slackened; he hesitates to even cite from the work (Origen, *Hom. Num.* 28.2.1). By the time Origen had composed *Against Celsus* (a work from his later years), he had become estranged from the book altogether. As proof that Jesus was not the only heavenly figure to

---

15. See 292–93, above.
16. Origen, *Princ.* 4.35: "For it is written in the same *Book of Enoch*, 'I beheld the whole of matter.'"

have descended to earth in human likeness, Celsus had previously pointed to Jewish traditions about the teachings of fallen angels. His reference to "sixty or seventy angels who descended … and fell into a state of wickedness" suggested to Origen that Celsus had in mind, if only dimly, Enoch's account of the fallen Watchers. If so, Origen says, Celsus had misinterpreted a story from a work whose authority was generally rejected. Scoring a point in a contest with an enemy of the church may partly account for Origen's disaffection from a work which he had earlier cited approvingly. But it may also reflect his heightened awareness that "books bearing the name of Enoch do not at all circulate in the churches as divine [ὡς θεῖα]" (Origen, *Cels.* 5.54).

If there is any broad direction in the evolution of Origen's thinking about apocrypha, it is in the pursuit of taxonomic precision. While Theodor Zahn's claim that the words ἀπόκρυφα βιβλία were Origen's own Greek rendering of the Hebrew ספרים חיצונים has not been widely embraced, we can say that recasting the loaded word apocrypha as a factual description of writings removed from public circulation in the synagogues enabled him to find a technical and neutral use for the word, relieved of its prejudicial connotations.[17] Interest in fashioning a useful set of analytical categories also lies behind Origen's nuanced distinction between apocrypha and "traditions" (παραδόσεις). For Origen, these traditions were vital to the authentication of material preserved in a more corrupt written form in the apocrypha. While conceding in his epistle to Africanus that Jewish tampering had cast doubt on an apocryphal book, he assures him that oral traditions conveyed to him from Jewish sages confirmed the book's testimony about the death of the prophet by being sawn asunder (Origen, *Ep. Afr.* 11.65).[18] A subcategory of oral traditions of special interest to Origen encompassed secret teachings, unattested in public scriptures, transmitted in Jewish schools from teacher to student, and dealing with more rarefied subjects like the transmigration of souls and their descent into bodies. He calls them τὰ ἀπόρρητα, a term elsewhere almost interchangeable with τὰ ἀπόκρυφα. But since the word apocrypha was now a formal designation

---

17. Zahn, *Geschichte des Neutestamentlichen Kanons*, 1:i, 126 n. 2. For discussion and critique, see Ruwet, "Les apocryphes dans les œuvres d'Origène," 146–51; Oepke, "Βίβλοι ἀπόκρυφοι in Christianity," 997–98.

18. For the distinction between oral traditions and apocrypha, see further Origen, *Comm. Jo.* 19.15.97: ἢ ἐκ παραδόσεως ἢ ἐξ ἀποκρύφων; Origen, *Comm. Matt.* 17.2: εἴτε ἐκ παραδόσεων [εἴτε καὶ] ἐπιβάλλοντες εἴτε καὶ ἐξ ἀποκρύφων.

of a corpus of writings, Origen no longer found it an apposite designation for this collection of esoteric oral doctrines. Apocryphal books may have contained τὰ ἀπόρρητα, but they were not one and the same.[19]

In all of this, we can see Origen's plan to fashion a system of technical and relatively neutral categories meant to advance the investigation of apocrypha. But how far Origen was willing to press the limits of his system is another question. A telling example of his own self-imposed limitations appears in his warnings to readers about the unreliability of the surviving texts of apocryphal compositions. On its face, Origen's differentiation between the original work and corrupt later witnesses speaks well of a scholar trained in Alexandrian higher criticism. Unlike the heresiologist's dismissal of apocrypha as pure fabrications, Origen's more fined-grained distinction adheres to the analytical categories set forth in his *Commentary on John*. He identifies here three possible ways to categorize what he calls a "little book" called the *Kerygma Petrou*: "authentic, spurious, or mixed" (γνήσιόν ἐστιν ἢ νόθον ἢ μικτόν) (Origen, *Comm. Jo.* 13.17.104). According to this three-fold taxonomy, the compositions making up Origen's collection of apocrypha would best belong in the class of mixed writings.

At least hypothetically, then, the trained literary critic could recover the intact original work, unspoiled by later tampering. But there is no indication that Origen ever took the challenge to heart. To actively pursue the full implications of his own characterization of apocrypha as mixed works risked raising a dangerously explosive issue. If it were possible to restore the genuine text of, for example, the Isaiah Apocryphon, what would this imply about its position and authority, especially in relationship to the recognized books of Jewish scriptures? In urging readers to test apocryphal books and find out what is "good in them," Origen was not laying the predicate for the recovery of some original text buried beneath layers of later corruptions. The distinction between the original work and later corrupt textual witnesses was more strategic than philological. While discouraging the use of these works by inexperienced readers, it also made room for their selective study by discerning biblical scholars like Origen himself.

---

19. See Ruwet, "Les apocryphes dans les œuvres d'Origène," 148. On secret tradition in Origen, see also Hanson, *Origen's Doctrine of Tradition*, 73–90.

14. Origen and the Old Testament Apocrypha

The Unraveling of a Category

1. Apocrypha and the New Testament

The shortcomings of what amounts to an apology for apocrypha were exposed, when, over time, Origen was required to explain his position to readers increasingly wary about their standing, especially in relationship to the recognized books of Jewish and Christians scriptures. One reason for the uncertainty involved a subject in which Origen, the biblical critic, took a special interest: references to apocryphal books by the apostles and evangelists. Even when the evidence was less decisive than the direct citation from the book of Enoch in the Epistle of Jude, Alexandrian scholarship had unearthed other passages in New Testament writings suggesting use of apocryphal books. In his *de Principiis*, Origen traces an extrabiblical tradition in the Epistle of Jude recounting a conflict between Satan and the archangel Michael over the body of Moses to the "little treatise" known as the Ascension of Moses (Origen, *Princ.* 3.4.1). In the Gospel according to Matthew, Origen noted that the evangelist attributed to Jeremiah the words: "And they took the thirty pieces of silver, the price of him on whom a price had been set by some of the sons of Israel" (Matt 27:9). Recognizing that nothing like this was found in "the book of Jeremiah received in the church," Origen hypothesized that the citation could have originated in an "apocryphal writing of Jeremiah" (Origen, *Comm. ser. Matt.* 117 [249.16–22]). Since publicly recognized Jewish scriptures were also silent about the names of the Egyptian magicians who opposed Moses, Origen believed that the identification of them by name in 2 Tim 3:8 originated in an apocryphal book he refers to as the Book of Jannes and Jambres. The apostle Paul was also quoting an apocryphal book of Elijah in 1 Corinthians when he said, "What no eye has seen, nor ear heard, nor the heart of man conceived, what God has prepared for those who love" (1 Cor 2:9) (Origen, *Comm. ser. Matt.* 28 on Matt 27:11).

When Origen assumed the mantle of the biblical critic and commentator, passages like these vindicated his claims about the value of apocrypha as an exegetical resource. To understand the words of Jesus or the apostles, the serious commentator was all but obliged to seek out the sources to which they were referring. But it was perhaps inevitable that he would find himself enmeshed in disputes about the wider implications of these references. Opponents of apocrypha apparently went well beyond merely denying that their use by a New Testament author was somehow validating. To Origen's evident dismay, they even challenged the authority of the New Testament works citing from them. Because of 2 Timothy's use of a work not found "in publicis libris, sed in libro secreto," some, he writes, "have had the temerity to reject the epistle." Suspecting an ulterior motive, Origen charges them with inconsistency in the application of their own rule. None of these fault-finders ever questioned 2 Corinthians because of its citation from the Apocryphon of Elijah. For Origen, their refusal to do so exposed their underlying intentions. The Epistle to the Hebrews, 2 Timothy, and Jude made vulnerable targets, because, unlike 2 Corinthians, the apostolic authorship of all of them was already in doubt (Origen, *Comm. ser. Matt.* ser. 117 [250.9–12]).

Origen's accusation of inconsistency appears after a learned exposition of the value of apocrypha in amplifying reports in the New Testament about the persecution of the prophets. If his tone rings of exasperation, it was probably because Origen saw in the rejectionist school a direct challenge to the biblical scholar interested in preserving access to this literature. But did the use of the book of Enoch, the Ascension of Moses, or an Elijah apocryphon by the apostles amount to an unqualified endorsement of their authority? Origen addresses this latter subject towards the conclusion of the prologue to his commentary on the Song of Songs. The occasion of his discussion was uncertainty about the meaning of the title of the work, a name that for some commentators presupposed the existence of many other songs. In support of this claim, they pointed to a passage in 1 Kings crediting Solomon with the composition of three thousand proverbs and five thousand songs (1 Kgs 5:12 [LXX]) (Origen, *Comm. Cant.* 32).

In his warning against drawing any ill-considered conclusions about the existence or legitimacy of other books of Solomon on the basis of a single verse in 1 Kings, Origen reminds his readers that references to extrabiblical writings permeate Scriptures, including the writings of the apostles and evangelists. It is common knowledge, he writes, that they have "put into the New Testament many things that are found in the apocryphal writings, and are quite obviously taken from them." But in no way did this mean that apocryphal books "are to be given a place." Even if a written witness to one of these works were to be located, it would be impossible to guarantee the integrity of a text containing "many things that are found to be corrupt and contrary to the true faith." It was for this reason that our predecessors "did not see fit … to admit them among those reckoned as authoritative works." In deciding how to read apocryphal books, readers of his own time should not "overstep the everlasting limits which our fathers have set" (Origen, *Comm. Cant.* 33–34).[20]

In his other writings, Origen would sometimes cite passages from apocryphal books whose authenticity could not be vouchsafed by New Testament authors. Here, however, he applies a more stringent standard. In determining authenticity, individual discretion is no longer an option. Adhere to the practice of the apostle and evangelists. "Infused with the Holy Spirit," they were able to discern "what was to be taken out and what must be rejected from these writing." "We," on the other hand, "who have no such abundance of the Spirit, cannot without danger, presume so to select" (Origen, *Comm. Cant.* 34).[21] Although the position Origen espouses here may seem atypically draconian, we need not blame the Latin translation for deliberate misrepresentation.[22] At its heart, his reflections on the textual corruptions of the apocrypha were never meant as a statement of a philological standard. When he invokes the principle, its purpose was simply to warn readers that whatever benefits could be derived from consulting apocryphal books needed to be measured against the uncertain state of their preservation. The application of the rule varied according to the circumstances.

2. The Apocrypha and Revealed Secret Wisdom

In the same prologue, Origen makes another observation about removed books seemingly at variance with the position he adopts elsewhere. If only in passing, he alludes to a second collection of extrabiblical books, separate from those belonging to the formal category of apocrypha. Unlike the works of mixed content removed and corrupted by human agents, these books were set apart by the Holy Spirit because "they contained

---

20. The admonition comes from Prov 22:28.
21. Translation from R. P. Lawson, *Origen: The Song of Songs, Commentary and Homilies*, Ancient Christian Writers 26 (New York: Newman Press, 1957), 56.
22. The text of Origen's commentary survives only in Rufinus's Latin translation. For discussion of the accuracy of Rufinus's translation of this passage, see Edmon L. Gallagher, "Writings Labelled Apocrypha," in *Sacra Scriptura: How "Non-Canonical" Texts Functioned in Early Judaism and Early Christianity*, ed. James H. Charlesworth and Lee Martin McDonald, Jewish and Christian Texts 20 (London: Bloomsbury, 2014), 7–8.

some matters beyond human understanding" (Origen, *Comm. Cant.* 34). Origen's postulation of this second class of hidden writings struck Adolf von Harnack as an uncharacteristic affirmation of an idea "from which Origen otherwise distances himself." In Harnack's judgment, Origen's recognition here of a division of apocryphal books "placed into hiding by the Holy Spirit because their contents exceed human intellectual capacities ... verged on a Gnostic understanding" of hidden wisdom.[23]

While Origen's recognition of hidden writings surpassing human understanding may seem incompatible with his more familiar disavowal of what Harnack calls a "förmliche Geheimtradition für die kirchlichen Gnostiker," Alexandrian Christianity was by Origen's time accustomed to treating parabiblical Jewish literature as deposits of secret revelations not meant for a wider readership. Their reception in this way was something encouraged by the sources themselves, most notably Jewish apocalypses and kindred writings. In the Testament of Moses, Moses, facing imminent death, instructs Joshua to anoint the books which he presents to him and conceal them in earthen jars "in the place which (God) has chosen from the beginning of the creation of the world."[24] Restrictions on readership are rather more exacting in 4 Ezra. After his fifth vision, Ezra is told to teach what he had learned to "the wise among your people, whose hearts you know are able to comprehend and keep these secrets" (4 Ezra 12:37–38). He is later ordered to dictate his revelations to five scribes, who record it in characters "which they did not know" for an interval of forty days. Ezra is then instructed by God "to make public the twenty-four books that you wrote first and let the worthy and the unworthy read them; but keep the seventy that were written last, in order to give them to the wise among your people. For in them is the spring of understanding, the fountain of wisdom, and the river of knowledge" (4 Ezra 14:42–48; trans. Bruce M. Metzger, *OTP* 1:555).

Like the other secret books circulating under the name of some ancient worthy in the second and third centuries, works like 4 Ezra made an appealing target for students of the Alexandrian allegorical

---

23. Harnack, *Der kirchengeschichtliche Ertrag*, 46.

24. T. Mos. 1.16–17: "But (you) take this writing so that later you will remember how to preserve the books which I shall entrust to you. You shall arrange them, anoint them with cedar, and deposit them in earthenware jars in the place which (God) has chosen from the beginning of the creation of the world" (trans. John Priest, *OTP* 1:919–33).

school seeking deeper wisdom meant only for religious elites. One of them was Clement. In his *Stromateis*, he refers to a parabiblical tradition about Joshua's vision of Moses's two bodies, the ultimate source of which was probably the Assumption of Moses or some related work. The story represented for him an allegory about the ability of the select few to penetrate beyond the "body of sacred scripture." In my opinion, he writes, the narrative shows "that knowledge is not the privilege of all" (δηλούσης, οἶμαι, τῆς ἱστορίας μὴ πάντων εἶναι τὴν γνῶσιν). Only the gnostic can see "through to the underlying thoughts and what is signified in scripture, seeking the Moses that is with the angels" (Clement, *Strom.* 6.15.132). Despite his own stated misgivings about apocryphal books, Origen himself never forecloses on the possibility that they may have contained, if only in a textually corrupt form, secret teachings about esoteric topics not found in more recognized scriptures. In, for example, his *Commentary on John*, Origen states that those who believed that Jesus was John the Baptist *redivivus* must have drawn this conclusion from a secret teaching they had learned "either from oral tradition or from apocrypha" (ἢ ἐκ παραδόσεως ἢ ἐξ ἀποκρύφων) (Origen, *Comm. Jo.* 19.15.97).[25]

But in postulating the existence of written and oral teachings about the transmigration of souls, "along with tens of thousands of other things unknown to the masses," Origen ran the risk of putting himself at odds with his own disavowal of a class of writings containing secret doctrines meant only for the Christian gnostic. In the *Commentariorum in Matthaeum Series*, Origen found one way to manage the dissonance, warning readers not to embrace the secret doctrines of "apocryphal and little-known books" cited by heretics and "outside of the faith and the rule of the church" (Origen, *Comm. ser. Matt.* 46 on Matt 24:23–28). In the prologue to his commentary on the Song of Songs, Origen seizes on another expedient. While not ruling out the existence of a class of secret books of inaccessible wisdom, Origen treats it here as little more than a hypothetical possibility, and not a viable one. Nor does Origen call these works apocrypha. He continues to reserve that formal label for texts removed from wider circulation in Jewish communities. *Pace* 4 Ezra, the removal of these writings by self-serving Jewish officials had nothing to do with preventing the unworthy from gaining access to the secrets contained in

---

25. See further Guy G. Stroumsa, *Hidden Wisdom: Esoteric Traditions and the Roots of Christian Mysticism*, 2nd ed. (Leiden: Brill, 2005), 119–21.

them. These latter works could be read and studied, but only with the requisite caution. Searching for works of the other class would be a transgression of a divine prohibition.

3. Apocrypha and the Autonomy of the Church

We turn finally to the question that comes to increasingly dominate Origen's thinking about the broader implications of his category of apocrypha. Did his understanding of apocryphal books as a body of writings removed from public reading in the synagogue subordinate the church's decisions about recognized and unrecognized works to Jewish practice?

In the prologue to the *Commentary on the Song of Solomon*, Origen skirted the question by limiting the question to those books of the apocrypha known and cited by New Testament writers. "It would be tiresome and irrelevant," he writes, "for us to enquire how many books are in the Divine Scriptures, of which nothing whatsoever has been handed down for us to read. Nor do we find that the Jews made use of lections of this kind" (Origen, *Comm. Cant.* 33). But for a scholar as invested as he was in the text of Jewish scriptures, it was impossible to overlook places where the church and synagogue diverged. From Jewish informants, he had learned that Judith and Tobit enjoyed no recognized standing in the synagogues, "not even among the apocrypha in Hebrew" (οὐδὲ γὰρ ἔχουσιν αὐτὰ καὶ ἐν ἀποκρύφοις ἑβραϊστί) (Origen, *Ep. Afr.* 13). And in his *Commentary on John*, he allows that the Prayer of Joseph, while not accepted in the churches, was included among "the apocryphal books current among the Hebrews." In commending this work for its affirmation of the doctrine of the descent of angels into bodies, Origen appends no disclaimers or warnings about consulting a book removed and possibly corrupted by Jewish leaders with a political agenda. To the contrary, he seems to consider the Prayer of Joseph's formal inclusion in the apocrypha of the Jews one more point in favor of a writing which, in his words, was "not to be despised" (οὐκ εὐκαταφρόνητον) (Origen, *Comm. Jo.* 2.31.192). Deference to Jewish practice is also his stated reason for hesitating to quote from the "many books circulating in the name of Enoch." "These books," he writes, "do not appear to be authoritative among the Hebrews" (Origen, *Hom. Num.* 28.2.1).

But Origen adopts a markedly different position on the regulatory role of the synagogue in his well-known later dispute with Julius Africanus over the standing of the story of Susanna, one of the three Greek additions to the book of Daniel. Observing that Origen had quoted the episode in a public debate, Africanus quite boldly challenges Origen to defend his appeal to a part of Daniel which he dismisses as "demonstrably a modern forgery" (νεωτερικὸν καὶ πεπλασμένον). In a deceptively short letter, Africanus assembled an impressive array of linguistic and historical arguments in support of his claim. He even objects to the work with an argument grounded in the phenomenology of religious experience. The prophetic inspiration ascribed to Daniel in the Susanna section differed from the visions and dreams the prophet experienced in the undisputed part of the work (Africanus, *Ep. Orig.* 1). But what Africanus calls the "foremost objection" to the work's authenticity appears towards the conclusion of the letter. "Along with the other two at the end of it, the Susanna section is not contained in the Daniel received among the Jews" (Africanus, *Ep. Orig.* 2).

Challenged here to defend a work "not received among the Jews," Origen casts himself in the role of defender of the church's right to regulate its own scriptures, unconstrained by the practices and the texts in use by the Jews. "Are we immediately to reject as spurious the copies in use in our churches, and enjoin the brotherhood to put away the sacred books current among them, and to coax the Jews, and persuade them to give us copies which shall be untampered with, and free from forgery!" (Origen, *Ep. Afr.* 4 [trans. Frederick Crombie, *ANF* 4:386–92]). There is a note of defensiveness when Origen insists, somewhat disingenuously, that the only motive for his painstaking critical annotation of the differences between the Hebrew and Greek texts of Jewish scriptures was to defeat the Jews in debate (Origen, *Ep. Afr.* 5).

That same defensiveness also shaped his advocacy of Christian autonomy in establishing the content of its scriptures. The fact that Tobit and Judith enjoyed no standing either among the recognized or apocryphal books of the Jews is now of no consequence to the reading practices of Christian communities. In defending the standing of Susanna, Origen does not explicitly number it among the apocrypha. But he does hold out the possibility that its unflattering depiction of the Jewish elders may explain why it suffered the same treatment as the Apocryphon of Isaiah and other works deemed threatening to the reputation of Jewish leaders. "We need not wonder," he tells Africanus, "if this history of the evil device of the licentious elders against Susanna is true, but was stolen away and subtracted from the Scriptures [ἐξέκλεψαν καὶ ὑφεῖλον ἀπὸ τῶν Γραφῶν] by men themselves not very far removed from the counsel of these elders"

(Orig. *Ep. Afr.* 9 [trans. Crombie]).²⁶ In his gospel commentaries, removal and corruption of apocryphal books by Jewish leaders formed the basis for his prescriptions on the proper handling of apocryphal books. But in the letter to Africanus, the same argument is put to a very different use: not to defend selective reading of apocryphal books, but rather to advocate for the church's independence in determining the text and the contents of its own sacred scriptures.

Origen's Legacy

Research on the reception of the Jewish pseudepigrapha in early Christianity tends to default to the assumption that after Origen, and largely in reaction to official interdictions, estimation of this literature suffered what Albrecht Oepke called a "sharp decline."²⁷ The evidence, however, does not always bear out the assumption. There were many reasons for continuing Christian interest in the study and preservation of this literature, especially in centers of monastic learning.²⁸ As with Origen, appreciation of this literature as an instrument of biblical scholarship seems to have played a role.²⁹

Nor did official lists of proscribed works deter biblical scholars from continuing to scour Jewish pseudepigrapha for the origins of contested New Testament quotations.³⁰ In the latter half of the fourth century, the

---

26. On the one occasion in which Origen does attempt to classify Susannah, he numbers it ἐν ἀπορρήτοις (not ἐν ἀποκρύφοις) (*Ep. Afr.* 12). For discussion of Origen's atypical use of the phrase ἐν ἀπορρήτοις in connection with a written text, see Ruwet, "Les apocryphes dans les œuvres d'Origène," 150.

27. Oepke, "Βίβλοι ἀπόκρυφοι in Christianity," 995.

28. For discussion, see Robert A. Kraft, "The Pseudepigrapha in Christianity," in *Tracing the Threads: Studies in the Vitality of Jewish Pseudepigrapha*, ed. John C. Reeves, EJL 6 (Atlanta: Scholars Press, 1994), 68–70.

29. If we may judge from the rather sizable number of references to the book of Jubilees in catenae commentaries, recognition of the work's value as a kind of narrative commentary on Genesis at least partially accounts for the surge in interest in a work that does not seem to have been widely embraced in the early church before the fourth century. For Jubilees citations in Greek catenae on Genesis, see Françoise Petit, ed., *La Chaîne sur la Genèse*, nos. 551, 553, 585, 590, 833, 857, 861, 867, 2270, Traditio Exegetica Graeca (Leuven: Peeters, 1991–1996).

30. On the dispute over the standing of apocrypha in the context of what he calls the conflict between "episcopal" and "academic" forms of Christianity in the fourth century, see David Brakke, "Canon Formation and Social Conflict in Fourth-Cen-

Spanish monk Priscillian of Avila complained of "canon-purists" whose policing of the reading habits of others constrained and undermined the work of the biblical scholar. "It is enough," they said, "for you to read what is written in the canon." In response, Priscillian defied these sticklers to explain the source of allusions in the New Testament to prophets whose words and writings are not recorded in the Old Testament. If only the witness of canonical books is subject to investigation, and "it is a sin to read anything else," then what was Jesus referring to when in Luke's gospel (Luke 11:50–51) he recalled the death of the prophets "since the foundation of the world, from the blood of Abel to the blood of Zechariah, who was killed between the altar and the sanctuary"?[31] In a learned study of the origins of extrabiblical witnesses cited in the epistles of the apostle Paul, the fifth century Alexandrian deacon Euthalius (later bishop of Sulca) supplemented Origen's own findings by tracing Paul's words in Gal 6:15 to a work he identifies as the Apocalypse of Moses. Euthalius also believed he had found in the Apocrypha of Jeremiah the source of Paul's reference in Eph 5:14: "Awake, O sleeper, and arise from the dead, and Christ shall give you light" (Euthalius, *Editio Epistolarum Pauli* [PG 85:721bc]). At around the same time, Jerome was also chasing down reports about the apocryphal sources of other citations in the Pauline epistles. He discovered two apocryphal sources of 1 Cor 2:9: not just the Apocalypse of Elijah, but the Ascension of Isaiah as well (Jerome, *Comm. Isa.* 17 on Isa 64:4, 5).[32] Despite his own doubts about Matthew's use of an apocryphal work at 27:9–10, Jerome knew of a "Hebrew of the Nazarene sect" who informed him of the existence of the disputed quotation in Matthew in a Jeremiah apocryphon. In that work, Jerome writes, "I discovered this passage written word for word" (Jerome, *Comm. Matt.* 4 on Matt 27:9, 10). All of these inquiries continued in the scholarly spirit of Origen: a pursuit for sources of the apostles and evangelists, no matter their origins, and a willingness

---

tury Egypt: Athanasius of Alexandria's Thirty-Ninth *Festal Letter*," *HTR* 87 (1994): 395–419.

31. Priscillian, *Tract.* 3.56 (44.19–20); 3.60 (47.3–18); 3.68 (53.3–5). See further Andrew S. Jacobs, "The Disorder of Books: Priscillian's Canonical Defense of Apocrypha," *HTR* 93 (2000): 135–59; Henry Chadwick, *Priscillian of Avila: The Occult and the Charismatic in the Early Church* (Oxford: Clarendon, 1976), 74, 80–83.

32. On Jerome's understanding of apocrypha, see most recently Edmon L. Gallagher, "The Old Testament 'Apocrypha' in Jerome's Canonical Theory," *JECS* 20 (2012): 213–33.

to seek out testimony from Jewish, or at least Jewish Christian witnesses, for confirmation and guidance.

A monk and scholar seeking further guidance on the proper handling of these sources could also find support in Origen's recommendations about the selective reading of apocrypha. One of them was the Byzantine universal chronicler George Syncellus. How Syncellus managed to obtain his excerpts from the Greek text of the books of Enoch, Jubilees, and various Adam books is far from clear. Alexandrian authorities probably had a hand in mediating some of these sources to him, including his excerpts from the Enoch corpus. Time spent in monasteries in Palestine may also have enriched Syncellus's familiarity with this literature. But when he arrived in Constantinople, Syncellus must have understood that his use of works that were far from household names in Constantinople of the early ninth century required justification. In a carefully-hedged endorsement of apocrypha following his second excerpt from Enoch's Book of the Watchers, Syncellus warns readers that the fathers of the church had sound reasons for preventing later generations from reading apocryphal books "as if they were the rest of divine scriptures." The fault lay with "Jews and heretics" who had corrupted the text of these works with "strange material [περιττά τινα] out of line with ecclesiastical teaching." It was also why inexperienced readers should settle for prescreened excerpts whose conformity with orthodox teaching had been tested and confirmed. But even while allowing for the uneven content in apocrypha, Syncellus assures readers that, used carefully, apocryphal books made a potentially valuable resource. And hadn't the apostle Paul himself quoted approvingly from apocryphal books circulating in the names of Jeremiah, Moses, and Elijah? (*Ecloga Chronographica* 27.12–18).[33]

Syncellus's warnings to readers about the dangers of apocrypha have the ring of tested clichés. The passages in the Pauline epistles he claims originated in apocryphal books were not the fruit of original study on his part. Euthalius had earlier discovered the same references. Nor can "conformity with church doctrine" count as a viable standard for differentiating genuine material from later corruptions by "Jews and heretics." Like Origen before him, Syncellus was chiefly interested in finding a way to continue quoting, however sparingly, from these sources. His cam-

---

33. For discussion of Syncellus's use of Jewish pseudepigrapha, see William Adler and Paul Tuffin, *The Chronography of George Syncellus* (Oxford: Oxford University Press, 2002), liv–lv.

paign seems to have succeeded. Once the learned monk and advisor to the patriarch Tarasius had given his qualified endorsement of them, later chroniclers felt free to quote from them and usually without apology.

Bibliography

Adler, William, and Paul Tuffin. *The Chronography of George Syncellus*. Oxford: Oxford University Press, 2002.

Bardy, Gustave. "Les traditions juives dans l'oeuvre d'origène." *RB* 34 (1925): 217–52.

Brakke, David. "Canon Formation and Social Conflict in Fourth-Century Egypt: Athanasius of Alexandria's Thirty-Ninth *Festal Letter*." *HTR* 87 (1994): 395–419.

Chadwick, Henry. *Priscillian of Avila: The Occult and the Charismatic in the Early Church*. Oxford: Clarendon, 1976.

Charles, R. H. *The Apocrypha and Pseudepigrapha of the Old Testament*. 2 vols. Oxford: Clarendon, 1913.

Gallagher, Edmon L. *Hebrew Scriptures in Patristic Biblical Theory*. VCSup 114. Leiden: Brill, 2012.

———. "The Old Testament 'Apocrypha' in Jerome's Canonical Theory." *JECS* 20 (2012): 213–33.

———. "Writings Labelled Apocrypha." Pages 1–14 in *Sacra Scriptura: How "Non-Canonical" Texts Functioned in Early Judaism and Early Christianity*. Edited by James H. Charlesworth and Lee Martin McDonald. Jewish and Christian Texts 20. London: Bloomsbury, 2014.

Hanson, R. P. C. *Origen's Doctrine of Tradition*. London: SPCK, 1954.

Harnack, Adolf von. *Der kirchengeschichtliche Ertrag der exegetischen Arbeiten des Origenes*. TUGAL 42.3. Leipzig: Hinrichs, 1918.

Jacobs, Andrew S. "The Disorder of Books: Priscillian's Canonical Defense of Apocrypha." *HTR* 93 (2000): 135–59.

Kraft, Robert A. "The Pseudepigrapha in Christianity." Pages 68–70 in *Tracing the Threads: Studies in the Vitality of Jewish Pseudepigrapha*. Edited by John C. Reeves. EJL 6. Atlanta: Scholars Press, 1994.

Lawson, R. P. *Origen: The Song of Songs, Commentary and Homilies*. Ancient Christian Writers 26. New York: Newman Press, 1957.

Lied, Liv Ingeborg. "Text—Work—Manuscript: What Is an 'Old Testament Pseudepigraphon'?" *JSP* 25 (2015): 150–65.

Metzger, Bruce M. "The Fourth Book of Ezra." *OTP* 1:517–59.

Oepke, Albrecht. "Βίβλοι ἀπόκρυφοι in Christianity." *TDNT* 3:987–1000.

Petit, Françoise, ed. *La Chaîne sur la Genèse*, #551, #553, #585, #590, #833, #857, #861, #867, #2270. Traditio Exegetica Graeca. Leuven: Peeters, 1991–1996.

Priest, John. "Testament of Moses." *OTP* 1:919–34.

Reed, Annette Yoshiko. *Fallen Angels and the History of Judaism and Christianity: The Reception of Enochic Literature*. New York: Cambridge University Press, 2005.

———. "The Modern Invention of Old Testament Pseudepigrapha." *JTS* 60 (2009): 403–36.

Reeves, John C., and Annette Yoshiko Reed. *Sources from Judaism, Christianity, and Islam*. Vol. 1 of *Enoch from Antiquity to the Middle Ages*. Oxford: Oxford University Press, 2018.

Ruwet, J. "Les *apocryphes* dans les œuvres d'Origène." *Bib* 25 (1944): 143–66.

Smith, J. Z. "Prayer of Joseph, a New Translation with Introduction." *OTP* 2:699–714.

Stroumsa, Guy G. *Hidden Wisdom: Esoteric Traditions and the Roots of Christian Mysticism*. 2nd ed. Leiden: Brill, 2005.

Zahn, Theodor. *Geschichte des Neutestamentlichen Kanons*. Erlangen: Deichert, 1888.

15
Pseudepigrapha Between Judaism and Christianity: The Case of 3 Baruch

John J. Collins

The title Old Testament pseudepigrapha properly refers to writings falsely attributed to Old Testament figures (Adam, Abraham, Moses, etc.).[1] The term is used loosely, however, to include writings about Old Testament figures, even if they are not presented as authors or speakers (e.g., the romance of Joseph and Aseneth) and pseudepigraphic writings attributed to figures who are not found in the Old Testament (e.g., the Sibylline Oracles). Since the late nineteenth century, these writings have been studied mainly for the light they may shed on Judaism in the late Second Temple period. The long-running Pseudepigrapha unit of the Society of Biblical Literature may fairly be said to have concerned itself with Jewish literature preserved in languages other than Hebrew and Aramaic, except for the apocrypha or deuterocanonical books and the lengthy writings of Philo and Josephus. Interest in the literature of this period had been stimulated by manuscript discoveries in the nineteenth century, and more recently by the discovery of the Dead Sea Scrolls.

The manuscript discoveries of the nineteenth century, which led to the first modern editions of such texts as 1 and 2 Enoch, Jubilees, the Apocalypse of Abraham, and 2 and 3 Baruch, revolutionized the study of ancient Judaism. Before these texts came to light, portrayals of Judaism around the turn of the era were heavily dependent on rabbinic writings. The newly discovered pseudepigrapha, many of which were apocalypses, disclosed a very different world, one that was much less focused on the law, that was

---

1. On the history of the category, see Annette Yoshiko Reed, "The Modern Invention of 'Old Testament Pseudepigrapha,'" *JTS* 60 (2009): 403–36.

peopled by angels and demons, and that was rife with expectation of a coming judgment.[2]

The apocalyptic pseudepigrapha provided the material for a new account of Jewish religion in this era by Wilhelm Bousset, whose *Religion des Judentums im neutestamentlichen Zeitalter* first appeared in 1903.[3] This work provoked a furious backlash. Bousset was accused of missing the center of Jewish religion by failing to give a systematic description of the normative Judaism represented by the rabbinic literature.[4] The great Christian scholar of ancient Judaism, George F. Moore, declared: "It is clear that the author ought not to have called his book *Die Religion des Judentums*, for the sources from which his representation is drawn are those to which, so far as we know, Judaism never conceded any authority, while he discredits and largely ignores those which it has always regarded as normative."[5]

Moore's concept of normative Judaism would come in for much criticism later in the twentieth century. Jacob Neusner would question whether notions of normativity are appropriate to the history of religion at all and go so far as to speak of Judaisms in the plural as a way of emphasizing the diversity of Judaism around the turn of the era.[6] More to the point, we might ask whether there was any controlling body in Judaism in this era that was capable of imposing the supposed norms. But notions of normativity survive in the discussion nonetheless, even if they are not as explicit as in Moore's formulation.

There have always been some Jewish scholars who refuse to accept the pseudepigrapha as "really Jewish," for reasons similar to those advanced by Moore, or insisted that they be interpreted in conformity with "essential biblical doctrines."[7] For most scholars, the discovery of portions of 1 Enoch and Jubilees at Qumran showed beyond dispute that at least some

---

2. See my essay, "Early Judaism in Modern Scholarship," in *Early Judaism: A Comprehensive Overview*, ed. John J. Collins and Daniel C. Harlow (Grand Rapids: Eerdmans, 2012), 1–29.

3. Wilhelm Bousset, *Religion des Judentums im neutestamentlichen Zeitalter* (Berlin: Reuther & Reichard, 1903).

4. Felix Perles, *Bousset's Religion des Judentums im neutestamentlichen Zeitalter kritisch untersucht* (Berlin: Peiser, 1903).

5. George F. Moore, "Christian Writers on Judaism," *HTR* 14 (1921): 244.

6. Jacob Neusner, *Judaism: The Evidence of the Mishnah* (Chicago: University of Chicago Press, 1981), 7.

7. E.g., Joshua Efron, *Studies on the Hasmonean Period* (Leiden: Brill, 1987); Paul

of the pseudepigrapha did indeed originate as Jewish works before the rise of Christianity, even if they were preserved by Christians and rejected by rabbinic Judaism. The Dead Sea Scrolls also showed the diversity of Judaism before the turn of the era and the existence of many texts that might at least loosely be called apocalyptic, even beyond those preserved in the pseudepigrapha. Nonetheless, the provenance of many of the pseudepigrapha has remained controversial.

Christian Transmission

The problem is that all these writings were preserved by Christians, often in translation, and are only found in manuscripts many centuries later than their supposed time of origin. Many of them contain explicit Christian references, which are often viewed as interpolations. Robert Kraft has argued repeatedly that texts that were preserved by Christians should be studied first in their Christian contexts.[8] "They are, first of all, 'Christian' materials, and recognition of that fact is a necessary step in using them appropriately in the quest to throw light on early Judaism. I call this the 'default' position—sources transmitted by way of Christian communities are 'Christian,' whatever else they may also prove to be."[9] There have indeed been several cases where scholars have argued convincingly that texts that had often been taken as Jewish with interpolations should rather be understood as Christian compositions. The showcase example is the Testaments of the Twelve Patriarchs, where the argument for Christian provenance was made by Marinus de Jonge already in 1953.[10] Other plausible cases are The Lives of the Prophets, The Ascension of Isaiah, and The Life of Adam and Eve.[11] Other attempted arguments along these lines,

---

Heger, *Challenges to Conventional Opinions on Qumran and Enoch Issues*, STDJ 100 (Leiden: Brill, 2012).

8. Robert A. Kraft, "The Pseudepigrapha in Christianity," in *Tracing the Threads: Studies in the Vitality of Jewish Pseudepigrapha*, ed. John C. Reeves, EJL 6 (Atlanta: Scholars Press, 1994), 55–86; and Kraft, "The Pseudepigrapha in Christianity Revisited: Setting the Stage and Framing Some Central Questions," *JSJ* 32 (2001): 371–95.

9. Kraft, "Pseudepigrapha and Christianity, Revisited," 36.

10. Marinus de Jonge, *The Testaments of the Twelve Patriarchs: A Study of Their Text, Composition, and Origin* (Assen: Van Gorcum, 1953); de Jonge, *Pseudepigrapha of the Old Testament as Part of Christian Literature: The Case of the Testaments of the Twelve Patriarchs and the Greek Life of Adam and Eve*, SVTP 18 (Leiden: Brill, 2003).

11. David Satran, *Biblical Prophets in Byzantine Palestine: Reassessing the Lives*

concerning 2 Baruch and Joseph and Aseneth, have been unpersuasive.[12] Kraft himself has done little to document his default position by case studies. While Kraft's student, Martha Himmelfarb, has claimed that Kraft's observations "have come to seem obvious and commonsensical,"[13] not all scholars agree. Richard Bauckham has argued cogently that the oldest manuscripts of a given work are still likely to be far removed from the original time and place of composition, and he has also questioned the value of having a default position at all.[14] The fact that a given text is preserved by Christians should not necessarily create a presumption in favor of Christian origin. Whether such works are Christian or Jewish must be decided on the merits of each individual case. Some pseudepigrapha in the name of figures known from the Hebrew Bible are demonstrably Jewish (e.g., several sections of 1 Enoch). Some are better understood as Christian compositions, even if they incorporate Jewish traditions (the testaments). But the provenance of many texts remains open to dispute.

The task of distinguishing Jewish and Christian compositions has been further complicated in recent decades by the recognition that the parting of the ways was neither as absolute nor as early as had previously been supposed.[15] Some followers of Jesus remained attached to Jewish traditions and may have thought of themselves as Jewish. Nonetheless, the acknowl-

---

of the Prophets, SVTP 11 (Leiden: Brill, 1995); Enrico Norelli, *Ascension du Prophète Isaïe* (Turnhout: Brepols, 1993); Marinus de Jonge and Johannes Tromp, *The Life of Adam and Eve and Related Literature* (Sheffield: Sheffield Academic, 1997).

12. Rivka Nir, *The Destruction of Jerusalem and the Idea of Redemption in the Syriac Apocalypse of Baruch* (Atlanta: Society of Biblical Literature, 2003); Ross S. Kraemer, *When Aseneth Met Joseph: A Late Antique Tale of the Biblical Patriarch and His Egyptian Wife, Reconsidered* (Oxford: Oxford University Press, 1998); Rivka Nir, *Joseph and Aseneth: A Christian Book* (Sheffield: Sheffield Phoenix, 2012). See my critique of Kraemer, "*Joseph and Aseneth*: Jewish or Christian?," in *Jewish Cult and Hellenistic Culture: Essays on the Jewish Encounter with Hellenism and Roman Rule*, JSJSup 100 (Leiden: Brill, 2005), 112–27.

13. Martha Himmelfarb, "3 Baruch Revisited: Jewish or Christian Composition, and Why It Matters," *ZAC* 20 (2016): 44.

14. Richard J. Bauckham, "The Continuing Quest for the Provenance of Old Testament Pseudepigrapha," in *The Pseudepigrapha and Christian Origins*, ed. Gerbern S. Oegema and James H. Charlesworth (London: T&T Clark, 2008), 9–29, especially 23.

15. Adam H. Becker and Annette Yoshiko Reed, eds., *The Ways That Never Parted: Jews and Christians in Late Antiquity and the Early Middle Ages* (Tübingen: Mohr Siebeck, 2003); Daniel Boyarin, *Border Lines: The Partition of Judeo-Christianity* (Berkeley: University of California Press, 2004).

edgement of Jesus as the Christ or Messiah remains a decisive point of difference. Since most Christian literature refers explicitly to Christ, the tendency has been to assume that any text that does not refer to Christ explicitly is Jewish by default.

Many scholars object to that tendency, however, and insist on looking for positive indications of Jewish authorship. James Davila argues that "no satisfactory definition of Judaism based on a *sine qua non* or core essence can be formulated."[16] Instead, he favors a polythetic approach: "Rather than attempting to find an essence common to every member, it is based on a broad grouping of characteristics or properties. A member of the class being defined must have many of these characteristics, but no single characteristic is necessarily possessed by every member."[17] So he offers a list of signature features, which need not all be present, but which provide reason to see a work as Jewish:

> substantial Jewish content and evidence of a pre-Christian date;
> compelling evidence that a work was translated from Hebrew;
> sympathetic concern with the Jewish ritual cult;
> sympathetic concern with Jewish law and halakah;
> concern with Jewish national interests.[18]

These signature features are helpful, but it is important to keep in mind that no single characteristic is decisive. Some Christians were surely torah-observant, while a lack of concern for halakah would disqualify most of the Enoch literature from being regarded as Jewish, even in cases where manuscripts were found at Qumran.

It is easy enough to recognize as Christian a work that praises Jesus as Lord. But can we conceive of a Christian writing that does not mention Christ at all? Or does so only in a single verse that fits awkwardly in its context? Conversely, it is easy to recognize as Jewish a book that has a stringent view of the law. But can we conceive of a Jewish work that does not refer to the law explicitly or regards it only as a source of general ethical norms? Our decisions about the provenance of a text inevitably depends on the profile of Judaism or of Christianity that we are willing to accept.

---

16. James R. Davila, *The Provenance of the Pseudepigrapha: Jewish, Christian, or Other?*, JSJSup 105 (Leiden: Brill, 2005), 19.

17. Davila, *Provenance of the Pseudepigrapha*, 19.

18. Davila, *Provenance of the Pseudepigrapha*, 65.

3 Baruch

The problems involved in determining the provenance of some pseudepigrapha may be illustrated from the example of 3 Baruch. This work describes the heavenly ascent of Baruch, scribe of Jeremiah. It begins with Baruch mourning the destruction of Jerusalem by the Babylonians. An angel tells him to cease his lamentation and offers to show him "the mysteries of God." The angel then accompanies Baruch in an ascent through five heavens. The first two contain the places of punishment of the builders of the tower of Babel. The third contains a serpent or dragon and also Hades. Baruch gets to see various cosmological wonders (the sun, a phoenix) and is told at length about the tree that caused Adam to stray, which is identified as the vine. In the fourth heaven, he sees birds around a lake and is told that this is where the righteous gather to praise God. In the fifth heaven, the archangel Michael presides while the angels present human merits. Michael alone ascends to the presence of God. In the end, Baruch returns to his place on earth and praises God.

This work was practically unknown until the end of the nineteenth century. Origen had referred to a book of "the prophet Baruch" that allegedly described seven heavens (*Princ.* 2.3.6). Whether this was in fact the book we know as 3 Baruch remains in dispute, since our pseudepigraphon only describes five heavens.[19]

The work is preserved in two recensions, Greek and Slavonic. The Slavonic manuscript N was published in 1886.[20] A German translation of that manuscript was published by G. N. Bonwetsch in 1896, and an English translation by W. R. Morfill followed in 1897.[21] Six more Slavonic manuscripts were subsequently discovered. The Greek came to light when a single manuscript was discovered in 1896 in the British Museum. It was published the following year by M. R. James, who assumed Christian

---

19. On the integrity of the ending, see Daniel C. Harlow, *The Greek Apocalypse of Baruch (3 Baruch) in Hellenistic Judaism and Early Christianity*, SVTP 12 (Leiden: Brill, 1996), 34–76.

20. See Alexander Kulik, *3 Baruch: Greek-Slavonic Apocalypse of Baruch*, CEJL (Berlin: de Gruyter, 2010), 9.

21. Gottlieb Nathanael Bonwetsch, "Das Slavisch Erhaltene Baruchbuch," *NGWG* (1896): 91–101; W. R. Morfill, "The Apocalypse of Baruch Translated from the Slavonic," in *Apocrypha Anecdota II*, ed. M. R. James, Texts and Studies 5.1 (Cambridge: Cambridge University Press, 1897), 95–102.

provenance.²² Only one more Greek manuscript has been discovered. It was published by J.-C. Picard in 1967.²³ There is consensus that the Slavonic was translated from a Greek text that is no longer extant and that Greek was the original language of composition. All the manuscripts are very late. The two Greek manuscripts date to the fifteenth/sixteenth century and the oldest of the Slavonic manuscripts to the thirteenth.²⁴

The suggestion that 3 Baruch was originally a Jewish apocalypse seems to have been made first by Emil Schürer already in 1886 on the basis of the newly discovered Slavonic manuscript.²⁵ Schürer's discussion was very brief. The first scholar to offer an argument for Jewish origin was Louis Ginzberg in the *Jewish Encyclopedia* in 1902.²⁶ Ginzberg argued on the basis of scattered parallels in rabbinic sources, and his treatment has not been influential in later scholarship. His contribution is worth noting, however, in view of occasional suggestions that attempt to claim 3 Baruch, and the view of Judaism it represents, as Jewish reflects a Christian prejudice. This was obviously not true in Ginzberg's case. The scholar whose treatment shaped the subsequent discussion most profoundly was H. M. Hughes, in R. H. Charles's edition of the pseudepigrapha.²⁷ Hughes argued that a second-century Jewish work had been taken up and redacted by Christians. In the century that followed, there have been only a few book-length treatments. A similar position to that of Hughes was defended at length by Dan Harlow in his 1996 monograph.²⁸ The most recent extensive treatment by Alexander Kulik claims that the Slavonic text witnesses to a pre-Christianized stage of transmission.²⁹

At the same time, some scholars have expressed reservations or objections to the supposed Jewish origin. Harry Gaylord, in the James H. Charlesworth edition of the pseudepigrapha, left the question open and

---

22. M. R. James, "Apocalypsis Baruchi Tertia Graece," in James, *Apocrypha Anecdota II*, 83–94.
23. Jean-Claude Picard, *Apocalypsis Baruchi Graece*, PVTG 2 (Leiden: Brill, 1967).
24. Harlow, *Greek Apocalypse of Baruch*, 10.
25. Emil Schürer, *Geschichte des jüdischen Volkes im Zeitalter Jesu Christi*, 2nd ed. (Leipzig: Hinrichs, 1886), 2:645. See Harlow, *Greek Apocalypse of Baruch*, 25.
26. Louis Ginzberg, "Baruch, Apocalypse of (Greek)," *JE* 2:551.
27. H. M. Hughes, "The Greek Apocalypse of Baruch, or III Baruch," in *The Apocrypha and Pseudepigrapha of the Old Testament*, ed. R. H. Charles (Oxford: Clarendon, 1913), 527–41.
28. Harlow, *Greek Apocalypse of Baruch*.
29. Kulik, *3 Baruch*, 14.

warned that "the scholarly dichotomy of Jewish and Christian writings in the first two centuries ... may be a misleading attempt to distinguish what is closely interrelated."[30] George W. E. Nickelsburg, who had treated 3 Baruch as a Jewish response to the destruction of Jerusalem in his 1981 introduction to *Jewish Literature between the Bible and the Mishnah*, quietly omitted it from the revised edition in 2005.[31] Harlow revised his position in an article published five years after this monograph and found it "difficult to say with any certainty," while allowing that a Christian setting "may prove to be the more secure foundation when this and other Pseudepigrapha are further studied as part of the literary heritage of Christianity."[32] In his latest discussion, he concludes that "the original authorship of the work must remain an open question."[33] The strongest proponent of Christian provenance has been Himmelfarb. In her monograph, *Ascent to Heaven*, she was "inclined to see [3 Baruch] as a Christian work."[34] In a review of Harlow's monograph, she questioned whether it was necessary to posit an original Jewish stage.[35] Most recently, she has renewed her critique of the view that any stage of the work was Jewish and offered a suggestion for an original Christian setting.[36] She concludes, however, with an admission: "I am by no means confident that the milieu I have just described is the one in which 3 Baruch was composed or reshaped."[37]

Christian Elements

There can be no dispute that 3 Baruch is Christian in its extant Greek recension. The passages that most clearly show Christian authorship or

---

30. Harry E. Gaylord Jr., "3 (Greek Apocalypse of) Baruch: A New Translation and Introduction," *OTP* 1:656.
31. George W. E. Nickelsburg, *Jewish Literature between the Bible and the Mishnah: A Historical and Literary Introduction* (Philadelphia: Fortress, 1981), 277–309.
32. Daniel C. Harlow, "The Christianization of Early Jewish Pseudepigrapha: The Case of 3 *Baruch*," *JSJ* 32 (2001): 416–44.
33. Daniel C. Harlow, "Baruch, Third Book of," *EDEJ* 429.
34. Martha Himmelfarb, *Ascent to Heaven in Jewish and Christian Apocalypses* (New York: Oxford University Press, 1993), 89.
35. Martha Himmelfarb, review of *The Greek Apocalypse of Baruch (3 Baruch) in Hellenistic Judaism and Early Christianity*, by Daniel C. Harlow, *RBL* (1998): https://tinyurl.com/SBL3550e.
36. Himmelfarb, "3 *Baruch* Revisited," 44.
37. Himmelfarb, "3 *Baruch* Revisited," 61.

editing, however, are lacking in the Slavonic. The evidence for Christian elements in the Slavonic is much less explicit.

Three passages in the Greek manuscripts are quite explicitly Christian. The first is in 3 Bar. 4.15, where Noah is told to plant the vine after the flood, because its fruit would become the blood of God, and that just as humanity had been condemned through the vine, so it would be saved by Jesus Christ. This passage is not found in the Slavonic. Moreover, it contradicts the negative view of the vine in the verses that precede and follow it. This passage, then, is clearly secondary on literary and textual grounds.

The other explicitly Christian elements are in 3 Bar. 13.4 and 15.4. In ch.13, the righteous ask to be separated from unrighteous people: "we have seen them enter into no church, nor (go) to the spiritual fathers nor to anything good." Again, this formulation is missing from the Slavonic. Whether the corresponding Slavonic statement is itself Christian is disputed. Gaylord translates, "their wives flee to the church."[38] Kulik translates "for their wives flee to the Temple,"[39] but 3 Baruch presupposes the destruction of the temple, so this is problematic. Third Baruch 15.24, in the Greek, seems to cite Matt 25:23: "Thus says the Lord: You have been faithful over a little, he will set you over much; enter into the delight of our Lord." This again is lacking in the Slavonic. Instead, it urges people to prostrate themselves in prayer in the holy church (Gaylord) or temple (Kulik). It may well be that these passages also show signs of Christian redaction in the Slavonic, but the formulation is different from the Greek, and this supports the view that all the explicitly Christian passages are secondary in both traditions. There are also possible echoes of New Testament language in a few other passages in the Greek (3 Bar. 4.17; 12.6; 13.2; 15.2; 16.2; 16.3). The only case, however, where the Slavonic has the same Christian terminology as the Greek is in the invocation at the end of its title, "may the Lord bless!," and titles are especially vulnerable to manipulation in the course of transmission. So even if we accept that the Slavonic has its own Christian elements, these elements appear to be secondary in both textual traditions. It is extremely unlikely that the common *Vorlage* of the Greek and Slavonic included Christian elements that were omitted by later Christian elements.

---

38. Gaylord, "3 (Greek Apocalypse of) Baruch," 676. Translations of 3 Baruch are from Gaylord, unless otherwise specified.

39. Kulik, *3 Baruch*, 355.

A Pre-Christian Stratum?

If the common *Vorlage* of the Greek and Slavonic texts contains no explicitly Christian elements, may we assume that it is Jewish? Here Harlow demurs in deference to the contention of Kraft and others that Christian writings need not contain any explicitly Christian language.[40] It is possible, conceivable, that 3 Baruch is Christian even without any specifically Christian elements, and it is also possible and conceivable that it is Jewish. The question, however, is not just possibility but relative degrees of probability.

The main reason why many scholars consider 3 Baruch to be Jewish and early is the setting in chapter 1. Baruch is lamenting the destruction of Jerusalem by the Babylonians. Grief over the destruction of Jerusalem is a quintessential Jewish concern, amply illustrated in writings from the late first and early second centuries CE, such as 4 Ezra, 2 Baruch, and the fifth book of Sibylline Oracles.[41] This motif is not characteristic of works that are clearly Christian. It may be argued that the book of Revelation's denunciation of Rome as Babylon bespeaks a deep anger over the destruction of Jerusalem, analogous to that of the Fifth Sibyl, although Revelation does not mention the destruction explicitly. But it may also be argued that John of Patmos was Jewish, albeit a follower of Jesus.[42] After the first century, such concern for Jerusalem is difficult to find in a Christian text. As Harlow puts it:

> Virtually nowhere in early Christianity—Jewish Christianity included—is the destruction of Jerusalem an occasion for lamentation. The restoration of Jerusalem does surface as an object of Christian hope, but only in connection with the millennial reign of Christ.... For the most part, what we find in Christian literature of the first four centuries of the common era are two types of relevant material: a spiritualizing appropriation of Jerusalem- and Temple-imagery, and the apologetic claim

---

40. Harlow, "Christianization of Early Jewish Pseudepigrapha," 426.

41. See my essay, "Jerusalem and the Temple in Jewish Apocalyptic Literature of the Second Temple Period," in *Apocalypse, Prophecy, and Pseudepigraphy: On Jewish Apocalyptic Literature* (Grand Rapids: Eerdmans, 2015), 159–77; Dereck Daschke, *City of Ruins: Mourning the Destruction of Jerusalem through Jewish Apocalypse*, BibInt 99 (Leiden: Brill, 2010), 103–86.

42. So John W. Marshall, *Parables of War: Reading John's Jewish Apocalypse*, Studies in Christianity and Judaism 10 (Waterloo: Wilfred Laurier University, 2001).

that the destruction of City and Temple signals God's punishment of the Jews for murdering Christ. All this is conspicuously absent in *3 Baruch*.[43]

Against this, Himmelfarb asks: "Might not a Christian author take over the setting associated with Baruch in 2 Baruch for his own purpose? That is, if the prologue places Baruch in a conventional setting, it may not be strong evidence for the concerns of its author or his intended audience."[44] Many things are possible, but is there any other evidence that 3 Baruch was influenced by 2 Baruch, or that its author even knew the latter work? If not, is there any evidence that this setting was conventional for Baruch? (Baruch is also depicted as mourning for Jerusalem in 4 Baruch, or Paraleipomena Ieremiou, which is clearly dependent on 2 Baruch but bears no demonstrable relation to 3 Baruch.)

Himmelfarb's main objection to Jewish provenance is that while "there are few Christian texts that demonstrate a deep concern for the loss of the temple, 3 Baruch is alone among putatively Jewish texts of the first centuries of this era in its equanimity about that loss."[45] *Equanimity* may not be quite the right word. In the Greek, the angel tells Baruch not to concern himself so much over the salvation of Jerusalem and proceeds to distract him by showing him cosmological mysteries. One might compare 4 Ezra, where Ezra is told not to concern himself so much over the fate of sinners and is eventually distracted by visions of the future. But the initial concern is real, and we should not assume that it is lightly set aside. The instruction not to be concerned for the fall of Jerusalem is admittedly extreme. The closest parallel I can think of is the Fourth Sibylline Oracle, also written after the destruction of Jerusalem, which begins by declaring that God "does not have a house, a stone set up as a temple ... but one which it is not possible to see from earth nor to measure with mortal eyes, since it was not fashioned by mortal hand" (Sib. Or. 4.8–11 [my trans.]). The Sibyl, however, goes on to note that Rome would "sack the Temple of the great God" (116), and while it places the blame on those who "commit repulsive murders in front of the Temple" (presumably the rebels), the destruction is still a matter of consequence. It should be noted that the formulation in the Slavonic text of 3 Baruch is much less extreme. The angel says simply "Jerusalem had to suffer this." Even here, the message is to move on rather

---

43. Harlow, "Christianization of Early Jewish Pseudepigrapha," 428–29.
44. Himmelfarb, review of *The Greek Apocalypse of Baruch*.
45. Himmelfarb, "*3 Baruch* Revisited," 49.

than dwell on hopes for restoration, but Jerusalem is not devalued as might be inferred from the Greek. The Greek formulation is not part of the common *Vorlage* and may be a Christian embellishment.

Baruch poses a question in the opening chapter: "Lord, in what way was King Nebuchadnezzar righteous? Why did you not spare your city Jerusalem, which is your vineyard of glory? Why have you acted so, Lord?" (3 Bar. 1.2 Slavonic). The Greek adds another question: "and why, Lord, did you not requite us with another punishment, but rather handed us over to such heathen so that they reproach us saying, 'where is their God?'" (an allusion to Deut 32:37). The latter question receives an answer in 3 Bar. 16.2, again alluding to Deut 32, this time to verse 21: "But since they have provoked me to anger by their deeds, go and provoke them to jealousy, and provoke them to anger, and embitter them against those who are no nation, against a people without understanding." Even though the antecedent here is "the sons of men," rather than specifically the people of Jerusalem, the implication is that the handing over of Jerusalem to the nations was punishment for sin. Harlow objects that "such specific identifications ... ill accord with the universalistic perspective that characterizes the entire tour."[46] But universalistic ethics are often combined with particularist interests in surprising ways, and it is difficult not to see here a response to Baruch's question in the opening chapter.[47]

Harlow also makes a weightier point that "Deut 32:21 is most often appealed to in Christian literature as a *testimonium* of Jewish unbelief and Gentile election," beginning with Rom 10:19.[48] This passage is not found in the Slavonic, and so it may well be part of the Christian expansion attested in the Greek.

Both textual traditions, however, identify those who are singled out for punishment in the second and third heaven as those who planned and built the tower, an allusion to Gen 11. Himmelfarb reasonably comments: "the reason things have gone so wrong in the world that started out 'very good' (Gen 1:31) is human unwillingness to accept the limits God

---

46. Harlow, *Greek Apocalypse of Baruch*, 156.
47. As argued by Nickelsburg, *Jewish Literature between the Bible and the Mishnah*, 302.
48. Harlow, "Christianization of Early Jewish Pseudepigrapha," 442, followed by Himmelfarb, "*3 Baruch* Revisited," 48.

has set."⁴⁹ But it can hardly be coincidental that the builders of the tower are Babylonians and that it was Babylon that destroyed Jerusalem. Even though the crimes for which they are indicted are cruelty and attempting to discover the nature of heaven, the people who destroyed Jerusalem are punished in the hereafter. This, again, qualifies the equanimity with which 3 Baruch views the destruction.

One other passage in 3 Baruch may pick up a motif from the opening chapter. There Baruch refers to Jerusalem as "your vineyard of glory" (3 Bar. 1.2, Slavonic). In chapter 4, however, the vine is the vine planted by Satanael (Slavonic) or Samael (Greek), which led Adam astray. After the flood, Noah hesitates as to whether he should plant it, but he is told to do so and to change it for the better. The Greek has an explicitly Christian digression at this point, saying how its fruit will become the blood of God, but this is not found in the Slavonic. There Baruch is warned that the tree still possesses its evil and warns against those who drink to excess, a warning also found in the Greek. Picard argued that the association of the vine with the vineyard Jerusalem amounted to a scathing condemnation.⁵⁰ In truth, an even more scathing rejection of Jerusalem, symbolized by a vine, is found in the Hebrew Bible, in Ezek 15, but that passage is not invoked here. Neither is the vine associated with Jerusalem in chapter 4, and so I am reluctant to accept Picard's suggestion.⁵¹

But while 3 Baruch provides for the punishment of the Babylonians, it does not provide a direct answer to Baruch's opening question. Instead, the angel proceeds by distraction, inviting Baruch to contemplate the mysteries of God. The technique is similar to that employed in 4 Ezra, where the angel distracts the visionary with the wonders of the end time. Here the wonders are cosmological rather than eschatological.⁵² Ultimately, however, they culminate in the fifth heaven, with the vision of the archangel Michael receiving the prayers of humanity. Michael takes these up to a

---

49. Himmelfarb, "*3 Baruch* Revisited," 45. She contrasts this with the use of the Watchers myth in 1 Enoch.

50. Jean-Claude Picard, "Observations sur l'Apocalypse grecque de Baruch I. Cadre historique et efficacité symbolique," *Sem* 20 (1970): 77–103.

51. John J. Collins, *Between Athens and Jerusalem: Jewish Identity in the Hellenistic Diaspora*, 2nd ed. (Grand Rapids: Eerdmans, 2000), 259.

52. See J. Edward Wright, *The Early History of Heaven* (New York: Oxford, 2000), 164–74.

higher heaven, where Baruch is not admitted. He brings back mercies for the virtuous but diseases and plagues for sinners.

The scene in the fifth heaven provides a replacement for the cult in the earthly temple, which has been destroyed. While Baruch does not enter the heavenly temple, he is transported to its gates. In the words of J. Edward Wright:

> Although the temple, the central institution of Judaism for centuries was in ruins, God was still active, hearing prayers for forgiveness and justice in his heavenly temple. Thus, Solomon's prayer is still being answered, and God is still attentive to his people.[53]

This scene provides consolation for the destruction of the temple. Unlike Solomon's temple, however, the heavenly temple is "a house of prayer for all peoples," as promised in Isa 56:7.

The discussion of the virtues and vices is Christianized, in both textual traditions, more obviously in the Greek. The Slavonic is quite laconic. The main sins denounced are fornication and failure to attend church (if the term is translated correctly). The Greek has a more elaborate list, including murder, adultery, theft, slander, perjury, idolatry, and so on. What is common to both textual traditions, however, is the idea that judgment is based on individual merits. At no point is there any suggestion that the distinctive markers of Judaism in the ancient world, such as circumcision or Sabbath observance, are of significance. It is this lack of Jewish specificity that leads Himmelfarb to conclude that this is not a Jewish composition.

3 Baruch in the Context of Diaspora Judaism

I have argued, to the contrary, that even though 3 Baruch is extreme, it can be viewed as the logical culmination of a trend in diaspora Judaism.[54] The literature that survives from the diaspora, written in Greek, generally, with few exceptions, is silent about the distinctive Jewish laws and emphasize matters of social and sexual morality.[55] A typical example is provided by Sib. Or. 3.762–766:

---

53. Wright, *Early History of Heaven*, 174.
54. Collins, *Between Athens and Jerusalem*, 259.
55. See most recently John J. Collins, *The Invention of Judaism: Torah and Jewish*

But urge on your minds in your breasts and shun unlawful worship. Worship the Living One. Avoid adultery and indiscriminate intercourse with males. Rear your own offspring and do not kill it, for the Immortal is angry at whoever commits these sins.

It may be argued that this passage, and much of the diaspora literature, is ostensibly addressed to gentiles and that this explains the failure to mention the Sabbath or circumcision. But the fact that so much of the diaspora literature is ostensibly addressed to gentiles is itself significant. It reflects the attempt of diaspora Jews to construe their identity in ways that gives priority to features that Greeks of goodwill could appreciate. This does not necessarily mean that the authors of these works had abandoned the distinctive laws. It is clear from the descriptions of Jews in Greco-Roman authors that the distinctive Jewish customs were widely observed.[56] The Letter of Aristeas provides an elaborate defense of the food laws, but it does so by arguing that they gave symbolic expression to things that any reasonable person would affirm.[57]

Himmelfarb protests that "our picture of Diaspora Judaism depends on the texts we attribute to it" and that several works that have been used to construct this profile of Jewish ethical monotheism, such as the Testaments of the Twelve Patriarchs, Testament of Job, and Testament of Abraham, are also of disputed provenance.[58] But even if we leave these works aside, the picture is not greatly altered. It holds true for such works as the Wisdom of Solomon, the Third Sibylline Oracle, and the Letter of Aristeas, although all of these works have distinctive Jewish characteristics.[59] The Jewish origin of the Sentences of Pseudo-Phocylides is betrayed

---

Identity from Deuteronomy to Paul (Oakland, CA: University of California Press, 2017), 135–42.

56. Shaye J. D. Cohen, "Common Judaism in Greek and Latin Authors," in *Redefining First-Century Jewish and Christian Identities: Essays in Honor of Ed Parish Sanders*, ed. Fabian Udoh, with Susannah Heschel, Mark Chancey, and Gregory Tatum (Notre Dame, IN: University of Notre Dame, 2008), 69–87.

57. See the commentary by Benjamin G. Wright III, *The Letter of Aristeas: 'Aristeas to Philocrates' or 'On the Translation of the Law of the Jews'*, CEJL (Berlin: de Gruyter, 2015), 246–313.

58. Himmelfarb, "3 Baruch Revisited," 51.

59. Davila, *Provenance of the Pseudepigrapha*, 225, finds nothing in the Wisdom of Solomon that prohibits or even renders unlikely its having been written by a gen-

only by a few sayings that clearly reflect the Septuagint.⁶⁰ Yet the Sentences of Pseudo-Phocylides share considerable material with Philo's *Hypoth.* 7.1–9 and Josephus's *C. Ap.* 2.190–219, both of which are explicitly presented as summaries of the law.

We have no way of measuring how widely or well the law was observed in the Egyptian diaspora. I would assume that observance was the norm in Jewish communities. But there were evidently some Jews in Alexandria who did not feel bound by literal observance. In a famous passage in his treatise on *The Migration of Abraham*, Philo writes:

> There are some who, regarding laws in their literal sense in the light of symbols of matters belonging to the intellect, are overpunctilious about the latter, while treating the former with easygoing neglect. Such men I for my part should blame for handling the matter in too easy and offhand a manner: they ought to have given careful attention to both aims, to a more full and exact investigation of what is not seen and in what is seen to be stewards without reproach. (*Migr.* 89 [trans. F. H. Colson and G. H. Whitaker])

Philo himself was observant, but he does not say that those he would blame were not Jews or not *real* Jews. There was evidently some range of opinion and practice in the Jewish communities in Egypt.

Himmelfarb, however, is "suspicious of a picture of diaspora Judaism or even a major strand of diaspora Judaism as lacking in concern for the markers of Jewish particularism."⁶¹ She suspects that scholars such as myself are motivated by "the search for a usable past for Christianity, whether in purely scholarly or theological terms."⁶² Perhaps, but herself is clearly motivated by her own view of Judaism, in which the markers of Jewish particularism are very important. What is at stake here is the importance of some kind of normativity and the degree of diversity that can be tolerated in a religious tradition. This has as much to do with identity and ethos in the twenty-first century as in antiquity. To Himmelfarb's

---

tile Christian in the second half of the first century CE. This position can only be described as eccentric.

60. For text and commentary, see P. W. van der Horst, *The Sentences of Pseudo-Phocylides* (Leiden: Brill, 1978); Walter T. Wilson, *The Sentences of Pseudo-Phocylides*, CEJL (Berlin: de Gruyter, 2005).

61. Himmelfarb, "3 Baruch Revisited," 52.

62. Himmelfarb, "3 Baruch Revisited," 51.

credit, she recognizes that it is impossible to escape the problem of circularity in this issue.[63]

The problem is further complicated by the realization that some Christians in the early centuries also considered themselves to be Jews. Himmelfarb insists that for her purposes what matters is not whether the authors of the works in question could have been Jews who were also Christians, but whether they could have been Jews who were not also Christians.[64] Let us look then at the common core of 3 Baruch, bracketing out the clearly Christian elements that are found in only one of the two textual traditions.

Third Baruch is an attempt to cope with the loss of the temple and the destruction of the mother-city of Judaism by diverting its attention to a heavenly cult and a judgment based on individual merits. This solution falls on one end of the spectrum of reactions to the fall of the temple, in contrast to works like 4 Ezra or 2 Baruch that hope for eschatological restoration. But the *aporia* that gives rise to the work only makes sense within Jewish tradition. Indeed, both the choice of Baruch as visionary and the initial concern for Jerusalem are clearer marks of Jewish tradition than we find in works like Pseudo-Phocylides. It seems clear, then, that 3 Baruch stands in the Jewish tradition, whether Christian or not.

But what indication is there that the author is a Jew who is also a Christian? There is no doubt at all that the Greek redactor is a Christian. For him, atonement is now achieved through "Jesus Christ Emmanuel" (3 Bar. 4.15). But the Slavonic says nothing of the atoning power of Christ, although this was the obvious Christian replacement for the temple sacrifices. There does not then seem to be positive reason for regarding the common core, the presumed *Vorlage* of both Greek and Slavonic recensions, as a Christian composition.

But would a Jew who believed that acceptance before God was now on the basis of individual merits and attached no great importance to the distinctive Jewish laws, whether he observed them or not, be accepted as Jewish in a synagogue? This question, I would think, could equally be asked of Philo's allegorizers. The answer might well vary, depending on the synagogue. We do not know that the allegorizers were repudiated by their communities. But it seems to me that the author stood in the Jewish

---

63. Himmelfarb, "3 Baruch Revisited," 52.
64. Himmelfarb, "3 Baruch Revisited," 53.

tradition and tried to make sense of the world in that tradition, without invoking Jesus as messiah or savior or appealing to distinctive Christian beliefs. I would think that his chances of acceptance would have been at least as good in a synagogue as in a church, if indeed he sought acceptance in either.

Himmelfarb closes her essay with a suggestion that 3 Baruch was composed by a monk, in fourth or fifth century Egypt.[65] The argument rests on parallels with the Apocalypse of Paul and the Ladder of Jacob. Himmelfarb herself claims no more than that the suggestion is an "experiment" that raises new possibilities. Fair enough. But the place of 3 Baruch in relation to other literature of late antiquity requires much more systematic exploration before any conclusions can be drawn from it. One intriguing aspect of such exploration might be the place of 3 Baruch in the development of the ascent apocalypses. The fact that the visionary is not admitted to the presence of God has often led to the supposition that the work is truncated. More recently, it has been explained as a corrective to an apocalypse like 2 Enoch, where the visionary is transformed into an angel. But we should bear in mind that the earliest Jewish ascents, like that of Enoch in the Book of the Watchers, do not have a numbered sequence of heavens at all. The earlier recension of the Testament of Levi has only three heavens, and Paul famously boasted of having been caught up to the third heaven, as if this were the highest one could go. It may well be that 3 Baruch is a relatively early ascent apocalypse, written before the ascent through seven heavens became standard. This issue, too, requires much further examination.[66]

Conclusion

I conclude, then, that the assumption that a pseudepigraphon like 3 Baruch should be presumed to be a Christian composition, because it was transmitted by Christians, is premature. To be sure, that possibility should be considered, but there is no virtue in adopting one position or the other as a default. What holds for 3 Baruch does not necessarily hold for the Testament of Job or the Testament of Abraham. Each of these works must be considered on its own merits. There is inevitably some circularity

---

65. Himmelfarb, "3 Baruch Revisited," 61.
66. See further Adela Yarbro Collins, "The Seven Heavens in Jewish and Christian Apocalypses," in *Cosmology and Eschatology in Jewish and Christian Apocalypticism*, JSJSup 50 (Leiden: Brill, 1996), 21–54.

involved in our views of what is acceptably Jewish or Christian, but we should beware of tendencies to impose norms whether ancient or modern on the material. The value of this material is precisely that it survived on the fringes without canonical endorsement and that it can now expand our view of the possible range of either tradition.

Bibliography

Bauckham, Richard J. "The Continuing Quest for the Provenance of Old Testament Pseudepigrapha." Pages 9–29 in *The Pseudepigrapha and Christian Origins*. Edited by Gerbern S. Oegema and James H. Charlesworth. London: T&T Clark, 2008.

Becker, Adam H., and Annette Yoshiko Reed, eds. *The Ways That Never Parted: Jews and Christians in Late Antiquity and the Early Middle Ages*. Tübingen: Mohr Siebeck, 2003.

Bonwetsch, Gottlieb Nathanael. "Das Slavisch Erhaltene Baruchbuch." *NGWG* (1896): 91–101.

Bousset, Wilhelm. *Religion des Judentums im neutestamentlichen Zeitalter*. Berlin: Reuther & Reichard, 1903.

Boyarin, Daniel. *Border Lines: The Partition of Judeo-Christianity*. Berkeley: University of California Press, 2004.

Cohen, Shaye J. D. "Common Judaism in Greek and Latin Authors." Pages 69–87 in *Redefining First-Century Jewish and Christian Identities: Essays in Honor of Ed Parish Sanders*. Edited by Fabian Udoh, with Susannah Heschel, Mark Chancey, and Gregory Tatum. Notre Dame, IN: University of Notre Dame, 2008.

Collins, Adela Yarbro. "The Seven Heavens in Jewish and Christian Apocalypses." Pages 21–54 in *Cosmology and Eschatology in Jewish and Christian Apocalypticism*. JSJSup 50. Leiden: Brill, 1996.

Collins, John J. *Between Athens and Jerusalem: Jewish Identity in the Hellenistic Diaspora*. 2nd ed. Grand Rapids: Eerdmans, 2000.

———. "Early Judaism in Modern Scholarship." Pages 1–29 in *Early Judaism: A Comprehensive Overview*. Edited by John J. Collins and Daniel C. Harlow. Grand Rapids: Eerdmans, 2012.

———. *The Invention of Judaism: Torah and Jewish Identity from Deuteronomy to Paul*. Oakland, CA: University of California Press, 2017.

———. "Jerusalem and the Temple in Jewish Apocalyptic Literature of the Second Temple Period." Pages 159–77 in *Apocalypse, Prophecy, and Pseudepigraphy: On Jewish Apocalyptic Literature*. Grand Rapids: Eerdmans, 2015.

———. "*Joseph and Aseneth*: Jewish or Christian?" Pages 112–27 in *Jewish Cult and Hellenistic Culture: Essays on the Jewish Encounter with Hellenism and Roman Rule*. JSJSup 100. Leiden: Brill, 2005.

Daschke, Dereck. *City of Ruins: Mourning the Destruction of Jerusalem through Jewish Apocalypse*. BibInt 99. Leiden: Brill, 2010.

Davila, James R. *The Provenance of the Pseudepigrapha: Jewish, Christian, or Other?* JSJSup 105. Leiden: Brill, 2005.

Efron, Joshua. *Studies on the Hasmonean Period*. Leiden: Brill, 1987.

Gaylord, Harry E., Jr. "3 (Greek Apocalypse of) Baruch: A New Translation and Introduction." *OTP* 1:653–79.

Ginzberg, Louis. "Baruch, Apocalypse of (Greek)." *JE* 2:551.

Harlow, Daniel C. "Baruch, Third Book of." *EDEJ* 428–30.

———. "The Christianization of Early Jewish Pseudepigrapha: The Case of 3 Baruch." *JSJ* 32 (2001): 416–44.

———. *The Greek Apocalypse of Baruch (3 Baruch) in Hellenistic Judaism and Early Christianity*. SVTP 12. Leiden: Brill, 1996.

Heger, Paul. *Challenges to Conventional Opinions on Qumran and Enoch Issues*. STDJ 100. Leiden: Brill, 2012.

Himmelfarb, Martha. "*3 Baruch* Revisited: Jewish or Christian Composition, and Why It Matters." *ZAC* 20 (2016): 41–62.

———. *Ascent to Heaven in Jewish and Christian Apocalypses*. New York: Oxford University Press, 1993.

———. Review of *The Greek Apocalypse of Baruch (3 Baruch) in Hellenistic Judaism and Early Christianity*, by Daniel C. Harlow. *RBL* (1998): https://tinyurl.com/SBL3550e.

Horst, Pieter W. van der. *The Sentences of Pseudo-Phocylides*. Leiden: Brill, 1978.

Hughes, H. M. "The Greek Apocalypse of Baruch, or III Baruch." Pages 527–41 in *The Apocrypha and Pseudepigrapha of the Old Testament*. Edited by R. H. Charles. Oxford: Clarendon, 1913.

James, M. R. "Apocalypsis Baruchi Tertia Graece." Pages 83–94 in *Apocrypha Anecdota II*. Edited by M. R. James. Texts and Studies 5.1. Cambridge: Cambridge University Press, 1897.

Jonge, Marinus de. *Pseudepigrapha of the Old Testament as Part of Christian Literature: The Case of the Testaments of the Twelve Patriarchs and the Greek Life of Adam and Eve*. SVTP 18. Leiden: Brill, 2003.

———. *The Testaments of the Twelve Patriarchs: A Study of Their Text, Composition, and Origin.* Assen: Van Gorcum, 1953.
Jonge, Marinus de, and Johannes Tromp. *The Life of Adam and Eve and Related Literature.* Sheffield: Sheffield Academic, 1997.
Kraft, Robert A. "The Pseudepigrapha in Christianity." Pages 55–86 in *Tracing the Threads: Studies in the Vitality of Jewish Pseudepigrapha.* Edited by John C. Reeves. EJL 6. Atlanta: Scholars Press, 1994.
———. "The Pseudepigrapha in Christianity Revisited: Setting the Stage and Framing Some Central Questions." *JSJ* 32 (2001): 371–95.
Kraemer, Ross S. *When Aseneth Met Joseph: A Late Antique Tale of the Biblical Patriarch and His Egyptian Wife, Reconsidered.* Oxford: Oxford University Press, 1998.
Kulik, Alexander. *3 Baruch: Greek-Slavonic Apocalypse of Baruch.* CEJL. Berlin: de Gruyter, 2010.
Marshall, John W. *Parables of War: Reading John's Jewish Apocalypse.* Studies in Christianity and Judaism 10. Waterloo: Wilfred Laurier University, 2001.
Moore, George F. "Christian Writers on Judaism." *HTR* 14 (1921): 197–254.
Morfill, W. R. "The Apocalypse of Baruch Translated from the Slavonic." Pages 95–102 in *Apocrypha Anecdota II.* Edited by M. R. James. Texts and Studies 5.1. Cambridge: Cambridge University Press, 1897.
Neusner, Jacob. *Judaism: The Evidence of the Mishnah.* Chicago: University of Chicago Press, 1981.
Nickelsburg, George W. E. *Jewish Literature between the Bible and the Mishnah: A Historical and Literary Introduction.* Philadelphia: Fortress, 1981.
Nir, Rivka. *The Destruction of Jerusalem and the Idea of Redemption in the Syriac Apocalypse of Baruch.* Atlanta: Society of Biblical Literature, 2003.
———. *Joseph and Aseneth: A Christian Book.* Sheffield: Sheffield Phoenix, 2012.
Norelli, Enrico. *Ascension du Prophète Isaïe.* Turnhout: Brepols, 1993.
Perles, Felix. *Bousset's Religion des Judentums im neutestamentlichen Zeitalter kritisch untersucht.* Berlin: Peiser, 1903.
Picard, Jean-Claude. *Apocalypsis Baruchi Graece.* PVTG 2. Leiden: Brill, 1967.
———. "Observations sur l'Apocalypse grecque de Baruch I. Cadre historique et efficacité symbolique." *Sem* 20 (1970): 77–103.

Reed, Annette Yoshiko. "The Modern Invention of 'Old Testament Pseudepigrapha.'" *JTS* 60 (2009): 403–36.

Satran, David. *Biblical Prophets in Byzantine Palestine: Reassessing the Lives of the Prophets*. SVTP 11. Leiden: Brill, 1995.

Schürer, Emil. *Geschichte des jüdischen Volkes im Zeitalter Jesu Christi*. 2nd ed. Leipzig: Hinrichs, 1886.

Wilson, Walter T. *The Sentences of Pseudo-Phocylides*. CEJL. Berlin: de Gruyter, 2005.

Wright, Benjamin G., III. *The Letter of Aristeas: 'Aristeas to Philocrates' or 'On the Translation of the Law of the Jews'*. CEJL. Berlin: de Gruyter, 2015.

Wright, J. Edward. *The Early History of Heaven*. New York: Oxford, 2000.

16
Pseudepigraphy as an Interpretative Construct

Hindy Najman and Irene Peirano Garrison

1. Introduction

Our starting point is that pseudepigraphy should not be understood primarily as forgery but rather as a reading practice which is fundamentally interpretative. The ensuing argument is a result of collaborative and comparative thinking across Jewish and Greco-Roman traditions and within a variety of linguistic and cultural registers: Hebrew, Greek, Aramaic, and Latin (among others). This premise emerges out of discussions over the nature of pseudepigraphy across texts that are conceived of as both marginal and canonical, as well as exceptional and normative.

We write with a shared commitment to the following aspects of what we consider to be central to pseudepigraphical composition and interpretation thereof:

- problematization of the author function;
- reevaluation of the center and the margin with respect to authoritative texts, collections, and reading lists;
- reexamination of scholarly assumptions with respect to canon-discourse and so-called pseudepigraphical texts.

Scholars have imposed contemporary assumptions about philological practices onto antiquity, with the result that the modern discourse of authenticity has in fact obscured the dynamics of the texts and literary traditions which scholarship seeks out to recover, rescue, and protect. These are the assumptions that we want to challenge as we seek to articulate a new agenda for the study of pseudepigraphy, to forge new paths that were not taken at the birth of classical and biblical philology and, additionally, to rethink text critical practices for the production of editions and the assembly of collections. It is important to highlight the fact that scholarly practices of establishing and evaluating authentic and inauthentic texts in post-Enlightenment discussions emerged at a time when classics and biblical studies were part and parcel of the same field. We want to continue to problematize the division between the sacred and the profane. We are inviting a reconfiguration of narratives of canonicity and authenticity and a new shift in focus onto the growth of corpora and the pluriformity of textuality. The philological processes that are in place often reinforce old assumptions, integrating new texts and new findings into old categories instead of rethinking the old and embracing new possibilities. Our goal is thus far more than comparative; it is integrative. We hope to reconnect the space between biblical studies, early Judaism, ancient Christianity, and the pagan world.

2. Terminology

The Greek term *pseudepigraphon* has an unusual history in modern scholarship. In ancient Greek, this word, originally belonging to the technical language of Hellenistic literary criticism, means both "wrongly attributed" and "deceitfully attributed," referring both to texts which purport to have a specific authorial provenance (primary pseudonymity) and to texts whose (mis)attribution results from the later intervention of editors, scribes, and readers.[1] By contrast, in its current usage the term Old Testament pseudepigrapha is by and large a function, not of authorial self-presentation or literary ascription, but of canonical status, with many canonical texts being in some way pseudepigraphic and some pseudepigrapha being anonymous but not necessarily fabricating a narrative about their authorship.[2] Similarly, standard reference works on Greco-Roman

---

1. Irene Peirano, "Authenticity as an Aesthetic Concept: Ancient and Modern Reflections," in *Aesthetic Value in Classical Antiquity*, ed. Ralph Mark Rosen and Ineke Sluiter, Penn-Leiden Colloquium on Ancient Values 6 (Leiden: Brill, 2012), 1–7; Wolfgang Speyer, *Die literarische Fälschung im heidnischen und christlichen Altertum: Ein Versuch ihrer Deutung* (Munich: Beck, 1971).

2. Kent D. Clarke, "The Problems of Pseudonymity in Biblical Literature and Its Implications for Canon Formation," in *The Canon Debate*, ed. Lee Martin McDonald and James A. Sanders (Peabody, MA: Hendrickson, 2002), 440–42. The confusion is compounded by the fact that extracanonical works excluded from the New Testament are traditionally labeled as apocrypha. This is, of course, also true for the Old Testa-

pseudepigrapha analyze together *adespota* (from the Greek "without a master")—anonymous texts of unknown date that may have become attributed to a given author—with texts which actively purport to be written by a great author such as Virgil or Sallust.[3] Thus, the term pseudepigrapha is now being used of a number of texts—Jewish, Christian, and pagan—which are not categorized as such in ancient sources and to which the discourse itself of pseudepigraphy is culturally alien. This repurposing of the Greek term *pseudepigraphon* to describe texts that are perceived to be somewhat related to the Bible but somewhat distinct is the product of the eighteenth century's anxiety about forgery and attribution in the wake of the dissemination of print and copyright.[4] Although we may not want to heed the call "to use 'pseudepigraphic' as a literary category, whether the book is regarded as canonical or apocryphal," we would do well to interrogate the entrenched assumptions about ancient literary and religious practice that underlie the deployment of Greek terminology to texts with different identities and different readerships and contexts of production.[5] Relatedly, we see an urgent and important corrective to ongoing nineteenth century attempts to recover the Urtext as a result of an—at times unwitting—impulse to recover *sola Scriptura*. Additionally, we also want to expose residual historicist trends in current departments of classics, religious studies, or theology.

Yet this well-acknowledged failure of the term pseudepigrapha to provide a stable umbrella under which to organize texts that do not seem to fit canonical narratives and/or identities should be taken as symptomatic. To

---

ment as well. On the history of the term and its relation to pseudepigrapha, see Loren T. Stuckenbruck, "Apocrypha and Pseudepigrapha," in *Early Judaism: A Comprehensive Overview*, ed. John J. Collins and Daniel Harlow (Grand Rapids: Eerdmans, 2010). On the relation between Old Testament pseudepigrapha and Old Testament apocrypha, see Clarke, "Problems of Pseudepigraphy in Biblical Literature," 441 n. 9.

3. For example, the *Appendix Vergiliana* contains both works such as the *Culex*, which purport to have been written by Virgil (see below), and works such as the *Elegies for Maecenas*, which cannot be by Virgil but were not composed with the intent of being passed off as Virgilian. See Peirano, "Authenticity as an Aesthetic Concept," 74–79.

4. Annette Yoshiko Reed, "The Modern Invention of 'Old Testament Pseudepigrapha,'" *JTS* 60 (2009): 403–36; and see Hindy Najman, *Second Sinai: The Development of Mosaic Discourse in Second Temple Judaism*, JSJSup 77 (Leiden: Brill, 2004), 6.

5. Bruce M. Metzger, "Literary Forgeries and Canonical Pseudepigrapha," *JBL* 91 (1972): 4.

begin with, practices of attribution and practices of composition cannot (and should not) be so easily disentangled. Examples of this challenge are the various anthologies, appendices, and other editorial compilations of works that belong to a famous author of antiquity and his imitators, readers, and continuators, such as the sylloge Theognidea, the Anacreontea, and the anthology of Meleager.[6] These anthologies, comprising as they do different kinds of pseudepigrapha—from anonymous poetry presented as the work of archaic poets to new poems written in their style and persona—shed light on the permeability of the roles of editor, author, and reader. Moreover, in selecting poems, the editor can in effect reauthor an anonymous poem, turn imitation into a forgery, and even construct a narrative by juxtaposing texts originally unrelated to each other. It is best to approach the inability to disentangle primary and secondary pseudonymity in these cases not as the result of philological failure but rather as a symptom of the permeability of categories that are firmly distinct in modern cultures and of the different strategies and effects to which the positionality of author could be occupied.[7]

In the field of biblical studies, distinctions between canonical and noncanonical, between authentic and inauthentic, or between authored and pseudonymous became ever more complicated after the discovery of the Dead Sea Scrolls in the middle of the twentieth century. At first, these findings were used to reinforce existing categories, as the Dead Sea scrolls were contextualized in terms of what was already known. In that sense, the Dead Sea Scrolls were placed in a straitjacket in order to accommodate what we *already knew* to be true—for the Hebrew Bible and also for the New Testament. Additionally, rabbinical categories and patristic categories constrained and overdetermined our readings and analyses. So, these new texts were *apocryphal, pseudonymous,* or *extracanonical.* They could not initially challenge the fault lines between the canonical and the non-

---

6. See Patricia A. Rosenmeyer, *The Poetics of Imitation: Anacreon and the Anacreontic Tradition* (Cambridge: Cambridge University Press, 1992); and Glenn Most, "The Virgilian *Culex*," in *Homo Viator: Classical Essays for John Bramble*, ed. Michael Whitby, Philip R. Hardie, and Mary Whitby (Bristol: Bristol Classical Press, 1987), 199–209.

7. Karen King, "'What Is an Author?' Ancient Author-Function in The Apocryphon of John and The Apocalypse of John," in *Scribal Practices and Social Structures among Jesus's Adherents: Essays in Honour of John S. Kloppenborg*, ed. William E. Arnal, Richard S. Ascough, R. A. Derrenbacker, and Phillip A. Harland, BETL (Leuven: Peeters, 2016), 15–42.

canonical. But these assumptions gradually and continuously have been changing and emerging to the surface, touching all aspects of biblical studies. Even the residual canonical positions have had to acknowledge the place and relevance of these texts that are nowhere in the Jewish or Christian canons (or Western canons, for that matter) as they are relevant to understanding the formation of ancient Jewish and early Christian communities as well as to Western culture.

When read for their own value and as testimony to the composition of new texts, to the pluriformity of biblical texts, and to the reality of ongoing growth of biblical traditions employing the pseudonym as a way of justifying and generating new texts, suddenly the Dead Sea Scrolls can function as a challenge to existing categories. The Dead Sea Scrolls reflect some of our earliest records of thinking about law, exegesis, and practices of prayer and communal ritual and should just be understood as part of ancient culture and thinking. The Hebrew Bible never ends—it is an ongoing process of production. Moreover, the Dead Sea Scrolls have come increasingly to have a voice in text critical debates about identity of particular textual traditions and books.

To emphasize the tension between the modern category and the ancient Greek word, we use pseudepigrapha for the modern category and *pseudepigraphon* for the transliterated Greek term. Moreover, by using the term *pseudepigraphy* for texts that refashion, interpret, and expand an older literary or religious corpus while claiming in some way to be chronologically and authorially part of the same tradition, we are inspired by Michel Foucault's notion of "discourse tied to a founder" or Friedrich Nietzsche's discussion of the "Homeric question."[8] Though the term pseudepigraphy serves an immediate function within the field, it also carries implications of deceit. For reasons that will become clear, we are purposefully choosing to stay away from a definition of pseudepigraphy as forgery, that is, as a *false* or *deceitful* claim to be distinguished from practices of misattribution and later redactional processes.[9] For one, while it is true that pseudepigraphy involves donning the garb of a famous author

---

8. Najman, *Second Sinai*, 1–40.

9. Contra Bart Ehrman, *Forgery and Counterforgery: The Use of Literary Deceit in Early Christian Polemics* (Oxford: Oxford University Press, 2012), 30. Ehrman uses pseudepigraphon as a term encompassing both misattributed texts and authorial and chronological fictions and considers a forgery any text "when an author claims to be someone else who is well known.... Forgeries involve false authorial claims."

or founder or stepping in a time sphere different from one's own, the question remains whether such acts of impersonation and chronological fiction should be evaluated as acts of deception or as something else. The issue has been vigorously debated in the fields of early Judaism, ancient Christianity, and classics with little to no cross-cultural and comparative angle.[10] How should we interpret pseudepigraphic attribution not as an obstacle blocking our apprehension of the ancient cultures under study, but instead as a site for reception of literary and religious corpora and composition of new texts?

By analyzing the lexicon of authenticity criticism in Greco-Roman antiquity and its repurposing for the texts of ancient Judaism and ancient Christianity, we want to shed light on what the Greco-Roman sources, from which this term has been adopted both by the early church fathers and by modern scholars, can tell us about the phenomenon of discourse tied to founder. While these ancient literary and religious traditions have unique histories and practices, the circulation of texts and ideas in the wider Mediterranean and the Near East in antiquity, as well as the deeply intertwined modern history of these scholarly fields, suggest that practices of attribution and composition are not culturally self-contained.[11] We think that there is an alternative way of understanding pseudepigraphy, not as deceit but as an interpretative construct. In this model, (1) the assumption of a persona or reworking of an exemplar functions as an act

---

10. The bibliography on this question is rich. For an effort at cross-cultural work, see David Brakke, "Early Christian Lies and the Lying Liars Who Wrote Them: Bart Ehrman's *Forgery and Counterforgery*," *JR* 96 (2016): 378–90; Karel van der Toorn, *Scribal Culture and the Making of the Hebrew Bible* (Cambridge: Harvard University Press: 2012), 27–49; Jed Wyrick, *The Ascension of Authorship: Attribution and Canon Formation in Jewish, Hellenistic, and Christian Traditions* (Cambridge: Harvard University Press, 2004); David G. Meade, *Pseudonymity and Canon: An Investigation into the Relationship of Authorship and Authority in Jewish and Earliest Christian Tradition* (Tübingen: Mohr Siebeck, 1986); Jörg Frey, Jens Herzer, Martina Janssen, and Clare K. Rothschild, eds., *Pseudepigraphie und Verfasserfiktion in frühchristlichen Briefen*, WUNT 246 (Tübingen: Mohr Siebeck, 2009); Armin Daniel Baum, *Pseudepigraphie und literarische Fälschung im frühen Christentum: Mit ausgewählten Quellentexten samt deutscher Übersetzung*, WUNT 2/138 (Tübingen: Mohr Siebeck, 2001). See also Najman, *Seconding Sinai*; Charles M. Stang, *Apophasis and Pseudonymity in Dionysius the Aeropagite: "No Longer I"* (Oxford: Oxford University Press, 2012); Peirano, "Authenticity as an Aesthetic Concept."

11. Van der Toorn, *Scribal Culture and the Making of the Hebrew Bible*.

of interpretation and participation in a tradition; and (2) the modality of true discourse is not confined to authorial originality but can also encompass ritual participation, historical actualization, exegesis, and fictional exploration.[12]

3. Pseudepigrapha and the Pseudepigraphic

The tradition of using anachronisms in texts to contest purported date of composition and authorship goes back to Hellenistic exegesis:[13] in his essay on the Attic orator Dinarchus, where the word is first attested in the context of a discussion of textual attribution, Dionysius of Halicarnassus uses *pseudepigraphon* of misattributed speeches. He writes thus:

---

12. Yakir Paz, "Re-scripturizing Traditions: Designating Dependence in Rabbinic Halakhic Midrashim and Homeric Scholarship," in *Homer and the Bible in the Eyes of Ancient Interpreters*, ed. Maren R. Niehoff (Leiden: Brill, 2012), 269–98; George J. Brooke, "From Florilegium or Midrash to Commentary: The Problem of Re-naming an Adopted Manuscript," in *The Mermaid and the Partridge: Essays from the Copenhagen Conference on Revising Texts from Cave Four*, ed. George J. Brooke and Jesper Høgenhaven, STDJ 97 (Leiden: Brill, 2011), 129–50; Loren T. Stuckenbruck, "Copying, Rewriting, and Interpretation in Community Formation: The Habakkuk Pesher from Qumran Cave 1," in *Scripture Interpretation and the Interface between Education and Religion*, ed. Florian Wilk, TBN (Leiden: Brill, 2018), 72–87; Philip Alexander, Armin Lange, and Renate Pillinger, eds., *In the Second Degree: Paratextual Literature in Ancient Near Eastern and Ancient Mediterranean Culture and Its Reflections in Medieval Literature* (Leiden: Brill, 2010); József Zsengellér, ed., *Rewritten Bible after Fifty Years: Texts, Terms, or Techniques? A Last Dialogue with Geza Vermes* (Leiden: Brill 2014); Ishay Rosen-Zvi, "Structure and Reflectivity in Tannaitic Legal Homilies, Or: How to Read Midrashic Terminology," *Prooftexts* 34 (2014): 271–301; Daniel Boyarin, *Intertextuality and Reading of Midrash* (Indiana: Indiana University Press, 1980); Hindy Najman, "The Idea of Biblical Genre," in *Prayer and Poetry in the Dead Sea Scrolls and Related Literature: Essays in Honor of Eileen Schuller on the Occasion of Her Sixty-Fifth Birthday*, ed. J. Penner, K. M. Penner, and C. Wassen, STDJ 98 (Leiden: Brill, 2011), 308–21; Hindy Najman, "Traditionary Processes and Textual Unity in 4 Ezra," in *Fourth Ezra and Second Baruch: Recpnstructions after the Fall*, ed. Matthias Henze and Gabriele Boccaccini, JSJSup 164 (Leiden: Brill, 2013), 99–117; Hindy Najman, Eva Mroczek and I. Manoff, "How to Make Sense of Pseudonymous Attribution: The Cases of 4 Ezra and 2 Baruch," in *Companion to Biblical Interpretation in Early Judaism*, ed. Matthias Henze (Grand Rapids: Eerdmans, 2012), 308–36.

13. For earlier examples of authenticity criticism see Herodotus's comments on the epic cycle with Irene Peirano, *The Rhetoric of the Roman Fake: Latin Pseudepigrapha in Context* (Cambridge: Cambridge University Press, 2012).

> There still remains one very necessary task, to determine [Dinarchus's] life-span in order to be able to say something definite on the matter of which speeches are genuinely his and which are not [περὶ τῶν λόγων τῶν τε γνησίων αὐτοῦ καὶ μή]. (Dionysius of Halicarnassus, *De Din.* 4 [trans. Stephen Usher])

Assuming that Dinarchus returned from exile when he was seventy years old, Dionysius works out that he began to write speeches at the age of twenty-six under the archonship of Pythodemus and that therefore:

> The claim suit concerning the myrtle and the smilax, On behalf of the Athmoneis"... is earlier than the prime of Dinarchus: for it was delivered during the archonship of Nicomachus, as becomes obvious from the speech itself. Dinarchus was then twenty-one years old. These, then, are the speeches falsely ascribed to him [ψευδεπίγραφοι λόγοι εἰσὶν οἵδε] which were in circulation before his prime. (Dionysius of Halicarnassus, *De Din.* 11 [trans. Stephen Usher])

The word *pseudepigraphon* obviously refers here to a work misattributed to the orator rather than to a text claiming Dinarchus as its author. Writing in Augustan Rome for an audience of students of Greek literature and rhetoric, Dionysius is using chronological inconsistencies to create and defend a canon of works deemed authentic. In so doing, he is following in the footsteps of the Alexandrian grammarians who first practiced authenticity criticism on texts and created bibliographical lists of works for the authors surviving from the Greek classical past.[14]

We would do well, however, not to retroject anachronistic notions about modern philological practice on the work of the Alexandrians. Writing in the first century CE, the Roman grammarian Quintilian summarizes thus the work of the Alexandrian grammarians:

---

14. The bibliographical work of the *Pinakes* by Callimachus is collected in R. Pfeiffer, *Fragmenta*, vol. 1 of *Callimachus* (Oxford: Clarendon, 1949), 429–53. Also see Rudolf Blum, *Kallimachos: The Alexandrian Library and the Origins of Bibliography*, trans. Hans H. Wellisch (Madison: University of Wisconsin Press, 2011). For authenticity criticism in the Homeric scholia, see Franco Montanari, "Correcting a Copy, Editing a Text: Alexandrian *Ekdosis* and Papyri," in *From Scholars to Scholia: Chapters in the History of Ancient Greek Scholarship*, ed. Franco Montanari and Lara Pagani (Berlin: de Gruyter, 2011), 1–15.

16. Pseudepigraphy as an Interpretative Construct 339

> Indeed, the grammarians of old employed their judgment in such a severe manner that they not only allowed themselves to mark verses with a sign of disapproval and take out of the family as if they were suppositious children [*tamquam subditos*] any books which appeared to be wrongly attributed [*qui falso viderentur inscripti*], but also included some authors in the canon, and excluded others altogether from the list. (Quintilian, *Inst.* 1.4.3 [our translation])

Quintilian is here translating the Greek technical vocabulary of authenticity criticism: *falso inscripti* renders the Greek *pseudepigraphos*, "wrongly entitled." The application of the language of paternity to books is also borrowed from Greek technical vocabulary: the Greek word *nothos* ("bastard," "illegitimate child") is often used of *pseudepigrapha*. Conversely, a work considered genuine is defined as *gnēsios* ("legitimate," "born in wedlock") or in Latin as *genuinus*. It is worth taking seriously the metaphorical implications of this lexicon, which implicitly configures *pseudepigrapha* not as complete outsiders but as children of lower status who still share a paternal line with the legitimate offspring of the author.

On the basis of these philological discussions of authenticity, it is often objected that because the ancients had a notion of literary fraud, all ancient texts that are demonstrably not written by the author or figure to whom they are ascribed should be called forgeries.[15] Yet, as we have seen, far from operating under the assumption of a straightforwardly dichotomous distinction between forged and authentic, Greco-Roman authenticity criticism constitutes a deeply problematic precedent for early Christian writers debating questions of canonicity and authorial attribution. Eusebius's account of the canon of scripture in his *Historia ecclesiastica* is often cited as one of the earliest sources for the existence of a developing canon of Christian texts deemed authentic and is one of the most interesting examples of the application of Hellenistic *Echtheitskritik* to scriptural texts:[16]

---

15. The term *pious fraud* is sometimes used by modern scholars to excuse texts that are written in the persona of a religious figure. Ancient discussions, however, do not mention ideas of fraud: e.g., Iamblichus, *Vit. Pyth.* 198–199: "it was a fine thing that they even attributed and assigned everything to Pythagoras and did not keep as their own any doctrines among those that they had discovered, except in rare cases; for there are in fact altogether very few people whose works are circulated with their own name attached to them."

16. Bruce M. Metzger, *The Canon of the New Testament: Its Origin, Development and Significance* (Oxford: Oxford University Press: 1987), 201–07.

1. Since we are dealing with this subject it is proper to sum up the writings of the New Testament which have been already mentioned. First then must be put the holy quaternion of the Gospels; following them the Acts of the Apostles.
2. After this must be reckoned the epistles of Paul; next in order the extant former epistle of John, and likewise the epistle of Peter, must be maintained. After them is to be placed, if it really seems proper, the Apocalypse of John, concerning which we shall give the different opinions at the proper time. These then belong among the *accepted writings* [καὶ ταῦτα μὲν ἐν ὁμολογουμένοις].
3. Among the *disputed writings* [τῶν δ' ἀντιλεγομένων], which are nevertheless recognized by many, are extant the so-called epistle of James and that of Jude, also the second epistle of Peter, and those that are called the second and third of John whether they belong to the evangelist or to another person of the same name.
4. Among the *rejected writings* [ἐν τοῖς νόθοις] must be reckoned also the Acts of Paul, and the so-called Shepherd, and the Apocalypse of Peter, and in addition to these the extant epistle of Barnabas, and the so-called Teachings of the Apostles; and besides, as I said, the Apocalypse of John, if it seem proper, which some, as I said, reject, but which others class with the accepted books.
5. And among these some have placed also the Gospel according to the Hebrews, with which those of the Hebrews that have accepted Christ are especially delighted. And all these may be reckoned among the *disputed books*. (Eusebius, *Hist. eccl.* 3.25.1–5 [trans. McGiffert, NPNF 2/1:156–57, emphasis original]).

Here Eusebius seems at first to follow Hellenistic terminology in distinguishing three categories of texts: genuine texts (literally, "accepted," ὁμολογύμενα), texts of disputed authorship (ἀντιλεγόμενα), and spurious texts (νόθα), such as the Acts of Paul or the Apocalypse of John.[17]

---

17. For this tripartite division in late antiquity in the context of both pagan and Christian exegesis, see Jaap Mansfeld, *Prolegomena: Questions to Be Settled before the Study of an Author or Text* (Leiden: Brill, 1994), 4–5 and 44–45. The question of pseudepigrapha was one of those tackled in the context of biography and commentary. See Jerome, *On Illustrious Men*, *praefatio* and passim for discussion of attribution and authenticity with Brakke, "Early Christian Lies and the Lying Liars Who Wrote Them," 389–90. In the *praefatio*, Jerome reveals his dependence on Suetonius and the tradition of Hellenistic biography; see Tomas Hägg, *The Art of Biography in Antiquity* (Cambridge: Cambridge University Press, 2012), 69.

Once again, it is important to stress that there are noticeable discontinuities between the modern philological method of the search for the historical author and the authentication and authorization of the earliest or original text and, by way of contrast, these ancient examples of attribution, authentication, and criticism. For example, at the end of the same section of Eusebius *Historia ecclesiastica* (3.25.5), it becomes clear that these three categories of texts—genuine, disputed, and spurious—ought to be distinguished from yet another set of texts:

> 6. But we have nevertheless felt compelled to give a catalogue of these also, distinguishing those works which according to ecclesiastical tradition are true and genuine and commonly accepted, from those others which, although not canonical but disputed, are yet at the same time known to most ecclesiastical writers—we have felt compelled to give this catalogue in order that we might be able to know both these works and those that are cited by the heretics under the name of the apostles, including, for instance, such books as the Gospels of Peter, of Thomas, of Matthias, or of any others besides them, and the Acts of Andrew and John and the other apostles, which no one belonging to the succession of ecclesiastical writers has deemed worthy of mention in his writings.
> 7. And further, the character of the style is at variance with apostolic usage, and both the thoughts and the purpose of the things that are related in them are so completely out of accord with true hortodoxy that they clearly show themselves to be the fictions of heretics. Wherefore they are not to be placed even among the rejected writings, but are all of them to be cast aside as absurd and impious [ὅθεν οὐδ' ἐν νόθοις αὐτὰ κατατακτέον, ἀλλ' ὡς ἄτοπα πάντῃ καὶ δυσσεβῆ παραιτητέον]. (Eusebius, *Hist. eccl.* 3.25.6–7 [trans. McGiffert, *NPNF* 2/1:157])

Eusebius's language here is redolent of the authenticity criticism of the "old grammarians" outlined by Quintilian; not just the vocabulary of genuine, spurious, and disputed, but also the appeal to the style (χαρακτήρ) of the author. Moreover, in Eusebius's formulation, "bastard" texts (νόθα), though authorially unstable, maintain something of a connection to the accepted texts such as to warrant their inclusion into a canon made of texts of unstable or debated origin, as opposed to texts that are demonstrably at odds with the church's true teaching.[18] Similarly, if we accept a more capa-

---

18. "Thus the *notha* occupy a peculiar position, being orthodox but uncanonical" (Metzger, *The Canon of the New Testament*, 205).

cious definition of what can constitute a text as belonging to the canon, we can better understand Origen's statement commending anyone who accepts the Epistle to Hebrews "as by Paul" (ὡς Παύλου), despite the fact that "the thoughts are those of the apostle, but the diction and phraseology are those of someone who remembered the apostolic teachings, and wrote down at his leisure what had been said by his teacher" (Eusebius, *Hist. eccl.* 6.25.13). Origen approves of those who call the epistle the work of Paul since it chimes with the νοήματα of the apostle.[19] We may compare similar attempts of Greco-Roman writers to frame a text belonging to an authorial corpus or textual tradition of a founding figure as the work of a close associate, blood relative, or lover of the author or founder.[20] There is a larger point at stake here: if we take seriously the familial rhetoric of Greco-Roman authenticity criticism, we can see pseudepigrapha not as foreign and false but as texts perhaps endowed with a lower genealogical pedigree and yet nevertheless deeply and legitimately connected to the father/author.

Finally, it is important to evaluate the *rhetorical context* in which these claims and discussions of (in)authenticity are found. While this philological sense of temporality is often portrayed as the dispassionate application of an uncontestable scientific method, it is important to note that this use of philology to debunk a text's date and with it its claim to moral and religious authority has a long history. According to Jerome, in his book *Against the Christians*, Porphyry, the second century follower of Plotinus and author of the *Homeric Questions*, denied that the book of Daniel

> was composed by the person to whom it is ascribed in its title, but rather by some individual living in Judaea at the time of the Antiochus [Antiochus IV in the second century BCE] who was surnamed Epiphanes [not by the prophet Daniel under Cyrus the Persian in the sixth century]. He further-

---

19. Pace Ehrman, for whom this passage is proof that Origen "will not say a book is by Paul unless Paul actually wrote it" (*Forgery and Counterforgery*, 88). Clearly, Origen is prepared to praise those who attribute the work to Paul.

20. See Servius *ad Buc.* 3.20, where the tragedy Thyestes, attributed to Varius, is presented as a *pseudepigraphon* (cf. Suetonius-Donatus, *Vit. Verg.* 48), originally a gift by Virgil to Varius's wife with whom the poet was having an affair. See also the anecdotes about composition of the poems of the Homeric cycle in Callimachus *Ep.* 6, Aelian *Varia Hist.* 9.15. See further Barbara Graziosi, *Inventing Homer: The Early Reception of Epic* (Cambridge: Cambridge University Press, 2002), 184–93; and Peirano, "Authenticity as an Aesthetic Concept," 48.

more alleged that "Daniel" did not foretell the future so much as he related the past [the revolt of the Maccabees and subsequent events], and lastly that whatever he spoke of up till the time of Antiochus contained authentic history, whereas anything he may have conjectured beyond that point was false, inasmuch as he would not have foreknown the future. (Jerome, *Expl. Dan.* prologue // *Porphyry*, frag. 43 [trans. Gleason L. Archer])

Greco-Roman chronography, in the works of Callinicus and others, is here put into the service of an unabashedly religious polemic aimed at debunking a Christian reading of the book of Daniel to justify the Christian claim that Jesus was the messiah prophesied in the Hebrew Bible.[21] The point is not, of course, that Porphyry was wrong but rather that this particular use of philology is not geared toward a sympathetic understanding of a culture but to the contrary has a long tradition of being used in the context of a polemical debunking of its core traditions and values.[22] The tradition of polemical deployment of philology is long lasting when one considers that Lorenzo Valla's *On the Donation of Constantine*, which many see as a foundational text in the history of the modern philological method, is in fact a political attack against the church.[23]

4. Pseudepigraphy as an Interpretative Construct

Greco-Roman, Jewish, and Christian writers in antiquity offer other useful perspectives for thinking about these texts not as false but as creative acts of interpretation. Thinking about pseudepigraphy as an interpretative construct rather than as fallacy or forgery allows us to overcome a hermeneutical impasse that arises when we constrict texts into prepackaged anachronistic categories.

The connection between creative continuation, impersonation, and interpretation is well evident across the different literary and religious tra-

---

21. In turn, see Ariane Magny, *Porphyry in Fragments: Reception of an Anti-Christian Text in Late Antiquity*, Ashgate Series (London: Routledge, 2014), on the hostile reception of Porphyry in Christian sources.

22. See Reed, "Modern Invention of 'Old Testament Pseudepigrapha,'" for a discussion of the religious agenda of Johann Albert Fabricius who first used the term pseudepigrapha in his *Codex Pseudepigraphus Veteris Testamenti* of 1716.

23. Christopher S. Celenza, "Lorenzo Valla's Radical Philology: The 'Preface' to the *Annotations of the New Testament* in Context," *Journal of Medieval and Early Modern Studies* 42 (2012): 365–93.

ditions that form the subject of our study. One could begin by highlighting the place of early biblical interpretation in the production of textuality and composition in Jewish antiquity. In addition to the reshaping of how we conceive of what is in and outside of the Hebrew Bible, scholars have also rethought the way we have come to understand the place of interpretation and reading practices within and beyond the so-called canon as a whole. As a result, the discourse around what constitutes the authentic or the genuine versus what is constituted as spurious or pseudonymous has also been called into question. At first, much of this was avoided as biblical scholars continued to insist upon canonical strictures. Moreover, the project of Jewish commentary was understood only to be late and subsequent to the formation and fixity of the Jewish canon of Scripture, and thus the Dead Sea Scrolls that exhibited commentary were considered either not genuinely commentary or nonnormative. Eventually and inevitably, scholars have come to accept that there was indeed a great deal of early commentary and interpretation from targum to pesher, from rewritten Pentateuch to entirely new compositions that reused and implemented biblical traditions.[24]

---

24. George J. Brooke, "Genre Theory, Rewritten Bible and Pesher," *DSD* 17 (2010): 361–86; Geza Vermes, *Scripture and Tradition in Judaism: Haggadic Studies*, 2nd ed., SPB 4 (Leiden: Brill, 1973); Najman, *Seconding Sinai*; Eugene Ulrich, "From Literature to Scripture: The Growth of a Text's Authoritativeness," *DSD* 10 (2003): 3–25; Daniel K. Falk, *The Parabiblical Texts: Strategies for Extending the Scriptures in the Dead Sea Scrolls*, CQS 8 (London: T&T Clark, 2007), 14–15; Emanuel Tov and Sidnie White Crawford, "Reworked Pentateuch," in *Qumran Cave 4. VIII: Parabiblical Texts, Part 1*, ed. H. Attridge et al., DJD 13 (Oxford: Clarendon, 1994), 187–351, for 4Q364-367. 4Q158 is also regularly included as an exemplar of this composition; see George J. Brooke, "4Q158: Reworked Pentateucha or 4QReworked Pentateuch A?," *DSD* 8 (2001): 219–41; Moshe J. Bernstein, "'Rewritten Bible': A Generic Category Which Has Outlived Its Usefulness?," *Textus* 22 (2005): 169–96; Philip S. Alexander, "Retelling the Old Testament," in *It Is Written: Scripture Citing Scripture; Essays in Honour of Barnabas Lindars, SSF* (Cambridge: Cambridge University Press, 1987), 99–121; William H. Brownlee, *The Midrash Pesher of Habakkuk*, SBLMS 24 (Missoula, MT: Scholars Press, 1979); Shani L. Berrin, *The Pesher Nahum Scroll from Qumran: An Exegetical Study of 4Q169*, STDJ 53 (Leiden: Brill, 2004); Markus Bockmuehl, "The Dead Sea Scrolls and the Origins of Biblical Commentary," in *Text, Thought and Practice in Qumran and Early Christianity: Proceedings of the Ninth International Symposium of the Orion Center for the Study of the Dead Sea Scrolls and Associated Literature, Jointly Sponsored by the Hebrew University Center for the Study of Christianity, 11–13 January,*

This aspect of the findings went much further as it came to impact upon the biblical texts themselves. The place of interpretation within the biblical canon became far more integrated and central to this work. Consideration of the place of interpretation in the very composition of the biblical texts themselves became central to the discourse of biblical studies. Our point is that it opened up pathways that had not been considered. Increasingly, the question was less about how to reconstruct the earliest layer of a text or the differentiation of sources and more, at least in the critical work of pentateuchal studies or Jeremiah, it was about charting the growth of tradition through interpretation and compositional variety and flexibility. This brings out a very dynamic, creative, and new picture of what biblical authorship might have looked like. The function and place of the author also became far less dominant, as the place of pseudepigraphical attribution was increasingly understood to be an interpretative gesture rather than an historical claim to authenticity. The picture was instead one of vitality, transformation, emergence, and pluriformity.[25]

Interpretation is also central to practices of impersonation in Greco-Roman texts that seek to expand and revise supposedly fixed authorial canons. Already in antiquity, the name of Virgil was associated not just with his three canonical works—*Eclogues*, *Georgics*, and *Aeneid*—but also with a fluctuating number of other minor poems of different date, origin, and genre, a portion of which are gathered in a collection that is known today as the *Appendix Vergiliana*.[26] The pseudo-Virgilian *Culex* is a poem in hexameters that belongs to this collection and was already widely quoted as Virgilian in the first century.[27] The poem tells the story of a shepherd who is warned of the imminent attack of a snake by a gnat, which he inadvertently kills and which later appears to him in a prophetic dream. The poem playfully teases the reader with a fictional young Virgil whose lighthearted epic self-consciously cites, recapitulates, and prefigures Virgil's three canonical works. Approaching this text as a biographical fiction, not as a failed forgery or as an act of deception but as a constructed and fictional identity, allows one to catch a glimpse of the interests that

---

2004, ed. Ruth A. Clements and Daniel R. Schwartz, STDJ 84 (Leiden: Brill, 2009), 3–29.

25. Hindy Najman, "The Vitality of Scripture within and beyond the 'Canon,'" *JSJ* 43 (2012): 497–518.

26. Most, "Virgilian *Culex*."

27. Peirano, *Rhetoric of the Roman Fake*, 74–79.

animated early Virgilian readers and the questions they brought to bear to the poet's work. Thus, the very narrative apparatus of the *Culex* develops out of a clue in the Virgilian text: a passage about snakes in *Georg.* 3, which is heavily imitated in the *Culex*, is in fact one of the very few places in the poem where Virgil breaks into the narrative and presents himself as a farmer and a potential recipient of his own advice. In this passage, the mature Virgil of the *Georgics* warns precisely against falling asleep when the snakes are out and about.[28] Rather than seeing the author of the *Culex* as convicting himself, we can see the pseudepigraphon as reflecting and creatively expanding upon the genesis of the parent text, interpreting the *Georgics* in this case as authoritative advice grounded in experience.

What seems just as important is the function of this text as a creative cultural aetiology, resting on important assumptions about human and historical development as the gradual unveiling of innate characteristics. The pseudepigraphon can be understood not as forged text but as an exploration of causation. What is more, we can track a precise parallel between the interpretation supplied by the *Culex* and that found in the exegetical tradition. The Virgilian commentator Servius gives us a note on the passage in the *Georgics* about snakes that specifically cautions against biographical reading: he states that when Virgil uses "you" he "means anyone" (Servius, *Georg.* 3.435 *cuicumque*). Yet the fact that Servius issued such a warning might lead one to believe that the passage was actually subject to the kind of reading that the scholiast is discouraging and upon which the poet of the *Culex* is building.

Analogously, the radical rewriting of the Genesis narrative known as the Genesis Apocryphon arises out of a need to interpret the unexplainable. A Dead Sea Scrolls text found in Cave 1 at Qumran, this narrative reworks the Genesis narrative in order to justify Abram's behavior apologetically, as though it is already a revealed prophecy (in a dream) that Abram must deliver his wife Sarai to Pharaoh in order to escape what would otherwise be an inevitable death. It tries to justify or to explain apologetically Abram's giving up of Sarai to Pharaoh, a story well known from the book of Genesis. It is clear that this text struggles with the ethical challenge that is put to Abram. How could he risk the honor and the life of his wife? The answer is that this action and necessary compro-

---

28. Servius, *Georg.* 3.435–438: *ne mihi tum mollis sub divo carpere somnos / neu dorso nemoris libeat iacuisse per herbas, / cum positis novus exuviis nitidusque iuventa / volvitur.*

mise are not only already determined through prophecy, but that Sarai, his own wife, calls for this act in order to spare her husband. Ethical rewriting and reworking is already evident in texts such as Chronicles and Daniel and perhaps even Joshua through the rethinking of Abram. The Genesis Apocryphon pushes readers to think and rethink the ethical implications and to interpret accordingly. It is also important to highlight here that this apologetic rewriting of Abram's ethical choice should be approached in the larger context of the idealization of the hero in the Hellenistic context (e.g., Plutarch's *Moralia*).[29] We want to suggest that the rewriting of these established textual traditions, whether of Virgil or of Genesis, is enacted through composition, authentication, and inclusion of new text—now self-authorized through association with and expansion of a prior exemplar.

5. Imitation

How, in light of the aforementioned issue of anachronism—that is, the contemporary scholar's charge of forgery against cultures in which rewriting is fundamental to the growth of scripture and at the heart of reading and reception of literary texts in a pagan context—can we reconsider practices of false attribution as a genuine gesture? The practice of imitation offers one important lens through which to consider pseudepigraphy as genuine. Because of the importance of literary imitation in Greco-Roman education, the line is often blurred between impersonation, fiction, forgery, and writing in the style of another. Impersonation and chronological fiction—temporarily stepping out of one's present tense persona to inhabit the past—were cornerstones of educational practice in Greco-Roman antiquity all the way from elementary education to advanced rhetorical training.[30] Imitation (Greek: *mimēsis*; Latin: *imitatio*) was not construed as unoriginal but rather as a means for stylistic and moral self-improvement in an agonistic spirit that invited rewriting,

---

29. E.g., D. A. Russell, "Plutarch and the Antique Hero," *Yearbook of English Studies* 12 (1982): 24–34.

30. Stanley Frederick Bonner, *Roman Declamation in the Late Republic and Early Empire* (Berkeley: University of California Press, 1949); Raffaella Cribiore, *Gymnastics of the Mind: Greek Education in Hellenistic and Roman Egypt* (Princeton: Princeton University Press, 2001).

retooling, and improvement of the past, all the while staging fictional explorations of alternative outcomes.[31]

Thus, it is important to stress that imitation in the realm of pseudepigrapha stands on a *continuum* of imitative practices that span ethics, religion, literature, and the visual arts across Jewish, Christian, and pagan traditions and as such must not be viewed in isolation as an aberrant phenomenon but rather considered in light of the role of mimetic practices in other areas of cultural relevance. In this regard, self-effacement for the purpose of imitating an exemplary figure plays a fundamental role as a spiritual discipline.[32] On the one hand, humanity is described as godlike or created in the image of God, and human beings are called upon to "be holy" and to be "godlike" in their behavior (e.g., the incomparability formula in Exod 15:11 and the call to be holy in Lev 20:26). On the other hand, crossing between the earth and the heavens is impossible (Isa 55). How then is the call to be godlike or to be holy like god or the call implicitly raised by texts to be like the exemplar who is godlike—even a divine human—remotely compelling or coherent?

Our response to this challenge and impasse is to look to texts from the Hellenistic period that construct a bridge between the possible and the impossible through wisdom and a journey towards coming to understand creation, the law of nature, and divine knowledge. How do these texts, which capture the challenge of defining oneself through an originary form (from creation or birth) that is unrepeatable but inevitably aspires to repeat, illuminate the way we think about imitation and the practice of so-called pseudonymity in the construction of new texts? Humans are continually invited to emulate through exemplars and by being godlike. Similarly, in the work of pseudepigraphy, the expansion, refinement, and extension of new texts (processes of editing and interpretation) is not a practice of transgression but one of ethical formation.

There are many different ways in which this pluriformity of mimetic practices is visible in our ancient Jewish texts. Imitation can be performed

---

31. D. A. Russell, "*De Imitatione*," in *Creative Imitation and Latin Literature*, ed. David A. West and A. J. Woodman (Cambridge: Cambridge University Press, 1979), 1–16.

32. Najman, "Vitality of Scripture," 235–42; for the theological implications of authorial self-effacement in gnostic texts, see David Brakke, "Pseudonymity, Gnosis, and the Self of Gnostic Literature," *Gnosis* 2 (2017): 194–211; Stang, *Apophasis and Pseudonymity in Dionysius the Aeropagite*.

through creating and building (e.g., Betzalel in Exod 31 and 35). But there are also imitative ways of reproducing the creation of humanity or of incomparable heroes such as Moses or Isaiah. This is done through pseudonymous attribution, which can (though it does not have to) have the effect of growing a corpus or attaching a much later work to an earlier author in the form of a pseudonym. This is thus done as a way of repeating an unrepeatable moment, but it also will have an effect on the self who defines herself through the originary form of the creation. So, for example, the second century CE work, the book of Jubilees, claims to be heavenly, written by Moses, dictated by the angel of presence. Jubilees describes itself as a copy of the heavenly tablets.

> These are the words regarding the divisions of the times of the law and of the testimony, of the events of the years, of the weeks of their jubilees throughout all the years of eternity as he related (them) to Moses on Mt. Sinai when he went up to receive the stone tablets—the law and the commandments—on the Lord's orders as he had told him that he should come up to the summit of the mountain.
> During the first year of the Israelites' exodus from Egypt, in the third month—on the sixteenth of the month—the Lord said to Moses: "Come up to me on the mountain. I will give you the two stone tablets of the law and the commandments which I have written so that you may teach them." So Moses went up the mountain of the Lord. The glory of the Lord took up residence on Mt. Sinai, and a cloud covered it for six days. When he summoned Moses into the cloud on the seventh day, he saw the glory of the Lord like a fire blazing on the summit of the mountain. Moses remained on the mountain for 40 days and 40 nights while the Lord showed him what (had happened) beforehand as well as what was to come. He related to him the divisions of all the times—both of the law and of the testimony. (Jubilees, prologue and 1.1-4 [trans. James C. Vanderkam])

Or, in the second century CE work of 4 Ezra (otherwise known as 2 Esdras), the biblical Ezra is said to struggle with the destruction of the first temple (not the second which was destroyed in 70 CE). He is confronted by destruction and overcomes that trauma with a new revelation, becoming Moses again.

> In the thirtieth year of the destruction of our country, I, Shealtiel, who is Ezra, was in Babylon. And I lay on my bed, I was upset and thoughts

welled up in my heart because I saw the destruction of Zion and the affluence of those who lived their lives in Babylon. (4 Ezra 3.1)

Then he (God) said to me, "I revealed myself in a bush and spoke to Moses when my people were in bondage in Egypt; and I sent him and led my people out of Egypt; and I led him up to Mount Sinai. And I kept him with me many days; and I told him many wondrous things, and showed him the secrets of the times and declared to him the end of the times. Then I commanded him, saying: 'These words you shall publish openly, and these you shall keep secret.' And now I say to you; Lay up in your heart the signs that I have shown you, the dreams that you have seen and the interpretation that you have heard; for you shall be taken up from among men, and henceforth you shall be with my servant and with those who are like you, until the times are ended." (4 Ezra 14.3)

And the Most High gave understanding to the five men, and by turns they wrote what was dictated, in characters which they did not know. They sat forty days, and wrote during the daytime, and ate their bread at night. As for me, I spoke in the daytime and was not silent at night. So during the forty days ninety-four books were written. And when the forty days were ended, the Most High spoke to me, saying, "Make public the twenty-four books that you wrote first and let the worthy and the unworthy read them; but keep the seventy that were written last, in order to give them to the wise among your people. For in them is the spring of understanding, the fountain of wisdom, and the river of knowledge." And I did so. (4 Ezra 14.42–48 [trans. James C. Vanderkam])

The repetition of Sinai and the reaccessing of figures who are long-deceased is part of a process that is at once interpretive but also creative with time. Pasts can be accessed as well as futures being constructed through texts which can be expanded, imitated, or even repeated (like events, under the right conditions of inspiration or writing).

The aspiration is not to *be Moses* or not to *be God*, but rather to be angel-like, god-like, and perhaps also to embody the law of nature or the law of Moses as that perfectionist aspiration.[33] This process of refiguring past exemplars is essentially a project about primordial perfection. To be like the gods, or godlike, or to extend, expand, and reinterpret the idealized figures of the past has a deep affinity with the concept of recovery. This

---

33. Hindy Najman, *Past Renewals: Interpretative Authority, Renewed Revelation, and the Quest for Perfection in Jewish Antiquity* (Leiden: Brill, 2010).

claim to having been written by a prior figure, who is then extended and transformed through the application and extension of that past, is about recovering the past, but also and at the same time it is about reinvigorating a new present. This is then catapulted into a new future which is a revised and transformed interpretive extension of that past.

6. Conclusion

In reframing pseudepigraphy as an act of interpretation or as a generative mechanism that enables growth of a tradition,[34] we can study these texts not as intruders or interlopers into the canon but as creative responses to their respective traditions. It is imperative that we look at pseudepigrapha outside of the disciplinary and intellectual limits inherited from post-Enlightenment scholarly discourses. Instead, we want to include pseudepigraphy into a larger reevaluation of practices of reading, interpretation, textual refinement, and extension in antiquity. Moreover, it is our thought that the interpretative construct through which pseudepigraphy can be seen to operate is a marker for compositional growth within and without of an inherited or authoritative tradition (be it Latin, Hebrew, Greek, or Aramaic). In reconsidering texts that are not normative from the point of view of a later canonical perspective, we can embrace a process that we want to call marginal. This marginal process dissipates the distinction between the canonical and the noncanonical, the margin and the center, and the sacred and the profane by essentially allowing so-called marginal texts do the work of reconstituting our understanding of the center and the very functioning of the canon.

Bibliography

Alexander, Philip S. "Retelling the Old Testament." Pages 99–121 in *It Is Written: Scripture Citing Scripture; Essays in Honour of Barnabas Lindars, SSF*. Cambridge: Cambridge University Press, 1987.

Alexander, Philip, Armin Lange, and Renate Pillinger, eds. *In the Second Degree: Paratextual Literature in Ancient Near Eastern and Ancient*

---

34. Hindy Najman, *Losing the Temple and Recovering the Future: An Analysis of 4 Ezra* (Cambridge: Cambridge University Press, 2014).

Mediterranean Culture and Its Reflections in Medieval Literature. Leiden: Brill, 2010.

Baum, Armin Daniel. *Pseudepigraphie und literarische Fälschung im frühen Christentum: Mit ausgewählten Quellentexten samt deutscher Übersetzung.* WUNT 2/138. Tübingen: Mohr Siebeck, 2001.

Bernstein, Moshe J. "'Rewritten Bible': A Generic Category Which Has Outlived Its Usefulness?" *Textus* 22 (2005): 169–96.

Berrin, Shani L. *The Pesher Nahum Scroll from Qumran: An Exegetical Study of 4Q169.* STDJ 53. Leiden: Brill, 2004.

Blum, Rudolf. *Kallimachos: The Alexandrian Library and the Origins of Bibliography.* Translated by Hans H. Wellisch. Madison: University of Wisconsin Press, 2011.

Bockmuehl, Markus. "The Dead Sea Scrolls and the Origins of Biblical Commentary." Pages 3–29 in *Text, Thought and Practice in Qumran and Early Christianity: Proceedings of the Ninth International Symposium of the Orion Center for the Study of the Dead Sea Scrolls and Associated Literature, Jointly Sponsored by the Hebrew University Center for the Study of Christianity, 11–13 January, 2004.* Edited by Ruth A. Clements and Daniel R. Schwartz. STDJ 84. Leiden: Brill, 2009.

Bonner, Stanley Frederick. *Roman Declamation in the Late Republic and Early Empire.* Berkeley: University of California Press, 1949.

Boyarin, Daniel. *Intertextuality and Reading of Midrash.* Indiana: Indiana University Press, 1980.

Brakke, David. "Early Christian Lies and the Lying Liars Who Wrote Them: Bart Ehrman's *Forgery and Counterforgery*." *JR* 96 (2016): 378–90.

———. "Pseudonymity, Gnosis, and the Self of Gnostic Literature." *Gnosis* 2 (2017): 194–211.

Brooke, George J. "4Q158: Reworked Pentateucha or 4QReworked Pentateuch A?" *DSD* 8 (2001): 219–41.

———. "From Florilegium or Midrash to Commentary: The Problem of Re-naming an Adopted Manuscript." Pages 129–50 in *The Mermaid and the Partridge: Essays from the Copenhagen Conference on Revising Texts from Cave Four*, ed. George J. Brooke and Jesper Høgenhaven. STDJ 97. Leiden: Brill, 2011.

———. "Genre Theory, Rewritten Bible and Pesher." *DSD* 17 (2010): 361–86.

Brownlee, William H. *The Midrash Pesher of Habakkuk.* SBLMS 24. Missoula, MT: Scholars Press, 1979.

Celenza, Christopher S. "Lorenzo Valla's Radical Philology: The 'Preface' to the *Annotations of the New Testament* in Context." *Journal of Medieval and Early Modern Studies* 42 (2012): 365–93.

Clarke, Kent D. "The Problems of Pseudonymity in Biblical Literature and Its Implications for Canon Formation." Pages 440–42 in *The Canon Debate*. Edited by Lee Martin McDonald and James A. Sanders. Peabody, MA: Hendrickson, 2002.

Cribiore, Raffaella. *Gymnastics of the Mind: Greek Education in Hellenistic and Roman Egypt*. Princeton: Princeton University Press, 2001.

Ehrman, Bart. *Forgery and Counterforgery: The Use of Literary Deceit in Early Christian Polemics*. Oxford: Oxford University Press, 2012.

Falk, Daniel K. *The Parabiblical Texts: Strategies for Extending the Scriptures in the Dead Sea Scrolls*. CQS 8. London: T&T Clark, 2007.

Frey, Jörg, Jens Herzer, Martina Janssen, and Clare K. Rothschild, eds. *Pseudepigraphie und Verfasserfiktion in frühchristlichen Briefen*. WUNT 246. Tübingen: Mohr Siebeck, 2009.

Graziosi, Barbara. *Inventing Homer: The Early Reception of Epic*. Cambridge: Cambridge University Press, 2002.

Hägg, Tomas. *The Art of Biography in Antiquity*. Cambridge: Cambridge University Press, 2012.

King, Karen. "'What Is an Author?' Ancient Author-Function in The Apocryphon of John and The Apocalypse of John." Pages 15–42 in *Scribal Practices and Social Structures among Jesus's Adherents: Essays in Honour of John S. Kloppenborg*. Edited by William E. Arnal, Richard S. Ascough, R. A. Derrenbacker, and Phillip A. Harland. BETL. Leuven: Peeters, 2016.

Magny, Ariane. *Porphyry in Fragments: Reception of an Anti-Christian Text in Late Antiquity*. Ashgate Series. London: Routledge, 2014.

Mansfeld, Jaap. *Prolegomena: Questions to Be Settled before the Study of an Author or Text*. Leiden: Brill, 1994.

Meade, David G. *Pseudonymity and Canon: An Investigation into the Relationship of Authorship and Authority in Jewish and Earliest Christian Tradition*. Tübingen: Mohr Siebeck, 1986.

Metzger, Bruce M. *The Canon of the New Testament: Its Origin, Development and Significance*. Oxford: Oxford University Press: 1987.

———. "Literary Forgeries and Canonical Pseudepigrapha." *JBL* 91 (1972): 3–24.

Montanari, Franco. "Correcting a Copy, Editing a Text: Alexandrian *Ekdosis* and Papyri." Pages 1–15 in *From Scholars to Scholia: Chapters in the*

History of Ancient Greek Scholarship. Edited by Franco Montari and Lara Pagani. Berlin: de Gruyter, 2011.

Most, Glenn. "The Virgilian *Culex*." Pages 199–209 in *Homo Viator: Classical Essays for John Bramble*. Edited by Michael Whitby, Philip R. Hardie, and Mary Whitby. Bristol: Bristol Classical Press, 1987.

Najman, Hindy. "The Idea of Biblical Genre." Pages 308–21 in *Prayer and Poetry in the Dead Sea Scrolls and Related Literature: Essays in Honor of Eileen Schuller on the Occasion of Her Sixty-Fifth Birthday*. Edited by J. Penner, K. M. Penner, and C. Wassen. STDJ 98. Leiden: Brill, 2011.

———. *Losing the Temple and Recovering the Future: An Analysis of 4 Ezra*. Cambridge: Cambridge University Press, 2014.

———. *Past Renewals: Interpretative Authority, Renewed Revelation, and the Quest for Perfection in Jewish Antiquity*. Leiden: Brill, 2010.

———. *Second Sinai: The Development of Mosaic Discourse in Second Temple Judaism*. JSJSup 77. Leiden: Brill, 2004.

———. "Traditionary Processes and Textual Unity in 4 Ezra." Pages 99–117 in *Fourth Ezra and Second Baruch: Recpnstructions after the Fall*. Edited by Matthias Henze and Gabriele Boccaccini. JSJSup 164. Leiden: Brill, 2013.

———. "The Vitality of Scripture within and beyond the 'Canon.'" *JSJ* 43 (2012): 497–518.

Najman, Hindy, Eva Mroczek and I. Manoff. "How to Make Sense of Pseudonymous Attribution: The Cases of 4 Ezra and 2 Baruch." Pages 308–36 in *Companion to Biblical Interpretation in Early Judaism*. Edited by Matthias Henze. Grand Rapids: Eerdmans, 2012.

Paz, Yakir. "Re-scripturizing Traditions: Designating Dependence in Rabbinic Halakhic Midrashim and Homeric Scholarship." Pages 269–98 in *Homer and the Bible in the Eyes of Ancient Interpreters*. Edited by Maren R. Niehoff. Leiden: Brill, 2012.

Peirano, Irene. "Authenticity as an Aesthetic Concept: Ancient and Modern Reflections." Pages 1–7 in *Aesthetic Value in Classical Antiquity*. Edited by Ralph Mark Rosen and Ineke Sluiter. Penn-Leiden Colloquium on Ancient Values 6. Leiden: Brill, 2012.

———. *The Rhetoric of the Roman Fake: Latin Pseudepigrapha in Context*. Cambridge: Cambridge University Press, 2012.

Pfeiffer, R. *Fragmenta*. Vol. 1 of *Callimachus*. Oxford: Clarendon, 1949.

Reed, Annette Yoshiko. "The Modern Invention of 'Old Testament Pseudepigrapha.'" *JTS* 60 (2009): 403–36.

Rosen-Zvi, Ishay. "Structure and Reflectivity in Tannaitic Legal Homilies, Or: How to Read Midrashic Terminology." *Prooftexts* 34 (2014): 271–301.

Rosenmeyer, Patricia A. *The Poetics of Imitation: Anacreon and the Anacreontic Tradition.* Cambridge: Cambridge University Press, 1992.

Russell, D. A. "*De Imitatione*." Pages 1–16 in *Creative Imitation and Latin Literature.* Edited by David A. West and A. J. Woodman. Cambridge: Cambridge University Press, 1979.

———. "Plutarch and the Antique Hero." *Yearbook of English Studies* 12 (1982): 24–34.

Speyer, Wolfgang. *Die literarische Fälschung im heidnischen und christlichen Altertum: Ein Versuch ihrer Deutung.* Munich: München Beck, 1971.

Stang, Charles M. *Apophasis and Pseudonymity in Dionysius the Aeropagite: "No Longer I".* Oxford: Oxford University Press, 2012.

Stuckenbruck, Loren T. "Apocrypha and Pseudepigrapha." Pages 179–83 in *Early Judaism: A Comprehensive Overview.* Edited by John J. Collins and Daniel Harlow. Grand Rapids: Eerdmans, 2010.

———. "Copying, Rewriting, and Interpretation in Community Formation: The Habakkuk Pesher from Qumran Cave 1." Pages 72–87 in *Scripture Interpretation and the Interface between Education and Religion.* Edited by Florian Wilk, TBN. Leiden: Brill, 2018.

Toorn, Karel van der. *Scribal Culture and the Making of the Hebrew Bible.* Cambridge: Harvard University Press: 2012.

Tov, Emanuel, and Sidnie White Crawford. "Reworked Pentateuch." Pages 187–351 in *Qumran Cave 4. VIII: Parabiblical Texts, Part 1.* Edited by H. Attridge et al. DJD 13. Oxford: Clarendon, 1994.

Ulrich, Eugene. "From Literature to Scripture: The Growth of a Text's Authoritativeness." *DSD* 10 (2003): 3–25.

Vermes, Geza. *Scripture and Tradition in Judaism: Haggadic Studies.* 2nd ed. StPB 4. Leiden: Brill, 1973.

Wyrick, Jed. *The Ascension of Authorship: Attribution and Canon Formation in Jewish, Hellenistic, and Christian Traditions.* Cambridge: Harvard University Press, 2004.

Zsengellér, József, ed. *Rewritten Bible after Fifty Years: Texts, Terms, or Techniques? A Last Dialogue with Geza Vermes.* Leiden: Brill 2014.

The Future of the Study of the Pseudepigrapha

17
The More Old Testament Pseudepigrapha Project

James R. Davila

Sometime in the spring of 2002, Professor Richard Bauckham, my colleague (now retired) at the University of St. Andrews, told me he wanted to meet with me to discuss a possible new research project. When we met for coffee at an outdoor cafe across the street from St. Mary's College, he handed me a written list and told me that he thought there was enough material for us to publish a volume of Old Testament pseudepigrapha supplemental to James H. Charlesworth's two volumes of pseudepigrapha published in the 1980s.[1] I still have the list. It is headed "Possible contents of a volume of 'More OTP.'" It contains thirty-seven individual items. Our list today is well expanded beyond that one, but most of the original items remain. Some have been published in 2013 in our first volume of texts and others are slated for the second volume.

We continued to develop the project over the next few years. We settled from the beginning on the title of the More Old Testament

---

In 2006, I presented papers on the More Old Testament Pseudepigrapha Project at the International Meeting of the Society of Biblical Literature in Edinburgh and the Ottawa Workshop on Christian Apocrypha. Then I presented an updated paper on the project at the Biblical Studies Seminar at the University of Edinburgh in 2009. The current essay borrows some of the language from the 2009 paper, but it is fully and completely revised and updated to reflect contents and progress of the project as of December 2017. I am grateful to Richard Bauckham, who read a draft of this article and provided some useful suggestions for improvement and saved me from some errors. Any problems or errors that remain are, of course, my responsibility entirely.

1. James H. Charlesworth, ed., *Old Testament Pseudepigrapha*, 2 vols. (New York: Doubleday, 1983–1985). Another major English collection of Old Testament pseudepigrapha was published shortly before this, Hedley F. D. Sparks, *The Apocryphal Old Testament* (Oxford: Clarendon, 1984).

Pseudepigrapha Project. We set out to assemble an international team of specialists in many fields who would provide excellent translations of texts from many languages along with introductions to these texts. These would give scholars a good understanding of the current state of the question, while at the same time remaining accessible to specialists in cognate areas and also to interested lay readers.

In 2005 we submitted an application to the Leverhulme Trust for funding for a postdoctoral fellow to work on the project. The application was successful and resulted in the appointment of Dr. Alexander Panayotov as the research fellow for the calendar years 2006 through 2008.[2] Progress on the project proceeded steadily, but on its own time, and our first volume of texts was published in October of 2013.[3] This coincided nicely, but coincidentally with the centenary of the publication of R. H. Charles's collection of pseudepigrapha in 1913 and the three-hundredth anniversary of the first such collection by Johann Fabricius in 1713.[4] Our first volume was dedicated to them. James H. Charlesworth was kind enough to write the preface to this volume.

We use the term *Old Testament pseudepigrapha* to mean ancient literary works that claim to be written by a character in the Hebrew Bible or to be set in the same time period as the Hebrew Bible, but which do not belong to any of the major (Jewish, Protestant, or Catholic) biblical canons.[5]

We apply the following criteria in collecting the texts to be included in the two More Old Testament Pseudepigrapha volumes. First, we generally include only texts that can be dated with some degree of confidence

---

2. We are grateful to the Leverhulme Trust for its generous funding of the project.

3. Richard Bauckam, James R. Davila, and Alexander Panayotov, eds., *Old Testament Pseudepigrapha: More Noncanonical Scriptures*, vol. 1 (Grand Rapids: Eerdmans, 2013).

4. R. H. Charles, ed., *The Apocrypha and Pseudepigrapha of the Old Testament in English: With Introductions and Critical and Explanatory Notes to the Several Books*, 2 vols. (Oxford: Clarendon, 1913); Johann Albert Fabricius, *Codex Pseudepigraphus Veteris Testamenti* (Hamburg: Lieberzeit, 1713).

5. There has been some criticism of our use of the term, but I do not wish to enter into that discussion here. See, for example, Hindy Najman's review of *Old Testament Pseudepigrapha: More Noncanonical Scriptures*, vol. 1, in *DSD* 22 (2015): 211–14. Our view is that it is more important to define our terms clearly and then to use them consistently than to toil endlessly to find the perfect terminology. For some comments on the term *pseudepigrapha* and our use of it, see Richard Bauckham and James R. Davila, "Introduction," *MOTP* 1:xviii–xix and xxvii.

17. The More Old Testament Pseudepigrapha Project   361

before the rise of Islam, that is, the early seventh century. After this period, the amount of material becomes unmanageably large. (As an aside, it is interesting to note that our oldest text is an Iron Age II inscription dating to around 700 BCE.) Second, we are translating texts of any origin (Jewish, Christian, traditional polytheistic [i.e., "pagan"], etc.). Thus our collection is somewhat more inclusive than previous ones. Third, for the most part we do not include texts that are already published in thematic collections and are thus already widely available in good translations: the Dead Sea Scrolls, the Nag Hammadi Library, the Hekhalot literature, and the like. In some cases fragments of our texts survive in the Dead Sea Scrolls, but important manuscripts are known from elsewhere as well. In those cases we have translated all the available material. Fourth, we are not including texts already translated in the Charlesworth and Hedley F. D. Sparks collections unless we have new and better manuscript data or we have some other reason to think that we can improve substantially on the earlier treatment. Fifth, we are translating a few texts that were written in their current form later than our upper chronological limit, but which have some sort of close relationship with earlier material. A final point is worth mentioning. We have chosen to publish the texts in the traditional biblical chronological order rather than dividing the material on the basis of genre.[6]

The More Old Testament Pseudepigrapha Project has become a major international endeavor. The first volume included contributions by thirty scholars from seven different countries. They translated ancient works from Arabic, Armenian, Aramaic, Coptic, Ethiopic, Greek, Hebrew, Old Irish, epigraphic Northwest Semitic, Latin, Church Slavonic, and Syriac. The contents of and contributors to the second volume are not yet fixed, but it will include a comparable number of contributors who are comparably international and who translate texts from a comparable range of languages. Its publication remains at least several years away at the time of the writing of this article.

In honor of the fiftieth anniversary of the Society of Biblical Literature's Pseudepigrapha unit, this essay will discuss briefly the contribution of the More Old Testament Pseudepigrapha Project to the field of pseudepigrapha studies and the study of antiquity and the Middle Ages more generally. I will not discuss every text that has been published or is to be

---

6. For a more detailed discussion of these points, see Bauckham and Davila, "Introduction," *MOTP* 1:xxvii–xxx.

published by the project, but what is covered below is more than representative of the contents of volume 1 and what is slated for volume 2. I will label the latter texts as "forthcoming."[7]

Contributions to the Study of Judaism

Literature Cognate with the Hebrew Bible

Our first volume is unique among pseudepigrapha collections in that it includes at least one and possibly more texts that belong to the preexilic (or Iron Age IIb) period. The Balaam Text from Tell Deir ʿAllā is an inscription excavated in Jordan in 1967.[8] It was painted on plaster on the wall of a building. It dates to around 700 BCE and is written in an otherwise unknown Northwest Semitic dialect with affinities to both Hebrew and Aramaic. It tells of a vision or visions of Balaam the seer, who is known also from Num 22–24 in the Hebrew Bible. The vision speaks of the gods and describes a world in chaos and ruin.

In addition, the Hebrew Bible itself purports from time to time to quote from various written sources. I have collected these and translated them together.[9] I have also included an excursus on quotations from lost books in the New Testament.

These two chapters have perhaps been the most controversial in the volume. It has been objected that the Balaam Text is a non-Israelite work independent of the Hebrew Bible and thus does not really count as an Old Testament pseudepigraphon. Some also doubt that the quotation fragments in the other chapter are of real lost ancient books.

Neither objection is without substance. Nevertheless, the Balaam Text, as an ancient noncanonical work written in the name of a biblical figure, does fit within our definition of Old Testament pseudepigrapha. We hope that our inclusion of it will invite specialists in Northwest Semitic epigraphy, the Hebrew Bible, and the Old Testament pseudepigrapha to think of

---

7. When possible, I will note the authors of forthcoming contributions, but in some cases the final assignment of these is still in progress. Likewise, the contents of volume 2 are still not completely fixed, and it is possible that there will be a few changes to what is indicated below.

8. Edward M. Cook, "The Balaam Text from Tell Deir ʿAllā," *MOTP* 1:236–43.

9. James R. Davila, "Quotations from Lost Books in the Hebrew Bible," *MOTP* 1:673–98.

it a little differently. And the scholarly literature has made the case that the quotation fragments are of genuine ancient works. To my knowledge, this is the first time that the quotations have been collected together along with the relevant scholarly arguments. If some or all of the quotations are not genuine, those arguments need to be addressed.

Second Temple Jewish Literature

Traditionally, the driving interest behind the study of the pseudepigrapha has been to uncover new Jewish literature of the Second Temple period, especially if it is somehow relevant as background to the New Testament. We included as many Second Temple-era Jewish texts as we found, but these are relatively few, so the relevance of our corpus for these areas is somewhat more limited than earlier collections.

Nevertheless, some of the texts we do publish in this category are of considerable interest. Volume 1 included my translation of an eclectic reconstructed text of Aramaic Levi, a work known from fragmentary manuscripts from the Cairo Geniza and Qumran.[10] It tells of the foundation of the priesthood of the patriarch Levi many centuries before the traditional foundation of the Aaronid (and later Zadokite) priesthood in the time of Moses. It raises intriguing questions about competing priestly lines as late as the Second Temple period.

Other texts from roughly this period are slated for volume 2. The Book of Giants (forthcoming) tells the story of the rise and fall of the offspring of the fallen angelic watchers and mortal women. They are known also from the Enochic literature and are hinted at in Gen 6:1–4. A tentative reconstruction contains the following elements. The watchers descend from heaven, seduce mortal women, and impregnate them with the giants (one of whom is named Gilgamesh and another Humbaba, names of characters in the Epic of Gilgamesh). Two giants have revelatory dreams. The patriarch Enoch interprets them: they warn of the coming flood. In due course, after more adventures, the angels slay the giants and the flood comes.

The reconstruction of Aramaic Levi was no easy matter, but the Book of Giants offers a considerably greater challenge. The original Aramaic book is partially preserved in very fragmentary manuscripts from Qumran. But it was also adopted as scripture by the gnostic prophet Mani,

---

10. James R. Davila, "Aramaic Levi," *MOTP* 1:121–42.

and very fragmentary manuscripts of it also survive in medieval Turkic and Manichean Iranian. We plan to translate all surviving fragments of it in any language in the first attempt ever at a comprehensive reconstruction of the content and transmission of the book. Loren Stuckenbruck is translating the Qumran Aramaic manuscripts, Peter Zieme the Medieval Turkic (Uigur), and Prods Oktor Skjaervø the Manichean Iranian.

Hazon Gabriel or the Revelation of Gabriel (forthcoming, by Matthias Henze) is one of the few texts discovered after the publication of the Charlesworth volumes. It is a very difficult Hebrew work, painted on stone and arguably dating to around the turn of the era, although some specialists still believe it may be a modern forgery. It mentions the angels Gabriel and Michael and appears to involve an eschatological oracle concerning Jerusalem.

We are also publishing (forthcoming, by Sze-kar Wan) translations of a number of sermons (about Jonah, Samson, and God) preserved only in Armenian, which are transmitted in the name of Philo of Alexandria. Philo is not the author of at least most of them, but they do seem to be genuinely ancient Jewish works.

In some cases the transmission and content of pseudepigrapha leave open an origin in the Second Temple period or in late antiquity or some combination of the two. The Songs of David translated in volume 1 are Hebrew poems written in the name of David that survive in a single tenth-century CE manuscript from the Cairo Geniza.[11] Some elements in them are consistent with the Qumran literature, but others point to an origin in late antiquity. The Aramaic Song of the Lamb is an acrostic poem that survives embedded in Targumic material associated with 1–2 Samuel.[12] It recounts a dialogue between David and Goliath during their confrontation. The song may preserve material from the Second Temple period. It has intriguing parallels with Josephus, the Liber Antiquitatum Biblicarum, and the book of Revelation. But it also contains ideas that may come from considerably later. The Nine and a Half Tribes survives only in a poetic work by Commodian, but it is probably based on a Jewish text from the

---

11. Geert W. Lorein and Eveline van Staalduine-Sulman, "Songs of David," *MOTP* 1:257–71.

12. Charles T. R. Hayward, "The Aramaic Song of the Lamb (The Dialogue between David and Goliath)," *MOTP* 1:272–86.

late Second Temple period.[13] The Latin Apocalypse of Ezra (see below) may be a Jewish work as well.

Nonrabbinic Judaism of Late Antiquity

Some of the works in our corpus preserve perspectives of Jews who lived in the rabbinic period but whose interests and viewpoints were often rather different from those of the rabbis as described in the Talmudic and Midrashic literature.

Two of these are apocalypses that were composed in Hebrew, probably late in the Talmudic era. Sefer-Zerubbabel contains eschatological and messianic oracles placed in the mouth of Zerubbabel.[14] These describe the future actions of the messiahs of the line of David and the line of Joseph and give names to the antichrist and the mother of the Davidic messiah. The Hebrew Apocalypse of Elijah (forthcoming, by David Levenson) describes a series of visions seen by the prophet Elijah and revelations delivered by the angel Michael. The text of both these works varies substantially in the manuscripts.

Another nonrabbinic Jewish work is Sefer HaRazim or The Book of the Mysteries (forthcoming, by myself). It is a magical tractate, a type of literature popular in late antiquity. It was composed in Hebrew and dates from the Talmudic era. It purports to record revelations vouchsafed to Noah by the angel Raziel and then transmitted eventually to Solomon. It gives instructions on how a magician may invoke the various angels of the seven firmaments to work the magician's will in matters of finance, the heart, and influence with important people; to heal various illnesses and infirmities; to harm the magician's rivals, creditors, and enemies; and to obtain revelations from the heavenly bodies and the dead. Although it is a monotheistic Jewish work, it shows considerable influence from traditional polytheistic magical literature known best to us from the Greco-Egyptian Greek magical papyri. Indeed, it goes so far as to invoke the pagan god Hermes in a necromantic incantation.

The Sword of Moses (Harba di-Moshe) (forthcoming, by Yuval Harari) again dates to roughly the Talmudic era, but it is a collection of magical traditions supposedly revealed to Moses. It consists of an opening Hebrew

---

13. Richard Bauckham, "The Nine and a Half Tribes," *MOTP* 1:346–59.
14. John C. Reeves, "*Sefer-Zerubbabel*: The Prophetic Vision of Zerubbabel ben Shealtiel," *MOTP* 1:448–66.

section of preparatory rituals, a middle section giving the divine names and *nomina barbara* that constitute the Sword of Moses proper, and a concluding Aramaic section that gives instructions for the use of these names for numerous specific purposes.

Jewish Reception of Traditions from Jewish Pseudepigrapha

We are including a number of Jewish works or passages from Jewish works that clearly date from the Middle Ages or perhaps even later. Some of these texts give good indication of transmitting otherwise lost or highly fragmentary material from the Second Temple period. Others show intriguing connections with such early material that deserve further exploration.

The medieval Hebrew Book of Asaph quotes a passage from The Book of Noah, which is similar to a reference to the Book of Noah in Jub. 10.1-4.[15] But there are some indications that Asaph draws on the source used by Jubilees rather than the passage in Jubilees itself. Another medieval work, Midrash Vayissa'u, tells the story of how Jacob and his sons fought wars with the Ninevites, the Amorites, and Esau and his sons.[16] These stories are not found in the Bible, but versions of the wars with the Amorites and with Esau and his sons appear in the book of Jubilees and the Greek Testament of Judah. The content of Midrash Vayissa'u does not seem simply to be a combination of the accounts in Jubilees and the Testament of Judah. Rather, it may be a retelling in medieval Hebrew of a Greek translation of the ancient source used by Jubilees.

The Treatise of the Vessels (Maasekhet Kelim—not to be confused with the Mishanic tractate) is a remarkable document, in terms both of its content and its preservation.[17] It purports to record the locations of the various treasures of Solomon's temple, which were hidden by Levites and prophets before the temple was destroyed by the Babylonians. It is a mixture of rabbinic-style exegesis of various biblical texts and ancient legends known in various forms from elsewhere. It also has parallels to the Qumran Copper Scroll, which may record the locations of hidden treasures from the second temple. One recension of the Treatise of the Vessels even relates that its contents were written down on a tablet of bronze. Its

---

15. Martha Himmelfarb, "The Book of Noah," *MOTP* 1:40-46.
16. Martha Himmelfarb, "*Midrash Vayissa'u*," *MOTP* 1:143-59.
17. James R. Davila, "The Treatise of the Vessels (*Maasekhet Kelim*)," *MOTP* 1:393-409.

date is uncertain. It is clearly no earlier than the Talmudic era, but our earliest source for it is a printed version from the seventeenth century. It also survived inscribed on a set of marble plaques, again, of uncertain date. These seem to have been associated with a similar set of plaques on which the entire book of Ezekiel is inscribed. The Ezekiel plaques are now on display at the Yad Ben Zvi Institute in Jerusalem. The plaques containing the Treatise of the Vessels were transcribed by J. T. Milik in Beirut, but their current whereabouts are unknown.

In the late nineteenth century, Moses Gaster collected a group of medieval texts in Hebrew and Aramaic that describe the postmortem punishments of the wicked and the rewards of the righteous. These have been retranslated in our first volume.[18] These nine texts include descriptions of otherworldly journeys of Moses to gehinnom (hell), the garden of Eden, and the throne room of God; a similar journey of Rabbi Yehoshua ben Levi; an apocalypse in which Rabbi Ishmael sees visions of the future glory of Israel and King David; and various traditions about the cosmography of gehinnom and the garden of Eden. These texts contain many parallels with earlier Jewish and Christian apocalypses that transmit material about the fate of the dead and the layout of heaven and hell.

The Midrash of Shemihazai and Aza'el (forthcoming) is a medieval Hebrew account in several versions of the rise of the watchers and the genesis and fall of the giants. It has some connection with the Book of Giants. The two angels named in the title are central to the giants tradition. As in the Book of Giants they descend from heaven and become sexually involved with mortal women. Their children, the giants, have revelatory dreams that predict the coming of the flood and the destruction of the giants and the human race apart from Noah and his sons. The giants are killed in the flood. Shemihazai repents and suspends himself upside down between heaven and earth. Aza'el refuses to repent and becomes a demon who entices human beings to corrupt deeds and who bears the sins of Israel on the Day of Atonement (cf. Lev 16:7–10).

Hebrew Naphtali (forthcoming, by Vered Hillel) is a medieval story about the patriarch Naphtali that survives embedded in the Chronicles of Jerahmeel. It has a close relationship of some sort to the Greek Testament of Naphtali, and they both seem to have developed from a common archetype from the Second Temple period. A fragment of this archetype,

---

18. Helen Spurling, "Hebrew Visions of Hell and Paradise," *MOTP* 1:699–753.

or something closely related, survives in 4Q215, a Qumran fragment in Hebrew which gives the genealogy of Bilhah. The eleventh-century author R. Moses the Preacher of Narbonne cites Naphtali material in Hebrew that also seems to stem ultimately from this lost work. All of these Hebrew sources will be included under the title Hebrew Naphtali.

Contributions to the Study of Christianity

Nonpatristic Christianity in Late Antiquity

None of the Christian works in our corpus go back to the period of the New Testament. But many of them preserve perspectives of Christians who lived in late antiquity, but whose interests and viewpoints were rather different from those of many of the patristic writers who were their contemporaries. These late-antique Christian works survive in many languages and contain a wide range of genres and interests.

We are reprinting a Coptic Enoch Apocryphon (forthcoming, by Birger A. Pearson). It features an angelic revelation to Enoch on a mountain, followed by an encounter between Enoch and his virgin sister, Tabitha. It develops that she is actually the sibyl, and she reveals to Enoch that both of them and the prophet Elijah will be assumed bodily into heaven.

The Story of Melchizedek is a Greek composition that was very popular and was translated into many languages.[19] It is a creative account of the life story of Melchizedek leading up to the time of his encounter with Abraham in the book of Genesis. As an appendix to this chapter we have also published a translation of a treatise on Melchizedek from the Chronicon Paschale. It traces Melchizedek's origin to "the tribe of Ham," from which God removed him to Canaan. It also describes his meeting with Abraham.

The Syriac History of Joseph is a retelling of the biblical Joseph story.[20] It was likely composed in Syriac in a Christian context. Its narrative expansions also show considerable awareness of Jewish traditions, as is not unusual for Syriac literature of late antiquity. The Ethiopic translation of

---

19. Pierluigi Piovanelli, "The Story of Melchizedek, with the Melchizedek Legend from the *Chronicon Paschale*," *MOTP* 1:64–84.

20. Kristian S. Heal, "The Syriac History of Joseph," *MOTP* 1:85–120.

this work had already been translated into English by Ephraim Isaac,[21] but this is the first English translation of the complete Syriac text.

We continue the tradition of including the pseudepigraphic works of traditional polytheistic prophets and sages who were adopted, so to speak, into the biblical tradition by Christians and Jews in antiquity. Such figures include the sibyls, Ahiqar, Zoroaster, and (see below) Hystaspes. The Tiburtine Sibyl is an apocalypse that was composed in Greek in the fourth century.[22] This early Greek version has not survived, but there is a Latin translation of it.[23] We have published a translation of a longer Greek recension dating to the sixth century. This work presents the Tiburtine Sibyl as interpreting a revelatory dream granted to one hundred Roman judges. She explains it as a series of *ex eventu* prophecies that begin roughly at the time of Alexander the Great, focus heavily on Jesus, describe a series of Roman and Byzantine emperors, and leave the reader expecting the eschatological battle sometime in the sixth century.

The Sibylla Maga (The Witch Sibyl; forthcoming, by Johannes Magliano-Tromp) is a Latin poem in which the sibyl warns humanity of the coming final judgment. It is an explicitly Christian work.

The Questions of the Queen of Sheba and Answers by King Solomon fills out the biblical story of the visit of the Queen to Solomon with a dialogue in which she asks him a series of scientific and theological questions and some riddles, which he answers wisely. We include a new translation of an Armenian version of this work, and we reprint a translation of a Syriac version.[24]

The fragment known as Jeremiah's Prophecy to Pashhur survives in Coptic, Ethiopic, and Arabic and still appears in the Coptic and Ethiopic liturgies today.[25] It indirectly addresses the notorious difficulty in Matt 27:9-10, which quotes a passage from Zechariah but attributes it to Jeremiah. Jeremiah's Prophecy to Pashhur solves the problem by providing

---

21. Ephraim Isaac, "The Ethiopic History of Joseph," *JSP* 6 (1990): 3-125.
22. Rieuwerd Buitenwerf, "The Tiburtine Sibyl (Greek)," *MOTP* 1:176-88.
23. This Latin version has been translated into English by Stephen J. Shoemaker, "The Tiburtine Sibyl," *MNTA* 1:510-25. It can reasonably be classed as a New Testament apocryphon as well as an Old Testament pseudepigraphon.
24. Vahan S. Hovhanessian, "Questions of the Queen of Sheba and Answers by King Solomon," *MOTP* 1:326-42 (Armenian version); Sebastian Brock, "The Queen of Sheba's Questions to Solomon," *MOTP* 1:343-45 (Syriac version).
25. Darrell D. Hannah, "Jeremiah's Prophecy to Pashhur," *MOTP* 1:367-79.

an apocryphal oracle of Jeremiah that contains the text quoted in Matthew. At the end of the fourth century, Jerome knew a Hebrew Apocryphon of Jeremiah that contained this passage as well, and there is a good case that our surviving text is a translated fragment of the document Jerome knew, a work that he tells us originated from the Jewish-Christian Nazoraean sect. If so, we have in Jeremiah's Prophecy to Pashhur a precious fragment of scriptural exegesis and storytelling from an early Jewish-Christian movement whose literature is otherwise virtually entirely lost.

There is a vast pseudepigraphic literature in the name of the biblical figure Daniel. We are including the works that can reasonably be dated no later than the early seventh century CE. The Seventh Vision of Daniel gives an *ex eventu* review of Byzantine history to the late fifth century, then culminates in the coming of the antichrist, the destruction of the world, and the final judgment.[26] It was composed in Greek but survives only in an Armenian translation. The Syriac Apocalypse of Daniel (forthcoming, by Matthias Henze) was composed in Syriac in the first half of the seventh century CE. It is presented as a first-person account by Daniel. In the first part, he relates some of his own adventures not found in the canonical version of Daniel. In the second part, he describes his vision of the end times. There will be various eschatological woes, followed by the earthly paradise, the resurrection of the dead, the coming of the messiah, and his enthronement in the New Jerusalem. The Danielic pseudepigraphon paraphrased by Papias is mentioned below.

A number of Greek Danielic pseudepigrapha (forthcoming, by Lorenzo DiTommaso) will be translated in the second volume. These include two apocalypses (at least by Byzantine-era standards, when the parameters of the genre were broader than in the earlier period), and some oracular works or *prognostica*. The latter include the Somnalia Danielis (dream-interpretations manuals) and Lunationes Danielis (with prognostications based on the movements or appearance of the moon). The *prognostica* were composed in Greek but now survive mostly in Latin translation.[27]

In our first volume, we have published a number of pseudepigrapha that circulated in Latin in the name of Ezra in late antiquity. Fifth Ezra (2 Esd 1–2) is a Christian oracular composition that may originally have

---

26. Sergio La Porta, "The Seventh Vision of Daniel," *MOTP* 1:410–34.

27. See Lorenzo DiTommaso, *The Book of Daniel and the Apocryphal Daniel Literature*, SVTP 20 (Leiden: Brill, 2005), esp. 87–307.

been written in Greek.[28] Sixth Ezra (2 Esd 15–16) is a similar work that survives in a complete Latin version and also in a Greek fragment that may reflect its original language.[29] Both works have been transmitted, respectively, as a prologue and epilogue to the Latin translation of the Jewish apocalypse 4 Ezra, although they clearly were not composed as part of it and they may not originally have been attributed to Ezra. Both were translated in the first Charlesworth volume as part of 4 Ezra.[30] We felt they were worth treating as compositions in their own right and have accordingly given each a chapter in our first volume.

A Greek Apocalypse of Ezra was also published in the Charlesworth and Sparks collections.[31] Shortly after the translation in the first Charlesworth volume came out, a manuscript containing a Latin version of a longer recension of the work was published.[32] It has since become clear that this long recension preserves the earliest surviving version of the work. The shorter Latin recensions are abbreviations of it and the Greek work used its (now lost) Greek original freely as its main source.[33] Accordingly, we have published a translation of the long Latin recension as The Latin Vision of Ezra.[34] It may be a Jewish composition although it and the works based on it only survive in Christian contexts. In it, Ezra the prophet is given a thorough tour of hell and a briefer tour of paradise. Ezra then intercedes with God for sinners, negotiates the terms of his own death with the angel Michael, and surrenders his soul to death. The work shows familiarity with the Jewish apocalypse 4 Ezra.

Christian Reception of Pseudepigrapha Traditions

Two longer works are of considerable interest as repositories of earlier pseudepigraphic and other traditions, now edited into Christian nar-

---

28. Theodore A. Bergren, "Fifth Ezra," *MOTP* 1:467–82.
29. Theodore A. Bergren, "Sixth Ezra," *MOTP* 1:483–97.
30. Bruce M. Metzger, "The Fourth Book of Ezra," *OTP* 1:517–59.
31. Michael E. Stone, "Greek Apocalypse of Ezra," *OTP* 1:561–79; Karl H. Kuhn, "The Apocalypse of Esdras," *AOT* 927–41.
32. Pierre-Maurice Bogaert, "Une version longue inédite de la 'Visio Beati Esdrae; dans le légendier de Teano (Barberini Lat. 2318)," *RBén* 94 (1984): 50–70.
33. Translations of the short Latin version were published by James R. Mueller and Gregory Allen Robbins as "Vision of Ezra," *OTP* 1:581–90, and by R. J. H. Shutt as "The Vision of Esdras," *AOT* 943–51.
34. Richard Bauckham, "The Latin Vision of Ezra," *MOTP* 1:498–528.

ratives. The Cave of Treasures survives in complete Syriac versions and fragments of a Coptic one.[35] It was composed in Syriac in the early seventh century. It is a retelling of the biblical narrative that begins with the six days of creation and ends with the resurrection of Christ and the coming of the Holy Spirit upon the apostles. It draws on earlier material including the Testament of Adam and rabbinic midrashic traditions—the latter mediated primarily through the works of Ephrem and Aphraat.

The Palaea Historica is a Byzantine Greek composition from the ninth century or later that retells the Old Testament story from creation to King David, along with material about Isaiah and King Uzziah, a garbled version of the story of Tobit ("Bit"), and material from the apocryphal additions to Daniel.[36] It includes a version of the Story of Melchizedek mentioned above and draws on a great deal of earlier Jewish and Christian biblical legend.

Other Contributions

Magical Traditions

Our collection includes a number of pseudepigrapha that are devoted to magical traditions. Such works are comparatively scarce in earlier pseudepigrapha collections, but they represent a subject of considerable interest in antiquity and late antiquity to Jews, Christians, and others. I have already mentioned the Jewish works Sefer HaRazim and Harba di-Moshe above. The Christian exorcistic text The Testament of Solomon is noted below. In addition we have published some collected Jewish and Christian exorcistic psalms of David and Solomon.[37] These include the incantations associated with David in 11Q11 (11QApocryphal Psalms); a hymn from Pseudo-Philo's *Biblical Antiquities*, also attributed to David; excerpted exorcistic hymns of David and Solomon from two amulets; and another hymn of David found in a Babylonian incantation bowl.

Aside from these works, whose provenance is clear, we are publishing a number of magical texts that draw on Jewish, traditional polytheistic, and sometimes Christian traditions.

---

35. Alexander Toepel, "The Cave of Treasures," *MOTP* 1:531–84.

36. William Adler, "*Palaea Historica* ('The Old Testament History')," *MOTP* 1:585–672.

37. Gideon Bohak, "Exorcistic Psalms of David and Solomon," *MOTP* 1:287–97.

The Selendromion of David and Solomon ties a traditional astrological genre that connects biblical personages and events to the fate of an individual on each day of a lunar month.[38] It is preserved in late-antique Koine Greek in medieval and early modern Christian manuscripts, but its content resembles an adaptation of traditional polytheistic traditions to a Jewish setting. The Hygromancy of Solomon, another late-antique work in Koine Greek, alludes briefly to the subject matter of the title, divination by means of water, but the rest of the work is a collection of astrological instruction containing a mixture of Jewish, Christian, and traditional polytheistic traditions.[39]

The Phylactery of Moses (forthcoming, by Roy Kotansky) is a late-antique copper lamella inscribed in Greek which claims to give the text of the protective amulet that Moses carried when he ascended Mount Sinai. It is aware of Jewish traditions, but its provenance is uncertain.

We have also included a traditional polytheistic (Greco-Egyptian) work that draws on Jewish and perhaps Christian traditions. The Eighth Book of Moses[40] survives in a single fourth-century Greek manuscript, one of those generally classed as Greek Magical Papyri. It preserves two somewhat variant sets of instructions for a ritual for experiencing a revelatory meeting with a god. We hope that including it in our collection as an Old Testament pseudepigraphon will help scholars think about it in a new way.

New Manuscript Material

As noted above, in general we have not republished texts already translated in the Charlesworth or Sparks collections unless we think they needed a fuller treatment (such as with 5–6 Ezra above) or we had access to new manuscript material for a text. The (Greek and Latin) Life of Adam and Eve/Apocalypse of Moses and the (Greek) Testament of Job were well covered in the Charlesworth and Sparks collections, but we have published fragmentary Coptic manuscripts of both.[41] The Coptic material for the

---

38. Pablo A. Torijano, "The Selendromion of David and Solomon," *MOTP* 1:298–304.

39. Pablo A. Torijano, "The Hygromancy of Solomon," *MOTP* 1:305–25.

40. Todd E. Klutz, "The Eighth Book of Moses," *MOTP* 1:189–235.

41. M. D. Johnson, "Life of Adam and Eve," *OTP* 2:249–95; Rudolph P. Spittler, "Testament of Job," *OTP* 1:829–68; L. S. A. Wells, revised by M. Whittaker, "The Life

Testament of Job is substantial. In both cases the Sahidic Coptic fragments (which are translations of the original Greek) seem to be the earliest manuscript attestations of the work. We also published new material associated with the fragmentary text the Apocryphon of Ezekiel.[42]

A translation of Chester Charlton McCown's eclectic Greek text of the Testament of Solomon was published in both the Charlesworth and the Sparks collections,[43] but we believe the earliest manuscript of this work is worthy of a treatment of its own. The so-called Vienna Papyrus is a fragmentary fifth- or sixth-century manuscript that seems to have been a scroll containing the material on the thirty-six decans (deities ruling the zodiac) of T. Sol. 18 redacted into a form somewhat differently organized than in the Testament of Solomon.[44] Dennis C. Duling has advanced redactional considerations to argue for this manuscript being an excerpt from the larger work rather than an independent source later incorporated into the Testament of Solomon. We shall publish a translation of the Vienna Papyrus in volume 2 (by Todd E. Klutz).

We shall also be translating new material from Jannes and Jambres in Greek and in an Ethiopic translation, as well as closely related new material in Coptic.[45]

Quotations and Fragments of Lost Works

Numerous fragments of lost ancient pseudepigrapha appear to survive in quotations in later works, sometimes supplemented with what appear to

---

of Adam and Eve," *AOT* 141–67; R. Thornhill, "The Testament of Job," *AOT* 617–48; Simon J. Gathercole, "The Life of Adam and Eve (Coptic Fragments)," *MOTP* 1:22–27; Gesa Schenke, "The Testament of Job (Coptic Fragments)," *MOTP* 1:160–75.

42. James R. Mueller and Stephen E. Robinson, "Apocryphon of Ezekiel," *OTP* 1:487–95; Benjamin G. Wright III, "The Apocryphon of Ezekiel," *MOTP* 1: 380–92.

43. Dennis C. Duling, "Testament of Solomon," *OTP* 1:935–87; John A. Emerton, "The Testament of Solomon," *AOT* 733–51.

44. Cf. Duling, "Testament of Solomon," 937 and n. 3. For further discussion see Dennis C. Duling, "The Testament of Solomon: Retrospect and Prospect," *JSP* 2 (1988): 87–112, esp. 91–96; Todd E. Klutz, *Rewriting the Testament of Solomon: Tradition, Conflict and Identity in a Late Antique Pseudepigraphon*, LSTS 53 (London: T&T Clark, 2005), 19–27.

45. Our translations in volume 2 will supplement Albert Pietersma and R. T. Lutz, "Jannes and Jambres," *OTP* 2:427–42. The Ethiopic material will be translated by Ted Erho and the Coptic material by Frederic Krueger.

be fragments of actual manuscripts of such works. We include the surviving fragments of a number of them. I have already mentioned lost books quoted in the Hebrew Bible, the Book of Noah, and the fragments of the Apocryphon of Ezekiel. Volume 1 also included chapters on Adam Octipartite/Septipartite (which survives complete in multiple recensions, but only embedded in other works), the Book of the Covenant, the Apocryphon of Seth, the Apocryphon of Eber, the Dispute over Abraham, the Inquiry of Abraham, Eldad and Modad, the Nine and a Half Tribes (see above), and A Danielic Pseudepigraphon Paraphrased by Papias.[46] In some cases there is doubt whether the proposed document ever existed as a separate work,[47] but we decided to include the texts for which we thought a reasonable case could be made. Volume 2 will include chapters on the surviving fragments of the Testament and Assumption of Moses, the (Greek) Apocalypse of Elijah (both by Richard Bauckham), the Book of Baruch by Justin the Gnostic (by Todd E. Klutz), and the apocalypses quoted in the Life of Mani (by John Reeves). It will also include (by Liv Ingeborg Lied and Matthew P. Monger) a chapter on Old Testament pseudepigrapha known only by title.

One chapter (forthcoming, by Vicente Dobroruka and Robert A. Kraft) collects the quotation fragments of the elusive Oracle of Hystaspes. Hystaspes is a royal figure associated with Zoroaster in Persian tradition and treated as a prophetic figure in ancient Christian tradition. The main sources for the Oracle of Hystaspes were probably composed early in the Common Era, but their provenance is uncertain and perhaps a complex mixture. It is unlikely that these quotations come from a single work.

---

46. Grant Macaskill with Eamon Greenwood, "Adam Octipartite/Septipartite," *MOTP* 1:3–21; James VanderKam, "The Book of the Covenant," *MOTP* 1:28–32; Alexander Toepel, "The Apocryphon of Seth," *MOTP* 1:33–39; James VanderKam, "The Apocryphon of Eber," *MOTP* 1:47–52; Richard Bauckham, "The Dispute over Abraham," *MOTP* 1:53–58; Bauckham, "The Inquiry of Abraham (A Possible Allusion to the Apocalypse of Abraham)," *MOTP* 1:59–63; Bauckham, "Eldad and Modad," *MOTP* 1:244–56; and Basil Lourié, "A Danielic Pseudepigraphon Paraphrased by Papias," *MOTP* 1:435–41. The Apocryphon of Seth seems to be a summary of a longer work on the Magi found embedded in the Syriac Chronicle of Zuqnin. See Brent Landau, "The Revelation of the Magi: A Summary and Introduction," *MNTA* 1:19–38.

47. Liv Ingeborg Lied, "Text—Work—Manuscript: What Is an 'Old Testament Pseudepigraphon'?," *JSP* 25 (2015): 159–65.

Conclusion: Reflections on the Contributions of the More Old Testament Pseudepigrapha Project

In our earlier planning of the More Old Testament Pseudepigrapha Project we did not set out very specific objectives for the use of the texts we intended to translate and publish. Our agenda was, first, to make these works widely available, in reliable translations with up-to-date introductions, to scholars and students working in the various fields to which they are relevant. This was to serve as a catalyst for much future scholarship and also to provide a rich resource for students, as well as to become a standard work of reference. We aimed, second, to offer the translations and introductions in a form that would be accessible to interested specialists in cognate fields as well as interested nonspecialists.

At the time of this writing, the first volume has been out for just over four years, and it is too early to get a clear picture of how it will be used over time. Anecdotally, I am aware of it being used in teaching at the university level and by lay readers. I am also aware of publications in progress that will cite it.[48] The More Old Testament Pseudepigrapha Project has already served as a direct inspiration for the undertaking of a parallel project in a cognate field. The More New Testament Apocrypha Project, headed by Tony Burke of York University and Brent Landau of the University of Texas at Austin, aims to produce two volumes of translations of and introductions to New Testament apocrypha as a supplement to the collection published by J. K. Elliott in the early 1990s.[49] Their project is patterned after the template of ours and shares many of its aims and objectives. It has so far produced an excellent volume of

---

48. Two of the editors have published articles on material published in volume 1: Richard Bauckham, "Apocalypses and Prophetic Works in Volume 1 of the New Pseudepigrapha," *Early Christianity* 5 (2014): 127–38; James R. Davila, "Scriptural Exegesis in the Treatise of the Vessels, a Legendary Account of the Hiding of the Temple Treasures," in *With Letters of Light: Studies in the Dead Sea Scrolls, Early Jewish Apocalypticism, Magic, and Mysticism in Honor of Rachel Elior*, ed. Daphna Arbel and Andrei Orlov, Ekstasis 2 (Berlin: de Gruyter, 2011), 45–61; and Davila, "Seven Theses Concerning the Use of Scripture in *4 Ezra* and the *Latin Vision of Ezra*," in *Old Testament Pseudepigrapha and the Scriptures*, ed. Eibert Tigchelaar, BETL 270 (Leuven: Peeters, 2014), 305–26. See also n. 47 above.

49. J. K. Elliott, *The Apocryphal New Testament: A Collection of Apocryphal Christian Literature in an English Translation* (Oxford: Clarendon, 1993).

texts,⁵⁰ and we look forward to the publication of their second volume in due course.

I shall close with some comments on how the More Old Testament Pseudepigrapha Project has received attention from the media and non-specialist readers. In January of 2014 *Live Science* published an online article about one of the texts translated in volume 1: The Treatise of the Vessels, discussed above.⁵¹ Despite the somewhat sensationalistic title, the article was a well-written and sober summary of my chapter on the work in volume 1. Doubtless because of the connection with the ark of the covenant, the article was widely noticed and was reprinted by *Yahoo News*, *Fox News*, *Discovery*, and *NBC News*. This led to a couple of phone interviews with journalists, resulting in an article in the *Daily Mail*.⁵² Again, the article accurately presented the text as entirely legendary and important only for its preservation of interesting Jewish legends about the ark and for its similarities to the Copper Scroll. Nevertheless, within the next week I received various letters and phone calls from people who had read the *Daily Mail* article and who were keen to tell me about their "research" that had uncovered the true hiding place of the ark. I even had one visitor to my office who informed me that the ark was located in St. Andrews and disclosed its hiding place to me. I shall not reveal that information here. Such communications continued to trickle in for the next year or so. I still get them occasionally.

Now, on the one hand, this sort of attention is exactly what we do not want for our research. It was disappointing that some people were so locked into their Indiana Jones framework that they failed to get the point that legends about the ark are not a good source of historical information. But, on the other hand, I think that overall the media attention had a more positive result. We should not ignore the teaching moment it provided. The people who contacted me were generally a small minority whose hobby or avocation was the recovery of the location of the ark of the covenant. The vast majority of the readers of the popular articles would

---

50. Tony Burke and Brent Landau, eds., *New Testament Apocrypha: More Noncanonical Scriptures* (Grand Rapids: Eerdmans, 2016).

51. Owen Jarus, "Fate of Ark of the Covenant Revealed in Hebrew Text," *Live Science*, 7 January 2014, https://tinyurl.com/SBL3550f.

52. Ellie Zolfagharifard, "King Solomon's Treasures Revealed: Newly Translated Hebrew Text Lists Legendary Riches—Including the Ark of the Covenant," *Daily Mail*, 9 January 2014, https://tinyurl.com/SBL3550g.

not have fallen into that category. True, they too would have come to the story with an Indiana Jones level of understanding of the ark legend. But at the very least they would have come away with the realization that the ark story was as entertaining to people in the past as it to us and that those people were making up diverting legends about it long before *Raiders of the Lost Ark*. One hopes that that understanding would inoculate them with some healthy skepticism toward the next biblical conspiracy theory they encounter.

To conclude, our project has widened the corpus of pseudepigrapha with new texts within a slightly wider explicit chronological horizon. We include some Second Temple Jewish texts, but our focus is broader than this. Accordingly, we anticipate that these volumes will be of less interest for background material to the New Testament than earlier collections. We anticipate that our volumes will be of considerable interest for the study of the exegesis of scripture and theological reflection in ancient Judaism and ancient Christianity outside the established corpora of rabbinic and patristic literature. Some of the material is useful for our understanding of late antique magic and mysticism. Some of it is also important for our knowledge of early medieval reception of apocryphal scriptural traditions. And it is clear that lay readers are receiving the publications with enthusiasm and, one hopes, coming away with at least a slightly better understanding of the importance of the Old Testament pseudepigrapha in the history of the Western religious tradition.

Bibliography

Adler, William. "*Palaea Historica* ('The Old Testament History')." *MOTP* 1:585–672.

Bauckham, Richard. "Apocalypses and Prophetic Works in Volume 1 of the New Pseudepigrapha." *Early Christianity* 5 (2014): 127–38.

———. "The Dispute over Abraham." *MOTP* 1:53–58.

———. "Eldad and Modad," *MOTP* 1:244–56,

———. "The Inquiry of Abraham (A Possible Allusion to the Apocalypse of Abraham)." *MOTP* 1:59–63.

———. "The Latin Vision of Ezra." *MOTP* 1:498–528.

———. "The Nine and a Half Tribes." *MOTP* 1:346–59.

Bauckham, Richard, and James R. Davila. "Introduction." *MOTP* 1:xvii–xxxviii.

Bauckam, Richard, James R. Davila, and Alexander Panayotov, eds. *Old Testament Pseudepigrapha: More Noncanonical Scriptures*. Vol. 1. Grand Rapids: Eerdmans, 2013.

Bergren, Theodore A. "Fifth Ezra." *MOTP* 1:467–82.

———. "Sixth Ezra." *MOTP* 1:483–97.

Bogaert, Pierre-Maurice. "Une version longue inédite de la 'Visio Beati Esdrae; dans le légendier de Teano (Barberini Lat. 2318)." *Rbén* 94 (1984): 50–70.

Bohak, Gideon. "Exorcistic Psalms of David and Solomon." *MOTP* 1:287–97.

Brock, Sebastian P. "The Queen of Sheba's Questions to Solomon." *MOTP* 1:343–45.

Buitenwerf, Rieuwerd. "The Tiburtine Sibyl (Greek)." *MOTP* 1:176–88.

Burke, Tony, and Brent Landau, eds. *New Testament Apocrypha: More Noncanonical Scriptures*. Grand Rapids: Eerdmans, 2016.

Charles, R. H., ed. *The Apocrypha and Pseudepigrapha of the Old Testament in English: With Introductions and Critical and Explanatory Notes to the Several Books*. 2 vols. Oxford: Clarendon, 1913.

Charlesworth, James H., ed. *Old Testament Pseudepigrapha*. 2 vols. New York: Doubleday, 1983–1985.

Cook, Edward M. "The Balaam Text from Tell Deir 'Allā." *MOTP* 1:236–43.

Davila, James R. "Aramaic Levi." *MOTP* 1:121–42.

———. "Quotations from Lost Books in the Hebrew Bible." *MOTP* 1:673–98.

———. "Scriptural Exegesis in the Treatise of the Vessels, a Legendary Account of the Hiding of the Temple Treasures." Pages 45–61 in *With Letters of Light: Studies in the Dead Sea Scrolls, Early Jewish Apocalypticism, Magic, and Mysticism in Honor of Rachel Elior*. Edited by Daphna Arbel and Andrei Orlov. Ekstasis 2. Berlin: de Gruyter, 2011.

———. "Seven Theses Concerning the Use of Scripture in *4 Ezra* and the Latin Vision of Ezra." Pages 305–26 in *Old Testament Pseudepigrapha and the Scriptures*. Edited by Eibert Tigchelaar. BETL 270. Leuven: Peeters, 2014.

———. "The Treatise of the Vessels (*Maasekhet Kelim*)." *MOTP* 1:393–409.

DiTommaso, Lorenzo. *The Book of Daniel and the Apocryphal Daniel Literature*. SVTP 20. Leiden: Brill, 2005.

Duling, Dennis C. "Testament of Solomon." *OTP* 1:935–87.

———. "The Testament of Solomon: Retrospect and Prospect." *JSP* 2 (1988): 87–112.

Elliott, J. K. *The Apocryphal New Testament: A Collection of Apocryphal Christian Literature in an English Translation*. Oxford: Clarendon, 1993.

Emerton, John A. "The Testament of Solomon." *AOT* 733–51.

Fabricius, Johann Albert. *Codex Pseudepigraphus Veteris Testamenti*. Hamburg: Lieberzeit, 1713.

Gathercole, Simon J. "The Life of Adam and Eve (Coptic Fragments)." *MOTP* 1:22–27.

Hannah, Darrell D. "Jeremiah's Prophecy to Pashhur." *MOTP* 1:367–79.

Hayward, Charles T. R. "The Aramaic Song of the Lamb (The Dialogue between David and Goliath)." *MOTP* 1:272–86.

Heal, Kristian S. "The Syriac History of Joseph." *MOTP* 1:85–120.

Himmelfarb, Martha. "The Book of Noah." *MOTP* 1:40–46.

———. "*Midrash Vayissaʻu*." *MOTP* 1:143–59.

Hovhanessian, Vahan S. "Questions of the Queen of Sheba and Answers by King Solomon." *MOTP* 1:326–42.

Isaac, Ephraim. "The Ethiopic History of Joseph." *JSP* 6 (1990): 3–125.

Jarus, Owen. "Fate of Ark of the Covenant Revealed in Hebrew Text." *Live Science*. 7 January 2014. https://tinyurl.com/SBL3550f.

Johnson, M. D. "Life of Adam and Eve." *OTP* 2:249–95.

Klutz, Todd E. "The Eighth Book of Moses." *MOTP* 1:189–235.

———. *Rewriting the Testament of Solomon: Tradition, Conflict and Identity in a Late Antique Pseudepigraphon*. LSTS 53. London: T&T Clark, 2005.

Kuhn, Karl H. "The Apocalypse of Esdras." *AOT* 927–41.

La Porta, Sergio. "The Seventh Vision of Daniel." *MOTP* 1:410–34.

Landau, Brent. "The Revelation of the Magi: A Summary and Introduction." *MNTA* 1:19–38.

Lied, Liv Ingeborg. "Text—Work—Manuscript: What Is an 'Old Testament Pseudepigraphon'?" *JSP* 25 (2015): 159–65.

Lorein, Geert W., and Eveline van Staalduine-Sulman. "Songs of David." *MOTP* 1:257–71.

Lourié, Basil. "A Danielic Pseudepigraphon Paraphrased by Papias." *MOTP* 1:435–41.

Macaskill, Grant, with Eamon Greenwood. "Adam Octipartite/Septipartite." *MOTP* 1:3–21.

Metzger, Bruce M. "The Fourth Book of Ezra." *OTP* 1:517–59.

Mueller, James R., and Gregory Allen Robbins. "Vision of Ezra." *OTP* 1:581–90.

Mueller, James R., and Stephen E. Robinson. "Apocryphon of Ezekiel." *OTP* 1:487–95.
Najman, Hindy. Review of *Old Testament Pseudepigrapha: More Noncanonical Scriptures*, vol. 1, by Richard Bauckam, James R. Davila, and Alexander Panayotov. *DSD* 22 (2015): 211–14.
Pietersma, Albert, and R. T. Lutz. "Jannes and Jambres." *OTP* 2:427–42.
Piovanelli, Pierluigi. "The Story of Melchizedek, with the Melchizedek Legend from the *Chronicon Paschale*." *MOTP* 1:64–84.
Reeves, John C. "*Sefer-Zerubbabel*: The Prophetic Vision of Zerubbabel ben Shealtiel." *MOTP* 1:448–66.
Schenke, Gesa. "The Testament of Job (Coptic Fragments)." *MOTP* 1:160–75.
Shoemaker, Stephen J. "The Tiburtine Sibyl." *MNTA* 1:510–25.
Shutt, R. J. H. "The Vision of Esdras." *AOT* 943–51.
Sparks, Hedley F. D. *The Apocryphal Old Testament*. Oxford: Clarendon, 1984.
Spittler, Rudolph P. "Testament of Job." *OTP* 1:829–68.
Spurling, Helen. "Hebrew Visions of Hell and Paradise." *MOTP* 1:699–753.
Stone, Michael E. "Greek Apocalypse of Ezra." *OTP* 1:561–79.
Thornhill, R. "The Testament of Job." *AOT* 617–48.
Toepel, Alexander. "The Apocryphon of Seth." *MOTP* 1:33–39.
———. "The Cave of Treasures." *MOTP* 1:531–84.
Torijano, Pablo A. "The Hygromancy of Solomon." *MOTP* 1:305–25.
———. "The Selendromion of David and Solomon." *MOTP* 1:298–304.
VanderKam, James. "The Apocryphon of Eber." *MOTP* 1:47–52.
———. "Book of the Covenant." *MOTP* 1:28–32.
Wells, L. S. A., revised by M. Whittaker, "The Life of Adam and Eve." *AOT* 141–67.
Wright, Benjamin G., III. "The Apocryphon of Ezekiel." *MOTP* 1: 380–92.
Zolfagharifard, Ellie. "King Solomon's Treasures Revealed: Newly Translated Hebrew Text Lists Legendary Riches—Including the Ark of the Covenant." *Daily Mail*. 9 January 2014. https://tinyurl.com/SBL3550g.

18
Encomium or *Apologia*? The Future (?) of the Society of Biblical Literature Pseudepigrapha Section

Randall D. Chesnutt

During my terms as cochair of the Society of Biblical Literature Pseudepigrapha Group (1996–1998) and Pseudepigrapha Section (1999–2003),[1] more than one esteemed colleague suggested that the time had come to disband the body and let its subject matter be absorbed into other units in the Society. No one doubted the value of the unit's attention over the years to little-known and underinvestigated Jewish sources. The concern rather sprang from two premises: (1) as a categorical label for this literature, *Pseudepigrapha* is inaccurate, disparaging, and misleading; and (2) under *any* label, compartmentalizing these works as a discrete literary corpus apart from other early Jewish writings skews their interpretation. In the reflections that follow I do not dispute these premises but question the conclusion. I contend that the inconvenient truth in these premises justifies sounding an alarm for methodological caution but not sounding the death knell for scholarly focus on what has come to be called the Old Testament Pseudepigrapha.[2]

---

1. Hereafter I use *unit* in the lower case for the long-standing Society of Biblical Literature unit that began in 1969 as a *project* and evolved into a *seminar*, a *group*, and finally a *section*. When I capitalize any of these latter terms I am referring to the unit by the name actually used at a particular time.

2. Throughout this essay, pseudepigrapha is used in in the lower case with reference to individual writings and in the upper case as a designation for a corpus or collection of writings.

A Problematic Label for an Arbitrary Corpus

Old Testament Pseudepigrapha and kindred terms as they are now used are the legacy of Johann A. Fabricius, who entitled his pioneering 1713 anthology *Codex pseudepigraphus Veteris Testamenti*.[3] Fabricius's preface makes clear that his project was no neutral act of anthologizing part of the ancient literary heritage and his use of Pseudepigrapha no arbitrary choice. Rather, he sought to expose what he called *pseudepigrapha, fabula*, and *fraudes* as spurious works written under false pretenses, thereby distinguishing them from the canonical Scriptures.[4] As a label for these writings, Pseudepigrapha is not only denigrating; it is also simply inaccurate. While a number of the works are written under a pseudonym, others are anonymous. Even for those with pseudonymous claims or attributions, foregrounding this aspect retrojects anachronistic notions of authorship and forgery.[5] Moreover, pseudepigraphy is hardly distinctive of these writings but was a widespread phenomenon in antiquity.

Despite these deficiencies, the label Pseudepigrapha has become entrenched, even normalized, in the three centuries since Fabricius, not least by its use in the more recent anthologies.[6] Many who express reservations

---

3. Johann A. Fabricius, *Codex pseudepigraphus Veteris Testamenti: Collectus, castigatus, testimoniisque, censuris et animaduersionibus illustrates* (Hamburg: Liebezeit, 1713). A second edition and a second volume were published as *Codicis pseudepigraphi Veteris Testamenti: Volumen Alterum Accedit Josephi Veteris Christiani Auctoria Hypomnesticon* (Hamburg: Felginer, 1722-1723).

4. See further Annette Yoshiko Reed, "The Modern Invention of 'Old Testament Pseudepigrapha,'" *JTS* 60 (2009): 403-36; and Eva Mroczek, *The Literary Imagination in Jewish Antiquity* (Oxford: Oxford University Press, 2016), 129-30.

5. See Hindy Najman, *Seconding Sinai: The Development of Mosaic Discourse in Second Temple Judaism*, JSJSup 77 (Leiden: Brill, 2003), 1-8; Annette Yoshiko Reed, "Pseudepigraphy, Authorship, and the Reception of 'the Bible' in Late Antiquity," in *The Reception and Interpretation of the Bible in Late Antiquity*, ed. Lorenzo DiTommaso and Lucian Turcescu, BAC 6 (Leiden: Brill, 2008), 467-90; and Mroczek, *Literary Imagination in Jewish Antiquity*, 51-85.

6. Emil F. Kautzsch, ed., *Die Apocryphen und Pseudepigraphen des Alten Testaments*, 2 vols. (Tübingen: Mohr Siebeck, 1900); R. H. Charles, ed., *Apocrypha and Pseudepigrapha of the Old Testament*, 2 vols. (Oxford: Clarendon, 1913); James H. Charlesworth, ed., *The Old Testament Pseudepigrapha*, 2 vols. (Garden City, NY: Doubleday, 1983-1985); and Richard Bauckam, James R. Davila, and Alexander Panayotov, eds., *Old Testament Pseudepigrapha: More Noncanonical Scriptures*, vol. 1 (Grand Rapids: Eerdmans, 2013).

about the term nevertheless persist in using it because of the momentum and convenience of custom and the lack of a suitable alternative.⁷ Indeed the Pseudepigrapha unit has retained the name by default, although in sessions of this unit one is likely to hear reference to the *so-called* Pseudepigrapha or some such qualification as often as the unmodified term.

Fabricius bequeathed to us not only the label Pseudepigrapha for the collection but also the very idea of such a collection.⁸ However convenient we find the assembling of these writings today, it must be remembered that the grouping is modern, not ancient, and etic, not emic. Nothing intrinsic in the writings suggests that they belong together as a corpus. They do not come to us from one author (as do the works of Philo and Josephus) or one community (as do the Dead Sea Scrolls and the Nag Hammadi Codices). They were not collected in antiquity (as the writings now called apocryphal or deuterocanonical were preserved in the Septuagint along with the works from the Hebrew Bible). Nothing in common as to genre, date, provenance, language, distinctive ideology, or special methodological requirements sets them apart from other early Jewish writings. Thus they are not a corpus at all, much less an ancient one, but a modern grab-bag of ancient Jewish writings that are not included in the other categories (except those also preserved among the Dead Sea Scrolls). And, of course, anthologizing literary works impacts how they

---

7. So, e.g., A.-M. Denis says the term is "amphibologique et d'allieurs impropre" but concludes "il est préférable de le garder." A.-M. Denis, *Introduction aux pseudépigraphes grecs d'Ancien Testament*, SVTP 1 (Leiden: Brill, 1970), xi. James H. Charlesworth finds the term "inappropriate" ("The Renaissance of Pseudepigrapha Studies: The SBL Pseudepigrapha Project," *JSJ* 2 [1971]: 113) but retains it because it "has been inherited and is now used internationally" ("Introduction for the General Reader," *OTP* 1: xxv). Bauckam, Davila, and Panayotov "retain 'Pseudepigrapha' despite its unsatisfactory associations, because none of the proposed replacement terms … yet commands general acceptance or is as widely recognized by the public" (Bauckham and Davila, "Introduction," *MOTP* 1:xxvii). Robert A. Kraft uses the term reluctantly, calling it "a category designation that I have come to view as inappropriate and/or misleading, without yet finding a more satisfactory substitute" (*Exploring the Scripturesque: Jewish Texts and their Christian Contexts*, JSJSup 137 [Leiden: Brill 2009], viii).

8. Fabricius referred to a prior collection, Johann A. Schmidt's *Pseudo-Veteri Testamento*, which was apparently limited in scope and quickly superseded by Fabricius's own (Reed, "Modern Invention of 'Old Testament Pseudepigrapha,'" 424 and n. 71). It is Fabricius's pioneering anthology that is the precedent for subsequent collections.

are received;[9] the selection, omission, arrangement, and naming of works can convey meaning, define disciplinary boundaries, and prejudice interpretation. Hence the growing discomfort about a branch of study that centers on an artificial (as well as quite fluid) literary category and uses a label that is itself objectionable.

In view of these reservations, what can be said in favor of prolonging the life of the Society of Biblical Literature Pseudepigrapha Section? The precursory answer that follows is both retrospective and prospective and as much anecdotal as systematic.

Looking to the Past: Precedents and Prospects

A Society of Biblical Literature unit devoted to the study of the Pseudepigrapha originated at the 1969 Annual Meeting in Toronto when Walter Harrelson convened a breakfast meeting to launch a Pseudepigrapha Project. Continuing as a breakfast in 1970 and constituted as the Pseudepigrapha Seminar in 1971, the unit began the practice of dealing each year with a particular work that was not well known. Early sessions dealt with the Paralipomena of Jeremiah (1971), the Testament of Abraham (1972), the Testament of Moses (1973), the Testament of Job (1974), the Testament of Joseph (1975), and Joseph and Aseneth (1976). "The textual orientation of the unit," a charter member later reflected, "was a conscious decision, intended to expose us to 'new' works and to keep us from wandering into predetermined categories."[10] Some sessions focused on a work for which a new text had become available recently; in other cases a preliminary edition grew out of the discussion. Thus began the Society of Biblical Literature Texts and Translations series, of which most early volumes were in a subseries called the Pseudepigrapha Series.[11] The working papers from

---

9. Reed, "Modern Invention of 'Old Testament Pseudepigrapha,'" 407–8; David Stern, ed., *The Anthology in Jewish Literature* (Oxford: Oxford University Press, 2004); and Mroczek, *Literary Imagination*, 128–29, 139, *et passim*.

10. Private correspondence from George W. E. Nickelsburg dated November 27, 2001. I am grateful to Nickelsburg for this correspondence and for supplying me with materials from the early meetings in hopes that someone would write a history of the unit when it reached age thirty-five or forty. Finally, this desideratum has come to fruition in connection with the unit's fiftieth anniversary, at least for the early years of the unit; see Matthias Henze's essay in this volume.

11. E.g., Robert A. Kraft and Ann-Elizabeth Purintun, *Paraleipomena Jeremiou*, SBLTT 1 (Missoula, MT: Society of Biblical Literature, 1972); Michael E. Stone, *The*

the early sessions, often collected in the Society of Biblical Literature Septuagint and Cognate Studies series, became the first significant published research on some works and set the agenda for subsequent investigation.[12] James H. Charlesworth, who was appointed project secretary, edited and circulated a Pseudepigrapha Newsletter for several years to report on current work and future plans. In a few years a small cadre of scholars had essentially carved out a new discipline[13] whose bailiwick was works that had tended to slip through the cracks even as the rich diversity of Second Temple Judaism was increasingly recognized from related studies, including the Dead Sea Scrolls and the new critical analysis of rabbinic literature. One may bemoan the unit's choice of a name and its further reification of an artificial category, but there is no doubt that it brought fresh attention and elucidation to many writings that needed to be factored into the emerging new understanding of ancient Judaism.

This is not the place to trace the history of the Society of Biblical Literature Pseudepigrapha unit beyond the early hunting-and-gathering phase.[14] Having operated continuously since 1969, it is one of the oldest units in the Society and has continued to advance our understanding of Judaism in the Second Temple period and beyond, not only on many individual writings but also on the bigger picture. One illustration is the remarkable advances over the past fifty years in the study of Jewish apocalyptic thought. Although the landmark publications on the apocalyptic tradition

---

Testament of Abraham: The Greek Recensions, SBLTT 2 (Missoula, MT: Society of Biblical Literature, 1972); Daniel J. Harrington, *The Hebrew Fragments of Pseudo-Philo's* Liber Antiquitatum Biblicarum *Preserved in the Chronicles of Jeraḥmeel*, SBLTT 3 (Missoula, MT: Society of Biblical Literature, 1974); and Robert A. Kraft, *The Testament of Job according to the SV Text*, SBLTT 5 (Missoula, MT: Scholars Press, 1974).

12. Thus, e.g., George W. E. Nickelsburg, ed., *Studies on the Testament of Moses*, SCS 4 (Cambridge, MA: Society of Biblical Literature, 1973); George W. E. Nickelsburg, ed., *Studies on the Testament of Joseph*, SCS 5 (Missoula, MT: Scholars Press, 1975); and George W. E. Nickelsburg, ed., *Studies on the Testament of Abraham*, SCS 6 (Missoula, MT: Scholars Press, 1976).

13. This is not to imply that the Society of Biblical Literature unit was the sole impetus for this development. On roughly contemporaneous projects in Europe, see Robert A. Kraft, "Jewish Greek Scriptures and Related Topics," *NTS* 16 (1970): 390; Charlesworth, "Renaissance of Pseudepigrapha Studies," 107; and Daniel J. Harrington, "Research on the Jewish Pseudepigrapha during the 1970s," *CBQ* 42 (1980): 142–59.

14. See the essay by Matthias Henze in this volume.

have come from other colloquia,[15] many of the contributors were at the same time actively engaged in the Society of Biblical Literature Pseudepigrapha unit, which laid essential groundwork for the larger conceptual studies by its regular focus on the texts themselves, their manuscript traditions, their literary evolution, and basic issues of interpretation, as well as by keeping in the mix apocalyptic works extant only in recondite languages not widely known in the West and therefore not always brought into the discussion.[16] Panels and papers on these matters almost every year in the Pseudepigrapha unit have not merely mirrored the momentous developments in the study of Jewish apocalypticism but have been a driving force behind them. The same could be said of the unit's contributions to many other areas of inquiry over the last half century, including literary conventions such as rewritten Scripture, motifs such as messianic and other ideal figures, and new strategies only beginning to gain traction, such as investigating manuscripts as textual artifacts in their own right and not merely as means to a putative *Urtext*.[17]

Critical Collaboration

Some years ago I was asked to write a review essay on George W. E. Nickelsburg's *Jewish Literature between the Bible and the Mishnah: A Historical*

---

15. E.g., John J. Collins, ed., *Apocalypse: The Morphology of a Genre*, Semeia 14 (1979), which grew out of the Apocalypse Group of the Society of Biblical Literature Genres Project; David Hellholm, ed., *Apocalypticism in the Mediterranean World and the Near East: Proceedings of the International Colloquium on Apocalypticism, Uppsula, August 12–17, 1979* (Tübingen: Mohr Siebeck, 1983); and more recently Carol A. Newsom, ed., *Seeking Knowledge: The Intellectual Project of Apocalypticism in Cultural Context*, HBAI 5 (2016).

16. Especially 2 Enoch and the Apocalypse of Abraham, first-century CE apocalypses preserved in Old Church Slavonic.

17. For examples of rewritten Scripture, see papers at the 1978, 1996, 1997, 2013, and 2016 sessions, among others. For examples of messianic and ideal figures, see papers at the 1980 meeting printed in John J. Collins and George W. E. Nickelsburg, eds., *Ideal Figures in Ancient Judaism: Profiles and Paradigms*, SCS 12 (Chico, CA: Scholars Press, 1980). On attention to individual manuscripts as artifacts of evolving traditions, see Liv Ingeborg Lied, "Media Culture, New Philology, and the Pseudepigrapha" (paper presented at the 2012 Annual Meeting), and the essays collected in Hugo Lundhaug and Liv Ingeborg Lied, eds., *Snapshots of Evolving Traditions: Jewish and Christian Manuscript Culture, Textual Fluidity, and New Philology*, TUGAL 175 (Berlin: de Gruyter, 2017).

and Literary Introduction.[18] A few years later, by invitation from the same editor, I followed with a review essay on the revised edition of this outstanding volume.[19] One of the things that struck me most about the changes since the first edition was the exponential growth of secondary literature in the intervening quarter century, especially on the works under consideration here. And because the early years of my involvement with the Pseudepigrapha unit coincided roughly with the interim between the two editions, I could not help but observe that much of the new research that Nickelsburg cited had seen the light of day first in sessions of this unit. Nickelsburg had attended almost every session from the beginning and continued to do so until quite recently. When he was not presenting, he regularly attended presentations by others. Often he was the first to raise a question, eager to sharpen his own understanding and to press the presenter and other colleagues to think further about this aspect or that, as he did pointedly after my own meager first paper at the 1984 meeting. In particular I remember his keenness to learn more about works extant in languages outside his own expertise, as when Michael Stone reported on Armenian sources or Andrei Orlov analyzed apocalyptic works preserved in Old Church Slavonic.[20] From its inception the Pseudepigrapha unit was a matrix that informed Nickelsburg's scholarly work as well as being informed by it—a fact he acknowledged in both editions.[21] The value of

---

18. George W. E. Nickelsburg, *Jewish Literature between the Bible and the Mishnah: A Historical and Literary Introduction* (Philadelphia: Fortress, 1981). The review essay appeared as "Chapter Eleven: George Nickelsburg's *Jewish Literature between the Bible and the Mishnah*: Retrospect and Prospect," in *George W. E. Nickelsburg in Perspective: An Ongoing Dialogue of Learning*, ed. Jacob Neusner and Alan J. Avery-Peck, 2 vols. (Leiden: Brill, 2003), 2:343–56.

19. George W. E. Nickelsburg, *Jewish Literature between the Bible and the Mishnah: A Historical and Literary Introduction*, 2nd ed. (Minneapolis: Fortress, 2005). The review essay is "A Good Book Made Better: An Encomium on the Second Edition of George Nickelsburg, *Jewish Literature between the Bible and the Mishnah*," *Review of Rabbinic Judaism* 11 (2008): 167–75.

20. E.g., Michael Stone at the 1988, 1998, and 1999 meetings and in numerous publications; and Andrei Orlov in sessions in 2000, 2002, 2004, 2005, 2007, and 2014. Of Orlov's numerous published studies, only *The Enoch-Metatron Tradition*, TSAJ 107 (Tübingen: Mohr Siebeck, 2005) appeared in time to be cited in Nickelsburg's second edition.

21. In his own words Nickelsburg, *Jewish Literature between the Bible and the Mishnah*, first edition, "the unfootnoted context of the project has been my work in the Pseudepigrapha Group of the Society of Biblical Literature and my teaching at

scholarly collaboration in exploring such diverse and complex materials was very much in evidence.

The need for such collaborative work has not subsided. Learned groups that deal with some or all of the same literature have emerged in professional societies besides the Society of Biblical Literature,[22] and within the Society of Biblical Literature some of these works now receive attention in other units as well as the Pseudepigrapha Section. Thus the Qumran Section and the Ethiopic Bible and Literature Consultation deal sometimes with Jubilees and 1 Enoch. Apocalyptic and related works are investigated regularly in the Wisdom and Apocalypticism Section and at times in the Religious Experience in Antiquity Section and the Ritual in the Biblical World Section, among others. Studies of the Letter of Aristeas show up in the International Organization for Septuagint and Cognate Studies and the Hellenistic Judaism Section. Poetic compositions such as the Psalms of Solomon have found occasional consideration in the Prayer in Antiquity Consultation and the Religious Experience in Early Judaism and Early Christianity Section. Studies of Joseph and Aseneth have appeared in several units, including the Ancient Fiction and Early Christian and Jewish Narrative Section, the Early Jewish and Christian Mysticism Section, and the Gender, Sexuality, and the Bible Group. The Ascension of Isaiah has gotten some attention in the Ancient Fiction and Early Jewish and Christian Narrative Section and the Esotericism and Mysticism in Antiquity Section, as well as others. The consideration of these writings in multiple venues is a very positive development but does not obviate the need for a section devoted specifically to them. These works need a home, a place to reside where they are not occasional visitors but the center of attention, where scholars address the most basic matters of text, literary form, social context, and interpretation as well as the implications for larger topics. The need is all the more pressing in the case of other works that have no conspicuous overlap with the purview of another Society of Biblical Literature unit; the Life of Adam and

---

the University of Iowa" (pp. xii–xiii). In the second edition, he named the Pseudepigrapha Group, the same Society's unit on Wisdom and Apocalypticism in Early Judaism and Early Christianity, and the Taskforce on Apocalypticism of the Wissenschaftliche Gesellschaft für Theologie as the professional bodies that continued to inform his work.

22. The Pseudepigrapha Seminar of the Studiorum Novi Testamenti Societas and the Enoch Seminar are two leading examples.

Eve, Pseudo-Philo's Liber antiquitatum biblicarum, the Testament of Job, and the Testament of Abraham are a few cases in point. These orphaned works, too, need a home in the Society.

The End Is Not Yet

The ideal of dispensing with etic categories and labels has some appeal, and the growing digitization of texts and manuscripts makes it possible now for extensive texts without borders to be amassed online. However, for printed compilations and collaborative scholarly research, some breakdown into manageable categories is needed, and categories require labels. The problems mentioned at the outset about how to classify and what to call the materials are real, but an even greater detriment to the appreciation of the works under discussion is the neglect that would follow from a methodological purism that suspends collection and systematic analysis until the issues of taxonomy and nomenclature are settled. The organized scholarly attention given to this literature over the last fifty years needs to continue. But where, and under what rubrics?

As currently configured in the humanities, academic disciplines that flourish entail some form of scholarly interaction wherein specialists gather periodically to contribute to, learn from, and be spurred on by the work of others. Here there must be some division of labor and assortment of subject matter, even if these are heuristic and the boundaries provisional and permeable. Within this prevailing system, it seems to me that the collection of the writings in view here under one heading is harmless enough, as long as it is taken no more seriously than what it is: a convenient assemblage of *the rest*, that is, the remainder of early Jewish writings besides those collected in the works of Philo, Josephus, the Septuagint, or (exclusively) in the Dead Sea Scrolls. Each of these corpora has a home among current Society of Biblical Literature units: the Philo of Alexandria Seminar, the Josephus Seminar, the Deuterocanonical and Cognate Literature Section, and the Qumran Section. Surely *the rest*, which by any definition are collectively more voluminous than any one of these, also deserve a place at the table.

As to the label Pseudepigrapha, I would welcome a viable replacement, but thus far those proposed have not commended themselves. *Parabiblical literature, parascriptural literature,* and *scripturesque writings* all take some biblical canon as the only starting point and standard over against which to denominate other writings; yet they neither apply equally to all of the Jewish writings that fall outside the canon(s) nor distinguish clear subsets among them. I would not propose as a serious heading my language above about "the rest" or the equivalent "everything else" that I also sometimes use informally, although these descriptors do indicate the only real grounds for bringing these works together. For all its deficiencies, Pseudepigrapha at least has the advantage of being widely recognized by both experts and informed nonspecialists to designate early Jewish writings that do not fit into any of the fixed categories and yet command attention as primary sources from Judaism around the turn of the eras. I would prefer to reserve pseudepigrapha (sg. pseudepigraphon) in the lower case for individual works that are actually written under a pseudonym. But on occasion when I seem unable to do without some designation for the larger hodgepodge of works outside the well-defined groupings, I reluctantly use "Pseudepigrapha" (uppercase) in the collective sense, soothing my qualms only slightly with unwieldy qualifiers: "the so-called Pseudepigrapha," or "the group of miscellaneous writings often called the Pseudepigrapha."

If, as I have suggested, we should not only welcome the *ad hoc* consideration of these writings in various units but also maintain a unit devoted specifically to them, perhaps the lesser of evils is to retain for this unit the inherited heading Pseudepigrapha—not, to be sure, on the merits of the term but for reasons of familiarity and expedience—until a suitable alternative is found. One thing is clear: collecting these writings for study even under a less-than-ideal heading is less harmful than *not* collecting them. Maintaining this loose collection of writings and a scholarly cadre to investigate them does not resolve the complicated issues of taxonomy and nomenclature, but it does provide a forum in which to continue work on these and other issues. The contours of the collection will continue to evolve, both because of further additions[23] and the growing consensus that a number of the supposed early Jewish writings are in fact Christian rather than (non-Christian) Jewish.[24] Refinement of nomenclature and modes

---

23. See Bauckam, Davila, and Panayotov, *Old Testament Pseudepigrapha: More Noncanonical Scriptures*, a second volume of which remains forthcoming.

24. Robert A. Kraft has championed the default view that works preserved in Christian communities (as most of the so-called pseudepigrapha certainly were) should be presumed to be originally Christian unless there is compelling evidence of a Jewish origin. See his "The Pseudepigrapha in Christianity," in *Tracing the Threads: Studies in the Vitality of Jewish Pseudepigrapha*, ed. John C. Reeves, EJL 6 (Atlanta: Scholars Press, 1994), 55–96; and Kraft, "The Pseudepigrapha and Christianity Revis-

of categorization will surely continue.[25] New and more sophisticated tools and interdisciplinary approaches will continue to emerge. Avoiding any isolation of these writings so that the heuristic borders do not become restrictive barriers must also remain a methodological priority.[26] But progress on these and other fronts is more likely to happen within the ongoing collaborative study of these works than as a prerequisite to it.

A primary motive for the Society of Biblical Literature's restructuring in 1969 (operationalized in 1970) from which came the basic model still in effect today was "to organize research work increasingly on a group basis" and foster broader and deeper research projects "which need doing but have failed to reach completion or even to find full conception because no base for ongoing work has existed."[27] A decade after this arrangement

---

ited: Setting the Stage and Framing Some Central Questions," *JSJ* 32 (2001): 371–95. Many others, including Daniel C. Harlow, have carried through on this approach with reference to individual works. See Daniel C. Harlow, "The Christianization of Early Jewish Pseudepigrapha: The Case of 3 Baruch," *JSJ* 32 (2001): 416–44; see also James R. Davila, *The Provenance of the Pseudepigrapha: Jewish, Christian, or Other?* JSJSup 105 (Leiden: Brill, 2005). Numerous sessions of the Pseudepigrapha unit have addressed the Jewish or Christian character of various works (the Testaments of the Twelve Patriarchs, 3 Baruch, Joseph and Aseneth, the Ascension of Isaiah, the Paralipomena of Jeremiah, and the Story of Zosimus, among others), as well as the need to investigate these in *both* their Christian contexts *and* the (possible or certain) Jewish settings that preceded.

25. I say "continue" because such has been integral to the Society of Biblical Literature unit's work all along. Papers on methodology were featured in the very first meeting in which the unit was constituted as a seminar in 1971 and have continued since, as in the 2008 session entitled "Problematizing 'Pseudepigrapha'" that was devoted precisely to these issues.

26. Again I say "remain" because from the beginning the unit has resisted such isolation and tried to keep in touch with diverse approaches and perspectives, as is evidenced by regular joint sessions over the years with units such as the Nag Hammadi Group (1977); the Qumran Section (1986, 2005, 2013); the Seminar on Early Christian Apocalypticism (1987); the Intertextuality in Christian Apocrypha Seminar (1992); the Nag Hammadi and Gnosticism Section (1998); the Quran and Biblical Literature Consultation (2004); the Aramaic Studies Section (2005); the Religious Experience in Early Judaism and Early Christianity Section (2006, 2008); the Hellenistic Judaism Section (2007, 2015); the Book of Daniel Consultation (2013); the Hebrew Scriptures and Cognate Literature Section (2016); and the Digital Humanities in Biblical, Early Jewish, and Christian Studies Section (2017).

27. Ernest W. Saunders, *Searching the Scriptures: A History of the Society of Biblical Literature, 1880–1990*, BSNA 8 (Chico, CA: Scholars Press, 1982), 101; George W.

by specialization, Ernest W. Saunders, in his history of the Society's first hundred years (1880–1980), discerned the opposite challenge:

> A major problem facing the Society in the second century will be to facilitate the process of communication between groups and individuals to develop languages of synthesis rather than separation and to emphasize the larger schemes and issues that will integrate atomized research activity.[28]

In my judgment the pursuit of these twin goals—providing a home base for ongoing collaborative work on oft-neglected sources while also synthesizing this work with other sources and studies rather than isolating or atomizing it—is ample reason for the unit now called the Pseudepigrapha Section to live on in some form well beyond its fiftieth anniversary. Thus I hope this brief essay and the larger jubilee volume will serve not as an *encomium* marking the expiration of the unit but an *apologia* for its long continuation.

Bibliography

Bauckham, Richard, and James R. Davila. "Introduction." *MOTP* 1:xvii–xxxviii.

Bauckam, Richard, James R. Davila, and Alexander Panayotov, eds. *Old Testament Pseudepigrapha: More Noncanonical Scriptures*. Vol. 1. Grand Rapids: Eerdmans, 2013.

Charles, R. H., ed. *Apocrypha and Pseudepigrapha of the Old Testament*. 2 vols. Oxford: Clarendon, 1913.

Charlesworth, James H., ed. "Introduction for the General Reader." *OTP* 1:xxi–xxxiv.

———. *The Old Testament Pseudepigrapha*. 2 vols. Garden City, NY: Doubleday, 1983–1985.

———. "The Renaissance of Pseudepigrapha Studies: The SBL Pseudepigrapha Project." *JSJ* 2 (1971): 107–14.

Chesnutt, Randall D. "Chapter Eleven: George Nickelsburg's *Jewish Literature between the Bible and the Mishnah*: Retrospect and Prospect." Pages 343–56 in vol. 2 of *George W. E. Nickelsburg in Perspective: An*

MacRae, ed., *Report of the Task Force on Scholarly Communication and Publication* (Missoula, MT: University of Montana Press, 1972), 17.

28. Saunders, *Searching the Scriptures*, 100.

Ongoing Dialogue of Learning. Edited by Jacob Neusner and Alan J. Avery-Peck. 2 vols. Leiden: Brill, 2003.

———. "A Good Book Made Better: An Encomium on the Second Edition of George Nickelsburg, *Jewish Literature between the Bible and the Mishnah*." *Review of Rabbinic Judaism* 11 (2008): 167–75.

Collins, John J., ed. *Apocalypse: The Morphology of a Genre*. Semeia 14 (1979).

Collins, John J., and George W. E. Nickelsburg, eds. *Ideal Figures in Ancient Judaism: Profiles and Paradigms*. SCS 12. Chico, CA: Scholars Press, 1980.

Davila, James R. *The Provenance of the Pseudepigrapha: Jewish, Christian, or Other?* JSJSup 105. Leiden: Brill, 2005.

Denis, A.-M. *Introduction aux pseudépigraphes grecs d'Ancien Testament*. SVTP 1. Leiden: Brill, 1970.

Fabricius, Johann A. *Codex pseudepigraphus Veteris Testamenti: Collectus, castigatus, testimoniisque, censuris et animaduersionibus illustrates*. Hamburg: Liebezeit, 1713.

———. *Codicis pseudepigraphi Veteris Testamenti: Volumen Alterum Accedit Josephi Veteris Christiani Auctoria Hypomnesticon*. Hamburg: Felginer, 1722–1723.

Harlow, Daniel C. "The Christianization of Early Jewish Pseudepigrapha: The Case of 3 *Baruch*." *JSJ* 32 (2001): 416–44.

Harrington, Daniel J. *The Hebrew Fragments of Pseudo-Philo's* Liber Antiquitatum Biblicarum *Preserved in the Chronicles of Jeraḥmeel*. SBLTT 3. Missoula, MT: Society of Biblical Literature, 1974.

———. "Research on the Jewish Pseudepigrapha during the 1970s." *CBQ* 42 (1980): 142–59.

Hellholm, David, ed. *Apocalypticism in the Mediterranean World and the Near East: Proceedings of the International Colloquium on Apocalypticism, Uppsula, August 12–17, 1979*. Tübingen: Mohr Siebeck, 1983.

Kautzsch, Emil F., ed. *Die Apocryphen und Pseudepigraphen des Alten Testaments*. 2 vols. Tübingen: Mohr Siebeck, 1900.

Kraft, Robert A. *Exploring the Scripturesque: Jewish Texts and their Christian Contexts*. JSJSup 137. Leiden: Brill 2009.

———. "Jewish Greek Scriptures and Related Topics." *NTS* 16 (1970): 384–96.

———. "The Pseudepigrapha in Christianity." Pages 55–96 in *Tracing the Threads: Studies in the Vitality of Jewish Pseudepigrapha*. Edited by John C. Reeves. EJL 6. Atlanta: Scholars Press, 1994.

———. "The Pseudepigrapha and Christianity Revisited: Setting the Stage and Framing Some Central Questions." *JSJ* 32 (2001): 371–95.

———. *The Testament of Job according to the SV Text*. SBLTT 5. Missoula, MT: Scholars Press, 1974.

Kraft, Robert A., and Ann-Elizabeth Purintun. *Paraleipomena Jeremiou*. SBLTT 1. Missoula, MT: Society of Biblical Literature, 1972.

Lied, Liv Ingeborg. "Media Culture, New Philology, and the Pseudepigrapha: A Note on Method." Paper presented at the Annual Meeting of the Society of Biblical Literature. Chicago, 19 November 2012.

Lundhaug, Hugo, and Liv Ingeborg Lied, eds. *Snapshots of Evolving Traditions: Jewish and Christian Manuscript Culture, Textual Fluidity, and New Philology*. TUGAL 175. Berlin: de Gruyter, 2017.

MacRae, George W., ed. *Report of the Task Force on Scholarly Communication and Publication*. Missoula, MT: University of Montana Press, 1972.

Mroczek, Eva. *The Literary Imagination in Jewish Antiquity*. Oxford: Oxford University Press, 2016.

Najman, Hindy. *Seconding Sinai: The Development of Mosaic Discourse in Second Temple Judaism*. JSJSup 77. Leiden: Brill, 2003.

Newsom, Carol A., ed. *Seeking Knowledge: The Intellectual Project of Apocalypticism in Cultural Context*. HBAI 5 (2016).

Nickelsburg, George W. E. *Jewish Literature between the Bible and the Mishnah: A Historical and Literary Introduction*. Philadelphia: Fortress, 1981. 2nd ed. Minneapolis: Fortress, 2005.

———, ed. *Studies on the Testament of Abraham*. SCS 6. Missoula, MT: Scholars Press, 1976.

———, ed. *Studies on the Testament of Moses*. SCS 4. Cambridge, MA: Society of Biblical Literature, 1973.

———, ed. *Studies on the Testament of Joseph*. SCS 5. Missoula, MT: Scholars Press, 1975.

Orlov, Andrei. *The Enoch-Metatron Tradition*. TSAJ 107. Tübingen: Mohr Siebeck, 2005.

Reed, Annette Yoshiko. "The Modern Invention of 'Old Testament Pseudepigrapha.'" *JTS* 60 (2009): 403–36.

———. "Pseudepigraphy, Authorship, and the Reception of 'the Bible' in Late Antiquity." Pages 467–90 in *The Reception and Interpretation of the Bible in Late Antiquity*. Edited by Lorenzo DiTommaso and Lucian Turcescu. BAC 6. Leiden: Brill, 2008.

Saunders, Ernest W. *Searching the Scriptures: A History of the Society of Biblical Literature, 1880–1990*. BSNA 8. Chico, CA: Scholars Press, 1982.

Stern, David, ed. *The Anthology in Jewish Literature*. Oxford: Oxford University Press, 2004.

Stone, Michael E. *The Testament of Abraham: The Greek Recensions*. SBLTT 2. Missoula, MT: Society of Biblical Literature, 1972.

19
Looking Ahead:
The Pseudepigrapha and the New Testament

John R. Levison

In 1980, I began my graduate studies at Duke University. I had wanted to study at Duke because of its emphasis upon the Jewish origins of early Christianity. W. D. Davies was still there, as were archaeologists Eric and Carol Meyers, along with James H. Charlesworth.

When it came time to choose a dissertation topic, I proposed exactly what I came to Duke to study. I decided upon "The Jewish Origins of the Christ and Adam Contrast in the Writings of Paul." My first step, of course, was to look seriously at the Jewish literature. This early Jewish literature proved to be so fascinating that I never emerged from it, at least not with respect to Adam and Eve. I never went on to write a dissertation on the writings of Paul but instead published *Portraits of Adam in Early Judaism: From Sirach to 2 Baruch*, a volume that includes Jubilees, 4 Ezra, 2 Baruch, and the Life of Adam and Eve.[1]

Thirty years have elapsed since that thesis was published in revised form. During those decades, I have become further aware of two *desiderata* of pseudepigrapha studies that emerged from my work on that doctoral thesis.

---

1. John R. Levison, *Portraits of Adam in Early Judaism: From Sirach to 2 Baruch*, JSPSup 1 (Sheffield: JSOT, 1988). In a telling development, the manuscript was first accepted in Sheffield Academic's Journal for the Study of the Old Testament Supplement series but then became the first volume in the brand new Journal for the Study of the Pseudepigrapha Supplement series (1988). The book is now in the Bloomsbury's Biblical Studies: The Hebrew Bible series (2015). This book has, then, gone from an Old Testament series to a pseudepigrapha series to a Hebrew Bible series.

Beyond Parallels

I do not regret that I did not turn my attention to the letters of Paul, but I do think there is much left undone on the connection between Jewish pseudepigraphical literature and the New Testament. With respect to Adam and Eve, for example, the relationship between Paul and other Jewish authors has yet to be explored and exploited with a level of rigor and detail the topic deserves. Many a parallel has been noted, but something more needs to be done: to establish *essential* connections between pseudepigraphical literature and the New Testament. In short, of what specific texts in the pseudepigrapha can it be said that an interpretation of the New Testament is incomplete and perhaps even inadequate without them? The answer to this question lies in discrete, detailed studies that demonstrate the *indispensability* of pseudepigrapha for interpreting the New Testament.[2]

Typically, however, the nature of the relationship between texts such as the Greek Life of Adam and Eve and Paul's letters is cursory, little more than a catalogue of possible parallels. Richard Kabisch, in the first detailed study devoted to the origin of the Life of Adam and Eve, concluded, "So our legend appears to have had influence on the formation of Paul's conceptual world."[3] Yet, the nature of that alleged influence proved difficult to pinpoint. L. S. A. Wells, in his contribution to R. H. Charles's volumes, ventured that "it seems at least tenable that S. Paul and the author of 2 Enoch were near contemporaries of the original author of Apoc. Mos. and moved in the same circle of ideas."[4] Words such as "at least tenable" and "circle of ideas" hardly inspire confidence about the significance of

---

2. To say this is not to minimize the reality that myriad issues face the study of the pseudepigrapha, including the creation of critical editions, the intractable issue of Christian transmission, the related questions of provenance and date of origin. Nevertheless, on a case-by-case basis, it is often possible to identify and isolate texts and traditions that date to the first century, as well as many that do not. In fact, taut correspondences with the New Testament, another Jewish corpus, may prove beneficial for pinpointing the date and provenance of pseudepigraphical texts. The illumination, in other words, may be mutual.

3. Richard Kabisch, "Die Entstehungszeit der Apokalypse Mose," *ZNW* 6 (1905): 134: "So scheint unsere Legende auf die Bildung der Vorstellungswelt des Paulus Einfluss gehabt zu haben."

4. L. S. A. Wells, "The Books of Adam and Eve," in *The Apocrypha and Pseudepigrapha of the Old Testament in English*, ed. R. H. Charles, 2 vols. (Oxford: Clarendon, 1913), 2:130.

pseudepigraphical texts for New Testament study. More recently, M. D. Johnson, in his translation of the Greek and Latin Life of Adam and Eve in Charlesworth's edition of the pseudepigrapha, agreed with Wells that Paul, 2 Enoch, and the Life of Adam and Eve reflect the same circle of ideas. Johnson noted "interesting parallels" yet concluded that "in spite of these parallels it is impossible to determine whether there is a relationship between the New Testament and our texts."[5] The list of scholars who have identified parallels but not demonstrated the *necessity* of some sort of connection, oral or written, can be expanded to include Daniel A. Bertrand, Otto Merk and Martin Meiser, and Jan Dochhorn, none of whom explores the relationship between the Greek Life of Adam and Eve and New Testament literature in any systematic or detailed way.[6]

A more thorough effort to illuminate Pauline theology through the Greek Life of Adam and Eve occurs in James D. G. Dunn's *Theology of Paul the Apostle*. Dunn asks, "Where did Paul draw his Adam theology from?" He responds, "from Genesis 1–3 itself and the theological themes opened up already there." He continues, "can we detect other influence from the long pre-Christian Jewish theological tradition?"[7] With this question, Dunn moves from Israelite texts to postbiblical ones; noting that Adam and Eve material is rare in Israel's literature, he suggests that this "situation changes ... in the writings of the postbiblical ... period."[8] Dunn includes the Life of Adam and Eve (both Latin and Greek) among those writings because it "shows some striking parallels with Paul." Yet at the end of the day, Dunn concludes cautiously that "Paul was entering into an already well-developed debate and that his own views were not uninfluenced by its earlier participants." Again, the choice of words—"were not uninfluenced"—hardly inspires confidence in the significance of the pseudepigrapha for understanding the New Testament.

One of the difficulties that confronts students of the pseudepigrapha is that parallels reflect general concepts rather than unique ones. As early as

---

5. M. D. Johnson, "Life of Adam and Eve," *OTP* 2:255.

6. Daniel A. Bertrand, *La Vie Grecque d'Adam et Ève* (Paris: Librairie Adrien Maisonneuve, 1987); Otto Merk and Martin Meiser, *Das Leben Adams und Evas*, JSHRZ 2.5 (Gütersloh: Gütersloher Verlagshaus, 1998); Jan Dochhorn, *Die Apokalypse des Mose: Text, Übersetzung, Kommentar*, TSAJ 106 (Tübingen: Mohr Siebeck, 2005).

7. James D. G. Dunn, *The Theology of Paul the Apostle* (Grand Rapids: Eerdmans, 1998), 82.

8. Dunn, *Theology of Paul the Apostle*, 84.

1900, in Kautzsch's edition of the apocrypha and pseudepigrapha, E. Fuchs identified several of these individual motifs: "revelation" in the Greek LAE 3 and Eph 3:2–3; "open heavens" in the Greek LAE 33–35 and Acts 7:55–56; 1 Cor 2:9; Rev 8:3, 31, 35, 42; Luke 23:46; John 16:20, 31; et cetera; "Satan's ability to disguise himself as an angel of light" in the Greek LAE 17 and 2 Cor 11:14.[9] Others can be added, such as "a loss of glory" in the Greek LAE 21.2, 6 and Rom 3:23; "the location of paradise in the third heaven" in the Greek LAE 37.5 and 2 Cor 12:4; and the reference to "desire as the origin of sin" in the Greek LAE 19.3 and Rom 7:7.[10] Unfortunately, these details are usually too general for the sake of comparison. They do not, therefore, provide *essential* links between a pseudepigraphon and the New Testament or, in this instance, between the Greek Life of Adam and Eve and Paul's theology.

Another difficulty besetting studies is that they often catalogue parallels without exploring their significance. For example, Dunn notes that "the thought of Adam's sin resulting in his deprivation of the glory of God" in Rom 3:23 "is already present in Apoc. Mos. 20.2 and 21.6. Correspondingly, the hope of the age to come could be expressed in terms of the restoration or enhancement of the original glory (Apoc. Mos. 39.2–3)." Is this parallel not too general to be of significance? What more can be garnered from the Greek Life of Adam and Eve than from 1QS IV, 21, with its hope that "all the glory of Adam will be theirs?"

Several years ago I did attempt to remedy the problem of parallels in a single instance by arguing that the Greek Life of Adam and Eve is *indispensable* for an adequate interpretation of Rom 1:18–25, a pivotal Pauline text.[11] Scholars tend to be dissatisfied, I noted, with the Hebrew or Septuagintal foreground of Rom 1. Paul's rhetoric and argument simply do not make sense in light of Israelite texts, such as Gen 1:24, 26–27; Deut 4:15–18; or LXX Ps 105:20. In contrast, the Greek Life of Adam and Eve—a fanciful iteration of Gen 1–5—provides a middle ground, of sorts, between the biblical text and the Pauline interpretation. The suppression of truth, the onslaught of divine anger, the inevitability of death, the exchange of glory for mortality and dominion for subservience to animals, and the presence of greed—all of these are central to the Greek Life of Adam and Eve and

---

9. E. Fuchs, "Das Leben Adams und Evas," in *Die Apokryphen und Pseudepigraphen des Alten Testaments*, ed. E. Kautzsch, 2 vols. (Tübingen: Mohr, 1900), 510.

10. See the list in Johnson, "Life of Adam and Eve," 2:254–55.

11. John R. Levison, "Adam and Eve in Romans 1.18–25 and the Greek *Life of Adam and Eve*," NTS 50 (2004): 519–34.

supply what is lacking in Paul's otherwise laconic argument. None of these, I noted, is an isolated or individual motif; together they comprise vital elements of the narrative of Adam and Eve, understood in a postbiblical key, which Paul presupposes in Rom 1:18–25. In short, the Greek Life of Adam and Eve alone makes sense of Paul's argument in Rom 1.

Whether I was successful must be left to readers of that study. The point I wish to make here is that this is a simple, solitary example of the sort of study that, in my opinion, needs to be undertaken more often in pseudepigrapha studies. Otherwise, this rich literary corpus will be sidelined, left to languish as a convenient background—rich in parallels but lacking in relevance—to the New Testament.

Beyond Speculation

The first point I wish to make, therefore, is that comparisons must be text-focused, concrete, and rooted in the literary shape and tenor of specific pseudepigraphical texts. Comparisons between the pseudepigrapha and the New Testament must be made one to one.

My second point is related to the first. The wealth and breadth of the pseudepigrapha offers ample opportunity to compare specific pseudepigraphical texts in their literary contexts with New Testament texts in their literary contexts. In this light, text-to-text comparisons are preferable to gathering citations extracted from their narrative and theological contexts as a putative foreground to the New Testament. It is much more important—and trustworthy—to compare specific texts embedded in literary contexts than to gather textual snippets from an array of contexts in order to construct an eclectic, hypothetical foreground to the New Testament. This sort of intensive form of comparison, text-to-text, also has the advantage of avoiding the potential problem of utilizing a later text, such as 4 Ezra or 2 Baruch, to establish a proposed eclectic foreground of a text of earlier provenance, such as Paul's Letter to the Romans.

It is all too easy, further, for these hypothetical foregrounds to serve the needs of New Testament interpreters at the expense of the authenticity of early Jewish literature. Pseudepigraphical texts, in other words, can too easily be combined with other select texts from early Judaism in order to compose the interpretative background that supports an interpreter's particular understanding of a Pauline letter. This was the point I tried to make in the introduction to *Portraits of Adam in Early Judaism*, in which I surveyed the scholarship of W. D. Davies, J. Jervell, C. K. Barrett, E. Brandenburger,

R. Scroggs, J. D. G. Dunn, and N. T. Wright in order to illuminate their deft but ill-advised ability to select an array of Jewish texts in support of their respective takes on Pauline theology.[12] Essentially, each of these scholars looked into the same reservoir of early Jewish literature and discovered there the image of Adam that reflected their perspective on Paul.

The ability to compare texts in contexts rather than in isolation from those literary contexts has the added advantage of simplifying the process of interpretation. By avoiding an alleged hypothetical Jewish Adam tradition, it is possible to opt for historical simplicity. According to those scholars who discern the presence of Adam in Rom 1, Paul's conception of Adam must be interpreted in light of a hypothetical Jewish Adam tradition—what Wright calls "Adam-speculation."[13] This requires the further step of reconstruction: piecing together disparate elements of literary texts which differ widely with respect to date and provenance. The approach I am recommending here is simpler: to identify correspondences that come from individual literary corpora, such as Rom 1 and the Greek Life of Adam and Eve. Though this is no easy task, it does at least avoid the elusive notion of a speculative Adam tradition.

This approach does not mean that texts cannot be connected. They can, but only if they are first interpreted within a narrative context and then compared with another text that is interpreted similarly within its narrative context. C. T. R. Hayward has done this with respect to the figure of Adam in early Judaism. Resolutely rejecting a hypothetical Adam myth, he nonetheless connects several texts in which Adam is portrayed as a priest.[14] This approach to texts is a far cry from Wright's Adam speculation, though it does allow for the identification of a web of connections in early Jewish texts that could prove fruitful for understanding Adam in New Testament texts.

Beyond the Past

When I first explored the pseudepigrapha, I did so with the proofs of Charlesworth's *The Old Testament Pseudepigrapha* draped over my knees

---

12. Levison, *Portraits of Adam in Early Judaism*, 14–23.

13. Dunn, *Theology of Paul the Apostle*, 79–101; N. T. Wright, *The Climax of the Covenant: Christ and the Law in Pauline Theology* (Minneapolis: Fortress, 1993), 19; see the full discussion in pages 19–40.

14. C. T. R. Hayward, "The Figure of Adam in Pseudo-Philo's Biblical Antiquities," *JSJ* 23 (1992): 1–20.

in his Duke University office. Since those early days of my career, felicitous developments have taken place in pseudepigrapha studies: critical editions of the texts themselves; ample attention to reception history; exceptionally well-executed scholarly commentaries; studies of pseudepigrapha alongside (or among) the Dead Sea Scrolls. Yet there is so much left to accomplish. It is possible to imagine, for example, a dedicated series with analyses of the grand themes of covenant, spirit, temple, messiah, heaven, kingdom of God, incarnation, persecution, Sabbath, light, exile, torah, worship—and a host of other themes that emerge from Israelite literature and permeate segments of ancient Jewish literature, both pseudepigraphical and New Testament. In a new era, these studies could be undertaken with an exquisite attention to detail, not just the detail of New Testament texts with catalogues of Jewish texts relegated to notes, but equally to *select* ancient Jewish texts and their New Testament counterparts. These generative studies would signal a new era, both in New Testament and pseudepigrapha studies. How? By being collaborative ventures, jointly written by scholars with expertise in pseudepigrapha and scholars with expertise in New Testament studies. I had a similar experience of writing a lengthy article on Plutarch and the book of Acts with doctoral student Heidrun Gunkel and Plutarch expert Rainer Hirsch-Luipold; the experience was enthralling, filled with fierce arguments and a fervent friendship with Rainer, and it led to the discovery of new borderlands in the relationship between Plutarch and the New Testament.[15] A succession of similar collaborations focused upon grand themes in the pseudepigrapha and the New Testament would mark a new day in the study of antiquity. It is time, perhaps, to imagine such a new venture and to welcome such a new day.

Bibliography

Bertrand, Daniel A. *La Vie Grecque d'Adam et Ève*. Paris: Librairie Adrien Maisonneuve, 1987.
Dochhorn, Jan. *Die Apokalypse des Mose: Text, Übersetzung, Kommentar.* TSAJ 106. Tübingen: Mohr Siebeck, 2005.

---

15. Heidrun Gunkel, Rainer Hirsch-Luipold, and John R. Levison, "Plutarch and Pentecost: An Exploration in Interdisciplinary Collaboration," in *The Holy Spirit, Inspiration, and the Cultures of Antiquity: Multidisciplinary Perspectives*, ed. Jörg Frey and John R. Levison (Berlin: de Gruyter, 2014), 63–94.

Dunn, James D. G. *The Theology of Paul the Apostle*. Grand Rapids: Eerdmans, 1998.
Fuchs, E. "Das Leben Adams und Evas." Pages 506–28 in *Die Apokryphen und Pseudepigraphen des Alten Testaments*. Edited by E. Kautzsch. 2 vols. Tübingen: Mohr, 1900.
Gunkel, Heidrun, Rainer Hirsch-Luipold, and John R. Levison. "Plutarch and Pentecost: An Exploration in Interdisciplinary Collaboration." Pages 63–94 in *The Holy Spirit, Inspiration, and the Cultures of Antiquity: Multidisciplinary Perspectives*. Edited by Jörg Frey and John R. Levison. Berlin: de Gruyter, 2014.
Hayward, C. T. R. "The Figure of Adam in Pseudo-Philo's Biblical Antiquities." *JSJ* 23 (1992): 1–20.
Johnson, M. D. "Life of Adam and Eve." *OTP* 2:249–95.
Kabisch, Richard. "Die Entstehungszeit der Apokalypse Mose." *ZNW* 6 (1905): 109–34.
Levison, John R. "Adam and Eve in Romans 1.18–25 and the Greek *Life of Adam and Eve*." *NTS* 50 (2004): 519–34.
———. *Portraits of Adam in Early Judaism: From Sirach to 2 Baruch*. JSPSup 1. Sheffield: JSOT, 1988.
Merk, Otto, and Martin Meiser. *Das Leben Adams und Evas*. JSHRZ 2.5. Gütersloh: Gütersloher Verlagshaus, 1998.
Wells, L. S. A. "The Books of Adam and Eve." Pages 123–54 in vol. 2 of *The Apocrypha and Pseudepigrapha of the Old Testament in English*. Edited by R. H. Charles. 2 vols. Oxford: Clarendon, 1913.
Wright, N. T. *The Climax of the Covenant: Christ and the Law in Pauline Theology*. Minneapolis: Fortress, 1993.

20
Fifty More Years of the Society of Biblical Literature Pseudepigrapha Section? Prospects for the Future

Judith H. Newman

Rounding the golden age of fifty, is the Society of Biblical Literature Pseudepigrapha unit facing a midlife crisis? If it is not, should it be? Has the Pseudepigrapha unit passed its prime, or can we anticipate another fruitful fifty years of scholarship originating from its sessions? Answering these questions requires some consideration of both the origins of the Pseudepigrapha unit and its current context in order to anticipate a future. Thinking about the past and future of the Pseudepigrapha unit should not be separated from the changing character of the Society of Biblical Literature itself. The section was born in the last century in which the composition and orientation of the Society of Biblical Literature was different in many ways. There are reasons to argue that the Pseudepigrapha unit has outlived its usefulness, but I think that is not so.

The Society of Biblical Literature and Shifting Institutional Contexts

Let us begin with a snapshot from fifty years ago: Walter Harrelson, a widely respected scholar and Professor of Old Testament at Vanderbilt Divinity School, initiated the idea of a Pseudepigrapha Group at a breakfast meeting in Toronto in 1969. The Toronto meeting of 1969 itself was a novum in that it was the first Annual Meeting of the Society of Biblical Literature held outside the United States, a sign of international dynamics yet to come. At that time, the membership of the Society of Biblical Literature numbered roughly 2,700. By the next year, papers appeared in ten categories: apocrypha and pseudepigrapha, biblical archaeology, Nag Hammadi library, Old Testament and New Testament theology, Hebrew and Greek grammar, history of American biblical interpretation, literary criticism and biblical criticism, eastern Mediterranean history and religions, textual criticism, and Septuagint and cognate studies. One hundred and fifteen items appeared on the program.[1]

Fifty years later, the Society of Biblical Literature has more than tripled in size. The 2018 Membership Report records 8,465 members.[2] The Society reflects an increasingly global scope. Currently almost 40 percent of the membership is international, drawing members from 102 countries outside the United States. The program of the Annual Meeting is likewise marked by great growth in comparison with 1969. In 2017 there were 171 program units, each of which offered a range of paper or panel presentations. Roughly half of the membership, over 4,200 members, attended its Annual Meeting in Boston in 2017, a year in which thirty-three books were published by SBL Press. While religious affiliation is nowhere recorded, it seems a shift and broadening of membership has occurred along with this growth. Whereas the predominant affiliation fifty years ago was Protestant Christian with smaller but growing numbers of Catholics and Jews, there is now a rich diversity of affiliations, from evangelical Protestant to Catholic to Latter-day Saints, scholars from the range of Jewish movements, to Muslim scholars and non-Muslims engaged in the study of the Qur'an. Many secular or nonreligiously affiliated scholars populate the membership as well.

Aside from the great membership growth, another important change since the Society's inception are the many methods and contexts through which its mission is pursued. In the late sixties, the predominant mode of scholarship was the range of historical-critical methods rooted in European scholarship, with a healthy dose of comparative religions and archaeological exploration as exemplified by the work of the Albright-Cross school (at least on the Hebrew Bible side.) By contrast, now a vast variety of approaches to the study of the Bible and related literature is fully apparent. The list of program units for the 2019 Annual Meeting includes African Biblical Hermeneutics, Animal Studies and the Bible, Art and Religions of Antiquity, Bible and Emotion, Bible and Popular Culture,

---

1. Information about the Society of Biblical Literature in 1969 is drawn from Ernest W. Saunders, *Searching the Scriptures: A History of the Society of Biblical Literature, 1880–1990*, BSNA 8 (Chico, CA: Scholars Press, 1982).

2. The membership report can be found online at the Society of Biblical Literature website (https://www.sbl-site.org/).

Biblical Exegesis from Eastern Orthodox Perspectives, Biblical Literature and the Hermeneutics of Trauma, Children in the Biblical World, Cognitive Linguistics in Biblical Interpretation, and Cultic Personnel in the Biblical World—and those are just ten options culled from titles beginning with the letters A, B, and C! There are also units devoted to specific books within the Bible but also literature outside the Bible, including attention both to the literature of Qumran and the Islamic Qur'an. Within such a wealth of approaches and literatures, the Pseudepigrapha unit now carries out its work. How can it best contribute to scholarship and learning in this context?

Philology and Beyond: An Interdisciplinary Future

There is no single answer to that question and no doubt the ingenuity of its current and future chairs will point in new directions and sessions will continue to bear fruit. I served for only two years as a cochair of the Pseudepigrapha unit, but my perspective on the future of the group is shaped by my engagement with Second Temple literature more broadly in both the sessions of Society of Biblical Literature meetings and in my own research. One approach that will remain essential in the field is traditional philology, even as more texts are identified, translated, and become the focus of study beyond the now "canonical" collections in English translation of R. H. Charles, James H. Charlesworth, H. F. D. Sparks, and Louis K. Feldman, James L. Kugel, and Lawrence H. Schiffman.[3] The expertise of scholars equipped with Hebrew, Aramaic, Ethiopic, Syriac, Greek, Latin, Arabic, Coptic, Old Church Slavonic, and/or Armenian who evaluate manuscripts in their original languages will continue to be crucial. So, too, traditional literary treatments that track themes and concepts in works remain important staples of the study of these ancient texts. This is true particularly as new works are considered such as those in the collection

---

3. R. H. Charles, *The Apocrypha and Pseudepigrapha of the Old Testament*, 2 vols. (Oxford: Clarendon, 1913); James H. Charlesworth, ed. *The Old Testament Pseudepigrapha*, 2 vols. (Garden City, NY: Doubleday, 1983–1985); H. F. D. Sparks, ed. *The Apocryphal Old Testament* (Oxford: Clarendon, 1984); and Louis K. Feldman, James L. Kugel, and Lawrence H. Schiffman, eds., *Outside the Bible: Ancient Jewish Writings Related to Scripture*, 3 vols. (Lincoln: University of Nebraska Press; Philadelphia: Jewish Publication Society, 2013).

of the More Old Testament Pseudepigrapha Project.[4] Yet beyond the traditional historical-critical approaches, a number of newer methods and approaches, some treated in this volume, offer continuing fruitful avenues for the future. I will point briefly to three approaches that show particular promise: reception history, new philology, and embodied approaches.

Tracing Traditions through the History of Reception

When I began graduate school at Harvard in 1988, the history of biblical interpretation was still a strange new world within the field of biblical studies. James L. Kugel convinced me, however, that there was much work to be down outside the canon and, indeed, that one could not properly understand the formation of the Bible without understanding ancient hermeneutics and the broad swath of traditional interpretations from which it crystallized.[5] Thirty years later, while there is some debate about the exact term that should be used to describe this now burgeoning area of inquiry, reception history has become mainstream. It is routine for many job openings to require this expertise or area of research interest. Evidence for its coming of age can be seen in part through publications. For example, de Gruyter now has three publishing initiatives in the area: the *Journal of the Bible and Its Reception*, launched in 2014; an associated monograph series, Studies of the Bible and Its Reception; and finally the *Encyclopedia of the Bible and Its Reception* (EBR). EBR is an ambitious and impressive resource available both in print and digitally that seeks to trace biblical reception in Judaism, Christianity, Islam, and other religions, as well as the impact of the Bible on literature, visual arts, music, and film.

The inclusion of such reception scholarship in the *Encyclopedia of the Bible and Its Reception* marks its complete integration into the field of biblical studies. In that sense it is like the new Eerdmans commentary series Illuminations (chief editor Choon-Leong Seow) with which I am involved that includes not just the traditional historical-critical and philological approaches to the text, but moves beyond to consider its diachronic inter-

---

4. The first volume: Richard Bauckham, James R. Davila, and Alexander Panayotov, eds., *Old Testament Pseudepigrapha: More Noncanonical Scriptures*, vol. 1 (Grand Rapids: Eerdmans, 2013).

5. James Kugel was at that time teaching his enormously popular undergraduate course, "The Bible and Its Interpreters," but had not yet published his seminal book *The Bible as It Was* (Cambridge: Harvard University Press, 1997).

action with culture, politics, and religion.⁶ The important hermeneutical affirmation that is signaled from that broadening of orientation is that the meaning of biblical texts does not inhere simply in a synchronic point of time. We cannot focus simply on one putative original composition or conversely only in the present as if a text has had no past. Rather it is in the cumulative layering of interpretation and meaning in different cultural and religious contexts through traditioning processes that the Bible has had such an enormous impact.⁷ The Old Testament pseudepigrapha form a large part of that textual traditioning process from antiquity onwards.

New Philology

Another important approach to the field that is now gaining traction is the so-called new philology.⁸ New philology is neither new nor concerned solely with the study of words. Borrowed from the field of medieval studies, new philology brings a poststructuralist perspective to the study of antiquity by means of detaching the concern for authorship from texts and embracing variance as a constant feature of textuality.⁹ It seeks to examine specific manuscripts and their material characteristics *in situ*. Rather than conceiving of a text as a fixed and bounded entity connected to a particular author or authors, new philology pays attention to the circumstances of a manuscript's production and transmission.

Such an approach to manuscripts might allow for better elaboration and integration of historical contexts so that we might learn more about lived religion in different regions where texts circulated. That might be from Jubilees manuscripts in the context of eighteenth-century Ethiopian monasteries or a single manuscript of 2 Baruch used liturgically at

---

6. C. L. Seow prefers the term *cultural consequences* of the Bible to describe the cultural and political impact of scripture through the ages. See his *Job 1–21: Interpretation and Commentary* (Grand Rapids: Eerdmans, 2013).

7. For this reason, Timothy Beal prefers the term *cultural history*. See his "Reception History and Beyond: Toward the Cultural History of Scriptures," *BibInt* 19 (2011): 357–72.

8. A sample of work from this perspective is found in Liv Ingeborg Lied and Hugo Lundhaug, eds., *Snapshots of Evolving Traditions: Jewish and Christian Manuscript Culture, Textual Fluidity, and New Philology*, TUGAL 175 (Berlin: de Gruyter, 2017).

9. A series of essays in the first issue of the journal *Speculum* 65 (1990) introduced new philology to the field of medieval studies.

Easter by medieval Syriac Christians.[10] Investigation of the manuscripts in their time can reveal quite surprising and illuminating information not only about the fluidity of textual traditions and the changing shapes of the scriptural, but about the practices of religious communities through the ages and their interaction. The Pseudepigrapha unit is by no means the only group involved in the study of the extracanonical literature, so joint sessions should be employed as much as possible to marshal relevant expertise and broaden perspectives. Collaborative sessions and projects with other scholars in the humanities or social sciences could also enrich such work.

Embodiment

A final avenue of approach is the newest and lies with a set of methods most broadly termed *embodiment* or *embodied cognition*. Under this umbrella, we can consider such varied theoretical frameworks as conceptual metaphor theory, ritual studies, liturgical practices, and the study of emotions. Much research on so-called pseudepigraphical texts has focused on literary aspects or ideas within the works as presumed fixed and final texts, but not on the specific social contexts in which the texts and manuscripts were deployed (as in new philology) or the effects the performance of these texts had on the formation of self and communities. In my recent book, I have tried to address that gap by focusing on the entwinement of texts and bodies, on Scriptures and their ongoing entanglement with prayer and other liturgical practices like study.[11] While my book does not focus on texts that are typically conceived as among the pseudepigrapha, the methodological approach I take could be adapted for other texts in antiquity. This perspective is cogent because we know that worship and liturgical contexts were a chief source of their ongoing vitality and indeed, the rationale for their transmission. The contexts for reading practices varied, but certainly one primary reason for reading texts was in order to shape individuals or communities and their character. In that regard, the cultivation

---

10. For which see Liv Ingeborg Lied, "Imagining and Re-imagining 2 Baruch: Syriac Christian Manuscripts—Ancient Jewish Text?" (paper presented at the Annual Meeting of the North American Patristic Society, Chicago, 25 May 2018).

11. Judith H. Newman, *Before the Bible: The Liturgical Body and the Formation of Scriptures in Early Judaism* (New York: Oxford University Press, 2018).

of proper emotions was important.[12] Thus the integration of embodied perspectives offers another large emerging field of inquiry that could continue to enrich the work of the Pseudepigrapha unit.

For the reasons laid out above, I would argue that the Pseudepigrapha unit, far from being outmoded, can continue to play an important and even path-breaking role in the Society of Biblical Literature as it changes with the times. Like all units at given points in their trajectory, the section perhaps could profit from some rejuvenation in part through a name change alongside a reevaluation of its role in relation to the rest of the guild. Like Abram, Sarai, and Jacob, the unit might benefit from wrestling a new name to represent its transformative coming of a golden age. Others within this volume have rightly pointed out the problems with the term. To use the term *pseudepigrapha* is to contribute to the continuing reification of an artificial category of literature that was conceived by those with a particular theological perspective that privileged the Christian canon.[13] We know, however, that there was continuing vitality of scripture within and beyond that canon.[14] Indeed, this volume may well help to enable and revitalize a venerable section of the Society of Biblical Literature.

Bibliography

Charles, R. H. *The Apocrypha and Pseudepigrapha of the Old Testament*. 2 vols. Oxford: Clarendon, 1913.

Charlesworth, James H., ed. *The Old Testament Pseudepigrapha*. 2 vols. Garden City, NY: Doubleday, 1983–1985.

Bauckham, Richard, James R. Davila, and Alexander Panayotov, eds. *Old Testament Pseudepigrapha: More Noncanonical Scriptures*. Vol. 1. Grand Rapids: Eerdmans, 2013.

Beal, Timothy. "Reception History and Beyond: Toward the Cultural History of Scriptures." *BibInt* 19 (2011): 357–72.

---

12. The recent work of Françoise Mirguet offers a model for such work, *An Early History of Compassion: Emotion and Imagination in Early Judaism* (New York: Cambridge University Press, 2017).

13. On the term's genealogy, see Annette Yoshiko Reed, "The Modern Invention of Old Testament Pseudepigrapha," *JTS* 60 (2009): 403–36.

14. I borrow directly from the title of Hindy Najman's article, "The Vitality of Scripture within and beyond the Canon," *JSJ* 43 (2012): 497–518.

Feldman, Louis K., James L. Kugel, and Lawrence H. Schiffman, eds. *Outside the Bible: Ancient Jewish Writings Related to Scripture*. 3 vols. Lincoln: University of Nebraska Press; Philadelphia: Jewish Publication Society, 2013.

Kugel, James L. *The Bible as It Was*. Cambridge: Harvard University Press, 1997.

Lied, Liv Ingeborg. "Imagining and Re-imagining 2 Baruch: Syriac Christian Manuscripts—Ancient Jewish Text?" Paper presented at the Annual Meeting of the North American Patristic Society. Chicago, 25 May 2018.

Lied, Liv Ingeborg, and Hugo Lundhaug, eds. *Snapshots of Evolving Traditions: Jewish and Christian Manuscript Culture, Textual Fluidity, and New Philology*. TUGAL 175. Berlin: de Gruyter, 2017.

Mirguet, Françoise. *An Early History of Compassion: Emotion and Imagination in Early Judaism*. New York: Cambridge University Press, 2017.

Najman, Hindy. "The Vitality of Scripture within and beyond the Canon." *JSJ* 43 (2012): 497–518.

Newman, Judith H. *Before the Bible: The Liturgical Body and the Formation of Scriptures in Early Judaism*. New York: Oxford University Press, 2018.

Reed, Annette Yoshiko. "The Modern Invention of Old Testament Pseudepigrapha." *JTS* 60 (2009): 403–36.

Saunders, Ernest W. *Searching the Scriptures: A History of the Society of Biblical Literature, 1880–1990*. BSNA 8. Chico, CA: Scholars Press, 1982.

Seow, Choon-Leong. *Job 1–21: Interpretation and Commentary*. Grand Rapids: Eerdmans, 2013.

Sparks, H. F. D., ed. *The Apocryphal Old Testament*. Oxford: Clarendon, 1984.

21

Future Trends for the Study of Jewish Pseudepigrapha: Two Recommendations

John C. Reeves

The past fifty years have been witness to enormous strides in the study of early Jewish pseudepigraphic writings, and much of this progress results from the important work done within or sponsored by the Pseudepigrapha program unit of the Society of Biblical Literature. It was, after all, not that long ago that works falling in this category were dismissively labeled as *intertestamental literature*, a rubric which verbally branded them as exotic outliers in the scholarly discipline of biblical studies as it was academically practiced throughout the nineteenth and much of the twentieth centuries. Standard introductions to Hebrew Bible or the New Testament rarely included excerpts or discussions of these writings among their lengthy treatments of canonical works or hypothesized scribal schools, usually relegating them instead to the ancillary anthologies of primary source materials deemed to be helpful for illuminating the historical, social, and cultural backgrounds out of which the biblical books emerged. They were conceptually and historically subjugated to their canonical peers: early Jewish pseudepigrapha like 1 Enoch or Jubilees were at best exegetical amplifications or at worst imitative, even parasitic rivals, of their presumed biblical prototypes. Under either scenario, though, the preeminence of Bible was unabashedly and uncritically foregrounded. Relatively little attention was given to the larger questions surrounding how religiously authoritative literature *tout court* might actually have been manufactured amidst the scribal circles who were operating within Second Temple and Roman era Jewish and early Christian religious communities.

This situation happily began to change during the last quarter of the twentieth and the initial decades of the twenty-first century. Thanks in large part to the full publication of the Dead Sea Scrolls and to a plethora of new critical assessments of the significance of their contents for the history of Jewish religious literature, previously unexamined assumptions about biblical priority rightly came under scrutiny. It was increasingly recognized that there was no compelling historical justification for privileging the study of the contents of the biblical books over those of contemporaneous noncanonical congeners. There was, it was realized, no fixed canon to speak of (apart from vague references to "the law of Moses" [e.g., 1QS V, 8; CD XV, 2] or what had been revealed by "his servants the prophets" [e.g., 1QS I, 3]) at the time when the Dead Sea Scrolls were being inked or even for some time thereafter, and this dawning realization has been confirmed by a reconsideration of the textual evidence stemming from other locales in the Mediterranean world where biblically based religions reveal their presence. Conceptions of what constituted Bible or sacred Scripture varied regionally among the different religious communities who staked a claim to an ethnic and/or a confessional affiliation with the heirs of Abraham. Unfiltered textual cues emanating ultimately from the Jewish diasporas in Mesopotamia, Syria, Asia Minor, North and East Africa, and the Arabian peninsula and which are sometimes also mediated through Christian and Muslim traditionists exhibit an extraordinarily broad range of traditions to which scripturally fixated communities and individuals would make appeal, and it is evident that a sizeable number of them do not fall within the anachronistically imagined boundaries of our Western biblical canon(s).

Wider acknowledgement of the significant ramifications of this necessary theoretical reorientation is now revolutionizing how we might responsibly reconstruct the history of early Jewish (and Christian) literature. Students of pseudepigrapha are thus uniquely positioned to be at the forefront of those efforts that seek to understand how Bible came to be and to assess whether older source-critical and redactional theories retain their utility as models for the production of scriptural books. Continued close scrutiny of written cosmogonic, epic, legal, ritual, prophetic, and sapiential traditions of the ancient Israelites underscores the wide variety of cultural materials treasured (and vilified) by those devoted to the cultic service of the God of Abraham, and the evidence that is provided by the pseudepigrapha can no longer be subordinated to what later Jewish and Christian groups proclaim to be Bible in light of this latter label's demonstrable editorial and textual volatility over much of the first millennium.

But in addition to coming to terms with this fundamental paradigm shift, students of pseudepigrapha also need to grapple more seriously and

21. Future Trends for the Study of Jewish Pseudepigrapha 417

systematically with issues pertaining to the continuing transmission of noncanonical writings and traditions within and across formal religious boundaries over the *longue durée*. Since the nineteenth century, scholars have remarked on the unexpected existence within medieval Jewish manuscripts of Semitic language versions of old biblically affiliated tales of Jewish origin such as Tobit, Judith, and Bel and the Dragon, works previously thought to exist only in Greek and later Christian language editions.[1] The initial years of research devoted to exploring the remains of the Cairo Genizah witnessed the astonishing discovery of several Second Temple Jewish literary products such as portions of Hebrew Ben Sira, the remains of an apparent Aramaic language predecessor of the Greek Testament of Levi, and the controversial Zadokite Fragments or so-called Damascus Document, a work eventually recognized as having originated among the Jewish sectarian community famous for their first-century deposit of what are now known as the Dead Sea Scrolls.[2] Citations from written works attributed to biblical characters such as Adam, Seth, Enosh, and Enoch occur among the literary productions of the third-century Mesopotamian prophetic religion founded by the infamous Christian heretic Mani, including one work, the so-called Book of Giants, whose Middle Iranian and Old Turkic versions are clearly indebted to a much older Aramaic composition recovered from the Dead Sea Scrolls.[3] Analogous hints to the likely existence of written works associated with antediluvian biblical characters are also extant in Mandaean and other Aramaic-language gnostic writings emanating in late antiquity amidst the Syro-Mesopotamian cultural sphere. Syriac language compilations of biblical legends and

---

1. For examples of such texts, see Adolf Neubauer, *The Book of Tobit: A Chaldee Text from a Unique Ms. in the Bodleian Library* (Oxford: Clarendon, 1878); Adolph Jellinek, *Bet ha-Midrasch: Sammlung kleiner Midraschim und vermischler Abhandlungen aus der ältern jüdischen Literatur*, 6 vols. (Jerusalem: Bamberger & Wahrmann, 1938), 1:130–31; 2:12–22; David Flusser, ed., *Sefer Yosippon*, 2 vols. (Jerusalem: Bialik, 1978–1980), 1:25–43; Eli Yassif, ed., *Sefer ha-Zikronot hu' Divrey ha-Yamim le-Yeraḥme'el* (Tel Aviv: Tel Aviv University, 2001), 231–79; and the references compiled by Alexander Marx, "An Aramaic Fragment of the Wisdom of Solomon," *JBL* 40 (1921): 57–69.

2. See especially the detailed discussion of Stefan C. Reif, *A Jewish Archive from Old Cairo: The History of Cambridge University's Genizah Collection* (Richmond, Surrey: Curzon, 2000), 70–120; also Flusser, *Sefer Yosippon*, 2:148–53.

3. Matthew Goff J., Loren T. Stuckenbruck, and Enrico Morano, eds., *Ancient Tales of Giants from Qumran and Turfan*, WUNT 360 (Tübingen: Mohr Siebeck, 2016).

interpretative expansions often attest the continued vitality among eastern Christian communities of older Jewish motifs, themes, and narrative cycles drawn from Second Temple era Jewish writings such as 1 Enoch, Jubilees, and the apocryphal Davidic psalms, or tale-cycles associated with biblical characters like Adam, Seth, and Abraham. Collections of biblically affiliated noncanonical lore are extant in Old Church Slavonic, Armenian, Georgian, Coptic, Ethiopic, and a host of European vernaculars, and they remain remarkably underutilized. Assemblages of so-called *Isrā'īliyyāt*, that is, "Israelite lore" within Muslim *ḥadīth*, *tafsīr*, and "tales of the prophets" (*qiṣaṣ al-anbiyā'*) collections often exhibit distinct cognizance of, and in certain cases a direct relationship to, the vocabulary, motifs, and themes found in early Jewish and Christian apocrypha and noncanonical legendry.[4] Finally, certain medieval Jewish literary compilations and testimonia produced in Western Europe, North Africa, and Byzantium arguably attest to the importation, circulation, and continuing promulgation of a wide variety of exegetical and speculative traditions which display ties with noncanonical traditions and themes.[5]

Over the past fifty years, scholars have produced a number of annotated anthologies, new Western language translations, critical textual editions, and an ever-expanding series of analytical studies probing the import of Jewish pseudepigrapha for reconstructing the intellectual history of early Judaism and nascent Christianity. By contrast, relatively little attention has been devoted to exploring the afterlife of these same works among literate circles in both the East and the West during late antiquity, the medieval centuries, and early modernity. This is an area of research that cries out for sustained attention. One might point, for example, to the Islamicate cultural sphere wherein Jewish, Christian, Muslim, and other scriptural communities were active contributors and interlocutors. Closer scrutiny might be given to the diverse traditions about prominent biblical

---

4. E.g., Steven M. Wasserstrom, "Jewish Pseudepigrapha and *Qiṣaṣ al-Anbiyā*'," in *Judaism and Islam: Boundaries, Communication and Interaction*, ed. Benjamin H. Hary, John L. Hayes, and Fred Astren (Leiden: Brill, 2000), 237–56; John C. Reeves, "Some Parascriptural Dimensions of the 'Tale of Hārūt wa-Mārūt,'" *JAOS* 135 (2015): 817–42.

5. E.g., collections such as *Sefer Yosippon* and the *Chronicles of Yeraḥme'el* (see n. 1 above) or the exegetical anthologies associated with the name of R. Moshe ha-Darshan. For the last named, note especially Martha Himmelfarb, "R. Moses the Preacher and the Testaments of the Twelve Patriarchs," *AJS Review* 9 (1984): 55–78.

figures, episodes, and themes that were allegedly introduced into early Islamic literature by shadowy figures like Ka'b al-Aḥbār (d. 652/53 CE?) and Wahb b. Munabbih (d. 728–732 CE?), infamous traditionists who enjoyed notoriety as exponents of Jewish learning.[6] Shining light on the shadows that obscure these purported textual exchanges and unraveling the tangled web produced by the intercultural sharing of extracanonical textual lore are urgent desiderata.

Scholars should also devote more time to tracing the history of the literary transmission of ancient Jewish extracanonical texts and nonbiblical lore among the Near Eastern religious communities of late antiquity and the early medieval period and then tracking their peregrinations from literate circles in the East to Jewish and Christian communities located in the West. Several plausible scenarios are beginning to emerge for explaining how such knowledge was communicated, the most promising of which seem to involve the migration or relocation of community leaders, teachers, and literati from Islamicate realms in the East and on the Mediterranean shores to the Byzantine orbit and to Christian Europe. Critical assessment of these (and other) models demands a careful comparative study of both manuscript and print resources in a variety of languages, such as Hebrew, Aramaic, Greek, Latin, Syriac, Arabic, Coptic, Armenian, Georgian, Old Church Slavonic, and Ethiopic. Happily the rapid growth in digital resources made available by libraries, museums, research institutes, and commercial vendors renders this a less daunting task than it would have been in the past. The Dead Sea Scrolls are now completely accessible in an electronic format, and the Friedberg Genizah Project provides web-based access to tens of thousands of images of Jewish manuscripts gleaned from the Cairo Genizah.[7] Many academic libraries and institutional special collections possess newly realized capabilities for producing accessible electronic versions of individual manuscript and rare print holdings. Several websites are dedicated to making rare specialist imprints of Hebrew, Aramaic, Syriac, and Arabic literature freely available for download and consultation.[8] Hence a number of the primary resources crucial for the

---

6. Roberto Tottoli, *Biblical Prophets in the Qur'ān and Muslim Literature* (Richmond, Surrey: Curzon, 2002), 89–92; 138–41.

7. Accessible at https://fjms.genizah.org/.

8. E.g., https://archive.org/; http://www.hebrewbooks.org/; http://www.bethmardutho.org/index.php/home.html. See also the resources surveyed by Kristian S. Heal, "Corpora, eLibraries, and Databases: Locating Syriac Studies in the Twenty-First Cen-

prosecution of these kinds of projects are now conveniently available in an unparalleled way.

Successfully realizing such a research program offers an important way forward for pseudepigrapha scholars to advance our discipline beyond a largely self-imposed scholastic insularity. It is becoming increasingly clear that the transmission, reception, and manipulation of extracanonical writings and traditions play critical, yet largely unheralded, roles in the more general realms of the history of ideas and of the history of speculative thought. By paying more attention to the ways in which Jewish pseudepigrapha have repeatedly percolated within wider intellectual movements and trends, we become vital contributors to the program of achieving a better understanding of our world and the cultural forces that have had a hand in shaping it.

Bibliography

Flusser, David, ed. *Sefer Yosippon*. 2 vols. Jerusalem: Bialik, 1978–1980.

Goff, Matthew J., Loren T. Stuckenbruck, and Enrico Morano, eds. *Ancient Tales of Giants from Qumran and Turfan*. WUNT 360. Tübingen: Mohr Siebeck, 2016.

Heal, Kristian S. "Corpora, eLibraries, and Databases: Locating Syriac Studies in the Twenty-First Century." *Hugoye* 15 (2012): 65–78.

Himmelfarb, Martha. "R. Moses the Preacher and the Testaments of the Twelve Patriarchs." *AJS Review* 9 (1984): 55–78.

Jellinek, Adolph. *Bet Ha-Midrasch: Sammlung kleiner Midraschim und vermischler Abhandlungen aus der ältern jüdischen Literatur*. 6 vols. Jerusalem: Bamberger & Wahrmann, 1938.

Marx, Alexander. "An Aramaic Fragment of the Wisdom of Solomon." *JBL* 40 (1921): 57–69.

Neubauer, Adolf. *The Book of Tobit: A Chaldee Text from a Unique Ms. in the Bodleian Library*. Oxford: Clarendon, 1878.

Reeves, John C. "Some Parascriptural Dimensions of the 'Tale of Hārūt wa-Mārūt.'" *JAOS* 135 (2015): 817–42.

Reif, Stefan C. *A Jewish Archive from Old Cairo: The History of Cambridge University's Genizah Collection*. Richmond, Surrey: Curzon, 2000.

---

tury," *Hugoye* 15 (2012): 65–78; Travis Zadeh, "Uncertainty and the Archive," in *The Digital Humanities and Islamic and Middle Eastern Studies*, ed. Elias Muhanna (Berlin: de Gruyter, 2016), 11–64.

Tottoli, Roberto. *Biblical Prophets in the Qurʾān and Muslim Literature.* Richmond, Surrey: Curzon, 2002.

Wasserstrom, Steven M. "Jewish Pseudepigrapha and *Qiṣaṣ al-Anbiyāʾ*." Pages in 237–56 in *Judaism and Islam: Boundaries, Communication and Interaction.* Edited by Benjamin H. Hary, John L. Hayes, and Fred Astren. Leiden: Brill, 2000.

Yassif, Eli, ed. *Sefer ha-Zikronot hu' Divrey ha-Yamim le-Yeraḥmeʾel.* Tel Aviv: Tel Aviv University, 2001.

Zadeh, Travis. "Uncertainty and the Archive." Pages 11–64 in *The Digital Humanities and Islamic and Middle Eastern Studies.* Edited by Elias Muhanna. Berlin: de Gruyter, 2016.

Contributors

William Adler
Distinguished University Professor of Religious Studies, North Carolina State University

Patricia D. Ahearne-Kroll
Assistant Professor in the Department of Classical and Near Eastern Studies, The University of Minnesota

James Hamilton Charlesworth
George L. Collord Professor of New Testament Language and Literature, Princeton Theological Seminary

Randall D. Chesnutt
William S. Banowsky Chair in Religion, Pepperdine University

John J. Collins
Holmes Professor of Old Testament Criticism & Interpretation, Yale Divinity School

James R. Davila
Professor of Early Jewish Studies, The University of Saint Andrews

Lorenzo DiTommaso
Professor of Religions & Cultures, Concordia University Montréal, Canada

Irene Peirano Garrison
Associate Professor of Classics, Yale University

Matthias Henze
Isla Carol and Percy E. Turner Professor of Hebrew Bible and Early Judaism, Rice University

Martha Himmelfarb
William H. Danforth Professor of Religion, Princeton University

Robert A. Kraft
Berg Professor of Religious Studies Emeritus, The University of Pennsylvania

John R. Levison
W. J. A. Power Professor of Old Testament Interpretation and Biblical Hebrew, Southern Methodist University Perkins School of Theology

Liv Ingeborg Lied
Professor of Religious Studies, MF Norwegian School of Theology, Religion and Society

Hindy Najman
Oriel and Laing Professor of the Interpretation of Holy Scripture, The University of Oxford

Judith H. Newman
Professor of Hebrew Bible and Early Judaism, Emmanuel College of Victoria University in the University of Toronto, Canada

George W. E. Nickelsburg
Emeritus Professor of Religion, The University of Iowa

John C. Reeves
Blumenthal Professor of Judaic Studies and Professor of Religious Studies, The University of North Carolina at Charlotte

Michael E. Stone
Emeritus Professor of Armenian Studies and of Comparative Religion, The Hebrew University of Jerusalem, Israel

Loren T. Stuckenbruck
Professor of New Testament (with emphasis on Second Temple Judaism),
The Ludwig Maximilian University of Munich, Germany

Hanna Tervanotko
Assistant Professor of Religious Studies, McMaster University, Canada

Eibert Tigchelaar
Professor of Biblical Studies, The KU Leuven, Belgium

Benjamin G. Wright III
University Distinguished Professor of Religion Studies, Lehigh University

Ancient Sources Index

Hebrew Bible/Old Testament		2 Kings	
		6:24–8:3	214
Genesis	141, 143, 180, 346–47		
1–3	401	1 Chronicles	137 n. 9, 347
1–5	402		
1:24	402	2 Chronicles	137 n. 9, 347
1:26–27	402		
1:31	320–21	Ezra	137 n. 9, 289
6:1–4	363		
11	320	Nehemiah	137 n. 9
Exodus	141, 143, 180	Esther	265, 274, 276–77
15:11	348		
31	349	Job	135, 213 n. 27
35	349		
		Psalms	
Leviticus	141	72:8	293
16:7–10	367	105:20	402
20:26	348		
		Proverbs	135
Numbers	141		
22–24	362	Qoheleth	105, 135–36
Deuteronomy	138, 141	Song of Songs	135
4:15–18	402		
32:21	320	Isaiah	212 n. 26
32:37	320	7:14	112
		55	348
Joshua	347	56:7	322
		64:4, 5	305
1, 2 Samuel	364		
		Jeremiah	63, 212 n. 26, 369
1 Kings	298		
5:12	298	Ezekiel	71, 289, 367
		15	321

Daniel 40, 105, 118, 121, 137 n. 9, 212 n. 26, 268–69, 276, 342–43, 347

Zephaniah 289

Zechariah 292, 369

Inscriptions from Ancient Israel

Tell Deir 'Alla 362

Apocrypha/Deuterocanonical Books

Tobit 69, 106 n. 9, 119, 136, 209 n. 15, 270–71, 281, 302, 303, 372, 417

Judith 2, 5, 34, 69, 106 n. 9, 182, 264, 274–79, 281, 302, 303, 417
4:8–15 276

Additions to Esther 106 n. 9, 277 n. 44

Wisdom of Solomon 69, 106 n. 9, 121, 136, 323

Ben Sira 2, 63, 70, 71, 106 n. 9, 121, 136, 138, 208, 209, 265, 274, 417

Baruch 63, 106 n. 9, 264, 274, 278
4:30–5:6 278

Letter of Jeremiah 106 n. 9

Additions to Daniel 106 n. 9, 302–3, 417

Susanna 302–3

1 Maccabees 63, 106 n. 9, 274

2 Maccabees 63, 106 n. 9
3:14–21 276
7 193 n. 57

1 Esdras 106 n. 9

Prayer of Manasseh 69 n. 36, 106 n. 9, 208, 214 n. 30, 215 nn. 33–34

Psalm 151 106 n. 9

3 Maccabees 88–89, 106 n. 9, 276–79, 281–82
1:10 276
1:16–25 276
3:4 277
3:8–10 281

2 Esdras 106 n. 9, 370–371

4 Maccabees 89, 106 n. 9, 116 n. 37

Dead Sea Scrolls

Apocryphal Psalms (11Q11) 372

Apocryphon of Jeremiah A–C (4Q385–386; etc.) 86, 119, 161, 165

Apocryphon of Joshua (4Q522) 165

Apocalypse of Jubilees (4Q392) 161 n. 9

Aramaic Apocryphal Work (4Q310) 86

Aramaic Levi Document (1Q21; 4Q213–214) 37, 70, 123, 160, 208, 270–72, 281, 363–62

Birth of Noah (4Q534–536) 86

Book of Giants (1Q23–24; 2Q26; 4Q203, 4Q530–533; 6Q8) 86, 163–64, 210, 363–62, 367, 417

Copper Scroll (3Q15) 366, 377

Damascus Document (CD) 70, 81, 116 n. 37, 208, 417
II,15 142
II,17–19 143

Ancient Sources Index   429

XV, 2	416
XVI,2–4	143
Daniel Apocryphon (4Q246)	86
David Apocryphon (2Q22)	86
Enoch (4Q201; 4Q208–209)	163
Four Kingdoms (552–553)	119
Genesis Apocryphon (1Q20; 6Q8)	86, 119, 161, 165, 346–347
Joseph Apocryphon (Mas1m)	86
Joshua Apocryphon^{a–b} (4Q380–381)	86
Melchizedek (11Q13)	86
Midrash Sefer Moses (4Q249, 4Q445)	86
Moses Pseudepigrapha (4Q377–378)	119
New Jerusalem (1Q32; 2Q24; 4Q554–555; 5Q15; 11Q18)	263–64
Prayer of Nabonidus (4Q242)	119, 161
Pseudo-Daniel (4Q243–245)	165
Pseudo-Ezekiel (4Q387–391)	119, 165
Reworked Pentateuch (4Q158; 4Q366–369)	141–42, 344 n. 24
Rule of the Community (1QS)	
I,3	416
IV,21	402
V,8	416
Temple Scroll (11QT)	14, 88, 119–20, 140
Testament of Amram. *See* Vision of Amram	

Testament of Benjamin (4Q538)	86
Testament of Jacob (4Q537)	86, 119
Testament of Joseph (4Q539)	86, 119
Testament of Judah ((3Q7; 4Q484)	86, 119
Testament of Levi (1Q21; 4Q213–214)	86, 119, 162, 271–72
Testament of Naphtali (4Q215)	86, 208, 368
Testament of Qohath (4Q542)	86, 119
Tobit (4Q196–200)	119
Vision of Amram (4Q543–544, 4Q546–548)	86, 119, 161
Words of Moses (1Q22)	119
Zadokite Documents. *See* Damascus Document	

Josephus and Philo

Josephus   85, 88, 137 n. 8, 206 n. 7, 309, 364, 391

Josephus, *Antiquitates judaicae*	
18.11–22	138
Josephus, *Bellum judaicum*	
2.119–166	138
6.196, 201–213	214
Josephus, *Contra Apionem*	
2.190–219	324

Philo   85, 109, 137 n. 8, 206 n. 7, 279, 309, 325, 364, 391

Philo, *De migration Abrahami*
89   324

Philo, *Hypothetica*
7.1–9   324

Pseudepigrapha

1 Enoch   2, 16, 17, 23, 25 n. 36, 26, 32, 35, 36, 45, 46, 63, 65–66, 67 n. 30, 86, 97–98, 107–8, 113–18, 121, 139–40, 142–43, 151, 157, 159–64, 204–5, 209, 211–212 n. 24, 213–14, 217, 222, 290–91, 294–95, 297, 298, 306, 309–10, 312, 390, 415, 418

1–5   163
1–36   205–6, 263–64, 266–73, 281, 306, 326
1:1–32:6   114 n. 31, 266
1:9   289
6–19   164
6:6   290
14:22   266
19:3–21:9   266–67
37–71   161, 163–64, 207, 212 n. 24
48:10   207
52:4   207
65:5   207
65:11   207
69:29   207
72   214
72–82   144, 148–49, 161, 163, 269–70
76–79   163
82   163
82–84   219
83–84   212 n. 24
83–90   121, 266, 268–70
89   219
91–105   206, 266, 268–69
91:11–17   121, 266
91:14   207
91:18–19   207
92:3   207
93:1–10   121, 266
94:1   207

99–100   219
103–104   219
105:2   207
106–107   269
106:1–18   214
108   212 n. 24

2 Baruch   16, 21, 107 n. 12, 115–16, 121, 123–24, 151, 204–5, 210 n. 20, 212 n. 26, 213–14, 217, 221–22, 309, 312, 318, 319, 325, 399, 403, 411–10
53   23
56–74   23
78–87   107, 113

2 Enoch   45, 113, 114 n. 31, 116 n. 37, 117 n. 43, 164, 211 n. 24, 217, 267, 169, 270, 309, 326, 400–99
3–9   267 n. 13
3–22   267 n. 13
6   269 n. 21
11–16   269 n. 21

3 Baruch   16, 21, 116 n. 37, 146–47, 211 n. 24, 213, 270, 279–80, 309, 314–27, 393 n. 24
1:2   320, 321
4   321
4:15   317, 325
4:17   317
12:6   317
13:2   317
13:4   317
15:2   317
15:4   317
15:24   317
16:2   317, 320
16:3   317

3 Enoch   68 n. 33, 85, 208–209

4 Baruch. *See* Paralipomena of Jeremiah

4 Ezra   2, 16, 23, 25 n. 36, 26, 32, 38, 63–64, 82, 99 n. 9, 107, 113, 116 n. 37, 121,

Ancient Sources Index

152 n. 48, 205, 210 n. 20, 212 n. 26, 213–15, 222, 301, 318–19, 321, 325, 371, 399, 403
3:1   350
8   215 n. 33
12:37–38   300
14:3   350
14:38–50   211
14:42–48   300, 350

5 Ezra   370, 373

6 Ezra (2 Esd 15–16) 371, 373

5 Maccabees   85

Adam Octipartite/Septipartite   375

Apocalypse of Abraham   117 n. 43, 211 n. 24, 309

Apocalypse of Adam   85

Apocalypse of Daniel 85

Apocalypse of Ezra   371

Apocalypse of Elijah 305, 365, 375

Apocalypse of Moses   23, 25 n. 36, 279, 305, 373, 400
20:2   402
21:6   402
39:2–3   402

Apocalypse of Sedrach   85

Apocrypha of Jeremiah   305

Apocryphon of Eber   375

Apocryphon of Elijah 298

Apocryphon of Ezekiel   71 n. 44, 374–73

Apocryphon of Isaiah   292, 296, 303

Apocryphon of Jeremiah 305

Apocryphon of Seth   375

Aramaic Levi Document   37, 70, 123, 160, 208, 270–72, 281, 363–62

Aristobulus   121

Artapanus   121

Ascension of Isaiah   85, 115, 305, 311, 390, 393 n. 24

Ascension of Moses   294, 297, 298, 301

Assumption of Moses. See Testament of Moses

Book of Asaph   366

Book of Baruch   375

Book of Noah   143 n. 20, 366, 375

Book of the Covenant 375

Books of Adam and Eve   116 n. 37, 148 n. 38, 182, 279, 306

Cave of Treasures   372

Dispute over Abraham 375

Eighth Book of Moses 373

Eldad and Modad   375

Enoch Apocryphon (Coptic)   368

Ezekiel the Tragedian   26

Fifth Ezra (2 Esd 1–2)   370

Fifteen Signs of Doomsday 250, 252

Hazon Gabriel 364

Hebrew Apocryphon of Jeremiah 370

Hebrew Naphtali 367–66

History of Joseph (Syriac) 368–67

History of the Rechabites 81

Hygromancy of Solomon 373

Inquiry of Abraham 375

Jannes and Jambres 297, 374

Jeremiah's Prophecy to Pashhur 369–68

Joseph and Aseneth 2, 5, 21, 31, 35, 45, 46, 61, 81, 97, 99, 108–12, 123–24, 152 n. 48, 182, 213, 279–80, 309, 312, 386, 390, 393 n. 24

Jubilees 2, 16, 23, 69, 107, 114 n. 31, 115–16, 117 n. 43, 118, 121, 140, 142–43, 148 n. 38, 157, 159–62, 169, 180–81, 205–6, 209, 212 n. 26, 213–15, 219, 241, 263, 266, 272, 304 n. 29, 306, 309–10, 349, 366, 390, 399, 411, 415
1:1–4 349
10:1–4 366

Ladder of Jacob 326

Latin Vision of Ezra 371

Letter of Aristeas 2, 41, 116 n. 37, 121, 138, 152 n. 48, 265, 279, 323, 390

Liber antiquitatum biblicarum 17, 69 n. 37, 81, 180–81, 189–90, 192–93, 364, 372, 391

Life of Adam and Eve 5, 16, 110, 117 n. 43, 148 n. 38, 279, 311, 373, 390–89, 399–405
17 402
19:3 402
21:2 402
21:6 402
33–35 402
37:5 402

Life of Mani 375

Lives of the Prophets 150, 311

Lunationes Danielis 370

Martyrdom of Isaiah 16, 85, 116 n. 37

Nine and a Half Tribes 364–63, 375

Odes of Solomon 16, 17, 26, 80, 89

Oracles of Hystaspes 369, 375

Palea Historica 372

Paralipomena of Jeremiah 2, 17, 25, 26, 27 n. 43, 59, 60 n. 1, 61, 97, 213, 319, 386, 393 n. 24

Penitence of Solomon 248–49, 251–52

Phylactery of Moses 373

Prayer of Jacob 81, 85

Prayer of Joseph 81, 290, 302

Psalms of Solomon 16, 113, 115, 116, 121, 264, 274, 277–79, 281, 390
11 278

Pseudo-Philo. *See* Liber antiquitatum biblicarum

Ancient Sources Index 433

Pseudo-Phocylides 323–24, 325

Questions of the Queen of Sheba
and Answers by King Solomon 369

Revelation of Gabriel. *See* Hazon Gabriel

Selendromion of David and Solomon 373

Seventh Vision of Daniel 370

Sibylla Maga 369

Sibylline Oracles 82, 111–12, 115–16,
  117 n. 43, 309
  3 323
  3:762–766 322–23
  4:8–11 319
  4:116 319
  5 318

Somnalia Danielis 370

Song of the Lamb 364

Songs of David 364

Story of Melchizedek 215–16, 220 n.
  44, 368, 372

Story of Zosimus 393 n. 24

Sword of Moses 365–366, 372

Syriac Apocalypse of Daniel 370

Testament of Abraham 2, 27 nn. 43–44,
  30, 37, 56, 61, 67 n. 29, 82, 97, 99, 270,
  279–82, 323, 326, 386, 391

Testament of Adam 71, 81, 83, 84, 372

Testament of Job 2, 21, 31, 45, 61, 97,
  189, 192, 213, 279–82, 323, 326, 373–
  72, 386

Testament of Joseph 2, 27 n. 44, 31, 61,
  85, 97, 99, 386

Testament of Judah 85, 366

Testament of Levi 85, 157, 159, 161,
  272, 326, 417

Testament of Moses 2, 17–18, 23, 26, 27
  n. 44, 30, 56, 61, 97, 98, 107, 113, 114
  n. 31, 115–16, 205, 217, 219, 300, 375,
  386
  1:16–17 300 n. 24

Testament of Naphtali 70, 85, 105 n. 6,
  161, 367

Testament of Solomon 81, 215 n. 34, 372,
  374

Testaments of the Twelve Patriarchs 16,
  21, 62–63, 85, 110–13, 115, 116 n. 37,
  117 n. 43, 118–19, 123, 145–46, 159–
  62, 209, 213, 272, 279 80, 311, 323,
  393 n. 24

Testaments of the Three Patriarchs 82, 85

Tiburtine Sibyl 369

Treatise of the Vessels 366–65, 377

New Testament

Matthew
  3:17 208 n. 11
  12:18b 208 n. 11
  13:57 291
  17:5 208 n. 11
  23:31 291
  23:35 291, 292
  23:37–39 293
  24:23–28 301
  25:23 317
  27:9 297

27:9–10	305, 369	Hebrews	55, 298, 342
27:11	297	5:5	208 n. 11
		11:37	292
Mark			
1:11	208 n. 11	James	340
Luke		2 Peter	340
3:22	208 n. 11	2:17	208 n. 11
11:50–51	305		
23:46		2 John	340
John	55	3 John	340
1:18	290		
16:20, 31	402	Jude	297, 298, 340
		14	289
Acts	340, 405		
7:52	292	Revelation	318, 340, 364
7:55–56	402	8:3, 31, 35, 42	402
Romans	138		
1	402–404	*Christian Literature*	
1:18–25	402–403		
3:23	402	Acts of Andrew	341
7:7	402		
10:19	320	Acts of John	341
1 Corinthians		Acts of Paul	340
2:9	297, 305, 402		
		Africanus, *Epistula ad Origenem*	
2 Corinthians	298	1	303
11:14	402	2	303
12:4	402		
		Aphraat	372
Galatians			
6:15	305	Apocalypse of Ezra	371
Ephesians		Apocalypse of Paul	326
3:2–3	402		
5:14	305	Apocalypse of Peter	266, 340
1 Thessalonians		Barnabas	340
5:21	293	4:3a	289
2 Timothy	298	Cave of Treasures	372
3:8	297		

Ancient Sources Index

Chronicon Paschale	368	History of Joseph (Syriac)	368–67
Clement, *Eclogae propheticae*		Infancy Gospel of Matthew	110
2.1	291		
53.4	289 n. 7, 291	Infancy Gospel of Thomas	110
Clement, *Paedagogus*		Irenaeus, *Adversus Haereses*	
1.9.84.2	289 n. 7	1.13.1	293
Clement, *Stromateis*	107, 289	Jeremiah's Prophecy to Pashhur	369–68
1.1.13.2–3	290		
3.4.29.1	289–90 n. 8	Jerome	370
3.16.100.4	289 n. 7		
6.6.53	289 n. 7	Jerome, *Commentariorum in Isaiam*	
6.15.132	301	17	305
Dersane Gabriel	212 n. 26, 213 n. 27	Jerome, *Commentariorum in Matthaeum*	
		4	305
Enoch Apocryphon (Coptic)	368		
		Jerome, *Explanatio in Daniele*	
Ephrem	372	Prologue	342–43
Epiphanius	272	Julius Africanus	272
Eusebius, *Historia ecclesiastica*	339	Kedrenos	272
3.25.1–5	340		
3.25.5	341	Latin Vision of Ezra	371
3.25.6–7	341		
6.25.2	274	Lunationes Danielis	370
6.25.13	342		
		Matthew Paris, *Chronica Majora*	110
Euthalius, *Editio Epistolarum Pauli*	305, 306		
		Melchizedek Codex (Nag Hammadi)	59
Gospel of Mary	55	Moses of Aggel	109
Gospel of Peter	266, 341	Origen	274, 288–307
Gospel of the Hebrews	340	Origen, *Commentariorum in evangelium Matthaei*	
Gospel of the Truth	55	10.18	290 n. 10
		10.18.50–53	292
Gospel of Matthias	341	10.18.56–60	292
		17.2	295 n. 18
Gospel of Thomas	341	23	293

Origen, *Commentarii in evangelium*
Joannis	294
2.31	290
2.31.188	291
2.31.192	302
6.42.217	291
13.17.104	296
19.15.97	295 n. 18, 301

Origen, *Commentarium series in evangelium Matthaei*
28	297
46	301
117 [249.16–22]	297
117 [250.9–12]	298

Origen, *Commentarius in Canticum* 301
32	298
33	302
33–34	299
34	299, 300

Origen, *Contra Celsum*
5.54	295

Origen, *De Principiis*
2.3.6	314
3.2.1	294
3.4.1	297
4.35	294 n. 16

Origen, *Epistula ad Africanum*
4	303
5	303
9	292, 303–304
11.65	295
12	304 n. 26
13	302

Origen, *Homiliae in Numeros*
28.2.1	294, 302

Palea Historica	372
Papias	370, 375

Priscillian of Avila, *Tractate*
3.56 [44.19–20]	305 n. 31
3.60 [47.3–18]	305 n. 31
3.68 [53.3–5]	305 n. 31

Pseudo-Augustine, "Sermon on the Jews"	110
Pseudo-Methodius	249–250
Pseudo-Zachariah Rhetor	109
Questions of the Queen of Sheba and Answers by King Solomon	369
Seventh Vision of Daniel	370
Shepherd of Hermas	340
Sibylla Maga	369
Somnalia Danielis	370
Story of Melchizedek	215–216, 220 n. 44, 368, 372

Syncellus, *Ecloga Chronographica* 107 n. 11, 267, 272
27.12–18	306

Syriac Apocalypse of Daniel	370
Tatian of Adiabene	89
Thunder, Perfect Mind	55
Tiburtine Sibyl	369

Vincent of Beauvais, *Speculum Historiale* 111

Vindicta Salvatoris	110

Ancient Sources Index

Greco-Roman Writers and Literature

Aelian, *Varia Historia*
9.15 — 342 n. 20

Alexander Polyhistor — 82, 89

Anacreontea — 334

Appendix Vergiliana — 345

Callimachis, *Epigrams*
6 — 342 n. 20

Callinicus — 343

Chaeremon — 279

Dionysius of Halicarnassus, *De Dinarcho*
4 — 337–38
11 — 338

Iamblichus, *De vita Pythagorica*

Meleager — 334

Plutarch — 405
Plutarch, *Moralia* — 347

Porphyry, *Adversus Christianos* — 342–43

Pseudo-Callisthenes — 69

Pseudo-Virgil, *Culex* — 345–46

Quintilian, *Institutio Oratoria*
1.4.3 — 339, 341

Sallust — 333

Servius, *Bucolica*
3.20 — 342 n. 20

Servius, *Georgics*
3.435 — 346

3.435–438 — 346 n. 28

Suetonius-Donatus, *Vita Vergiliana*

Theognidea — 334

Varius — 342 n. 20

Virgil — 333, 342 n. 20, 345, 347

Virgil, *Eclogues* — 345

Virgil, *Georgics* — 345
3 — 346

Virgil, *Aeneid* — 345

Rabbinic and Nonrabbinic Works and Authors of Late Antiquity

Ahiqar — 116 n. 37

Babylonian Talmud
Bava Batra 140b — 177 n. 5
Bekhorot 42b — 177 n.5
Nazir 12b — 177 n. 5
Yevamot 72a — 177 n. 5

Book of Asaph — 366

Book of the Mysteries. *See* Sefer HaRazim

Chronicles of Jerahmeel 69, 367, 418 n. 5

Eldad ha-Dani — 209 n. 15

Fables of Aesop — 209 n. 15

Harba di-Moshe. *See* Sword of Moses

Hebrew Naphtali — 367–368

Hebrew Visions of Hell and Paradise 367

Josippon — 69, 418 n. 5

Maasekhet Kelim. *See* Treatise of the Vessels

Megillat Antiochus	69
Midrash of Shemihazai and Aza'el	367
Midrash Wa-yissa'u	70, 366
Pirqe Avot	81, 116 n. 37
Pirqe di Rabbi Eliezer	69
Proverbs of Sandabar	209 n. 15
Proverbs of Solomon	209 n. 15
R. Moshe ha-Darshan	418 n. 5
Sefer Asaf HaRofe	69
Sefer Eliyyahu	70 n. 43
Sefer HaRazim	365, 372
Sefer Zerubbabel	365
Speech of Aphar and Dinah	209 n. 15
Sword of Moses	365–366, 372
Treatise of the Vessels	366–367, 377

Muslim Works and Authors

ḥadīth, tafsīr	418
Isrā'īliyyāt	418
Ka'b al-Aḥbār	419
Wahb b. Munabbih	419

Modern Scholars Index

Abercrombie, John R. 54
Adams, Sean A. 274 n. 36
Adelman, Rachel 69 n. 35
Adler, William   7, 8, 29, 64, 65, 65 n. 24, 107 nn. 10–11, 115 n. 36, 170 n. 36, 216 n. 35, 220 n. 44, 223 n. 51, 287, 306 n. 33, 372 n. 36
Ahearne-Kroll, Patricia D.   6, 103, 124 n. 65, 133 n. 1, 181 n. 20, 184 n. 30
Albert, Lee S. H. 185 n. 35
Alexander, Philip S.   68, 68 n. 33, 337 n. 12, 344 n. 24
Allen, Garrick 231
Amihai, Aryeh 71 n. 44
Ammann, Sonja 184 n. 32
Anderson, Bernhard W. 12
Anderson, F. 82
Anderson, Gary A.   148 n. 38, 182 n. 24
Anderson, Hugh 88, 89
Andrews, Tara 231 n. 2
Arcari, Luca   267 n. 11, 273, 273 n. 35
Archer, Gleason L. 343
Atkinson, Kenneth 121 n. 53
Attridge, Harold 60, 96
Bader, Mary 184 n. 31
Bailey, Ryan 215 n. 34
Ballaban, S. A. 69 n. 35
Barclay, John M. G.   121 n. 54, 279, 279 n. 54, 280, 280 n. 57, 281, 281 n. 60
Bardy, Gustave 289 n. 6
Barr, James 268, 268 n. 14
Barrett, C. K. 403
Batalova, Stilyana 231 n. 2
Bauckham, Richard   2, 65, 65 n. 25, 105, 106 n. 8, 123 n. 64, 136 n. 8, 166 nn. 24–25, 167 n. 28, 212 n. 25, 312, 312 n. 14, 359, 360 n. 3, 361 n. 6, 365 n. 13, 371 n. 34, 375, 375 n. 46, 376 n. 48, 384 n. 6, 385 n. 7, 392 n. 23, 410 n. 4
Baum, Armin D. 336 n. 10
Baynes, Leslie 107 n. 12
Beal, Timothy 411 n. 7
Beare, Frank W. 12 n. 5, 13
Becker, Adam H. 312 n. 15
Bell, David 253 n. 68
Ben-Dov, Jonathan 149, 149 n. 39
Benoit, Pierre 84, 91
Bergren, Theodore   29, 371 nn. 28–29
Bernstein, Moshe J.   165 n. 23, 344 n. 24
Berrin, Shani L. 344 n. 24
Bertrand, Daniel A. 401, 401 n. 6
Betz, Hans D. 16 n. 17,
Birnbaum, David J. 231 n. 2
Black, Matthew   19, 21, 89, 122 n. 57, 206 n. 6, 264 n. 2, 267 n. 9, 269 n. 18
Blum, Rudolph 338 n. 14
Boccaccini, Gabriele   65, 138 n. 12, 180 n. 15
Bockmuehl, Markus 344 n. 24
Bogaert, Pierre-Maurice   21, 21 n. 30, 190 n. 47, 371 n. 32
Bohak, Gideon   68 n. 32, 183 n. 25, 372 n. 37
Bohlinger, Tavis A. 185 n. 35
Bondarev, Dmitry 254 n. 71
Bonde, Sheila 231 n. 2
Bonner, Stanley F. 347 n. 30
Bons, Eberhard   277, 277 n. 46, 278, 278 n. 50

-439-

Bonwetsch, Gottlieb Nathanael 234, 314, 314 n. 21
Borchardt, Francis 185 n. 35, 187 n. 41, 188, 188 n. 43
Born, R. E. 84
Böttrich, Christfried 219, 267 n. 13
Bousset, William 116, 116 n. 39, 117, 125 n. 67, 310, 310 n. 3
Boyarin, Daniel 312 n. 15, 337 n. 12
Boyd-Taylor, Cameron 149 n. 40
Boyle, Jennifer E. 231 n. 2
Breech, Earl 99
Brakke, David 304 n. 30, 336 n. 10, 340 n. 17, 348 n. 32
Brandenburger, E. 403
Bremer-McCollum, Adam 206 n. 9, 215 n. 33
Brenna, Christopher E. J. 184 n. 32
Brenner-Idan, Athalya 183 n. 27, 190 n. 50
Brisson, Luc 177 n. 5
Brock, Sebastian P. 21, 21 n. 29, 66, 66 n. 28, 216 n. 37, 369 n. 24
Brooke, George J. 141 n. 17, 337 n. 12, 344 n. 24
Brooten, Bernadette 183 n. 28
Brown, R. E. 84
Brownlee, William H. 344 n. 24
Buitenwerf, Rieuwerd 112 n. 25, 369 n. 22
Burchard, Christoph 109 n. 16
Burgess, Helen J. 231 n. 2
Burke, Tony 376, 377 n. 50
Burkhardt, Frederick 24, 24 n. 33
Butler, Judith 176 n. 4
Calabro, David 231
Callaway, Phillip R. 141 n. 17
Campagnolo, Alberto 258 n. 82
Celenza, Christopher S. 343 n. 23
Ceriani, Antonio M. 113 n. 31, 218 n. 38
Chadwick, Henry 305 n. 31
Chalmer, David J. 253 n. 69
Charles, Robert H. 26, 26 n. 39, 60, 61 n. 2, 80, 80 n. 3, 81, 84, 113 n. 31, 115,

116 n. 37, 136 n. 8, 138 n. 11, 180, 180 n. 14, 212 n. 25, 234, 287, 287 n.1, 288, 288 n. 2, 288 n. 5, 315, 360, 360 n. 4, 384 n. 6, 400, 409, 409 n. 3
Charles, Ronald 152 n. 48
Charlesworth, James H. 2, 6, 16, 16 nn. 16–17, 17 nn. 18–19, 18, 18 n. 21–23, 19, 21, 22, 23, 23 n. 32, 24, 24 n. 34, 25, 25 n. 36–38, 26, 26 nn. 40–41, 27, 27 n. 42, 28 n. 45, 30, 59, 61, 61 n. 9, 62, 62 n. 12, 70, 70 nn. 41–42, 79, 79 n. 1, 80 n. 2, 86 n. 5, 87, 88, 88 n. 7, 90 n. 8, 92, 96, 106 n. 9, 118 n. 44, 121, 121 n. 55, 136, 136 n. 8, 157 n. 1, 158 n. 2, 175 n. 1, 189 n. 46, 212 n. 25, 315, 359, 359 n. 1, 361, 371, 373, 384 n. 6, 385 n. 7, 387, 387 n. 13, 399, 409, 409 n. 3
Charlesworth, Jean H. 88
Chesnutt, Randall D. 8, 11, 29, 88, 183 n. 25, 269 n. 19, 270 n. 24, 383
Childs, Brevard S. 12
Cioată, Maria 170 n. 36, 213 n. 28
Clark, Andy 253 n. 69
Clark, Kenneth W. 16 n. 17
Clark, Mark J. 251 n. 64
Clarke, Kent D. 332 n. 2
Clivaz, Claire 231 n. 2
Coblentz-Bautch, Kelley 30, 266 n. 6
Cohen, Shaye J. D. 323 n. 56
Cohn, L. 69 n. 37
Collins, Adela Yarbro 326 n. 65
Collins, John J. 2, 8, 27, 29, 30, 60, 61 n. 8, 63, 64, 80, 82, 96, 97, 98 n.7, 121 n. 54, 122 n. 56, 125 n. 67, 144 n. 23, 158, 158 nn. 3–4, 279, 279 n. 55, 280, 280 n. 56, 281, 281 n. 61, 309, 310 n. 2, 312 n. 12, 318 n. 41, 321 n. 51, 322 nn. 54–55, 388 n. 15, 388 n. 17
Colson, F. H. 324
Conroy, Charles 240 n. 29
Coogan, Jeremiah 214 n. 30
Cook, Edward M. 362 n. 8
Cowley, Roger 66, 66 n. 28
Cranz, F. Edward 236 n. 15
Craven, Toni 182 n. 23

Crawford, Sidnie White   120 n. 50, 142 n. 18, 182 n. 23, 344 n. 24
Crenshaw, Kimberle   178 n. 8
Cribiore, Raffaella   347 n. 30
Crombie, Frederick   303, 304
Cross, Frank M.   88, 91, 159, 163 n. 14
Daniel-Nataf, Suzanne   54
Daschke, Derek   318 n. 41
Davila, James R.   2, 8, 65, 65 n. 25, 105, 106 n. 8, 123 n. 61, 123 n. 64, 136 n. 8, 146 n. 28, 166 nn. 24–25, 167 n. 28, 169 n. 35, 212 n. 25, 239 n. 24, 280 nn. 58–59, 313, 313 nn. 16–18, 323 n. 59, 359, 360 n. 3, 361 n. 6, 362 n. 9, 363 n. 10, 365, 366 n. 17, 376 n. 48, 384 n. 6, 385 n. 7, 392 n. 23, 392 n. 24, 410 n. 4
Davies, W. D.   23, 79, 84, 88, 399, 403
Davies, Philip R.   135, 135 n. 6, 141 n. 17
Davis, Stacy   189 n. 45
Day, Peggy L.   191 n. 51
Deane, William J.   115, 115 n. 35
Delisle, Léopold   255 n. 73
Denis, Albert-Marie   20, 20 n. 27, 21, 22, 25, 25 nn. 36–37, 27, 30, 62, 62 n. 12, 70, 70 n. 41, 96, 385 n. 7
Dervensis, Adso   249 n. 58
DesCamps, Mary T.   192 n. 57
Desreumaux, Alain   214 n. 32
Dillmann, August   113 n. 31, 207, 207 n. 10, 234
Dimant, Devorah   119 n. 46, 120 nn. 49–50, 143 n. 20, 165 n. 22, 270, 270 nn. 26–27, 271 n. 28
DiTommaso, Lorenzo   7, 62 n. 12, 65 n. 24, 68, 68 n. 34, 170 n. 36, 211 n. 24, 218 n. 38, 219 n. 40, 220, 220 n. 45, 234 n. 9, 240 n. 27, 247 n. 51, 248 n. 54, 249 n. 56, 250 n. 59, 251 n. 64, 254 n. 72, 370, 370 n. 27
Dobroruka, Vicente   375
Dochhorn, Jan   401, 401 n. 6
Dorival, Gilles   265 n. 3
Drawnel, Henryk   272 n. 33
Drint, Adrina   211 n. 22
Dugan, Elena   267 n. 10

Duling, Dennis C.   374, 374 nn. 43–44
Dumville, David   64, 63 n. 19
Dunn, James D. G.   401, 401 nn. 7–8, 402, 404, 404 n. 13
Dykstra, Trisha   88
Eckhardt, Benedikt   278, 278 n. 48, 278 n. 51
Edrei, Arye   209 n. 18, 211 n. 23
Efron, Joshua   278, 278 n. 51, 310 n. 7
Ehrensberger, Kathy   175
Ehrman, Bart   335 n. 9, 342 n. 19
Elliott, J. K.   376, 376 n. 49
Emerton, John A.   80, 374 n. 43
Erho, Ted M.   66 n. 28, 149 n. 39, 208 n. 13, 213 n. 27, 219 n. 40, 222 n. 50, 374 n. 45
Eshel, Esther   271 nn. 32–33
Even-Shmuel, Yehuda   69, 69 n. 38
Fabricius, Johan A.   67 n. 29, 70, 104, 104 n. 3, 105, 106, 112, 112 n. 26, 113, 113 nn. 27– 28, 203 n. 2, 212 n. 25, 233, 233 n. 7, 234, 256, 343 n. 22, 360, 360 n. 4, 384, 384 n. 3, 385 n. 8
Falk, Daniel   167, 167 n. 26, 344 n. 24
Feldman, Louis H.   66 n. 27, 136 n. 8, 409, 409 n. 3
Fiensy, David   88
Fiorenza, Elisabeth Schüssler   176 n. 3, 181 n. 18, 188 n. 42, 189, 189 n. 45, 191, 191 n. 51
Fisher, Loren   16 n. 17
Fitzgerald, Katharine   175
Flusser, David   69 n. 37, 417 nn. 1–2
Fonseca-Quezada, Channah   175
Fontaine, Carol   183 n. 27
Fortna, Robert T.   95 n.1
Foucault, Michel   335
Fraade, Steven D.   64, 64 n. 21, 149 n. 40, 182 n. 24
Freedman, Noel   91
Frey, Jörg   336 n. 10
Fröhlich, Ida   208 n. 14
Funk, Robert W.   12, 12 n. 4, 13, 14, 14 n. 13, 15 n. 14, 24, 24 n. 33, 26, 96, 97
Fuchs, E.   402, 402 n. 9

Gallagher, Edmon L. 289 n. 6, 299 n. 22, 305 n. 32
Gamble, Sarah 178 n. 6, 178 n. 9, 190 n. 49
García Martínez, Florentino 142 n. 19
Garrison, Irene Peirano 8, 331, 332 n. 1, 333 n. 3, 336 n. 10, 337 n. 12, 342 n. 20, 345 n. 27
Gathercole, Simon J. 373 n. 41
Gaylord, Harry 315, 316 n. 30, 317 n. 38
Geiger, Abraham 104, 114, 115 n. 33, 117, 125 n. 67
Gera, Deborah L. 275, 275 nn. 37–41, 276, 276 n. 43, 277 n. 44
Gifford, Carolyn D. 179 n. 13
Ginzberg, Louis 104, 117, 117 nn. 42–43, 122, 315, 315 n. 26
Giorgi, Dieter 59
Goff, Matthew J. 210 n. 19, 417 n. 3
Gold, Victor 18, 18 n. 20
Gooding, Paul 257 n. 80
Graf, George 67 n. 29
Grafton, Anthony 108 n. 13, 112 n. 24
Graybill, Rhiannon 186 n. 37, 191 n. 52
Graziosi, Barbara 342 n. 20
Greenfield, Jonas C. 160 n. 6, 271 nn. 31–33
Greenwood, Eamon 375 n. 46
Grenfell, Bernhard P. 205 n. 5
Gunkel, Heidrun 405, 405 n. 15
Gutman, Ariel 214 n. 30, 215 nn. 33–34
Hacham, Noah 277 n. 44
Haelewyck, Jean-Claude 70 n. 41
Hagen, Joost L. 267 n. 13
Hägg, Tomas 340 n. 17
Halpern-Amaru, Betsy 180, 180 nn. 15–17
Hanson, Paul 63, 63 n. 14
Hammershaimb, Erling 21, 83, 84 n. 4
Hamrick, James 213 n. 27
Hannah, Darrell D. 369 n.25
Hanneken, Todd R. 206 n. 6, 219, 219 n. 42, 231, 241 n. 32
Hanson, Paul 89
Hanson, R. P. C. 290 n. 9, 296 n. 19

Harari, Yuval 365
Harnack, Adolf von 145 n. 27, 293 n. 14, 300, 300 n. 23
Harl, Marguerite 265 n. 3
Harlow, Daniel 146, 146 n. 31, 147, 147 n. 32, 148, 148 nn. 36–37, 213 nn. 28–29, 220 n. 46, 314 n. 19, 315, 315 n. 24, 315 n. 28, 316, 316 nn. 32–33, 318, 318 n. 40, 319 n. 43, 320, 320 nn. 46–48, 392 n. 24
Harrelson, Walter J. 1, 3, 5, 6, 12, 13, 13 n. 8, 14, 14 n. 13, 15, 15 nn. 14–15, 16, 16 n. 17, 17 n. 19, 18, 18 n. 21–23, 19, 19 n. 24, 20, 20 nn. 25–28, 21, 22, 23, 23 n. 31, 24, 25, 25 n. 36, 26, 26 n. 41, 27, 27 n. 42, 29, 53, 54, 59, 79, 82, 95, 95 n.1, 96, 96 n. 2, 386, 407
Harrington, Daniel J. 2, 17 n. 18, 25 n. 36, 27, 69 n. 37, 96, 190 n. 47, 386 n. 11, 387 n. 13
Hartog, Pieter B. 169 n. 33
Hawk, Brandon W. 231, 254 n. 71
Hayward, Charles T. R. 364 n. 12, 404, 404 n. 14
Heal, Kristian S. 231 n. 2, 368 n. 20, 419 n. 8
Heger, Paul 310 n. 7
Heist, William 250, 250 n. 60
Hellholm, David 63, 63 n. 15
Hengel, Martin 88, 89
Henning, W. B. 210 n. 19
Henze, Matthias 1, 5, 6, 11, 30, 65 n. 24, 99 n. 10, 122 n. 56, 133, 182 n. 21, 231, 266 n. 6, 364, 370, 386 n. 10, 387 n. 14
Herzer, Jens 336 n. 10
Heschel, Susannah 114 n. 32, 115 n. 33, 116 n. 38, 117 n. 40, 125 n. 67
Hicks-Keeton, Jill 152 n. 48, 185 n. 35
Hilgenfeld, Adolph 125 n. 67
Hillel, Vered 63 n. 13, 71 n. 44, 184 n. 31, 367
Himmelfarb, Martha 2, 7, 27, 29, 64, 209 nn. 17–18, 216 n. 36, 263, 271 n. 31, 280 n. 58, 312, 312 n. 13, 316, 316 nn. 34–37, 319, 319 nn. 44–45, 320, 320 n.

48, 321 n. 49, 323, 323 n. 58, 324, 324 nn. 61–62, 325, 325 nn. 63–64, 326, 326 n. 65, 366 nn. 15–16, 418 n. 5
Hirsch-Luipold, Rainer   405, 405 n. 15
Hodgson-Wright, Stephanie   178 n. 9
Hogan, Karina M.   121 n. 53, 144 n. 23, 184 n. 32
Hollander, Harm   62 n. 11, 99, 99 n. 11
Hollywood, Amy   184 n. 30
Horst, Pieter W. van der 180 n. 17, 192 n. 57, 324 n. 60
Houten, Christiana de Groot van 182 n. 24
Hovhanessian, Vahan S. 369 n. 24
Huffmon, Herbert B.   16 n. 17
Hughes, H. M.   315, 315 n. 27
Hunt, Arthur S.   205 n. 5
Ilan, Tal   191 n. 54
Ir-Shai, Oded   69
Isaac, Ephraim   113 n. 31, 369 n. 21
James, Montague R.   70, 70 n. 40, 71, 97, 145 n. 27, 180 n. 17, 234, 235, 235 n. 13, 255 n. 73, 314, 314 n. 21, 315 n. 22
Jacobs, Andrew S.   305 n. 31
Jacobson, Howard   69 n. 37, 180 n. 17
Janssen, Martina   336 n. 10
Jellinek, Adolph   69, 69 n. 38
Jervel, Jacob   403
Johnson, Michael   231, 257 n. 79
Johnson, M. D.   373 n. 41, 401, 402 n. 10
Johnston, Sarah Iles   184 n. 30
Jonge, Marinus de   3, 20, 20 n. 27, 21, 21 n. 29, 22, 25 n. 37, 27, 30, 62, 62 n. 11, 63, 89, 96, 99, 99 n. 11, 110 nn. 19–20, 111 n. 23, 123, 123 n. 60, 123 n. 63, 145, 145 n. 24, 146, 146 n. 29, 151, 162 n.12, 169 n. 35, 220 n. 46, 272 n. 33, 280 n. 58, 311 nn. 10–11
Joosten, Jan   265 n. 3, 275, 275 n. 42, 277 n. 45, 278, 278 n. 49, 279 nn. 52–53
Kabisch, Richard   400, 400 n. 3
Käsemann, Ernst   158, 158 n. 4
Kaup, Matthias   231

Kautzsch, Emil F.   80, 80 n. 3, 84, 137, 138 n. 11, 212 n. 25, 384 n. 6, 402
Keady, Jessica M.   186 n. 37
Keck, Lee   90
Kee, Howard C.   89, 182 n. 22
Kestemont, Mike   231 n. 2
King, Karen   334 n. 7
Kister, Menachem   69 n. 35, 209 n. 17
Klawans, Jonathan   138 n. 12
Klutz, Todd E.   373 n. 40, 374, 374 n. 44, 375
Knibb, Michael A. 17 n. 18, 62, 164 n. 17
Knierim, Rolf   16 n. 17,
Koch, Klaus   63, 63 n. 14, 158, 158 n. 4
Koester, Helmut   55, 56 n. 1, 59
Kolenkow, Anitra B.   23
Koningsveld, P. Sj. van   210 n. 20
Korteweg, Theodore   99 n. 11
Kotansky, Roy   373
Kraft, Robert A.   2, 3, 6, 12, 17 nn. 18–19, 18, 21, 22, 24, 25, 26, 27, 27 n. 43, 53, 54, 59, 60 n. 1, 61, 61 n. 3, 63, 64, 64 n. 22, 71, 79, 82, 89, 96, 97, 97 n. 3, 99, 99 n. 10, 108 n. 13, 122 n. 57, 123 n. 59, 136 n. 8, 145, 145 nn. 25–27, 146, 146 n. 28, 147, 151, 169 n. 35, 188 n. 44, 223 n. 52, 236 n. 16, 240 n. 29, 263 n.1, 280 n. 59, 304 n. 28, 311 nn. 8–9, 312, 318, 375, 385 n. 7, 386 n. 11, 387 n. 13, 392 n. 24
Kramer, Ross   123 n. 62, 183 n. 25, 193 n. 58, 280 n. 58, 312 n. 12
Krueger, Fredric   374 n. 45
Kugel, James L.   66 n. 27, 136 n. 8, 409, 409 n. 3, 410, 410 n.5
Kuhn, Karl H.   371 n. 31
Kulik, Alexander   66, 66 n. 28, 146, 146 nn. 30–31, 147, 147 nn. 33–35, 211 n. 24, 213 n. 28, 314 n. 20, 315, 315 n. 29, 317 n. 39
Kümmel, Werner G.   84, 84 n. 4
Kutsko, John F.   12 n. 6
Kynes, Will   136 n. 7
Labendz, Jenny R.   209 n. 17
Lakoff, George   184, 184 nn. 32–33

Landau, Brent 375 n. 46, 376, 377 n. 50
Lanfer, Peter T. 184 n. 31
Lange, Armin 165 n. 23, 188 n. 44, 337 n. 12
Langlois, Michael 67 n. 30, 163 n. 14
La Porta, Sergio 370 n. 26
Larson, Erik W. 267 n. 9, 268, 268 nn. 15–17, 273 n. 35
Laurence, Richard 113 n. 31
Laurey, Marc 249, 249 n. 57
Lawrence, Beatrice 179 n.10
Lawson, R. P. 299 n. 21
Legaspi, Michael 133, 135 n. 6
Leicht, Reimund 69, 69 n. 36
Levenson, David 365
Levine, Amy-Jill 88, 181, 181 n. 19, 182 n. 23, 183 n. 25
Levison, John R. 8, 29, 184 n. 30, 399, 399 n. 1, 402 n. 11, 404 n. 12, 405 n. 15
Lied, Liv I. 1, 7, 1, 30, 67, 67 n. 30, 107 n. 12, 108 n. 15, 121 n. 53, 123 n. 62, 124 n. 65, 133, 151 n. 57, 168 n. 31, 170 n. 36, 182 n. 21, 188 n. 43, 203, 206 n. 6, 206 n. 8, 213 n. 27, 214 n. 30, 215 n. 33, 220 n. 44, 220 n. 46, 223 n. 53, 231, 231 n. 2, 251 n. 64, 254 n. 71, 288, 288 nn. 3–4, 375, 375 n. 47, 388 n. 17, 411 n. 8, 412 n. 10
Lim, Timothy H. 140 n. 15
Lion, Brigitte 192 n. 55
Lorein, Geert W. 364 n. 11
Lourié, Basil 375 n. 46
Lovering, Eugene G. 182 n. 24
Lundhaug, Hugo 151 n. 57, 168 n. 31, 206 n. 8, 231, 251 n. 64, 256 n. 76, 388 n. 17, 411 n. 8
Lunt, H. 82
Lutz, R. T. 374 n. 45
Macaskil, Grant 375 n. 46
Macé, Caroline 231 n. 2
MacRae, George W., S. J. 2, 6, 17 n. 19, 21, 23, 24, 25, 26, 53, 54–58, 59, 61, 80, 82, 83, 84, 96, 98, 182 n. 22, 393 n. 27
Magny, Ariane 343 n. 21
Mai, Angelo 255 n. 73
Manoff, I. 337 n. 12
Mansfeld, Jaap 340 n. 17
Marshall, John W. 318 n. 42
Martin, Raymond 99
Marx, Alexander 417 n. 1
May, Herbert G. 12 n. 5
McCutcheon, Russell T. 134, 134 n. 4, 135 n. 5
McNamara, Martin 64, 64 n. 20, 66, 66 n. 28
Meade, David J. 336 n. 10
Meiser, Martin 401, 401 n. 6
Mendels, Doron 88, 89, 92, 209 n. 18, 211 n. 23
Merk, Otto 401, 401 n. 6
Metzger, Bruce 2, 16 n. 17, 17 n. 19, 21, 23, 24, 26, 53, 54, 79, 82, 84, 96, 300, 333 n. 5, 339 n. 16, 341 n. 18, 371 n. 30
Meyer, Paul 234
Meyers, Carol 399
Meyers, Eric 399
Michel, Cécil 192 n. 55
Migne, Jacques-Paul 67 n. 29, 70
Milik, Józef T. 7, 97, 98 n. 6, 159–165, 160 nn. 5–6, 161 nn. 8–10, 162 nn. 11–13, 163 nn. 14–16, 165 nn. 19–21, 205 n. 4, 268, 268 n. 14, 367
Millar, Fergus 122 n. 57
Miller, Troy A. 184 n. 31
Miltenova, Anisava 67 n. 29
Minov, Sergey 211 n. 24
Mirguet, Françoise 184 n. 32, 413 n. 12
Mittmann-Richert, Ulrike 165 n. 23
Momigliano, Arnoldo D. 234 n. 11
Monger, Matthew P. 118 n. 45, 169 n. 34, 170 n. 36, 215 n. 33, 254 n. 71, 375
Montanari, Franco 338 n. 14
Moore, Carey A. 182 n. 23, 271 nn. 29–30
Moore, George F. 116 n. 38, 310
Morano, Enrico 210 n. 19, 417 n. 3
Morfill, W. R. 314, 314 n. 21
Most, Glenn 334 n. 6, 345 n. 26
Mroczek, Eva 218 n. 39, 337 n. 12, 384 nn. 4–5, 386 n. 9

Mueller, James R.   29, 88, 371 n. 33, 374 n. 42
Muilenburg, James   16 n. 17
Munnich, Olivier   265 n. 3, 265 n. 5
Murdock, Brian O.   66, 66 n. 28
Murphy, Frederick J.   180 n. 17
Murphy, Roland E.   84, 88
Najman, Hindy   8, 29, 120, 120 n. 51, 143 n. 21, 144 n. 23, 152 n. 48, 167 n. 29, 331, 333 n. 4, 335 n. 8, 336 n. 10, 337 n. 12, 344 n. 24, 345 n. 25, 348 n. 32, 350 n. 33, 351 n. 34, 360 n. 5, 384 n. 5, 413 n. 14
Nasrallah, Laura   176 n. 3
Naveh, Joseph   68 n. 32
Nebe, G.-Wilhelm   269 n. 22
Neubauer, Adolph   417 n. 1
Neusner, Jacob   66 n. 26, 310 n. 6
Newman, Judith H.   8, 29, 407, 412 n. 11
Newsom, Carol A.   388 n. 15
Nickelsburg, George W. E.   2, 6, 11, 18 n. 22, 25 n. 36, 26, 26 n. 40, 27, 27 n. 44, 29, 59, 61, 61 n. 6, 63, 63 n. 18, 64, 65, 80, 82, 85, 95, 97 n. 3, 97 n. 5, 98 nn. 7–8, 99, 99 n. 10, 107 n. 12, 121 n. 52, 122 nn. 57–58, 164, 164 n. 17, 182 n. 23, 266 nn. 7–8, 267 nn. 11–12, 269 n. 18, 269 n. 20, 270 n. 23, 316, 316 n. 31, 320 n. 47, 386 n. 10, 387 n. 12, 388, 388 n. 17, 389, 389 nn. 18–21
Nietzsche, Friedrich   335
Nievergelt, Andreas   258 n. 82
Nir, Rivka   123 n. 62, 184 n. 31, 312 n. 12
Nisse, Ruth   110, 110 nn. 17–18, 111 nn. 20–22
Norelli, Enrico   311 n. 11
Odeberg, Hugo   209 n. 15
Oegema, Gerbern   192 n. 57
Oepke, Albrecht   289 n. 6, 295 n. 17, 304 n. 27
Orlinsky, Harry M.   2, 12 n. 5, 16 n. 17, 21, 24, 26, 27, 53, 54, 96, 98
Orlov, Andrei   108 n. 14, 211 n. 24, 240 n. 29
Palmer, James   249
Panayotov, Alexander   2, 65 n. 25, 106, 106 n. 8, 123 n. 64, 136 n. 8, 166 n. 24, 212 n. 25, 360, 360 n. 3, 384 n. 6, 385 n. 7, 392 n. 23, 410 n. 4
Parks, Sarah   187 n. 40
Patton, Corrine L.   182 n. 24
Paz, Yakir   337 n. 12
Pearson, Birger A.   59, 60, 368
Peirano, Irene. See Garrison, Irene Peirano
Perles, Felix   117, 117 n. 41, 125 n. 67, 310 n. 4
Perrin, Andrew W.   231
Perrot, Charles   190 n. 47
Pervo, Richard I.   182 nn. 22–23, 183 n. 25
Petit, Françoise   304 n. 29
Peursen, Wido van   214 n. 30, 215 nn. 33–34, 231 n. 2
Pfeiffer, R.   338 n. 14
Phelps, Michael   219
Picard, J.-C.   21, 315, 315 n. 23, 321, 321 n. 50
Pietersma, Albert   149 n. 40, 374 n. 45
Philonenko, Marc   21, 21 n. 30, 83, 84, 84 n. 4
Pick, Bernhard   103, 103 n. 1, 104, 106 n. 9, 125
Pillinger, Renate   337 n. 12
Piovanelli, Pierluigi   368 n. 19
Popović, Mladen   169 n. 33
Portier-Young, Anathea   121 n. 53
Pregill, Michael   210 n. 21
Priest, John   23, 84, 89, 113 n. 31, 300 n. 24
Puech, Émile   269 n. 22
Purintun, Ann-Elizabeth   2, 17 n. 18, 26, 27 n. 43, 54, 60, 60 n. 1, 61 n. 3, 97, 97 n. 3, 386 n. 11
Quenzer, Jörg   254 n. 71
Rabin, Ira   219 n. 43, 231, 241 n.32
Rabinowitz, Nancy S.   192 n. 55
Radini, A.   105 n. 7
Raffaelli, Enrico   231
Raphael, Rebecca   152 n. 48

Reed, Annette Yoshiko 65, 65 n. 23, 104 n. 4, 108 nn. 13–14, 112 n. 26, 113 nn. 28–30, 115 nn. 34–35, 123 nn. 63–64, 133 n. 1, 175 n. 1, 181 n. 20, 203 n. 2, 210 n. 21, 211 n. 24, 218 n. 38, 287 n.1, 291 n. 13, 309 n. 1, 312 n. 15, 333 n. 4, 343 n. 22, 384 nn. 4–5, 385 n. 8, 386 n. 9, 413 n.13
Reeves, John C. 8, 29, 64, 65, 65 n. 23, 68, 68 n. 31, 123 n. 64, 209 nn. 17–18, 220 n. 46, 291 n. 13, 365 n. 14, 375, 415, 418 n. 4
Reif, Stefan C. 417 n. 2
Renan, Ernest 114, 114 n. 32
Rengstorf, Karl H. 19, 21
Renninger, Jesse B. 16 n. 17,
Rhodes, Erroll F. 16 n. 17
Richlin, Amy 192 n. 55
Riessler, Paul 66 n. 27, 80, 80 n. 3, 84
Robinson, James M. 19, 19 n. 24, 20, 20 n. 25, 24, 59
Robinson, Stephen E. 71, 71 n. 45, 88, 374 n. 42
Roddy, Nicolae 67 n. 29
Roitman, Adolfo D. 182 n. 23
Rosenmeyer, Patricia A. 334 n. 6
Rosen-Zwi, Ishay 337 n. 12
Rotschield, Clare K. 336 n. 10
Ruiten, Jacques van 30
Russell, D. A. 347 n. 29, 348 n. 31
Russell, David S. 63, 63 n. 14
Ruwet, J. 289 n. 6, 293 n. 14, 295 n. 17, 296 n. 19, 304 n. 26
Sacchi, Paulo 83, 84 n. 4
Sakel, Dean 251 n. 64
Sanders, James 16 n. 17, 82, 91
Sanders, Valerie 178 n. 9
Sandmel, Samuel 87, 87 n. 6
Satran, David 71 n. 44, 150, 150 nn. 44–46, 220 n. 46, 311 n. 11
Saunders, Ernest W. 11, 11 n. 1, 12 nn. 2, 4, 5, 14 nn. 11–12, 393 n. 27, 394, 394 n. 28, 408 n. 1
Schechter, Ronald 253 n. 68
Schenke, Gesa 373 n. 41
Schilbrack, Kevin 134 n. 4
Schmidt, Johann A. 385 n. 8
Scholer, David M. 16 n. 17,
Schottroff, Luise 179 nn. 11–13
Schroer, Silvia 179 nn. 11–13
Schürer, Emil 115 n. 34, 122 n. 57, 125 n. 67, 315, 315 n. 25
Scrimgeour, Andrew D. 11, 12 n. 4
Scroggs, R. 404
Segal, Michael 169 n. 34
Sergew Hable Selassie 27
Schiffman, Lawrence H. 66 n. 27, 120 n. 48, 136 n. 8, 271 n. 31, 409, 409 n. 3
Schmidt, Francis 99
Scholem, Gershom 68
Seow, Choon-Leong 410, 411 n. 6
Sgambati, Scipione 233, 233 n. 7, 234, 256
Shaked, Saul 68 n. 32
Sharpe, John L., III 16 n. 17, 17 n. 18, 18, 23, 25 n. 36, 26, 30
Sheinfeldt, Shayna 175
Sherwood, Yvonne 178 n. 7
Shoemaker, Stephen J. 369 n. 23
Shutt, R. J. H. 371 n. 33
Sibley Towner, W. 16 n. 17
Sjöberg, Birgitta L. 176 n. 3
Skehan, Patrick 159
Skjaervø, Prods Oktor 364
Smith, Edgar W. 182 n. 22
Smith, Jonathan Z. 60, 79, 90, 99, 182 n. 22, 290 n. 11
Smith, Morton 16 n. 17
Sobisch, Jan-Ulrich 254 n. 71
Sparks, Hedley F. D. 19, 21, 136, 136 n. 8, 212 n. 25, 359 n. 1, 361, 371, 373, 409, 409 n. 3
Speyer, Wolfgang 332 n. 1
Spittler, Rudolph P. 373 n. 41
Spurling, Helen 367 n. 18
Staack, William A. K. 16 n. 17
Staalduine-Sullman, Eveline van 364 n. 11
Standhartinger, Angela 123 n. 62, 183 n. 25

Stang, Charles M. 348 n. 32
Stanton, Elizabeth Cady 179, 179 n. 12
Stendahl, Krister 59
Stern, David 386 n. 9
Stern, Menachem 88
Stewart, Columba 218 n. 38
Stinespring, William F. 16 n. 17, 23, 82, 88
Stone, Michael E. 3, 6, 25, 25 nn. 36–38, 26, 26 nn. 40–41, 27 n. 43, 30, 31, 59, 61 nn. 4–7, 63 n. 13, 63 n. 18, 64 n. 20, 65 n. 24, 70 nn. 43–44, 80, 82, 84, 87, 96, 97, 97 nn. 3–4, 104 n. 4, 108 n. 15, 116 n. 38, 117 nn. 42–43, 119 nn. 46–47, 122 n. 57, 124 n. 66, 136 n. 8, 137 n. 10, 139, 139 n. 14, 144 n. 22, 148 n. 38, 149, 149 n. 42, 150 n. 43, 151, 160 n. 6, 165 n. 23, 169 n. 35, 209 n. 17, 211 n. 24, 213 n. 27, 219 n. 40, 220 n. 46, 231, 233 n. 6, 234 n. 8, 236 n. 16, 271 nn. 31–33, 371 n. 31, 386 n. 11, 389 n. 20
Stone, Nira 182 n. 23
Strauss, David 114
Stroumsa, Guy G. 301 n. 25
Strugnell, John 17 n. 19, 21, 25 n. 36, 26, 27 n. 43, 53, 59, 61, 63, 70, 70 n. 43, 79, 82, 84, 86, 89, 91, 161 n. 9
Stuckenbruck, Loren T. 7, 66, 66 n. 28, 106 n. 9, 119 n. 46, 149 n. 39, 165 n. 22, 165 n. 23, 167, 167 n. 27, 203, 203 n. 2, 208 n. 13, 210 n. 19, 219 n. 40, 219 n. 43, 220 n. 47, 222 n. 50, 231, 332 n. 2, 337 n. 12, 364, 417 n. 3
Suciu, Alin 231
Sundermann, Werner 210 n. 19
Svärd, Saana 194 n. 59
Szold, Henrietta 117 n. 43
Taddesse Tamrat 27
Talmon, Shemaryahu 84, 89
Talshir, Zipora 54
Tarchnishvili, M. 67 n. 29
Terry, Milton S. 103 n. 2
Tervanotko, Hanna 5, 7, 175, 178 n. 7, 183 n. 28, 184 n. 32, 185 n. 34, 190 n. 48

Thomson, S. H. 111 n. 23
Thornham, Sue 178 n. 9
Thornhill, R. 373 n. 41
Thoutenhoofd, Ernst D. 231 n. 2
Tigchelaar, Eibert 7, 118 n. 45, 157, 163 n. 16, 165 n. 18, 165 n. 23, 168 n. 30, 168 n. 32, 169 n. 34, 181 n. 20
Tikhonravov, Nikolai 234
Tischendorf, Constantin von 234
Toepel, Alexander 372 n. 35
Toorn, Karel van der 192 n. 56, 336 nn. 10–11
Torijano, Pablo A. 373 nn. 38–39
Tottoli, Roberto 419 n. 6
Toury, Gideon 149 n. 40
Tov, Emanuel 63, 63 n. 17, 265 n. 4, 344 n. 24
Treharne, Elaine 251 n. 64
Tromp, Johannes 311 n. 11, 369
Trumbower, Jeffrey A. 182 n. 24
Tucker, Gene 13, 13 n. 7
Tucker, James 241 n. 31
Tuffin, Paul 306 n. 33
Ulrich, Eugene 344 n. 24
Urbach, Ephrem E. 88
VanderKam, James C. 2, 27, 29, 63 n. 18, 64, 66, 66 n. 28, 96, 107 n. 12, 113 n. 31, 120 n. 49, 205 n. 4, 269 n. 21, 272 n. 34, 350, 375 n. 46
Vaux, Roland de 91
Verhelst, Daniel 249, 249 n. 57
Vermes, Geza 80, 84, 122 n. 57, 344 n. 24
Vikan, Gary 182 n. 22
Vine, Agnus 252 n. 66
Wacholder, Ben Zion 276, 276 n. 43
Wacker, Marie-Theres 179 nn. 11–13, 183 n. 27, 183 n. 28
Wagner, Norman E. 12
Wan, Zse-kar 364
Ward, R. B. 30
Wassen, Cecilia 183 n. 28
Wasserstrom, Steven M. 418 n. 4
Weeks, Stuart 136 n. 7
Weel, Adriaan van der 231 n. 2

Welch, Claude	14
Wells, L. S. A.	373 n. 41, 400, 400 n. 4, 401
Werline, Rodney	99 n. 10
Wermann, Cana	169 n. 34
West, Candace	194 n. 59
Whiston, William	113, 113 n. 29
Whitaker, G. H.	324
Whittaker, M.	373 n. 41
Wiese, Christian	104 n. 5, 115 n. 34, 116 n. 38, 125 n. 67
Wilckens, Jens	210 n. 19
Wills, Lawrence M.	122 n. 56
Wilson, Robert M.	19, 21
Wilson Walter T.	324 n. 60
Wright, Benjamin G., III	7, 64, 71, 71 nn. 44–45, 133, 138 n. 13, 149 n. 40, 204 n. 3, 323 n. 57, 374 n. 42
Wright, Charles D.	238 n. 21, 240 n. 29
Wright, Charles W.	231
Wright, J. Edward	321 n. 52, 322, 322 n. 53
Wright, N. T.	404, 404 n. 13
Wyrick, Jed	336 n. 10
Xerawitz, Géza G.	278, 278 n. 47
Yadin, Yigael	14
Yassif, Eli	69 n. 37, 105 n. 6, 417 n. 1
Young, Stephen L.	185 n. 35
Zadeh, Travis	419 n. 8
Zahn, Theodor	289 n. 6, 295, 295 n. 17
Zervos, George	88
Ziegler, Joseph	63 n. 16
Zieme, Peter	364
Zimmerman, Don H.	194 n. 59
Zsengellér, József	337 n. 12

www.ingramcontent.com/pod-product-compliance
Lightning Source LLC
Chambersburg PA
CBHW021926290426
44108CB00012B/742